African American Psychology

Fourth Edition

Sara Miller McCune founded SAGE Publishing in 1965 to support the dissemination of usable knowledge and educate a global community. SAGE publishes more than 1000 journals and over 800 new books each year, spanning a wide range of subject areas. Our growing selection of library products includes archives, data, case studies and video. SAGE remains majority owned by our founder and after her lifetime will become owned by a charitable trust that secures the company's continued independence.

Los Angeles | London | New Delhi | Singapore | Washington DC | Melbourne

African American Psychology

From Africa to America

Fourth Edition

Faye Z. Belgrave

Virginia Commonwealth University

Kevin W. Allison

Virginia Commonwealth University

Los Angeles | London | New Delhi
Singapore | Washington DC | Melbourne

FOR INFORMATION:

SAGE Publications, Inc.
2455 Teller Road
Thousand Oaks, California 91320
E-mail: order@sagepub.com

SAGE Publications Ltd.
1 Oliver's Yard
55 City Road
London EC1Y 1SP
United Kingdom

SAGE Publications India Pvt. Ltd.
B 1/I 1 Mohan Cooperative Industrial Area
Mathura Road, New Delhi 110 044
India

SAGE Publications Asia-Pacific Pte. Ltd.
3 Church Street
#10-04 Samsung Hub
Singapore 049483

Printed in the United States of America

Library of Congress Cataloging-in-Publication Data

ISBN 978-1-5063-3340-3

Acquisitions Editor: Lara Parra
Editorial Assistant: Zachary Valladon
Production Editor: Andrew Olson
Copy Editor: Jared Leighton
Typesetter: C&M Digitals (P) Ltd.
Proofreader: Ellen Howard
Indexer: Sylvia Coates
Cover Designer: Candice Harman
Marketing Manager: Katherine Hepburn

This book is printed on acid-free paper.

MIX
Paper from
responsible sources
FSC
www.fsc.org   FSC® C008955

19 20 21 22 10 9 8 7 6 5 4 3 2

DETAILED CONTENTS

SECTION II • SOCIAL SYSTEMS AND STRUCTURES

SECTION IV • ADJUSTMENT AND ADAPTATION

PREFACE

The completion of this fourth edition of *African American Psychology* is at a time of tremendous division and challenges in this country. A very contentious election with a president unpopular among many, coupled with increases in overt displays of bigotry, has impacted all Americans. High-profile police violence has continued and has been shared on all media, especially social media. Disparities remain for African Americans across most indicators, including education, employment, housing, incarceration, and health, among others. The toxic water in Flint, Michigan, is a notable example of systematic racism's impact on African Americans' health. Many other recent examples are discussed throughout this book.

While there are several troubling problems that continue to affect African Americans, there is some progress to report. The Black Lives Matter movement, formed in 2012 following the acquittal of Zimmerman in the Trayvon Martin case, has become a large social justice movement involving people of all racial and ethnic groups. The White supremacist terrorist attack in Charlottesville, Virginia, (August 2017) also brought together people of all races and ethnicities, religions, and ages and furthered the commitment of many to work against bigotry and racism. Barack Obama, the first African American president, served two terms (2009–2017) and moved the country out of a recession that started in 2007 and that had devastating effects on African Americans. While disparities remain, the economy and employment of African Americans are better than it was prior to Obama taking office. As of this writing, the Patient Protection and Affordable Care Act (Obamacare) is still in effect and continues to provide health care for many African Americans who otherwise would not have received it. While much more is needed, there have been some initiatives to address some of the concerns of specific African American populations (e.g., My Brother's Keeper Initiative on African American boys and adolescents). Understanding the psychology of African Americans is closely linked to understanding what is happening in the institutional systems in this country and is a continuing theme in this fourth edition.

Our purpose for writing this fourth edition largely remains the same as for the first edition. We wanted a text that would provide comprehensive and integrated coverage of the field of African American psychology. We also desired a book that would address and consider both African and American cultural perspectives. We also wanted this book to capture and reflect upon contemporary issues African Americans face. There have been notable advances and developments in African American psychology over the past several years, and these updates are included in this fourth edition.

Who should use this book? This book is for students interested in African American psychology. It is designed to be used as a semester-long textbook and covers 15 focal areas in African American psychology. The text can be used as a mid- to advanced-level undergraduate textbook and can also be used at the graduate level. In addition, those interested in understanding the psychology of African Americans may use the book in support of other courses and disciplines.

What are the unique aspects of this book? There are several unique features in this book. We begin each chapter with an African proverb that provides a perspective on the issue and a departure point for considering the material within the chapter. Proverbs enrich us with lessons, rules, and wisdom for living our lives. We also begin each chapter with a cover story that demonstrates the applicability of African American psychology to everyday life. The cover stories in this edition include blogs as well as articles from news outlets. Each chapter contains five to eight learning objectives that, if met, will provide the student with knowledge of key concepts and an overview of the research and literature on topics covered in the chapter. We also added a text box to each chapter that highlights a contemporary issue. The contemporary issues introduce the student to a new idea, an emerging area of research, and/or information that is interesting and relevant to African American psychology but that may not be covered in the psychological literature. In each chapter, we provide a historical context that includes relevant information and literature from Africa, during the enslavement period, and at other critical historical points in time. Because we believe in the concept of Sankofa—that it is important to look to the past to understand the present and consider the future—we relate the historical context of Africans and African Americans to the psychology of contemporary African Americans.

Each chapter begins with an introduction that defines terms and concepts. We have attempted to describe attributes of African and African American culture that impact the psychology of African Americans. Where applicable, we include research that covers Blacks throughout the diaspora. Each chapter has a research and methodological section that highlights methodological issues relevant to topics discussed in the chapter.

Each chapter also has a section on best practices or empirically supported practices. These sections recognize the importance of moving beyond discussions of research and literature to highlight effective ways and promising strategies to address problems and to improve well-being for African Americans. A section on critical analysis provides our insights on topics covered in each chapter. This section also includes discussion of noteworthy research, new and innovative ideas, and directions for future work.

The book is organized in four sections. The first four chapters provide an introduction to and a foundational framework for the remainder of the book. Chapter 1 focuses on African American psychology as a discipline and provides a historical account of African Americans in the larger discipline of psychology. Chapter 2 is on African-centered psychology, which provides the framework for the study of people of African descent. Chapter 3, on self and identity, is considered foundational to the psychology of African Americans, as self-attributes such as self-concept and ethnic identity define our thoughts and beliefs about who we are. Chapter 4, on race and racism, is also included as a foundational chapter because race and racism have an all-encompassing influence on every aspect of being African American.

The second section of the book focuses on social systems and structures and includes chapters on family, community, and educational and work institutions and related processes. Chapter 5 describes the African American family and kinship, the primary agents of socialization. Educational systems and processes, including schools and other institutions of learning, are discussed in Chapter 6 along with work and related topics, such as careers and employment. African Americans live, work, and go to school in neighborhoods and communities; this is the topic of Chapter 7.

The third section of the book covers individual and developmental processes and includes chapters on interpersonal and close relationships; cognition, learning, and language; religion and spirituality; and life span development. Our relationships with others are central to who we are and how we function. Interpersonal relationships, including relationships with friends, romantic partners, and others, are the focus of Chapter 8. Chapter 9 describes unique features of cognition, learning, and language among African Americans and discusses the relevance of these to creating positive learning environments for African American youth. Religion and spirituality are central beliefs of people of African descent; this topic is covered in Chapter 10. Chapter 11 covers developmental issues of African Americans throughout the life span.

The fourth and final section of the book focuses on adjustment and adaptation and includes chapters on health, illness, and disability; psychosocial adaptation and mental health; drug use and abuse; and prosocial and antisocial behavior. Chapter 12 discusses health, illness, and disability from the perspective of African Americans attending to cultural and structural conditions that impact health conditions and how we adapt to chronic illness and disability. Psychosocial adaptation and mental health are the subjects of Chapter 13, which provides an assessment of mental health conditions, mental health functioning, and culturally congruent models of mental health and adaptation. Drug use and abuse have serious adverse consequences for African Americans. These consequences are discussed, along with strategies to prevent drug use and abuse, in Chapter 14. Chapter 15 focuses on both the positive aspects of prosocial behavior and the adverse consequences of antisocial behavior, such as aggression. The Kenyan proverb, "Having a good discussion is like having riches," exemplifies what we desire for the readers of this book. We hope that the readers of this book will have many riches as they read, review, challenge, and think about the materials in this book.

ACKNOWLEDGMENTS

We are honored that this book continues to be used in many universities throughout the United States to educate students about African American psychology. We appreciate the instructors who chose this book and students who allowed us to share our knowledge. The staff, especially Deborah Butler, at the Center for Cultural Experiences in Prevention at Virginia Commonwealth University forgave our absences and filled in for us on work tasks so that we could spend time on the book. Our research assistants, Joi Hamm and Yunjung Chung, provided numerous hours and commitment to seeing this project to completion.

Several Sage personnel contributed to this project. Lara Parra (acquisitions editor) greatly facilitated the completion of this fourth edition by providing encouragement, keeping us on schedule, and attending to all of our requests. Zachary Valladon provided much technical assistance in a cheerful and prompt manner. Other SAGE editors (Jared Leighton, copy editor, and Andrew Olson, production editor) also contributed much to the completion of this project. Thank you. Several reviewers who were anonymous to us provided critical and instructive feedback regarding the third edition and what was needed in the fourth edition. We appreciate and used your instructive wisdom.

The writings and ideas of several psychologists have made a strong impact on each of us. Thank you, Reginald Jones, whom we will always admire for leading the way and writing the first comprehensive book on African American psychology. The Egyptian scholar Asa Hilliard was influential and inspirational to so many of us. Robert Guthrie provided us with a comprehensive history of Blacks in psychology. We are eternally grateful to James Jones and Dalmas Taylor for supporting us and countless other African American psychologists through the American Psychological Association's Minority Fellowship Program. We would also like to thank scholars such as Robert Williams, Margaret Spencer, and William Cross for their conceptual and empirical contributions, scholarship, and support. And thank you, Na'im Akbar and Fred Phillips, for your influential writings and commentaries on African-centered psychology. We have learned so much.

The authors and SAGE gratefully acknowledge the contributions of reviewers who have used the previous edition of this book and provided valuable suggestions for how to improve the book.

Finally, thanks to all the friends, family, students, and colleagues who have cheered us along the way. *Asante sana*.

ABOUT THE AUTHORS

Faye Z. Belgrave, PhD (University of Maryland), is professor of psychology at Virginia Commonwealth University and founder and director of the Center for Cultural Experiences in Prevention. Her programmatic and research interests are in the areas of HIV and substance abuse prevention. Her research focuses on the role of culture and context in preventive interventions and on issues of gender and women. Dr. Belgrave has published extensively and is an invited speaker on these topics. In collaboration with community partners, she has implemented several prevention programs targeting African American adolescents, young adults, and women. These programs have been beneficial in increasing cultural attributes and in preventing and/or decreasing drug use and associated negative behaviors. Dr. Belgrave serves as an expert advisor on several national committees and agencies, including the American Psychological Association, the National Institute of Drug Abuse, the Substance Abuse and Mental Health Services Administration, and the Center for Substance Abuse Prevention. She is the recipient of many national awards for her work with African American populations, including the Association of Black Psychologists's Distinguished Psychologists Award and the American Psychological Association's Distinguished Career Award for a distinguished career in psychology. Additionally, she is the recipient of the Substance Abuse and Mental Health Service Administration's (SAMHSA) Addie Jane Key Prevention Award in recognition of her outstanding contributions to prevention, and the State Council of Higher Education for Virginia (SCHEV) Outstanding Faculty Award.

Kevin W. Allison, PhD (DePaul University), is senior assistant to the president of Virginia Commonwealth University (VCU) and professor in the Department of Psychology and the Wilder School of Government and Public Affairs. He completed his undergraduate degree in psychology at the University of Notre Dame and his graduate work in clinical-community psychology at DePaul University in Chicago. Prior to joining the VCU faculty, Dr. Allison worked at the Pennsylvania State University and served as the clinical director of City Lights in Washington, DC. Dr. Allison's work has focused on understanding and addressing processes that support positive developmental outcomes for African American children and youth. This has included the examination of life skills and culturally informed interventions for youth and work with community-based human services providers. In addition, Dr. Allison works extensively with nonprofit organizations and public agencies to use research and evaluation in strengthening programmatic and community-level change in urban neighborhoods.

INTRODUCTION AND HISTORICAL FOUNDATION

INTRODUCTION TO AFRICAN AMERICAN PSYCHOLOGY

If you know the beginning well, the end will not trouble you.

—Wolof proverb

LEARNING OBJECTIVES

- To define and conceptualize African American psychology
- To become familiar with some of the historical events in African American psychology
- To become knowledgeable about critical events in the development of African American psychology
- To identify influential African American psychologists
- To identify the status of African American psychology today
- To identify methodological issues in studying African American psychology

ETHNICALLY IDENTIFIED PSYCHOLOGICAL ASSOCIATIONS

The annual convention of the Association of Black Psychologists (ABPsi) has the cutting-edge workshops and networking opportunities that other psychology conventions offer. But it also offers an emphasis on African-American-focused research and practice too often ignored by so-called mainstream psychology, and a worldview steeped in African-American culture and traditions that might seem surprising at other psychology conferences, such as the pouring of libations, the honoring of elders and ancestors and other rituals rooted in African heritage.

(Continued)

(Continued)

"The emphasis on tradition is a reminder of the importance of who we are and why that's important for our psychological well-being," says ABPsi member Kevin Cokley, PhD, a psychology professor at the University of Texas at Austin. That focus on African-American identity is also why Cokley and others consider the association their "professional home."

ABPsi is one of four ethnic-minority psychological associations. The three others are the Asian American Psychological Association, the Society of Indian Psychologists and the National Latina/o Psychological Association. Each group is invited to send a nonvoting delegate to the APA Council of Representatives; all of them except ABPsi send such a delegate.

What the organizations have in common are efforts to recruit and keep ethnic-minority students in psychology's pipeline, professional development activities and intimate networking opportunities. "Each of the associations has a different history, but in general they began in order for people to have a place to focus on the unique research, training and treatment issues related to ethnic-minority psychology," says APA President Melba J. T. Vasquez, PhD. "When these organizations were established, APA wasn't seen as a place that provided that. But even when APA started to become more open and inclusive, these associations have continued because they offer a unique place to address those issues."

You don't have to be a particular ethnicity to join any of these groups. "Ethnic-minority psychological associations tend to be welcoming of allies—people who share an interest in ethnic-minority psychology," Vasquez says.

But not enough psychologists and students know about the ethnic-minority psychological associations, says Cokley. "There needs to be more of an effort made," he says. "The ethnic-minority associations need to communicate to the world what we do, and APA and others need to try to get to know us and our work."

Source: Clay (2011). Copyright 2002 by the American Psychological Association. Reprinted with permission.

INTRODUCTION, DEFINITIONS, AND CONCEPTUAL FRAMEWORKS

African American psychology encompasses many topics. In this chapter, we provide definitions and discuss conceptual frameworks for studying and understanding African American psychology. We then examine historical influences on the study of African American psychology. The contributions of African American psychologists in defining and conceptualizing African American psychology are discussed in a section on self-determination. As noted by the cover story, the Association of Black Psychologists (ABPsi) has been instrumental in defining and promoting the psychology of Black people. Following the section on "Self-Determination," we review the current status of African American psychology. Methodological issues are addressed, followed by a critical analysis. The chapter ends with a summary.

What Is African American Psychology?

Who Are African Americans and Other Racial/Ethnic Groups?

Prior to defining African American psychology, we define and provide data on African Americans and other racial/ethnic groups. The U.S. Census (2018b) defines *Black* or *African American* as "a person having origins in any of the Black racial groups of Africa." It includes people who indicate their race as "Black, African American, or Negro" or who provide written entries such as African American, Afro American, Kenyan, Nigerian, or Haitian. In this book, the term African American is generally used. However, in some cases, the term Black is used to retain the intent of authors in literature cited. African Americans may identify with other racial groups, and people of any race may be of Hispanic/Latino ethnic background.

Other racial/ethnic groups will be referred to in this book, and definitions of these groups are provided.

White—a person having origins in any of the original peoples of Europe, the Middle East, or North Africa; American Indian or Alaska Native—a person having origins in any of the original peoples of North and South America (including Central America) and who maintains tribal affiliation or community attachment; Asian—a person having origins in any of the original peoples of the Far East, Southeast Asia, or the Indian subcontinent including, for example, Cambodia, China, India, Japan, Korea, Malaysia, Pakistan, the Philippine Islands, Thailand, and Vietnam; Native Hawaiian or Other Pacific Islander—a person having origins in any of the original peoples of Hawaii, Guam, Samoa, or other Pacific Islands. Hispanic refers to people whose origin is Mexican, Puerto Rican, Cuban, Spanish-speaking Central or South American countries, or other Hispanic/Latino, regardless of race (U.S. Census, 2016b). See Table 1.1 for statistics on percentage of racial/ethnic groups in the United States. The terms "White," "Latino," and "Asian" will generally be used in this book. However, other terms (e.g., non-Latino White, Hispanic) may be used to retain the intent of authors in information cited.

Individuals may identify with two or more racial groups. The United States' biracial and multiracial population has grown over the past 20 years, and about 9 million Americans are considered multiracial, 2.1% of the population. However, Pew estimates about 6.9% of the population in the United States could be considered biracial and multiracial if the race/ethnicity of one's parents and grandparents were considered (Pew, 2015). Between 2000 and 2010, the number of White and African American biracial Americans more than doubled. Among African Americans with a multiracial background, 69% report that most people would view them as Black

TABLE 1.1 ■ Race and Ethnicity of Unites States Population

Race/Ethnicity	Percentage
White alone	77.1
Black/African American alone	13.3
Asian alone	5.6
American Indian/Alaskan Native	1.2
Native Hawaiian/Other Pacific Islander	.2
Two or more races	2.9
Hispanic/Latino	17.6

Source: United States Census (2016a).

or African American—and thus, their experiences, attitudes, and social interactions tend to be associated with the Black community. For example, African American multiracial individuals report experiencing discrimination to the same extent as those who are single-race African American. African American and White biracial adults are also 3 times as likely to report that they have a lot in common with people who are Black than they do with people who are White. It is important to note that African Americans are diverse and may identify as African American, Black, Black American, Afro-Caribbean, African, or some other designation. Research discussed in this book examines similarities and differences among Blacks based on whether they were born in this country or not.

African American Psychology Defined

African American, Black, and African psychology have been defined by several scholars. J. A. Baldwin (1986)—aka Kambon—defines Black psychology this way:

> African (Black) Psychology is defined as a system of knowledge (philosophy, definitions, concepts, models, procedures, and practice) concerning the nature of the social universe from the perspectives of African cosmology. Black psychology is nothing more or less than the uncovering, articulation, operationalization, and application of the principles of the African reality structure relative to psychological phenomena. (p. 242)

Fairchild (2000) defines African American psychology as follows:

> African American psychology is the body of knowledge that is concerned with the understanding of African American life and culture. . . . African American psychology focuses on the mental, physical, psychological, and spiritual nature of humanity. It is the collection of works that has been produced by African psychologists in the United States (African Americans) and throughout the world (p. 93).

African American psychology has been studied primarily from two perspectives. The first perspective is that psychological concepts and theories are universal and, thus, African Americans can be studied using universal laws and principles. Research on topics such as minority stress, stereotype threat, and identity assume that people across diverse cultural groups will exhibit similar behavior in similar situations and contexts. The second perspective, taken from African-centered scholars, is that African American psychology is the psychology of people of African descent and African beliefs and behaviors are central to the study of African Americans. In this book, we use a convergent approach that captures both perspectives.

Baldwin's definition encompasses an African-centered perspective. African-centered psychology is discussed in more detail in Chapter 2. African-centered psychology considers core values, beliefs, and behaviors found among people of African descent that are central to understanding African Americans. Likewise, Azibo (1996) considers African American psychology to be African or Black psychology. He writes, "All human life processes including the spiritual, mental, biological, genetic, and behavioral constitutes African psychology" (pp. 6–7). In these definitions, Baldwin and Azibo do not make a distinction between African psychology and African American psychology, arguing that all people with origins in Africa are African.

One way of understanding the two perspectives in the psychology of African Americans is to consider differences between two schools of thought regarding

Black or African psychology (Azibo, 1996). One school of thought is pro-Black, and the other is African. In contrasting the two, Azibo notes that the pro-Black school of thought has focused on the African in the U.S. experience and has not used the African structure to provide the framework for interpreting the experience of African Americans. Although this Black school of thought has been useful in changing myths about African Americans based on a deficit model, it does not capture the core of the African experience. To capture the core of the African experience, Azibo advocates that an African-centered proactive school of thought be taken. This school takes the position that African philosophy is critical to understanding the psychology of Black or African people. To understand African American behavior, one must understand the behavior of Africans.

Baldwin similarly makes a distinction between Black psychology and African psychology (Baldwin, 1991). According to Baldwin, Black psychology was formed as a reaction to Western psychology. The Black psychological approach concerns itself with the psychological consequence of being Black in America. However, Baldwin argues that because African people existed before European people as a distinct cultural group, it follows that a distinct African psychology existed, irrespective of when and how it was articulated by social scientists. Baldwin makes the point that indeed Black psychology is African psychology.

Convergent Perspectives

There are convergent viewpoints in conceptualizing the psychology of African Americans. Both perspectives acknowledge that African American psychology is a science and, consistent with a Western conceptualization of psychology, it is organized and structured. This means that there is a systematic approach to understanding the psychology of African Americans, although there may be disagreement on the methods used for conducting scientific work. Both perspectives consider the scope and content of African or African American psychology to be fairly broad and diverse. African or African American psychology includes the study of behaviors as well as thoughts, feelings, beliefs, attitudes, and social interactions. All perspectives underscore the importance of self-definition and self-determination. For example, from the perspective of African-centered scholars, self-knowledge is a requisite for achieving well-being. Similarly, other psychological perspectives emphasize that striving for self-determination is basic to human well-being (Bandura, 1982; Jenkins, 2005).

African and Western Psychology

African American psychology can be distinguished from Western psychology not only by the population studied (i.e., African Americans) but also by the nature of the discipline. Azibo (1996) distinguishes African psychology from Western psychology by its nature and essence. According to Azibo, the essence of African psychology was seen in the practice of the people from Kemet (i.e., ancient Egypt, the cradle of one of the first civilizations). The Kemet approach to understanding humans was through self-realization, whereas Western psychology's approach was through domination (Kambon, 1998).

One feature of Western psychology is the importance that is placed on observable behavior. Although Freud's influence made the unconscious a part of the scope of Western psychology, psychology has primarily focused on that which can be observed. The focus on observable behavior is attributed to the great weight that Western psychology has placed on prediction and control of the behavior of people.

African psychology considers self-knowledge and intuition to be as important as that which is observable (Grills, 2004; Myers, 1992).

In summary, there is no one definition of African American psychology. The definition depends on the perspective that is taken regarding the influence of African and American or Western cultures on the psychology of African Americans. We acknowledge both African and American or Western influences on behavior.

HISTORICAL PERSPECTIVE ON THE PSYCHOLOGICAL STUDY OF AFRICAN AMERICANS

Origins of African Psychology

According to Azibo (1996), African American psychology began in ancient Kemet (now called Egypt), a civilization that began around 3200 BC. Azibo writes that African psychology can be traced to the period during which Africans produced an "organized system of knowledge (philosophy, definitions, concepts, models, procedures, and practice) concerning the nature of the social universe" (p. 4). From this perspective, African American psychology preexisted Western psychology. African psychology is discussed in more detail in the next chapter.

On the other hand, Greek philosophy is credited as the origin of Western psychology. The word *psychology* is derived from the Greek work *psych*, which means "soul or mind" and *ology*, which means "study of."

European Scientists' Contribution to Racism

In 1976, Robert Guthrie published the seminal book *Even the Rat Was White*. A second edition was published in 1998. This book reviews the contributions of the European scientific community in influencing American psychology and beliefs about Blacks and how Blacks have been studied over the past two centuries. The book illustrates how scientific racism contributed to the perception of the inferiority of Blacks and provided justification for racism and oppression. Contributions from Guthrie's book are highlighted next.

Comparative Studies in Physical Anthropology

Studies by physical anthropologists in the late 18th century and in the 19th century compared differences in the physical attributes of Blacks and Whites (Guthrie, 1976/1998). These included skin color, hair texture, skull shape and size, facial structure, and posture. Observed differences were always found in favor of the superiority of Whites and the inferiority of Blacks. Studies that looked at skull size as an indicator of intelligence concluded that the Black man's skull and brain were smaller and therefore less complex than the White brain.

In 1898, the Cambridge Anthropological Society began a cooperative venture between psychology and anthropology. When scientists were sent to New Guinea to study the mental attributes of its residents, they concluded that the natives of the South Pacific were inferior to Westerners on all traits, including intelligence. This study was the beginning of studies of racial differences.

Darwin's Survival of the Fittest

In 1859, Darwin published his theory on the survival of the fittest. The key assumption of this theory was that only the strongest and most intelligent could survive. According to Guthrie (1976/1998), this doctrine greatly influenced American psychology by emphasizing individual differences, an assumption that currently underlies much of the work in psychology. The vast majority of research on African Americans within the field of psychology during the first half of the 20th century looked at individual differences in the psychological attributes of African Americans and Whites. The findings were generally used to support a perspective describing African Americans to be inferior on individual difference variables.

Galton's Eugenics

Galton's work in the 19th century also contributed to promoting a belief in the racial inferiority of Blacks. Galton's theory was that intelligence and other personality attributes were inherited. If intelligence was inherited, then one would not expect those of lower intelligence to improve in ability (Guthrie, 1976/1998). Galton's theory of eugenics was promoted to improve the race through selective mating and sterilization. The improvement of the human race could be achieved by genetic control of those who were of inferior intelligence and those who were social deviants. The application of eugenics resulted in Blacks and other ethnic minorities being disproportionately included among those who were inferior and unfit. Recent effort by a nonprofit organization, Project Prevention, to pay certain groups of women to submit to sterilization or to use other long-term forms of birth control is considered by some to be eugenics. These women are targeted supposedly because they are addicted to drugs, but they are usually poor and African American (Project Prevention, n.d.).

American Scientists' Contributions to Scientific Racism

Like their European counterparts, American scientists also conducted research to support the intellectual inferiority of African Americans (Guthrie, 1976/1998). The implication of this research on social policy has adversely affected African Americans.

Jensen's (1969) work on intelligence encouraged the belief that some people were genetically inferior to others. According to Jensen, intelligence was essentially determined at birth, and genetics or inheritance accounted for about 80% of intelligence. This theory is notably similar to that of eugenics. In regard to public policy, using a theory that intelligence is predetermined works to adversely affect people who may need environmental and social supports to improve their conditions. For example, compensatory programs such as Head Start were designed to provide economically disadvantaged children an academic boost prior to beginning school. However, if the reasoning is that intelligence is fixed at birth, there is little that can be done to change one's ability, and compensatory programs are not likely to do much good.

Research on the intellectual inferiority of African Americans is seen in more contemporary times in Herrnstein and Murray's (1994) book, *The Bell Curve*. These authors presented data suggesting that intelligence differs among racial groups and that African Americans are at the lowest end of the bell curve. A major point of their book is that most social problems, especially those found among economically and socially marginalized people, cannot be solved because they are linked to intelligence, which is mainly inherited. Therefore, environmental supports put in place to solve these problems will not be useful if the social problem is due to intelligence. A broad implication of *The Bell Curve* is that the poor, the uneducated, and the unemployed—among whom African Americans constitute a sizable percentage—will live unproductive lives. Social programs cannot help these individuals, due to their lower intelligence (Haynes, 1995). Another implication of *The Bell Curve* is that people who are socially and intellectually inferior cause many of the social problems in this country.

The Bell Curve has been subject to intense scrutiny and criticism because of its erroneous assumptions and methodological flaws (Fairchild, 1994; Haynes, 1995). The inference of causality based on correlational data is a major methodological flaw, as is the importance given to what an intelligence test means. That is, to assume that lower intelligence scores cause social problems is erroneous when cross-sectional correlational data are used to make these assumptions. Also, the assumption that an intelligence test score is the best indicator of intelligence, adaptability, and general life success is flawed.

Intelligence Testing

Intelligence testing, according to Guthrie (1976/1998), was an important factor in perpetuating scientific racism during the first part of the 20th century. Binet and Spearman's work contributed to scientific racism in that intelligence testing was used to show intellectual differences between Blacks and Whites.

In 1904, Alfred Binet, a French physician, developed the Simon-Binet Scale, the forerunner of the Stanford-Binet test of intelligence that is still in use today. Charles Spearman developed the two-factor theory of intelligence that says that mental tests measure two factors: a general factor and a specific factor. The assumption is that the general factor measures general intellectual capability. The problem with this conception of a general factor of intelligence is that it emphasizes the general intellectual capacity while deemphasizing other mental attributes that may be more contextual or culturally specific (Williams, Williams, & Mitchell, 2004).

The earliest test of racial differences in intelligence was done using the Binet scales in 1912. In this study, Alice Strong measured the intelligence of 225 White children and 1,125 Black children. Black children were also categorized according to skin color (dark, medium, and light). Strong (as quoted in Guthrie, 1976/1998) noted that the "colored children excelled in rote memory. . . . However, they are inferior in aesthetics judgment, observation, reasoning, motor control, logical memory, use of words, resistance to suggestion, and in orientation or adjustment to the institutions and complexities of civilized society" (p. 64). In other words, the Black children were inferior to Whites on conceptual and intellectual attributes.

In 1916, G. O. Ferguson published a study titled *The Psychology of the Negro: An Experimental Study*. This study was considered a classic. It reported that the Negro had deficits in abstract thinking but was very capable in sensory and motor abilities. Given capacity in these types of skills, Negroes should be useful for doing manual work. Overall, much of the early work of American scientists perpetuated the myth of Black inferiority.

Intelligence testing of African American youth continues to be a debated topic, especially considering that African American children are overrepresented in special education for intellectual disabilities (Graves & Nichols, 2016). See Chapter 6 for more discussion of intelligence testing.

STUDY OF AFRICAN AMERICANS IN AMERICAN PSYCHOLOGY

In American psychology, studies of Negroes, Coloreds, Blacks, Afro-Americans, and African Americans have been conducted throughout the last century in the United States. Often, theories and conceptual frameworks that may be useful for Western psychology have been erroneously applied to the psychology of African Americans. For example, consider the concept of *self-esteem*, a frequently studied topic in Western and American psychology. In understanding what self-esteem is from an African and Western perspective, one must understand the difference between Western and African conceptions of the self. Using a Western perspective, self-esteem can be defined as a feeling of liking and regard for one's *self.* From an African-centered perspective, the personal self is indistinguishable from the self that is derived from membership in the African community (Nobles, 1991). Therefore, one's affiliation with one's group defines one's view of self. The African proverb, "I am because we are, and because we are, I am," characterizes this notion of the self. Thus, the conceptualization of people of African descent may be different from that of Whites, and it also may function differently for African Americans than how it functions for Whites (see Chapter 3 for a more detailed discussion).

Another approach taken by American psychology has been to use information gathered from White populations as the norm and then to compare African Americans with Whites. This approach is seen with the use of measures that have been developed to assess individual difference traits. For example, continuing with the example of self-esteem, a measure of self-esteem that does not include the collective nature of self-esteem may not be relevant for some African Americans. Given the problem of non-normative data, it is important to include African Americans and other ethnic and cultural groups within normative samples when measures are developed. Fortunately, this is changing, and more contemporary research recognizes the importance of including diverse racial/ethnic groups when measures are developed. For example, the National Institutes of Health (NIH) requires researchers to include information about the inclusion of ethnic/racial minority groups in its application package (NIH, 2016). Alternatively researchers have developed culturally specific measures for African Americans (Belgrave, Abrams, Hood, Moore, & Nguyen, 2016; Utsey, Adams, & Bolden, 2000).

A related problem is when methods that are based on Western psychology are used to study African Americans. As will be discussed in Chapter 2, the method for acquiring knowledge may differ for different cultural groups. According to Africentric scholars, self-knowledge is the most important type of knowledge and is the basis for all knowledge. Self-knowledge then is more important than knowledge that is acquired from the external environment. In this regard, understanding how a person who participates in a research project perceives himself or herself may be just as important as seeing how he or she responds to external stimuli. Within American psychology, the preferred methodology for conducting research has been the experiment. Experiments are believed to be superior to other research methods in producing valid and factually correct information. Experiments also provide a context in which predictions—and subsequently, control—can be more exact. Yet experimentation may not be the best way to obtain information about African Americans. Other, more naturalistic methods, such as interviewing and systematic observations, may be more useful singularly or in conjunction with experimental approaches. A large percentage of studies done in American psychology have focused on differences between African Americans and Whites. During the first part of the 20th century, most of the research conducted on African Americans involved comparative studies that contrasted African Americans and Whites on individual difference traits (Guthrie, 1976/1998).

This focus on differences led to African Americans being viewed as having deficits on many psychological characteristics. And in fact, as stated previously, much of the earlier work in psychology focused on deficits among African Americans when compared with Whites. Studies that examine within-group differences among African Americans are just as important to aid us in understanding why some African Americans do well and others do not. In the next section, we provide an overview of earlier comparative studies done on African Americans.

Comparative Studies

The vast majority of the studies conducted by psychologists on African Americans during the first half of the 20th century were studies that compared Coloreds, Negroes, and Blacks with Whites. For the most part, these studies examined differences between African Americans and Whites on intelligence, mental ability, and personality. Studies were conducted with children, adolescents, and adults. Studies on intellectual differences employed standard individual intelligence tests such as the Stanford-Binet, as well as group tests to assess mental functioning. One test used was the Army Classification Battery (ACB). The ACB was developed by the Army to assess soldiers' aptitude on different assignments. The ACB test was used in several studies that examined differences in mental ability and intelligence between African Americans and Whites. One study that examined differences between Negroes and Whites on the ACB found that Negroes scored lower than Whites on intelligence (Roen, 1961).

Other studies conducted during the first half of the 20th century investigated differences between African Americans and Whites on personality attributes, traits, and temperaments. Findings from representative studies are reviewed next. The methods used to carry out these studies were influenced by the social and political climate of the time, with most findings reflecting negatively on African Americans. These studies, which almost always found inferior traits among African Americans, contributed to the climate of racism and discrimination against African Americans.

A study published in the 1920s is illustrative of the studies of this era. Peterson (1923) tested White and Negro children using several group intelligence tests and individual learning tests. He found significant race differences, with White children scoring higher on both group and individual tests. He noted in his findings that the White 8-year-old children scored higher than the Negro 10-year-old children. Peterson pointed out that these differences were especially salient because of the fact that 60% of the White 8-year-old children came from poor sections of the city, whereas 97% of the 10-year-old Negro children came from one of the best Negro schools in the city. He reported that about 83% of the Whites were smarter than the Negroes, and that only 15% to 18% of the Negroes were as smart as the Whites. According to Peterson, differences between the two groups were most striking on tasks that required abstract and logical thinking. In making recommendations stemming from his findings, he suggested that there be less abstract and conventional types of education for Negro children. Peterson did not mention that even though the Negro children may have attended one of the best Negro schools in town, these schools had substantially fewer resources than the poor White schools. In addition, access to community resources beyond the school might have been more available to White than Negro children.

Findings of inferior functioning among African Americans were also seen in early studies on personality traits. Roen (1961) found that Negroes in his study lacked self-confidence more than was the case with Whites. Furthermore, low self-confidence among Negroes was associated with lower intelligence test scores. Roen speculated that the lack of pride in historical achievement, coupled with a negative socioenvironmental context, led to internalized, intellectually defeating personality traits that contributed to lower intelligence scores.

Many studies found that African Americans had elevated scores for problem behaviors. For example, Hokanson and Calden (1960) found even when Negroes and Whites both came from predominantly Northern working-class settings, Negroes had personality deficits higher in several areas of the Minnesota Multiphasic Personality Inventory (MMPI). The authors suggested that special norms be developed for Negro and White subjects. Regarding general adaptation to society, studies found that White and Negro adolescents of similar mental ability differed in personal and social adjustment (Pierce-Jones, Reid, & King, 1964).

In a review of psychological studies published between 1943 and 1958, Dreger and Miller (1960) found that Whites were superior to Negroes on several attributes, including psychophysical, psychomotor, intelligence, and temperament traits (i.e., neuroticism). They noted that differences between Negroes and Whites were smaller among young children. In none of these studies did the authors find superior performance among African Americans.

Given the findings from psychological studies, it is no wonder there was an assumption of African American racial inferiority during most of the 20th century. These studies were conducted by researchers at prestigious universities who had the authority of their position and "scientific" credibility for their work (Guthrie, 1976/1998).

In spite of the reports of inferior psychological attributes found in most psychology publications, some scholars as early as the 1940s were questioning the racial bias of psychological tests, especially intelligence tests. In commenting on why test items that differentiate between Blacks and Whites should be replaced, Pastore (1946) pointed out that test items that differentiate between boys and girls are eliminated because they are unfair. However, items that differentiate between Whites and Blacks have not been eliminated in intelligence testing. He concluded that this leads to no differences being seen between boys and girls but differences being seen between Negroes and Whites. Such item selection procedures in this early work systematically support the finding of differences between racial groups and are based on values and other attitudinal assumptions regarding race and intelligence.

A large amount of research on African Americans published during the first half of the 20th century was concerned with whether the results of differences between Blacks and Whites were due to genetic inferiority or the environment. Studies were cited to provide evidence for both positions. Those who made the argument that the environment was the cause of inferior performance among African Americans presented evidence that African Americans could learn when provided an opportunity to do so. Witty (1945) argued that the scores for the Army General Classification test, a test of intelligence, were associated with educational opportunities for soldiers within their local communities. To support this argument, Witty provided evidence that Negroes improved in performance when given the opportunity. In a special training unit, people who were illiterate were given an 8-week course to develop fourth-grade skills. The essential skills were attained by 87% of the Negroes and 84% of the Whites. He concluded that these findings showed evidence that Negroes are equal to Whites in the ability to learn.

In accounting for environmental influences on low Negro self-concept, Grambs (1965) wrote,

> It does not take much imagination to understand what generations of being told one is unworthy will do to a group's own validation of its worth. . . . The self-esteem of the Negro is damaged by the overwhelming fact that the world he lives in says, "White is right; black is bad." The impact on the Negro community is to overvalue all those traits of appearance that are most Caucasian. Evidence is clear that in almost every Negro family, the lighter children are favored by the parents. (p. 14)

The first part of the 20th century saw much work devoted to justifying the inferiority of Blacks within American psychology. However, during the second half of the century some began to question this assumption.

Contemporary Research in African American Psychology

Contemporary writings and research on African American psychology are diverse, as will be seen throughout this book. Some topics have received more attention (e.g., racial identity, racism) than others. The methods used to conduct research are varied and include both quantitative and qualitative studies and studies with college, community, work, and clinical samples. Several studies have included national representative samples (e.g., National Survey of Black Americans) and have examined U.S.-born African Americans and Blacks born in other countries. Notably, more recent studies focus on within-group differences among African Americans rather than comparing African Americans with other racial/ethnic groups. More recent research has also focused on identifying strengths and resiliencies that promote well-being.

SELF-DETERMINATION

Several critical events provided the impetus for the development of a contemporary psychology of African Americans. A pivotal assumption was that African Americans had to define for themselves what constitutes the psychology of African Americans. The emergence of a voice among African American psychologists (albeit few in number) occurred during the sociopolitical struggles of the 1960s for civil rights and equality in all aspects of life. The demand for civil rights was seen in all institutions, including educational institutions. Black Nationalism and the Black Power movement were also driving forces for self-determination during the 1960s. These sociopolitical movements set the stage for self-determination.

African American Psychologists in the Early 20th Century

During the first part of the 20th century, a few African Americans were beginning to enter the field of psychology. Despite many obstacles, African Americans managed to become psychologists (Guthrie, 1976/1998). Two of the major obstacles for African Americans were geographical location of graduate programs in psychology and the cost of graduate school. Most graduate-level universities in the South, where the majority of African Americans lived, did not admit African Americans. This meant that African Americans had to go North in order to attend graduate school. However, out-of-state tuition was expensive, as were travel costs to get there. This situation, along with the low incomes of most African Americans during this period, made it very difficult for African Americans to go to graduate school even if they were accepted.

At this time, most African Americans attended predominantly Black colleges. White universities required African Americans who had received their bachelor degree from a predominantly African American university to complete an additional year of undergraduate school to demonstrate that they had the ability for graduate school. This resulted in a longer period of matriculation for African Americans than for Whites (Guthrie, 1976/1998).

Despite these obstacles, a few African Americans managed to obtain a doctoral degree (PhD) in psychology during the first quarter of the 20th century. Francis C. Sumner was the first Black to receive a PhD in psychology in the United States; he received it in 1920 from Clark University in Massachusetts. Because of this distinction, Sumner is referred to as the "Father of Black Psychology." Sumner conducted his dissertation research on the psychoanalysis of Freud and Adler. He became chair of the Department of Psychology at Howard University in Washington, DC. Howard became a leading university for providing training in psychology to African Americans at both undergraduate and graduate levels. Charles Henry Thompson was another early recipient of the PhD in psychology. He received his PhD in educational psychology from the University of Chicago in 1925. Dr. Thompson conducted his dissertation research on teacher curriculums. In 1933, Inez Beverly Prosser received a PhD in educational psychology from the University of Cincinnati and became the first Black female to receive a doctorate in psychology. In 1938, Herman Canaday at West Virginia State College convened Black professionals interested in Black psychology and established a Black psychologists committee within the American Teachers Association (ATA). The ATA was the professional organization for Black educators.

The Association of Black Psychologists

The Association of Black Psychologists (ABPsi) is featured in the cover story and is the membership organization for people interested in Black psychology. ABPsi is now 50 years old and was organized in 1968 when African American psychologists attending the predominantly White American Psychological Association (APA) conference reacted to what they felt were nonsupportive, if not racist, positions regarding ethnic minority concerns. A group of African American psychologists met during the 1968 APA meeting in San Francisco and generated a list of demands (Guthrie, 1976/1998). The reactionary position of African American psychologists at this meeting was consistent with the self-determination and protest ideology of the 1960s. African American psychologists were tired of being ignored and were fed up with research, policies, and programs that were discriminatory to African Americans.

The demands that African American psychologists made included the following:

1. The APA must integrate its own workforce with more African Americans.

2. The APA should work to gain the admittance of more African Americans in psychology graduate schools.

3. Racist content found in APA journals should be eliminated.

4. The APA should establish programs so that concerns specific to each minority group can be addressed.

Following the 1968 meeting, African American psychologists in attendance decided to form their own organization rather than to try to effect change within the APA. Robert Williams, one of the founding fathers of ABPsi chronicled the history of the organization in a book published on the *History of the Association of Black Psychologists* (Williams, 2008). The thrust of ABPsi today remains similar to that articulated 50 years ago. See http://www.abpsi.org for more information on ABPsi. Some of the agendas of the ABPsi today are as follows: One, to provide training and support to African American psychology students. The ABPsi encourages and promotes the professional development of African American undergraduate and graduate students through scholarships, support of students in their research activities, and publications directed at assisting students in their graduate education. The student committee (known as the Student Circle) of ABPsi provides support to and a forum in which students can address important topics facing them, the universities they attend, and communities in which they live. The Student Circle of ABPsi has been especially beneficial to students who attend predominantly White universities, as it introduces them to African American psychologists.

Two, ABPsi has been engaged in strong advocacy against racist and discriminatory practices within the discipline of psychology, as well as in other arenas. The ABPsi has emphasized the need for culturally competent practices, treatment, and services. As early as 1969, the year after the formation of ABPsi, African American psychologists were arguing against the use of culturally biased tests. Robert Williams, then president of ABPsi, asked for an end to using tests that were not standardized on African Americans, arguing that they were not valid. To illustrate what he perceived as cultural bias in testing, Williams developed a test labeled the "Bitch" test: the Black Intelligence Test of Cultural Homogeneity. Williams showed that when the Bitch test was administered to White samples, they fared poorly in comparison with African Americans. The discriminatory nature of testing as it affects African Americans continues to be one of the major issues addressed by ABPsi.

A more recent example of ABPsi's advocacy is its criticism of the National Institutes of Health's (NIH's) discriminatory policies that result in African American researchers being less likely than any other ethnic and racial group to obtain funding (Psych Discourse, 2011). The NIH is the United States' premier federal agency for funding and conducting research, including psychological research. Citing a study published on race, ethnicity, and NIH research awards (Ginther et al., 2011), ABPsi wrote in a position statement,

> In considering the potential for research funding to contribute heavily to the body of scholarly work, it is of utmost importance for the Association of Black Psychologists (ABPsi) to respond to alarming new evidence suggesting inherent racial bias within the funding process of the NIH. The researchers discussed findings that illustrated a significant difference in the racial/ethnic make-up of individuals receiving R01 research grants, even after all other factors had been controlled for. (Psych Discourse, 2011)

ABPsi offers several suggestions to remediate this disparity. ABPsi and/or its members have articulated positions on several other practices that are discriminatory against Black people and have promoted agendas that aid in improving the mental, physical, social, economic, and political status of all people of African descent. In this regard, ABPsi has developed position papers and press releases and has provided information to the public on racist research, practices, and policies. For example, a special issue of the official journal of ABPsi, the *Journal of Black Psychology*, was dedicated to exposing the fallacies found in the book *The Bell Curve*, which promoted racial inferiority (*Journal of Black Psychology*, 1995). A 2004 issue of the *Journal of Black Psychology* was devoted to HIV/AIDS epidemiology, prevention, and treatment for people of African descent (*Journal of Black Psychology*, 2004).

Three, ABPsi has been active in addressing social, psychological, and health problems found among people of African descent through training, education, and programs at the local, state, and national levels. Training in topics related to mental health, substance abuse, inequity in the criminal justice system, HIV, and children and families are offered by local chapters, at the national convention, and by members throughout the country. ABPsi and its members provide health screenings, mental health assessments, expert testimony, consultation to agencies, and other activities in communities throughout the United States.

Four, ABPsi has promoted an awareness of the problems and concerns facing Blacks throughout the Diaspora. A related mission is to increase connections and collaborations among Blacks throughout the world. For example, ABPsi has publicized racial apartheid in South Africa, tribal conflict, and famine in African countries. Annual national conferences of the ABPsi have included Blacks from other countries, and there have been collaborative activities with Blacks from other countries, including those in the Caribbean, Africa, and South America. Two ABPsi annual conferences have been international conferences, one held in Jamaica and one held in Ghana.

Toward a Black Psychology

A seminal message that contributed to the recognition of the field of Black psychology was articulated by Joseph White (1970) in an *Ebony* magazine article titled "Toward a Black Psychology." (An update of this article appeared as a chapter in the fourth edition of Reginald Jones's book *Black Psychology* [2004].) In this article, Dr. White, a professor at the University of California, Irvine, explained how it was difficult, if not impossible, to understand the psychology of Black people using theories that were developed by White psychologists to examine White people (Guthrie, 1976/1998). In this article, White strongly advocated a Black psychology defined by Blacks.

This article received a lot of attention from the public. Some felt that Joseph White's position was polarizing for African Americans. Others felt that this position dichotomized psychology into Black and White disciplines. Still others felt that a psychology formulated from the experiences of Blacks would marginalize Black psychology. The perspective that Black psychology was in some way different from White psychology was perceived by some as creating a lower-class psychology for Blacks. Others felt just as strongly as Professor White that it was time for Black psychology to be formulated for the authentic experiences of Blacks.

Over the next several years (until present), several books on Black psychology or African American psychology were written. Some of the earlier books included Reginald L. Jones's *Black Psychology* (1972), Lawrence Houston's *Psychological Principles and the Black Experience* (1990), and White and Parham's (1990) *The Psychology of Blacks*. The *Handbook of African American Psychology* was published in 2008 (Neville, Tynes, & Utsey, 2008).

The Journal of Black Psychology

The *Journal of Black Psychology* is the official journal of the ABPsi. The journal began in 1974, 6 years after the formation of the ABPsi, and has grown from publishing issues twice a year to publishing issues four times per year. In addition, special issues that focus on specific topics are published on a periodic basis. Some of the more recent special issue topics have included sickle cell disease, racial identity, African American children, African American girls, HIV prevention, substance abuse prevention, and health disparities. The *Journal of Black Psychology* publishes contributions within the field of psychology that are directed toward the understanding of the experience and behavior of Black populations. The major disciplines of psychology are represented in the journal, including clinical, counseling, social, educational, organizational, and cognitive psychology. Journal articles tend to be empirical but also include theoretical reviews, commentaries, case studies, and book reviews. The authors relied on the *Journal of Black Psychology* extensively in gathering research and literature for this book.

Studies of African Americans in Other Journals

There have been an increasing number of studies on African Americans published in journals other than the *Journal of Black Psychology*. This includes journals whose focus are on Blacks or African Americans (e.g., *Journal of Black Studies*), journals with an ethnic minority focus (e.g., *Cultural Diversity and Ethnic Minority Psychology*), and journals that are not targeted specifically to African Americans (e.g., *Journal of Counseling Psychology*). This increase has been partially due to the increase in African American psychologists, as well as to an increasing awareness of cultural diversity. Publications have expanded the knowledge of African Americans and informed the psychological community on culturally congruent approaches to studying African Americans. Recent writings have also focused on understanding African American behaviors from a positive, culturally appropriate framework rather than a negative, culturally deviant framework.

Influential African American Psychologists

Several African American psychologists have influenced the field of African American psychology. Next, we highlight individuals who have made important contributions. We selected these individuals based on several considerations: (a) These individuals were the first African Americans to obtain a doctorate in psychology or the first in other accomplishments, (b) they developed new theories and conceptual frameworks, and (c) they have conducted research that has impacted social policy and improved conditions for African Americans. Some have been influential because they have advanced theories that have been a catalyst for others who have followed them; still others have had a large impact because of how prolific they were. Some are listed because they have directly and indirectly influenced our teachings and writings.

Francis C. Sumner

Sumner, the first African American to receive a PhD in psychology in the United States (in 1920), is regarded as the "Father of Black Psychology" (Guthrie, 1976/1998). This accomplishment is noteworthy because at the time he received his degree, only 11 Blacks out of a total of 10,000 recipients had earned a PhD between 1876 and 1920 in the United States. Working against many barriers, Francis Sumner earned his degree at Clark University in Massachusetts. At the age of 15, he enrolled as a freshman at Lincoln University in Pennsylvania after having passed an examination in lieu of a high school diploma. He enrolled in Clark College in 1915 and also received a degree in English. Sumner joined the faculty at Howard University,

Washington, DC, in 1928 and was chair of the Department of Psychology from 1928 to 1954. During this period, he established strong graduate and undergraduate programs in psychology. Under his leadership, the department produced many influential Black psychologists and provided training, especially at the bachelor's and master's levels. Both Mamie Clark and Kenneth Clark, two other influential African American psychologists, received training at Howard University.

Inez Beverly Prosser

Inez Beverly Prosser, born in 1895, was the first African American woman to receive her PhD in psychology. She obtained a doctorate in educational psychology in 1933 from the University of Cincinnati. Her dissertation, which received much recognition, was titled *The Non-Academic Development of Negro Children in Mixed and Segregated Schools*. It was one of the earliest studies that examined personality differences in Black children attending either voluntarily segregated or integrated schools. Dr. Prosser concluded that Black children were better served in segregated schools. This research was one of several studies in the 1920s and 1930s that was part of the debate on segregated schools as maintained in the United States under the separate but equal doctrine of *Plessy v. Ferguson* concerning school environments of African American children (Warren, 1999). Inez Prosser is included because her achievement is notable and inspiring considering the immense barriers during her era for women and Blacks in education. Dr. Prosser served in teaching and administrative positions at Tillotson College in Austin, Texas, and Tougaloo College, in Tougaloo, Mississippi. Her influence would have been even greater had she not been killed in a tragic accident in 1934 at the age of 39.

Mamie Clark and Kenneth Clark

This husband-and-wife team is best known for their work on racial preferences among Black children. Their classic doll studies were published in the 1930s and early 1940s (Clark & Clark, 1939, 1947). In these studies, Black children were shown Black and White dolls and told to choose the one that looked like them, the one they preferred, the one that was a good doll, and the one that was a bad doll. The Clarks concluded from their findings that Black children preferred White dolls. This classic study led the Clarks to argue that Black children who attended segregated schools had low self-esteem. The findings were used in arguments against racial segregation, the most famous of which was the 1954 landmark case *Brown v. Board of Education*. Prior to this, Blacks had received inferior education in segregated schools. The *Brown v. Board of Education* landmark decision ruled that separate but equal education was unconstitutional. That is, schools could not be separate and equal at the same time. Although there were several subsequent methodological criticisms of the Clark and Clark doll studies, they continue to be classic studies of racial identity and preferences. Kenneth Clark was the first African American to be president of the APA.

William E. Cross

William Cross's model of the development of racial and ethnic identity has generated a considerable amount of work over the past four decades and continues to do so today. Cross's model was labeled a nigrescence model. (Nigrescence, a word with Latin roots, means to become black.) Nigrescence models accounted for the progression of African Americans through sequential stages to arrive at a mature racial identity (Cross, 1978, 1991). These stages were subsequently labeled as pre-encounter, encounter, immersion-emersion, internalization, and internalization commitment.

Each stage is characterized by certain affective, cognitive, and behavioral reactions. Racial identity theory is discussed more extensively in Chapter 3. Cross's model has been revised and augmented by several other scholars, including Janet Helms (also included as an influential psychologist) and Thomas Parham. Dr. Cross is also known for his book, *Shades of Black: Diversity in African-American Identity* (Cross, 1991). His model provided a framework for other models of identity development (e.g., Native American identity, women's identity, gay-lesbian identity, Asian identity). Dr. Cross is professor emeritus at the City University of New York. He spent many years on faculty at Cornell University and Penn State University.

Reginald L. Jones

Reginald Jones is included as an influential psychologist because of the large amount of work he published on African American or Black psychology. Jones published more than 20 books on African American psychology and related topics, and his books have provided comprehensive coverage of Black psychology. Many of his works are edited volumes that include a variety of authors, perspectives, and topics. His book on Black psychology was the first to be published on the topic. The first edition of *Black Psychology* was published in 1972, and the fourth edition was published in 2004. *Black Psychology* includes chapters on several topics, including African philosophy, personality, assessment, intelligence assessment, counseling, racism, racial identity, cognition, and language. We frequently consulted all editions of Jones's *Black Psychology* while writing this book.

Some of the other books on African American psychology that R. Jones edited include *African American Identity Development* (1998b); *Advances in African American Psychology* (1999); *African American Children, Youth, and Parenting* (1998a); *African American Mental Health* (1998c); *Black Adolescents* (1989); and *Handbook of Tests and Measurement for Black Populations* (1996). The books authored and edited by Dr. Jones have been used in African American psychology classes and similar courses throughout the country. Dr. Jones died in 2005 while a professor emeritus at Hampton University in Hampton, Virginia.

James M. Jones

James Jones is included as an influential African American psychologist for two reasons. First, his book on *Prejudice and Racism*, originally published in 1972 and revised in 1997, is a classic examination of prejudice and racism. In this book, Jones provides an analysis of the different types of racism—that is, individual, institutional, and cultural. A more recent book on the topic is *The Psychology of Diversity: Beyond Prejudice and Racism* (with Jack Dovidio and Deborah Vietze) (Jones, Dovidio, & Vietze, 2013).

Second, Dr. Jones substantially impacted African American psychology in his role as the director of the APA's Minority Fellowship Program for over 30 years. In this position, Dr. Jones was responsible for managing a program to increase the number of African American and other ethnic minority scholars who obtain doctorates in psychology. The mission of the minority fellowship program is to improve the quality of mental health treatment and research on issues of concern among ethnic minority populations in psychology by offering financial support and by providing guidance and training in becoming a psychologist. More than 1,500 students of color have benefitted from this program. The minority fellowship program began in 1974 with Dalmas Taylor as the first director. James Jones became director in 1977 and directed the program for many years. Dr. Jones is professor of psychological and brain sciences and director of the Center for the Study of Diversity at the University of Delaware.

Janet E. Helms

Janet Helms is an influential African American psychologist because of her vast contributions to multiracial counseling, race relations, and racial identity theory and development. Dr. Helms has written prolifically on the topics of race, racial identity, and multicultural counseling. She developed the Racial Attitude Identity Scale (RAIS), which is one of the most widely used measures in psychology. Her book, *Black and White Racial Identity: Theory, Research and Practice*, published in 1990, was one of the first published books on racial identity and is considered a classic. Other books include, *A Race Is a Nice Thing to Have* (Helms, 2008) and *Using Culture in Counseling and Psychotherapy: Theory and Process* (Helms & Cook, 1999).

Dr. Helms was on the faculty of the University of Maryland College Park for 20 years, where she trained more than 40 doctoral students who have become influential psychologists in their own right. In 2000, Teachers College, Columbia University, established an award in her name, the Janet E. Helms Award, in recognition of her mentoring. In 2000, she joined the faculty at Boston College and founded the Institute for the Study and Promotion of Race and Culture. Dr. Helms is a professor in the Department of Counseling, Developmental, and Educational Psychology. She continues to write and publish on topics in counseling psychology, including racial identity.

Margaret Beale Spencer

Margaret Beale Spencer has played a significant role in supporting our understanding of the development of African American children and adolescents. Dr. Spencer graduated from the University of Chicago's Child and Developmental Psychology Program, where her studies included the replication of the Clark and Clark doll studies. This work further clarified our understanding that children as young as 3 years of age are influenced by and have awareness of societal racial bias but that early in development, knowledge of these societal attitudes is unrelated to African American children's sense of self.

Dr. Spencer is known for the Phenomenological Variant of Ecological Systems Theory (PVEST), which uses a strength and resiliency framework to understand African American youth. Her work largely focuses on issues of identity, resiliency, and adaptive development within challenging developmental contexts. This has included work measuring the influence of neighborhood factors on the development of African American adolescents, as well as examining the ways in which the social ecology of African American youth plays a role in their construction of meaning and in their developmental outcomes (see discussion of PVEST, phenomenology, and ecological systems theory in Chapter 11). Her recent work focuses on the use of incentive programs for low- and high-achieving high school students and the role of skin tone in self-perception. Dr. Spencer is the Marshall Field IV Professor of Urban Education at the University of Chicago. Prior to this she was a professor within the University of Pennsylvania's Graduate School of Education.

Claude M. Steele

Claude Steele is best known for his work on stereotype threat and how it affects performance among minority groups beginning with his classic study, "Stereotype threat and the intellectual test performance of African Americans" (Steele & Aronson, 1995).

Stereotype threat occurs when a person believes that he or she is at risk of confirming a negative stereotype of his or her social group. The anxiety arising from stereotype threat can undermine performance of a task that may be viewed as nondescriptive of one's group. This classic study showed that Black students underperformed on an achievement test when their race was made salient. When race was not salient, there was no difference in the performance of Black and White students. This study has been replicated with other cultural groups (e.g., women, Latinos, Asians) and stereotypes (Spencer, Steele, & Quinn, 1999). Dr. Steele has also conducted research on self-affirmation and self-image and the role of self-regulation in addictive behaviors. His book, *Whistling Vivaldi and Other Clues to How Stereotypes Affect Us* summarizes research on stereotype threat and the underperformance of minority students in higher education (Steele, 2010).

Dr. Steele is a professor of psychology at the University of California, Berkeley where until recently he was the executive vice chancellor and provost for the University of California, Berkeley. He held leadership positions at several other universities including dean of the School of Education at Stanford (from 2011–2014) and provost of Columbia University (2009–2011). Dr. Steele has taught at several other universities, including the University of Utah, the University of Washington, and the University of Michigan.

Jennifer Lynn Eberhardt

Jennifer Eberhardt has made significant contributions to understanding how the race of African Americans impacts their treatment in the criminal justice system. Her research has shown that police officers are more likely to classify African American faces than White faces as criminal. She has further shown that the race–crime association implicitly leads people to attend more closely to crime-related images. In an experiment, people who were exposed to Black faces subsequently were more quickly able to identify a blurry image as a gun than those who were exposed to White faces or no faces (Eberhardt, Goff, Purdie, & Davies, 2004). Dr. Eberhardt's research has also demonstrated the impact of Africentric facial features. Her research showed that among defendants convicted of murdering a White victim, defendants whose appearance was more Africentric (e.g., darker skinned, with a broader nose and thicker lips) were more likely to be sentenced to death than if their features were less Africentric. A study on juveniles and sentencing found that simply bringing to mind a Black (versus a White) juvenile offender led them to view juveniles in general as more similar to adults and therefore deserving of more severe punishment (Rattan, Levine, Dweck, & Eberhardt, 2012). Finally, Dr. Eberhardt's work has considered how dehumanizing African Americans (i.e., implicit association as ape-like) alters judgments in criminal justice contexts (Goff, Eberhardt, Williams, & Jackson, 2008). Dr. Eberhardt has applied her research by working with police departments to recognize and address racial bias. She is professor of psychology and law at Stanford University. She was awarded the MacArthur "genius" award in 2014 for her work on stereotypes and criminal sentencing.

African-Centered Psychologists

Beginning in the 1970s, several African American psychologists began writing and educating people about the importance of understanding African philosophy as a basis for understanding African American psychology. These include Na'im Akbar, Asa Hilliard, Wade Nobles, Joseph Baldwin (aka Kobi Kambon), Daudi Azibo, Amos Wilson, Linda James Myers, Cheryl Grills, and Shawn Utsey. The work of these psychologists is often published in the *Journal of Black Psychology*. Chapters were also published in Reginald Jones's edited book *Black Psychology* (1972, 2004) and Neville et al.'s (2008) edited book, *Handbook of African American Psychology*. Several of these psychologists are highlighted in Chapter 2.

African Americans' Presence Within the American Psychological Association

The APA is a membership organization of approximately 116,000 members. The mission of APA is to advance the creation, communication, and application of psychological knowledge to benefit society and improve people's lives (APA, 2017a). Divisions within APA operate that are geared to disciplines and interests of APA members.

Several components of APA represent the professional interests of African American psychologists. APA's Division 45, the Society for the Psychological Study of Ethnic Minority Issues, encourages research on ethnic minority issues and the application of psychological knowledge to address issues of ethnic minority populations. One distinction between APA's Division 45 and the ABPsi is that APA's Division 45 supports issues of all ethnic minority groups while ABPsi is more specifically focused on Black issues. The official journal of Division 45 is *Cultural Diversity and Ethnic Minority Psychology*.

The Office of Ethnic Minority Affairs at APA seeks to increase the scientific understanding of how culture pertains to psychology and how ethnicity influences behavior. It also focuses on promotion, recruitment, retention, and training opportunities for ethnic minority psychologists, increasing the delivery of appropriate psychological services to ethnic minority communities, and promoting better inclusion of ethnic minorities in organized psychology (APA, 2017b).

STATUS OF AFRICAN AMERICAN PSYCHOLOGY TODAY

Teaching African American Psychology

Today, African American psychology is taught at many colleges and universities. The course is often cross-listed with African American studies. Increased interest in African American psychology is attributed to several factors. These include the growing appreciation for cultural diversity, increased enrollment of African American students, recognition of the contributions of African American psychology to general psychology, and increases in the number of African American faculty who can teach this course.

African American Psychologists

African Americans and other racial- or ethnic minority groups compose a relatively small percentage of the active psychology workforce (APA, 2015). The active psychology workforce is defined as psychologists with doctoral or professional degrees. In 2013, the racial and ethnic distribution of active psychologists was as follows: White (83.6%), Black/African American (5.3%), Hispanic (5%), Asian (4.3%), and other racial or ethnic groups (1.7%). While African Americans and other racial minorities compose a relatively small percentage of the active psychology workforce, there has been some improvement over the past eight years. African American psychologists doubled in the workforce from 2.7% in 2005 to 5.4% in 2013.

A large gender disparity exists among African American psychologists, and this disparity is greater than for other racial or ethnic groups. Among African American active psychologists, for every male there are 5.8 females. Among active psychologists of all racial and ethnic groups, females outnumbered male psychologists such that for every male there are 2.1 females. Among active psychologists, 66.1% are female, and 32.2% are male.

African American males are fairly rare in psychology. Only 5.3% of the psychology workforce is African American, and African American men compose a small percentage of this group. These statistics highlight a great need for African American male psychologists. One of the reasons for this disparity is that males do not pursue graduate studies in psychology at the rate of females. African American males are less likely than females to obtain a bachelor's degree, a prerequisite for enrolling in a doctoral program (Turner & Turner, 2015).

African American Faculty and Graduate Students in Graduate Departments of Psychology

African American Faculty

The presence of African American faculty in psychology departments, specifically graduate departments, is important. Graduate departments provide training at the doctoral level. African American faculty are important insofar as they generally tend to encourage research on issues of concern to African Americans, assist in recruitment and retention of African American students, and teach classes and integrate material on African Americans in the curriculum of courses taught. An APA survey of departments of psychology gathered demographic data on faculty and graduate students (Hart, Wicherski, & Kohout, 2011). From 2010 to 2011, out of the 520 U.S. graduate departments of psychology that responded to an APA-administered survey, fewer than 14% of their total full-time faculty were ethnic minority (Hart et al. 2011). Because all ethnic minority faculty are included in this figure, the number of African American faculty is much lower.

African American Graduate Students

Ethnic and racial diversity among graduate students is also important. In addition to being trained as a psychologist, graduate students fulfill many other roles. They are teaching assistants and instructors in courses; they advise and mentor undergraduate students around careers and personal and professional issues; in doctoral programs, they engage and train undergraduate students in conducting research; they work with faculty to conduct research; and they serve as role models for ethnic minority undergraduate students. Many African American graduate students, especially those in doctoral programs, study issues that are directly related to African American psychology. Our graduate students have been involved in HIV and substance abuse prevention programs and education in the local community, conducting research on eliminating health disparities, and conducting research on cultural attributes (e.g., racial identity, gender roles) and youth well-being.

Similar to faculty, the number of students enrolled in graduate programs is not representative of the racial and ethnic group representation in the United States. APA conducted a survey of 520 psychology departments with graduate programs (Cope, Michalski, & Fowler, 2017). Racial and ethnic minorities composed about 30% of the graduate students in psychology, and African Americans composed about 9.1% (see Figure 1.1). There was an increase among all ethnic and racial minorities in graduate programs from 2005 to 2015, from 26.3% in 2005 to 30% in 2015. African Americans in graduate programs

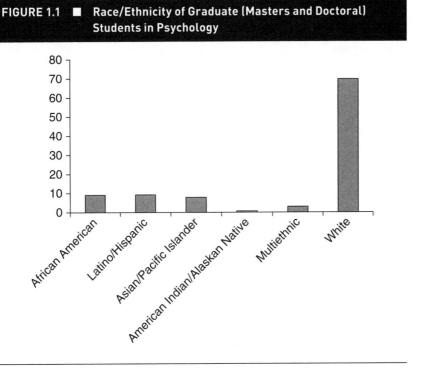

FIGURE 1.1 ■ Race/Ethnicity of Graduate (Masters and Doctoral) Students in Psychology

Source: Cope, Michalski, and Fowler (2017).

increased by 14% over this time period. Consistent with faculty, there were more women enrolled than men; 75% of graduate students were female, and 25% were male.

One of the barriers to the enrollment of African Americans in doctoral programs in psychology is the lack of mentoring at the undergraduate level in preparation for graduate school. When undergraduate students are not mentored or advised by faculty (or graduate students), they may not realize until it is too late (usually their senior year) what they need to do to gain admission to a doctoral program. Requirements for a master's program are generally not as competitive. Undergraduate students also may not have been involved in research experiences that are often required for graduate school.

Once enrolled in doctoral programs in psychology, African American students face several barriers; some of which are similar to and some of which differ from those faced by other racial and ethnic groups. Some of the barriers include microaggressions (i.e., everyday exchanges that send demeaning messages to people based on racial or ethnic group membership) (Sue et al., 2007), lack of culturally competent and culturally sensitive faculty who can mentor African American students, lack of faculty with expertise in topics related to African American psychology, and the lack of peers who share values and lifestyle.

METHODOLOGICAL AND RESEARCH ISSUES

Some of the methodological issues that were historically problematic in studying African Americans remain while there has been a shift in others. The best methods for studying African American populations may differ from the methods for studying

CONTEMPORARY ISSUES
WHY DO WE NEED MORE AFRICAN AMERICAN FACULTY?

When we have argued for more African American faculty who represent the student body, the community, and the "subject/participant" population, colleagues, particularly those who are not faculty of color, have reacted with surprise and challenged our assumption that African American faculty and researchers should be representative of the people studied, taught, and worked with. This is not to imply that those who are not of African descent cannot do good research, programming, teaching, and so forth with people of African descent but that people of African descent bring a lived perspective that is likely to inform research, teaching, and other aspects of behavior and interpersonal relationships. Still others in academia view African American psychology as a subfield of multicultural psychology and argue that attentiveness should be directed toward all diversity and multicultural issues rather than African American psychology specifically. While multiculturalism and attentiveness to diversity are important and indeed increase openness and appreciation for all cultural groups, a basic premise of multiculturalism is to know yourself and those with whom you are working. As the statistics in this chapter point out, the field of psychology has significantly fewer African American psychologists than are represented in the population. There are also significantly fewer African American graduate students than White graduate students who are studying to become psychologists. This is partially attributable to the low number of African American faculty at graduate training universities in the country. As will be seen throughout this book, African American researchers and teachers bring experiences and perspectives that are meaningful to the training of all students. All students, not just African American students, benefit from a diverse and representative faculty.

other ethnic groups. For example, the experimental method is the favored method in psychology and has been considered the gold standard for conducting research. However, it may not always be the best way to arrive at an understanding of the psychology of African Americans. Other methods, such as interviewing and observation, may be more appropriate, depending on what is being studied. African psychology (discussed in Chapter 2) considers self-knowledge and intuition to be as important a source of knowing as observable data. Self-knowledge is derived from asking people about themselves, not from observing them under experimental conditions.

Another methodological consideration is the relevance of the constructs that are being examined. A construct may not hold the same meaning for African Americans as for other ethnic groups. An earlier example we used was how the concept of self-esteem is used. For people of African descent, the concept of self includes the collective as well as the individual self. From a Western psychological perspective, the self is individualized. Another construct that may differ is that of the family. Who constitutes the African American family, and where are its boundaries? What is effective family functioning? The answers to these questions for African Americans may be different from answers for other groups. More research is needed to better understand when constructs are universal and when constructs are culturally specific to African Americans.

Another major concern in many studies, past and present, involves the issue of defining and sampling African Americans. When studies are presented focusing on African Americans, who are the individuals in the sample? Are they college students? Urban children, youth, and their families living in challenged communities? Suburban youth attending integrated schools? Recently migrated children or youth living in segregated communities with variable access to educational resources? First-generation African immigrants? A person's self-identification as Black, African American, or Afro-American also may impact study findings. Understanding, identifying, and describing the experience, history, and context of African Americans as a diverse group and considering this variability within our research samples is critically important in strengthening our understanding of the psychology of African Americans. From an Africentric perspective, this also raises questions regarding whether there is the need for pan-African psychology that includes, integrates, and compares work involving participants from the United States, Africa, and other settings relevant to the Diaspora.

The relatively low percentage of African American psychologists contributes to some of these methodological issues. The problems and questions of interest are often identified and studied by those least affected and who may not understand the right questions to ask and the methods to use. We return to methodological and conceptual issues throughout this book, pointing out how these issues affect the validity and practicality of studies conducted on African Americans.

Another methodological issue concerns the actual researcher or investigator. We all hold values about what is important to study. The investigator is, in a sense, an independent variable. Acknowledging what these values are is a necessary step in conducting research. For example, our values have been to focus more on positive attributes of African American psychology, not on negative attributes. This may be considered a reactionary stance given that we have seen so much published on negative attributes. At the same time, the range of functioning among African Americans is negative as well as positive.

CRITICAL ANALYSIS

We offer our analysis on several perspectives in African American psychology, including where we see the need for more research and writings.

The divergent perspectives on whether African American psychology should be based on African-focused or Western-focused psychology is long standing; this book will not resolve those perspectives. At the same time, we believe there is much to be gained by generating more theoretical literature and research concerning how both perspectives can continue to inform our understanding of African Americans, including areas where convergence and the integration of these perspectives is useful. Research on positive psychology may provide an area of convergence as this area of research focuses on topics of interests to Western- and African-centered psychology (i.e., prosocial behavior, spirituality, gratitude, and so on).

Within the field of African American psychology, a considerable amount of work has been done in the area of identity—ethnic identity, racial identity, and other aspects of the self. We have devoted a chapter in this book to the topic of identity. Several of the African American psychologists we consider influential (e.g., K. B. Clark, M. K. Clark, W. E. Cross, J. E. Helms) are best known for their work on identity. At the same time, we can also study the identity of the discipline of African American psychology. The same questions that are asked regarding individual identity development can be extended to the identity of African American psychology. What were key milestones in the development of African American psychology? What were the socioenvironmental and political factors that contributed to the development of African American psychology? What are some of the core topics that the discipline is concerned with? What will the discipline look like 20 years from now? It is our expectation that these and other questions will be addressed as African American psychology develops and maintains its identity.

Another issue concerns the influence of African American psychology on Western psychology. Just as Western psychology has had an influence on African American psychology, African American psychology has made a contribution to Western psychology. A core premise of African American psychology is that consideration must be given to understanding the values, culture, and ways of being of a group of people. This is certainly true, whether the group differs racially and ethnically or by age, disability and socioeconomic status, or sexual orientation. African American psychology has insisted on the acknowledgement of ways of being that are fundamental to our cultural group. Other groups can also benefit from this perspective.

Although Western psychology is sometimes criticized for its emphasis on universal perspectives and reductionistic strategies that ignore culture and context, it is also important that African American and Africentric psychological perspectives critically consider these factors in their psychological perspective on African Americans. To what extent and in what ways are other disciplinary perspectives on culture and context, especially history, important, made explicit, and integrated in our work in understanding African Americans? To what extent are interdisciplinary social science perspectives and strategies critical to pushing forward our knowledge base?

As we will see throughout this book, much of the study of African American psychology has been the study of differences between African Americans and Whites. In fact, we report many of these differences in this book. However, we need more research on how African Americans have survived and thrived individually, as groups, and as a people. We need more research on optimal functioning of individuals, families, and communities. We have attempted to highlight some of the areas where more research is needed throughout the book.

Summary

The proverb at the top of this chapter suggests that when the beginning is understood, the end will be successful. This chapter was written to inform the reader about African American psychology, its origins, and historical events and people. By so informing the reader of the history, we hope that the reader will be successful in learning about this field of psychology.

The origin of the study of African American psychology can be traced to Kemet: It is during this period that Black people produced a systematic body of knowledge. European theories, including Darwin's survival of the fittest doctrine and Galton's doctrine of eugenics, contributed to the belief in the inferiority of Blacks. This belief perpetuated discrimination and racism. Contemporary scientific work on racial inferiority is seen in Herrnstein and Murray's (1994) *The Bell Curve*.

During the first half of the 20th century, the study of African Americans in American psychology was largely comparative, and findings showed African Americans to be inferior to Whites on intelligence, personality, and general adaptation. Obtaining a PhD in psychology was very difficult for Blacks. Francis Sumner obtained his degree in 1920 and is known as the "Father of Black Psychology" because of this achievement. In 1968, a period of self-determination began. The ABPsi was formed by African American psychologists who felt that the predominantly White APA did not address the concerns of Black people. Since then, there has been an increase in culturally appropriate publications within APA and in general. There has also been an increase in the number of African American psychologists and an increase in awareness of cultural diversity in psychology. The APA has offices (e.g., the Office of Ethnic Minority Affairs) and programs targeted at African American professionals and students. More college students are becoming familiar with African American psychology because many colleges and universities teach courses in it.

2

AFRICAN-CENTERED PSYCHOLOGY

Wood may remain ten years in the water,
but it will never become a crocodile.

—Zarian proverb

LEARNING OBJECTIVES

- To define and understand African-centered psychology
- To understand the origins of African psychology
- To understand worldview dimensions found among people of African descent
- To appreciate the contributions of African-centered psychologists
- To become familiar with research in African-centered psychology
- To become familiar with programs that use an African-centered approach

ON THE NEED FOR EUROCENTRICS ANONYMOUS: AN ASSESSMENT OF THE JULY 2000 KEYNOTE ADDRESS

BY HALFORD FAIRCHILD

On July 31, 2000, Dr. Asa G. Hilliard provided the Keynote Address to the Annual International Convention of The Association of Black Psychologists in Accra, Ghana. At one point in the address, he suggested that Africans need a 12-Step Program to solve our addiction to Eurocentric thinking. We need a "Eurocentrics Anonymous."

Hilliard magnificently encapsulated the mission of Black psychologists: to rescue and

(Continued)

(Continued)

reclaim the African mind. His historically contextualized address relied on novelist Armah's *Two Thousand Seasons*, which suggested that the struggles of African people—throughout the world—have stretched through the millennia.

Hilliard makes no distinction between continental Africans and those throughout the Diaspora: We are one people—united in our history, in our struggles, and in our (eventual) liberation. Africans have been at war with invaders who sought to invalidate their humanity. Africans have endured many forms of genocide—physical onslaughts (murder, captivity, enslavement), and the destruction of culture. The cultural genocide robbed Africans of their names, religions and memories. Because of Divide and Conquer, Africans learned to hate each other and themselves.

And yet, despite the odds, Africans have survived. Hilliard celebrated the return of Africans from America through the "Door of (No) Return." But the emphasis on overcoming historical oppression isn't about the past, it is about the future.

The Sankofa symbol—a bird with its head turned toward the rear, with an egg in its beak—has future generations in mind. To acknowledge the tens of thousands of years of African development is to reclaim the past in order to chart a future course. As Marcus Garvey said, "Up you mighty race! What you have done before, you can do again!"

Hilliard illustrated that the liberation psychology literature already exists—in the works of Akbar, Nobles, Ani, Wright, Kambon, Armey, Garvey, Woodson—it is up to us to read it. We must study the success stories of African liberation: the Haitian revolution (and Toussaint L'Overture), Marcus Garvey (and the United Negro Improvement Association), Steve Biko (and the ANC [African National Congress]), Septima Clark (and literacy training), and others.

As Biko said, "The most potent weapon in the hands of the oppressor is the mind of the oppressed." What we need, Hilliard intones, is to break the chains of conceptual incarceration. We need Eurocentric Anonymous.

Source: Fairchild (2011). Used with permission of Psych Discourse.

INTRODUCTION TO AFRICAN-CENTERED PSYCHOLOGY AND THE AFRICENTRIC WORLDVIEW

The news story that opens this chapter provides an assessment by Dr. Halford Fairchild of how Dr. Asa Hilliard, a prominent Africentric psychologist, encouraged Black psychologists to reclaim their African identity by ridding themselves of Eurocentric thinking.[1] The focus on African-centered psychology is on African values and on ways of thinking and behaving that are indigenous to Blacks throughout the Diaspora. In this chapter, we discuss the influence of African culture and the Africentric worldview on the psychology of African Americans. The terms *African-centered*, *Africentric*, *African*, and *Black* psychology are used interchangeably in this chapter according to the usage by scholars cited. Likewise, the terms *Africentric* and *Afrocentric* are used interchangeably, following the spelling used by the scholar cited. In this chapter, we begin with a definition of African psychology followed by a discussion of *worldview*, including the Africentric worldview and its origins. We then describe the contributions of several African-centered psychologists. Africentric worldview dimensions are discussed next, and the question as to whether an Africentric worldview can exist among contemporary African Americans is addressed. In the section on African-centered research, we discuss two areas of research: (1) research on differences between African and European Americans on Africentric dimensions and (2) studies on the relationship between Africentric values and other variables. Methodological and research issues are addressed, including a review of some Africentric measures, followed by a discussion of empirically based programs. We then raise issues relevant to African-centered perspectives and contributions in our critical analysis. The chapter concludes with a summary.

What Is African Psychology?

Grills (2004) conceptualized African psychology by its focus on defining psychological experiences from an African perspective. According to Grills, African psychology consists of African values, ways of accessing knowledge, ways of defining reality, ways of governing and interpreting behavior, social relations, and designing environments to sustain healthy, adaptive functioning among people of African descent. African psychology is rooted in African culture and based on philosophical assumptions indigenous to African-descent people (Utsey, Belvet, & Fischer, 2009). African-centered psychology is a discipline whose purpose is to address the mental health needs of people of African descent from a self-empowering perspective (Obasi & Smith, 2009). Although these conceptualizations reflect some variation, the underlying and primary consensus reflected in these ideas is that African culture undergirds the behavior of people of African descent. African American psychology, in contrast, has been traditionally limited to understanding the values, beliefs, and behavior of Blacks in the United States. This book encompasses both African-centered and African American psychology.

What Is a Worldview?

A *worldview* is a way of thinking that organizes all aspects of one's life, including intra- and interpersonal thoughts and behaviors and one's functioning in social systems and institutions in the community (e.g., family, school, job, religious institutions) and in larger society. Intrapersonal thoughts refer to one's attitudes, beliefs, values, and expectations. Interpersonal behaviors refer to one's interactions with others. Worldviews provide us with guidelines for living: They affect our perceptions, thoughts, feelings, inferences, and behaviors and how we experience the external world. Simply put, a worldview provides us with a framework for interpreting events and understanding the world.

An Africentric worldview finds its base and foundation in the worldview of African peoples. It consists of the values, beliefs, and behavior of the indigenous people of Africa and those in the Diaspora who share in this cultural heritage. Butler (1992) characterizes the African worldview as follows:

> It represents a general design for living and patterns for interpreting reality. It is how someone makes sense of their world and their experiences—it determines which events are meaningful and which are not and provides the process by which those events are made harmonious with their lives. (p. 29)

Asante (2003) defines Afrocentricity as an attitude and actions that promote the well-being of people of African descent. "Afrocentricity is a mode of thought and action in which the centrality of African interests, values, and perspectives dominate. . . . It is the placing of African people in the center of any analysis of African phenomena" (p. 2).

The Africentric worldview has been contrasted with a Eurocentric worldview that is derived from European culture. The Africentric worldview differs from a Eurocentric worldview along several dimensions, including spirituality, interdependence and collectiveness, time orientation, death and immortality, and kinship (Akbar, 1991a; Nobles, 1991, 2015). These dimensions will be discussed later. In general, the Eurocentric worldview provides a cultural template for people of European descent, whereas the Africentric worldview provides a cultural template for people of African descent. Worldviews are, of course, not limited to people of African and European descent but exist among all ethnic and cultural groups.

It is important to note that there are variations across Africentric and other worldviews, and individuals may function along a continuum, with some people of African descent holding some Eurocentric worldview beliefs and some people of European descent having some Africentric worldview beliefs. However, from an African-centered perspective, it is expected that Africentric worldview dimensions will be found, in some degree, among most people of African descent.

Beginnings and Current State of African-Centered Psychology

African-centered psychology in the United States, as a topic and a perspective, is fairly recent. Most literature on African-centered psychology has been published within the past 50 years. However, the study of African psychology as an organized and systematic study of African people has existed since Kemet (3400–600 BCE) (Azibo, 1996). Although much of the scholarship on the Africentric worldview has come out of African studies, several African American psychologists have also contributed significantly to our understanding of the Africentric worldview.

During the 1960s and early 1970s, African American psychologists began to write about African-centered psychology and the Africentric worldview and how it could be used to understand the psychology of African Americans (Azibo, 1983; Nobles, 1976, 1986; White, 1972, 1984). These early writings coincided with other historical events such as the civil rights movement and the Black Power movement. Much of this earlier work focused on articulating what the Africentric worldview was and how it differed from the Eurocentric worldview.

Over the past 40 years, there has been considerable theoretical and empirical work directed at better understanding the Africentric worldview. African American scholars from various academic disciplines have contributed. Much of the work produced by African American psychologists has been published in the *Journal of Black Psychology*, the official journal of the Association of Black Psychologists (ABPsi). Other sources of information on African-centered and Africentric psychology include journals such as the *Western Journal of Black Studies* and the *Journal of Black Studies*. Several books have also been written. A notable work is Molefi Asante's classic book, *Afrocentricity: The Theory of Social Change*, first published in 1980 and updated in 2003. Azibo's (1996) *African Psychology in Historical Perspective and Related Commentary* was an earlier addition to the understanding of Africentric psychology. Kobi Kambon's book *African-Black Psychology in the American Context: An African-Centered Approach* (1998) also contributed to African-centered psychology. Representative African-centered research will be discussed later in the chapter.

Although African-centered psychology has borrowed heavily from African traditions and culture, psychology on the continent of Africa has encountered challenges similar to those faced by African American psychology in this country. Mpofu (2002), in an article titled "Psychology in Sub-Saharan Africa: Challenges, Prospects, and Promises," discusses several issues relevant to psychology in Africa.

Mpofu notes that most of the mainstream theories in Africa are Western and represent a minority worldview based on a heritage that does not contain the worldviews of the majority of the population. He identifies several challenges with the adoption of a Western worldview by psychologists in Africa. One limitation is that these mainstream theories are individualistic for the most part and do not reflect the psychological well-being of an African who would include the family and community. Practices are adopted from Western countries and often applied to African communities without cultural adaptation.

Regarding Africans' discourse with mainstream theorists, Mpofu notes that the conversations between Westerners and Africans have been unequal and in favor of Western cultures. He notes that the majority of the psychological works by European and North American scholars lack coauthorship with African professionals. According to Mpofu, this suggests that the work is written with European and North American audiences in mind, which may misrepresent African perspectives. Furthermore, there are concerns that these perspectives are not readily available for scrutiny by African audiences and may lead Africans to become dependent on Europeans and North Americans for knowledge.

At the same time, Mpofu does not advocate totally eliminating mainstream theories: He believes that human societies have similarities as well as differences. Similarly, mainstream Western theories could encourage the development of theories unique to Africans. Psychological constructs indigenous to Africa (and other developing countries) also have the potential to (a) reveal limitations in Western psychological constructs, (b) add to an understanding of psychological theories and social constructions, and (c) inform culturally sensitive psychological practices in African settings.

In contrast, Nobles (2015) advocates for a Black psychology in Africa devoid of Western psychology. He writes, "The discipline and practice designed to assist in the healing and management of the human affairs of African people must be uncompromisingly African centered and grounded in the philosophy and wisdom tradition of African people" (p. 402). Noting that Western paradigms have been used to demean, demoralize, and oppress African people, Nobles rejects their use in the psychology of Black people. He describes instead a psychology based on an African Grand Narrative, which would capture personhood, synergy, interconnectedness, circularity, holism, and collectivism. This practice of psychology would be a pan-African Black psychology that would involve Black psychologists throughout the African world.

In general, there is limited research and study of African psychology in Africa, and more research is needed, especially considering the diversity of people on the continent. Currently, there are only two major journals devoted to African psychology. These are the *South African Journal of Psychology* and the *Journal of Psychology in Africa*. Papers published in these journals are diverse and range from those that have used Western frameworks to those that have incorporated frameworks indigenous to African cultures. Bojuwoye and Edwards's (2011) paper on integrating ancestral consciousness into conventional counseling published in the *Journal of Psychology in Africa* is an example of the latter.

A related concern is the limited scholarship on people of African ancestry throughout the Diaspora. There are few psychology journals and books specific to Blacks in the Caribbean and Afro-Latinos, although papers on these populations are occasionally published in the *Journal of Black Psychology* and the *Journal of Black Studies*.

AFRICAN AMERICAN PSYCHOLOGISTS AND AFRICAN-CENTERED PSYCHOLOGY

Several African American psychologists have contributed to an understanding of African-centered psychology and the Africentric worldview. Seven psychologists and their contributions are discussed next.

Joseph White

Joseph White (1932–2017) was one of the most influential African-centered psychologists of our time. White's chapter on the psychology of Black people (White, 1972) is an important early work that challenged the use of traditional theories and frameworks to study African Americans. White is credited for the establishment of Black psychology as a discipline. His work helped to reshape thinking of how African Americans should be studied. White wrote,

> It is very difficult, if not impossible, to understand the lifestyles of Black people using traditional theories developed by White psychologists to explain White people. Moreover, when these traditional theories are applied to the lives of black folks many incorrect, weakness-dominated, and inferiority oriented conclusions come about. (p. 5)

White's work captured the attention of African Americans in the general public, as well as in academia. A paper he authored, published in *Ebony* magazine (1970) provided a convincing argument for why Black psychology was needed. *Ebony* is a popular magazine targeting Black readership. White's book on Black psychology (coauthored with Thomas Parham, 1990), *The Psychology of Blacks*, was also widely read by the general public, as well as the academic community. This book advanced an understanding of the psychology of African Americans long before it was recognized as a discipline in psychology. A theme throughout the book is that Western models of human behavior are not appropriate for studying African Americans and that African Americans must define their paradigms. The book is now in its fourth edition (Parham, White, & Ajamu, 2008).

Dr. White also has made significant contributions to establishing programs for helping college students succeed. He established the Educational Opportunity Program (EOP) while on faculty at the California State University at Long Beach. This program expanded from Long Beach to other universities in the state and provided more than 250,000 low-income and first-generation college students with opportunities for success.

Asa Hilliard

Asa Hilliard (1933–2007) was influential in many ways in promoting African-centered psychology. Dr. Hilliard was a historian and master teacher as well as a psychologist. At the time of his death, he was a professor of educational psychology at Georgia State University. Hilliard was instrumental in the development of systems for testing African American children and consulted with many school systems that were challenging these systems to eliminate testing bias against African American children. As a consultant to schools and teachers, he provided training on cultural competency and pluralistic education.

Asa Hilliard is also well known for his work on the study of ancient African civilization. He was a founding member of the Association for the Study of Classical African Civilization and served as its first vice president. He believed that the teaching of Black psychology must include an understanding of the ancient history of Africans and advocated for an African-centered education when educating African American children. He led many students and professionals on tours to Egypt, teaching them of the connection between ancient African civilization and contemporary issues facing African Americans. Although he received many accolades during his lifetime, he was also regarded as a humble and gracious individual who gave of his wisdom and time freely to others, especially to students.

Wade Nobles

Nobles advanced the understanding of the study of Black psychology in several ways, and his writings on African philosophy serve as the foundation for Black psychology (Nobles, 1980, 1991, 2004). Prominent in Nobles's contributions is his work on African philosophy and how it operates in Black cultures. Nobles's writings contribute to our understanding of several aspects of African philosophy, including religion and philosophy, notion of unity, concept of time, death and immortality, and kinship. His work addressed how these African perspectives were maintained by Blacks in this country. Nobles proposed that an orientation stemming from a particular indigenous African philosophy could be maintained only when its cultural carriers were isolated from alien cultural interaction and if their behavioral expression of the orientation did not openly conflict with the cultural–behavioral elements of the host society (Nobles, 1991, pp. 47–63). Consequently, in the United States, isolation of Blacks through slavery and other oppressive conditions helped to preserve African values. Nobles's contribution to African-centered psychology can also be found in his conceptualization of the self from an African-centered perspective. According to Nobles, the individual self-concept is intricately linked to the collective self. Hence, the individual self cannot exist independently from the collective self. One's personal identity, esteem, and worth are tied to one's identity as a person of African descent. Nobles's work has encouraged several scholars to study the relationship between individual and collective selves among African Americans (Townsend et al., 2007; Townsend & Lunphier, 2007).

Nobles's work has also focused on culturally grounded African-centered programs that address the problems of substance abuse and HIV in Black communities (Nobles, Goddard, & Gilbert, 2009). The Healer Women Fighting Disease (HWFD) Integrated Substance Abuse and HIV Prevention Program for Black Women is an example of one such program. It is discussed later in this chapter.

Na'im Akbar

Akbar has written and spoken extensively on the effects of oppression on African Americans and other Blacks. According to Akbar, many mental illnesses among African Americans are due to attempts to function within an oppressive and alien environment. Akbar classified and described some of the mental conditions that result from functioning within an alien environment. One such disorder is called an *alien-self disorder*. This disorder is found among people who behave in ways counter to their natural disposition. A symptom of this would be materialism. On materialism, Akbar (1991b) writes, "African Americans have been socialized with materialistic goals and evaluate their worth by the prevalence of material accomplishments" (p. 343). Another disorder is the *anti-self disorder*. This disorder is found among persons who identify with the oppressor and who are hostile to and reject members of their own groups.

Akbar (1991a, 2004) is also known for his work on the developmental stages of the study of Black or African psychology. He notes that African American psychology has been studied from three perspectives—Eurocentric, Black, and African. The Eurocentric perspective holds as normative a model of the middle-class Caucasian male. When this model is used, African Americans are seen as deficient and inferior.

The approach of the Black perspective is to prove that Blacks are not inferior. However, this perspective is reactive rather than proactive. Psychologists taking this perspective assume that differences between African and European Americans are due to environmental and sociological differences. The socioenvironmental context for African Americans is primarily labeled as "low class" and "ghetto." This perspective does not recognize the vast diversity among African Americans. It also does not recognize that not all Blacks are from urban, low-income, inner-city environments.

According to Akbar, the African perspective is "nature-centric" and can be described as natural psychology. This perspective assumes that there are standards and principles governing human behavior. One such principle is collective survival. From the perspective of this principle, a wide range of human behavior can be understood. In his most recent writing and speaking engagements, Akbar has addressed several social issues such as Black male–female relationships, African-centered education, alcohol and drug counseling, and counseling African American clients.

Kobi K. K. Kambon (aka Joseph Baldwin)

Kambon's contributions to Africentric psychology have been numerous. One major contribution has been in work on the African personality. Kambon distinguishes African-centered and non-African-centered theories of the African personality. African-centered theories assume that the African personality is core to people of African descent.

Another important contribution has been his development of measures that provide empirical support of African-centered principles (Jamison, 2016). To measure the African personality, Kambon developed the African Self-Consciousness Scale (ASC) (Baldwin & Bell, 1985). This scale has been used extensively in studies of Blacks (Baldwin, Duncan, & Bell, 1992; Pierre & Mahalik, 2005; Witherspoon & Speight, 2009). Several studies have examined and confirmed the validity of this scale and/or its subscales (Bhagwat, Kelly, & Lambert, 2012; Kambon & Bowen-Reid, 2009). The African Self-Consciousness Scale assesses how African Americans feel about African or African American culture and societal issues that are related to racism. Using this scale, Kambon and others have examined the prevalence of African self-consciousness among African American college students in both predominantly White and predominantly Black universities and within African American male–female relationships (Baldwin et al., 1992; Hamlet, 1998).

Kambon's (2003) book, *Cultural Misorientation*, discusses forms of cultural misorientation found among contemporary African Americans. According to Kambon, cultural misorientation is a condition that drives African people to engage in anti-Black, racially disempowering, and self-destructive behaviors. It represents the basis for Black personality disorder. Examples of cultural misorientation can be seen in education, religious practices, and the media. For example, regarding the media, Kambon posits that media in America are controlled by and based on Eurocentric imagery. Africans subsequently accept Eurocentric media and perpetuate its imagery in Black-owned media as well.

Linda James Myers

Myers's contribution is found in her writings on an optimal worldview and African psychology (Myers, 1988, 2009). Although Myers examines the oppression of African Americans, her theory is not exclusive to this group. Rather, she promotes social change for all oppressed groups. Myers's optimal worldview theory helps to promote an appreciation of human diversity by encouraging an investigation of both human behavior and social roles such as gender and ethnicity.

In introducing an optimal worldview, Myers notes that our orientation is influenced by how we perceive the world. The world we see, hear, and feel through our senses is not an external world but our own projection of reality. According to Myers, understanding the perceptual system of the dominant European culture is critical for understanding how knowledge about the external world is acquired.

The Eurocentric worldview places importance on the acquisition of material objects. Furthermore, external knowledge is assumed to be the basis for all knowledge. One acquires knowledge by attending to the external world. These values result in an identity or self-worth that is based on external criteria (e.g., what one owns, status symbols, job title). Myers maintains that these assumptions are the basis for racism and other -isms, all of which are suboptimal. According to Myers, not everyone of European descent is racist, but rather, anyone buying into these assumptions is at risk for consequences that naturally follow.

On the other hand, according to Myers, African knowledge is based on the ideas that reality is both spiritual and material, interpersonal relationships are valued, and self-knowledge is the foundation for all knowledge. Myers maintains that these assumptions result in an optimal worldview with resulting peace and happiness. Not everyone of African descent has this worldview, but this optimal worldview may be generalized across many people of African descent.

Myers also contributed to the development of the Belief Systems Analysis Scale (BSAS), which measures an optimal Afrocentric worldview (Montgomery, Fine, & James-Myers, 1990). The scale has been used in research that has examined Africentric worldviews in relation to other variables among African Americans, including ethnic identity (Brookins, 1994), depression (Neblett, Hammond, Seaton, & Townsend, 2010), and the imposter syndrome (feeling that one is faking being smart) (Ewing, Richardson, James-Myers, & Russell, 1996).

Cheryl Tawede Grills

Cheryl Grills has made important contributions to Africentric psychology through her theoretical work on African-centered psychology, her methodological work on the assessment of Africentric values, and community work that uses the principles of African-centered psychology to address social and economic problems. Her writings on African-centered psychology have identified and defined key components of an African-centered psychology such as ma'at, maafa, and Sankofa (these are discussed later in this chapter) (Grills, 2004).

Grills developed the Africentrism Scale with Longshore (Longshore & Grills, 1996). This scale is based on the principles of Nguzo Saba (discussed later in this chapter) and has been used in several studies that assess Africentric beliefs and values. For example, this measure has been used to examine Africentric values and variables such as academic self-concept (Williams & Chung, 2013), drug use (Brook & Pahl, 2005), and help-seeking behaviors (Wallace & Constantine, 2005).

Grills has successfully used an African-centered approach in community work to address problems in the Black community. These include programs and interventions aimed at reducing relapse among drug abusers (Longshore & Grills, 2000). Her most recent work with community groups involves creating healthy environments to improve health conditions in African American communities (e.g., obesity, access to healthy foods [Grills, Villanueva, Subica, & Douglas, 2014]).

These seven African-centered psychologists have all made unique contributions to understanding Africentric psychology. They share several common features: They all assume that the study of African American psychology has to be based on an understanding of the African worldview and that this worldview is adaptive and functional for people of African descent. They all assume that people of African descent are the best prepared to define and study Black people. Furthermore, they all believe that the methodology for conducting research and acquiring knowledge cannot be based on Western paradigms. Six are past national presidents of the ABPsi (J. L. White, Nobles, Akbar, Kambon, Myers, and Grills). Three have advanced Africentric psychology by developing valid and culturally relevant measures of Africentric beliefs and personality (Kambon, Myers, and Grills).

African-centered psychologists have been strong vocal advocates for social, political, and economic justice within the African American and pan-African community. They have been at the forefront fighting against oppression, domination, and racism and have spoken about how these conditions contribute to poor mental health among Blacks. The work of several early African-centered psychologists influenced their thinking and writing. These include Bobby Wright, who wrote in the early 1970s about Black menticide (refers to destruction of the Black mind; Rashid, 2005), and Amos Wilson, who chronicled in his classic book *Blueprint for Black Power* a detailed strategy for African American and Caribbean Blacks to gain economic power in the 21st century (Wilson, 1998). More recently, Shawn Utsey's work on Africultural coping and counseling people of African descent has spawned much research (Utsey, Abrams, Opare-Henaku, Bolden, & Williams, 2015; Utsey et al., 2009; Utsey, Brown, & Bolden, 2004).

AFRICAN PHILOSOPHY

Several African scholars have written on African philosophy, which provides a foundation for African-centered psychology. A thorough discussion of African philosophy is beyond the scope of this chapter but can be found in the *African Philosophy Reader*, edited by Coetzee and Roux (2003). This reader contains 49 papers, most of them written by African scholars, on the nature and discourse of African philosophy. A brief overview of some of the central assumptions of African philosophy written by African scholars is discussed next.

First, African scholars caution against making general statements regarding all Africans but believe that there are some broad generalities among people across the continent. Teffo and Roux (2003) write that there is diversity regarding metaphysical thinking in Africa, but the views are alike in a fairly large part of Africa, which can serve as representative of metaphysical thinking in Africa. They identify religious beliefs related to the African conceptions of God, the universe, and their interrelations as central to Africans. Also, African metaphysics are holistic in nature, and reality is a closed system so that everything bands together and is affected by any change in the system. Regarding dualism, Teffo and Roux note that dualism found in Western thought, such as a distinction between the natural and the supernatural and the material and spiritual, is absent from African metaphysics. Related issues are considered in greater detail in Chapter 10. In Western thinking, knowledge is the possession of a particular individual, and the central cultural focus becomes how this knowledge can be accounted for or assessed. In African thinking, the starting point is social relationships. One's selfhood is seen and accounted for from a relational perspective.

In considering epistemology, Kaphagawani and Malherbe (1998) discuss this topic in terms of how an African might come to know how knowledge is acquired. One way is through sages who, in African traditional society, are a rich source of knowledge. Sages may or may not hold formal education but are indeed possessors of knowledge; others look up to them and respect them for their knowledge. There are such individuals in every community; most often these individuals are considered elders.

Other African philosophical foundations are relevant to our consideration of African-centered psychology and Africentric worldview dimensions. African philosophy, as described by several African scholars, has provided the foundation for African American psychologists' description of the Africentric worldview dimensions (Akbar, 1991a; Azibo, 1996; Kambon, 2003; Myers, 1988, 2009; Nobles, 1991, 2004).

Although the dimensions of the Africentric worldview are discussed separately here, for the sake of clarity, these dimensions should not be considered independent. In fact, they are interdependent and highly correlated with one another. Central to Africentric thinking is the concept of holism. Holism provides an overarching framework for Africentric beliefs. All aspects of one's being are integrated, in harmony, and in balance.

The Africentric dimensions discussed next are not unique to people of African descent. See Table 2.1 for an overview of differences and examples of Africentric and Eurocentric world-view dimensions. Many of these dimensions are characteristic of other cultural groups. In sociological and psychological literature, the distinction has been made between individualistic cultures, such as that of the United States, and collectivist cultures, such as those found in Asia (Triandis, 1995). Individualistic cultures are those where people are oriented to look out for themselves and their immediate families, whereas in collective cultures, people are oriented toward the needs of the groups to which they belong (Shiraev & Levy, 2010). Africentric dimensions are likely to be found among people in collective cultures. Several non-Western cultural groups and ethnic minority groups in this country, including Latinos, Native Americans, and Asians, may hold worldview dimensions that are similar in some respects to the dimensions discussed next (Zea, Quezada, & Belgrave, 1996).

Spirituality

Spirituality is a fundamental Africentric dimension and is interwoven in the lives of African people. Mattis and Watson (2009) define spirituality as a relationship between transcendent forces (e.g., God, spirits) and humans that results in the individual's recognition of the sacredness of all things and a conscious commitment to live a life of virtue. In the United States, spirituality is seen in religious worship and rituals, such as attending Church, prayers, and celebration of religious holidays. Within Western culture, spirituality is reflected in religiosity and is kept separately from other aspects of one's life. This separation is, in part, due to the separation of Church and state. (See Chapter 10 for a fuller discussion of religion and spirituality in Africa.)

TABLE 2.1 ■ Contrasting an Africentric With a Eurocentric Worldview		
Belief System	**African-Centered**	**Eurocentric**
Spirituality	Spirituality is interwoven in all aspects of life. There is no separation of spirituality and everyday activities.	Spirituality is seen in practice of religious worship and rituals. There is separation of religion from other aspects of life.
Example	*It is ok to offer a prayer during a routine meeting.*	*I pray during religious services.*
Collectivism	Well-being of the group to which one belongs is most important. Emphasis is placed on maintaining harmony within the group.	Well-being of the individual and those closest to the individual is most important. Emphasis is placed on individual achievement.
Example	*I will make a career decision based on what is in the best interest of my family.*	*I will make a career decision based on what is best for my career.*
Time Orientation	Time is cyclical rather than linear. Time is flexible and is to be used rather than be dictated. The past is as important as the present and the future.	Time is a commodity and a resource. Time is exact, and precise time dictates when events start and end. Emphasis is on the future.
Example	*The party begins when I get there.*	*I have to be at the party at 8 p.m.*
Orality	Oral communication is important in conversation. Oral communication from sages and elders is valued.	Written communication is most credible, especially when information is delivered by experts.
Example	*Face-to-face discussions with an elder is useful for helping me be a better parent.*	*I find a scientific study on parenting to be useful in helping me be a better parent.*
Sensitivity to Affect and Emotional Cues	Attention is given to the emotional state of others, and it is important to recognize and share the joy and pain of others.	Attention is focused on one's own emotions, and the emotional state of others does not impact one's own emotional state.
Example	*I am ok if you are ok. If you are sad, I am sad.*	*Your being sad does not make me sad.*
Verve and Rhythm	One prefers movement and stimulation and changes in stimuli in environment.	Preference for consistency and routine environment.
Example	*I cannot sit down when the music is playing.*	*I am not moved to get up by music.*
Balance and Harmony With Nature	Preference is to live in harmony with nature and appropriately use nature's resources.	Preference is for the control and mastery of nature.
Example	I must not waste natural resources.	I can collect all the natural resources I can afford.

According to Wiredu (2003), the Ghanaian scholar, the Akans, as well as other African people, have a religious aspect to their culture and an unmistakable belief in a supreme being. He writes, "There is virtual unanimity in particular, on the report that Africans have a strong belief in the existence of God" (p. 21). Spirituality is not separated from other aspects of one's life in African culture. One's spirituality is woven into one's daily activities.

According to Nobles (1991), in traditional African culture, spirituality was such an integral part of one's existence that it could not be separated from the person. Spirituality was central in one's life from conception to post–physical death. One's being was, in fact, a religious experience. According to Akbar (1996), man is essentially spirit at the highest form of life. Spiritual beliefs have been compared with materialistic beliefs. The highest fulfillment for those with a spiritual worldview is the development of the self into a spiritual being that exists in harmony with other aspects of the universe. In contrast, the fulfillment of a material worldview is the acquisition of material goods and services. Societies that have reached the highest levels of human refinement, sensitivity, and cultural dignity are those with a widely accepted and powerful image of God (Akbar, 1996). Although spirituality and religiosity differ, they are associated. Spiritual people are likely to engage in religious practices, such as praying and attending Church. According to a study by the Pew Forum on Religion & Public Life (Pew Forum, 2009), African Americans are more religious than the U.S. population as a whole. African Americans have higher levels of religious affiliation, religious service attendance, and beliefs in the importance of prayer and religion in their lives. Eighty-seven percent of African Americans report belonging to one or more religious groups (Pew Forum, 2009).

Religious practices among African Americans are reflected in several ways. African Americans, when compared with other racial or ethnic groups, spend more time in Church and other places of worship (Taylor, Chatters, & Jackson, 2007). African Americans are also more likely to use spirituality to provide comfort (Taylor, Mattis, & Chatters, 1999) and as a framework for coping with stressful circumstances brought about my family, work, health, and financial problems (Holt, Clark, Debnam, & Roth, 2014; Mattis & Watson, 2009). African Americans report that in times of stress, faith (e.g., attending religious services, praying, using religious coping strategies, using ministerial support) is important (Mattis & Watson, 2009). Among people of African ancestry, spirituality and religious behaviors exist across all socioeconomic levels, age groups, and geographical locations.

Collectivism

A collective orientation is an Africentric dimension that reinforces interdependence, cooperation, and the motivation to work for the survival of the group rather than for that of the individual. Significant others are considered in one's thoughts and actions.

The collectivistic orientation differs from the individualistic and competitive orientation found in Western culture. The collectivistic orientation is reflected by the saying, "I am because we are, and because we are I am" (Mbiti, 1970). In a collectivistic culture, the experiences of the individual influence the experiences of the group and vice versa. The individual does not exist apart from the group (Nobles, 1991). Competition is minimized in collective cultures, and harmony within the group is emphasized. The collectivistic orientation values interpersonal relationships. Relationships with other persons are important because one's own well-being is interwoven with that of significant others. Okolo, the African philosopher, writes, "Bantu psychology cannot conceive of man as an individual as a force existing by itself and apart from its ontological relationship with other living beings and from its connection with animals or inanimate forces around it" (Okolo, 2003, p. 213). In African cultures, the collectivistic orientation helped to ensure the survival of the tribe. African tribes' strong commitment to kinship included the sharing of common beliefs, which helped sustain all members of the tribe (Nobles, 1991). When one member suffered, all suffered, and when one member did well, all did well. Loneliness and alienation are not found in African cultural groups because the members of each tribe are interconnected: Members have concern for and take responsibility for one another (White & Parham, 1990). Aggression and violence are minimized within tribes. From a collectivistic perspective, an act of aggression against another member of the tribe is viewed as an act of aggression toward oneself (Nobles, 1976). A mistaken notion involves too broadly defining the group within which the collective orientation is seen. Among collective groups, this collectivism is not extended to all persons but to the tribe or group to which one belongs.

Among many contemporary African Americans, collective orientation is reflected through strong commitment to the family, the extended family, and fictive kin (McAdoo, 2007; Nobles, 1991). Fictive kin are those individuals who are not related biologically or through marriage but who are treated as though they are. This collective orientation is reflected in African Americans' frequent contact with the immediate and extended family, the tendency of family members to live near one another, and the care provided for elderly and family members with disabilities.

The collectivistic orientation has important implications for studying and understanding the behavior of African Americans. The family and significant other members of the "family tribe" should be considered when one attempts to understand, diagnose, or treat individual-level problems. Within Western psychology, the unit of analysis has been based on the Eurocentric dimension of individualism. Consequently, much of Western psychology has focused on understanding and addressing problems at an individual level. This focus on individuation is not always appropriate for African Americans because significant others should be considered in diagnosis and treatment. For example, within African American communities, persuasive health care messages promote good health practices by appealing to the family or community rather than to the individual.

However, findings from research on collectivism versus individualism orientations among African Americans is equivocal. A study by Oyserman, Coon, and Kemmelmeier (2002) found that African Americans were more individualistic than European Americans and Latinos, especially concerning individualistic traits such as value for personal uniqueness, privacy, and competition, traits traditionally associated with individualism. Perhaps these components of individualism are different from other aspects of individualism, such as focus on self and exclusion of others. More research is needed to discern the different components of individualistic beliefs among African Americans.

Time Orientation

Time is viewed differently in Western as opposed to African cultures. Time within Western culture is future oriented, whereas time within African culture is past, present, and future oriented (Akbar, 1991a). Time for West Africans was experienced through the life of the tribe that goes back many generations (Nobles, 1991). Time in African cultures is cyclical rather than linear. The past is important in African cultures because it shapes the direction for present-day life experiences. African cultures make future decisions based on what has happened in the past.

In European culture, time is a concrete commodity to be bought and sold (Akbar, 1991a). It is seen as mathematical and bound by the clock. In contrast, time among

Africans is flexible and elastic and exists to meet the needs of the people. Africans experience time subjectively, which reduces the need to impose one's own time on others. According to Akbar (1991a), Eurocentric future orientation creates urgency and pressure because it is essentially impossible to ever catch up with the future. Future time orientation is reflected in Western psychology's emphasis on prediction and control.

Among African Americans, time orientation can be captured by the expression "colored people's time" (CPT). CPT means that arriving late is acceptable or that time must be experienced to be valid. A CPT orientation is found among Blacks throughout the Diaspora. Jones (2003) commented on experiences with time in Trinidad. He noticed that people from Trinidad have personal control over time; they are not driven or made a slave by it. Things start when people arrive and end when they leave. Accordingly, present-time orientation is not just a failure to value time and the future.

There is evidence of elastic and flexible use of time by African Americans when compared with European Americans. Rubin and Belgrave (1999) investigated differences in European and African American college students' responses to when they were likely to arrive at certain events (e.g., to meet a professor, go on a job interview, arrive at a social dinner). They found that African American students used time in a more flexible way, and European American students used time in a more mathematical or exact way. African Americans were more likely to respond that they would arrive at an event at an approximate time in contrast to European Americans, who indicated that they would arrive at an event at the exact time.

Hofstede (2001) surveyed respondents from 36 countries on their time orientation—that is, whether it was predominantly short or long term. People who live in cultures or countries with long-term time orientations tend to delay gratification of material, social, and emotional needs and think more about the future (Matsumoto & Juang, 2013). People who live in countries with short-term time orientation think less about the future and act more in the immediate present. Hofstede categorized the 36 countries into one of the three groups of 12 each: short-term time orientation, long-term time orientation, and time orientation that is neither short nor long. Seven of the twelve countries that he categorized as short term were in Africa (Botswana, Ghana, Malawi, Nigeria, Sierra Leone, Zambia, and Zimbabwe). Interestingly, the United States was also one of the 12 countries categorized as short term. None of the countries categorized as long term was in Africa.

Orality

Orality is a preference for receiving stimuli and information from the external world orally. This orientation may be contrasted with one that prefers written stimuli. African cultures, compared with Western cultures, are more oral in orientation.

Orality is used in Africa when information is handed down from elder to younger members of the tribe. The culture of a tribe was thus orally transmitted from generation to generation. On coming to the New World, the oral orientation helped slaves to retain their African culture and to function in the New World since they frequently were not allowed to read or write. The oral orientation is reflected in present-day African Americans' storytelling, rap music, and spoken word performance. With technologically advanced ways of transmitting information (e.g., Facebook, Twitter, Instagram, Tumblr), it is possible to receive virtually all types of information without oral communication. These means of communication allow for faster dissemination of information but may be counter to the oral preference of some people of African descent. More research on preferences for oral versus non-oral methods for communicating and obtaining information among African Americans is needed.

Sensitivity to Affect and Emotional Cues

The sensitivity to affect and emotional cues is an orientation that acknowledges the emotional and affective states of self and others. This dimension is related to the collective orientation as it includes a consideration of other people. Among people of African descent, there is an extended sensitivity to the emotional and affective states of others (Boykin & Ellison, 1995; Randolph & Banks, 1993). This orientation places emphasis on emotional receptivity and expression. It is seen when one empathizes with and relates to others. From this perspective, we have the ability to feel the pain and the joy of others and to expect others to feel our own pain and joy. Similarly, an individual's affective states are linked to the feelings and emotional experience of significant others. The sensitivity to affect and emotional cue orientation leads to synchronicity between one's emotions and affective states and others' thoughts and behaviors. For example, if a person feels happy, he or she is more likely to engage in positive behavior. If unhappy, he or she is less likely to engage in positive behavior.

Sensitivity to others' orientation can be contrasted to an emotionally isolated orientation whereby one's affective state is determined by one's individual and personal level of functioning. Here, one's emotional and affective state is determined in isolation from the emotional state of others.

Verve and Rhythm

The verve and rhythm dimension is reflected in behavior that is rhythmic and creative. This may be seen in movement, posture, speech patterns, and behavior. Verve can be considered an improvisational style among African Americans (Boykin, 1983; Chimezie, 1988). Verve and rhythm orientations are related to time orientations insofar as natural rhythm dictates how one functions and presents oneself (Nobles, 1991). A person with verve walks, talks, and presents himself or herself in a creative and expressive way. Rhythm is a recurring pattern of behavior that gives energy and meaning to one's experiences of the external environment (Jones, 2003).

Verve suggests a preference for the simultaneous, complementary, coordinated, or novel experience of several stimuli rather than a singular and routine stimulus. It is characterized by an increased appeal for stimuli that changes by increases in energy level and pace. According to Boykin (1983), verve is important in terms of how children learn. The didactic "teacher talks and students listen" mode of learning may not work as well with African American children as it does with European American children because of differences in preferences for verve and rhythm. African American children might learn better through multiple teaching and learning methods (interactions with each other, movement, touching, etc.) (Cole & Boykin, 2008). In speaking of rhythm and music, Ramose, the African scholar, expresses a conceptualization of rhythm and verve through a discussion of music and "be-ing." With music, there is the notion of participation rather than being a passive observer. For the Africans, the invitation of the dance of be-ing is indeclinable; there is a saying among Bantu-speaking languages that "you don't listen to music seated" (Ramose, 2003, p. 235).

Balance and Harmony With Nature

African thought is the continual quest for consensus aimed to establish harmony (Ramose, 2003). In African philosophy, it is important to have balance and harmony with nature (Nobles, 1991; Parham, 2009). Balance and harmony are necessary for one's well-being, and it is necessary to have balance between one's mental, physical, and spiritual states. Within the African tradition, this assumes that the various aspects of one's self are intricately connected. Spiritual imbalance is reflected by a physical and mental imbalance and vice versa.

The importance of living in harmony with nature is also seen in African cultures. Nature includes the animals, plants, and natural phenomena that constitute the environment in which humans live. The desired goal of life is not to conquer nature and the physical elements but rather to live in harmony with them (Ramose, 2003). According to Nobles (1991) and Parham (2009), everything in nature, including humans, animals, and plants, is interconnected. Therefore, control and mastery over nature, which is a prominent theme in Western philosophy, does not exist in African philosophy. Although these dimensions are not the only characteristics found among people of African descent, they are core to rendering this group distinct (Randolph & Banks, 1993).

Other Aspects of Africentric Psychology

In a thoughtful review of African psychology, Grills (2004) discusses seven related concepts that anchor and frame the study of African psychology.

1. *Ma'at* is a cardinal principle that governs the dynamic functioning of the universe and refers to balance and cosmic order. There are seven cardinal virtues of *ma'at*: truth, justice, compassion, harmony, balance, reciprocity, and order. The more one practices these virtues, the more developed one's self becomes.

2. *Maafa* is the word used to describe the enslavement of Africans by Europeans. The *maafa* was designed to oppress, humiliate, and destroy African people. Critical to *maafa* is the denial of the humanity of Africans. It is seen today in oppressive and discriminatory actions against African Americans.

3. *Veneration of the person* assumes the value of all living beings. A person's life is interwoven with the lives of everyone else. This includes both the living and the departed. In short, life is venerated, cherished, and celebrated.

4. *Spiritness* is a concept whose meaning is to be full of life—to have a mind, soul, energy, and passion. From the Africentric perspective, spirit is both real and symbolic and is the divine spark that makes humans who they are.

5. *Human authenticity* is the condition of being sincere and being who you are meant to be. It is the quality of being genuine and free of imitation. When authenticity is absent, one is not sure who to trust or rely on.

6. *Inclusive metaphysical epistemology* refers to the use of both affective and cognitive syntheses of information as a way of knowing. Reality is not limited to what is understood by the five senses, and rational logic is not the only way of obtaining knowledge.

7. *Sankofa* is an Akan Adrinka symbol that means in order to go forward, one must look back. In contemporary African American culture, this means that one must look back at historical events to learn from them and to plan for the future. Sankofa also symbolizes one's return to African culture and identity for guidance.

According to Grills (2004), understanding the concepts of Ma'at, *maafa*, veneration of the person, spiritness, human authenticity, inclusive metaphysical epistemology, and

Sankofa, along with Africentric worldview dimensions, are central to understanding African psychology.

One other aspect of African philosophy is that of reverence for the dead. The African scholar Oruka (2002) writes that one cultural value found among traditional African culture is the reverence for and communication with the dead. From this perspective, the wishes and expectations of the dead are to be advanced by the living.

Can an African Worldview Exist Among Contemporary African Americans?

The belief that an African worldview exists among African Americans has been questioned for two reasons. One, people on the African continent are diverse and thus not likely to hold universal beliefs and values. Two, Africans in America have been socialized for several centuries in this country and may have lost African traditions in the socialization process. In addressing these issues, Nobles (1991) wrote that although many West African tribes have different languages and religions and many unique customs, there are many similarities that suggest a common ethos among persons of African descent.

In the New World, enslaved Africans held on to the African worldview because it provided a familiar pattern of beliefs, habits, and ways of behaving that were adaptive in an oppressive environment (Nobles, 1991). Physical and environmental isolation helped Africans in the New World retain their culture. Blacks were cut off from the civilization of Europeans, and their culture was retained as a means of survival. Enslaved Africans were frequently not allowed to read or write, and there were none of our contemporary means—televisions, radio, Internet, cell phones, or other modes of transmission—by which they could assimilate European culture.

CONTEMPORARY ISSUES:
HIP-HOP: FROM WEST AFRICA TO THE BRONX

When we think about the origins of hip-hop music, we often cite the South Bronx during the mid-1970s as the time when contemporary hip-hop music emerged. Yet hip-hop goes back much farther to traditions and manners of expression that have existed for centuries in West Africa (Keyes, 2002). Payne and Gibson (2009) provide a thoughtful analysis of West Africa's influence on contemporary hip-hop in a paper on hip-hop music and culture. According to Payne and Gibson, the character and foundations of hip-hop can be seen in the musical expressions of griots of West Africa who were involved in the bardic tradition. Bards were believed to be able to display the spirit of Nyama; Nyama is the transference of positive and negative energy through speech, music, and movement. Bards also used poetry and folklore known as the animal trickster tales. The animal trickster tales made their way to the slave quarters and evolved in the United States into the slave trickster tales (Levine, 1977). These tales revolved around the theme of the powerless (that is, the slave) developing ways to outsmart and defeat the oppressors (that is, White slaveholders). These tales have similar messages to the unique and rebellious lyrics that took root in hip-hop music and culture. West African traditional and contemporary expressions highlight the salience of the oral tradition, a core defining attribute for people of African descent. Hip-hop music is here to stay and, with it, linkages to oral traditions in West Africa.

We see the continued physical and geographical isolation of African Americans in many urban areas today. African Americans almost exclusively populate some inner cities or specific urban neighborhoods.

A second way of transmitting African culture and worldview has been through the oral tradition. Enslaved Africans brought their oral tradition with them to the New World. Laws that did not permit slaves to read and write reinforced the retention of this tradition. Oral communication became essential for survival. This tradition has been passed down through the generations and can be seen in contemporary music and expressions, including hip-hop (see "Contemporary Issues: Hip-Hop").

Spirituality also helped Africans in the New World to maintain the African worldview. Under harsh and oppressive conditions, spirituality provided a reason for living. This ideology continues in present-day beliefs. The fulfillment of the spiritual self is not linked to external criteria but rather to a relationship with God or a similar higher power. One's life is meaningful if one is spiritual and if one lives for a higher calling, regardless of social status.

The extended family and fictive kin also supported Africans in the New World in maintaining African beliefs and preferences. In Africa, members of a tribe worked and lived interdependently. On the plantation, biological families were separated and sold. Once sold, families often did not see each other again. Therefore, biologically unrelated slaves on the plantation related to one another as family. The inclusion of nonbiologically related persons as family is known today as "fictive kinship" (McAdoo, 2007; Nobles, 1991). African American families and kin have had to rely on each other due to economic hardships, and this reliance has fostered collectivism.

Acculturation affects the extent to which African Americans have assimilated to the Eurocentric worldview. Acculturation is the degree to which a minority culture adopts the values and customs of the majority culture. There is a fair amount of acculturation among African Americans, with some individuals being more acculturated than others. The degree to which enslaved Africans were acculturated was determined by their geographical location. For example, the Geechees (also known as the Gullahs), a geographically isolated group of African Americans who live on the Sea Islands off the coast of Georgia, have behaviors and language patterns in which African culture is highly evident. Their geographic isolation has resulted in lower levels of acculturation relative to other African Americans (White & Parham, 1990). Residents on the Gullah Islands retained much of the culture from West Africa because of segregation until bridges connected the islands and the mainland in the 1950s. In more integrated and acculturated settings, the Africentric worldview may be present but more limited.

In an interesting analysis of traditional African values in American society, Jenkins (2006) describes how African values have been used in informal dispute resolutions among people living in the Gullah Islands of South Carolina. Restorative justice is a means to deal with social problems within a community and is similar to African tribal practices in which disputes were settled by elders and tribal chiefs. Use of traditional forms of dispute resolution is still present in African countries, although the dominant legal system now is most likely to be one with European roots. Here, the elders of the tribe or village arbitrate the dispute between parties, with the goal being to restore the relationship between the parties and obtain spiritual harmony in the community. This method of resolving conflict is contrasted with the use of formal laws, which assume that legal guidelines and rules are needed because people cannot control themselves.

Jenkins (2006) conducted interviews with 33 residents of the Gullah Islands who ranged in age from 15 to 89. Jenkins found that there were two forms of justice on the Gullah Islands: "just law," which was akin to distributive justice (similar to African tribal practices), and "unjust law." The just law is the law of the Church, with rules within the Bible that dictate where there is a violation and what the punishment will be. This informal process of dispute resolution was made formal through the Churches and praise houses located throughout the Gullah Islands after slavery ended. There was no involvement of the state in this form of dispute resolution. Disputes were handled through an informal process that used just laws as the foundation. The primary goals of just laws were reparations for the harmed party, community peace, and an assurance that individuals would follow either Church or community norms. The just laws seemed similar to the laws that governed tribal disputes in traditional West African culture. However, among younger participants (ages 15–18), the only accepted approach to resolve disputes was found within what was called unjust law, the more traditional form of law that we know as the judicial system.

Some scholars note that acculturation and deviation from an African-centered perspective is at the root of many of the social problems African Americans face today, including problems with drugs and violence, as well as child abuse and neglect (Akbar, 1991b; Azibo, 1996; Kambon, 2003). The loss of core Africentric values is attributed to many factors, including expansive indoctrination of European culture through the mass media. Conceptual models of acculturation and assimilation are discussed in greater detail in Chapter 3.

AFRICAN-CENTERED RESEARCH WITH AFRICAN AMERICANS

Although research in African-centered psychology is limited, there has been a growing body of work on this topic over the past 50 years. Studies have (a) examined differences between African Americans and European Americans on Africentric worldview dimensions (Allen & Butler, 1996; Grills & Longshore, 1996; Rubin & Belgrave, 1999) and (b) examined the relationship between the Africentric worldview and other psychological and sociological variables, such as racial identity (Brookins, 1994; Jagers, Smith, Mock, & Dill, 1997), self-esteem (Constantine, Alleyne, Wallace, & Franklin-Jackson, 2006), mental health (Azibo & Dixon, 1998), and drug use (Belgrave, Brome, & Hampton, 2000a). Prevention and intervention programs that are framed using an Africentric worldview are discussed later in this chapter.

Studies on Differences Between African Americans and European Americans on Africentric Dimensions

A few studies have looked at differences between African Americans and European Americans on Africentric dimensions. Others have examined whether Africentric worldview dimensions relate to adaptive functioning among African Americans and European Americans. One would expect favorable outcomes to be correlated with Africentric values for African Americans more so than for European Americans. A study by Ellison, Boykin, Tyler, and Dillihunt (2005) is typical of this research.

Ellison et al. (2005) examined classroom learning preferences among African American and White elementary school students. They administered the Social Interdependence Scale, which assesses cooperative, competitive, and individualistic learning preferences, to 138 fifth and sixth graders attending a school in a low-income community. Although, overall, all students preferred cooperative learning to competitive and individualistic learning, African American students reported significantly higher preferences for cooperative learning than did their White counterparts. White students preferred more individualistic and competitive learning than did African American students.

Other studies conducted on differences between people of African descent and people of European descent have revealed findings that are both supportive of and unsupportive of differences in worldview dimensions (Gaines, Larbie, Patel, Pereira, & Sereke-Melake, 2005; Komarraju & Cokley, 2008). For example, Gaines et al. compared cultural values among people of African descent and people of European and Asian descent in the United Kingdom. Two hundred twenty-seven individuals participated in this study. The authors found differences, with persons of African descent scoring higher on measures of collectivism, familism, and romanticism than persons of European descent. However, there were no differences between African-descended people and European-descended people on measures of individualism or spiritualism. African-descended people also did not differ from Asian-descended people on any of the variables. The finding of no difference between persons of African descent and persons of Asian descent was not surprising, given the "we" and "collective" orientation of both Asian and African cultural groups. These studies suggest there may be differences in worldview and related behavioral dimensions among people of African descent and people of European descent, but it is important to note that the studies are few. More research is indicated with larger and more diverse samples of people of African descent.

The Relationship Between Africentric Beliefs and Other Variables

Studies have examined the relationship between Africentric beliefs and other psychological and sociological variables. Africentric worldview constructs have been associated with racial and ethnic identity (Brookins, 1994; Townsend et al., 2007), academic attitudes (Jagers et al., 1997), self-esteem (Constantine et al., 2006; Ewing et al., 1996), and drug attitudes and use (Belgrave, Brome, & Hampton, 2000; Nasim, Belgrave, Jagers, Wilson, & Owens, 2007a).

Africentric beliefs have been linked to self-esteem and self-worth. High Africentric beliefs may be linked to self-esteem through involvement in positive family and community activities that promote feelings of self-worth and well-being. In addition, Africentric beliefs might positively influence ethnic identity, and ethnic identity might positively influence self-esteem. Constantine et al. (2006) investigated the relationship among Africentric cultural values and self-esteem and other variables in 147 African American adolescent girls (mean age = 15). Constantine et al. administered the Africentric Value Scale for Children (described later) and the Rosenberg Self-Esteem Scale, a global measure of self-esteem, and a measure of life satisfaction along with other measures. They found that greater adherence to Africentric cultural values were predictive of higher levels of self-esteem, perceived social support, and life satisfaction.

Thomas, Townsend, and Belgrave (2003) used data collected from 106 African American children to examine the linkages among Africentric values, self-esteem, and racial identity and how these factors affect adjustment to school. Adjustment to school was assessed by self-ratings and teacher ratings. The authors found significant associations between Africentric values, racial identity, and self-esteem. Moreover, Africentric values and racial identity were significantly correlated with teachers' ratings of the children. The authors summarized that the nature of the relationship was such that Africentric values were associated with higher self-esteem and racial identity, which, in turn, promoted psychosocial functioning that was more adaptive.

Similarly, Africentric values were found to be related to more favorable academic outcomes among African American college students. Using a sample of 119 African American college students, Williams and Chung (2013) found a significant relationship between an Africentric cultural orientation and academic self-concept. In this same study, the authors found a significant relationship between Africentric cultural orientation and involvement in culturally relevant school and community activities. The findings from this study suggest that Africentric values are linked to engaging in culturally congruent behaviors.

A few studies have examined Africentric beliefs and drug use, mostly among African American youth. A study by Nasim, Belgrave, et al. (2007) is illustrative. Nasim, Belgrave, et al. found a significant relationship between Africentric beliefs and other cultural variables (e.g., ethnic identity, religiosity) and alcohol use among African American adolescents who lived in low-resource communities. One hundred and fourteen youth ages 13 to 20 participated in the study. The authors found that Africentric beliefs delayed alcohol initiation: That is, adolescents with higher levels of Africentric beliefs initiated alcohol use later than those with lower Africentric beliefs. Africentric beliefs were also linked to lower lifetime alcohol use.

An Africentric worldview may also have indirect or protective effects, as well as direct effects, on drug use. Nasim et al. found that Africentric beliefs (along with religiousness) were especially beneficial in reducing alcohol use when participants lived and attended school in communities in which their peers were involved in deviant and problem behaviors.

With regard to mental health outcomes, Wang, Wong, Tran, Nyutu, & Spears (2013) investigated the influence of an Africentric worldview on reasons for living, an indicator of suicidal ideation. They also investigated the role of depression in this relationship. Two hundred and eighty nine African American college students completed a survey that assessed reasons for living, an Africentric worldview, and other variables. They found that strong Africentric values predicted lower depression, which predicted greater reasons for living. Neblett et al. (2010) also found a significant relationship between Africentric worldview beliefs and depressive symptoms with strong Africentric worldview beliefs linked to less depression.

In overview, there is some empirical (albeit limited) support for differences between African Americans and Whites on Africentric worldview dimensions. Africentric values seem to be linked to better outcomes, such as higher self-worth and less drug use. However, most studies have been conducted on adolescent and college samples. Research using diverse African American samples, including adult samples, is needed.

METHODOLOGICAL AND RESEARCH ISSUES

There are two central methodological issues to consider in African-centered psychology. One revolves around how we study people of African descent. The second issue is how we measure Africentric values, beliefs, and constructs. These are discussed next.

Methods for Studying People of African Descent

The psychology of African Americans cannot be studied with the same methodology used to study European Americans. Carruthers (1996) argues specifically against the use of the experimental method to study African Americans, noting that this method, with its emphasis on control and prediction, has been used to control oppressed people.

Kambon's (1998) analysis of Africentric and non-Africentric theories of African personality suggests another concern with the scientific method. The scientific method, in its attempt to isolate discrete cause-and-effect relationships between variables, may be inherently biased toward Eurocentric or non-Africentric explanations or perspectives of African behavior. Kambon asserts that non-Africentric (e.g., Eurocentric) theories of personality focus exclusively on the individual. Within Eurocentric psychology, each individual is seen as unique, with a personalized biopsychological condition that makes the person a distinguishable significant entity. Persons outside this unique individual are not considered as they are in African psychology.

Semaj (1996) also rejects the use of the experimental method as the scientific method to study Black people. Semaj rejects as a myth that science is objective, culturally universal, and unemotional. He disputes the notion that science leads systematically to truth. According to Semaj, the knowledge gained from studying society can never be passive but is always active in maintaining or in destroying a social system. Semaj further points out that despite the many academic degrees awarded, the problems of society remain relatively unchanged. Semaj (pp. 198–199) offers alternative guidelines for conducting research with people of African descent:

1. Self-knowledge should be of primary importance. "Know thyself."

2. There should be no artificial divisions via discipline; such divisions do not allow for the collective efforts that come about through diversity.

3. There should be no limitations on issues studied and methodologies used to study them. Scholars should be free to study that which is important and not just that which is dictated by one's discipline.

4. There should be no scientific colonization. Research should be conducted that will serve the interests of people rather than to advance a career or satisfy individual interests.

5. There should be concern with interpretation and application of data. The scientist should make sure that his or her findings are appropriately interpreted and applied.

6. The publication and dissemination of work should be done by those who share the vision of liberation.

7. Researchers should practice what they preach. The lifestyle of the researcher should be consistent with his or her work.

How Is the Africentric Worldview Measured?

Increased interest in the Africentric worldview has raised attention to methods of measuring this construct and its relevant dimensions. There have been several scales developed to assess Africentric constructs over the past two decades. Before describing the measures and the theoretical frameworks used to develop these measures, we make a distinction between the Africentric worldview and racial identity attitudes, as these terms are sometimes used interchangeably. Both are relevant to understanding the beliefs, attitudes, and behavior of African Americans. As noted previously, an Africentric worldview involves the set of cognitive and perceptual structures that organize our understanding that are derived from people of African descent and include those values and related beliefs that are reflected by the dimensions discussed previously (i.e., spirituality, collectivism, flexible time orientation, and so on). Ethnic identity consists of thoughts, behaviors, and feelings about being a member of a racial and ethnic group and feelings of belonging and affiliation with one's ethnic group.

Substantially more work has been done on the conceptualization and measurement of ethnic and racial identity than on Africentric worldview and values (Byrd, 2012; Cokley & Chapman, 2009; Helms, 1990; Roberts et al., 1999). We discuss some of the work on measurement of the Africentric worldview next.

African Self-Consciousness Scale

Baldwin (aka Kambon) developed the African Self-Consciousness Scale (ASC) to assess dimensions of Black personality (Baldwin & Bell, 1985). This scale is the most well-known among all such scales and has been widely used with African American populations. According to Baldwin, the core of the Black personality is oneness of being that is reflected in an extension of self and a communal orientation. The ASC assesses self-extension and communal orientation.

Several dimensions core to African self-consciousness are captured in this measure, including awareness that one is of African heritage, priorities placed on Black survival and liberation, priorities placed on activities directed at self-knowledge and self-affirmations, and resistance toward anti-Black forces and threats to Black survival. These dimensions cover educational, family, religious, and cultural activities; interpersonal relations; and political orientation areas.

The scale consists of 42 items. One such item is, "I don't necessarily feel like I am also being mistreated in a situation where I see another Black person being mistreated." A Likert-type format that ranges from 1 = "strongly disagree" to 8 = "strongly agree" is used. Higher scores represent stronger African self-consciousness.

The scale has been used in several studies, including studies of Africentric values and racial identity and psychological well-being (Pierre & Mahalik, 2005); community responsibility and achievement (Robinson & Biran, 2006); help-seeking behavior (Duncan, 2003); and counselor preference (Duncan & Johnson, 2007). More recent validation studies conducted with the ASC supports the validity of the scale or some of its subscales (Bhagwat et al., 2012; Simmons, Worrell, & Berry, 2008).

Asante Afrocentricity Scale

Pellebon (2011) developed a scale based on Molefi Asante's Afrocentric paradigm, believing it to be the most logical starting point for an Afrocentric Scale because Asante is the founder of Afrocentricity. Interestingly, Pellebon notes that according to Asante, while empiricism is not theoretically Afrocentric, since an Afrocentrist is a scientist, any critical analysis and study of human behavior must be supported by reason and evidence. The Asante Afrocentricity Scale has three main dimensions: (a) cultural centeredness (e.g., "If someone from my race is treated unfairly, everyone in my race has been treated unfairly"); (b) spirituality and ancestral connection (e.g., "My spirit is connected to all things in the universe"); and (c) Afrocentric epistemology (e.g., "An important source of knowledge and truth for me is my ancestor's culture and traditions"). The scale has 24 items and uses a Likert-type 5-point format that ranges from strongly agree to strongly disagree. The development of the Asante Afrocentricity Scale involved data collected on university students and faculty. More research with other samples is indicated.

The Communalism Scale

The Communalism Scale, developed by Boykin, Jagers, Ellison, and Albury (1997), assesses the Africentric dimension of communalism. Communalism is akin to collectivism. It reflects interdependence among people and is associated with cooperation, shared interests and activities, and concern for others. Communalism places greater emphasis on the survival of the group than on the individual. Communalism is a central dimension because it reinforces the other Africentric worldview dimensions.

The Communalism Scale measures how connected the respondent feels to others in his or her family, community, and other environments. The scale consists of 31 items that are rated based on Likert-type responses that range from 1 = "completely false" to 6 = "completely true." Nine filler items are included to reduce response set and social desirability. An example of a scale item is, "I place great value on social relations among people." The Communalism Scale has been used in several studies that have examined communalism and its relationship to other variables among African Americans (Bediako & Neblett, 2011; Schwartz et al., 2010).

Africentrism Based on the Principles of Nguzo Saba

The Africentrism scale was developed by Grills and Longshore (1996) to assess the principles of the Nguzo Saba, the seven principles of Kwanzaa. Kwanzaa is a 7-day celebration from December 26 to January 1. It was founded by Dr. Maulana Karenga in 1966 as an African American holiday, and Kwanzaa is based on the African Swahili word that means first fruits of the harvest. The principles of Nguzo Saba were originally intended to be celebrated during Kwanzaa, among African Americans; however, the principles are believed to be universal guidelines, and their usage is not restricted to African Americans or Kwanzaa celebrations.

The seven principles of Nguzo Saba represent a set of guidelines and a value system for healthy living that African Americans should strive for and live by (Karenga, 1988). The principles of Nguzo Saba are as follows:

Umoja (unity): To strive for and maintain unity in the family, community, nation, and race

Kujichagulia (self-determination): To define ourselves, name ourselves, create for ourselves, and speak for ourselves

Ujima (collective work and responsibility): To build and maintain our community together by sharing our sisters' and brothers' problems and making an effort to solve them together

Ujamaa (cooperative economics): To build and maintain our own stores, shops, and other businesses and to profit from them together

Nia (purpose): To make our collective vocation the building and developing of our community and to restore our people to their traditional greatness

Kuumba (creativity): To always do as much as we can, in the way we can, to leave our community more beautiful and beneficial than we inherited it

Imani (faith): To believe with all our heart in our people, our parents, and our teachers, along with the righteousness and victory of our struggle

The Africentrism Scale consists of 17 items. A 4-point Likert-type scale format is used, and items range from 1 = "strongly disagree" to 4 = "strongly agree." An example of a scale item is, "My family's needs are more important to me than my own needs."

Africentric Value Scale for Children

The measures discussed thus far are used with adolescents and adults. Much less has been done to assess Africentric constructs among children. This is partially due to the fact that children and adults understand differently. At the preadolescent stage, children are ego centered. It may be difficult for them to respond to concepts of spirituality, unity, and collectivism if they have not yet formed a personal identity. On the other hand, there may be some internalization of Africentric beliefs, especially in a cultural context where children are socialized and surrounded by significant others who hold these beliefs.

The Africentric Value Scale for Children (AVS-C) was developed to meet the need for a measure to assess Africentric values following an Africentric-based program designed to infuse Africentric values among youth (Belgrave, Townsend, Cherry, & Cunningham, 1997). Like the Africentrism Scale developed by Grills and Longshore (1996), items composing the scale were written to correspond to the seven principles of Nguzo Saba (Karenga, 1988). Factor analysis of 18 items resulted in three distinct factors: collective work and responsibility, cooperative economics, and self-determination. The collective work and responsibility subscale assesses the belief that African Americans are responsible for one another and should work together to improve their families and communities. The cooperative economics subscale assesses the belief that resources should be shared and maintained within the African American community. The third subscale, self-determination, assesses the belief that African Americans should make decisions about what is best for them, their families, and their communities. A Likert-type scale format is used with three response categories: "yes," "sometimes," and "no." An example of a scale item is, "African Americans should shop in African American–owned stores whenever possible." The scale has been used with children between the ages of 9 and 14.

The AVS-C has been used in studies that have examined the relationship between Africentric values and other constructs (Constantine et al., 2006; Kekwaletswe, 2008; Shin, 2011; Thomas et al., 2003). The scale has also been used in studies that have assessed program effects derived from Africentric-based programs for children and adolescents (Belgrave et al., 1997; Burlew et al., 2000).

Africentric Home Environment Inventory

The Africentric scales discussed thus far rely on self-report. Caughy, Randolph, and O'Campo (2002) developed an Africentric observational scale that assesses racial socialization in the home. According to Caughy et al., the sociocultural context of the home is one of the most important socializing environments for young children, especially children under the age of 5. Messages children receive in the home are often subtle and may promote pride in one's African heritage. Therefore, the Africentric Home Environment Inventory (AHEI) was developed to assess these messages.

There are 10 items on which to rate the home environment: (1) child has African American toy, (2) there is Black artwork in the home, (3) there are Black religious or other figurines, (4) there are African American children's books, (5) there are 10 or more African American books, (6) there is a variety of music, (7) there are toys to learn about African American history, (8) there are pictures of family members, (9) the family has subscriptions to African American periodicals, and (10) there is African fabric or print clothing. The AHEI was developed with 200 primary caregivers, the majority of whom were mothers. The instrument was found to be valid as indicated by a significant correlation with a racial socialization scale.

In the Caughy et al. (2002) study, the authors also correlated the AHEI with other measures collected from the child. They found that a home rich in African

American culture (as measured by the AHEI) is associated with greater factual knowledge and better problem-solving skills among African American preschoolers, even after adjusting for income and parental involvement. The measure can be used while in the home but can also be used in nonhome observations through a phone interview. The measure has been used in studies examining the home environment and racial socialization of African American children (Caughy, O'Brien, Nettles, O'Campo, & Lohrfink, 2006; Caughy, Nettles, & Lima, 2011).

In summary, some measures for assessing the Africentric worldview exist. These measures are based on the Africentric dimensions and the principles of Nguzo Saba. In general, these measures are valid and reliable. Research on measuring Africentric constructs is likely to continue.

EMPIRICALLY BASED PROGRAMS IN AFRICENTRIC PSYCHOLOGY

Research on the effectiveness of programs based on Africentric theory remains fairly limited. There have been more programs targeted at African American youth than adults. Increased interest in Africentric beliefs should encourage work in this area.

Africentric Programs for Youth

Jones and Neblett (2016) provide a comprehensive review of prevention and intervention programs targeted at positive youth development among African Americans that integrated Africentric principles in program format and activities. According to S. C. Jones and Neblett, culturally sensitive prevention and intervention programs provide additional benefits to those that use standard interventions. Articles selected for the review covered the years from 1995 to 2012. Programs that targeted racial or ethnic identity and racial socialization were also included in the review.

Seventeen programs were identified that focused on African American youth under the age of 18 and that integrated Africentric principles, racial or ethnic identity, or racial socialization. Out of the 17 programs, 15 integrated Africentric principles most often by using the principles of Nguza Saba. An example of such a program is one developed and implemented by Thomas, Davidson, and McAdoo (2008). The aim of this after-school program for high school females was to increase positive cultural factors such as ethnic or racial identity, racism awareness, youth activism, and a collective orientation. The 10-week program emphasized expressions of collectivism and unity and the shared historical experiences of Black people in the United States, along with the principles of Nguzo Saba. For example, Ujima was infused by having the group work collectively to complete group projects. Ujamaa was demonstrated by having participants hold a bake sale to raise money for a field trip to the African American museum. An evaluation of the program found significant improvements among intervention girls (and not comparison girls) on measures of racial identity, awareness of racism, and endorsement of Africentric values.

Africentric-based programs for children and youth often (1) use African proverbs and symbolism to relate to contemporary issues (e.g., when the cock is drunk the rooster will come to illustrate the dangers of drugs); (2) use African American adults as respected elders so youth participants can practice showing respect for elders; (3) educate participants about African and African American culture and history; and (4) use Rites of Passage rituals to formally recognize transitions from childhood to adolescence and transitions from adolescence to adulthood (e.g., a naming ceremony that bestows the child with an African name to symbolize what the child is like and can become) (Cherry et al., 1998). These programs are often used in conjunction with programs that seek to increase racial identity. Africentric-based programs have shown improvement among participants in several areas, including improved grades (Gordon, Iwamoto, Ward, Potts, & Boyd, 2009), increased family communication (Caldwell, Rafferty, Reischl, De Loney, & Brooks, 2010), increased drug use efficacy (Belgrave et al., 2004), decreased drug use and decreased sexual risk (Ferguson, 1998), increased self-esteem (Harvey & Hill, 2004), and increased ethnic identity (Lewis et al., 2012).

African-Centered Programs for Adults

Only a few African-centered programs for adults could be identified. Longshore and Grills's research demonstrated how an African-centered approach can be integrated into interventions and programs to reduce drug use among African American drug users (Longshore & Grills, 2000). Three hundred sixty-four African American drug users were recruited from community service providers, the streets, and jails for a one-session intervention. The intervention's content and format were based on the Africentric values of communalism and group process. The session began with a traditional African American meal. During the meal, participants were joined by an intervention team consisting of a counselor and a peer, who was a former drug user. A video that depicted African Americans was then shown. The final step was a counseling session that focused on the participant's recovery and specific needs. The video and the counseling session portrayed drug use as a personal problem but also a community problem rooted in cultural and power differences. The discussions acknowledged that there were negative experiences (e.g., racism, few job opportunities) for the participants and for all African Americans. The findings showed that drug use 1 year after the intervention was significantly less among participants in the intervention than the control group.

Nobles and Goddard's Healer Women Fighting Disease (HWFD) Integrated Substance Abuse and HIV Prevention Program for Black Women (Nobles et al., 2009) used African philosophy for framing and delivering HIV and substance abuse intervention activities. This program assumes that dysfunctional behavior among Blacks can be corrected through a process called culturalization, which involves cultural realignment, cognitive restructuring, and character refinement. An example of cultural realignment might be a shift from an individualistic value of personal responsibility to a collective value of collective and mutual responsibility. Cognitive restructuring involves changing how one thinks about one's self in relation to the world that one lives in. Character refinement allows the person to develop her own character in accordance with what is natural to her. The HWFD program has four core components: (a) the African Centered Behavioral Change HIV/AIDS & Substance Abuse Prevention Curriculum; (b) the Zola Ngolo Healing Ritual; (c) the Self-Healing Practice: Loving Oneself; and (d) Journaling. The intervention is delivered by trained women who are supported by a licensed mental health professional. There are 16 sessions that are carried out in 2-hour modules. An evaluation of 149 women who participated in the intervention group and the comparison group revealed significant changes for intervention participants in cultural realignment (e.g., increasing motivation, decreasing depression), cognitive restructuring (e.g., increasing HIV knowledge and self-worth), and character development (e.g., adopting less risky sexual behaviors).

Programs that use Africentric approaches tend to be better received by African American participants than those that do not (Chipungu et al., 2000). Chipungu reviewed 12 drug prevention programs that targeted African Americans. Chipungu et al. found that African American youth liked their Africentric prevention programs more than African American youth who were in other programs and non–African American program participants. Participants were also likely to view the program as more important to them if it used Africentric methods than if it did not. In summary, studies that use Africentric methods in programs are increasing. This early work suggests a positive benefit to children and adults using these methods. However, much more work is needed.

CRITICAL ANALYSIS

In this critical analysis, we discuss issues related to conceptualizing, understanding, and using African-centered psychology. We also discuss the Africentric worldview, programs and practices based on the Africentric worldview, and ways of conducting Africentric research.

African-centered psychology is based on African philosophy, and as we discuss in this chapter, there has been limited but emerging research on this topic. This research has been conducted mostly by African American psychologists. At the same time, we have seen much less work on African psychology conducted by scholars on the continent of Africa and in other countries with people of African descent (e.g., Caribbean countries). Mpofu (2002) raised a concern about ways in which Western and African psychology has been used in Africa and challenged us to think of ways in which Western psychology can learn from African psychology. Along these same lines, work done in Africa may be fruitful in helping us understand how African-centered approaches can be used with African Americans in this country. In deepening our understanding of African Americans through an African-centered lens, we must appreciate the complexity of both the continental and the American experience. The consideration of universal, regional, and ethnic variations across the continent; the historical and contemporary role of the colonial experience on the continent; and the differences between majority and minority experiences as social groups may further our understanding of complex influences on the psychology of African Americans.

We also raised the issue about the limited scholarly research on the Africentric worldview. Although there has been some theoretical and conceptual discussion of what the Africentric worldview is, there is a need to better elucidate how this worldview is manifested among contemporary African Americans. In reviewing the literature for this chapter, we could identify only a few published studies that have found differences in Africentric worldview dimensions among African Americans, Whites, and other ethnic groups. This is not to say that these differences do not exist, but this is an empirical question that needs to be addressed. For example, the study by Oyserman et al. (2002) found that African Americans scored higher on certain aspects of individualism than did Whites and members of other ethnic groups. This would seem counterintuitive, and a closer look at exactly what individualism and collectiveness means to African Americans might be instructive for future research. Although we do not encourage comparative studies between African Americans and other ethnic groups, more research is needed to elucidate how Africentric worldview values are manifested among African Americans.

As we further explore empirically the Africentric worldview, we have the increasing benefit of access to many useful and promising indices. We have the opportunity to use these measures to deepen our understanding, noting with specificity the relevant construct or dimension of focus. These measures can help us clarify whether what we believe or what we do is most important in our well-being and is most relevant to our intervention efforts. How are cognitive factors such as worldview, values, and beliefs relevant to life course outcomes? Are these cognitive factors more important than behavioral indices, attitudes about cultural group membership, individual ethnic identity, or cultural practices? How do measures of context, as opposed to social and relational preferences, inform our work?

In some psychological literature, we have begun to see authors encourage Africentric programming (Gilbert, Harvey, & Belgrave, 2009). These scholars have advocated using an Africentric framework as a best practice for programs and intervention work with African Americans. But there is limited published work on the efficacy of Africentric approaches, and most of these programs have targeted youth. In order to make judgments and recommendations that an Africentric approach is an empirically supported best practice, we will need to conduct more work in this area. This will include addressing core questions such as, what additional benefits (if any) do participants gain when programs are implemented using an Africentric framework?

Assuming that using Africentric principles in programming is more effective than not incorporating these cultural factors in intervention, a different question is how do we infuse this in our programs and work with African Americans? For example, what would a reading program look like for African Americans if it used an Africentric framework? How would clinical treatment incorporate an Africentric framework when working with a depressed African American adult male? While the work of Boykin et al. (e.g., rhythm and verve and collective orientation among children) and Wade Nobles has addressed these questions, additional research is needed. While core features of an Africentric approach have been identified by some scholars, are there other aspects that should be attended to in programs? In one sense, evaluation of the effectiveness of these programs would lend support (or lack of support) for the Africentric framework. If programs with an Africentric framework produce better outcomes for African Americans than those that do not use this framework, then we would have evidence that this framework is more useful for understanding the psychology of African Americans.

Yet another important consideration is how we obtain knowledge and understanding about African Americans. The majority of studies cited in this chapter have used Western methods to gather information about African-centered psychology. The vast majority of these studies have been conducted using paper-and-pencil surveys or questionnaires. Yet as noted, the nature of knowledge acquisition might differ for African people. For example, from an Africentric framework, sages (elderly and wise people in the community) are often the source of knowledge and truth and not data generated from a questionnaire. Qualitative and ethnographic research methods, methodologies typically not used in psychology, are encouraged. In addition, exploring the regional, historical, and cultural variability within and across the African American experience may also support a richer understanding by avoiding assumptions of the monolithic nature of the African American community. How do we understand the commonality and uniqueness of the African worldview of a 14-year old Jamaican American in Flatbush, a 60-year-old African American man in Tulsa, a 30-year-old Somali refugee in San Diego, and a 75-year-old Black woman in Birmingham?

Many of the African-centered theorists and researchers have contrasted an Africentric view with a Eurocentric view for illustrative purposes. At the same time, there are similarities and differences among all cultural and ethnic groups. Research that compares and contrasts the worldview of people of African descent with the worldview of other ethnic and cultural groups (Asian, Latino, and Middle Eastern) would be informative.

In terms of future work, there is much left to do. This includes more theoretical work examining Africentric constructs, work on understanding how Africentric values function in the lives of African Americans, and work that involves using culturally congruent methods for gathering data.

Summary

The proverb at the beginning of this chapter, "Wood may remain ten years in the water, but it will never become a crocodile," conveys the idea that although time and conditions change, core features of the person will remain the same. This is true of persons of African ancestry living in America.

The Africentric worldview is found among most people of African descent. A worldview consists of the values, beliefs, and behaviors of a group of people. African American psychologists began to write about the Africentric worldview in the late 1960s and early 1970s. Several psychologists have advanced our understanding of the Africentric worldview. Among them are Joseph White, Asa Hilliard, Na'im Akbar, Wade Nobles, Kobi Kambon, Linda James Myers, and Cheryl Grills. Much of the work on African-centered psychology has been published in The *Journal of Black Psychology*.

The Africentric worldview is characterized by several dimensions that differ from the Eurocentric worldview. Although there is a great deal of diversity among African Americans, the following dimensions are assumed to exist among most people of African descent to some degree: spirituality, collectiveness, flexible and past time orientation, orality, sensitivity to the emotional and affective state of others, verve and rhythm, and an orientation toward balance and harmony. Grills (2004) identified other concepts relevant to understanding African psychology: ma'at, maafa, veneration of the person, spiritness, human authenticity, and Sankofa. Several conditions helped Africans in the New World to maintain African values and traditions.

African-centered research has examined differences between African Americans and European Americans on Africentric dimensions and the relationship between Africentric dimensions and other psychological and social variables. Several measures have been developed to assess Africentric worldview dimensions. Research on empirically based programs suggest that programs that use an Africentric framework promote better psychosocial outcomes among both African American youth and adults than those that do not. Although there has been very promising work in extending our understanding of the Africentric worldview, we have much exciting work and deeper knowledge ahead.

Note

1. An earlier version of this chapter was published as a supplement by authors Belgrave, Logan, and Tademy (2000b).

SELF-ATTRIBUTES AND IDENTITY

The fowl does not act like the goat.

—Ghanaian proverb

LEARNING OBJECTIVES

- To appreciate the ways in which our understanding and construction of "the self" have changed over time

- To recognize the multiple dimensions of identity that are relevant to African Americans' understandings of themselves

- To understand the ways in which African Americans develop identity and self

- To understand why intersectionality of identities is important

- To become aware of the associations between dimensions of self and identity constructs and well-being and adaptation among African Americans

- To develop familiarity with measures used to assess racial/ethnic identity and related constructs

- To consider the effectiveness of programs that support the positive development of racial, cultural, and ethnic identity and positive self-concepts

"I'M NOT JUST BLACK!": EXPLORING INTERSECTIONS OF IDENTITY

BY FAYE Z. BELGRAVE AND SARAH J. JAVIER

Through a very complete body of research, the field of psychology has established that a person's identity is composed of several different parts. However, psychological research projects often focus on only one or two aspects of identity. As we move toward a more complete picture of human behavior, we must remember to keep in mind that the *intersections* of identity are a vital piece of that picture.

"Intersectionality" is a term that is coming to the forefront in psychological research. It encompasses race, ethnicity, gender, socioeconomic status, sexual orientation, and other intersecting, categorical dimensions that describe groups of people. For example, think about different parts of your identity. You may describe yourself as a single, older, African American female who makes a modest income. Or perhaps you are a young, White male who identifies as gay. These different parts of our identities make us who we are, and professionals interested in intersectionality have come to understand that these different components of identity are integral to why individuals do the things they do.

Intersectionality in National Data Sets

Data collection on the intersections of identity and how they affect health is of utmost importance. By examining combinations of identities (e.g. Gender × Race, Race × Sexual Orientation), researchers can more completely understand why some groups do better on certain health outcomes than others.

For instance, research on the intersecting identities of Race × Gender yields findings that there are different outcomes among African American males compared to, not only White males, but also African American females, including lower levels of academic achievement and higher levels of incarceration. These data can then be used to create culturally and identity-appropriate programs to decrease disparities and promote wellness among African American males.

But data aren't perfect. And often, these identities get lost, even in well-known national data sets. For example, because it is politically charged, sexual orientation may be omitted completely from national data sets, based on the idea that children and adolescents should be protected from this information. However, research indicates that sexual orientation may develop anywhere between middle childhood and early adolescence, and being a sexual minority is associated with a host of worsened physical and mental health disparities (e.g., higher levels of suicidality, depression, substance use, risk for sexually transmitted infections). What's more, not asking these questions limits the amount of research that can be done in exploring how sexual orientation intersects with other identities.

Youth Risk Behavioral Surveillance Survey

On August 11, 2016, the Centers for Disease Control and Prevention released sexual minority youth data from the Youth Risk Behavioral Surveillance Survey (YRBSS). The YRBSS is a survey collected from thousands of 9th through 12th grade students in the continental U.S. bi-annually. The survey asks questions about a diverse array of health behaviors, including violence, sexual activity, sexually transmitted infections including HIV infection, alcohol, tobacco, and other drug use, and physical activity.

One key feature of the YRBSS is its inclusion of identities in asking these questions. For instance, the survey asks items on race, gender, grade, and includes questions on sexual orientation. Research that can come from this report includes how the intersection of sexual orientation and other identities (i.e., race/ethnicity) affect these outcomes, if at all. Individuals at intersections of identity in adolescence are especially at high risk for mental and physical consequences, and intersecting identities may be a vital component to risk for these consequences. Data from the YRBSS may also help us understand whether certain intersections of identity act as protective factors that will help to combat negative health outcomes. For instance, African American adult females on the whole have been shown to smoke cigarettes at lower rates compared with both African men and White women. With the YRBSS, researchers can determine if this is true at a younger age, and whether this varies by grade, gender, sexual orientation, or any combination of these identities.

Source: Belgrave & Javier (2016). Blog from the APA Public Interest Directorate, Psychology Benefits Society, American Psychological Association (see https://psychologybenefits.org/2016/09/08/im-not-just-black-exploring-intersections-of-identity).

INTRODUCTIONS, DEFINITIONS, AND CONCEPTUAL FRAMEWORK

The study of self-esteem and self-concept has played an important role in the history of African Americans. Self-attributes such as self-esteem, self-concept, and racial identity have been studied more than any other topic in African American psychology. The popular notion that African Americans suffer from low self-esteem because of a history of oppression has not been supported. Not only are these self-attributes interesting to study in their own right, but perhaps more important is to study the relations between these constructs and the well-being and functioning of African Americans across several domains (i.e., academic achievement, social relations, and mental and physical health).

We begin this chapter by considering conceptualizations and definitions of the self and identity, with attention to cultural differences therein. Historical and contemporary models of self-concept among African Americans are then discussed. Identity development and change are discussed next because identity is not static across the life span. We also describe models of racial identity and review the research on variables related to high and low levels of racial and ethnic identity. We discuss other forms of identity and self-attributes, including sexual identity, gender role beliefs, feminism, and masculinity. As seen in the cover story, we also address the importance of intersectionality in this chapter. Intersectionality allows us to consider multiple aspects of identity at the same time. We show that racial socialization and acculturation are cultural constructs that, like racial identity, influence functioning and well-being. Research and methodological issues related to measuring identity and related constructs are examined, followed by a discussion of best practices for increasing racial identity and related constructs. A critical analysis is provided, and the chapter ends with a summary.

Defining Self-Esteem and Self-Concept

The self has been studied extensively in psychology. Many of the early studies in African American psychology were on the topics of self-concept and self-esteem (Clark & Clark, 1939). Self-concept involves beliefs and knowledge about the self. Our self-concept organizes and manages information about how we see ourselves (Baumeister, 1999). The self-concept is a component of our self-schema. A self-schema is a cognitive representation of the self. It organizes how we process information about the self and others (Fiske & Taylor, 1991). A question one may ask relevant to self-concept is, "Do I believe I am a smart person?" In contrast, self-esteem is one's affective or emotional reaction toward and feeling about oneself that is also evaluative. The question, "Do I like myself?" is relevant to self-esteem.

Cultural Differences in Self-Conceptualization

Conceptualization of the self depends on culture and socialization. Cultures can be categorized as collective, where people have an interdependent view of the self, or individualistic, where people hold an independent view of the self. Interdependent cultures include many from Africa, Asia, and Latin America. Independent cultures include the cultures of Europe and the United States. Differences in self-attributes among members of interdependent and independent cultures have been observed (Markus & Kitayama, 1999; Vignoles et al., 2016). Many of these self-attributes are described throughout this book. People of African descent are likely to have interdependent conceptualizations of the self, as are members of Latino, Asian, and Native American cultural groups.

In interdependent cultures, the self is seen as connected to and linked within the surrounding social context, and the self is considered in relation to others. This means that one's thoughts and behaviors are influenced by the relevant others in one's social context. For example, if I am a member of an interdependent culture, I cannot make a decision about employment without considering members of my family. Fitting in, attentiveness to others, and harmonious relationships are important.

Within individualistic cultures, emphasis is placed on the uniqueness of the self. If I am a member of an individualistic culture, my self-interest and well-being are more likely to direct my thoughts and actions than are the well-being of or my relationship with others. In addition, I will be less likely to care about the consequences of my actions for others. I will want to stand out as an individual. An example of cultural differences in self-attributes can be found in commercial advertisements in interdependent and individualistic cultures. In individualistic cultures, an ad might show how a product can be used to make a person "stand out from the crowd." This ad would appeal to one's need to be separate from others and to be unique. In interdependent cultures, an advertisement might emphasize that others use this product and that the use of this product would make one "fit in."

In interdependent cultures, relationships are important, and maintaining a connection to others means being constantly aware of others' needs, desires, and goals. The assumption here is that one needs to consider the goals of others in order to meet one's own goal.

In summary, one's beliefs and feelings about the self may be linked more to one's social group for those from interdependent cultures than for those from independent cultures.

Social Identity

Social identity is that part of an individual's self-concept that is derived from his or her membership in and adherence to the values associated with that culturally defined social group (Tajfel, 1981, 2010). Identity may be thought of as an adaptation to a social context (Baumeister & Muraven, 1996). Identity focuses on self-ascribed definitions that include social roles, reputation, values, and possibilities. Social identity may include one's self-concept with relation to nationality, religion, gender, sexual orientation, age, health status, and racial and ethnic identity. The latter two types of identity have been studied extensively among African Americans because of the physical salience of race in the American context.

Conceptualization of identity focusing on race can be contrasted with conceptualization of identity among other salient personal attributes (e.g., gender). Racial identity models have most often emphasized that race is the key defining feature of one's social identity group. Salience models assume that race is only one of several other types of referent factors that may determine salience of one's social identity group. Other factors might include ethnicity, religion, sexual orientation, or gender. Whether one's identity is based on race or some other attribute is likely to be influenced by contextual factors. For example, race is likely to be salient for a lone African American in a White group, whereas gender is likely to be salient for a lone female in an all-male group.

There is a difference of opinion regarding the terminology that best describes the identity of African Americans. Some scholars prefer the term *racial identity* because race is seen as the single most important aspect of the person's social identity (Helms, 1990). Others prefer the term *ethnic identity* because of the lack of clarity regarding what constitutes a race. Ethnicity is culturally prescribed, whereas race is conceptually linked to biologically based characteristics.

Many people have multiple social identities. W. E. B. Du Bois wrote about double identity, a term he called double consciousness, among African Americans more than a century ago (Du Bois, 1903). Research supports the notion of double consciousness among African Americans, as African Americans have conceptualizations of identity as an African American and also as an American (Brannon, Markus, & Taylor, 2015). Research by Brannon and colleagues showed that African American college students shifted self-conceptualization depending on the situational context. They behaved in more independent ways when primed with mainstream American culture, and they behaved in more interdependent ways (e.g., they were more cooperative) when primed with African American culture.

Racial Identity and Ethnic Identity

Racial identity is based on the perception of a shared racial history. Helms (1990) defines racial identity as "a sense of group or collective identity based on one's perception that he or she shares a common racial heritage with a particular racial group" (p. 3). Racial group orientation is the psychological attachment to the social category that designates the racial group to which one is a member (Helms, 1990). Ethnic identity is defined by involvement in the cultural practices and activities of a particular ethnic group and by positive attitudes toward, attachment to, and feelings of belonging to that group (Phinney, 1995).

In this chapter, the usage of one term over the other (i.e., racial identity vs. ethnic identity) corresponds to that of the particular author and literature being cited.

Other Forms of Identity and Related Constructs

Other aspects of identity include sexual identity, gender identity, and gender roles. Sexual identity is generally thought of as sexual orientation and one's beliefs and feelings about the individual or individuals to whom one is sexually and romantically attracted. Gender role beliefs are the expectations and beliefs that people hold as to how males and females are supposed to feel, think, and act (Bem, 1993). Gender identity involves the individual's sense of being psychologically male or female. Related constructs are acculturation, racial socialization, and Africentric values. Acculturation refers to both individual and group-level changes in behaviors, attitudes, and values that take place over time as two or more cultural groups come into contact (Berry, 1990). Racial socialization is a process involving messages and behaviors about race that parents or other members of a person's social context transmit to children and adolescents (Stevenson, 1995). Africentric values are the beliefs, attitudes, and worldview that come from people of African descent. See Chapter 2 for a discussion of the Africentric worldview.

Intersectionality

Intersectionality was coined by Crenshaw (1989) to address the continued absence of the unique situation of African American women in the single frameworks found in both antiracist and feminist theory. Intersectionality is a theoretical framework that seeks to understand how multiple social identities, including race, gender, sexual identity, and disability, among others, intersect within the individual in considering multiple interacting levels of social inequality (Bowleg, 2013). Since Crenshaw's conceptualization, intersectionality has been applied to the consideration of various social identities simultaneously (Cole, 2009). For African Americans, this means that being both African American and a woman or an African American and a sexuality minority (or an African American and a person with a disability or an African American and a Latina) results in unique experiences that otherwise could not be completely understood if these social identities were examined in isolation (Chow, Segal, & Tan, 2011). Intersectionality helps us understand how multiple identities work together rather than independently in relation to well-being of African Americans. The cover story highlights the importance of considering multiple identities and provides an example of one national data set (the Youth Risk Behavioral Surveillance Survey) that allows researchers to consider intersectional identities.

Intersectionality theory has been applied to understanding how race of African Americans and other social identities interact within several contexts. Some applications of intersectionality theory include African American women's success in vocational contexts (McDowell & Carter-Francique, 2017); African American women and relationships (Lashley, Marshall, & McLaurin-Jones, 2017); African American lesbians and transgender women (Brooks, 2016); African American men and discrimination (Bowleg et al., 2016); African American men and women and smoking (Aguirre et al., 2016); and African American girls and health outcomes (Townsend & Hargrove, 2016).

SELF-CONCEPT AMONG AFRICAN AMERICANS

The self-concept of African Americans has been extensively discussed and researched. In fact, popular literature would implicate challenges with self-concept to be the root of many problems in the African American community. Self-concept is a multidimensional construct, and self-concept among African Americans is generally positive. The research and literature have provided evidence of positive self-esteem among various African American populations, including adolescents (Birndorf, Ryan, Auinger, & Aten, 2005), African American women (Patterson, 2004), and African American men (Phares, Fields, Watkins-Clay, Kamboukos, & Han, 2005). Some of these studies have been comparative, showing higher levels of self-esteem, especially when African Americans are compared with Whites (Gray-Little & Hafdahl, 2000; Negy, Shreve, Jensen, & Uddin, 2003). Other studies, of which have included only African American samples, have also found high levels of positive self-esteem and self-concept (Corneille & Belgrave, 2007; Kiecolt, Momplaisir, & Hughes, 2016; Patterson, 2004).

Historical Perspectives on Black Self-Concept

Historically, African Americans in the United States have been described as having a negative self-concept and a tendency to self-denigrate as a result of inferior status in this country. Kardiner and Ovesey (1951, 1962) wrote about the impact of oppression on the self-concept of Blacks. Their classic work, *The Mark of Oppression: A Psychosocial Study of the American Negro*, makes the point that Blacks have a negative self-concept because of oppression, discrimination, and inferior status. In another early book on the Negro self-concept, Grambs (1965) explains why Negroes perceive themselves as inferior and have negative self-concepts: "The self-concept of the Negro is contaminated by the central fact that it is based on a color-caste complex" (p. 13); "The self-esteem of the Negro is damaged by the over-whelming fact that the world he lives in says, 'White is right; Black is bad'" (p. 15). The author goes on to cite instances of the manifestation of low self-concept, including increased Black-on-Black crime, aggression, low levels of educational achievement, and unstable household and parenting practices.

A central premise in the landmark *Brown v. Board of Education* (1954) case, which outlawed school segregation, was that Blacks who attended Black schools not only suffered educationally but also socially and psychologically from low self-concept. The findings from the doll studies conducted by Mamie and Kenneth Clark were cited as evidence of this. Clark and Clark (1939) conducted studies with African American preschool children using dolls as stimulus materials. Children were asked to choose the doll that they would like to play with, the doll that was the prettiest, the doll that was the smartest, and the doll that most looked like them. Children were more likely to select the White doll as the one that they would most like to play with and the one that was the prettiest. A conclusion from this study was that the historical context of separatism and racism had affected the self-esteem and racial identity of Black children.

There were several methodological concerns with the doll study that later replications have addressed, and these later studies have yielded different results concerning Black self-concept. One concern was that asking children to select a doll that is most like them did not take into account the diversity of complexion among African American children. Lighter-complexioned children may see themselves as more similar to the White doll than to the Black doll. Another problem was that the Black dolls were very similar in appearance to the White dolls and only differed in skin color. Additional research (e.g., Cross, 1991; Powell-Hopson & Hopson, 1992; Spencer, 1982) has further clarified the distinction between young children's feelings of self-worth and their racial self-awareness and knowledge of cultural biases. Although young children understand racial categories and biases by the time they are of school age, their self-esteem is not directly linked to this awareness, and they do not necessarily feel negatively toward themselves.

IDENTITY: DEVELOPMENT AND CHANGE

The development of identity is a process that involves personal insight and observation of oneself in a social context. The observation might make one realize that members of one's ethnic group are treated differently from members of other ethnic groups.

CONTEMPORARY ISSUES

WHAT'S IN A NAME? IDENTITY AND HISTORY

Does it mean the same thing to be "Black" today as it did 50 years ago? Our theoretical perspectives on identity have been shaped by cultural changes within the African American and the broader American community and by the ways in which members of the community understand and name themselves. From the U.S. Constitution's "three-fifths of all other Persons" guidelines for enumeration for the U.S. Census to the various and changing terms used across the years since 1790, constructions of race have evolved. Free inhabitants. Slave inhabitants. Mulatto. Color "B." Negro. Colored. Black. Afro-American. African American. African Caribbean and Afro-Caribbean. Black alone. These varied terms reflect the changing sociocultural and political constructions of race and ethnicity within the United States.

For African Americans, there has been rich historical significance and power in choosing names for oneself as well as the name for one's group, but as these names and constructions of race and ethnicity have changed over time, there have been important tensions around our understandings of race and ethnicity as they have changed and shifted.

Whether tensions over the claiming and use of the "N" word in rap music, emerging considerations of the potential metabolic significance of race in ethno-pharmacology, or differing constructions of the racial and ethnic identification of individuals of mixed or biracial heritage—the contemporary construction of race is ongoing. Is Halle Berry Black? Jordin Sparks? Barack Obama? Is Drake African American because he says so or because the African American community does? What about Will Demp, Tony Parker, or Tim Duncan? What about the White person who feels culturally Black?

As many young African Americans grow up in communities different from those of their parents and grandparents, we can ask ourselves how the identities of African Americans might continue to evolve and change. In addition, as Americans of Hispanic origin, who may also be of African descent, become the largest ethnic minority group in the United States, there will likely be continuing fluidity in our understanding of what it means to be African American. Perhaps we will need future editions of Baratunde Thurston's *How to Be Black* (2012) or perhaps, more accurately, *How to Be What Used to Be Black*.

The self-observation may also make salient how the behavior of one's ethnic group differs from the behavior of other ethnic groups. Overall, African Americans and Caribbean Blacks have more positive than negative racial identity (Kiecolt et al., 2016). As we discuss next, ethnic identity is important and serves many functions. Ethnic identity is not static: It changes throughout the life span.

Identity Development

Identify formation begins at birth and continues throughout the life course. Young children's understanding of ethnicity and race is mainly derived from the family and the community (Spencer & Markstrom-Adams, 1990). As children's social cognitive development progresses, they move from understanding and describing themselves based on individual external characteristics to increasingly emphasizing more internal, multidimensional, psychological, and situational factors (Damon & Hart, 1982). American children develop an understanding of racial categories, their group membership, and the broad cultural attributions and biases associated with race and ethnicity during their preschool years. This understanding appears to be shaped, in part, by their general social cognitive development (Loyd & Williams, 2017; Spencer, 1982; Swanson, Spencer, Dell'Angelo, Harpalani, & Spencer, 2002).

It is during the adolescent years that identity formation is emphasized, as explained by the psychosocial stage theory of Erik Erikson (1963, 1968). With developmental increases in cognitive ability, dramatic physical changes, and the impending transition to adulthood, the question of "Who am I?" becomes increasingly important. Identity development is dependent on prior experiences, developmental context, and historical period.

Building on Erikson's perspective of adolescent identity exploration and commitment, Marcia (1966, 1980) articulated four identity statuses for adolescents: identity achievement, moratorium, foreclosure, and diffusion. Moreover, African Americans' experiences of these statuses may differ from those of majority youth.

Identity *achievement* is the status reflecting the exploration of and commitment to an identity. At this stage, adolescents understand and accept who they are in terms of their racial and ethnic background. For example, individuals may refer to themselves as Black and be committed to being African American. Identity *moratorium* occurs when there has been or there is an ongoing exploration of identity, but no commitment has been made to a specific identity. Individuals may have some confusion about their ethnicity during this stage. They may know that they are African American but may not necessarily feel committed to this aspect of their identity and subsequently may not participate in activities of their ethnic group. Identity *foreclosure* is when individuals have clarity about their ethnicity but have not explored this aspect of their self-concept. Feelings about their ethnicity may be positive or negative depending on the socialization process. Individuals in this status may be clear that they are African American but do not think deeply about what it means to be African American. Identity *diffusion* is a status in which the individual has neither explored his or her identity nor developed a clear understanding of identity-related issues. An individual in this status has not significantly thought about or experienced aspects of being African American.

A considerable proportion of the research on identity development has been conducted with adolescents. These studies have generally involved administering identity scales to adolescents of different age groups to infer their identity status. Less research has been conducted on the process or the manner in which identity develops. French, Seidman, Allen, and Aber (2006) addressed this issue by conducting a longitudinal study of ethnic identity over two critical transitional periods during adolescence. They also investigated whether patterns of ethnic identity were similar to or different for African Americans, Latinos, and Whites. The authors used data collected from a large study called the Adolescent Pathways Project, a longitudinal study of youth attending urban public schools in the eastern part of the United States. Data at Time 1 were collected from students in elementary and junior high during the late spring. Time 2 data were collected 10 to 12 months later, after students' transition from elementary to junior high and junior high to high school. Time 3 data were collected 1 year later. Measures included students' self-identification of racial or ethnic label, group esteem, and an exploration (achievement) measure of ethnic identity. The authors reported that the group esteem component of identity increased for both early and middle school adolescents. However, the exploration component of ethnic identity increased only for the middle school adolescent students. The authors also found that the increase in the exploration dimension of ethnic identity occurred more when students went from ethnically homogeneous middle schools to more ethnically diverse high schools. They noted that perhaps this transition served as an encounter that increased racial salience.

In other work on identity development, Yip, Seaton, and Sellers (2006) explored the four identity statuses among African Americans of different age groups (i.e., adolescents, college students, and adults). Their sample consisted of 940 African Americans distributed among the three groups. They found that the four identity statuses—diffused, foreclosed, moratorium, and achieved—existed among this sample. Individuals from all three age groups were in each of the four identity statuses. The authors noted that this finding is consistent with research that suggests recycling occurs. Recycling occurs when an individual in a later identity status returns to an earlier status and vice versa. The concept of recycling will be discussed in more detail later in this chapter. There were some differences across age groups such that 27% of the adolescents, 47% of the college students, and 56% of the adults were classified as achieved, suggesting developmental differences. More of the adolescents were in the moratorium status of exploration, which was consistent with where they were developmentally. Relatively few of the participants were classified as having diffused identities.

Ethnic Identity Change

Situational and environmental factors have an impact on one's ethnic identity. Identity change may occur if an individual moves into a new situation or a new environment or has a change in life circumstances, such as relocation, marriage, new job, new school, and so on. When a new situation is encountered, the individual is prompted to search for a new source of support. The new support may move the individual into another context in which he involves himself in activities and organizations that support that new identity. For example, students in the Yip et al. (2006) study changed in one identity status when they went from an ethnically homogenous to an ethnically heterogeneous environment. Before students start college, they may have support for their identity within their community or Church environment. However, once in college, they may have to find new sources of support for their identity through greater involvement in African American clubs and organizations. This may be the case especially if they attend a predominantly White college. In fact, research has shown that ethnic minority students' feelings of belonging to a group and commitment to their ethnic group increase when they go from a predominantly minority community to a predominantly White college (Saylor & Aries, 1999). We next turn to a discussion of two of the major models of racial identity.

MODELS OF RACIAL IDENTITY

Interest in racial and ethnic identity led some of the early researchers to develop models of racial identity. One of the earliest and most studied models of racial identity is the nigrescence model. The multidimensional model of racial identity is a more recent identity model and provides a framework for understanding the importance of race and the meaning of being a member of a racial group.

Nigrescence Models of Racial Identity

The earlier racial identity models assumed that people progress through phases or stages of identity. Individuals in a particular stage have certain attitudes, beliefs, and behaviors that are distinct from those that emerge within other stages. Nigrescence models of racial identity have been widely studied, and these models have undergone refinement.

Nigrescence models take into account the process by which Blacks become aware of being Black in the United States. (Nigrescence, a word with Latin roots, means to become black.) Nigrescence models and measures have been developed by African American psychologists, including Charles Thomas, William Cross, Janet Helms, and Thomas Parham. These models provide a template of what happens during each of the stages that African Americans go through to reach racial awareness. Each of these stages is characterized by certain affective, cognitive, and behavioral features. A description of the stages, as articulated by Helms (1990), follows. Also see Table 3.1 for examples of behaviors at each stage.

Stage 1: Pre-Encounter

In the pre-encounter stage, there is an orientation toward White culture and away from Black culture. People in this stage may feel ashamed and embarrassed about being African American and may hold the values of the White culture. These individuals may feel that Blacks are responsible for their own oppression and fate. Correspondingly, they may hold individualistic views about opportunities, seeing the individual and not the environment as responsible for what happens to people. Individuals in this stage may believe that Blacks who do not do well are responsible for their lack of success and that the historical background of slavery and discrimination are not relevant factors. Individuals in this stage are likely to engage in activities with Whites or activities that they assume are culturally White.

Emotional behaviors during this stage may be defensiveness, avoidance, and anxiety. The individual in this stage is looking for acceptance among Whites, which may or may not be available. Compliance and conformity to societal norms are also seen in this stage.

Individuals in this stage may hold beliefs and behaviors that are not overtly anti-Black and pro-White (especially if they want to be seen as politically correct) but that may be inferred from unobtrusive and indirect indicators. This may be seen, for example, when individuals prefer to buy from White merchants over Black merchants and rationalize that White merchants provide better products, service, or both.

Stage 2: Dissonance

During the dissonance or encounter stage, individuals encounter an event or series of events that shatter the perception of themselves or the perception of the conditions of Blacks in America. This experience, described as "pulling the rug from under one's feet" (Cross, Parham, & Helms, 1998, p. 9), makes salient the consequences of being Black. An example might be when a person realizes that he was charged a higher price for an automobile because of his race or when an individual realizes that there was no justice in the murder of a Black man. Dissonance may also be experienced when an individual is transitioning from one environment to another. This might occur when a person leaves a predominantly African American high school to attend a predominantly White school. In the transition process, his race becomes salient to him and to others.

During the dissonance stage, the person begins to wonder what it might be like to have an identity as a Black person. This person may begin reading and seeking out information about Blacks and may begin to question what she had previously believed to be true about Blacks and Whites. The emotional state associated with this stage is one of vigilance and anxiety. The person in this stage is motivated to learn about Blacks and actively seeks out information about being Black. For example, she may begin to learn more about Black Lives Matter and other social activist movements.

Stage 3: Immersion and Emersion

The immersion and emersion stage is characterized by a new way of thinking and a new identity that incorporates being Black. Immersion is the beginning phase and emersion the end phase of this stage. Individuals in this stage may have over-valued beliefs about the goodness of being Black. Dichotomous thinking is used, and Black is good, and White is bad. Persons in this stage want to affiliate only with other Blacks. Individuals in this stage attend events and participate in activities that affirm and support their African American identity. The first part of this stage has been described as total immersion into Blackness, with individuals experiencing the emotions of energy and elation. During the second part of this stage, called emersion, there is some leveling off of energy and elation.

Stage 4: Internalization

During this stage, the individual has internalized a new identity. The conflicts between the old and the new identity have been resolved and the anxiety, emotionality, and defensiveness of the prior stages are gone. The individual feels more calm and secure. This person knows who he is, and he does not have to display his Blackness in order to prove that he is Black. Blacks are still seen as the primary reference group, but friendships and interactions with Whites are possible. Furthermore, persons in the internalization stage do not participate in Black organizations exclusively. Their thinking is more flexible, and they are more accepting of people from other cultural groups.

Stage 5: Internalization-Commitment

At the fifth stage, called internalization-commitment, the individual possesses all of the characteristics of the internalization stage. However, not only does she have a firm self-identity about what it means to be Black, but also she is likely to work for the liberation of all oppressed people. For example, a person in the internalization-commitment stage might work to support the civil rights of other oppressed groups (e.g., lesbian, gay, bisexual, transgendered, and queer [LGBTQs]).

The Racial Attitude Identity Scale (RAIS) has been the most widely used scale to measure racial identity attitudes (Parham & Helms, 1981). This scale is discussed in more detail in the research and methodological section of this chapter.

Adaptations and Refinements of Nigrescence Theory

The nigrescence theory of racial identity has been modified since its original conceptualization over 35 years ago. These modifications more accurately reflect identity among contemporary African Americans.

Parham (1992a) modified the nigrescence theory to include a life span perspective on racial identity. His adaptation addresses how the stages of racial identity are manifested in three phases of life: (a) late adolescence/early adulthood, (b) midlife, and (c) late adulthood. Each of these phases has a central theme that relates to a particular stage of racial identity. Parham's adaptation of the model accounts for how one would experience nigrescence during the three developmental periods.

During childhood and late adolescence, parents and the immediate environmental context (e.g., schools, neighborhoods, churches) have greater influence than during later developmental stages. This means that individuals might be more likely to progress through stages during adolescence and early adulthood. For example, leaving home during late adolescence and going to a new school environment might trigger the dissonance stage. One's immediate sociocultural environment and close

TABLE 3.1 ■ Behavioral Examples of Contemporary Racial Identity Status	
Status	**Behaviors**
Pre-encounter	• Exclusively using White service providers (e.g., physicians, accountants, therapists) • Hanging out with White friends only • Making a negative comment about an all-Black neighborhood
Dissonance	• Going to a talk to learn more about the history of Confederate monuments • Reading a Facebook post about housing inequality • Questioning a friend about a microaggression encountered from a teacher
Immersion and emersion	• Exclusively attending only Black-organized events • Making a negative remark about a person because he is White • Criticizing Black people for having White friends
Internalization and internalization-commitment	• Being a participant in movements that promote equity for various oppressed groups (e.g., Black Lives Matter, Equality Federation) • Teaching youth about the history of African Americans and other racial/ethnic minority groups in this country • Reading and learning from womanist literature

contact and collaborations with other African Americans might also encourage the immersion-emersion stage.

A life span approach to identity also recognizes that recycling occurs. In recycling, the individual goes back to an earlier completed stage. Parham (1992a) defines recycling as the reinstatement of the racial identity struggle and resolution after having achieved it at an earlier time in one's life.

During midlife, changes and transitions might cause one to reevaluate racial attitudes and return to an earlier stage and/or move forward to another stage. Events such as child-rearing, marriage, and new or changing jobs may serve as catalysts for a particular attitude.

The life span perspective also assumes that a person's initial identity can be at any of the stages and that it does not always have to begin at the pre-encounter stage. For example, if a child is immersed in a culture of pro-Black activities and beliefs based on his parents and other socialization influences, he may never hold pre-encounter attitudes.

The life span perspective on nigrescence holds that identity resolution can occur in one of three ways: (a) stagnation or failure to move beyond one's initial identity stage, (b) through the sequential linear stage progression described previously, and (c) by recycling.

Multidimensional Model of Racial Identity

In contrast to stage or developmental models, Sellers, Smith, Shelton, Rowledy, and Chavous (1998) have developed a model that emphasizes the multidimensional nature of racial identity. The multidimensional model of racial identity (MMRI) builds on symbolic interactionism and outlines four primary dimensions of racial identity: salience, centrality, ideology, and regard.

Salience involves the extent to which individuals emphasize race as an important dimension of their self-concept at a specific point in time. Sellers et al. (1998) note that the salience of racial identity may vary over time and from situation to situation. Centrality refers to the extent that race is core to an individual's self-concept and how she normally defines herself. Ideology is the third dimension of the MMRI and describes four different sets of beliefs and attitudes: (a) nationalist, (b) oppressed minority, (c) assimilationist, and (d) humanist. The nationalist perspective emphasizes "the importance and uniqueness of being of African descent." The oppressed minority ideology focuses on oppression and commonalities with other oppressed groups. The assimilationist perspective emphasizes "commonalities between African Americans and the rest of American society," and, the humanist perspective underlines "the commonalities of all humans" (Sellers et al., 1998, p. 28). The fourth dimension of identity, regard, involves both the individuals' feelings about group membership (private regard) and their sense of others' evaluations and feelings about their group (public regard). The MMRI model seeks to address a variety of research and conceptual issues on racial identity. We discuss the Multidimensional Inventory of Black Identity (MIBI), which is based on the MMRI, later in the chapter.

The extensive research on racial and ethnic identity has led to numerous studies that have investigated the correlates or consequences of high and low racial and ethnic identity. Other self-attributes have been investigated along with ethnic identity.

Correlates of Racial Identity and Self-Concept

There are causes and effects of having high and low racial and ethnic identity. We discuss next the relationship between racial identity and demographic variables and then the relationship between racial and ethnic identity and other variables.

Racial Identity Status and Demographic Variables

Several studies have examined the nigrescence stages of racial identity (described previously) and their correlations with demographic variables. One question is whether certain demographic characteristics are more likely to be found among persons in a specific racial identity status. A study that used data from the National Survey of Black Americans (NSBA) and the National Election Panel Study (NEPS) addressed this question (Hyers, 2001). The authors found that some demographic variables correlated with different identity stages. Respondents were classified into one of three racial identity types—pre-encounter, immersion, or internalization—based on their responses to questions on the NSBA and the NEPS. Persons were classified into the pre-encounter stage if they answered yes to a question such as, "Do you think what happens generally to Black people in this country will have something to do with what happens in your life?" An immersion-type question was, "How much say or power do you think Black people have in American life and in politics?" A question aimed at internalization was, "How close do you feel in your ideals and feelings to White people in this country?" The study found that most of the respondents (80% in the NEPS and 84% in the NSBA) could be classified into the pre-encounter, immersion, and internalization stages. The percentage categorized as pre-encounter in the NEPS survey was 44% and in the NSBA survey 35%. Immersion types represented 16% of the NEPS sample and 21% of the NSBA sample. Internalization types represented 40% of the NEPS sample and 28% of the NSBA sample.

The findings indicated that socioeconomic status is a predictor of identity status. Less educated and lower-income respondents were more likely to be in the pre-encounter than the immersion stage. In addition, respondents in the NEPS from urban areas were more likely to be in the pre-encounter than in the immersion stage. Data from the NEPS showed that men and older participants were more likely to be in the internalization than in the immersion stage.

Individuals classified in the pre-encounter stage were the least likely to blame the system for the problems Black people had, were most likely to have White friends, and were least likely to self-label as Black. Those in the pre-encounter stage, compared with those in the immersion and internalization stages, were least likely to report experiencing racism or having a family member who had experienced racism, and they were least likely to report feeling discriminated against in hiring and other situations. Regarding psychological well-being, individuals in the pre-encounter stage were the most satisfied, those in the internalization stage were the second most satisfied, and individuals classified within the immersion stage were the least satisfied with their lives. Although pre-encounter types reported high psychological well-being, they had the lowest level of global self-esteem. Internalization types had the highest level of global self-esteem.

Racial and Ethnic Identity and Psychological Well-Being

High racial and ethnic identity have been found to be associated with positive psychosocial well-being (Loyd & Williams, 2017). The positive effects of racial identity on psychological well-being are both direct and indirect and seen across diverse groups. Pierre and Mahalik (2005) examined psychological well-being among African American male college students and community members. They found that pre-encounter and immersion racial identity attitudes were associated with higher psychological distress (as measured by a psychological distress checklist) and lower self-esteem. On the other hand, internalization racial identity attitudes were associated with higher self-esteem.

Sellers, Copeland-Linder, Martin, and Lewis (2006) reported that different components of racial identity had direct and indirect effects on psychological functioning and well-being in a sample of 314 African American adolescents. Participants who reported attitudes that are more positive (labeled positive regard beliefs) about African Americans reported higher psychological well-being (i.e., self-acceptance, positive relationships with others, and so on). They also found an indirect effect such that the belief that other groups had negative attitudes toward African Americans (labeled the low public regard component of racial identity) lessened the impact of perceived racial discrimination on psychological well-being.

In another study showing indirect effects of racial identity, Jones, Cross, and DeFour (2007) studied racial identity among 144 Caribbean women. They found that racial identity attitudes had a protective effect on racial stress appraisal and events regarding depression. That is, when racist events were appraised as high, women with higher racial identity were not as depressed as those with lower racial identity. Similarly, Kiecolt et al. (2016) found among African Americans and Afro-Caribbeans a protective effect of ethnic identity on depression for participants who perceived discrimination from others.

Similarly, ethnic identity has also been shown to be a protective factor against online discrimination-related stress. A contemporary source of stress for African

American adolescents involves online discrimination (e.g., race-based exclusion in social networking settings, overt racial attacks or exchanges, exposure to text or imagery reflecting prejudice). Tynes, Umaña-Taylor, Rose, Lin, and Anderson (2012) found that higher levels of self-esteem and ethnic identity buffered the effects of online discrimination on self-reported anxiety in a sample of 125 African American high school students (mean age = 16.1).

Neighborhood context may also make a difference when considering the impact of racial identity and well-being. Hurd, Sellers, Cogburn, Butler-Barnes, and Zimmerman (2012) found that African American adolescents and young adults with more positive feeling about Blacks had lower symptoms of depression but that this relationship was stronger in neighborhoods with fewer Black residents. In neighborhoods with fewer Black residents, believing others held less positive view of Blacks was associated with less depression, while in neighborhoods with a greater presence of Blacks, believing others held less positive view of Blacks was associated with greater depression.

Racial and Ethnic Identity and Academic Achievement

Findings regarding the relationship between ethnic identity and school achievement are mixed. On one hand, high ethnic identity should foster achievement-related activities, such as studying and affiliating with peers who have high academic success. On the other hand, Fordham and Ogbu (1986) note that high achievement among African American youth may be viewed as "acting White" by their peers. For some, high achievement may be seen as selling out the Black culture. This occurs when students do not see academic achievement as a core defining attribute for themselves and their peers; consequently, high academic achievement is not a positive accomplishment. Beyond the linkage between ethnic identity and academic achievement, accusations of "acting White" may carry their own toll for African American youth. In a study of 101 African American high school students with a mean age of 15.9, Murray, Neal-Barnett, Demmings, and Stadulis (2012) reported that those who were indirectly accused of acting White (e.g., "Because of my friends, my peers don't think I'm Black enough," or, "The kids around me say I talk proper"), as well as directly accused of acting White (N = 52), reported higher levels of anxiety than those who experienced only the indirect accusation (N = 45). Only four participants indicated that they had experienced neither direct nor indirect accusations.

The devaluing of educational achievement has a historical context. Historically, White America has doubted African Americans' capabilities to perform well, and some African Americans subsequently bought into this belief, doubting their own capabilities. In order to maintain self-esteem, African Americans have thereby defined success for Whites as based on school achievement and defined success for African Americans as based on other attributes. From this perspective, students who are strongly connected to their culture and who have high racial identity may not be successful in school. In one study, Neblett, Philip, Cogburn, and Sellers (2006) found results that were consistent with this hypothesis. The authors studied 548 students in Grades 7 through 10 and found that racial pride messages were correlated with lower grades and less academic curiosity.

In contrast, studies have more frequently identified ethnic or racial identity as a positive factor for academic success (Rivas-Drake et al., 2014; Witherspoon, Daniels, Mason, & Smith, 2016). Hughes, Witherspoon, Rivas-Drake, and West-Bey (2009) found, among students in early adolescence, that higher ethnic affirmation was associated with higher academic engagement. Spencer, Noll, Stoltzfus, and Harpalani (2001) found African American youth who scored high on Eurocentric identity to have lower academic achievement and those who scored higher on Africentric identity to have higher achievement. They challenge the "acting White" hypothesis, and discuss several problems with it. They note, for example, important individual differences among African Americans in their conceptions of identity. Another challenge to the acting White hypothesis is that many African Americans are bicultural and can code-switch while negotiating American culture. Finally, many African American youth and parents have positive values regarding education.

In another study with similar findings, Adelabu (2008) studied ethnic identity and grade point average (GPA) in a sample of 661 African American adolescents in Grades 7–12. The findings showed that ethnic identity was positively correlated with grade point average within the total sample. The correlation was stronger for females than for males.

Ethnic identity may affect academic achievement, such as grades, through its impact on other attributes, such as academic expectations and orientation. Kerpelman, Eryigit, and Stephens (2008) examined ethnic identity and future education orientation. Their study included 374 African American adolescents who were in Grades 7–12. Ethnic identity was a significant factor in future education orientation for both male and female students.

Racial and Ethnic Identity and Problem Behaviors

Several studies have examined ethnic identity in relation to problem behaviors including drug use, risky sexual activity, juvenile delinquency, and violence. Much of this research has been conducted with adolescents. These studies have generally found ethnic identity to be a protective factor for youth. Ethnic identity provides an alternative to poor behaviors and a more appropriate way of resisting negative forces that lead to problem behaviors.

There are several other ways in which positive ethnic identity protects against problem behaviors (Brook, Balka, Brook, Win, & Gursen, 1998). One way is that a positive ethnic identity may support adolescents' identification with their parents. Identification with parents, in turn, may lead to better problem-solving skills. Rather than seeking approval from deviant peers, adolescents seek and receive support from parents. This support may include socialization in culturally sanctioned, prosocial coping strategies. Another way that high ethnic identity protects against problem behaviors is that high ethnic identity buffers against poor self-esteem, which could be a risk factor for drug use and other problem behaviors. Youth with high ethnic identity are not likely to have poor self-esteem and feelings of incompetence, which lead to problem behaviors.

Corneille and Belgrave (2007) examined the impact of ethnic identity on drug and sex attitudes and intentions in a sample of 175 African American girls in middle school. Attitudes and intentions were targeted rather than behaviors because the sample was young and largely not using drugs or engaging in sex. The researchers examined both direct and indirect effects of ethnic identity. They were also interested in whether ethnic identity was a protective factor under conditions of neighborhood risk. The authors found that higher ethnic identity was correlated with higher sexual refusal efficacy, higher disapproval of drug use, and less intention to use drugs. They also found a protective effect of ethnic identity under conditions of neighborhood risk. Adolescents who lived in high-risk neighborhoods reported fewer intentions to use drugs when they had high rather than low ethnic identity.

In another study, the relationship between ethnic identity and drug use was examined among youth of diverse ethnic backgrounds. The sample of over 34,000 included students who were African Americans, Hispanic, Multiracial, and White in Grades 4–12 (Zapolski, Fisher, Banks, Hensel, & Barnes-Najor, 2017). Higher ethnic identity was correlated with lower past-month drug use for African American, Hispanic, and multiracial youth. Higher levels of ethnic identity were associated with increased drug use for White youth. The findings are important and implicate high ethnic identity as a protective factor for ethnic minority but not White youth. In overview, the majority of the research suggests that racial and ethnic identity is a positive attribute. Ethnic and racial identity is generally associated with increased self-esteem, psychological well-being, academic performance, and reduced problem behaviors.

Media and Technology Influence on Self and Identity

Much has been written on the influence of the media on self and identity. Most of this research has been conducted outside of psychology in fields such as sociology and communication. Overall, research suggests a negative impact of the media on self and identity. This negative impact is partly attributed to the fact that images of African Americans portrayed in the media, especially television, are based on negative stereotypes that perpetuate society's pejorative view of African Americans (Martin, 2008). The impact of the television media may be especially damaging during childhood and adolescence, the period in which identity is developing. Contributing to this is the fact that African Americans watch more television than other Americans (Common Sense Media, 2015). Among teens, Black youth consume about 11 hours 10 minutes of media a day compared with 8 hours 51 minutes for Hispanic teens and 8 hours 27 minutes for White teens. Martin (2008) describes some contemporary images that, although subtle, are still damaging portrayals of African Americans in the media. These include television characterizations as perfect entertainers and athletes, delinquents and criminals, devoted sidekicks, and/or individuals who need saving by White counterparts. These stereotypical images are generally identifiable by African American males and females.

Music videos have been implicated as a negative force for positive self and identity. Stephens and Phillips (2003) provide a thoughtful discussion of how hip-hop music, along with other media forces, has contributed to negative sexual scripts (roles and beliefs about behavior) for African American adolescents. They identify eight sexual scripts that can be seen in television and hip-hop music depictions. These scripts include the diva, the gold digger, the freak, the dyke, the gangsta's bitch, the sister savior, the Earth mother, and the baby mama. They propose that adolescent identification with these scripts is universal and likely influences their behaviors. Sexually explicit videos may be especially problematic: They have shown negative effects on sexual risk-taking behaviors, such as increases in number of partners and reductions in contraceptive use (Wingood et al., 2003).

Coleman, Butler, Long, and Fisher (2016) explored two sexual scripts found in hip-hop music and reality television shows by engaging African American women ages 19 to 28 years in focus groups. The authors found that the freak and the gold digger scripts were very salient for the women in their study. Women reported that there were unique and shared features of both sexual scripts represented in hip-hop and reality television shows. Participants commented that they had been affected by the negative images and shared examples from their own lives of how these negative scripts had affected them. For example, women reported that the freak script may have negatively influenced African American men's expectations of African American women.

As media and technology evolve, considerations of interactive technology and media, including Facebook and Twitter, are becoming important venues that can expand our examination of media and technology in influencing identity. For example, Lee (2012) and Grasmuck, Martin, and Zhao (2009) report that within their Facebook profiles, African Americans and Latinos shared information that reflected aspects of their cultural selves (e.g., a quote, favorite songs, artists) more frequently than did their White or Vietnamese counterparts. Lee reports, however, that ethnic identity and self-esteem were not related to time spent on Facebook in a sample of students at a historically Black college.

On the other hand, recent research by Maxwell, Abrams, and Belgrave (2017) suggests there are potential negative implications of social media usage among young African Americans. In a study of 199 young African American adults (ages 18–29), Maxwell et al. found that the more young African Americans perceive racism and discrimination via social media, the more anger they experienced. Closer examination of the impact of social media on self and other identity attributes is warranted.

SEXUAL IDENTITY

There has been limited research in psychology on sexual identity among African Americans. Most of the research describing the identity process has been conducted on White LGBTQ (lesbian, gay, bisexual, transgender, and queer) women and men (Parks, Hughes, & Matthews, 2004). A stage process somewhat similar to the ethnic identity process has been used to describe identity development among LGBTQ persons. Persons in the first stage may have beliefs about the superiority of heterosexuality (akin to pre-encounter), and persons at the internalization stage may have acceptance and support for all types of diversity. The committed state of sexual identity development seems to be the most favorable stage or status with respect to psychological well-being (Troiden, 1993). This stage, akin to the internalization stage, has been described as a blending of sexuality and emotionality into a significant whole, believing and feeling that a gay identity is valid and not inferior to a heterosexual identity, initiating and maintaining relationships with same-sex partners, and disclosing to the public.

Perspectives used to examine identity among African American LGBTQ individuals have generally not considered the multiple contexts in which they live and work. Although some historical changes to more tolerant and accepting attitudes have occurred, there remain variations in different cultural groups. African Americans who are LGBTQ must contend with the values and expectations of the communities in which they live and work. Family and religious institutions can be both supportive and nonsupportive systems for African Americans. In fact, some researchers have suggested that the combined effects of racism in lesbian and gay communities and homophobia in racial or ethnic communities may limit (among some) the internalization of a sexual identity and also the disclosure of sexual identity (Greene, 1997; Parks et al., 2004).

The lack of internalization of a sexual identity may be one of the reasons why some men who are behaviorally bisexual do not identify as gay or bisexual. Qualitative interviews were conducted with 33 African American men to understand why these men identified as straight when they were behaviorally bisexual (i.e., they had sex with both men and women) (Duffin, 2016). Duffin found that these men thought of being gay in ways that excluded them from believing that gay was feminine or being exclusively with the same sex or playing the receptive role in sex. These men chose not to identify with bisexual identity because it was not distinguished from gay identity, at least not in their minds. The findings indicate the complexity of one's sexual identification.

Intersectionality of Racial/Ethnic and Sexual Identity

As noted previously, intersectionality theory focuses on overlapping identities that differ from each one in isolation. Intersectionality allows one to understand that racial and ethnic minority people have unique experiences as members of multiple marginalized groups (Bowleg, 2013). As will be discussed later, these overlapping systems of identity have implications for mental health.

Bowleg used intersectionality as a theoretical framework to examine the intersections of race, gender, and sexual identity in a qualitative study of Black gay men living in the Washington, D.C., area. The sample consisted of nine men who identified as gay and three who identified as bisexual. Interview questions were aimed at understanding how Black gay and bisexual men describe and experience the intersections of race, gender, and sexual identity. Bowleg found support for intersectionality of gender, race, and sexuality and also identified barriers and benefits these men faced. Several themes emerged. One, participants both implicitly and explicitly were able to describe intersectionality (e.g., "It is hard for me to separate my identities" [p. 758]). Two, the vast majority of participants ranked their identity as Black and/or Black men as primary. Bowleg notes that the social construction of race based on phenotypic features, along with prejudice and racism, may have prompted an early awareness of Blackness for the majority of the men—an awareness that preceded awareness of sexual identity. Three, all but one of the participants reported that it was challenging to be Black men in general and to be Black gay or bisexual men in particular. These men commented on negative stereotypes about Black men and Black gay men, racial macroaggressions in White LGB communities, heterosexism in Black communities, and pressure to act masculine. A fourth theme was the benefits of being Black gay or bisexual men. Men commented that being Black and gay or bisexual had led to their psychological growth, their freedom to not conform to traditional gender roles, and to be able to use their outsider status to explore new opportunities. These men evidenced both resiliencies and challenges in being Black and gay and bisexual.

Balsam et al. (2015) compared experiences among 967 White, Latina, Asian American, and African American sexual minority women (ages 18 to 25) who were recruited using online advertisements. Participants completed measures of racial/ethnic and LGB identity, mental health, stressors, trauma, and demographic questions, along with other measures. There were racial/ethnic group differences with regard to outness of sexual orientation to family. The study found racial/ethnic minority groups were significantly less "out" than Whites. In terms of demographic characteristics, African American women were less likely to be employed and also more likely to live with their parents or have a history of homelessness relative to White sexual minority women. In terms of trauma differences, African American women were more likely to have more sexual assault and Asian American women less sexual assault when compared with White women. There were few differences between the groups in terms of LGB identity characteristics, and there were few racial/ethnic differences with regard to health behaviors (e.g., drinking, smoking). The authors note that there were more similarities than differences among the four racial/ethnic groups. Given the lack of differences, overall, the findings suggest resilience among young sexual minority women of color, despite additional stressors.

Conflicting Identities

There are sometimes conflicting identities, and LGBTQ African Americans might be discriminated against because they have two stigmatized identities (McLean, 2003). The resolution of the dual identity status, as both African American and LGBTQ, may be a factor in identity development.

A term that has been used to describe conflicting identities is *conflicts in allegiance* (CIA). Conflicts in allegiance refers to feelings of conflict between one's ethnic/racial identity and one's LGB identity, along with a fear of betraying either of these identities (Morales, 1989). A measure of CIA between one's LGB identity and one's ethnic/racial identity was developed by Sarno, Mohr, Jackson, and Fassinger (2015) to better understand this construct.

Santos and VanDaalen (2016) studied multiple identities of LGB racial/ethnic minority individuals by examining the associations of LGB identity commitment, ethnic-racial identity commitment, and conflicts in allegiances (CIA) between these two identities and depression. The authors recruited a sample of 208 participants who identified as LGB racial and ethnic minority for a web-based study. The sample was 50% male, 45% female, and 5% other gender/ungendered, with an average age of 27.5. Regarding sexual orientation, 21.2% identified as lesbian, 43.3% identified as gay, 24.5% identified as bisexual women, 7.7% identified as bisexual men, and 3.4% identified as bisexual other gender/ungendered. For race/ethnicity, 22.1% identified as African American, 23.6% identified as Asian American, 31.3% identified as Latino/Latinx, 2.9% identified as Native American, and 20.2% identified as other race/ethnicity or of mixed race. Measures of ethnic/racial identity commitment, LGB commitment, conflicts in allegiances, and mental health were administered. The significant findings were (1) LGB identity commitment was associated with lower levels of depression, and (2) conflicts in allegiances were negatively associated with both LGB and ethnic/racial identity commitment. The authors speculated that individuals with a committed sense of identity are less likely to have feelings of conflict in allegiance between ethnic/racial identity and LGB identity perhaps due to having already worked through resolving these identities. The study also found that conflicts in allegiance were associated with higher levels of depression. This study highlights the negative effects of conflicts in identity for LGB individuals who are racial/ethnic minorities.

ACCULTURATION, RACIAL SOCIALIZATION, GENDER ROLES, AND MASCULINITY

Concepts related to identity include acculturation and racial socialization. These processes, like racial identity, are affected by family and other sociocultural and environmental processes. Other aspects of identity include what it means to be a man or a woman in this society, or gender roles.

Acculturation

Acculturation refers to the extent to which ethnic minorities participate in the cultural traditions, values, beliefs, and practices of their own culture versus the mainstream White culture (Landrine & Klonoff, 1996a). Ethnic minorities function on an acculturation continuum, with traditional on one end and acculturated on the other end. In the middle are those who are bicultural. Traditional individuals retain the values, beliefs, and practices of their indigenous cultural group. Individuals who are highly acculturated have assimilated the beliefs and behaviors of the majority White culture. Bicultural individuals hold the beliefs and practice the behaviors of their traditional culture but have also assimilated the beliefs and practices of the dominant culture. In a series of studies, Landrine and Klonoff (1996a) investigated the relationship between acculturation and mental health, physical health, and other variables among African Americans. They report that acculturation is associated with the amount of racism experienced, with more traditional African Americans experiencing more racism than more acculturated African Americans. Experiencing racism, in turn, predicted health-related problems, such as smoking and hypertension.

Other studies have also assessed the impact of acculturation on health outcomes. Everhart, Miadich, Leibach, Borschuk, and Koinis-Mitchell (2016) examined acculturation and quality of life of African American caregivers of children with asthma. Parents with more traditional (and less acculturated) African American religious beliefs and practices reported higher overall quality of life and better emotional functioning. Everhart noted that less acculturation may play a protective role in helping African American caregivers with chronically ill children.

Other studies have looked at the impact of acculturation on problem behaviors, such as substance use. Nasim, Corona, et al. (2007) examined components of acculturation in relation to tobacco and marijuana use among 145 African American college females. Their findings showed that traditional religious beliefs and practice were protective factors against tobacco smoking. Also, traditional family-related and religious beliefs and practices were protective factors against marijuana smoking. However, in the same study, the authors found that traditional health beliefs were associated with more, not less, smoking of cigarettes and marijuana. The authors speculated that perhaps acculturated individuals who used traditional health practices were less likely to believe mainstream information on the harmful effects of smoking. Similarly, Abdullah and Brown (2012) found in a sample of 203 African American college students that acculturation was linked to alcohol use. Participants who were assimilationists (i.e., those who rejected African culture in favor of Eurocentric U.S. culture) drank more frequently.

More recent research has been conducted on remote acculturation. Ferguson and Bornstein (2015) described a form of nonimmigrant acculturation, called "Americanization," among early adolescent Jamaicans. They studied 222 Jamaican adolescents (mean age = 12.08 years); 62% were traditionally Jamaican, and 38% were Americanized. Americanized Jamaican adolescents reported a stronger European American cultural orientation, lower Jamaican orientation, lower family obligations, and greater conflict with parents. Watching more U.S. media and less local Jamaican media and local sports seemed to be the mechanism for Jamaican adolescents becoming more acculturated to American culture. As social media use becomes more prevalent, it is likely that this form of acculturation will become more prevalent among other African-descent people living outside the United States.

Racial Socialization

One process that supports ethnic identity development is racial socialization. Racial socialization involves messages and practices that provide information concerning one's race as it relates to (a) personal and group identity, (b) intergroup and interindividual relationships, and (c) position in the social hierarchy (Hill, 1999; Thornton, Chatters, Taylor, & Allen, 1990). Racial socialization is the process by which messages are communicated to children to bolster their sense of identity in light of the fact that their life experiences may include racially hostile encounters (Stevenson, 1995). Racial socialization messages are more likely communicated by mothers than by fathers. In addition, older and more educated parents provide more racial socialization messages than do younger and less educated parents. Those who live in more racially mixed neighborhoods are more likely to provide racial socialization messages than those who live in predominantly African American neighborhoods (Hughes et al., 2006). Finally, racial socialization messages are more likely to be provided to older than to younger children and youth.

What types of socialization do parents provide? Parents socialize their children in several ways. Parents may socialize their children into the mainstream of American society, they might socialize them as to their minority status in the country, and they might socialize them in orientation to their Black culture (Thornton, 1997). Different types of socialization experiences promote different messages. When parents socialize their children regarding minority status, they socialize them to, for example, "Accept your color." Mainstream socialization messages might be something like, "Hard work will pay off in a good life." Parents who provide socialization messages related to the Black experience might convey to their children, "It is important to study Black culture and history."

Gaylord-Harden, Burrows, and Cunningham (2012) describe racial socialization, in addition to ethnic identity and cultural-based coping, as an asset available to African American youth to promote positive adaptation when they face stress. Within this framework, racial socialization is described as the pathway through which youth gain resources for the development of their racial identities, as well as coping strategies that may be specific to African Americans in handling unique stressors such as racial discrimination. In addition, racial socialization supports youths' understanding of the availability of adult support (Jones & Neblett, 2016).

Racial socialization is associated with better functioning among African American children and adolescence. Racial socialization is correlated with less negative emotions and greater social emotional competence (Dunbar, Leerkes, Coard, Supple, & Calkins, 2017). Racial socialization teaches problem-solving skills so that children can solve racial-related problems. It tends to increase racial identity and competence (Brown, 2008; Coard & Sellers, 2005). Neblett et al. (2008) examined how patterns of racial socialization were linked to psychological adjustment among 361 African American adolescents. They found that adolescents who reported high positive types of racial socialization reported the most positive psychological adjustment. Moreover, high positive racial socialization had a buffering effect. It protected adolescents who had experienced racial discrimination, lowering their perceived stress. Adolescents who reported low and negative racial socialization reported the worse psychological adjustment.

Similarly, Blackmon, Coyle, Davenport, Owens, and Sparrow (2016) found, among 191 African American college students, that childhood racial socialization was linked to several positive mental health outcomes. Racial socialization messages were linked to adaptive culturally specific coping mechanisms such as spiritual-centered, collective, and ritual-centered coping. Racial socialization messages on how to cope with racism were negatively associated with prolonged, active high-effort coping, a coping style known as John Henryism, which has been linked to poorer health outcomes.

Racial socialization is also correlated with academic achievement, either directly or indirectly, through its association with ethnic identity (Bennett, 2006). In a review of racial socialization and academic achievement, Hughes et al. (2006) reported that racial socialization may contain messages about opportunity that may influence youths' academic motivation and efforts. Further messages about preparation for racial bias may reduce youths' susceptibility to stereotypes about lower academic performance among African Americans, resulting in higher academic performance. Racial socialization messages may also highlight significant African Americans who have achieved and make salient to youth that academic achievement is necessary for success. The impact of racial socialization remains when adolescents leave home. Anglin and Wade (2007) found that racial socialization was positively linked to academic adjustment among African American students attending a predominantly White university. Other research found that racial socialization messages help youth to better understand African American history when taught in high schools (Thornhill, 2016).

Racial socialization messages are protective against discrimination and racism (Neblett, Rivas-Drake, & Umaña-Taylor, 2012). When African American children and adolescents experience racism, discrimination, they are less likely to develop poor mental health (e.g., depression, anxiety) when they have been racially socialized. Racial socialization prepares them to evaluate the situation and to respond appropriately. Wang and Huguley (2012) found that cultural socialization by parents buffered the effects of perceived discrimination by peers and teachers on grade point averages in a sample of 630 African American adolescents (mean age = 14.5). When there were low levels of cultural socialization by parents, teacher discrimination was more strongly associated with lower GPA. Parental cultural socialization also served to protect youth from the negative impact of perceived teacher discrimination on educational aspirations.

Mothers may give certain racial socialization messages to their daughters; these messages may consider both race and gender. Thomas and King (2007) interviewed 36 mother–daughter pairs and administered a racial socialization scale. Daughters were asked, "What are the specific messages that your mother gives you on being an African American woman or girl?" Mothers were asked, "What are the specific messages that you teach your daughter on race and gender?" Thomas and King found that daughters and mothers reported similar messages, especially concerning the importance of self-determination and self-pride. Mothers did not want the race and gender of their daughters to be a barrier for success. There was a negative correlation between racial socialization messages that embraced the mainstream culture and self-esteem, suggesting that messages that deny racial heritage may have a negative influence on self-esteem.

Gender Roles

Gender roles and beliefs shape our identity in many ways. Gender roles are the expectations of roles and positions that males and females hold in this society (Stockard & Johnson, 1980). Gender roles can be categorized as masculine or independent, feminine or expressive, undifferentiated (i.e., neither feminine nor masculine), or androgynous (high on both feminine and masculine) (Bem, 1993). Feminine gender roles are linked to more traditional feminine behaviors, such as taking care of others, showing concern for others, and careers such as teaching, social work, and nursing. Masculine gender roles are linked to behaviors such as leadership and independence, and to careers such as construction and engineering. In general, females score higher on feminine gender roles, and males score higher on masculine gender roles. However, this is not always the case with African Americans. Research suggests that among African American adolescents, both boys and girls identify with stereotypically masculine traits (e.g., assertive, dominant) (Palapattu, Kingery, & Ginsburg, 2006). African American females (and to a lesser extent males) also tend to have androgynous gender roles, meaning they possess beliefs and behaviors that are typically assertive and nurturing and also independent and assertive (Belgrave & Brevard, 2014; Corneille, Ashcraft, & Belgrave, 2005; Harris, 1996). Androgynous gender role beliefs have been useful for African American women, given their need to take care of self and family under the historical context of racism and oppression. As employment opportunities have often not been as good for African American men as for African American women, androgynous gender roles may support vocational success (Abrams, Maxwell, Pope, & Belgrave, 2014).

Research suggests that the gender roles that women hold affect the causes of their stress and how they respond to stress. Littlefield (2003) investigated the relationship between gender role identity and stress in African American women. Data collected from 481 women in the Norfolk (Virginia) Area Health Study were used. Littlefield found that 16.6% of the women could be classified as masculine, 17.2% as feminine, 33.1% as androgynous, and 33.1% as undifferentiated. She found that women who were classified as androgynous reported the lowest stress level. Undifferentiated women had the highest level of stress. Her findings suggest that programs and activities that promote androgynous gender roles could potentially buffer African American girls and women against stressful life conditions.

Given racial/ethnic differences in gender role beliefs, measures of gender roles specific to African American women are warranted (Belgrave et al., 2016). A scale that measures gender role beliefs among African American women is described in the "Methodological and Research Issues" section of this chapter.

The Strong Black Woman

One set of gender role beliefs among African American women can be described as the "Strong Black Woman Schema." The Strong Black Woman Schema, endorsed by many African American women, is characterized by dedication to caring for others, resilience, ethnic pride, obligation to embrace multiple roles, determination to succeed, and a perceived obligation to exude strength and suppress emotions (Abrams et al., 2014; Woods-Giscombé, 2010). These themes emerged in interviews and focus groups conducted by Abrams et al. with 44 African American women who ranged in age from 18 to 91 ($M = 44.23$, $SD = 19.63$). Although there are some benefits (e.g., resiliency, ethnic pride) of having a Strong Black Woman Schema, there are also negative consequences to the health and well-being of African American women. African American women with the Strong Black Woman Schema may neglect self-care in lieu of caring for others, suppress their own feelings and emotions in order to appear strong, and not ask others for support. In fact, research has shown that the Strong Black Women Schema has been associated with emotional difficulties and eating disorders (Harrington, Crowther, & Shipherd, 2010), postponement of self-care (Black & Woods-Giscombé, 2012), and increased anxiety and depression (Watson & Hunter, 2015).

Feminism and Womanism

Feminism and womanism are also aspects of identity among African American women. *Merriam-Webster's Collegiate Dictionary* (Merriam-Webster, 2003) defines feminism as "the theory of the political, economic, and social equality of the sexes" (p. 461). Women's feminist identity and its meaning may vary depending on race and ethnicity (Harnois, 2005).

Robnett and Anderson (2017) examined feminist orientations among 1,140 undergraduate students (men and women) who were African American, Asian American, European American, and Latino. The authors were interested in whether the meaning of feminism differed depending on ethnicity or gender and whether there were differences in rates of feminist identity. Overall, 80% of the participants provided a definition of feminism that included equality (e.g., fight for women's rights), and these definitions of femininity were consistent with operational definitions of feminism. Twenty percent of participants provided a definition of feminism that was not consistent with the operational definition of feminism (e.g., equated feminism with femininity, with aggression toward men). Asian American participants (compared with other racial/ethnic groups) were significantly more likely to provide definitions of feminism that did not include gender equality. The second question was whether identification as a feminist varied according to ethnicity and gender. Seventeen percent of participants reported that they identified as feminists, 53% reported they did not identify as feminist, and 30% were unsure. There were no racial/ethnic differences in terms of identification as a feminist among males. However, among females, European Americans (34%) were more likely to report that they identified as feminist compared with African American (15%), Asian American (13%), or Latina (19%) women. Among women who reported that they did not identify as feminist, African American women were overrepresented, with 58% reporting that they did not identify as feminist. The study findings suggest that identification with feminism may not be as prevalent among African American women as White women but similar to women in other racial/ethnic groups. Paths to feminism and identification with being a feminist likely account for differences for African American and other women of color than White women. A study by Harnois (2005) addresses this point.

Harnois (2005) conducted a study using data from a national survey to examine the meaning of feminism among ethnically diverse women. The sample included 1,619 women, 270 of whom self-identified as African American and 1,272 who self-identified as White. The author found that African American women embraced feminism. However, African American women's self-identification as feminists did not reflect the importance of feminism in their lives to the extent that it did for White women. For example, paying attention to women's issues was related to self-identification of feminism, but it was more significant for White than African American women. The authors also found that African American and White women followed different paths to feminism. Education, marital status, and religiosity significantly predicted the extent to which White women embraced feminism. However, none of these factors predicted whether African American women embraced feminism. The author noted that the path to feminism might be shaped more by labor or work and family relationships for African American women than for White women.

Harnois also found feminism meant something different for African American and White women. The importance of feminism for White women was associated with their support for gay and lesbian issues, along with nontraditional gender ideology. On the other hand, African American women's gender beliefs and support for gay and lesbian issues was unassociated with the importance of feminism in their lives. African American feminism may be associated more with social and economic justice issues, such as educational equality and economic equalities, than it is with attitudes or beliefs about sexual orientation.

There have been a few studies on feminism among African American men. White (2006) conducted research on feminism among African American males, calling these beliefs and attitudes "feminist Black masculinities" (p. 256). Scholars who study feminist masculinities examine the representation of male power and privilege with the goal to promote equalitarianism. The assumption is that men are harmed themselves when they hold patriarchal and heterosexual views. These scholars study how alternative feminist ideas and practices can benefit both men and women. White conducted interviews with 25 African American men who fit the criteria for being a feminist (i.e., they had participated in a feminist activity) and had provided the name of an African American feminist woman who would judge him as feminist. White reported that the narratives from these men helped to understand how key life events helped to shape their feminist ideology. Some of these included events such as (a) attendance at a conference on gender relationships, (b) involvement with a feminist nonprofit agency that works with men who batter women, (c) becoming aware of sexual exploitation of women through friendship with a sex worker, and (d) strengthening of the relationship with a feminist daughter who went through a divorce.

Womanism

Womanism is a term coined by Alice Walker (1983). Walker defines a womanist as a Black feminist or feminist of color who is committed to the survival and wholeness of entire people, male and female. A womanist does not create a hierarchy between the fight against racism and sexism but embraces both as necessary. Womanism goes beyond separating out the Black women's experience as may be seen in feminism and addresses racism, ethnocentrism, and poverty as well as gender issues (Bryant-Davis & Comas-Díaz, 2016). Womanism is holistic in recognizing the various aspects of Black women's identity. Moreover, womanists are communal and community oriented, as the focus goes beyond the well-being of the individual to the well-being of the community. This conceptualization of womanism reveals a similarity between African psychology and womanism. Womanism is culturally and strengths based and, like African psychology, emphasizes optimal psychological and collective well-being of African-descended women and all of humanity across race and gender (Harrell, Coleman, & Adams, 2014).

Womanism also emphasizes the importance of gender roles in African American women's psychosocial adaptation, and assumes that gender roles for African American women incorporate both nurturing and economic-providing functions (Littlefield, 2003). Models of womanist identity have proposed that the development of identity occurs in sequential stages similar to that of racial identity. For example, Helms's four-stage model of healthy identity development in women involves movement from external to internal standards of gender identity (Ossana, Helms, & Leonard, 1992). Measures of womanism follow the general structure of status measures of racial identity (i.e., womanist pre-encounter, encounter, immersion-emersion, and internalization). The stages of womanist identity include lack of awareness of the realities of gender oppression, encounters with oppressive agents, immersion and exploring one's gender (e.g., striving for sisterhood), and an internalized secure sense of self that recognizes oppression but is not defined by it (Bryant-Davis & Comas-Diaz, 2016).

Womanism is correlated with racial identity (Wyatt, 2006). In addition, context may impact womanist identity. In one study, Wyatt found that women at a historically Black coeducational college scored higher on the emersion womanist identity status than those at a single-sex college. This is the status similar to the emersion racial identity status in which women begin to idealize women and reject male supremacist ideals of womanhood. It is also the status in which women affirm themselves as women. Women at single-sex colleges (compared with coeducational colleges) may have more opportunities to see and discuss what it means to be a woman and subsequently have more resolved feelings about being a woman. Women at coeducational campuses may have to look more actively for opportunities for identity resolution.

Masculinity and Hypermasculinity

Among African American men, research has been mixed as to whether African American men hold more traditional or stereotypic views of masculinity than their White peers (Wade & Rochlen, 2012). Popular constructions of hypermasculinity and "cool pose" among African American men may reflect tendencies to approach the African American community as a monolith and to minimize the potential within-group variations among African American men. Norwalk, Vandiver, White, and Englar-Carlson (2011) report higher levels of gender role stress among African American male college students compared with their White peers. In a qualitative study of masculine identity development among African American young adults, Roberts-Douglass and Curtis-Boles (2012) found that respondents reported that they were exposed to multiple images of Black masculinity during their adolescence. Beyond expectations of hypermasculinity presented in media and images of toughness reinforced by peers, study participants described fathers, community members, and teachers as influences, models and resources for the construction and understanding of Black male identity. Athletics, as well as academic success and taking responsibility (i.e., "taking care of business"), were also described as pathways and markers of masculinity.

Research has suggested that masculine identity, along with ethnic identity, among African American men may influence attitudes about both relationships and sexual behavior. Corneille, Fife, Belgrave, and Sims (2012) studied the relationship between these constructs in a sample of 92 Black male college students with a mean age of 19.8. Higher ethnic identity and less traditional masculine ideology were predictive of higher relationship mutuality. In addition, less traditional attitudes about masculinity were associated with fewer sexual partners.

Hypermasculinity is an exaggerated form of masculinity characterized by physical and emotional toughness, aggressiveness, and an emphasis on wealth (Hunter & Davis, 1994). Hypermasculinity develops as a coping mechanism for threats to one's safety in neighborhoods with elevated crime and violence and, over time, becomes a part of one's identity (Seaton, 2007). For African American males, especially adolescents who reside in urban inner-city neighborhoods, toughness may be perceived as necessary for survival (Belgrave & Brevard, 2014).

Seaton (2007) examined school context, fear, and hypermasculinity in a sample of African American adolescent males and found that the level of neighborhood chaos and disorganization significantly predicted neighborhood fear. Males in disorganized neighborhoods with high crime and drug rates had higher levels of hypermasculinity. According to Seaton, hypermasculinity is one way of showing manhood when traditional ways of achieving manhood (e.g., education, employment) are difficult to obtain.

In another study Cunningham, Swanson, and Hayes (2013) examined hypermasculinity and reactive coping among 241 African American adolescent males (ages 12–17). The authors also assessed the extent to which hypermasculinity is influenced by youth perception of how adults in their school and community perceive them. They found that hypermasculine attitudes develop from negative perceptions about the community and school contexts. Research has also shown that hypermasculine attitudes are associated with problem behaviors such as risky sexual behaviors (Lapollo, Bond, & Lauby, 2014). In summary, research on gender roles, feminism, womanism, and hypermasculinity highlight that there are differences in these identity attributes and the meaning of these for African Americans and for members of other racial and ethnic groups.

METHODOLOGICAL AND RESEARCH ISSUES

Research and methodological issues include the measurement of racial and ethnic identity and related constructs. Although the terms *racial identity* and *ethnic identity* are often used interchangeably, they are different constructs and require different measures. In this section, we review measures of both racial identity and ethnic identity, along with measures of other cultural constructs, including racial socialization.

Measures of Racial and Ethnic Identity

Several good measures of racial and ethnic identity exist for both adolescent and adult populations. The RAIS, developed by Helms (1990), is the most widely used racial identity scale for adults. There are four subscales of the RAIS that correspond to the racial identity attitudes described previously. An example of a pre-encounter item is, "I feel very uncomfortable around Black people." A dissonance item is, "I find myself reading a lot of Black literature and thinking about being Black." An immersion item is, "I believe that everything Black is good, and consequently, limit myself to Black activities." An internalization item is, "People, regardless of their race, have strengths and limitations." The 50-item scale uses a Likert-type format whereby respondents indicate the degree of agreement from 1 = "strongly disagree" to 5 = "strongly agree."

The Multi-Ethnic Identity Measure (MEIM) is a measure of ethnic identity and not of racial identity. The MEIM was developed to measure ethnic identity in ethnically diverse populations. It has been extensively used with several ethnic minority adolescent populations. The measure assesses young people's identification with unique characteristics of their ethnic group (Phinney, 1992).

The three subscales of the MEIM are (a) affirmation and belonging, (b) ethnic identity achievement, and (c) ethnic behaviors. There are 14 items on a 4-point scale that goes from "strongly agree" to "strongly disagree." An example of an item that measures affirmation and belonging is, "I am happy to be a member of the group I belong to." An item that measures ethnic identity achievement is, "In order to learn more about my ethnic background, I have often talked to other people about my ethnic group." An ethnic behavioral item is, "I am active in organizations or social groups that include mostly members of my own ethnic group." Respondents are also asked to indicate their ethnicity and the ethnicity of their mother and father.

Smith and Brookins (1997) developed a measure of ethnic identity specifically for African American youth. The Multi-Construct African American Identity Questionnaire (MCAIQ) is used with youth from 11 to 18 years of age. Four components of ethnic identity are included in the measure. The social orientation subscale assesses the youths' affinity toward socializing with members of their own or other racial and ethnic groups. An item from this subscale is, "I prefer White friends." The appearance orientation subscale assesses values regarding physical characteristics ("Black is beautiful"). The attitudinal subscale assesses the degree to which respondents accept or reject stereotypical portrayals of African Americans ("Blacks can do anything if they try"). The other group orientation subscale assesses preferences for working with people other than Blacks ("I like working with other people better").

The Multidimensional Model of Black Identity (MIBI) is based on the multidimensional model of racial identity (MMRI) and has 56 items assessing three stable dimensions of racial identity: centrality, ideology, and regard (Sellers, Rowley, Chavous, Shelton, & Smith, 1997). Centrality is measured with eight items (e.g., "Being Black is important to my self-image"). Regard is measured using two subscales: a six-item scale for private regard (e.g., "I feel good about Black people") and a six-item scale measuring public regard (e.g., "Overall, Blacks are considered good by others"). There are four nine-item scales examining ideology. These subscales include assimilation (e.g., "Blacks should try to work within the system to achieve their political and economic goals"), humanism (e.g., "Blacks would be better off if they were more concerned with problems facing all people than just focusing on Black people"), minority (e.g., "The same forces that have led to the oppression of Blacks have led to the oppression of other groups"), and nationalism (e.g., "White people can never be trusted where Blacks are concerned").

The measures of racial and ethnic identity described here are valid and reliable and have been used in many studies. For example, in a longitudinal study of ethnic identity, Seaton, Yip, and Sellers (2009) found relative stability in identity centrality and private regard within a sample of 219 African American adolescents followed for 3 years (with a mean age of 13.8 at Time 1 and 15.8 at Time 3). There were declines in public regard across time. In addition, perceived racial discrimination at Time 1 predicted lower public regard at Time 3, which, in turn, was predictive of higher perception of discrimination at Time 3.

Measures of Other Cultural Constructs

Measures of racial socialization are important insofar as racial socialization has been linked to positive functioning across several domains among African American youth. Racial socialization has been studied by asking adolescents what messages they have received from parents and grandparents. Stevenson (1995) developed a 45-item Racial Socialization Scale that measures these processes. The scale is used with adolescents and has four components. The spiritual and religious coping component includes items about messages that recognize spirituality and religion as helpful to surviving life's experiences. A second component is extended family care. These items express attitudes and interactions that promote the role of the extended and immediate family in child-rearing and caretaking. A third component is teaching children African American history, culture, and pride. This component is called cultural pride reinforcement. The fourth component is racism awareness teaching. These items focus on messages and attitudes that promote cautious and preparatory views regarding the presence of racism in society. In addition to the adolescent scale, there is a recently developed parental racial socialization scale.

Given that gender role beliefs differ for African Americans and other racial and ethnic groups, Belgrave et al. (2016) developed a gender role measure specific to African American women. The development of the scale involved interviews and focus groups with African American college and community samples, as well as the administration of a survey. The final measure consists of two subscales labeled "agency" and "caretaking." Items on the "agency" subscale include "independent versus dependent," "weak versus strong," and "resilient versus cannot bounce back easily." Items on the "caretaking" scale include "supportive of others versus not supportive of others" and "a caregiver versus not a caregiver." Participants circle the extent to which bipolar attributes describe them. The Belgrave Gender Role Belief Scale has acceptable reliability and validity.

BEST PRACTICES FOR INCREASING POSITIVE RACIAL AND ETHNIC IDENTITY AND RACIAL SOCIALIZATION

Racial and ethnic socialization is important for African Americans, especially children and adolescents. Culturally relevant programs and activities that seek to improve racial socialization provide an opportune space for African American youth to talk with adults and peers about social issues that affect their lives (e.g., community violence, racial profiling) in a youth-centered environment

(Loyd & Williams, 2017). These programs transmit messages to African American youth about race (e.g., cultural heritage, preparation for bias) and ways to manage racism and discrimination. Racial socialization leads to ethnic identity that serves many functions. Racial identity (a) provides a sense of group belonging and affiliation; (b) acts as a buffer against stress that may arise from prejudice, racism, and discrimination; and (c) serves as a link to a larger social group. Being part of a group that shares one's history, perspectives, and values is important in developing a positive sense of self-worth. Because of the benefits of having a positive ethnic identity, there has been a growing interest for programs to improve racial socialization and ethnic identity among ethnic minority youth. These programs seek to increase or improve ethnic identity using culturally appropriate methods and topics. Jones and Neblett (2016) identified 17 programs that integrated racial and ethnic protective factors into program components. These included programs that increased racial socialization, racial and ethnic identity, and Africentric beliefs. We next discuss rites-of-passage programs and programs aimed at increasing racial socialization.

Rites-of-Passage Programs

Rites-of-passage programs have been used as a vehicle for promoting positive identity. Rites of passage have been used in both historical and contemporary times as a mechanism for encouraging youth to develop the attitudes and behaviors necessary for productive citizenship. Many of the rites-of-passage programs for African Americans are modeled after those in Africa. For example, in some traditional African cultures, male youth are taken away from the village to learn skills that contribute to the survival of the village (e.g., hunting, food gathering). Contemporary rites-of-passage programs do this symbolically by asking parents for permission to take their youth away from their community environment. Generally, this is done in a weekend or overnight retreat. Often, the youth participants are taken to naturalistic environments outside of their home environment (e.g., farm settings, peaceful retreat settings).

In contemporary times, rites-of-passage programs have been used to provide the structure to promote a change in the lives of participants. Rites-of-passage programs may help African American youth to clearly define their gender roles, and they may be used to initiate males and females into adult social roles and responsibilities. Rites of passage can be viewed as a developmental progression that separates individuals from their previous identity and facilitates their transition into a new identity that incorporates their new role, responsibilities, and status.

Brookins (1999) describes four stages in a rites-of-passage program called the adolescent developmental pathway paradigm (ADPP). The first stage is one of preparation and awareness, in which individuals are encouraged to become aware of their personal and ethnic characteristics. There is an initial ceremony that provides information on what is involved in the rites-of-passage process. During this stage, the beginner is introduced to community members who will serve as adult role models and be responsible for guiding the youth through the process.

The second stage is one of separation, in which individuals are provided with opportunities to increase their awareness of the need to develop a new identity. The formal beginning of the transition process begins during this stage. Youth are urged to evaluate their previous beliefs, roles, and responsibilities. There may be some anxiety during this stage, as youth are encountering new values and behaviors that may be foreign to them. Activities are designed to help them understand their fears and to begin the official training in the roles and responsibilities of adulthood. Genealogical and ancestral information may be discussed in terms of how it relates to the youths' current situation and their hopes and possibilities for the future. Life-management training sessions may focus on skills, knowledge, and values associated with responsible adulthood, such as careers and social success. Group-based community service projects may be carried out in order to help individuals develop an understanding of the social and political factors within their environment.

The third stage is one of transition. It is during this stage that adolescents may begin to adapt to new ways of thinking and behaving. They begin to understand their abilities and future possibilities in the vocational, academic, and personal realms. Attitudes and feelings toward their own and other ethnic groups become more salient. During this stage, adolescents begin to develop psychological resistance strategies. These strategies are developed through an understanding of the historical struggle of African people and the culturally derived means by which African people have counteracted oppression. These strategies are useful to help African American youth deal with experiences of prejudice and discrimination.

Reincorporation is the final stage, in which the individual and the community acknowledge that the old identity and peer group have been abandoned, and a new identity has developed along with a new support group. During this stage, the community is recognized formally as important and influential to the adolescent.

In summary, rites-of-passage programs can be used to enhance identity and other positive values and beliefs among African American youth.

Increasing Racial Socialization

Parents, along with other less proximal sources, can influence children's identity development. Rowley, Cooper, and Clinton (2005) discuss ways in which parents, schools, and communities can promote positive racial identity development in African American youth through racial socialization. Parents can support racial socialization by having discussions about the achievements of African Americans and engaging in activities that support these messages. Activities may involve visiting African American cultural exhibits, having dinner in an African American restaurant, celebrating Kwanzaa, and purchasing books by and about African American authors. The authors note that when socializing their children about their African American heritage, parents should also discuss respect and tolerance for all.

Schools can also contribute to positive identity and well-being among African American children. Rowley et al. (2005) note that some of the ways in which schools can achieve this are structural, such as by emphasizing equity and access, and by offering programs that promote positive school climate and healthy relationships. Other strategies include increasing the visibility of high-achieving students of color. Schools also should recognize that a standardized test in which African American children's ability may be underrepresented may lead to omission of African American children in programs for the gifted and talented. Cooperative learning environments in which students of different ethnic groups work together may decrease stereotypes. Multicultural curriculums that are truly integrated and include people of color in everyday lessons should also be used to promote racial pride.Schools should go beyond the obligatory discussion of African Americans during Black History Month. Finally, Rowley et al. note that schools that attempt to adopt a colorblind policy may inadvertently accept low expectations for African American students (Lewis, 2001). School and community-based programming to support ethnic identity development has also been promising (e.g., Belgrave, Cherry, Butler, & Townsend, 2008), but continued attention in this area of work is warranted because not all school-based efforts have resulted in desired outcomes (Hill, Mance, Anderson, & Smith, 2012; Lewis et al., 2012).

CRITICAL ANALYSIS

Self-concept and racial and ethnic identity have been studied more than any topic in African American psychology. The long tradition of studying these topics began with the early doll studies (Clark & Clark, 1939, 1947) and continues today. The search terms "Racial Identity and African American" and "Ethnic Identity and African American" in *Psych-INFO* abstracts resulted in 1,493 citations for racial identity and 1,058 for ethnic identity. Perhaps scholars study and report on what is most salient to them. Many of the studies have been conducted by African American psychologists who are on the faculty at predominantly White institutions. Given this widespread interest, the study of racial and ethnic identity will likely continue.

Fortunately, there has also been more attention devoted to understanding the complexities of racial and ethnic identity, including research that has focused on components of racial identity (notably the work by Sellers et al. [2006]). Other studies have sought to determine the processes or mechanisms through which high or low ethnic identity leads to positive (or negative) psychological, social, academic, and health outcomes. In spite of the voluminous amount of research on racial and ethnic identity, the amount of translational and intervention work lags. There have been few evidence-based programs that show us how to improve and increase ethnic and racial identity.

Within the past 20 years, we also have seen more literature on racial socialization, which is believed to precede racial identity. This body of research on how families socialize their children about being an African American in this country is important because this research highlights the family's role in the identity and socialization process. One of the methodological limitations of studies on racial socialization is that racial socialization is often assessed from the youth's perspective and not the parents'. Hughes et al.'s (2006) work on racial socialization suggests that racial socialization is dependent on the context in which African American families live and work. More research on the process and outcomes of racial socialization for families who reside in different community contexts (i.e., urban vs. rural, South vs. North, poor vs. affluent, and so on) would allow us to understand more about the conditions under which racial socialization occurs. Finally, similar to research on ethnic identity, it would be nice to move research on racial socialization from theory to practice. Family and parenting programs that teach and reinforce best racial socialization practices would be a great contribution to raising healthy and competent African American children.

Since the last edition of this book, there has been increased attention to other aspects of the African American identity, including sexual identity, gender roles, and feminist and womanist identity. A few studies have considered the intersectionality of multiple identities among LGBTQ African Americans. In overview, an understanding and examination of self and identity is likely to dominate the field of African American psychology. It is our hope that additional study be given to moving beyond theory to practice.

Summary

The study of self-attributes, such as self-esteem, self-concept, racial identity, and ethnic identity, has a long-standing history in African American psychology. Aspects of the self relate to well-being and functioning across several domains.

Conceptualization of the self depends on culture and socialization experiences. Historically, Blacks in this country were described as having a negative self-concept and were believed to engage in self-denigration as a result of inferior status in this country. However, more contemporary models of Black self-concept are affirming and indicate that the self-concept of African Americans is not negative. The development of identity is a process that involves personal insight and observation of oneself in a social context. Nigrescence models are the most common models of racial identity. Nigrescence models account for what happens during each of the stages African Americans go through to reach racial awareness. New models emphasize that there are multiple dimensions important to understanding racial identity. In general, studies have found that high ethnic identity is associated with better self-concept, better mental health, higher achievement, and fewer problem behaviors. Research has pointed to a negative impact of the media, especially television, on self and identity.

Identity development among African American LGBTQ individuals is a complex process that is affected by the family and community systems. Intersectionality theory helps to explain this process. African Americans who have both positive racial and sexual identities tend to function better psychologically; identity conflict is associated with poorer mental health functioning.

Acculturation, racial socialization, and gender role beliefs are other aspects related to identity. Research regarding the positive and negative impacts of acculturation on variables such as substance use and health is mixed. Racial socialization is the process by which African American parents socialize their children to what it means to be African American in the United States.

Gender roles are the beliefs and expectations about how men and women should act. African American women (and to a lesser extent African American men) tend to have gender role beliefs that are androgynous and not exclusively feminine or masculine. Feminism and womanism have also been discussed as aspects of identity among African American women. Hypermasculinity, an exaggerated form of masculinity is associated with problem behaviors among male African American adolescents.

Several good measures of racial and ethnic identity and racial socialization exist. Strategies to increase racial and ethnic identity and racial socialization include rites-of-passage programs, along with programs that increase racial socialization and racial identity.

In conclusion, the Ghanaian proverb, "The fowl does not act like the goat," implies important lessons about what it means to be African American in our commonality, in our uniqueness, and with our individual differences.

RACE AND RACISM

Until the lion has his or her own storyteller,
the hunter will always have the best part of the story.

—Beninese proverb

LEARNING OBJECTIVES

- To understand how race is conceptualized

- To understand the different forms of racism

- To become familiar with discrimination and racial disparities in the criminal justice system, in health, in housing, and on physical and psychological well-being

- To become familiar with ways of coping with racism

- To become familiar with the concept of colorism

- To become familiar with measures of racism and race-related stress

- To understand different approaches for reducing prejudice and racism

EMBRACING NEW APPROACH, AFRICAN-AMERICAN FAMILIES HELP KIDS DEAL WITH RACISM

BY ANNE HOFFMAN

Among the difficult discussions parents have with their children, talking about racism and inequality in one of the toughest.

A Philadelphia program is acting as a resource to help African-American families have honest conversations about those issues—and help them improve coping skills.

When Barbara Ellis was younger, growing up in small town West Texas, she remembers dancing with a white friend.

(Continued)

(Continued)

"And some of his friends were saying horrible things to him for dancing with me," she recalled. "And he kept that from me, I don't think he told me for like a year later."

But when she did find out, it was hard for her family and friends to have a larger conversation about the painful experience.

"Those weren't conversations that we had. It was just, 'That person is awful,' and forget about it," said Ellis who now lives in Delaware County.

Ellis has just finished the EMBRace program with her 13-year-old son, Peirce.

Formally known as Engaging, Managing and Bonding through Race, the five-week program—with an additional week at the beginning and the end for intake and evaluation—includes individual and family therapy. The program unpacks common responses to racism and gives families different coping tools.

Kids who are not prepared often bottle up frustration and anger, said Riana Anderson, developer and director of the program.

"You're going to internalize quite a bit, and think about all the things you did wrong . . . what it is about me as a person? . . . rather than this is what this person sees about a whole group of people," she said.

Part of helping kids process racist acts or prepare for them is an exercise families do in sessions—formulating comebacks.

"The racial comebacks are a way of saying 'I know you are, but what am I?'" said Anderson.

But before program participants come up with the comeback they might really use, they get a chance to say the first thing that would come to their mind. After that unfiltered reaction, they have an opportunity to think about what actually would work well for them in that situation, a response that's usually more tempered and assertive.

Anderson illustrated the prescription with a comeback of her own.

For instance, what if someone said to her there's no need to talk about race because we live in a post-racial society?

"So the comeback to that is, 'Oh, when were we racial?' And just ending it there, because people will ask you, 'Haven't we already dealt with this?'

"And they'll try to put it on you. So I just like to say, 'When is it that we did do this? Can you tell me?'" she said.

Turning a Situation Around

During the classes, Peirce thought about a recent painful situation. While he waited for his mom to pick him up from orchestra practice one night, he saw a man on the street with a companion.

"And he pulled his wife or fiancee closer, he was like, 'Let's hurry up, I don't want to get robbed.' And he was looking right at me, and I was the only person there," Peirce said. "So I felt like that was directed toward me."

Barbara Ellis said her first instinct as a parent would be to go into advocacy mode or parrot the responses she used to hear as a kid.

"What I would have said is, 'Oh, don't listen to him.' Which erases [her son's] emotions in that moment," she said.

Through the program, Ellis discovered that sort of a response made Peirce feel like she didn't totally see him.

She's shifted her reaction to a more curious, "How do you feel?" and "What would you like to do about it?"

Peirce said he's noticed the change. So, he thought about the fact that, in reality, he had cause to be afraid because he was carrying an expensive viola on his back.

Thinking up that comeback—with the knowledge that his mother supports his emotional reaction—Peirce said, "I think it makes me feel more supported in what I'm doing. Like getting reassurance that I didn't do anything wrong."

The hardest week of the program for Ellis was when the discussion touched on police killings of unarmed black men and the kinds of conversations she'll need to have with her sons.

"Just to even have to have that conversation with my 13-year-old is hard," she said. "When I think about it, it makes me want to cry."

"I've heard it said, and I think it's kind of common within black families, 'Just do what you need to do to come home,'" she said of her previous reaction.

But EMBRace helped her shift from that orientation, to exercises where kids can actually talk through these possibilities with their families and what they could reasonably do. They talk about how to stand up for oneself and how to become more empowered.

"I think that's more hopeful than conversations that are shrouded in a level of fear," Ellis said.

Anderson agreed.

So many things are beyond someone's control and no one can really know if a situation is fully safe, she said. But she said her program can help families assert their voices. And that, in itself, is powerful.

Source: Ann Hoffman (2017). WHYY/NewWorks.

INTRODUCTION, DEFINITIONS, AND HISTORICAL OVERVIEW

Racism has been the subject of extensive discussion and research in psychology, especially social psychology. Most African Americans are aware of the pervasive nature of racism and, as the news story indicates, engage in strategies to cope with racism. Others, mostly White Americans, are less likely to believe that racism still exists. Political affiliation also affects perception of racism. In the 2016 election, there were marked differences between Clinton and Trump supporters regarding whether racism was still prevalent. Over two-and-a-half times as many Clinton supporters (53%) as Trump supporters (21%) believed that racism was a very big problem in our country (Pew Research, 2016). The need to understand and reduce prejudice and racism was one of the reasons the first author of this text decided to enter the field of psychology. On the other hand, research and writings on race have most often been carried out in other social and biological sciences, including anthropology and genetics.

Race, racism, and race relations affect everyone in this country, especially African Americans but also other ethnic minorities and Whites. However, African American and other racial minorities can learn how to cope with and to even thrive in the face of racism as the opening covering story shows. Racism and discrimination have long-standing and pervasive effects on African Americans across almost every life domain (i.e., education, health, housing, politics, and physical and psychological well-being). The relationship between racism and certain life domains will be explored in this chapter.

The first section of this chapter provides definitions and conceptualizations of race, followed by definitions and conceptualizations of racism. This is followed by sections on types of racism, consequences of racism, and psychological perspectives on coping with racism. The next sections address methodological and research issues and then focus on empirically based approaches and practices for reducing racism. A critical analysis is provided, and the chapter ends with a summary and conclusion.

Definition and Conceptualization of Race

There are many definitions of race. *Merriam-Webster's Collegiate on-line Dictionary* (Merriam-Webster, n.d.) defines race as a "family, tribe, people, or nation belonging to the same stock; a class or kind of people unified by shared interests, habits, or characteristics; a category of humankind that shares certain distinctive physical traits"

(p. 1024). The most commonly used human racial categories are based on visible characteristics, such as skin color, facial features, and hair texture; other categories include self-identification.

The distinction is often made between race and ethnicity. Ethnicity refers to clusters of people who have common cultural traits that they distinguish from those of other people. People who share a common language, geographic locale or place of origin, religion, sense of history, traditions, values, beliefs, food habits, and other social behaviors are perceived and view themselves as constituting an ethnic group (Smedley & Smedley, 2005). Race, on the other hand, is based on biological ancestry.

Race and African Americans

The U.S. Census Bureau (2016a) defines a person's race based on that person's self-identification of the race or races with which he or she most closely identifies. According to the U.S. Census, racial categories are sociopolitical constructs and should not be interpreted as scientific or anthropological in nature. The Census Bureau defines "Black or African American" as, "a person having origins in any of the Black racial groups of Africa." It includes people who indicate their race as "Black, African American, or Negro" or provide written entries such as "African American, Afro-American, Kenyan, Nigerian, or Haitian" (Census Bureau, 2016a). Individuals can also self-identify as having two or more races by providing multiple write-in responses or by some combination of check boxes and write-in responses.

African American is the term currently preferred by most people of African ancestry in this country. However, many people of African ancestry do not self-identify as African American, but use terms such as African, Afro-Caribbean, Afro-Latino, and so on to describe their ancestry.

Historical Perspective on Racial Groups

Historically, racial differences have been used as an indication of biological differences. Banton (1987) locates the first use of the term *race* in early 1500s Europe. Between the 16th and the 18th centuries, *race* was used as a general categorizing term, similar to and interchangeable with such terms as *type, kind, sort*, and *breed* (Smedley, 1999). Toward the end of the 17th century, race had begun to be used as a term that referred to populations in North America—European, Africans, and Native Americans (or Indians) (Smedley, 1999). In the early 18th century, the use of race as a term increased in the written record and became standardized and uniform (Poliakov, 1982).

Beginning in the 19th century, races were viewed as subdivisions of the human species that differ from one another by phenotype, or by the physical expression of genes (Smedley, 1999). The genetic notion of race surfaced in the mid-20th century, and this idea persists today among many Americans. However, as discussed in the next section, most anthropologists believe that there are no neutral conceptualizations of race in science, nor have any of the definitions ever satisfactorily fully explained the phenomenon of race. When geneticists emphasized the similarities among races (e.g., humans are 99.9% genetically alike), the small amount of real genetic differences between defined racial groups (0.1%), and the difficulties of recognizing the racial identity of individuals through their genes, doubts about the biological reality of race appeared (Littlefield, Lieberman, & Reynolds, 1982).

Thus, in the 20th century, two conceptions of race existed: one that focused on human biogenetic variation exclusively and the other, a more popular conception, that merged together both physical features and aspects of social and cultural behavior. Skin color, hair texture, nose width, and lip thickness have remained primary markers of racial identity in the United States (Smedley, 2002).

As discussed in Chapter 1, African Americans have been historically viewed as "inferior" across all attributes. As noted in Guthrie's (1976/1998) seminal book *Even the Rat Was White*, much of the study of Blacks and African Americans in early psychology was done to confirm the inferiority of the Black race.

Conceptualizing Race

Janet Helms, a psychologist, defines race based on a definition provided by Casas (1984, cited in Helms, 1990): "Race is defined as a sub-group of people possessing definite combination of physical characters, of genetic origin, the combination of which to varying degrees distinguishes this sub-group from others" (p. 3). Although this definition is biological, she notes that there are no psychological, behavioral, or social implications arising from a person's race.

Geneticists and anthropologists agree that race is not a meaningful biological category. The position of the American Anthropological Association is that the concept of race is a social and cultural construction. This position asserts, "It has become clear that human populations are not unambiguous, clearly demarcated, biologically distinct groups," and there is greater variation within "racial" groups than there is between them (American Anthropological Association, 1998).

The American Association of Physical Anthropologists (Hagen, 2009) similarly makes these points concerning race: (a) All humans living today belong to a single species, Homo sapiens, and share a common descent. (b) Biological differences between human beings reflect both hereditary factors and the influence of natural and social environments. (c) There is great genetic diversity within all human populations. Pure races, in the sense of genetically homogenous populations, do not exist in the human species today, nor is there any evidence that they have ever existed in the past. (d) There are physical differences between populations living in different geographic areas of the world. Some of these differences are strongly inherited, and others, such as body size and shape, are strongly influenced by nutrition, way of life, and other aspects of the environment. (e) Physical, cultural, and social environments influence the behavioral differences among individuals in society.

In spite of consensus regarding the sociopolitical construction of race, it remains problematic as a concept. Several reasons have been offered for why race is problematic as a concept. A first reason is because there may be inconsistency between official and legal designations and how individuals define themselves. In an interesting case from the early 1980s, Ms. Susie Phipps, raised White, was surprised to find out that her birth certificate identified her as colored (Jaynes, 1982). The reason was a 1970 Louisiana law that required anyone with more than 1/32nd Black blood to be classified as Black. Ms. Phipps learned that her great-great-great-great grandmother had been a Black slave. Ms. Phipps sued the state of Louisiana to change her racial designation to reflect the way she self-identified, "White." She lost the case as the State Supreme Court denied her motion and the U.S. Supreme Court refused to review the case.

A second reason is that many individuals are biracial or multiracial and want to identify with all of the racial designations of all of the racial groups to which they belong. Most notable is Tiger Woods, who has refused to be pigeonholed as being either African American or Asian and has referred to himself as a "Cablinasian," a Caucasian-Black-Indian-Asian. The Census allows for the self-identification of two or more ethnic groups, but other documents may only request one racial and ethnic designation.

A third reason for the problematic nature of the concept of race is that it is often treated as a valid construct and used as a general explanatory factor (Fairchild, Yee, Wyatt, & Weizmann, 1995). We see this use of race in psychological studies where race is treated as an independent variable, most often without specifying or conceptualizing whether race is being viewed as a biological, cultural, or sociopolitical factor.

Relationships are tested between race and psychological and personality constructs, such as intelligence, emotional stability, help-seeking attitudes, depression and anxiety, and locus of control, with the assumption that race is a meaningful grouping variable to use. But there is a great deal of variability in identification with one's racial group even when one primarily identifies with this group. Our discussion in the previous chapter on racial and ethnic identity highlights this point. For example, one may check off African American as the racial group to which one belongs but not identify with the cultural values and norms associated with African Americans.

Helms, Jernigan, and Mascher (2005) also argue that racial categories should not be used to explain psychological phenomena because the categories have no conceptual meaning. Assignment of research participants to a racial category reveals something about the researchers' beliefs about race but nothing about the behaviors or attributes of the research participants. Nor does such assignment mean that persons in one category have more or less racial attributes than those in another category.

But should we throw out the baby with the bathwater? Recognition of race as a sociopolitical and not a biological construct is of concern, especially considering the limitation of the construct. The use of the term race may have negative implications in that it continues to reinforce simplistic notions of race. However, researchers such as Krieger (2000) maintain that these concerns should not prevent us from using race as a way to identify and hopefully improve life opportunities and outcomes for African Americans. Krieger argues that it is not whether race is biologically determined but how we use societal categories of race and ethnicity to help us understand determinants of racial or ethnic disparities in health and in other arenas (e.g., education, income, housing). With this in mind, a good reason for measuring racial status is to be able to monitor progress in reducing disparities, especially in the health arenas.

Diversity Among African Americans

No discussion of African Americans as a racial group would be complete without acknowledging the heterogeneity and diversity among African Americans. Diversity among African Americans is due, in part, to the large increase in the number of Black immigrants over the past 40 years. Today, 3.8 million Black immigrants live in the United States, more than 4 times the number in 1980 (Anderson, 2015). Black immigrants now compose close to 9% of the Black population in the United States, while accounting for only 3% in 1980. Half of the Black immigrants are from the Caribbean, with the majority coming from Jamaica (about 682,000 Black immigrants born there), followed by Haiti (586,000 Black immigrants). There have also been notable increases in Blacks from Africa, with 1.8 million African immigrants living in the U.S. in 2013, substantially up from 80,000 foreign-born Africans living in the United States in 1970 (Pew Research Center, 2015). Among Black immigrants from Africa, the majority come from Nigeria, Ethiopia, and Egypt. One reason for this increase is the Refugee Act of 1989, which made it easier for Africans leaving conflict-ridden areas, such as Somalia and Ethiopia, to relocate in the U.S. There are some demographic differences between foreign-born Blacks and U.S.-born Blacks. Foreign-born Blacks are more likely to have a bachelor's degree, to have higher household incomes, and to be married. Foreign-born Blacks are also less likely than U.S.-born Blacks to live in poverty (Anderson, 2015).

An African American born and raised in the Midwest, a Trinidadian raised in Washington, D.C., and a Haitian raised in Miami are all Black but likely differ in terms of cultural beliefs, social behaviors, and health outcomes. Several studies have shown that health outcomes favor foreign-born over U.S.-born Blacks, at least when they first immigrate to the U.S. (Doamekpor & Dinwiddie, 2015; Ford, Narayan, & Mehta, 2016; Mehta, Elo, Ford, & Siegel, 2015). For example, Read and Emerson (2005) found differences in health statuses among U.S.-born African Americans and Black immigrants. They found that among Black immigrants, those from Africa fared the best, followed by Blacks from South America, and then West Indians, with European Blacks having the poorest health. We might also anticipate differences among African Americans from the Southern United States and the Midwest, differences among African Americans from rural and urban areas, and differences among African Americans who are of high versus low socioeconomic class. Any discussion of African Americans as a racial group should always recognize within-group diversity.

Definition and Conceptualization of Racism

Definition of Racism and Related Constructs

Racism involves negative beliefs, actions, and emotions based on race. African Americans face racism individually and within many institutions. African Americans have faced and continue to face racism in the education, housing, employment, political, social, criminal justice, and health arenas.

Racism has been defined in several ways. One working definition is that racism includes the beliefs, attitudes, institutional arrangements, and acts that tend to denigrate individuals or groups because of phenotypic characteristics or ethnic group affiliation (Clark, Anderson, Clark, & Williams, 1999). Jones (1997) defines racism as the transformation of race prejudice through the exercise of power against a racial group perceived as inferior. This exercise of power can be expressed by both individuals and institutions and can be either intentional or unintentional. Other definitions of racism also capture the systematic privilege of one group over another, along with the power of one group over another. In this country, Whites have privilege because they have control over many of the economic, political, and social systems in operation. As will be discussed, Whites also hold advantages over African Americans in just about every life domain (e.g., higher income, better health, better housing, less criminal justice involvement). Because of this privilege, Whites, as a group, hold power that is not possessed by African Americans. When power and privilege are used to define racism, the assumption is that African Americans (and other ethnic minorities) cannot be racist because they lack power, specifically on a global scale. Some disagree with this definition and subscribe to the view that anyone who has negative feelings, behaviors, and actions toward a racial group can be racist.

Racism at the individual level comes about because of stereotypes and prejudice: that is, beliefs about the characteristics of groups of individuals. Stereotypes are generalizations that people make about the characteristics of all members of a group, based on an image (often faulty) about what people in that group are like. These characteristics are cognitively associated with a social category label in long-term, semantic memory (Stangor & Lange, 1994). Gordon Allport (1988) defined prejudice as an aversive or hostile attitude toward a person who belongs to a group simply because that person belongs to that group and is therefore presumed to have the objectionable qualities ascribed to that group. Implicit bias occurs when we have negative associations linked to a member of a certain group without conscious knowledge of these associations (Fiske, 2014). For example, criminality is automatically associated with African Americans.

CONTEMPORARY ISSUES

DO WE LIVE IN A POSTRACIAL AMERICA?

The election of Barack Obama brought with it a strong notion of a postracial America, a sense that Blacks were no longer discriminated against because of their skin color, and a belief that Blacks had as much of an opportunity to reach their dreams as any other ethnic or racial group. A postracial America is the belief that race is no longer a problem in the United States and that Blacks can succeed if they work hard and take advantage of opportunities. This topic has been extensively discussed and debated, especially since the election of Obama in 2008, and several books have been written on the topic (Parks & Hughey, 2011; Wise, 2010). The concept of equal opportunity for Blacks is not new. Tim Wise (2012) comments on this in an opinion essay for CNN titled, "What is post-racial? Reflections on denial and reality." According to Wise, postracial is "little more than a nonsense term devised by people (mostly white, frankly), who would simply rather not deal with the ever-present reality of racism and ongoing racial discrimination." Wise provides several statistics that show racial disparities for African Americans. These disparities are discussed in this chapter and throughout this book. Wise goes on to say,

> Though some sincerely believe this describes America's reality—especially since a man of color was elected president—the illogic of believing this signals the veritable death of racism should be apparent: after all, we certainly wouldn't claim that sexism and patriarchy had been smashed in Pakistan, India, Great Britain, Israel or the Philippines just because they all have elected women as heads of state.

The election of Donald Trump in 2016 squelched the notion of a postracial society for many, as this was a very racially divisive election. Moreover, African Americans and Whites differ greatly with regard to whether racially based discrimination still exists. Among African Americans, 46% reported that a lot of discrimination exists, and 42% reported some discrimination exists. Only 16% of Whites reported a lot of discrimination exists, and 41% reported some exists (Doherty, 2013).

Experiencing Racism

Most African Americans have experienced racism. The recipient of racial discrimination may not even be aware of such racism, as racism occurs collectively, unconsciously, and in very subtle and pervasive ways within institutions. Moreover, the degree and severity of racist experiences are not universal, as exposure is modulated by socioeconomic status and other factors. For example, although racism affects all African Americans, it may have less of an impact among African Americans of higher socioeconomic status because they have resources to buffer against some of the negative effects of racism. As will be discussed later in this chapter, experiences of racism are also affected by how an individual perceives and copes with racism. Subtle and covert forms of institutional racism affect almost all African Americans, and more direct, obvious forms of racism may less frequently affect those African Americans who have access to wealth, power, and influence.

As an example of current racism, consider the pervasive experience of racism on college campuses. College students might be viewed as more or less immune from racism, given the sociopolitical and relatively liberal and tolerant environment of most college campuses. However, this is not always the case.

Harwood, Huntt, Mendenhall, and Lewis (2012) interviewed students about racial microaggressions they experienced in residence halls at predominantly White universities. Microaggressions are subtle and sometimes automatic exchanges, behaviors, and processes in which African Americans and other ethnic minorities are stereotyped and put down by others (Pierce, 1978). The authors conducted 11 focus groups with 85 students of color, including African Americans, Asian Americans, and Latinos, focusing on both individual-level racial microaggressions and environmental racial microaggressions. Participants reported several racial microaggressions at an individual level, including racial jokes. Racial jokes that came from a roommate or friend were especially challenging for the students because of their relationship. Nevertheless, these jokes highlighted the student's minority status and made him or her feel like an outsider. Students also reported encountering racial slurs in shared spaces and feeling sometimes that responses (from administrators) to these racial slurs were not as quick as they should be. Students also reported racial microaggressions at an environmental level, believing that their living space was segregated and unequal. They believed that students of color were placed in dorms that were inferior. Interestingly, these types of racist events are not only encountered by students but also by resident advisors: In a study conducted by Harper et al. (2011), African American resident advisors reported similar subtle types of racism.

Swim, Hyers, and Cohen (2003) found that many students perceived racism within the class setting. This racism constituted not only negative but also positive compliments. For example, when someone compliments an African American college student or professional by saying he or she is articulate, it assumes that the person expressing this sentiment has the expectation that being articulate is not normative among African Americans. A well-meaning racist comment was made by Bill O'Reilly on his cable news talk show. The talk show host was complimenting Sylvia's, a well-known Black restaurant in Harlem, New York. Apparently her restaurant did not fit his expectation for what an African American restaurant would be like. He commented, "And I couldn't get over the fact that there was no difference between Sylvia's restaurant and any other restaurant in New York City. I mean, it was—it was exactly the same, even though it's run by Blacks, primarily Black patronship; it was the same" (O'Reilly, 2007).

These insidious forms of racism on college campuses and elsewhere are linked to distress and emotional, interpersonal, and academic difficulties (Banks, 2010; Chao, Mallinckrodt, & Wei, 2012). Chao et al. conducted a study of 1,555 African American clients seen at counseling centers at seven predominantly White Midwestern universities. They found that perceived racial discrimination was associated with a large range of other problems, including academic problems (e.g., performance anxiety), interpersonal problems (e.g., dating concerns), and emotional problems (e.g., depression).

Other more divisive types of racism are experienced when words that degrade and insult are used to describe African Americans. This type of racism is reflected in the comments made on the April 4, 2007, edition of MSNBC's *Imus in the Morning* show. Host Don Imus referred to the Rutgers University women's basketball team, which comprised eight African American and two White players, as "nappy-headed hos." This statement was made immediately after the show's executive producer, Bernard McGuirk, called the team "hard-core hos" (Chiachiere, 2007).

Although there was an outpouring of outrage following the comments of Don Imus, most racism is not of this variety but is just as insidious and harmful. Regardless of the expression of racism, experiences of racism, real and perceived, are likely to elicit anger, frustration, and sometimes helplessness.

A large student protest movement against racism occurred across the country following the lead of students at the University of Missouri (UM). UM's president,

Tim Wolfe, stepped down following demands from students citing inadequate responsiveness and nonresponsiveness to racial complaints at the university (Izadi, 2015). Some of these events included lack of response to Ferguson, a swastika etched onto a dorm wall, the student body president called the N-word, and Black students' play rehearsal interrupted by racial slurs. During the fall of 2015 and spring of 2016, students across the country, including students at our university (Virginia Commonwealth University), led similar protests, citing the small number of African American faculty, insensitive and racist comments made by professors, and lack of responsiveness to national events affecting Black lives.

The cover story speaks to issues parents have when their children and adolescents experience a great deal of racism. Seventy-five African American adolescents aged 14–18 completed daily surveys for 14 days (Seaton & Douglass, 2014). Participants were asked to report the frequency with which daily discriminatory experiences occurred involving them because of their race on a scale that ranged from "0" (none) to "2" (two or more times today). Participants reported an average of 26 discriminatory experiences based on race. Over the 14 days, 97% of the adolescents reported at least one incident.

TYPES OF RACISM

There are several ways of conceptualizing and measuring racism. We discuss two different typologies for understanding different types of racism and bias next. The first one makes the distinction between racism at individual, institutional, and cultural levels. The second one distinguishes between obvious and subtler forms of racism.

Individual, Institutional, and Cultural Racism

Jones identified three types of racism: individual, institutional, and cultural (Jones, 1997). Individual-level racism is synonymous with racial prejudice. This type of racism assumes the superiority of one's own racial group and rationalizes the dominance and power generally of Whites over African Americans. This racism would be targeted at an individual, although a person holding race prejudice beliefs can also engage in institutional or cultural racism. An example of this type of racism might be a comment made by a teacher about the intellectual capability of an African American student.

Institutional racism is revealed by policies and practices within organizations and institutions that contribute to discrimination for a group of people. In this context, one does not have to be an individual racist in order for racism to occur in institutions. Institutional racism can also be thought of as structural or systematic racism that continually leads to adverse outcomes for African Americans. Institutional racism is a primary reason for racial inequalities. An example of this type of racism might be the criteria used for placement tests that lead to African American youth being underrepresented in gifted and talented programs within a school system.

Nowhere do we see greater evidence of institutional racism than when considering the health outcomes of African Americans. Studies show health disparities for almost every health outcome and indicator when African Americans are compared with Whites, even when income, education, and other socioeconomic factors are controlled. These health disparities are due to differential access to health care, utilization of health services, attitudes and practices of health providers, and institutional policies. More on health disparities is included in a later section of this chapter and in Chapter 12.

Cultural racism is seen in the assumed superiority of a language or dialect, values, beliefs, worldviews, and cultural artifacts dominant in a society. This racism is perhaps the most insidious of all in terms of identification and change because culture, by its nature, is institutionalized, with pervasive effects on all aspects of life. An example of cultural racism might be the assumed superiority of classical music to hip-hop.

Understanding whether racism is at an individual, institutional, or cultural level has implications for how racism can be reduced. For example, individual-level race prejudice may focus on changing beliefs about members of a racial group through increased contact and education. Changing institutional racism would require changes in policies and procedures within organizations and within larger societal institutions that result in discrimination against African Americans. This might require, for example, educating more African American health care professionals. Affirmative action policies are another example of an institutional strategy used to reduce institutional racism. Changing cultural racism is most difficult because cultural beliefs and attributes are embedded in the fabric of everyday life. We will return to what the research says about effective ways of changing racism later in this chapter.

Symbolic and Aversive Racism vs. Old-Fashioned Racism

Other scholars have made the distinction between old-fashioned (e.g., overt) racism and modern-day, subtler forms of racism that have been called aversive racism and symbolic racism or modern-day racism (Henry & Sears, 2002). Old-fashioned racism is the type of racism seen in Whites' beliefs in the inferiority of African Americans (e.g., Blacks and Whites should not attend school together). Symbolic racism is reflected in beliefs among Whites that racial discrimination is no longer a problem in this society and that African Americans have not obtained success because they simply have not worked hard enough for it. The term *symbolic* is relevant because it highlights the fact that these beliefs are symbolic of an abstract system of learned moral values and ideals. Later in this text, we discuss a method for measuring symbolic racism. This type of racism has also been called modern racism (McConahay, 1982).

Both symbolic and old-fashioned racism were used to explain voting behaviors of Whites in the 2012 election. Obama won the 2012 election with the lowest percentage of the White vote received by a winning presidential candidate (Knuckey & Kim, 2014). Obama's presidency in 2008 appeared to have activated old-fashion racism in the 2012 election. According to Knuckey and Kim, since 1972, only George McGovern (1972), Jimmy Carter (1980), and Walter Mondale (1982) received fewer White votes than Obama in 2012. Using data from the American National Election Study (ANES), Knuckey and Kim examined old-fashioned racism, along with racial resentment (akin to symbolic racism), in relation to whether the respondent voted for Obama. Old-fashioned racism was measured by asking respondents to rank different racial groups on a seven-point scale with terms such as "hardworking versus lazy." Racial resentment was measured with questions such as, "Irish, Italian, Jewish, and many other minorities overcame prejudice and worked their way up. Blacks should do the same without any special favors." The authors examined the two forms of racism for both Southern and non-Southern voters. They found among Southern voters, racial attitudes (old-fashioned racism) influenced voter choice; respondents with negative old-fashioned racial attitudes were not likely to vote for Obama. Among non-Southern voters, both racial resentment and old-fashioned racism were associated with not voting for Obama. These findings show the influence of subtle symbolic forms of racism in the voting process.

A similar type of racism is known as aversive racism (Dovidio & Gaertner, 1991). Aversive racism is seen in subtle ways that allow racist individuals to hold views of themselves as equalitarian and fair. Gaertner and Dovidio (2000) use the term *aversive racism* to describe the type of racial attitudes that they believe characterize many White Americans who possess strong equalitarian values. Aversive racists are likely to endorse the statement, "When I see people, I don't see color." When statements such as this are made, it may be a way for Whites to avoid thinking that they are also a member of a racial or ethnic group, something they typically do not have to think about. Fundamental to understanding aversive racism is the assumption that individuals in the United States hold norms that are egalitarian regarding the treatment of people. At the same time, some White Americans hold deeply ingrained biases against African Americans. These biases are socially and historically grounded but also can be linked to the basic social cognitive process of categorization. Physical appearance is especially salient in categorizing African Americans because physical appearance is readily apparent. Simply, the process of categorization leads to in-group favoritism relative to the out-group (Stangor, 2000). In the case of White categorization, Whites are the in-group and African Americans are the out-group.

Aversive racism assumes that Whites will treat African Americans poorly when it is ambiguous or unclear about what type of evaluation is the norm (Dovidio & Gaertner, 1991). Subsequently, to understand aversive racism, one must distinguish between equalitarian and ambiguous contexts. An equalitarian context is one in which norms and expectations promote equal treatment. Ambiguous situations are those in which it is not clear what sort of behavior or evaluation is normative. For example, studies have shown that when a highly qualified African American job candidate is evaluated, and equalitarian evaluation is normative, African American job candidates are rated comparably, in fact sometimes slightly higher than White applicants. If, on the other hand, it is not clear whether an applicant is qualified, African Americans are more likely to be rated less favorably than Whites. Aversive racists endorse equalitarian values and deny negative and discriminatory attitudes toward African Americans. They do not discriminate openly. However, they will discriminate when discrimination is justifiable and based on factors other than race (Dovidio & Gaertner, 2000). Several studies have shown that aversive racism occurs within the domain of helping behavior (Frey & Gaertner, 1986) and evaluating job applications (Dovidio & Gaertner, 2000). When norms are ambiguous, African Americans are helped less and also evaluated less favorably than are Whites.

Aberson and Ettlin (2004) conducted a meta-analysis looking at aversive racism and responses favoring African Americans. They analyzed studies to determine the conditions that promoted favoritism for White and African American targets. This was done under conditions in which normative behaviors or expressions of attitude clearly favored egalitarian responses and when evaluative criteria were ambiguous. The meta-analysis was conducted on 31 studies and included more than 5,000 participants. Aberson and Ettlin concluded that when norms were ambiguous, African Americans received worse treatment than Whites, supporting the presence of aversive racism. However, under situations where African Americans are clearly positive, White individuals correct for their prejudice and inflate their ratings of African American targets so that African American targets are rated even higher than White targets. The authors, however, caution against inflated evaluations, noting that they may ultimately hurt African Americans. These inflated evaluations may not provide realistic feedback on performance and may ultimately deprive African Americans of opportunities and equal performance expectations.

Recent studies have found evidence of aversive racism across several contexts, including jury decisions (Mannes, 2016); media coverage of African Americans following natural disasters (Johnson, Dolan, & Sonnett, 2011); public funding for medical conditions disproportionally affecting African Americans (Bediako & King-Meadows, 2016); and for African Americans interactions with medical providers (Penner et al. 2010). Understanding the underlying motives for racism and modern-day expressions of racism is important in addressing racism and its effects. Theories of aversive and symbolic racism assume that most Whites will not engage in overt racist behavior, but when such behavior can be attributed to a reason other than racism, Whites are more likely to engage in such behavior.

CONSEQUENCES OF RACISM

As noted previously, the effects of racism are direct and subtle, pervasive and institutional, and evidenced in all of our institutions, including housing, politics, education, health, the law, and transportation. In the next section, we discuss the effects of racism within five major domains: (a) police violence against African American men, (b) criminal justice, (c) health, (d) housing, and (e) mental and psychological well-being. Racism has long-term deleterious effects on almost all indicators of life quality.

Police Violence Against African American Men

African Americans and African American men have been disproportionally killed. Some of the African American men who have died from police violence include Amadou Diallo, Manuel Loggins Jr., Ronald Madison, Sean Bell, Eric Garner, Michael Brown, and Alton Sterling. These are just a few of the many deaths; many deaths do not make the news headlines and are not discussed in social media. According to a story in the Huffington Post, police killed at least 258 Black people in 2016 (Craven, 2017). Thirty-nine were unarmed. Thirty-four percent of the unarmed people killed in 2016 were African American males. These are only the men who were killed and not the thousands who have been subjected to other forms of violence.

How acceptable is police violence against African American men, and who is more likely to be tolerant of such violence? A study by Hadden, Tolliver, Snowden, and Brown-Manning (2016) answered this question using a national sample of 1,974 (75% White) participants. Whites approved of a police officer showing violence against a citizen at higher rates than did other ethnic groups. In this same study, respondents were also asked to check off the reasons for differences in employment, income, and housing between African Americans and Whites. Those with attitudes supportive of police violence were more likely to believe reasons for racial inequities were because of lack of motivation and will. The majority of White respondents believed that inequities for African Americans are due to lack of motivation or will-power and ability to learn rather than to racial discrimination. On the other hand, the majority of African Americans perceived that police violence against African American men were linked to societal problems of discrimination and inequities for African Americans. This is also the opinion of African American police officers (Morin, Parker, Stepler, & Mercer, 2017). African American compared with White police officers were more likely to believe that deaths of Black men from police are an indicator of a bigger problem in the United States and not isolated incidents. Gramlich (2017) used data from a survey conducted on behalf of the Center for the National Research Platform. Approximately 8,000 officers were included in the survey. About twice as many African American officers (57%) than White officers (27%) reported that recent deaths of African Americans during incidents with the police are symptoms of a larger problem (see Table 4.1). A larger percentage of

TABLE 4.1 ■ Racial Differences in Perceptions of Deadly Black–Police Encounters Among Police, and the Public: % Saying the Deaths of Blacks During Encounters With Police in Recent Years Are		
	Isolated Incidents	**Signs of a Broader Problem**
Among Whites		
Officers	72	27
The Public	44	54
Among Blacks		
Officers	43	57
The Public	18	79

Source: Pew Research Center. Survey of law enforcement officers conducted May 19–August 14, 2016 and Survey of U.S. adults conducted August 16–September 22, 2016.

African Americans in the general public also report that deaths of Black men during police encounters are a sign of larger societal problems (79% for African Americans and 54% for Whites). This and the previous study support differences in racial perception surrounding violence against African Americans.

Blacks Lives Matter (BLM)

The BLM movement has been active and vocal against police violence in many cities throughout the United States. The movement began in 2013 following the acquittal of George Zimmerman who killed Black Florida teenager Trayvon Martin (Black Lives Matter, 2017). The BLM describes itself as "an ideological and political intervention in a world where Black lives are systematically and intentionally targeted for demise. It is an affirmation of Black folks' contributions to this society, our humanity, and our resilience in the face of deadly oppression."

The BLM movement grew into a large movement following the death of Michael Brown, who was killed by Ferguson, Missouri, police officer Darren Wilson in 2014. Today, there are BLM chapters in many cities throughout the United States and also a chapter in Canada. College students, young adults, and other adults from all walks of life and from all ethnic groups have joined this movement, which has included actions such as cultural and artistic expressions, education and empowerment activities, conferences, and organized protest and marches against inequities, among other activities.

Racial Trauma

Frequent negative police exposure results in trauma for many African Americans but especially for African American men (Aymer, 2016). Racial trauma is the feeling of danger from real or perceived experience of racial discrimination, threats of harm, and humiliating events. Racial trauma can also occur when witnessing harm to others of the same racial group (Smith, 2010).

Racial trauma occurs when African Americans are surrounded by constant reminders of the danger of being African American (Williams, 2016). Constantly reliving images of violence as television news and social media show videos of unarmed African Americans being killed across many contexts—in stores, in homes, in the streets, and even in Church—contributes to trauma. These constant images are reminders of the vulnerability of being harmed simply because of race, and there is a heightened fear and anxiety. Thus, when the death of an African American goes viral, it can trigger post-traumatic stress disorder (PTSD) (Downs, 2016).

In a study of police encounters and mental health, Geller, Fagan, Tyler, and Link (2014) surveyed 1,261 young men aged 18 to 26 years in New York City. Men were asked about interactions with the police and their mental health status (e.g., anxiety, PTSD) following these interactions. Eighty percent were racial or ethnic minorities. Eighty-five percent reported at least one police stop, and 46% reported being stopped at least once in the year prior to the survey. Respondents who reported more police contact, particularly more intrusive contact, reported higher levels of anxiety. PTSD symptoms were especially high when police intrusion levels (e.g. frisked or searched them, used harsh or racially tinged language, threatened or used physical force) were high.

Criminal Justice

African Americans, especially males, are disproportionately represented in the criminal justice system; this over-representation is most likely due to institutional racism. Although it is a myth that more African American males are involved in the criminal justice system than in college, a large percentage are, and a discussion of racism would be remiss without commenting on the link between education (or lack of education) and criminal justice involvement (Toldson, 2013). Two examples of racism within the criminal justice system are especially relevant— "driving while Black" and incarceration.

Driving While Black

Research on race and vehicle stops by police show that African American drivers are disproportionately stopped by police for traffic law violations (Kowalski & Lundman, 2007). The disproportionate number of African Americans, especially males, who are stopped by police has become known as the "driving while Black" phenomenon. According to research by Miller et al. (2017), African American and Latino men are more likely to be stopped by police, and this is what accounts for the increased number of deaths at the hands of police discussed previously (Miller et al., 2017).

Disproportionate stops are also known as racial profiling, which refers to the practice of targeting or stopping an individual primarily because of his or her race rather than because of a specific suspicion (Weitzer & Tuch, 2002). Racial profiling during automobile stops by officers shows racial and ethnic differences in whether the officer initiates a stop, whether the officer applies formal sanctions or coercion, and whether the officer searches drivers (Fallik & Novak, 2012). Research shows that Blacks and Hispanics are stopped at higher rates than their representation within the community (Roh & Robinson, 2009). Roh and Robinson looked at 333,760 traffic stops in 121 beats in which the driver's ethnicity was White, Black, or Hispanic. They found that Black drivers were stopped more than White or Hispanic drivers. Black drivers were also more likely than White or Hispanic drivers to be stopped for both nonmoving traffic reasons (13.9% more) and moving traffic reasons (7.6% more).

Regarding the decision to search, research suggests that Blacks are more likely than Whites to be searched by officers (Durose, Smith, & Langan, 2007; Tillyer, Klahm, & Engel, 2012). Durose et al. found that 9.5% of Black and 8.8% of Latino drivers reported being searched during traffic stops, compared with 3.6% of White drivers.

Incarceration

There are large racial disparities in incarceration and related detainments for African Americans. African Americans are more likely to be under the supervision of the Department of Corrections than any other racial or ethnic group. The correctional population includes persons incarcerated (either in prison or jail) or supervised in the community (probation or parole) (West, Sabol, & Greenman, 2010). According to data compiled by the Sentencing Project, racial minorities are more likely than Whites to be arrested, convicted, and given more severe sentences than Whites (Ghandnoosh, 2015). African American males are 6 times more likely to be incarcerated than White males and 2.5 times more likely than Hispanic males. If the current rate of incarceration continues, 1 of every 3 Black American males born today will go to prison in his lifetime, compared with 1 of every 17 White males. Racial and ethnic disparities among women are less substantial than among men but remain prevalent.

Some notable racial or ethnic disparities are pointed out by the Sentencing Project (Nellis, Green, & Mauer, 2008). African American youth account for 17% of youth but account for 46% of juvenile arrests and 31% of referrals to juvenile court. Ten percent of Black men in their 30s are in prison or jail. Although the number of African American men and women in state and federal prison declined slightly from 2000 to 2006, in 2009, African Americans still made up the majority of prisoners (West et al., 2010). There are three main factors that contribute to incarceration disparities. One is policies and practices such as the harsher drug laws and police policies such as "stop, question, and frisk" that give police broad discretion to stop a person. Two, implicit bias and stereotyping in decision making lead to more and higher periods of incarceration. The third factor is structural disadvantages associated with high rates of offending and arrests in African American and other communities of color (Nellis, 2016).

The policy of harsher sentencing for crack versus cocaine resulted in a disproportionate number of African American prisoners producing a 510% increase in the number of incarcerated drug offenders during the period 1983–1993. The Supreme Court in 2007 (Meehan, 2007) ruled that judges had flexibility in their use of sentencing guidelines articulated by the Sentencing Commission that had previously supported substantial differences between sentencing for crack cocaine and powdered cocaine. Current sentencing recommendations are expected to be less severe for African Americans, who typically are sentenced for a crack-related charge. Still, there remain other clear racial differences in arrest rates, incarceration rates, and length of sentences between African Americans and Whites. Implicit bias in decision making, which disadvantages African Americans, is also a major contributor to incarceration disparities.

Most of the research investigating racial or ethnic disparities has attended to the role of the jury in sentencing recommendations. However, most cases do not go to trial. Instead, a vast majority of convictions are determined through plea agreements. Edkins (2011) studied the extent to which race plays a role in the plea agreement process. Participants were 101 mostly White (91%) practicing defense attorneys. Participants were asked to respond to a case summary of a crime, suspect, and evidence. The race of the defendant was either African American or White. Findings revealed significant racial differences in the recommended plea bargain sentences. On average, the defense attorneys recommended longer prison terms for African American defendants than for White defendants. Defense attorneys reported that they would recommend an average of 2.88 years for the African American client and 2.22 years for the White client.

Race and Capital Punishment

Implicit bias and stereotyping occurs in capital punishment cases, where racial disparities are especially prevalent (Sentencing Project, 2013). There are two factors affecting capital punishment. One, Black defendants are more likely to be sentenced to death regardless of the race of their victims. Two, defendants convicted of the homicide of a White victim are substantially more likely to face capital punishment than those convicted of killing a non-White person. White people represent half of murder victims in the United States each year, but 77% of persons executed since 1976 were convicted of killing White victims. On the other hand, Black people also represent half of murder victims, but only 13% of persons executed since 1976 were convicted of killing Black victims.

Evidence of Racism From Experimental Studies

Other evidence of implicit bias has been in experimental studies that provide evidence that African Americans (compared with Whites) are more likely to be perceived as threatening, to be perceived as criminals, and to be shot (Greenwald, Oakes, & Hoffman, 2003; Sadler, Correll, Park, & Judd, 2012). Donders, Correll, and Wittenbrink (2008) showed that Black faces captured attention longer than White faces due to the perception of White participants about the threat of Blacks: that is, Whites' beliefs in the stereotypes that African Americans were dangerous.

Sadler et al. (2012) studied implicit racial bias among both college students and police officers in the decision to shoot males of different ethnic groups in a first-person shooter (FPS) task. This task is named FPS because participants have to take the first-person perspective of a police officer who must make rapid judgments about whether to shoot target suspects who appear on the screen holding either a gun or a nonthreatening object, such as a wallet or cell phone (Correll, Park, Judd, & Wittenbrink, 2002). In the first study, participants were college students attending a university in the Midwest. Stimulus materials were presented via a video game in which target suspects were holding or not holding a gun. The authors found that participants were especially likely to favor the "shoot" response over the "don't shoot" response when the target was Black than when the target was any other race (e.g., White, Latino, Asian). Furthermore, it took less time for the participant to shoot when the target was Black. The authors found that participants were significantly faster to correctly "shoot" a Black armed target than a White, Latino, or Asian armed target but slower to correctly "not shoot" a Black unarmed target than a White, Latino, or Asian unarmed target.

The second study involved police officers recruited from the Southeast, Southwest, and Northwest. The authors found evidence of racial bias in response time among this sample consistent with the college students. They found that police officers correctly responded more quickly to guns but more slowly to nonguns held by Black targets than to those held by targets of any other race.

Structural Disadvantages in African American Communities

Disparities in incarceration also exist because of structural conditions within communities in which many African Americans live (Nellis, 2016). These include disproportionate amounts of poverty, unemployment, inadequate housing, criminal activities, and higher levels of school dropouts. These disadvantages begin early in life and contribute to greater juvenile delinquency as well as school dropout.

Health

Health disparities are also created by racism. Although health outcomes have improved for African Americans, disparities have not. African Americans have the highest rates of morbidity and mortality for almost all diseases, the highest disability rates, shortest life expectancies, and the least access to health care of all major racial and ethnic groups (Miniño, Murphy, Xu, & Kochanek, 2011; National Center for Health Statistics, 2015). The health disparity gap between African Americans and Whites has remained the same and for some conditions become greater (Williams, 2000). Steven Woolf, Johnson, Fryer, Rust, and Satcher (2008) highlighted the role of racial disparities in mortality in a paper titled, "The Health Impact of Resolving Racial Disparities: An Analysis of US Mortality Data." In this paper, the authors argue that the U.S. health system spends much less money on achieving equity in health care than on the technology of care (e.g., use of medical devices and drugs). Using mortality data from the National Center for Health Statistics (NCHS), they estimated the number of deaths that did not occur by improving technology of care and the number of avoidable deaths among African Americans that would not have occurred if they were White. Analyses revealed that medical advances prevented 176,633 deaths, but had the mortality rates of Whites and African Americans been equal, 886,202 deaths would have been prevented. Miniño et al. (2011) similarly found that the average risk of death for the Black population is 26% higher than for the White population.

Smedley and Smedley (2005) summarize some areas of health disparities for African Americans and other ethnic groups:

1. African Americans and Hispanics receive lower quality health care across a range of diseases (including cancer, cardiovascular disease, HIV/AIDS, diabetes, mental health, and other chronic and infectious diseases) and clinical services.

2. Disparities are found even when clinical factors, such as stage of disease, presentation, comorbidities, age, and severity of disease are taken into account.

3. Disparities are found across a range of clinical settings, including public and private hospitals and teaching and nonteaching hospitals.

4. Disparities in care are associated with higher mortality among minorities who do not receive the same services as Whites.

5. There are significant racial differences in the receipt of appropriate screening and diagnosis services (e.g., cancer diagnostic tests, HIV tests).

6. Racial and ethnic disparities also are seen in access to and treatment of mental health illness.

Socioeconomic status alone does not explain the racial gap in health disparities. African Americans have worse health than Whites, even when factors such as education and income are taken into consideration (Smedley, Stith, & Nelson, 2003). Racism is a prime factor in these disparities, existing not just at the individual level but also at institutional levels in ways that impact health for African Americans (Smedley, 2012). For example, racism limits access to socioeconomic resources through housing segregation, which, in turn, determines access to education and employment opportunities. Discrimination in medical treatment triggers stress, which affects both physical and mental well-being (Read & Emerson, 2005).

Several studies show deleterious effects of racism on cardiovascular health, hypertension, and infant mortality (Adelman et al., 2008; Entringer, Buss, & Wadhwa, 2015), among other health conditions, which contribute to health disparities (Chou, Asnaani, & Hofmann, 2012). Several studies have been conducted on the relationship between race-related stress and cardiovascular diseases, such as hypertension. Dolezsar, McGrath, Herzig, and Miller (2014) summarized the findings from 44 published studies on the relationship between perceived racial discrimination and hypertension. Participants included mostly Blacks (62.2%) but also other ethnic groups, including Whites (13.6%), Hispanics (11.8%), and other (12.14%). The authors found a significant relation between perceived discrimination and hypertension. This relationship was stronger among Blacks, men, older participants, and those with lower education.

Racism and discrimination also contribute to poor health outcomes among African Americans within the treatment or health care environments (Hill et al., 2017; Parker, Kinlock, Chisolm, Furr-Holden, & Thorpe, 2016). For example, in an ethnically diverse sample of 1,699 persons recruited from Chicago's communities, 31% of African Americans versus 4% of Whites reported some level of discrimination in receiving health care.

Housing

In 1968, the federal government enacted the Fair Housing Act, which prohibits discrimination by direct providers of housing, such as landlords and real estate companies. The Fair Housing Act also prohibits discrimination by banks or other lending institutions and homeowners' insurance companies. Discriminatory practices that make housing unavailable to persons because of race or color, religion, sex, national origin, familial status, or disability are illegal. In spite of this federal law, housing discrimination continues to occur.

Although the more blatant (refusal to provide information to a minority applicant) forms of housing discrimination have declined, other more subtle forms of housing discrimination still exist. The Housing Discrimination Study (Turner et al., 2013) assessed housing discrimination. Turner conducted more than 8,000 housing discrimination tests in a nationally representative sample of 28 metropolitan areas. In each test, two trained individuals, one White and the other Black, Hispanic, or Asian, contacted a housing provider and asked about a housing unit for sale or rental. The two testers were matched on gender and age, and both presented themselves equally as qualified to rent or buy the advertised unit. African Americans, along with Hispanics and Asians, were told about and shown fewer units than Whites.

Another indicator of racism in the housing industry is the disproportionate rates of foreclosures among African Americans following the massive housing crisis that started in 2008. Rugh and Massey (2010) used data obtained from RealtyTrac, the nation's largest provider of foreclosure listings, to study ethnic or racial differences in foreclosures. They compiled the number of properties with foreclosures in the nation's largest metropolitan areas and looked at the impact of several variables on these foreclosures. They found that segregation of African Americans increased the number and rate of foreclosure. The impact of segregation on foreclosures was greater than other variables such as home buildings and house price booms. Foreclosures tended to occur in metropolitan areas where neighborhoods were largely segregated. They wrote, "Segregation therefore racialized and intensified the consequence of the American housing bubble. Hispanic and black home owners, not to mention entire Hispanic and black neighborhoods, bore the brunt of the foreclosure crisis" (p. 645).

Mental and Psychological Well-Being

Racist events also affect mental health and psychological well-being. Pieterse, Todd, Neville, and Carter (2012) conducted a meta-analysis of 66 studies that examined the association between racism and mental health among Black Americans. The sample size across these studies totaled 18,140. The authors found that the greater the perceived racism, the greater the likelihood of mental distress, including depression and anxiety. In fact, the authors noted that negative psychological responses to racism seemed to have some of the same reactions as responses to trauma.

Chao et al. (2012) found that African American students' perceptions of racism precipitated secondary emotional, interpersonal, and academic problems that led to the students being seen at a university counseling center. Using data collected from students at seven predominantly White Midwestern universities, the authors found that perceived racial discrimination was related to several co-occurring social and emotional problems. For men, perceived racism was most strongly related to increased irritability and anger. Pittman (2011) also found among African Americans that when anger was used to cope with racial discrimination, it impacted well-being and mental health.

In a study on race-related stress and life satisfaction among 247 African Americans, Driscoll, Reynolds, and Todman (2014) examined three types of race-related stress: individual (interpersonal experiences of racism); institutional (racism related to institutional policies and practices; and cultural (denigration of Black culture). Race-related stress was measured using a scale developed by Utsey (1999). Satisfaction with life was assessed using items from the Satisfaction with Life Scale (Diener, Emmons, Larsen, & Griffin, 1985). A sample item is, "If I could live my life over, I would change almost nothing." High levels of all three forms of race-related stress were linked to less life satisfaction.

Given the effects of race-related stress on psychological distress, Utsey and Hook (2007) were interested in examining physiological factors that might moderate or buffer this relationship. Higher heart rate variability (HRV) has been shown to be associated with good health outcomes. The authors investigated whether HRV might buffer African Americans against race-related stress with regard to psychological distress. Participants were 215 African American college students. Utsey and Hook found support for their study for males but not for females. They found that resting HRV moderated the relationship between race-related stressors and psychological distress. Men who had higher HRV reported less psychological distress even while reporting race-related stressors.

Racism affects the psychological well-being of children and adolescents as well as of adults. Priest et al. (2013) conducted a systematic review of the literature on the relationship between racial discrimination and the well-being of ethnic/racial minority children, including African Americans, Latino/as, and Asian Americans aged 12–18. One hundred and twenty-one studies across six countries were included in the review. The majority (71%) of the studies were conducted in the United States. Several mental health outcomes were significantly associated with reported discrimination: anxiety, depression, and negative self- esteem were associated with higher levels of discrimination. Higher levels of resilience, self-worth, psychological adaptation, psychological adjustment, and social and adaptive function were associated with less reported discrimination. In overview, studies show that racism has deleterious effects on health, including physical and psychological well-being, distress, disease, and other health indicators. Although racism has many adverse effects on health, many African Americans cope and do not show negative effects from racism. More recent research has focused on the moderators or factors that reduce the negative impact of racism on health and well-being. Coping with racism is discussed next.

COPING WITH RACISM

African Americans use various coping strategies to deal with racism stressors. These strategies are both general (i.e., support from family and friends) and culturally specific (i.e., racial socialization, spirituality, and so on). The cover story discusses a program specifically designed for parents to help them learn how to talk to their children when racist incidents occur. The EMBRace (Engaging, Managing, and Bonding through Race) is a 5-week program for African American families (Hoffman, 2017). Given the pervasive and chronic nature of racism, these types of programs are needed in communities throughout the United States. Other forms of coping are maladaptive (e.g., using tobacco, alcohol, other drugs). Culture-specific coping is the means by which ethnic minority individuals use knowledge of their culture to interpret and assign meaning to a stressful event in order to identify resources for dealing with the stressor (Slavin, Rainer, McCreary, & Gowda, 1991).

Utsey et al. (2000) define Africultural coping "as an effort to maintain a sense of harmony and balance within the physical, metaphysical, collective/communal, and the spiritual/psychological realms of existence" (p. 197). We next discuss methods that African Americans use to cope with stressors, including Africultural coping styles and other strategies.

Africultural Coping

Africultural coping has four primary components (Utsey et al., 2000): (a) cognitive or emotional debriefing, (b) spiritual-centered coping, (c) collective coping, and (d) ritual-centered coping. *Cognitive* or *emotional debriefing* is an adaptive reaction by African Americans to manage perceived environmental stressors. It might involve having a discussion with a supervisor about a coworker who is contributing to racial stress. *Spiritual-centered coping* is a coping behavior based on a sense of connection with spiritual elements in the universe and with the Creator. It could involve connecting to one's higher power and praying as a way of dealing with racial stress. Getting together with other African Americans and discussing and planning an activity would be an example of *collective coping*. These coping behaviors rely on group-centered activities. *Ritual-centered coping* is the use of rituals to manage a stressful situation. It might involve rituals such as playing certain types of music and lighting candles to deal with stress.

Utsey et al. (2000) developed the Africultural Coping Systems Inventory to measure the multidimensional nature of Africultural coping. The four subscales correspond to the four components of Africultural coping and include items such as, "Went to church or other religious meeting to get help from the group" and "We spent more time than usual doing things with family and friends."

Clinical Approaches for Coping With Racial Trauma

While most of research has focused on individual strategies for coping with racism, other work has attended to ways in which clinicians can help to reduce the impact of racism. Comas-Díaz (2016) describes a race-informed approach clinicians can use to help survivors of racial trauma. This approach is intended to give voice to participants, help them to see themselves as a source of authority, and help them to develop crucial consciousness to transform themselves and their circumstances. Comas-Díaz describes four steps that can be taken. The first step is an assessment of the race-related stress and trauma. Survivors are asked to tell their story within a safe environment; this exercise contributes to agency and power. The second step is one of desensitization, whereby the therapist helps the survivor to self-regulate her or his traumatic reactions after giving voice in the first step. Survivors are taught techniques such as safe-place imagery, healthy visualizations, and the practice of mind–body healings (e.g., yoga, relaxation, mediation). The third step is reprocessing, whereby clinicians support survivors in reprocessing negative thoughts and substituting these with positive thoughts. Here, the therapist helps the survivor find meaning and growth following traumatic events (e.g., adversity can teach one a life lesson). The fourth and final step is one of psychological decolonization, where critical consciousness is raised by asking questions such as, "Who benefits from racism?" Social action (giving testimony, advocacy, and community involvement) is also advocated in this step.

Other Strategies for Coping With Racism

Other forms of coping with racism range from both active and passive coping strategies, such as confrontation to withdrawal (Clark, 2004; Feagin, 1991; Landrine & Klonoff, 1996b; Plummer & Slane, 1996). Franklin (1999) describes a type of coping mechanism used by African American males called the "invisibility syndrome." Drawing from the earlier writing of Ralph Ellison in *The Invisible Man*, Franklin notes that some African American males may try to become invisible to cope with the adverse consequences of being noticed. However, Franklin notes that being invisible is not without its own adverse consequences. Invisibility, in fact, negates one's sense of identity and being, which creates other psychosocial problems. Finally, some African Americans engage in unhealthy behaviors, such as increased drinking, smoking, and other drug use to cope with racism and discrimination (Hudson et al., 2016).

As discussed earlier, racial trauma is particularly stressful, especially for African American men. A study by Brooms and Perry (2016) addressed how men coped with this type of race-related stress. The authors interviewed 25 Black men about how they responded to the killing of Black men. Several themes emerged. One theme titled, "I Try to Help Them See Me as a Human Being," involved men behaving in ways that represented mainstream values so as to not reinforce negative stereotypes. Others, aware of being policed and surveilled by White citizens, reported being mindful of the ways in which their physical stature and tone of voice could be perceived as menacing. Some other men used the strategy of modeling and representing respectability, believing it was their responsibility for changing perceptions of Whites. At the same time Black men expressed hurt, sadness, disbelief, and anger at the killing of Black men, realizing that these killings could happen to them.

In summary, African Americans cope with racism in several ways. Afrocultural coping strategies involve using African-centered ways of coping. Parents may also racially socialize their children to cope with racism. Coping with racial trauma due to the killing of African American men involves African American men behaving in ways to decrease negative perceptions. Other coping strategies, such as being invisible and using alcohol and other drugs, may have negative consequences.

Colorism and Africentric Features

Up to now, this chapter has focused on racism from the perspective of African Americans being the recipients of racism. However, assumed superiority based on skin color also exists within the African American community, as well as outside the African American community. Colorism is inequality based on skin color, hair texture, and facial features and an overall preference for Eurocentric physical attributes over African physical attributes (Wilder, 2010). Colorism is not unique to African Americans but is found throughout the world in most African, Asian, and Latin American countries. Colorism, in effect, supports the cultural assumption that White is superior to Black. Research on colorism is increasing as a scholarly body of work. One of the earliest studies on colorism was conducted by Keith and Herring (1991), who found that African Americans with very light skin had, on average, more than 2 years of education than did African Americans with dark skin.

Colorism operates within society at several levels and, like racism, is reflected in differentials and disparities among African Americans based on skin color (Hall, 2005). At a cultural level, colorism is reflected in African Americans with dark skin, especially African American women, being seen as less attractive and desirable than women with lighter skin tones (see Chapter 8 on "Interpersonal Relations"). Light-skin preferences are notably highlighted in the media, which are channels for cultural values. Although there are some recent exceptions in the media (e.g., popularity of Viola Davis, Tika Sumpter, Lupita Nyong'o), overall media depictions seem to favor African American women who have light skin and long straight hair.

At the institutional level, colorism is seen in disparities across several domains, including income, education, and incarceration. Hunter (2002) examined the relationship between skin tone and education among a national sample of African American women. She found that skin tone was a significant predictor of education. In this study, skin tone was measured using a 5-point scale, where "1" was darkest and "5" was lightest. Hunter found for every additional gradation of lightness, educational level increased by one-third of a year, so that the African American woman with the lightest skin had 1 additional year of education beyond a woman of a similar background with darker skin. In this same study, skin color was found to be significant predictor of African American women's annual income.

Research also supports differences in health outcomes based on skin color and other Africentric features among African Americans. Monk (2015) used data from the National Survey of American Life to investigate how skin color and discrimination are linked to health. A nationally representative sample of 3,570 Blacks responded to several questions. Discrimination was measured by perceived discrimination from both Whites and Blacks. Skin tone was assessed via interviewer rating of skin tone, as well as self-report. Health was measured by self-report physical health and whether the respondent was hypertensive. Monk found that skin tone was a predictor of both forms of discrimination; the darker Blacks were, the more discrimination they reported experiencing in their everyday life. However, when considering discrimination from African Americans only, it was the medium-tone African Americans who reported significantly less discrimination from other Blacks. Both very light-skinned and very dark-skinned Blacks reported significant amounts of discrimination due to their skin tone. Skin color discrimination from Blacks was a significant predictor of self-reported physical health, with darker skin tone linked to worse health. Skin color also predicted hypertension, with darker-skin African Americans more likely to report hypertension.

Other physical attributes of African Americans have been examined in relation to health outcomes. Hagiwara, Penner, Gonzalez, and Albrecht (2013) examined two

Africentric features (lip thickness and nose width) in relation to African Americans' health status. In the Hagiwara et al. study, 90 participants were shown a video-recorded interaction with patients and their physicians. The video recording allowed raters to measure lip thickness and nose width. These same participants completed a questionnaire that asked about their physical and mental health. Hagiwara and colleagues found that African Americans with both very strong Africentric features and very weak Africentric features reported poorer health than those with more moderate Africentric features. The link between weak Africentric features and poor health was unexpected but explained by the fact that African Americans who look more White may be subject to social ostracism by other African Americans. This finding is consistent with work on skin color that shows that being on either extreme of the color continuum is stigmatizing (Hunter, 2005).

Returning to the perceptions of Whites, Blair, Judd, and Chapleau (2004) found that Afrocentric features predicted longer prison sentences. This was true even when factors such as seriousness of crime and prior offenses were accounted for. Research has found that the more stereotypically Black a person's looks, the more of a criminal that person is perceived to be (Eberhardt et al., 2004). This extends to capital punishment. In an interesting two-part study, Eberhardt, Davies, Purdie-Vaughns, and Johnson (2006), obtained photos of 600 death-eligible cases that advanced to the penalty phase between 1979 and 1999. Study 1 involved 44 Black male defendants convicted of murdering White victims. Undergraduate students (mostly White) served as the raters and were asked to rate the stereotypicality of each Black defendant's appearance using features such as lips, nose, skin tone, and hair texture. The researchers controlled for other factors that typically affected sentencing (e.g., aggravating circumstances, mitigating circumstances, defendant's socioeconomic status). The results showed that above and beyond the covariates, defendants whose appearance was perceived as more stereotypically Black were more likely to receive a death sentence than defendants who appearance was seen as less stereotypically Black. Study 2 looked at whether this finding would be the same if the victims were Black. The authors found that a defendant's perceived stereotypicality made a difference when Blacks murdered White but not Black victims. Those who were more stereotypically Black received more death sentences when the victim was White and not Black. The researchers suggested that the interracial character of cases involving a Black defendant and a White victim may have made race especially salient and jurors more likely to think about race as a relevant heuristic for determining the blameworthiness of the defendant.

Research on skin color shows biases within and outside the African American community. And while this field of research is growing, further research is needed to assess how these biases affect not only socioeconomic status variables such as income and education but also aspects of the self, including self-worth and competence. Colorism is also discussed in Chapter 8.

METHODOLOGICAL AND RESEARCH ISSUES

Although there are several methodological and research topics to consider when discussing race and racism, we focus on the assessment and measurement of racism and reactions to racism. Measurement of racism has had a long history in psychology. This includes both direct and indirect ways of measuring racism, including recent studies on brain imaging.

Measures of Racism

Racism has been assessed using both direct and indirect strategies. Direct measures ask respondents about their attitudes and reactions toward a racial or ethnic group. Indirect measures assume that participants are not always motivated to be honest about racial bias and use other indicators for assessing race reactions. Several methods assume that automatic processes are better ways to assess racism than more thoughtful and more controlled processes. Priming and reaction time studies use these types of methods. Field studies include those that use paradigms such as the one described previously by Dovidio and Gaertner (1991), which showed that subjects are more reluctant to help Blacks relative to Whites. Physiological measures assume that subtle changes in one's physiological reactions are indicators of racial bias. Brain imaging is a more recent technique to assess reactions to different racial groups.

Paper-and-Pencil Surveys

Many paper-and-pencil surveys directly ask participants about their attitudes, beliefs, and behaviors toward a racial group. One example is Katz and Hass's (1988) pro-Black and anti-Black scales. Katz and Hass developed these scales based on the notion that Whites held conflicting attitudes toward Blacks, with feelings of friendliness and rejection toward Black people often existing side by side. A pro-Black statement from the scale is, "Blacks do not have the same employment opportunities as Whites." An anti-Black scale item is, "On the whole, Blacks do not stress education or training."

Implicit paper-and-pencil measures are more subtle and do not directly ask questions about race but rather present stimuli and ask for responses that allow one to infer whether there is racial bias. For example, the Racial Argument Scale (Saucier & Miller, 2003) measures racial attitudes indirectly by measuring how much respondents believe that arguments support positive and negative conclusions related to Blacks. Participants do not indicate whether they agree with these arguments but whether the arguments support the conclusion. Participants are presented with a paragraph description of an argument on a contemporary topic relevant to Blacks. Arguments advocate positions that are either positive or negative toward Blacks (e.g., African American studies in college, lack of Black actors, apology toward slavery, IQ scores). A conclusion statement follows each paragraph. Participants are asked to read each argument and then to rate how well the argument supported the conclusion. The measure assumes that since the items do not ask for the participant's own level of agreement, they would not be inclined to inhibit racist responses. If they indicate that they support an argument for a position that is against Blacks, there is some level of racial bias.

The Symbolic Racism Scale is a scale that measures aversive and symbolic racism described earlier. Henry and Sears (2002) describe symbolic racism as a form of racism that represents prejudice toward Blacks with four themes: (a) the sense that Blacks' failure to progress is due to their unwillingness to work hard enough, (b) the sense that Blacks are demanding too much, (c) a denial that racial discrimination exists today, and (d) the sense that Blacks have gotten more than they deserve.

The Symbolic Racism Scale has been primarily used to measure political attitudes. Some of the items in this scale are, "It's really a matter of some people not trying hard enough: If Blacks would only try harder, they could be just as well off as Whites," and, "How much discrimination against Blacks do you feel there is in the United States today, limiting their chances to get ahead?" According to Henry and Sears, the attitudes measured by these items justify (or do not justify) the status quo for Whites.

Priming and Reaction Time Measures

Priming and reaction time studies are other indirect ways of measuring prejudice and racism. These studies assume that automatic responses are better indicators of racial bias than are more controlled conscious responses. In reaction time studies, priming is often used, whereby White subjects respond to a Black stimulus that is presented via computer in millimeters of a second. These studies reduce the problems of self-report and social desirability bias.

A substantial amount of research has shown that White participants react differently to Black stimuli than they do to White stimuli. An example of this study is the classic study conducted by Dovidio, Evans, and Tyler (1986). College students were presented with category labels "Black" and "White" on a computer screen, followed by trait descriptors known to be stereotypical of the groups (ambitious and musical). Descriptors that were nontypical were also presented (i.e., drafty). The participant's task was to indicate as quickly as possible on the computer screen whether this characteristic could ever be true of the individual. For example, could musical ever be true of Blacks? The racial category activated the associated stereotypes, and participants were significantly faster in responding "yes" to stereotypical traits than they were to saying "yes" to nonstereotypical traits. Variations of this paradigm have been used in many studies (Lepore & Brown, 2000).

The Implicit Association Test (IAT) is also based on the assumption that people do not always know or speak their honest opinion. The IAT provides a method by which to assess conscious and unconscious preferences for several topics ranging from pets to political issues, ethnic groups to sports teams, and entertainers to styles of music. The IAT assesses reaction time when African American or Black and White are paired with both good and bad terms and concepts. Different versions of this test assess not only implicit Black and White race attitudes but also attitudes toward weight, skin tone, age, sexuality, and so on. The test can be self-administered over the Internet by going to https://implicit.harvard.edu/implicit/demo/selectatest.html.

Physiological Indicators and Measures

Physiological indicators can provide continuous, covert measures of psychological states during racial interactions (Cacioppo & Tassinary, 1990). These methods capture subtle physiological information, such as changes in cardiovascular reactivity, facial movement, and startle eye blinks, to assess racial bias. Research has shown that when Whites are exposed to Black targets, there are several physiological responses, including increased heart rate (Blascovich, Mendes, Hunter, Lickel, & Kowai-Bell, 2001) and contraction of facial muscles and eye blinking (Amodio, Harmon-Jones, & Devine, 2003). The results from physiological measures of White participants show reactions to African Americans that differ from when racial attitudes are directly assessed.

Vanman, Paul, Ito, and Miller (1997) had White participants simply imagine an interaction with a Black partner. Physiological change was noted relative to imagining an interaction with a White partner. On facial electromyography indicators, Whites showed more responses known to show negative affect, such as increased brow activity and decreased cheek activity. However, in the same study, on a self-report measure, Whites reported more favorable ratings of Black than of White partners. The findings from this study show that physiological responses are not always consistent with self-report responses.

The tool of neuroscience has also been used to examine racial responses. Eberhardt (2005) reviewed several studies that showed differences in brain imaging when participants (mostly Whites) were exposed to Blacks. These studies focus on the effects of race on the amygdala, an area of the brain that has been implicated in learned emotional responses. An earlier study on brain imaging exposed Black and White participants to the faces of Black and White people with neutral facial expressions while recording neural activity in the amygdala (Hart et al., 2000). The researchers found that during the early presentation of these racial stimuli, there was no difference in amygdala activation between in-group and out-group faces. However, during later presentations, amygdala activation declined more for in-group faces than for out-group faces. This was seen as an indicator of heightened habituation toward in-group faces.

In summary, there are many ways of measuring racism. Measures that are indirect will most likely provide more valid responses. These include reaction time studies, physiological measures, and, more recently, brain imaging.

Measures of Reactions to Racism

Most measures have been developed to assess racism toward ethnic minority populations. There are a few measures that assess reactions to racism. Utsey and Ponterotto (1996) developed the Index of Race-Related Stress (IRRS) to assess the stress experienced by African Americans in their daily experiences with racism and discrimination. The IRRS is a 46-item scale that consists of four subscales: the Cultural Racism subscale, which measures the experience of racism due to one's culture being denigrated; the Institutional Racism subscale, which taps into how institutional policies can lead to stress; the Collective Racism subscale that assesses racism due to organized efforts to harm or restrict the rights of African Americans; and the Individual Racism subscale that assesses racism that is interpersonally based.

Another measure that captures coping reactions to racism is the Racism-Related Coping Scale (RRCS; Forsyth & Carter, 2014). The measure assesses specific strategies African Americans use when coping with racism. The RRCS is a 59-item measure with eight subscales including the following: (1) racially conscious action ("I work to educate others about racism"); (2) hypervigilance ("I become more careful about what I say and do around people who are not Black"); (3) confrontation ("I expressed my anger to the person involved"); (4) empowered action ("I made a formal complaint"); (5) resistance ("I only did the bare minimum to get by in my job as a form of resistance"); (6) bargaining ("I tried to make something positive out of it"); (7) spiritual coping ("I prayed about it"); and (8) anger regulation ("I fantasized about getting revenge").

Reaction to racism scales have been used in studies of college student and community and medical samples (Brown & Tylka, 2011; Neblett & Carter, 2012). The scales were developed based on the assumption that understanding reactions to racism can aid in the development of interventions and programs to support individuals who are exposed to racism.

EVIDENCED-BASED AND PROMISING PRACTICES FOR REDUCING RACISM

Most empirical studies in psychology have targeted the individual in programs to decrease prejudice and racism. A large amount of this research comes from social psychology. Research on interracial attitudes has been conducted in labs under controlled experimental conditions, as well as in the field, most often in school settings. The majority of these studies do not make the distinction between prejudice and racism and, in general, have targeted the reduction of prejudice and/or improvement of intergroup relations.

School is an ideal place in which to change intergroup attitudes. The vast majority of youth attend school, and changes in race attitudes or preventing negative racial attitudes early on are likely to have long-lasting effects. Banks (2006) reviewed several intergroup relations and prejudice reduction strategies conducted in school over the past 60 years. School-based interventions include using multicultural textbooks and materials, role-playing, and other kinds of simulated experiences. This research indicates that the use of multicultural textbooks, other teaching materials, and cooperative teaching strategies that enable students from different racial and ethnic groups to interact positively is effective in helping children to develop more positive racial attitudes. These kinds of materials and teaching strategies also lead to students choosing more friends from outside their racial, ethnic, and cultural groups.

Ponterotto, Utsey, and Pedersen (2006), in their book *Preventing Prejudice*, offer several research-based practices for ways in which teachers, counselors, and parents can improve race attitudes among elementary, middle, high school, and college students. Based on the contact hypothesis (discussed next), they recommend that teachers develop learning tasks that encourage interdependence, whereby each student's contribution is equally important to the success of the task. Another activity might be to have students spend time interacting with individuals from a different ethnic and cultural group. A curriculum of inclusion would involve exposing students to multicultural materials that reflect the diversity of all experiences.

Contact Hypothesis

Much of the work done in school settings on reducing prejudice and racism has been derived from the contact hypothesis (Allport, 1954). This research emphasizes the importance of increasing contact between different racial groups. Increased contact is believed to lead to more positive racial attitudes and less prejudice and racism when four conditions are met: (a) Members of both groups have common goals. (b) There is intergroup cooperation. (c) There is equal status. (d) There is support from the larger social environment. Ellison and Powers (1994) and Sigelman, Bledsoe, Welch, and Combs (1996) found that interracial contact, especially if it occurs early in life and in school, leads to a greater likelihood that racially different groups will have close interracial friendships as adults. Multiracial relationships incorporate not only the ties between the individuals but also the ties of each person's social network (see Chapter 8 on interpersonal relations for further discussion on interracial relationship). Thus, multiracial social networks can promote cooperation, generate reciprocity norms, reduce segregation, and increase life opportunities (Emerson, Kimbro, & Yancey, 2002). Dixon, Durrheim, and Tredoux (2007) found similar support for the contact hypothesis in a study of almost 2,000 Black and White South Africans. The authors found that White contact with Blacks was associated with practices aimed at achieving racial justice.

Superordinate Group Memberships

Superordinate groups for African Americans, Whites, and other ethnic groups would be those in which all groups work together for a common goal. When superordinate group membership is salient, differences on other attributes (e.g., race, class) are less relevant (Stephan, 1999). Superordinate groups promote team activities and bonding and reduce stereotypes and potential conflicts. Examples of superordinate groups include sports teams, study groups, and social organizations.

Research shows that when students from diverse cultural, ethnic, and language groups have a superordinate identity in common, cultural differences diminish. Students are able to form positive relationships and friendships with others who are culturally different (Stephan & Stephan, 2004).

Societal Approaches to Decreasing Racism

Societal approaches to decreasing racism have been studied in the field of sociology more so than psychology. These approaches focus on changing norms, laws, and policies that support racism. Societal ways of changing racism would involve changes at an institutional or societal level. For example, racism in health disparities could potentially be reduced if there were uniform health coverage for all, one of the intents of the Affordable Care Act. Improvements in community infrastructure, such as community and police policies that support the reduction of crime and increases in employment opportunities, would reduce racism within the criminal justice system. An example of a policy change regarding disparities in the criminal justice system is changes in the recommended sentencing guidelines for crack cocaine and powdered cocaine. These guidelines give judges more discretion for sentencing of crack and powdered cocaine convictions. Previously, the differentials in sentencing favored powdered over crack cocaine.

CRITICAL ANALYSIS

In spite of the volumes of literature and research on race and racism, there are some remaining gaps in the literature and areas in which more research and efforts are needed. In this section, we identify some of these gaps and point to some promising frameworks for understanding race and racism.

First, we acknowledge that the use of the concept of race remains problematic in psychology. Race is still often used as an independent variable, with little recognition given to the context in which it is used. Is race being used to clarify associations or relationships relevant to the sociopolitical, cultural, or biological bases of this construct? Continuing arguments on the importance of race as a construct are not likely to be resolved. However, if race can be used to identify and ameliorate health and other disparities among African Americans, then some good can come out of its use. It is most likely that the increased utility of the construct will be linked with greater thoughtfulness and specificity in the measurement and conceptualization of race.

Throughout the literature, and indeed in this chapter, we have tended to focus on the negative consequences of racism. We have paid less attention to resiliency and how African Americans have survived and even thrived historically and contemporarily. Research on coping with racial stress provides additional information on how African Americans have managed their lives and how resiliency is evident. We hope to see more research on positive ways of coping with racism.

The study of racism in psychology has mostly been the study of White racism and White individuals' reactions to African Americans and other ethnic minorities. Research has also focused on changing attitudes and behaviors of Whites toward African Americans and not vice versa. Understanding the attitudes and beliefs African Americans hold toward Whites and other ethnic groups is also important in terms of intergroup relations. Similarly, less research has been devoted to the negative consequences of racism for Whites (Ponterotto et al., 2006).

We applaud the work that has begun to examine the variability within African Americans in their experience of racism. One line of research that has increased over the past 5 years is research on colorism and Africentric features. Both colorism and Africentric features are linked to disparities within and outside the African American community.

It is also important to consider the United States and its construction of race and racism in a broader global context and in historical perspective. Potential regional variations in racism and the salience of race must be acknowledged and considered when studying racism. Also, the increasing relevance of biracial and multiethnic individuals and historical changes in our sociopolitical construction of race are important considerations in ongoing empirical work focusing on race and racism.

Finally, it is important to note the importance of recent movements such as Black Lives Matter in addressing racism and social injustices. This movement, akin to the civil rights movement 60 years ago, is likely to continue, especially in the current climate where racial disparities and injustices seem to be increasing.

Summary

Racism is pervasive and affects everyone in this country. The concept of race remains problematic, although race is still frequently used in psychology. According to the U.S. Census Bureau (2016a), a Black or African American is "a person having origins in any of the Black racial groups of Africa."

Common to all definitions of racism is the assumption of implicit or explicit superiority of one group over another. Almost all African Americans have experienced racism—if not directly, then through institutions that systematically discriminate. Jones (1997) identified three major types of racism as individual, institutional, and cultural. Other scholars point to differences between old-fashioned racism and newer, subtler forms of racism, such as aversive or symbolic racism.

The effects of racism are both direct and subtle, pervasive, and seen in all of our institutions, including housing, politics, education, health, law, and transportation. Racism has an especially powerful and deleterious impact on African Americans in the criminal justice system, on health outcomes, in housing, and on psychological and mental health outcomes. African Americans use Africultural coping styles to deal with racist events. Racism has been measured both directly and indirectly. Indirect measures include priming and reaction time studies, field studies, and the use of physiological indicators, such as electrocardiograms and facial movements. More recent brain imaging studies show differences in brain activation when Black and White stimuli are presented. Ways of reducing racism include individual-level approaches, such as increasing interracial contact, and societal approaches, such as changing institutional practices.

SOCIAL SYSTEMS AND STRUCTURES

SECTION II

KINSHIP AND FAMILY

The ruin of a nation begins in the homes of its people.

—Ashanti proverb

LEARNING OBJECTIVES

- To be able to define the African American family
- To become aware of how the African American family has been historically studied
- To understand critical events affecting African American families historically and contemporarily
- To understand what the African American family looks like
- To become familiar with strengths and coping patterns of African American families
- To become aware of research and methodological issues when studying African American families
- To be able to identify best practices for working with African American families

MORE COMMITTED TO BABY MAMAS THAN A WIFE

BY DR. OBARI ADÉYE CARTMAN (2016, MAY 9)

Some cringe at the term baby mama. It connotes a low class, almost shameful position in Black communities where family structure has transitioned over the past few decades. Black folk in this country have always had remixed configurations of extended family systems.

(Continued)

(Continued)

The baby mama age was born from a decrease in marriage, increase in divorce, and no change in sex frequency. Although it literally means the exact same thing, saying "mother of my child" sounds more respectable. Beyond the semantics, and considering a wide variety of circumstances, I think we need to have more open conversations about healthy co-parenting, rooted in more sincere ways to celebrate mamas.

Let's start with definitions:

co-par·ent

kō'pe(ə)rənt/

noun: coparent

1. a divinely appointed assignment to engage in a long term relationship with another adult equally responsible for providing comprehensive care for one or more child.

Men invented "baby mama drama." It's a magician's sleight of hand trick. We say ooh look over there → women are crazy, and hope you don't see the mischief we tucked behind our ear. Baby mama drama becomes an asylum for male confusion, irresponsibility, miscommunication and selfishness. Replace that guy that with a man who presents his intentions with clarity, has the skills discipline and motivation to sustain himself and others, and is mature enough to make decisions like don't not sleep with her because you're lonely and she's familiar—and voilá! Baby mama drama disappears.

Marriage is old school. I'd probably be married by now if I wasn't afraid of forever. To have and to hold from this day forward, for better, for worse, for richer, for poorer, in sickness and in health, until death do us part. That vow makes so much more sense for our children. Why don't we make vows to our children? Write them out. Have public ceremonies and ask the community to hold us accountable for maintaining them? One of the dangers of patriarchy is superficially (or not at all) valuing children and women. Societies that prioritize men function from a level of imbalance that will always diminish the potential of human achievement. Maybe it all stems from men's envy of the power of women—and that resentment turns into control. I digress.

When I've asked myself why I'm not married (yet) I know it's certainly not for lack of marriageable women in my life. It's also not because I don't think marriage is important. The only reason left seems quite simple—I'm not married because I don't want to be. Our wants are informed by lots of things: community expectations, family pressure, fears, internal values, cost benefit analysis, but at the end of the day it's a decision to make. Choosing to get and stay married is the base. Sure, you gotta add all the other ingredients to it: patience, wisdom, shared values, communication, community support, etc. but none of that matters without two adults choosing to do it. Which isn't true for co-parenting. The choice is made (assuming the sex was consensual) the moment that child is conceived—no, actually, the moment the mother decides to give birth to it.

Source: Cartman (2016).

DEFINITIONS AND HISTORICAL BACKGROUND ON AFRICAN AMERICAN FAMILIES

African American families are varied and diverse. The cover story highlights the importance of fathers' coparenting, whether or not they are married to the child's mother. Many disciplines, including sociology, anthropology, history, and psychology, are interested in the African American family and kinships. The family is the most proximal influence for youth and the primary institution for socializing them. In this chapter, we examine structural (i.e., who the family consists of and what the family looks like) as well as functional (i.e., what purposes the family serves) aspects of the African American family. First, we provide definitions of terms relevant to family; then, we provide a historical overview of how African American families have been studied; and then, we describe the functional and structural characteristics of the social structures within which Africans lived in the New World during the period of enslavement. We provide a snapshot of what contemporary African American families look like. We also explore strengths and coping patterns among African American families. We review research and methodological issues relevant to studying African American families. Then, evidenced-based practices for working with African American families are discussed. Finally, we give a critique and summary of the main ideas of the chapter.

Definitions

More than half a century ago, the sociologist Murdock (1949) defined the family as a social group characterized by common residence, economic cooperation, and reproduction. Murdock defined a family as a male and female cohabiting adults who had a sexual relationship, and one or more children, biological or adopted. Murdock described the nuclear family as the most basic family structure, which consisted of a married man and woman with their offspring. Murdock's definition captures what has been thought of within contemporary American culture and social science as a traditional family. As we will see, African American families differ substantially from the family described by Murdock. Reiss's (1965) definition of the family focuses on its functional aspects. According to Reiss, the one universal function of the family is the socialization of the young. Reiss defines the family as a small, kinship-structured group with the key function of providing nurturance and socialization of the newborn. He acknowledges that this group is commonly the parents in a conjugal relationship, but occasionally, it is the mother and/or other relatives of the mother. Robert Hill's (1998) definition of the Black family emphasizes both functional and structural aspects. According to Hill, the Black family is a household related by blood or marriage or function that provides basic instrumental and expressive functions to its members. Families serve instrumental functions by providing for the physical and material needs of the family members, such as providing clothing, shelter, and food. The expressive functions of a family take into account the emotional support and nurturance needs met by the family.

The family network can include biological relations as well as nonbiologically related members. The African American family is characterized as an extended family (Hill, 1998). The *extended family* is a network of functionally related individuals who reside in different households. The *immediate family* consists of individuals who reside in the same household, regardless of the number of generations within that household. Akin to the extended family is the notion of the *augmented family*. The augmented family is defined as a family group where extended families and/or non-relatives live with and provide significant care to one or more children. The presence of additional adult care providers distinguishes the augmented family from nuclear and single-parent families (Barnes, 2001).

Fictive kin are often included as members of African American families. *Fictive kin* are those members of the family who are not biologically related nor related through marriage but who feel as if they are family and function like family. Friends who are fictive kin are incorporated into the extended family network and are seen socially and emotionally as kin. A person who is considered fictive kin may be seen as a father, mother, grandmother, grandfather, uncle, aunt, sister, brother, or cousin, depending on the role he or she plays (Scott & Black, 1989). Fictive kin may be referred to as play mother, play father, play cousin, play aunt, and so forth. The notion of fictive kin is also prevalent in African culture whereby all members of a tribe or community are considered family (Stewart, 2007). It is common in African culture for friends to refer to each other as brother or sister and use other terms denoting family relations.

Historical Approaches to Studying Black Families

Much of the early writings on the Black family are found in the domains of history and sociology. W. E. B. Du Bois authored the first books on the Black family, *The Philadelphia Negro* (1899) and *The Negro American Family* (1908). In these books, Du Bois draws on African and slave experiences in discussing differences between Black and White families. Du Bois disputes the then-existing myth that Africa was not a source of culture and civilization. He describes the cultural survival of Africans in the New World and discusses how their language, religion, and practices survived the Middle Passage to the United States (Gadsden, 1999).

Frazier's book, *The Negro Family in the United States* (1939), is one of the first scholarly works to examine Black family life in the United States. In this book, Frazier describes the negative consequences of slavery on the disorganization of the Black family. According to Frazier, slavery created an unstable family unit that resulted in lasting damage to the African American family. During slavery, the biological family unit was not sacred. Children were sold from their biological parents, and male and female partners were kept from legal unions. The economic structure of slavery forced separations of male and female partners from each other and from their children.

The lack of family stability, with its resulting problems among African Americans, continued after slavery as Blacks began the migration from the South to the North. According to Frazier (1939), social welfare measures to combat poverty in the 1930s had many negative consequences for families. Families became dependent on welfare and handouts and did not achieve self-sufficiency. Furthermore, many of the practices that were grounded in African traditions and useful in Southern life were not functional in the urban North. Frazier recommended that these traditional African practices be eliminated. He believed that a different approach was needed for these families to survive in the urban North and that African American families could not progress until they changed their way of living. At the same time, welfare programs that were intended to help African American families in poverty were, in fact, detrimental to the well-being of the African American family. One such program was the man-in-the-house rule. The man-in-the-house rule denied payments to a child who qualified for welfare benefits if the child's mother was living with or having relations with an able-bodied man (Man-in-the-House-Rule, 2008; Neubeck & Cazenave, 2001). This rule was struck down in 1968.

The study of the African American family during the 1960s and 1970s was conducted in the context of the many social and economic barriers African Americans faced during this period. Two types of literature on the family were written during this period (Gadsden, 1999). One group of studies focused on the conditions and circumstances that prevented Blacks from social and economic upward mobility. Moynihan's (1965) commissioned paper, "The Negro Family: The Case for National Action," is illustrative of this approach. This paper portrayed Black families as pathological, with a structure that differed from the normative family structure within the United States. Normative family structure was based on middle-class European

American family structure. According to Moynihan (1965), in essence, the Negro community has been forced into a matriarchal structure, which, because it is so out of line with the rest of the American society, seriously retards the progress of the group as a whole and imposes a crushing burden on the Negro male and, in consequence, on a great many Negro women as well (p. 7).

The theme in Moynihan's paper is congruent with Frazier's disorganization theme in accounting for the conditions of Black families. Moynihan's main point is that the deterioration of the Black family is responsible for the deterioration of Black society. Moynihan was assistant secretary of labor at the time this paper was written. By writing this paper, he advanced the notion that civil rights legislation alone would not guarantee racial equality since it was the breakdown in family structure that was largely responsible for poverty among Blacks. Moynihan went on to become an advisor to President Nixon and a senator representing New York for four terms.

The second type of literature that emerged during the 1960s and 1970s used a strength model to describe Black families. These writings used new ways of understanding the experiences of African American families (Billingsley, 1968). The patterns and styles that had come to be associated with African American families were seen as adaptive and functional for the survival and well-being of members of the family. This new work viewed flexible family structure, such as the extended family, as functional. Authors of this type of literature discussed the dynamic and positive interactional patterns and support systems within African American families (McAdoo, 1998, 2007). Robert Hill's work on the Black family began in the 1970s and, like Billingsley's, focused on resiliency and strength within the Black family. Hill's work is discussed later in this chapter. The strength-based approach to studying Black families started by Billingsley and Hill continues today.

Research on Black families in the 1990s and beyond also tended to focus on structural factors, such as the marriage rate of African Americans (Gadsden, 1999). These studies include studies of structural patterns and socioeconomic indicators, such as female-headed households, poverty, and adolescent mothers. Current research on African American families is diverse and spans several areas. These include topics on child-rearing and socialization practices, family communication and support, family strengths and resiliency, and African American fathers.

AFRICAN AMERICAN FAMILY STRUCTURE

Historical Perspective

Families in Africa

It is impossible to describe African culture without reference to the family. While African families are diverse (e.g., a few African cultures still practice polygamy while most do not), as with families of all cultural groups, there are key characteristic and unique aspects of the African family. The Ghanian scholar Gyekye (1996) describes the role of the family in a communal society. According to Gyekye, when one speaks of the family in an African context, one is referring not to the nuclear family but to the extended family. The communal values of solidarity, mutual helpfulness, interdependence, and concern for the well-being of every individual member of society are most often expressed in the institution of the family. Each member of the family is responsible for maintaining the cohesion of the family; within the family system, children have obligations to their parents, and parents have obligations to their children.

On the topic of marriage, Gyekye notes that marriage is essential to the development of kinship ties, and every adult man and woman is expected to marry and procreate. In traditional Africa, marriage is not only an affair between two persons who may be in love but also is a marriage between the families of each. Marriage is contracted only after each family is satisfied regarding the worthiness of each of the marriage partners. Marriage, in effect, in many African societies is considered a union of families.

The importance of marriage is seen in African puberty rites, in which young people are educated on sex, marriage, and family life in preparation for marriage. An unmarried woman in Africa is almost an anomaly: Marriage is a requirement of the society and an obligation that every man and woman must fulfill.

In many African societies, when a young man has gained employment, he is expected to marry because marriage symbolizes respect and social status. In the traditional Akan society of Ghana, if a man who has reached the age at which he is expected to marry does not do so, he will be regarded as a *kwasia* (Akan translation is "fool") and considered to be unwise and irresponsible.

Although, in general, the family unit is seen as a primary way of furthering the communal structure, there is variability. Western influences and new technology have begun to impact African families. The African family is seen as both resilient and troubled (Nkosi & Daniels, 2007). Akande, Adetoun, and Tserere (2006) describe some of the challenges, noting that the emerging South African family can best be described as a *saturated family*. The authors note that technologies (e.g., car, ill-gotten wealth, TV, cell phones) have contributed to family turmoil and a sense of discontinuity and fragmentation. The home is no longer a refuge of harmony, understanding, and peace but instead the site of disputes and violence between individuals of different ages and both genders.

Also of note is the impact of AIDS on the family system in Africa, especially sub-Saharan Africa. For example, in 2011, in South Africa and Zambia, the prevalence of adults living with HIV/AIDS was 17.3% and 12.5%, respectively (World Health Organization [WHO], 2012). Because of the high incidence of HIV among families in some countries, family systems have been disrupted and torn apart. Women who are the care providers in Africa have higher prevalence rates of HIV than men; in South Africa, three women in the 15- to 24-year-old age group are infected for every one man (AIDS Foundation, South Africa).

Caring for children orphaned due to AIDS can be especially burdensome for members of the immediate and extended family (Govender, Penning, George, & Quinlan, 2012). Govender et al. compared caregivers of children orphaned due to AIDS with caregivers who cared for nonorphans. Participants included orphan (N = 224) and nonorphan (N = 395) caregivers. Caregivers of orphans (compared with nonorphans) tended to be grandmothers who were mostly unemployed, which added to financial strain. These caregivers were also more likely to care for more children and to have less help from other adults. Seventy-five percent of the orphan caregivers had been the child's caregiver since birth. Caregivers of orphans also reported more health problems for themselves, as well as for their orphaned children. One of the implications of this study is that the extended family in South Africa may not be able to provide the support needed because of the AIDS epidemic. A related change in family systems due to HIV/AIDS is that children in households affected by HIV have had to become involved in caregiving. This is because there may not be a responsible adult to perform the caregiving role (Olang'o, Nyamongo, & Nyambedha, 2012).

In overview, we see similarities and differences between African and African American families in contemporary society, with some similarity in how families are conceptualized. However, the HIV epidemic, along with technological changes, is affecting the structure and the well-being of the family in Africa.

Families During Enslavement

Although it has been assumed that there were no two-parent families during enslavement, Burgess (1995) writes that many families of African descent living in the United States in the 1700s and 1800s were two-parent households. By examining plantation records, Gutman (1976) observed the presence of nuclear families among enslaved Africans that resembled those of the slave masters. Using 1880–1885 census data collected from Blacks in several cities, Gutman found that the majority of Blacks of all social classes were in nuclear families. Gutman believed that slavery did not destroy the Black family and that, in fact, enslaved families were stronger than had been thought. Although there were nuclear families, other family forms also existed because enslaved families were often separated through sales.

Enslaved Blacks tried to provide for their families financially, as well as spiritually (Hallam, 2004). Prior to slavery becoming a legal institution, some slaves were able to make arrangements for their families (e.g., some contracted the release of children after so many years of service). As the plantation dictated how the South functioned, in the late 17th and early 18th centuries, slavery became legalized in law, and it became very challenging for Blacks to form families as the laws forbade Blacks to marry each other. However, by the early 1700s, plantation owners became aware of the economic benefits of having slaves marry. Marriage led to less discontent among slaves, more stable unions, and, importantly, reliable reproduction cycles (Hallam, 2004).

The lives of the enslaved family depended on the needs of the agrarian region. In tobacco-planting regions, fewer slaves were needed, which led to families having different "owners" and living apart. Husbands in these unions would visit their wives and children once or twice a week. However, on large cotton plantations, which required many slaves, it was more common for families to live on the same plantation (Hallam, 2004).

During slavery, the mother–child relationship rather than the husband–wife relationship was primary to family life. Within slave communities, members helped to raise children of single mothers. When parents were sold to other slave owners, other adults in the slave community took care of the children left behind. The biggest fear of families was that a child would be sold.

Although enslaved families were able to function as adaptively as feasible given their circumstances, the consequences of slavery were nevertheless devastating to the African American family (Burgess, 1995). Enslavement had several pervasive, institutional, and long-term effects on the family. These included earlier ages of intercourse, childbearing, and establishment of a household. In African communities, natural spacing techniques, such as breastfeeding and polygamous unions, allowed women to space childbearing. Within the New World, there was an emphasis on increased economic production and, consequently, an emphasis on human reproduction. Therefore, enslaved African women began parenting at earlier ages and had greater numbers of children than did their foremothers in Africa.

Permanent unions and marriages were not possible because slaves could be sold at any time. Marriages between Africans in the United States received no legitimacy from slave owners. Enslaved Africans were required to get permission from their owners before they could marry, even though their marriages were not legally recognized.

Black Families During Emancipation and Reconstruction

During the period of emancipation, family life changed for African Americans. African American families could stay together, and legal marriage was possible. Fathers who had been sold and separated prior to emancipation reestablished relationships with their families. After slavery, there was an increase in two-parent households, as fathers rejoined their families, and couples were legally able to marry (Burgess, 1995).

However, most African Americans in the rural South lived in poverty, and economic conditions forced many to become sharecroppers. Sharecroppers paid rent by giving a portion of their crop to the landowners, who also often owned the house they lived in. Although education was now legal for Blacks, often children as young as 10 or 11 were unable to attend school because they had to work on the farm.

During the period from 1865 to 1898, African Americans began to own small businesses and farms and to develop Churches and some banking systems. Colleges were created, and some literacy was achieved. These advances helped to shape the African American family, as some children were able to get an education.

The Great Migration

From 1916 to 1970, African American families began to leave the South for what they thought would be a better life in cities in the North, Midwest, and West. These cities included New York, Chicago, Philadelphia, and Detroit. Although there were harsh conditions and Blacks could only obtain menial jobs, for the most part, they were able to find some form of employment. Some African Americans developed businesses and were able to take care of their families (Burgess, 1995). Others were able to obtain jobs in factories, slaughterhouses, and foundries, although these jobs had very poor working conditions. Black migration declined during the period of the Great Depression in the 1930s but increased with the coming of World War II. When the Great Migration ended, in 1970, the geographical distribution of Blacks had changed considerably. In 1900, roughly 9 out of every 10 Blacks lived in the South. By 1970, the South was home to less than half of the country's Blacks. Today about 55% of Blacks live in the South (Black Demographics, n.d.)

The Black family migration and growing urbanization changed the makeup of the Black family (Staples, 1999). By 1925, Blacks in the urban North, Midwest, and West no longer had the cultural practices that had enabled them to survive in the South. During this time and the decades that followed, new phenomena surfaced: children reared by mothers only, welfare dependency, juvenile delinquency, and drug addiction. According to Staples, about 10% to 15% of all Black families experienced these problems in the 1950s. Social policies that included welfare and poverty programs were developed during the period of the 1950s. However, many of these programs did not consider other factors that affected the African American community. For example, social policies were based on a "breadwinner" model that assumed that husbands would provide the basic needs for their families. This model did not consider the low wages and the high level of unemployment among African American men that made it impossible for them to take care of their families (Burgess, 1995). Consequently, some of the early programs that were intended to benefit families may have encouraged fathers to be absent from the home. For example, public assistance requirements prohibited male presence in homes in which public assistance was received, as discussed previously (i.e., man-in-the-house rule).

WHAT DOES THE AFRICAN AMERICAN FAMILY LOOK LIKE?

Structural aspects of the contemporary African American family have been described by scholars (e.g., McAdoo, 2007; Vereen, 2007). These papers focus on the individuals with whom African American children live, the composition of the family, who lives in the household, marriage and divorce, family structure and poverty, and differences between African American and White family structure. Other studies focus on social and psychosocial outcomes related to family structure. Vereen advocates the need for a paradigm shift in how African American family structure is categorized in order to meet the needs of this population. We discuss structural aspects of the family next.

Single-Parent-Headed Households

There has been an increase in single-mother families over the past few decades for both White and African American households. Reasons for the increase in single-female-headed households differ for African Americans and other ethnic groups. For example, among White women, there has been an increase in divorce and a decrease in remarriage. Among African American women, the increase in single-parent-headed households is due to the fact that there has been an increase in the number of never-married mothers. Never-married women tend to have less economic stability than married women because they are more likely to be younger and to have less education.

Family Structure of Households With Children

There has been a decline in the two-parent households among all racial and ethnic groups (Pew, 2015). In the 1960s, 73% of all children lived in a family with two married parents in their first marriage. By 1980, this percentage had dropped to 61%, and today, less than half (46%) live in this family arrangement. The decline in the number of children who live in the "traditional" family of the 1960s is due to children living with single or cohabitating (unmarried) parents.

The household structure of the family that the child lives in is important to consider; household structure has implications for the well-being of the child. For example, households with only one adult are more likely to be poor and to have fewer resources than households where there is more than one adult. Table 5.1 provides statistics on household structure by race and ethnicity.

As reflected in Table 5.1, slightly more than half (51.5%) of African American children live in mother-alone households, whereas 25.2% of Hispanic children and 18.1% of White children live in a household with a single mother as the only adult. A small proportion of African American children, 3.9%, live in single-father-headed families (U.S. Census, 2016b). The percentage of single-father-headed households is comparable across the three ethnic groups. Single-father-headed families tend to be more economically advantaged than single-mother-headed families and to have more support from others in the household than do single-mother-headed families (Mason, Skolnick, & Sugarman, 2002).

African American children are also more likely to reside in a home where one or more grandparents are present than are White children or Hispanic children (U.S. Census, 2016c). This was seen in the White House, where Michelle Obama's mother, Marian Robinson, resided in order to help care for her granddaughters.

Family Structure and Childhood Poverty

Childhood poverty is linked to family structure. Poverty among children is highest among those who live in single-mother-headed families. Children who live with their mothers only are much more likely to be poor than are children who

TABLE 5.1 ■ Percentages of Children With Both and Single Parents by Race and Ethnicity

Characteristic	White	Black	Hispanic
Mother alone	18.1	51.5	25.2
Father alone	4.0	3.9	0.09
Two parents	74.3	38.6	67.2

Source: U.S. Census (2016b).

Note: Households are headed by a mother or a father but may include other adults. Black and White includes children whose race was reported only as Black or White and not in combination with one or more other races.

live with both parents (DeNavas-Walt & Proctor, 2015). Across all racial and ethnic groups, 6% of married-couple families live in poverty, 16% of couples with male head of households live in poverty, and 31% of female-headed households live in poverty (DeNavas-Walt & Procter, 2015).

Table 5.2 provides information on child poverty among children by household structure and ethnicity (U.S. Census, 2016d). As seen in Table 5.2, both African American, White, and Hispanic children who live in married-couple families experience less poverty than those who live in single-parent households. For example, in 2015, 10.9% of African American children in married-couple families lived in poverty, compared with 46.1% of children in female-headed households. These large differences in poverty rates for female-headed households are also seen for other racial and ethnic groups.

TABLE 5.2 ■ Families 100% Below Poverty by Family Structure and Race and Ethnicity

Type of family	White	Black	Asian	Hispanic
All families	6.7	22.2	8.1	20.4
Married couple (with children under 18)	6.0	10.9	9.0	19.5
Female-headed household (with children under 18)	34.8	46.1	26.5	48.7
Male-headed household (with children under 18)	17.1	40.3	29.1	29.5

Source: U.S. Census Bureau (2016b).

Consequences of Family Structure on Children's Outcomes

Although many children reared in mother-only households do well, there may be adverse consequences for others (Gonzalez, Jones, Kincaid, & Cuellar, 2012; Mather & Adams, 2006). Research suggests that children who live in single-mother-headed households do not do as well on several social indicators. For example, there is a higher school dropout rate among these children, and daughters are at higher risk of becoming teen parents themselves. Juvenile delinquency may also be higher because there may be less parental supervision. Research suggests that fewer resources, economic instability, and poverty, not family structure, account for these differences. Poor economic conditions led to parental stress, and it is stress that contributes to decreased well-being among children (Cain & Combs-Orme, 2005). Many of these adverse social indicators can be moderated by support from extended family and friends, community resources, and decent employment. Also, involvement of the child's biological father attenuates potential negative youth outcomes (Langley, 2016). About 26% of single mothers report that the child's biological father is the primary coparent, and others report that other adults help with parenting (Jones, Zalot, Foster, Sterrett, & Chester, 2007).

Births to Teen Mothers

Teen mothers may experience special challenges, in that they are more likely to have more economic problems when compared with older mothers. The teen years also involve significant developmental transitions relevant to a range of social, emotional, and physical factors. The birth rate for African American females between the ages of 15 and 19 is about 34.9 per 1,000, compared with a national rate of about 24.2 per 1,000. Teen births across all ethnic groups have declined substantially over the past 25 years (Table 5.3; Martin, Hamilton, & Ventura, 2015). The largest decline since 1991 within a racial group was for African American females. The birth rate for African American and Hispanic teens ages 15 to 19 was reduced from 118.2 and 104.6 per 1,000 in 1991 to 34.9 and 38 per 1,000 in 2014. The birth rates of both Hispanics and African Americans, however, remain higher than for Whites.

Foster Care and Adoption

When parents are unable to care for a child or should they decide that there may be family options that are in the better interest of their child, there are multiple family and living situations in which children might be raised. For African American

TABLE 5.3 ■ Teen Birth Rates by Race and Ethnicity for 1991 and 2014			
Year	White	Black	Hispanic
1991	43.4	118.2	104.6
2014	17.3	34.9	38.0

Source: Martin et al. (2015).

Note: Rate per 1,000 women ages 15–19 years in the specified group.

children, these include placement of child with kin, placement in foster care, or placement for adoption.

Kinship Care

African American children are more likely than any other racial or ethnic group to live in kinship care (Washington, Gleeson, & Rulison, 2013). Kinship care involves a relative caring for children who cannot remain in the home of their biological parents (Messing, 2006). Three types of kinship care are (a) informal kinship care, (b) formal kinship care, and (c) legal guardianship or adoption. Most children are placed in the home of a relative informally. Here, the relative caregiver takes on primary care for the child outside of the child welfare system. Children placed into formal kinship care are under the supervision of a child welfare agency. Another option for kinship care is legal guardianship, where the relative is appointed by the court to take on the legal rights, responsibilities, and decision-making power of a parent. Relatives are often reluctant to adopt the child in their care because of the possible conflict that may arise with the child's biological parents. Children placed with relatives are more likely to have contact with birth parents than are those in traditional foster care. In addition, kinship care arrangements tend to be more stable than nonrelative arrangements.

Kinship care has been seen as an important and culturally congruent way in which some African American families have been preserved (Messing, 2006; Murphy, 2008). There is a long history of extended kin networks within traditional African communities, during enslavement, and in the modern era. Therefore, the presence of these networks has been of particular benefit to children whose biological parents cannot care for them.

Child Welfare System: Foster Care and Adoption

Beyond family-based kinship care, children might be placed in foster care by public social service and court systems when their families cannot care for them. These placements are sometimes temporary and—depending on the situation, circumstances, and systems—sometimes permanent.

African American children are overrepresented at every stage of the child welfare and child protective service systems (Anyon, 2011; Knott & Giwa, 2012). The first level of involvement often involves removal of the child from the home because of abuse, neglect, or endangerment. Abuse or neglect among ethnic minority children are twice as likely to be substantiated as abuse or neglect among White children despite research findings that abuse or neglect risk is no greater for an African American child than for a White child (Sedlak & Schultz, 2001). Once child abuse reporting has been confirmed, African American children are more likely than children from other racial and ethnic groups to be removed from the homes of their biological families, and they are less likely to return. African American parents are also more likely than parents of other ethnic groups to have their parental rights terminated. African American children in the child welfare system are more likely to be older and to be a part of sibling groups or to have behavioral problems than are children from other ethnic groups. All of these factors contribute to their being less attractive to potential adoptive parents. Despite the adoption initiatives created by the Adoption and Safe Families Act of 1997, racial differentials still exist in the adoption timeline for minority children (McRoy, Mica, Freundlich, & Kroll, 2007).

African American children are 3 times more likely than White children to be in foster care. African American children compose 16% of the total population under the age of 18, yet the Administration on Children, Youth, and Families reported that

24% of the children in foster care in 2014 were African American (see Table 5.4a; U.S. Department of Health and Human Services [DHHS], 2015). Also, African American children experience longer stays in foster care than children from other ethnic groups (see Tables 5.4b, 5.4c; DHHS, 2015). As shown in Tables 5.4b and 5.4c, a disproportionately higher number of African American children do not exit the foster care system and are not placed in adoption.

There are several reasons why African American and other ethnic minority children are overrepresented in the child welfare system (Boyd, 2014; McRoy et al., 2007). First, there may be more socioeconomic needs as African American families experience higher levels of individual, household, and structural poverty and financial stress, along with more single-parent-headed households. Second, racial bias may play a role in decision-making processes within child welfare systems (i.e., removal of children from biological parents). Differential provisions of services to African Americans and

TABLE 5.4A ■ Children in Foster Care by Race

Race	Percentage
White (non-Hispanic)	42
Black	24
Hispanic	22
Two or more races	7
American Indian/Alaskan Native	2
Asian	1
Other	2

Source: U.S. Department of Health and Human Services, Administration for Children and Families (2015).

TABLE 5.4B ■ Children Who Exited Foster Care by Race and Ethnicity

Race	Percentage
White	45
Black	23
Hispanic	21
Two or more races	6
American Indian/Alaskan Native	2
Asian	1
Other	2

Source: U.S. Department of Health and Human Services, Administration for Children and Families (2015).

TABLE 5.4C ■ Children Who Were Adopted From Public Foster Care System by Race and Ethnicity	
Race	**Percentage**
White	48
Hispanic	22
Black	19
Two or more races	8
American Indian/Alaskan Native	1
Asian	0
Other	2

Source: U.S. Department of Health and Human Services, Administration for Children and Families (2015).

other families of color by caseworkers that affect placement and resources available is another factor. Still another reason for the overrepresentation of African American children in the child welfare system is the incarceration of parents. Approximately 1 in 9 (11.4%) African American children have an incarcerated parent, compared with 1 in 28 (3.5%) Hispanic/Latino children and 1 in 57 (1.8%) White children (Pew, 2010). The majority of incarcerated parents are fathers. Cultural competence has also been cited as contributing to these disparities (Boyd, 2014).

Transracial Adoption

Over the past 30 years, the adoption of African American children, especially their adoption by White parents, has been the subject of debate (Bradley & Hawkins-Leon, 2002). This interracial placement is a process referred to as transracial adoption. Most of the contention has focused on whether African American children are able to develop healthy racial and cultural identities within White families (Alexander & Curtis, 1996). The basis for much of this discussion is attributed to a position paper (Simon & Alstein, 1977) drafted by the National Association of Black Social Workers that opposed the placement of African American children with White families. The paper went on to refer to this type of placement as a form of "cultural genocide" (p. 202). The paper emphasized that the socialization process for African American children is best met within an African American home environment and that the absence of this environment is likely to lead to detrimental social and psychological well-being. Other scholars have also noted that some transracially adopted children may experience racial identity and adjustment problems (Adkison-Bradley, DeBose, Terpstra, & Bilgic, 2012; Goss, Byrd, & Hughey, 2017).

A report issued by the Evan B. Donaldson Adoption Institute (Donaldson Report, 2008) also questioned whether transracial adoption is truly in the best interest of the child, igniting new controversy over transracial adoption. The concerns outlined in this report, consistent with the concerns of the National Association of Black Social Workers (NABSA), were that White parents, no matter how well intended, may not be able to help African American children develop the identity they need to live in a racist society. Most transracially adopted youth are adopted by middle-class or upper-middle-class White parents and reared in predominantly White neighborhoods. Racism continues to be central in the lives of the children but not in the lives of their White adoptive parents (Smith, Juarez, & Jacobson, 2011). White parents may not socialize their children to have a strong ethnic identity necessary to counter racism. In interviews with African American youth and their White adoptive parents, Smith et al. found that the socialization of White adoptive parents involved emphasizing the privilege of the individual (over the collective) and the notion that being White is good and right rather than that White does not have to be the norm.

Several studies on transracial adoption have been conducted over the past 30 years. The findings from these studies are equivocal but tend to show that African American adoptees adjust well in transracial home environments for the most part. However, these studies have been challenged on methodological, analytical, and interpretative grounds. One concern was that the adjustment of White youth was used as the norm. Other studies have shown transracial adoptees have problems with racial or ethnic identity during adolescence (Adkison-Bradley et al., 2012; Goss et al., 2017).

Butler-Sweet (2011) argues that class also influences the development of Black identity and that comparisons are often made between African American youth with middle-class White parents and African American youth who have grown up in poor households. Butler-Sweet explored Black identity among Black youth who were raised in middle-class families with two Black parents (monoracial), one White and one Black parent (biracial), and two White parents (transracial). Thirty-two Black young adults between the ages of 18 and 30 were interviewed. Butler-Sweet found some similarities between the three groups in that all three groups felt different from other Black youth while growing up. This difference was mainly due to enhanced academic achievement and acting White or not acting Black enough. Also, the racial socialization of acting White and acting Black were explained by class indicators, as the youth believed that "acting White" was associated with middle-class and suburban culture while "acting Black" was associated with urban poverty. One difference between the three groups was that biracial and transracially adopted informants tended to endorse racial stereotypes. Also, parents of biracial and transracially adopted children tended to involve their children in urban street culture activities (e.g., hip-hop dance classes) more so than Black middle-class organizations. Youth from middle-class monoracial families were involved in middle-class Black organizations (e.g., Jack and Jill) that focused on Black achievement. Youth from monoracial families were also exposed to middle-class Black role models more than biracial and transracial youth. Overall, the findings from the interviews suggested that youth with two Black parents developed a broader image of "Blackness" than youth raised in biracial and transracial homes.

The issue of the well-being of children from transracial adoption is not resolved and will likely continue. We have seen little to no research on African American families adopting White children and children from other ethnic groups.

Marriage, Divorce, Remarriage, and Cohabitation

Overall, marriage rates have declined for both African Americans and other racial and ethnic groups. Marriage rates among African Americans have substantially declined since 1950. In 1950, 64% of African American men and 62% of African American women were married, compared with marriage rates in 2016 in which 37.5% of African American men and 31.7% of African American women were married (U.S. Census, 2016e). Slightly more African American males over the age of 15 are married than African American females.

There are substantial differences in the marriage rates of African Americans and other ethnic groups. Among women ages 15 and older, African American women are almost twice as likely to have never married as White and Asian women (see Table 5.5). See the "Contemporary Issues" text box for further discussion of lower marriage rates among African Americans. African Americans are also more likely than Whites to be separated or divorced. When African Americans do separate, they tend to wait longer than Whites before they divorce (Copen, Daniels, Vespa, & Mosher, 2012). Only 30% of African American women divorce within a year of separating, whereas 59% of White women divorce within a year of separating (Copen et al.). On the other hand, 36% of African American men divorce within a year of separating, as compared with 69% of White men who divorce within a year of separating. The longer period of separation among African Americans may be because remarriage is not as likely to occur, so there may be less motivation to divorce. The chance of the first marriages of African American women lasting 20 years (37%) was significantly lower than White women (54%) (Copen et al., 2012). However there were no significant differences in the probability of first marriage lasting 20 years between White (54%) and African American (53%) men (Copen et al., 2012).

The African American Extended Family

The African American family is often extended and multigenerational, with a cooperative and collective family structure (Wilson et al., 1995). Historically, participation in extended kinship or family networks has been important to the survival and advancement of African Americans (Stewart, 2007).

TABLE 5.5 ■ Marital Status by Race and Ethnicity, 15 Years and Older (percentage)			
Characteristic	Married	Unmarried	Never Married
Male			
White	55.8	44.1	32.3
Black	37.5	62.5	50.4
Asian	61.6	38.3	34.7
Hispanic	47.9	52.0	44.0
Female			
White	53.6	46.3	25.8
Black	31.7	68.2	47.8
Asian	62.76	37.2	26.3
Hispanic	49.8	50.1	36.3

Source: U.S. Census (2016e).

CONTEMPORARY ISSUES

WHY ARE AFRICAN AMERICAN MARRIAGE RATES SO MUCH LOWER THAN OTHER ETHNIC GROUPS?

As the statistics in this chapter show, the majority of African Americans are not married, and many will never get married. The majority of African American children do not grow up in households with both parents present. The reasons for this situation are complex, and there are more questions than answers. However, accumulated wealth (or lack thereof) is likely to play some role. In an interesting study, Daniel Schneider of Princeton University found that African Americans and those with less than a high school education marry far less and much later (Schneider, 2011). Since African Americans have less education than Whites and are more likely to face discrimination in the job market, this accounts for some of the gap. However, a low level of accumulated wealth among African Americans is another reason for the gap.

Schneider examined if accumulated wealth (e.g., stocks and bonds, money in savings account, car ownership, home ownership,

other financial assets) played a role in marriage among African Americans. Wealth was defined as what people own, not just what they earn. If accumulated wealth plays a role, then existing inequalities in wealth between Blacks and other ethnic groups might account for the differentials in marriage rates. Schneider found wealth was a significant factor and a prerequisite of marriage, especially for men. African Americans have substantially less wealth than other ethnic groups. In 2011, Whites had 20 times more wealth than African Americans (Kochhar, Fry, & Taylor, 2011). The wealth for Whites was $113,149, for Hispanics, $6,325, and for African Americans, $5,677 (Luhby, 2012). The recession of 2008 and the economic downturn are partially responsible for these differentials in wealth. Also, African Americans are less likely to inherit wealth and may be more likely to share what wealth they have with members of their extended family.

Included within the family network are immediate family members, extended members, friends, neighbors, fictive kin, and Church members. There is diversity in living arrangements that goes beyond marriage, parentage, and children to include other adults and children in shared residence situations. African American children may live in households with grandparents and other adults who are not members of the immediate family. Elderly African Americans are likely to be living with grandchildren. Young, low-income, and single mothers also are likely to be sharing a residence with other family members.

Stewart (2007) conducted a study on the definitions and understanding of family and kinship among African American participants. An ethnographic approach was taken with one African American family from a rural community. Questions that addressed aspects of family interaction, definition, and function were asked during 42 interviews of 38 family members and 4 community informants. The youngest family member interviewed was 15, and the eldest family member interviewed was 80 years old. The family was also diverse by socioeconomic status and education. The author found that the family reported a strong commitment to the extended family system. When asked who belongs, they were likely to say things such as, "anybody that's a 'B' or 'K'" (letters represent family or surnames). There were some differences in responses based on socioeconomic status. Those of higher socioeconomic status acknowledged all of their family connections but began by distinguishing immediate (nuclear) family from other relationships. Members of families of lower socioeconomic status were less likely to make this distinction. The family members also acknowledged the importance of fictive kin, although this was not a term that they used. One of the respondents described fictive kin as people who are "grafted" into families. Once in the family, they became a functioning part of the group. Romantic relationships were sometimes the reason for a person to become fictive kin. Even when romantic relationships dissolve, fictive family members remained close to the family. Others become fictive kin when they moved to a new community and found family that functioned like their biological family. Although this ethnographic study included only one large family, it illustrated how African American families in contemporary society function as they did historically during enslavement and, before that, in Africa.

African American extended family members provide support to one another in several ways, including emotional and psychological support and economic and financial support, as well as tangible support (e.g., providing transportation, child-care). Support from the extended family is linked to better psychological well-being and fewer mental health problems (Chatters, Taylor, Woodward, & Nicklett, 2015; Nguyen et al., 2016b). Support from extended family members is reciprocal, and 80% of African Americans report involvement in reciprocal support exchanges (Taylor, Mouzon, Nguyen, & Chatters, 2016).

Richardson (2009) conducted research on one group of members of the extended family, uncles. His work highlighted the often neglected but vital role uncles play in the provision of social support to adolescent males living in single-female-headed households. Richardson collected data over 4 years using an ethnographic approach to study the social context of 15 adolescents who were around 12 at the beginning of the study. Richardson found that uncles played a vital role in supporting their sisters' children and fostered positive adolescent development by attending activities of the youth, providing adult supervision, and being surrogate fathers.

The Role of the Grandmother

As noted previously, grandparents are present in the homes of many African American families. Grandmothers may provide an especially important form of assistance in child-rearing (Robbins, Briones, & Schwartz, 2006; Sumo, Dancy, Julion, & Wilbur, 2016; Wilson et al., 1995). Grandmothers may be the primary caregiver of the children, as well as the secondary caregiver. Maternal grandparents are more likely than any other group to coparent with single parents (Parent, Jones, Forehand, Cuellar, & Shoulbert, 2013).

Grandmothers are a key source of support for their parenting adolescent children (Sumo et al., 2016). Sumo et al. conducted interviews with 20 African American maternal and paternal grandmothers about the type of support they provided. Grandmothers were, on average, 48 years of age, and their parenting children's age ranged from 16 to 19. Several types of support were provided by grandmothers to their adolescent child. These included babysitting support, providing advice and mentoring, daily caregiving to the adolescent child and the grandchild, financial support, and purchasing needed items for the grandchild and the child. Support from maternal grandmothers contributes positively to well-being, adolescent parenting skills and competencies, and completion of high school and vocational training of their daughters (Sumo et al). Grandmothers' support for their adolescent parenting son also has a positive influence, resulting in more responsible fatherhood, including involvement in the child's life.

Grandparents also provide support that may help to increase cognitive competence of their grandchildren. In one study, researchers found that the presence of grandparents increased African American children's cognitive scores at age 2 (Mollborn, Fomby, & Dennis, 2012); this increase in cognitive scores was not found for White children living with grandparents. The improvement in cognitive skills might be due to increased financial and social resources.

However, grandparents may feel some strain and resistance when they are solely responsible for rearing grandchildren. Ross and Aday (2006) found in a study of 55 African American grandparents with a mean age of 63 that 94% were significantly stressed. Grandparents often are placed in situations where they have to raise their grandchildren because of complex family problems, including drug abuse, neglect, and parental incarceration (Waldrop, 2003). Incarceration and drug use are of particular concern: Grandparents not only have to care for their grandchildren but also have to deal with special needs and circumstances surrounding their son or daughter. In interviews with 37 grandparents, Waldrop found that grandparents experience both burdens and benefits from their role as grandparents. In another study, Waldrop and Weber (2001) identified several burdens for grandparents. These include family stress such as marital problems brought on by exacerbated stress, work–family strain due to balancing the demands of a job with the needs of a grandchild, legal problems concerning parental custody issues for their grandchild, and financial burdens.

The findings from other studies also suggest that children raised by grandmothers alone may have more conduct and behavioral problems than do children raised by parents. Kelley, Whitley, and Campos (2011) studied 2,309 mostly African American children ages 2 to 16 who were being raised by grandparents in homes with no parent present. They found that almost one-third (31.3%) of the children scored in the clinical range for behavioral problems. Children's behavioral problems were linked to increased psychological stress among grandmothers, a less supportive home environment, and fewer family resources.

African American Fathers

There has been an increase in research on the role of fathers in families over the past 15 years (Behnke & Allen, 2007; Burns & Caldwell, 2016; Choi & Jackson, 2012). Traditional portrayals of African American men as husbands and fathers have often been negative, focusing on stereotypical images that include uninvolved and financially irresponsible fathers. Some research has been consistent with this portrayal. Many studies have been conducted on social problems of adolescent fatherhood, out-of-wedlock paternity, and child support enforcement, with a focus on young men or young fathers (Taylor & Johnson, 1997). This focus does not account for the broad diversity of family, spousal, and parental roles found among African American men.

A substantial line of research shows the diversity among African American fathers, including research on middle-income fathers (McAdoo, 1988). Research indicates that African American fathers are actively involved in the socialization of their children. A study by Leavell, Tamis-LeMonda, Ruble, Zosuls, and Cabrera (2012) found that Black fathers (compared with Latino and White fathers) provided the highest levels of caregiving, play, and visiting activities with their children. When African American fathers engage with their children, their children show higher academic achievement. Young children of fathers who engaged in home literacy practices, such as having books in the home, reading books with their children, telling stories, and singing, at 24 months had higher reading and math scores in preschool than children whose father was not engaged in literacy activities (Baker, 2014).

Other studies have shown that when African American fathers do not live with their children, they still remain emotionally involved in their children's lives (Behnke & Allen, 2007; Burns & Caldwell, 2016). African American fathers generally are more involved with their children when they are infants and again when they enter early adolescence, when compared with other developmental periods. Research has shown that adolescent sons engage in less risky behavior when nonresidential fathers are involved in their lives (Burns & Caldwell, 2016). Involvement includes providing racial socialization messages, monitoring their sons' whereabouts, involvement in school and extracurricular activities, and communication.

In interviews about parenting conducted with 30 African American biological fathers of preadolescent sons at risk for developing aggressive behaviors and poor mental health (Doyle et al., 2015), four major themes emerged that reflected African American men's views about parenting. One theme communicated by fathers was that it was important to assist their child in learning how to regulate and express emotions. Fathers encouraged their sons to verbalize rather than suppress their emotions. Fathers reminded their sons that challenging situations were temporary and of the importance of maintaining a positive outlook. A second theme was encouragement. Fathers encouraged their sons to develop interest and skills in sports and hobbies and to remain motivated in the face of setbacks. Fathers showed encouragement by "being there" and "being present." A third theme was discipline. Fathers viewed discipline as very important to helping their sons develop into healthy African American adults. They used a variety of discipline, including spanking; removing privileges, such as phones and computers; and providing rewards for desired behaviors. Other parents disciplined their sons by lecturing or explaining the consequences of their sons' negative behaviors. The forth theme was monitoring. Fathers monitored their sons' activities in several ways. They monitored homework completion; television, video game, and cell phone usage; their sons' friends; and their sons' activities and whereabouts. Fathers reported that they knew their sons' friends and the parents of their friends and tried to influence the type of friends their sons had.

Some African American fathers also have personal challenges that may affect their relationships with and involvement with their children. These include low educational attainment and occupational success (Behnke & Allen, 2007). These barriers may be exacerbated when fathers do not contribute to child support, which may result in child support enforcement consequences. When fathers cannot contribute to the financial needs of their families, they may become isolated from their families.

African American fathers also face incarceration to a larger extent than fathers in other ethnic minority groups (Pew, 2010). Higher rates of imprisonment make separation from their children more likely and can make involvement in their children's lives difficult. However, incarceration does not mean that African American fathers do not desire a role in their children's lives. Fathers who had been previously incarcerated and who were part of a reentry program were interviewed to learn more about their experiences of fatherhood (Dill et al., 2015). These fathers spoke of wanting a second chance to be more involved in their child's life, acknowledging mistakes they had made and lessons learned. These fathers were very invested in forming positive relationships with their children and appreciated that they now had more time to spend with their children.

African American fathers returning from incarceration desire to be better parents but sometimes do not have the skills to do so. To address this concern, there has been an increase in parenting programs in prison, so when fathers leave prison, they will be equipped with better parenting skills (Purvis, 2011).

Parenting Among Lesbian, Gay, Bisexual, and Transgender (LGBT) Couples

Although there has been more recent research on lesbian, gay, bisexual, and transgender (LGBT) families, the amount of writing and research on African American LGBT families remains sparse. About 19% of same-sex couple households include children under the age of 18; this includes 27% of female couples and close to 11% of male couples (Gates, 2013). Parenting among same-sex couples is higher among racial and ethnic minority couples, including African American couples. About 34% of African American same-sex couples are raising children (Kastanis & Gates, 2013). The question has been raised as to whether children of same-sex parents can have successful child outcomes or whether a set of gender-neutral characteristics, such as nurturance, protection, and guidance, are critical ingredients for parental competence. In 2005, the APA reviewed 59 published studies on same-sex parenting and children's outcomes and issued a brief that stated, "Not a single study has found children of lesbian or gay parents to be disadvantaged in any significant respect relative to children of heterosexual parents" (Patterson, 2005, p. 15). This brief suggested that the psychosocial outcomes of children raised by same-sex parents were similar to those raised by heterosexual parents.

However, this APA brief was criticized because the 59 studies used samples that were small and not culturally, ethnically, and socioeconomically diverse (Marks, 2012). Most of the participants in the research reviewed by APA were White mothers with high incomes and not ethnic minorities, including African Americans. Other researchers have noted that children of lesbian or gay parents have similar experiences of family life and that they are doing about as well as children normally do (Meezan & Rauch, 2005). There has been very little published on African American same-sex parenting. One challenge faced by children of same-sex parents is possible stigmatization by others. This may be even more of an issue among African American families, which tend to be less accepting of gay and lesbian relationships and parenting than other racial and ethnic groups (Newport, 2008).

Rural Families

The majority of the research on African American families has been conducted on urban and suburban families. Both minority status and being in a rural community are associated with increased risk among children and families. Thus rural minority families may be exposed to higher risk than nonrural families (Crockett, Carlo, & Temmen, 2016). In rural communities, there are fewer employment opportunities, and available employment may consist of minimum-wage jobs that do not provide for a living wage. Poverty rates tend to be higher in rural communities than nonrural communities, and poverty rates for minorities are even higher than for Whites (Crockett et al.). More than half of all rural African Americans live in high-poverty counties, mostly in the South (Lichter, Parisi, & Taquino, 2012). Adults living in rural areas also tend to have lower levels of education than those in nonrural communities (Vernon-Feagans & Cox, 2013). The lack of financial stability may contribute to family strain and poor quality of family relationships (Cutrona, Clavél, & Johnson, 2016).

Ethnic minority individuals in rural communities sometimes have increased stress due to racism and discrimination (Crockett et al., 2016). African American families in these communities may be subject to racial segregation, less access to quality health care, social services, and recreational activities, which contribute to increased stress and mental health problems (Cunningham & Francois, 2016).

Higher teen birth rates among rural teens than urban teens is one indicator of how rurality affects youth well-being. In 2015, teen birth rates were highest in rural counties and lowest in large urban counties for White, African American, and Hispanic females (Hamilton, Rossen, & Branum, 2016). In 2015, teen birth rates among non-Hispanic black females ranged from a low of 29.1 births per 1,000 females in large urban counties to a high of 39.6 in rural counties. Rural youth are more likely to use alcohol and cigarettes and to drive after drinking than urban youth, although urban youth are more likely to use illicit drugs such as marijuana and methamphetamine (Jiang, Sun, & Marsiglia, 2016). In overview, research suggests rural African American families may face certain challenges over and beyond that of families in other geographical regions.

STRENGTHS, COPING, AND PARENTING PATTERNS

Strength and Resilience Among African American Families

Over the past few decades, family scholars have moved from a deficit view of African American families to a strengths-based view. Strengths are viewed as culturally based beliefs and values unique to African Americans. Hill (1998) defines family strengths as those attributes that enable the family to meet both the needs of its members and the demands made on the family by outside forces.

Hill (1971) describes five strengths of African American families: (a) strong achievement orientation, (b) strong work orientation, (c) flexible family roles, (d) strong kinship bonds, and (e) strong religious orientation. According to Hill, these attributes are functional for the survival, stability, and advancement of African American families. Although these attributes are found among other ethnic groups, they are likely to be expressed differently among African Americans because of their unique experiences in this country.

According to McAdoo (1998, 2007), there are several cultural attributes that support strong African American families. These include social networks that are supportive, flexible roles and responsibilities within the family, a high level of religiosity and spirituality, and extended family and fictive kin. McAdoo also believes that cultural attributes that have been historically present have diminished because of poor economic conditions. Given changes in the urban communities in which many African Americans live, the historical strengths of African American families described by Hill must be reassessed in contemporary times.

Coping and Adjustment Among African American Families

Strong support from the family can help family members who are experiencing stress. Support can be emotional, such as affirmation and acceptance; instrumental, such as lending money or helping with childcare; or cognitive, such as giving advice. Examples of these types of support are seen among African American families who assist family members to cope with chronic illnesses and disabilities (Ha, Greenberg, & Seltzer, 2011) or to care for an elderly family member (Dilworth-Anderson & Goodwin, 2005). Many African American families have developed successful mechanisms for coping with stress caused by environmental challenges.

The family is the most important system within which health is maintained, and health decisions are made for the African American elderly by their families (Bowles & Kingston, 1998). The family is the primary source of social support and care of the African American elderly. African American elderly represented 8.5% of the total U.S. population ages 65 and older (U.S. Census Bureau, 2010b).

There may be fewer economic and social resources available for African American elderly because of restricted economic opportunities this cohort faced in their earlier life. African American elderly have less income and experience more poverty and more inadequate health care than do White elderly. In 2013, the poverty rate for those 65 and older was 22% for Blacks, 28% for Hispanics, and 12% for Whites (Cubanski, Casillas, & Damico, 2015). Informal social support from family and friends can attenuate poverty and other risk factors and contribute to the well-being of older African Americans (Nguyen, Chatters, Taylor, & Mouzon, 2016a).

There may be no greater strain on the family unit than caring for a member with dementia or Alzheimer's disease. African Americans are 2 times more likely to develop late-onset Alzheimer's disease than Whites and less likely to have the disease diagnosed (Alzheimer's Association, n.d.). A review of the literature shows ethnic difference in the caregiving experiences of African Americans, especially when compared with Whites (Na'poles, Chadiha, Eversley, & Moreno-John, 2010). Compared with White caregivers of family members with dementia, African American caregivers report better psychosocial health, more positive feelings about caregiving, and the use of spirituality and prayer. African American caregivers also reported more social support, a stronger sense of responsibility to extended family networks, and more of a dislike for institutionalizing relatives. Kosberg, Kaufman, Burgio, Leeper, and Sun (2007) examined differences and similarities in the experiences of 141 African American and White family caregivers of patients with dementia living in rural Alabama. White caregivers were more likely to be married and older, used acceptance and humor as coping styles, and had fewer financial problems. African American caregivers provided more hours of care and used religion and denial as ways with which to cope with the stress of caregiving. They also reported feeling less burdened.

Parenting Attitudes and Practices

African American parenting practices are both similar to and different from those of other cultural groups. For example, African American and White parents do not differ in the level of warmth and acceptance directed toward their children and in parenting inconsistency (Dexter, Wong, Stacks, Beeghly, & Barnett, 2013). Nor do they differ in limit-setting behaviors (LeCuyer, 2014). However, there are some differences. Some of these differences may be attributed to class differences, insofar as many studies have used African American samples comprising parents of low socioeconomic status. However, studies that have controlled for socioeconomic status suggest that some differences still exist between parenting practices of African Americans and other ethnic groups. Moreover, the relationship between parenting practices and child well-being may differ for African Americans and other ethnic groups.

Discipline

African American parents use a variety of disciplinary strategies. They are more likely than White parents to use authoritarian parenting and punitive methods, such as physical punishment and assertion of authority (Gershoff, Lansford, Sexton, Davis-Kean, & Sameroff, 2012; Lorber, O'Leary, & Smith, 2011). Although African American parents use all forms of discipline, spanking is at least used sometimes by the majority of African American parents. Spanking is defined as striking the child on the buttocks or extremities with an open hand without inflicting physical injury (McLoyd, Kaplan, Hardaway, & Wood, 2007). The use of more physical and authoritative discipline among African American parents has its origin in slavery. During slavery, the responsibility of the parent or family was to instill in children that they were to be compliant and subservient slaves. The method for maintaining docility and obedience was shown by the White slave masters' methods of disciplining slaves. Punishment was swift, harsh, and violent, no matter what the infraction (Lassiter, 1987). Consequently, African American parents used harsh discipline as a survival strategy: In order to teach children how to avoid violent punishment at the hands of the White slaveholder, adults had to use a less severe but still harsh form of punishment with children.

Enslavement also impacted how children reacted to adverse conditions. Enslaved parents socialized their children to behave in ways that were sometimes age inconsistent in order to keep them alive. For example, children were not allowed to cry out loud when they were hurt or in pain. Children were expected to assume adult responsibilities, including caring for younger children and doing chores in the house and in the field. Following slavery, the pattern of harsh and physical discipline continued as a mechanism for maintaining docility and compliance so that the child could survive in a racist society. African American scholars have noted that the use of physical punishment can be purposeful, controlled, and appropriate and useful in protecting African American children and instructing them how to behave and survive within a racist society (Thomas & Dettlaff, 2011).

Earlier research suggested that physical discipline is not linked to externalizing problem behaviors, such as aggression and acting out, for African American children, as is the case with White children (Lansford, Deater-Deckard, & Dodge, 2004). However, more recent research suggests that there is a relationship between physical discipline, such as spanking and behavior problems, among African American children. In one study, maternal spanking predicted long-term internalizing (e.g., withdrawal, depression, anxiety) and externalizing (e.g., aggression, rule breaking, destructive behaviors) behaviors among African American children (Coley, Kull, & Carrano, 2014). Mothers' endorsement of spanking when their child was 3 years of age predicted increased internalizing and externalizing behaviors at 9 years of age. Another study found no differences among White, Black, Hispanic, and Asian American families in spanking and externalizing behavior. More spanking at 5 years of age led to externalizing behavior at 8 years of age among children of all ethnic groups (Gershoff et al., 2012). Thus, more recent research suggests a negative impact of parental spanking on children's problem behaviors.

Parenting Attitudes and Involvement

Studies on parenting attitudes have looked at factors such as parental support for their children, warmth, acceptance, and expectations. In general, the literature reviewed by Magnus, Cowen, Wyman, Fagen, and Work (1999) suggests few differences between African American and White parents in parental attitudes. One difference is on the variable autonomy. African American parents are more likely than White parents to value and stress autonomy among their children. One positive implication of this is that children may be socialized to function independently, which may be useful when parents are not immediately available. However, parents who stress autonomy may be less likely to attend to minor distress signals from their children.

Another ethnic or racial difference is how parents respond to their child's negative emotions. Research has found that African American parents (relative to White parents) may respond to their child's negative emotions with less explanation and encouragement and more control and admonishment (Nelson, Leerkes, O'Brien, Calkins, & Marcovitch, 2012). African American parents may also be more likely to minimize emotionally distressing experiences of their children and punish them for outward displays when compared with White parents. In a study by Nelson et al., African American and White parents' responses to their children's negative emotions were correlated in different ways with their children's academic performance and socioemotional competence. White children whose parents helped them to address the problem causing their emotional distress performed better academically and had better social skills. However, African American children who were encouraged by their parents to express their negative emotions had poorer academic performance and less positive social skills than those who were not encouraged (Nelson et al., 2012). The outward display of emotions may not be adaptive for African American children who live and attend school in racially biased environments.

African American parents are also more likely than White parents to make decisions for adolescent children. A study by Gutman and Eccles (2007) found parental decision making to be normative in African American families, particularly during early adolescence. In this same study, more White adolescents than African American adolescents reported more decision-making opportunities during early adolescence. However, the authors found that as adolescents matured, there was more opportunity for decision making among both groups.

Racial Socialization

The process of racial socialization is the process by which parents and families socialize African American children in how to function in this society. This process involves making children aware of their race and of themselves as Black or African American as opposed to simply being American. Parents who racially socialize their children assume that their children will be in a hostile environment, at least at some times in their lives, and that they must be comfortable with being African American. Racial socialization includes specific messages and behaviors that families provide children about being African American, including group and personal identity, intergroup interactions, and their positions within the social hierarchy. These messages are both implicit and explicit (Thornton et al., 1990). Hughes and Johnson (2001) use the term *cultural socialization* and define it as messages and practices that teach children about racial and ethnic heritage and provide them with a sense of ethnic pride (p. 983). See Chapter 3 for further discussion of racial socialization.

Certain demographic factors influence the extent of racial socialization (Thornton, 1998). Mothers more than fathers socialize their children about race issues. This is attributed to general levels of maternal responsiveness in preparing children to function in the world. Parents with higher levels of education are more likely to socialize their children than those with lower levels of education.

According to Boykin and Toms (1985), the socialization process is related to identity. African Americans are socialized through three experiences in order to acquire a racial identity. First, they must participate in mainstream American culture. In order to achieve this, African American parents teach their children that which is American. Within this context, parents teach their children necessary life skills, including personal qualities such as confidence, respect, and achievement. An example of this strategy is when parents teach children the importance of studying in school.

The second method of socialization used by African American parents is to teach their children about being an ethnic minority and to prepare them for an oppressive environment. African American parents prepare their children for what may be an unsupportive world by building their self-confidence and helping them learn how to cope with prejudice and discrimination. These parents also teach their children the value of a good education and that injustice may occur because of their skin color.

The final strategy identified by Boykin and Toms (1985) is to socialize their children within the Black cultural experience. These parents socialize their children to value and identify with what is African centered. An example of this is when parents discuss historical events in their family's life or discuss famous Blacks and Africans. Racial socialization can serve as a protective role for African American children because it provides support and affirmation for being Black in a racist world (Stevenson, Cameron, Herrero-Taylor, & Davis, 2002).

Racial socialization is linked to positive youth development and well-being, including higher competence, connection, and confidence (Evans, Simons, & Simons, 2012). Youth who report more racial socialization have more confidence in academic achievement, higher racial identity, and higher self-esteem. Racial socialization provides youth not only with awareness of racism but also with coping mechanisms for dealing with racism (Dunbar et al., 2017; Neblett, Rivas-Drake, Umaña-Taylor, 2012).

METHODOLOGICAL AND RESEARCH ISSUES

There are several methodological issues to consider when studying African American families. Many studies have examined African American families over a short period and have failed to consider historical perspectives when examining contemporary African American families (Hill, 1998). One cannot truly understand African American families without considering historical, cultural, social, economic, and political factors and institutional practices. The period of enslavement had a profound impact on the African American family, an impact that continues today; no study of African American families can be complete without considering that impact.

Another methodological problem is that socioeconomic class has been confounded with ethnicity in studies of the African American family and child-rearing (McLoyd et al., 2007). Research has oversampled low-income African American families and generalized findings to all African American families. Also, studies have tended not to consider within-group differences among African American families. But within-group differences among African Americans do affect child well-being. McLoyd et al. found physical discipline to be moderated by characteristics of African American mothers, such as whether the parent is stressed. Another study found African American mothers more likely to use intense disciplinary methods than African American fathers (Adkison-Johnson, Terpstra, Burgos, & Payne, 2016). Although a fair amount of research and literature was identified in this chapter, there remains a need for more research and programming on African American families. It is sometimes difficult to recruit African American families in studies, and the reason for this is not always clear. African American families may have other, more pressing needs and may be turned off to being "studied" by academic researchers. In our own work, it has been especially difficult to recruit and retain African American families, especially if their involvement is over several weeks. A related issue is recruitment and study of African American families of all socioeconomic groups.

Breland-Noble, Bell, Burriss, and Poole (2012) provide a model of how to engage African American families in research. Breland-Noble et al. describe how they used a systematic community participatory research approach to recruit African American families for project AAKOMA (Breland-Noble et al., 2012). AAKOMA is a mental health intervention for African American females. Some of their strategies involved appointing an active and engaging community advisory panel that represented key stakeholders from the community (e.g., ministers, teachers, community advocates). They also used many recruitment sources that included community seminars, community liaisons, the university health system website, and participant-to-participant referrals. Using comprehensive recruitment strategies resulted in the recruitment of more African American families than the targeted number.

Typically, studies have focused on low-income families and families whose youth might be at high risk for a problem such as substance abuse and/or early sexual activity. But we also need to learn more about the challenges and strengths of working- and middle-class African American families.

EVIDENCED-BASED PRACTICES FOR STRENGTHENING AFRICAN AMERICAN FAMILIES

Over the past several years, there has been a stronger call for family-based programs. Advocates of family-based programs argue that youth outcomes will be better when the family rather than the individual child is targeted. Some of these programs specifically target African American families and attend to unique features of African American families in content and format. We discuss two family-based programs and an African-centered approach for African American families next.

Strong African American Family Program

As discussed in the section on rural families, poverty, financial strain, and unemployment are problematic for many rural African American families. African American youth from rural communities engage in risky behaviors, such as substance use, and risky sex at rates equal to or greater than their counterparts in urban and suburban communities. The Strong African American Families (SAAF) program was developed to provide a culturally congruent program for families in rural communities who were affected by poverty and financial distress (Brody et al., 2004, 2012a). The SAAF program is a skills training program for preadolescent (11–12 years) children and their caregivers. The program strengthens positive family interactions and increases parents' ability to help their children set and reach positive goals during the critical transition period between childhood and adolescence. Facilitators of the SAAF program are African American community members who are trained to teach the SAAF curriculum. Specifically, the SAAF curriculum is intended to (1) support parents and caregivers in learning how to use nurturing skills when interacting with their children; (2) teach parents and caregivers effective ways to discipline; (3) help youth to obtain a healthy future orientation and to increase their appreciation of their parents and caregivers; and (4) to teach youth skills to deal with stress and peer pressure.

The SAAF program consists of seven weekly, 2-hour meetings. Parents and youth are engaged in separate skill-building sessions for 1 hour. This is followed by a family session in which parents and youth jointly practice the skills that they learned in their separate sessions. The curriculum is presented on videotapes that show family interactions illustrating key points. Parents are taught how to be involved in their children's life and to use vigilant caregiving practices. Youth learn how to respond when faced with racism, how to develop future goals, and how to resist peer pressure to use alcohol and other drugs. Jointly, family youth and parents learn and practice communication skills and engage in activities that increase cohesion and positive interactions. An evaluation of the SAAF program showed several significant findings for SAAF youth and parents when compared with youth in control groups. Youth who participated in the SAAF program reported fewer conduct problems (e.g., theft, school suspension) and significantly less alcohol use at a 29-month follow-up. They also increased in protective beliefs and behaviors (e.g., negative attitudes about alcohol and sex, goal-directed future orientation, drug resistance efficacy, acceptance of parental influence, negative images of drinkers). Among parents, there were increased positive changes in parenting communication and monitoring (e.g., involved-vigilant parenting, racial socialization, communication about sex, establishment of clear parental expectations) at follow-up (Brody et al., 2012a).

REAL Men

REAL (responsible, empowered, aware, living) Men is another example of an evidenced-based intervention program (Dilorio, McCarty, Resnicow, Lehr, & Denzmore, 2007). The program was designed as an HIV prevention intervention for African American adolescent boys. The study involved 277 fathers or father figures and their sons. The inclusion of father figures is consistent with a perspective in which fathers do not have to be biologically related or related through marriage. Father figures were eligible if they were ages 18 years or older, were identified by the boy's mother as a significant influence in the adolescent's life, and had at least a 1-year relationship with the adolescent and the mother. In this intervention, fathers and other supportive adult males were presented information on communicating with adolescents, parental monitoring, and improving adolescent peer relations; they were also presented information on HIV and the prevention of HIV and AIDS. The program provided videotapes of fathers talking to their sons about sexual topics. Fathers and father figures had the opportunity to practice communication behavior through role-plays.

The intervention consisted of seven 2-hour sessions for the adult males. Fathers and father figures attended the first six sessions alone and attended the last session with their sons. The last session also included a completion celebration, and fathers, father figures, and sons received certificates of completion. The control group participated in a seven-session nutrition and exercise program that met for 2 hours. Fathers and the supportive adult males in the control group also attended the first six sessions alone and with their son for the last session. The primary outcomes in this study were adolescent sexual abstinence and father–son communication about sex. The findings were consistent with the hypothesis. Boys in the intervention group had higher rates of abstinence at the 6-month follow-up than did boys in the control group. These boys also were more likely to use a condom each time they had sexual intercourse.

African-Centered Approaches to Strengthening African American Families

Parham, White, and Ajamu (1999) offer several recommendations for building healthy African American families derived from an African-centered perspective. The approach of Parham et al. is based on counseling and education work with African American families and does not involve a curriculum per se. According to Parham et al., current family structures differ from the family structure of the past in that modern families do not necessarily begin with marriage or living together. Therefore, building healthy families must start with appropriate socialization of African American youth. Parham et al. offer several tips that can be used when working with African American families:

1. Socialize youth to love themselves and to understand their relationship with the Creator.

2. Help youth to develop an identity and perspective of what it means to be a man or a woman that is culturally congruent and that affirms both males and females.

3. Teach youth to recognize and model healthy family functioning; youth are often exposed to dysfunctional family functioning that provides a distorted view of how a healthy family should function.

4. Teach youth how to be successful in male–female relationships; youth must be taught to relate to members of the opposite sex in a sincere, respectful, caring, and loving way and not to first focus on their own needs.

5. Teach children that relationships should be sustained through difficult periods; when relationships are challenged during stressful and difficult times, tolerance and perseverance are needed.

6. Teach youth to develop personal insights into themselves, and help them to understand how past experiences affect their current ways of behaving.

We have discussed two programs developed specifically for African American families. Both programs were developed to improve functioning across a number of parenting and youth domains, and both have shown improved functioning for parents and children. Parham et al. (1999) offer general guidelines for families to use when raising African American children.

CRITICAL ANALYSIS

We provide our comments on the state of research and literature on African American family structure, parenting, the roles of father-husbands, and the inclusion of African American LGBT families in research.

Although there have been some changes, there continues to be a fair amount of literature and research published regarding the negative impact of African American family structure on family well-being, especially the well-being of children. This work has continued despite the fact that most scholars recognize that African American family structure differs from that of other ethnic groups. Moreover, socioeconomic background is often confounded with family structure as single-parent-headed households tend to be households with less money and fewer resources. Two-parent households tend to have more income and resources.

Vereen (2007) studied more than 301 African American women and found no differences in three categories of family: married or living together with or without children or other family members in the household; single with no children or family members living in the household; and single with children or other family members living in the household. Vereen found no effects for family structure on social indicators (e.g., social support), psychological indicators (e.g., self-esteem), and economic indicators (e.g., income). According to Vereen, what appears to be true with regard to psychosocial outcomes seemed to have more to do with income and opportunities than with family structure.

More research on differing types of family structure is needed to more clearly elucidate what family structure looks like for the African American family. For example, Vereen included "single with no children or family members living in the household" as one type of family structure. Another type of family structure might be "adult children living with parents and/or grandparents." Another might be to recognize coparenting by nonresidential fathers as a type of family structure as seen in the opening blog. Information on the differing ways in which African American families manifest themselves will help us better understand African American families.

In recent years, the focus on African Americans and other ethnic minority children has shifted away from looking at White and African American differences in developmental outcomes. More and more, we see research that focuses on an understanding of the positive and adaptive strategies African American families use. Research in the area of racial socialization is an example of this. This new paradigm recognizes the value of within-group analyses with African Americans as a legitimate research strategy and refocuses attention away from merely documenting group differences to an emphasis on understanding the processes that may account for differences in outcomes for different children in the same group.

Also, on a positive note, there has been some empirical research that has demonstrated that family- and parenting-based programs can improve parenting outcomes, youth outcomes, and family outcomes. These programs have been developed to be culturally specific and can be implemented in a variety of settings.

A growing body of research now focuses on African American fathers who remain with and are involved in the lives of their children. These studies show that African American fathers, including nonresidential fathers, desire to be and are a part of their children's lives (Burns & Caldwell, 2016; Cartman, 2016). We applaud this work, and others may find that this research can be useful in understanding father roles and responsibilities within other ethnic groups. Additional research is also needed on African American family composition and function with regard to LGBT parents. Despite the fact that many children are raised in LGBT-parented households, there has been little published on what promotes optimal functioning for these children and their parents. We could find no published research on transgender African American families. Moreover, we could not identify any intervention studies that specifically supported parental programs for these families. Given some continued stigma for LGBT families, these programs may be indicated.

Summary

Hill (1998) defined the African American family as a household related by blood or marriage or function that provides basic instrumental and expressive functions to its members. The family is important in African culture, and communalism is most often expressed in the family. In this chapter, we have examined historical, cultural, and economic patterns as they affect African American families. For example, understanding that enslaved African women were made to procreate early helps us to set a historical context for understanding the earlier age of childbirth among contemporary African American females. Understanding economic conditions assists in explaining lower marriage rates among African American men and women.

African American family structure differs from the family structure of other ethnic groups and is likely to be extended and female headed, with a larger presence of grandparents. African American children are more likely to be in foster care and less likely to be adopted than are children from other ethnic groups. African American fathers are involved in their children's lives whether or not they reside with their children.

African American child-rearing practices are both similar to and diverse from other racial and ethnic groups. Compared to other ethnic groups, African American parents may use more discipline and a more authoritarian parenting style. Strengths of the African American family include the extended family and religious beliefs. African American families have been useful in supporting the care of children of younger parents, as well as elder family members and members with disabilities. African American families living in rural communities face unique challenges due to increased poverty and unemployment.

Some of the methodological and research challenges to studying African American families include confounding race with socioeconomic status and challenges in recruiting African American families in research and programming. The Strong African American Family and REAL Men are culturally sensitive programs that have shown effectiveness for increasing positive child and parent outcomes.

EDUCATION AND WORK

He who learns, teaches.

—African proverb

LEARNING OBJECTIVES

- To consider the sociocultural importance of education in the lives of African Americans

- To understand significant historical factors that have shaped educational access and achievement of African Americans

- To examine educational data and research on the educational experiences of African Americans

- To consider the role of culture in the education of African Americans

- To consider the linkage between education, employment, and careers

- To examine measurements used for understanding the educational experiences, and employment of African Americans

- To examine interventions for improving positive educational outcomes for African American students

IN AFRICAN-AMERICAN EDUCATION, TOO, PARENTS KEY

BY BILL MAXWELL (2013, APRIL 12)

I never believed that racial desegregation was necessary for black children to excel. In other words, African-American children didn't need to be in the classroom with white children to learn.

My position is the result of my own experience as a student in underfunded Jim Crow public schools. Even with the benign neglect heaped upon us, we had our secrets for

(Continued)

(Continued)

success: We had parents and other adults at home who understood the value of education and who insisted that we succeed. We had principals and teachers, whose salaries were much less than those of their white peers, who cared about us.

Our service personnel—food preparers, janitors and landscapers—had children in our schools. They watched out for us. We knew that education was the key to the good life.

No, this is not a column about black history. It's about history repeating itself and about what education can be for black schoolchildren today when caring, wise, dedicated adults are in charge.

This time-tested formula is working at Urban Prep Academies in Chicago, the nation's first all-male and all-black charter high school. For the fourth consecutive year, all of its graduating seniors have been accepted to four-year colleges. This year, there are 167 seniors. They have been awarded more than $6 million in scholarships and grants.

It's a remarkable achievement in a city of high crime rates where black males are the lowest-performing demographic in public schools.

Tim King, Urban Prep's co-founder and CEO, opened the first campus in 2006 in the violent Englewood neighborhood. One of his main goals was to shut off the neighborhood's school-to-prison pipeline. When the school opened, only 4 percent of the boys were reading at grade level. Most had been written off by their teachers.

A lot of boys still enter Urban Prep socially and academically ill-prepared, but they undergo a metamorphosis. All staff members, from teachers to janitors, have a firm grasp of black culture, its weaknesses and strengths. When I visited the Englewood campus several years ago, I saw what King refers to as the "four R's": ritual, respect, responsibility and relationships.

Many of the teachers are black males, a phenomenon not seen elsewhere in Chicago schools. Staff members address students formally by their last names, and the students wear blue blazers, khakis and ties. Teachers are available after school hours. Students are required to perform community service.

At Urban Prep, "college is not a dream," King said. "It's reality. . . . It's a lot of hard work to get all the seniors into college. It's a combination of things, but I think most importantly, it's creating a positive school culture. From the day these boys come to us, we make sure we focus hard on letting them know that their job is to prepare for college. And our job, as the adults, is to make sure we're doing the right thing to help them along the way."

The school has adopted the nickname "Hogwarts in the Hood," a reference to the school for wizards in the Harry Potter saga.

And there's that other essential factor: parental responsibility. From the initial interview, parents must sign a contract affirming they will be involved in their children's education.

King makes it clear that Urban Prep—where 85 percent of the boys come from low-income families—is not in the business of rearing children. That's the parents' responsibility.

Urban Prep's story is one of hope. It is evidence of what is possible for black children when smart adults who care are at the helm.

Source: Maxwell (2013).

INTRODUCTION AND OVERVIEW

From early educational experiences at home and preschool through advanced professional and graduate training, education plays an important role in the individual development, cultural socialization, employment, and economic opportunities of African Americans. Academic experiences, achievement, and attainment shape African

Americans' access to social and career advancement. As a group, African Americans have historically experienced many challenges and barriers to accessing quality and equitable educational resources. However, as the opening story illustrates, some schools are meeting the challenges of providing high-quality education for African American children.

Understanding the role of education includes consideration of the academic experiences relevant to African Americans, the role that education plays in the life course of African Americans, and what educational resources support the most positive outcomes for African American children, youth, and adults. Several questions face us regarding education and African Americans: What assets do African American parents and families contribute to the learning and associated outcomes for their children? What characteristics of schools and educational settings (e.g., school and classroom size, ethnic composition) and educational processes (e.g., student–teacher relationships) play a role in the educational outcomes of African Americans? What role do specific educational factors play in the lives of African Americans, and how does culture influence education? Should employment and career be the primary goals of education for African Americans, or should their individual and cultural development be the desired goal? Educational outcomes include learning and mastery, grades and academic performance as measured by standardized test scores, and level of educational attainment.

Schools play a central role in preparing youth for their transitions to adult economic roles, whether this is based on a young person continuing to postsecondary education or vocational training. Education also plays a critical role in our ideas of an American "meritocracy," where an individual, though persistence and hard work, can access upward mobility. Education also serves as a key factor in an individual's access to a career and to his or her ability to care for self and family.

In the United States, the experience of individuals of African descent has been shaped significantly by their role in the American economy. Whether as individuals enslaved for the exploitation of their labor and service or persons achieving or marginalized in their pursuit of the "American Dream," work, employment, and economic roles are notably important in the experience of African Americans. American cultural characterizations of African Americans have often focused on economic and work issues and ranged from pejorative images of "welfare queens" and characterizations of African Americans as "shiftless" to the images of a powerful John Henry and the "hardest-working man." These images underline that work and employment roles of African Americans have shaped many cultural ideas, both outside and within the African American community. In addition, with the linkage of education to economic resources and access to health care through employment, our consideration of employment and careers is also critical to our understanding of the lives, experiences, and well-being of African Americans.

In this chapter, we consider the educational experiences of African Americans, including a specific focus on the transitions to careers and vocational opportunities. We begin with a demographic portrait that helps us understand current educational experiences. Next, we provide overviews of historical perspectives on the education of African Americans. We then review research on the educational experiences of African Americans. We also consider methodological issues in research and evidence-based practices informing our discussion and the education of African Americans. Because of the explicit role of schools in shaping an individual's access to career and vocational opportunities, we also note and describe the linkages of education and schooling to career and employment experiences. Finally, we critically examine issues relevant to the educational experiences of African Americans and end the chapter with a summary.

A Demographic Portrait of the Educational Status of African Americans

To understand psychological factors in the education of African Americans, it is helpful to first examine the historical and current status of the education of African Americans. According to data from DeNavas-Walt, Cleveland, and Roemer (2001) and the National Center for Education Statistics ([NCES]; Snyder, Dillow, & Hoffman, 2009), African Americans have shown increases in educational attainment since the 1940s. Although only 31.4% of African Americans age 25 or older had a high school diploma or GED in 1970, by 2016, 91.1% of African Americans 25 to 29 had graduated high school (Aud et al., 2012; U.S. Census, 2016f). Educational attainment at the high school level was generally comparable between African American men (91.7) and women (90.7). For African Americans age 25 or older, 2015 data indicate that 87.7% had completed high school or more, and 22.9% had attained a bachelor's degree or higher (U.S. Census, 2015). This compares to 93.3% of Whites having attained a high school diploma and 36.2% having attained a bachelor's degree or higher in 2015.

Based on Current Population Survey (CPS) data, in 2015, 6.5% of African Americans between ages 16 and 24 were classified as status dropouts (i.e., those not enrolled in school and who have not earned a GED or other high school credential) in comparison to 4.6% of Whites (U.S. Census, 2016g). These figures represent declines since 1992, when 13.7% of African Americans and 7.7% of Whites were classified dropouts.

Over time, more African American students have made an immediate transition to a 2- or 4-year college (e.g., 41.7% in 1975, 55.6% in 2015) (American College Testing Program, 2016). Of youth ages 16 to 24 who graduated from high school between January and October of 2016, 58.2% of African American students enrolled in college, compared with 69.7% of Whites, 92.4% of Asians, and 72% of Hispanics (BLS, 2017). For African American students who began their first full-time, 4-year college experience in 2010, 38% graduated within 6 years, compared with 62% of their White peers (Shapiro et al., 2017). In 2015, 14.1% of college students were African Americans (NCES, 2016a).

Since the early 1990s, women have been enrolled and completed college at higher rates than males. Gender differences have been especially notable among African Americans, where Black females have higher levels of postsecondary educational attainment than African American males (U.S. Census, 2016). While there has been a general positive trend in the enrollment of African American males in postsecondary degree-granting institutions (e.g., 17.5% in 1980, 34.1% in 2015), the enrollment for African American females has declined (e.g., 20.9% in 1980, 41.9% in 2009, 35.7% in 2015).

Educational attainment is important because it is associated with employment and income, which often defines a person's access to resources, such as housing and health care. Income is correlated with educational attainment; however, at the same level of educational attainment, income levels of males remain higher than for females and are higher for Whites than for African Americans. For example, in 2015 the average White adult age 25 to 34 with a high school diploma or GED working full time year-round earned $34,570, compared with $27,580 for the average African American adult at the same educational and employment status (U.S. Census Bureau, 2016h).

Historical Perspectives on the Education of African Americans

To understand current perspectives on educational systems and the experience of African Americans within them, it is useful to briefly consider historical perspectives. In 1831, Nat Turner, an enslaved man, led a rebellion to free slaves in Southampton

County, Virginia. Some attributed access to inflammatory abolition ideas as a contributor to the rebellion, and there were additional concerns about spreading ideas of rebellion among slave populations. In response, many states enacted or began to more vigilantly enforce laws that made it illegal to teach slaves to read and write. The fear was that education and the ability to read abolitionist writings would encourage and support slave rebellion. Education was seen as a tool and resource of resistance and liberation.

Prior to the Civil War, only 28 Blacks had received degrees from a college or university in the United States. Free Blacks established schools, many affiliated with Churches, following the American Revolution. Following the Civil War, in 1865, the Freedmen's Bureau was established by the U.S. federal government as a relief agency. It had success in establishing schools and providing educational funding for Blacks. Northern missionary societies also worked to increase access to educational opportunities for former slaves, and Blacks themselves spent more than $1 million on private education (Foner, 1988).

But education to what end and for what purpose? Historical discourse on the educational needs of African Americans is illustrated in the tension between the perspectives of Booker T. Washington and W. E. B. Du Bois. Born in 1856 and having early childhood experiences as a slave in Virginia, Washington was educated at the Hampton Institute. He established the Tuskegee Institute based on the principles of "thrift, economy and push" (Washington, 1896, p. 324) that prepared men and women for economic roles in industry, agriculture, and service. Washington felt that educational experiences should link practical applications with instruction in mathematics and the sciences. Washington's perspective emphasized the educational needs of Blacks in the "Black Belt" of the post–Civil War South, a context where wealth was largely based on agricultural production and land possession, as opposed to manufacturing. In this setting, the practices of mortgaging crops had left many Blacks in debt. Washington believed that "friction between the races will pass away in proportion as the black man, by reason of his skill, intelligence, and character, can produce something that the white man wants or respects in the commercial world" (Washington, p. 326).

In contrast to Washington, Du Bois was born in 1868 in Massachusetts to free parents. Following his parents' marital separation, he attended school as a young child and eventually became the first African American to receive a PhD from Harvard University. Du Bois felt that education purely to support industrial and economic roles was not the single or ultimate goal of education for Blacks. Du Bois (1903) believed that for Blacks to truly progress, the community needed the "Talented Tenth"—that is, the top 10% of Blacks—to pursue professional and other higher education to provide the African American community with teachers, ministers, lawyers, and doctors.

Challenges for Equal Access

Following emancipation, access to educational opportunities continued to be an important issue in the African American community and has been a central issue from Reconstruction and throughout the civil rights struggle. In challenging the legal principle of "separate but equal" established by the 1896 *Plessy v. Ferguson* decision, Thurgood Marshall, in the 1954 *Brown v. Board of Education* case, used the doll research by Mamie and Kenneth Clark (1939, 1947). This research presented evidence of the negative effects of segregation on the development of Black children. (An overview of Clark and Clark's work is presented in Chapters 1 and 3.)

Although the *Brown* decision struck down the legality of the separate but equal doctrine, the decision was clearly not the end of the struggle for equitable access to

CONTEMPORARY ISSUES

ENRICHMENT OR EMPLOYMENT: WHAT ARE THE GOALS OF EDUCATION FOR AFRICAN AMERICANS?

Is the goal of a college experience the cultural and personal development of the individual for their betterment and for the benefit of society? Or is the goal of a college education the preparation for entry into the workforce and improving one's chances of gaining desirable employment? At some level, this tension is not completely unlike the philosophical tensions between Du Bois and Washington. But this difference may seem less meaningful for many African American male youth who have experienced challenges in both educational and community settings. With continuing challenges with school failure and incarceration rates, young Black males, even if they have completed serving time, may face the additional challenge of obtaining "legitimate" employment.

City Startup Labs (CityStartupLabs, n.d) is a nonprofit organization that was established in 2012 in New York to support entrepreneurship education and the development of small businesses by young men, often ex-offenders, and allow them to create opportunities for self-employment. Henry Rock, the executive director of CLS, suggests that not only does this entrepreneurial perspective offer hope for the young men who can channel their talents to their personal, family, and community's development, but also, considering

the depressed job market, these entrepreneurial efforts present hope for the American economy.

Although this effort to create one's own path and sets of possibilities is laudable, it does raise important issues for African American communities to consider. We have not been successful at addressing the community and educational circumstances that undergird the developmental and contextual challenges that pave pathways to incarceration for many young African American males. We also understand that there are important gender discrepancies reflected in academic achievement, Does loving our sons and raising our daughters translate into our educational settings? How does the acceptance of mainstream cultural images and norms that support materialism place young men at risk, and what are the implied individual developmental, educational, and cultural needs of males within the African American community? Although we have important ongoing discussions of the relative merits and benefits of educational opportunities for African American males (e.g., single-sex schools; see Noguera, 2012), there is the critical need for additional research to inform our perspectives.

educational opportunities for African Americans. Southern public school systems were slow to desegregate, and the courts frequently ordered school redistricting or busing to remedy unequal access to educational opportunity. For example, in Virginia, a political movement called Massive Resistance (1956–1959) led to the closing of public schools in opposition to desegregation. The Virginia General Assembly, in 1958, passed a series of laws allowing local decisions in student placement, making public education optional and cutting off state funding for schools that allowed Black and White students to attend the same schools. Although the effort was legally squelched in 1959, some schools in Virginia did not begin integration efforts until 1968. Whites in New Orleans boycotted integrated schools, and governors in Arkansas, Mississippi, and Alabama attempted to block the entrance of Black students to White colleges and universities as late as 1963. The flight of Whites to suburbs in the 1950s and 1960s led to the de facto segregation of most urban-suburban government jurisdictions. Later court decisions (e.g., *Belk v. Charlotte-Mecklenburg Board of Education*, 2001; *Freeman v. Pitts*, 1992; *Missouri v. Jenkins*, 1995; *Oklahoma v. Dowell*, 1991) released school systems from court supervision of their desegregation efforts. Such court decisions are the cause, consequence, or correlate of the return of school integration levels comparable to those of the late 1960s.

Several books and studies have examined changes in and the effects of desegregation efforts. Kain and Singleton (1996) document racial disparity in students' access to equal opportunity in Texas schools. Their analysis provides an updated and more recent historical perspective on the 1966 Coleman Report, a study commissioned by Congress to examine the equality of educational opportunity following the Civil Rights Act of 1964. The Coleman report unexpectedly found limited racial differences in students' access to resources in suburban versus inner-city schools and reported limited school-level effects on student educational outcomes. The study suggested that family educational levels were important and reanalysis of the data and further research indicated that students of lower income benefit from an economically diverse student body (e.g., Kahlenberg, 2001).

Downey and Condron (2016) considered research and theory during the 50 years since the Coleman report and note that schools may work to reproduce or exacerbate social inequalities, may have limited effects on students, or may work in a compensatory fashion. These authors add that the Coleman report may not have measured key critical variables (e.g., teacher quality), or may not have considered ways the United States structures and supports children's educational experiences that may differentially disadvantage low-income students. For example, other countries, such as Canada, provide more robust early educational supports, which result in higher cognitive performance when students enter school.

In his book *Savage Inequalities*, Jonathan Kozol (1991) provides an analysis of urban and suburban public schools in six metropolitan areas. He describes dramatic differences in access to resources and infrastructure between urban schools and their suburban counterparts. Kozol poignantly notes the urban students' awareness of the gross inferiority of their schools and school resources. He describes states' local property tax funding strategies that disadvantage urban school systems. These urban school districts most often have higher proportions of nontaxable properties and higher numbers of students who may require costly special services. These services, when unavailable within the public school system, have to be paid for with public school funds. In some settings, upper-income individuals disproportionately access these services and resources such that public dollars are utilized to finance the special needs of middle- and upper-income children in private settings, further impoverishing public school districts.

RESEARCH ON THE EDUCATIONAL EXPERIENCES OF AFRICAN AMERICANS

Considerable research has been conducted examining the educational experiences of African Americans. Ongoing research underlines the importance of early stimulation in the brain development of infants and children that supports later cognitive development and academic achievement. Children born to teen mothers may receive less optimal parenting (Mollborn & Dennis, 2012), and African American children are more likely than their White peers to be born into low-income families or to teen moms (Hamilton et al., 2010). Although research has implicated lower academic performance of children to early parenting, other research raises questions as to whether these effects are linked to early childbearing itself or to the factors that predict and lead to early parenting (e.g., Hofferth & Reid, 2002; Levine, Emery, & Pollack, 2007). Decisions about childbearing appear to influence the educational opportunities for young parents. Delaying childbearing increases the likelihood of college attendance among African American females and delaying the birth of a second child, and having familial or educational supports enhance the likelihood of educational attainment (Cooley & Unger, 1991; Hofferth, Reid, & Mott, 2001).

Childhood Educational Experiences

Experience with structured, out-of-home educational settings begins relatively early for many African American children. African American children ages 3 to 5 are more likely to be enrolled in an early childhood care center or educational program than either their White or their Hispanic peers. For example, in 2015, 51.5% of African American children were enrolled in full-day preprimary programs, with an additional 14.6% of African American children in some type of structured part-day day care program. In contrast, 40.5% of White children ages 3 to 5 were in full-day programs and 25.8% in part-day preprimary programs; and 35.3% of Hispanic children were in full-day and 23.3% in part-day structured day care programs (U.S. Census, 2016c).

Quality early childhood experiences support later educational outcomes among low-income children and may be an important developmental resource and opportunity for children growing up in lower-resourced settings. For example, from 1958 to 1962, the Perry Preschool Project in Ypsilanti, Michigan, provided 30 hours of weekly high-quality active learning experiences for 123 low-income children ages 3 to 4 at risk for school failure. The long-term benefits of participation in such a program included fewer special education placements, greater school attainment, lower adult arrest rates, and higher incomes (Schweinhart, Barnes, & Weikart, 1993). Although early evaluations of Head Start (e.g., the Westinghouse in 1969) suggested that cognitive outcomes, such as IQ gains, were time limited, additional research suggests that students who attend Head Start are less likely to be held back in grades and less likely to be placed in special educational services (Barnett, 1995; Zigler, Taussig, & Black, 1992).

There has been additional work aimed at fully understanding the benefits of participation in Head Start and other early educational programming, such as the Abecedarian Project (Campbell & Ramey, 1995; Campbell, Ramey, Pungello, Sparling, & Miller-Johnson, 2002). Developmental research suggests that although young children who are not as well prepared to begin kindergarten or first grade show clear developmental gains once they begin school, they may not "catch up" to or make the same level of cognitive or academic gains as their peers. This may leave these students, although capable, at a cumulative disadvantage over their school careers.

Parent and Teacher Relationships and the Education of African Americans

Exchanges between children and their parents, their teachers, and other members of their social environment are important to their educational experiences and outcomes. Research has suggested that authoritative or democratic parenting (characterized by high parental warmth and control) has a positive effect on the academic performance of White and Latino adolescents but less impact on the educational outcomes of African and Asian American youth (Steinberg, Dornbusch, & Brown, 1992). In examining the effect of parenting behavior on academic achievement, Bean, Bush, McKenry, and Wilson (2003) studied maternal behavioral and psychological control and academic achievement among 80 White and 75 African American adolescents. White and African American adolescents were from Midwestern public high schools and were matched for family structure, parental education, gender, age, and grade level. Maternal support was found to be predictive of the achievement of the African American students but not of the White students. Fathers' parenting behaviors were unrelated to academic achievement.

Interpersonal exchanges may explicitly or implicitly shape students' expectations and understanding of the performance expected of them. Rosenthal and Jacobson (1968) examined the idea of the self-fulfilling prophecy and provided teachers with erroneous information about students in their classrooms. The researchers found that student performance conformed to teacher expectations; that is, if a teacher thought a student was smart and interacted with the student as if she or he was smart, then the student performed well. Although the study was controversial, subsequent research has established that teachers tend to pay less attention to students they perceive as low achievers, call on them less, criticize and interrupt them more, offer insincere praise, provide less feedback, and seat them farther from themselves (Good & Brophy, 1987). Research indicates that students are aware of different expectation and support from teachers. For example, in contrast to 54% of White males, only 20% of Black male senior high school students reported that their teachers "support me and care about my success in their class" (Noguera, 2003).

Parental racial socialization and racial attitudes are related to the academic performance of their children. Enrique Neblett, Chavous, Nguyen, and Sellers (2009) conducted a study involving 144 African American male adolescents in Grades 7 to 11 (mean age = 13.79). Analyses indicated four patterns of racial socialization: "Positive socialization (characterized by high racial pride, awareness of racial barriers, and self-worth)," "Moderate negative (relatively high negative messages and lower frequency of self-worth messages)," "Self-worth (high self-worth and lower racial socialization)," and low frequency. Racial socialization predicted academic performance and persistence over time. Specifically, those whose socialization experiences were characterized by self-worth messages had greater persistence than adolescents in the negative or low-frequency socialization groups. Youth in the self-worth group had higher grades than those who reported positive socialization and moderate negative socialization. Parental SES was also associated with academic achievement, with higher SES correlated with higher academic achievement.

Depending on how defined, *resources* may not be the most important predictors of educational experiences for African Americans. Lynn, Bacon, Totten, Bridges, and Jennings (2010) conducted a study in a wealthy African American suburban school district. Focus groups and classroom observations with 56 educators and administrators identified a culture of blame focused on parents, families, and communities for students' academic performance. Approximately 80% of teachers placed the responsibility for the low academic achievement of African American students on low motivation, class attendance and focus, limited preparation, poor classroom behavior, and engagement with street culture. Respondents also cited lack of parental engagement and limited confidence in their own ability to be successful in teaching Black students.

Disciplinary Actions and Treatment in Schools

African American males are disproportionately represented among students receiving disciplinary actions, including expulsions. The U.S. Department of Education Office for Civil Rights (2014) reports that Black students are 3 times more likely to be suspended or expelled from school than are White children. These disparities are reflected among preschool as well as older children, with African American children representing 18% of the student population but 48% of those experiencing more than one school suspension.

African American students are disproportionately likely to be referred to law enforcement officials, and students with a disability are more likely to be restrained. Black girls are more likely to be suspended compared with all other girls and other ethnic groups of boys. Smith and Harper (2015) found that 13 Southern states accounted for 55% of expulsions for African American students in the United States. B. Townsend (2000) and Morris and Perry (2016) remind us that expulsions result in more limited access to learning opportunities. Townsend links the higher levels of disciplinary actions to cultural conflicts, including lack of cultural knowledge among instructors (e.g., focusing on strict, hierarchical compliance to the teacher's desire for students' posture, as opposed to focusing on the primacy of the learning task). Townsend proposes several factors that may contribute to the improvement of these disciplinary problems, including greater focus on building relationships and cultural bridges and linking schools to families and communities. Using longitudinal data, Morris and Perry found that 17% of the differences in Black–White performance in math achievement and 20% in reading achievement may be due to the effects of school suspensions. With the enactment of zero-tolerance policies, additional concerns have been raised regarding the inequitable enforcement of these disciplinary guidelines (e.g., Polakow-Suransky, 1999).

Students' relationships with teachers are relevant both to their achievement and referrals for behavioral challenges. Decker, Dona, and Christenson (2007) conducted a study of 44 African American students (ranging from kindergarten to sixth grade) and 25 teachers from suburban and urban elementary schools. Teacher perspectives of the quality of their relationship with the students predicted the students' engagement and student self-reported social competence. Although teachers tended to rate their relationships with students somewhat negatively, at-risk students indicated interest in being close to teachers and rated their relationships with teachers relatively positively. Teacher perspectives on relationships also predicted suspensions and behavioral referrals. Positive student perspectives on the emotional quality of their relationships with teachers were associated with greater time on academic tasks and fewer behavioral referrals.

Discrimination and Educational Experiences

Interpersonal experiences of discrimination and racism play a role in the educational experiences of African American students. Wong, Eccles, and Sameroff (2003) present findings on experiences of discrimination reported among 336 African American male and 293 African American female participants in a longitudinal study beginning in the seventh grade. Students' perceived discrimination by teachers and peers was negatively associated with students' achievement motivation and beliefs about self-competence. Perceived discrimination was also negatively related to youths' sense of resiliency and feelings of self-esteem. Student problem behaviors, depressive symptoms, and anger were positively related to both perceived discrimination by teachers and by peers. Adolescents' connection to their ethnic group was a buffer to the effect of perceived discrimination on school achievement, feelings of self-competence, and behavior problems.

Wang and Huguley (2012) found that cultural socialization protected or buffered students from the negative effects that both teacher and peer discrimination can have on grade point average (GPA). In addition, teacher discrimination appeared to have a more negative effect on the cognitive engagement of males than of females in this sample of African American adolescents.

Chavous, Rivas-Drake, Smalls, Griffin, and Cogburn (2008) also found that the relationships among experiences of discrimination and academic performance varied by gender. For example, even if they experienced discrimination in the classroom or from peers, African American adolescent boys were more likely to have higher GPAs and to find school to be important if their racial identity was more central to their sense of self. In addition, boys from lower socioeconomic status families appeared at greater risk for negative effects of discrimination. For African American adolescent girls, racial identity was not correlated with good grades or the importance of school if the girls experienced classroom discrimination; if girls experienced discrimination from peers, however, they saw school as more important if they had a strong sense of racial identity. These findings support the utility of interventions that support African American youths' ethnic and cultural identity development and also underline that there are important gender factors in the educational experiences of African Americans.

Nasir and Shah (2011) examined feelings about achievement using interviews of middle and high school grade African American students. Students' racialized narratives about achievement reflected their perceptions of a "racial hierarchy" of academic achievement. Two primary narratives emerged in the study: (a) Blacks are not good at school or math, and (b) Asians are good at math. The students reported the tension between working from or countering stereotypical narratives and the need for them to engage in their social environment regarding these pejorative narratives. Youth were highly aware of these racial narratives and of being treated negatively by educators and described their efforts to counter and respond to these narratives.

Similarly, Tyrone Howard (2008) utilized narratives of 10 African American middle and high school students from five schools located in a metropolitan area on the West Coast to inform perspectives on the experiences of African American students. This work was grounded in a critical race theory perspective, which "interrogates the positionality and privilege of being White in the U.S., and seeks to challenge ideas such as meritocracy, fairness, and objectivity in a society that has a legacy of racial discrimination and exclusion" (p. 23).

Participants shared their experiences at schools through interviews. They reflected their awareness of pejorative stereotypes and their intentional effort to counter. Students were aware of structural racism and also reported the experience of lacking support due to racial stereotypes. One respondent described the following situation:

> We got into this fight. I said he started it, he said I started it, but the principal believed him. I had never been in trouble at school before, and this kid got in trouble a lot. But I am the one who got kicked out, and he stayed at the school. They said that I was 'too hostile and aggressive', and I never caused trouble, but it was like they didn't want to hear nothing me and my mother had to say. (p. 975)

Participants also reported experiencing expressions of racism despite their academic achievement. One student described the following scenario:

> We had an assembly at school for all the seniors who were going to college. They had the students come up on stage and said what college they were going to. For whatever reason, they forgot to call me up during the assembly, so I asked Mr. Matthews (the assistant principal) after the assembly why I didn't get called up, and he said that they were only calling up the kids who were going to 'good colleges,' and they didn't think that Morehouse was a really good college. That was like a slap in the face to me. Morehouse is a good college. I'm one of the first kids to go to college in my family, and he says that, it is not a good school. How does that make me feel? (pp. 973–974)

Students also described facing microaggressions reflective of low teacher expectations.

> On the first day in class, I showed up a little late to this AP Chemistry class. The teacher said, "You must be in the wrong class, this is AP Chemistry." I said, "No, I am in the right class," and showed her my schedule. She looked at it, and said, "this must be wrong, you cannot be in here." She didn't even know me, but she assumed that I didn't belong in her class. She called down to the office, and took about fifteen minutes calling down to the placement center, talking to counselors and everything, and when it was all over, I was in the right class. Am saying, if I was Asian would she have gone through all of that? (p. 974)

The study provides a compelling and troubling perspective on the experience and important voice of Black male youth in understanding their experiences of differential treatment.

Considering these challenging experiences, it is important to consider how discrimination factors may influence African American academic expectations and beliefs. Using a sample of 315 African American college students, Brown, Rosnick, and Segrist (2016) found internalized racial oppression to be associated with lower valuing of education and a greater sense of external control relevant to academic issues. For male participants, internalized racial oppression predicted a more external academic locus of control. An external locus of control implies that one's academic performance is outside of one's personal control. An external locus of control, in turn, predicted a lower valuing of education.

Testing and Accountability

With the enactment of legislation such as the No Child Left Behind Act in 2002, there was increased interest in the role and effect of high-stakes testing and accountability efforts in public education. High-stakes testing involves testing required for receiving a high school diploma. Based on a qualitative study of Chicago's experience with high-stakes testing and accountability in educational reform, Lipman (2002) suggests that these policy efforts promote and even exacerbate unequal educational access. Lipman describes extensive focus on test preparation in schools with low scores. This preparation includes redirecting resources from arts programs to purchase test preparation booklets, pep rallies, and announcements supporting student performance on the relevant accountability assessment. These efforts to improve test performance result in an overall narrowing of the educational opportunities available to students in lower-performing schools because these institutions increase their focus on test performance. In these settings, young teachers who are initially enthusiastic about learning are lost as the school focus turns to test preparation. In addition, Lipman describes how some school system workshops advised teachers about which students not to focus on. Teachers were advised to reduce their focus on both students who will clearly pass tests and students with little potential to pass so that the school could achieve its goals in test performance. In contrast, at higher-performing schools, teachers are described as focusing on developing richer curricula and promoting the value and love of learning. Orfield, Losen, Wald, and Swanson (2004) raise concerns that educational testing policies may exacerbate dropout problems among ethnic minority students (e.g., Haney et al., 2004), as school districts may have incentives to "push out" students who are perceived to bring down passing test score levels.

Former president Obama enacted the Every Student Succeeds Act (ESSA) in 2015. This act sought to reinforce learning for disadvantaged and high-needs students.

This act required that all students be taught standards that prepared them for careers and college. The act also expanded preschool investments and maintained expectations for change among low-performing schools. With Secretary of Education Betsy DeVos of the Trump administration, there appear to be potential shifts in perspectives on the implementation of ESSA reflected in feedback on states' educational plans.

Data on reading and math achievement tests indicate that discrepancies in scores between African American and White children have been decreasing over the past several decades. For example, while there was a 32-point difference in fourth-grade math achievement scores on the National Assessment of Educational Progress (NAEP) between Blacks and Whites in 1990, the gap was 24 by 2015 (see Table 6.1 below). Similarly, the reading achievement difference decreased modestly, from a 32-point difference in 1990 to a 24-point gap in 2015.

With current Secretary DeVos's prior support of charter schools, some have voiced concern that there may be possible shifts in education policy to favor charter schools, which some contend may divert already strained public educational resources to these alternatives. Research from the Center on Research on Education Outcomes has reflected mixed results (CREDO, 2013, 2015). In their study of charter schools

TABLE 6.1 ■ Average Reading and Math Achievement Scores and Long-Term Trends in the National Assessment of Educational Progress (NAEP), by Grade and Race/Ethnicity: Various Years, 1990–2015

Test Grade	Reading Achievement Scores				Math Achievement Scores			
	4th Grade		8th Grade		4th Grade		8th Grade	
Race	Black	White	Black	White	Black	White	Black	White
1990	NA	NA	NA	NA	187	219	236	269
1992	191	223	236	265	192	227	236	276
1994	184	222	235	265	NA	NA	NA	NA
1996	NA	NA	NA	NA	198	231	239	279
1998	192	223	242	268	NA	NA	NA	NA
2000	189	223	NA	NA	203	233	243	283
2002	198	227	244	271	NA	NA	NA	NA
2003	197	227	244	271	216	243	252	287
2005	199	228	242	269	220	246	254	288
2007	203	230	244	270	222	248	259	290
2013	206	232	250	276	224	250	263	294
2015	206	232	248	274	224	248	260	292

Source: NCES (2013, 2015).

across 26 states, there were no differences in learning gains for reading between charter schools and traditional schools in the majority (56%) of cases. In 29% of charter schools, performance was greater, and in 19%, performance was lower. For math, 40% of schools showed no differences, with 31% shower weaker performance and 29% showing stronger gains. Results for urban schools suggest more positive outcomes for charter schools but also noted variability.

Educational Contexts and Settings

In addition to interpersonal factors and processes on educational experiences, structural factors in schools, various educational settings, and neighborhoods also shape educational experiences and outcomes for African Americans. Research has shown that racial factors in the United States play an important role in shaping students' access to educational opportunities and experiences. Access is influenced by parental school choice, parents' residence options, and school classroom placement strategies. For example, when schools use ability grouping or tracking, African American students are more likely to be placed in lower tracks. Also, with the increasing focus on preparation for college and career and growth of employment opportunities in STEM (science, technology, engineering, and math) areas, African American high school graduates (6.1%) were less likely to have taken calculus than were their White (17.5%) or Asian/Pacific Islander (42.2%) peers in 2009 (Aud et al., 2012).

In a survey of 1,391 charter and 529 public school parents, Tedin and Weiher (2004) found that although school academic performance was the most important predictor of parental school choice, the racial composition of the school also played a significant role in parental selection of educational setting. Historically, Giles (1978) suggested that once a school's enrollment reaches 30% African American, White parents begin to move their children out of the school at an exponential rate. Further research suggests that Whites leave schools completely once those schools have student enrollments greater than 80% African American (Clotfelter, 1976). Data from U.S. Department of Education (NCES, 2016b) indicates that 57% of African American children in 2014 attended schools that were characterized by more than 75% minority student enrollment, whereas 52% of White students attended schools with less than 25% minority student enrollment.

Desegregation has shown some select positive effects on African American students' academic outcomes, as well as later income and job status (Schofield, 2001; Trent, 1997). Supreme Court rulings (e.g., *Parents Involved in Community Schools v. Seattle School District No. 1*, 2007 and *Meredith v. Jefferson County Board of Education*, 2006) have the potential to limit student access to desegregated settings. These court rulings have limited the explicit use of race by public school systems in voluntarily enacting strategies to support the desegregation of schools. The historical focus on desegregation and its relative benefits continue to raise important questions regarding the academic performance and access to educational resources (e.g., teaching effectiveness) of African American students. Clayton (2011) conducted a study of performance on state education accountability assessments in Virginia. The author noted that because many predominantly African American schools are characterized by having higher proportions of students living in poverty, as well as poorer teacher quality, it can be difficult to tease out the role of school racial composition alone in understanding academic achievement and progress. African American elementary school students are less likely to achieve advanced English pass scores in high-poverty schools and schools with lower ratings of teacher quality.

Neighborhood Influence

Research suggests that when considering academic and cognitive outcomes, White adolescents appear to benefit more than African American adolescents from having higher-income neighbors. The influence of neighborhood and the relevance of specific neighborhood factors may also differ between African American boys and girls. Several cognitive and academic indicators (e.g., school achievement, graduation rates, college attendance) suggest that affluent neighbors and ethnically diverse neighborhoods benefit African American males (Duncan, 1994; Ensminger, Lamkin, & Jacobson, 1996; Halpern-Felsher et al., 1997) more so than females.

Neighborhood cohesion also affects academic outcomes. Plybon, Edwards, Butler, Belgrave, and Allison (2003) found that positive perceptions of neighborhood cohesion were positively associated with school self-efficacy and self-reported grades among a sample of 84 urban African American adolescent females

Special Education

Data suggest that African Americans are more likely to be identified for specific learning disabilities (5.32% versus 3.42%), mental retardation (1.56% versus 0.60%), and emotional disturbance (1.27% versus 0.62%) than are their White peers ages 6 to 21 (Aud, Fox, & Kewal Ramani, 2010).

Data for 2014–2015 suggest that 15% of African Americans, as compared with 13% of Whites, between ages 3 and 21 receive services under the Individuals with Disabilities Education Act (IDEA; Office of Special Education Programs, 2016). Rates of identification for special education services have varied by region, with the highest rates in the South. In addition, although counterintuitive, overidentification of African Americans for special education services occurs most frequently in the wealthiest school districts (Losen & Orfield, 2002).

Problems with overidentification for services have often been tied to the role of assessment in the identification of students in need of special education. Problems appear to be linked not as much to test construction or cultural bias of test items as to the role of subjectivity in the processes by which students are identified and assessed. Court cases such as *Hobson v. Hansen* (1967/1969) challenged and limited the use of IQ testing in educational placement and tracking of African Americans. Cases such as *Larry P. v. Riles* (1972/1974) and *PASE v. Hannon* (1980) limited the use of IQ tests for placing African American students in classes for the mentally retarded (Hilliard, 1983). Legislation such as Public Law (P.L.) 94–142 (Education for All Handicapped Children Act, 1975) and its reauthorization as P.L. 101–476 (Individuals with Disabilities Education Act, 1990) protects students' rights to a free and appropriate education. P.L. 99–457 (1986), which extended this legal protection to children ages 3 to 5 and its reauthorization (P.L. 105–117, 1997) were based on many of the underlying tenets established by the earlier legal rulings. These laws require that student assessments for placement in special education services be based on multidisciplinary teams with expertise in the areas of the student's presumed deficits. They also require that assessment be culturally appropriate, that parents have the right to participation, and that students be placed in the least restrictive educational environment possible.

Many educational and civil rights advocates are concerned with the apparent weakening of an individual's legal recourse under Title VI of the Civil Rights Act of 1964. In 2001, the decision rendered by the Supreme Court in *Alexander v. Sandoval* indicated that such cases should be pursued by the Office of Civil Rights and not by private individual action. The courts have played and will continue to play an important role in shaping the educational experiences of African Americans.

Later in this chapter, we cover other roles that the courts and legislation have played in the educational experiences of African Americans.

Role of Race in Gifted and Talented Programs

Research by Ford (Ford, 1996; Ford, Harris, Tyson, & Trotman, 2002) and Worrell (2003) shows another domain in which African Americans face challenges within American educational systems: educational opportunities for the gifted and talented (GT). Ford et al. suggest that African Americans are underrepresented in GT programs by 50%. The authors note that biased beliefs about the cognitive abilities of African Americans and the use of intelligence tests as the primary method of identifying youth for participation in GT programs places these youth at a disadvantage. The singular use of IQ tests may be particularly inappropriate as IQ scores predict only a portion of the variance in academic performance. In addition, standardized tests have less predictive validity in relation to the academic performance and outcomes of African Americans. More comprehensive analysis of capabilities and use of assessments based on multidimensional models of intellectual capacity may be warranted. Card and Guiliano (2015) found that when a universal testing and screening program was used to identify and refer students to gifted educational opportunities, there was an 80% increase in the gifted rate among African American students.

Worrell (2003) notes, in particular, that potential biases in recruitment processes may play a role in the underidentification of African American youth for GT programs. In his study of participants in a summer program for GT students, Worrell notes that GT African American youth may come from homes that are less affluent, and this raises concerns that these youth and families may not be aware of opportunities for GT students. Ford also raises questions as to what types of educational experiences are engaging for, relevant to, and supportive of the retention of GT African American students. Additionally, Ford raises questions about training needed to support GT teachers and program designers in developing and using appropriate assessment, recruitment, and retention strategies. The use of teacher discretion may be especially problematic. Even after taking reading and other factors into account, Grissom and Redding (2016) find that African American students are less frequently referred for GT programming, especially in reading, when taught by non–African American teachers.

Educational Alternatives

Although research continues to document disparities in the educational resources and experiences available to African Americans, many African American students access high-quality educational opportunities and experiences in public and other educational settings. In *Dispelling the Myth Revisited*, Jerald (2001) presents an analysis of almost 90,000 public schools in the United States in the year 2000. Findings reveal 4,577 high-poverty (at least 50% low-income) or high-minority (at least 50% African American and Latino) enrollments in schools nationwide that had student reading and/or math scores in the top third of all schools within the state. Other African American parents choose private academic options, such as independent Black institutions, Catholic schools, and private (predominantly White) elite schools (Slaughter & Johnson, 1988).

Beyond traditional public and private schools, parents may choose to send their children to schools that specifically focus on the holistic education of children of African descent. The Council on Independent Black Institutions (CIBI) was established in 1972 as an umbrella organization for schools that are Afrikan centered and advocate Afrikan-centered education. CIBI defines *Afrikan-centered education* as "the means by which Afrikan culture—including the knowledge, attitudes, values, and skills needed to maintain and perpetuate it throughout the nation-building process—is developed and advanced through practice. Its aim, therefore, is to build commitment and competency within present and future generations to support the struggle for liberation and nationhood" (CIBI, 1996/2001, p. 3).

Data suggest that decreasing numbers of African American parents are choosing to homeschool their children. Data from the National Center on Education Statistics on homeschooling indicated that about 1.3% of African Americans were homeschooled in 2003 (Redford, Battle, & Bielick, 2016). However from 2001 to 2012, while 3.3% of White students were homeschooled (up from 2% in 1999), fewer than 1% of African American students (0.7%) were homeschooled. There is little existing research on the experiences and educational outcomes specific to African Americans who are homeschooled. However, a number of organizations, including the National Black Home Educators (NBHE, n.d.), have developed networks and resources targeting African American families interested or involved in homeschooling.

Higher Education

Blacks' access to higher education continues to be addressed in courts and legislation. The 1978 Supreme Court decision in the *Bakke* case (*Regents of the University of California v. Bakke*) supported the continuation of affirmative action in higher education, citing the educational benefits of diversity. In the 2003 cases of *Grutter v. Bollinger et al.* and *Gratz v. Bollinger et al.*, regarding admissions policies at the University of Michigan, the U.S. Supreme Court decided that race can be used as a factor in admissions in college and professional degree programs. The issue was recently addressed in the *Fisher* case involving the University of Texas. Race cannot be used if it is based on explicit quotas or rigid procedures (e.g., adding a specific number of points to the admissions score of an individual from a particular ethnic or racial group). In 2016, the Supreme Court upheld that Texas's inclusion of race as a factor within their admissions policy passed the strict scrutiny test (i.e., proving that alternatives to diversifying the student body were not viable) and was constitutional. Colleges and universities continue to craft both admissions policies and procedures for the distribution of financial aid that meet these legal guidelines. Some states, including California, Michigan and Oklahoma, do not allow race to be used as a factor in decisions such as university admissions, public employment, or the awarding of public contracts.

Research has raised serious questions as to whether public schools are adequately preparing African American students for higher education opportunities. Subject area test scores were used to predict whether a student would achieve a C or above in a first-year credit-bearing course in college. Data from the ACT indicate that among African American students who took the test, 36% were college ready in English, 22% in reading, 15% in math, 7% in science, and only 5% in all four subjects. In contrast, 77% of White students scored at levels reflecting college readiness in English, 62% in reading, 54% in Math, 38% in science, and 32% in all four subjects (ACT, 2012).

Factors That Predict Academic Success of African American College Students

Supportive relationships in college are linked to academic success. Strayhorn (2008) reports results from a sample of 231 African American males from a nationally representative random sample of college students. Having supportive relationships in the college environment was associated with greater student satisfaction with college. Satisfaction was also associated with higher academic performance. Strayhorn (2010), using data from the National Educational Longitudinal Study, tracked participants from an original sample of 27,394 individuals and followed them from the eighth grade in 1990 through 2000, when they had been out of high school for 8 years. Approximately 12,150 participated in all three follow-ups, resulting in a sample that was 9% African American and 13% Hispanic.

High school performance in math and science, discussions with parents about college, and participation in precollege programs predicted college GPA for both Latino and African American males; however, socioeconomic status and mother's expectations for academic persistence were more important predictors of African American male college student GPA. In contrast, participation in a pre-college program and high school GPA were more important predictors of college GPA for Latino males. African American males had lower levels of both college and pre-college academic achievement than Latino males and less frequent discussions about college with their parents than Latino males. Participation in student government and volunteer activities were associated with higher college GPA for African American males; however, involvement with fraternities was associated with lower college performance.

One question that has been relevant to higher education in general is whether there is benefit to having diverse and inclusive student bodies. Gurin, Dey, Hurtado, and Gurin (2002) analyzed data from 1,528 students who took part in the Michigan Student Survey and national data on 11,383 students attending 184 different colleges or universities from the Cooperative Institutional Research Program. Both data sets were collected during the late 1980s. The findings indicate that an ethnically diverse environment contributes positively to educational outcomes for all college students. Gurin et al. examined indices such as the diversity of the institution, opportunities for informal interaction with students from diverse cultural backgrounds, and exposure to diversity in course content or activities. These indices were examined in relation to outcomes such as intellectual engagement, academic skills, perspective taking, and attitudes about cultural awareness and diversity. Results suggest that campus diversity supports educational outcomes, especially for White students, and that these effects are achieved through student experiences.

The role of the far right (including White supremacy groups) in African Americans' higher educational experiences must be raised. Student protest at the University of Missouri, murder of an African American student at the University of Maryland, and White nationalists carrying torches on the campus of the University of Virginia raise important questions on the tension between free speech and the development of a hostile learning and work environment. These events on campus raise a series of important questions as to what types of learning and developmental environments are available and optimal for the educational and holistic development of African American college students. How do these crises affect our discussions and considerations of "safe spaces" on campus?

Finally, student loan debt is a factor that affects the lives of students after they leave college. Over the past 10 to 15 years, in part exacerbated by the recession, states have decreased the level of public support to cover the costs of higher education. Colleges and universities, in turn, have shifted these costs to students and families. African American families, on average, have more limited financial assets and may rely more heavily on student and private loans. Addo, Houle, and Simon (2016) report, using data from the National Longitudinal Study of Youth 1997 (NLSY97), that African Americans report 68.2% more debt than their White peers. Notably, parental assets do not appear to buffer the level of debt for African American students, and those who complete college have higher levels of debt than those who do not. Foundations such as Gates and Lumina are engaged in important programmatic and policy questions to address growing concerns about college accessibility, including the financial barriers, and college completion.

Historically Black Colleges and Universities (HBCUs)

At the college and university level, students and parents may also choose a historically Black college or university (HBCU). Lincoln and Wilberforce were the only two private colleges for Blacks established prior to the Civil War. From schools supported by the Freedmen's Bureau, Northern Churches, and post–Civil War Blacks, several teachers colleges emerged. By 1890, college courses and programs were being offered by 40 private colleges or universities for Blacks. Sixteen additional public HBCUs that still operate had been established by 1890 (Roebuck & Murty, 1993). There are currently approximately 100 HBCUs. In 2014, approximately 8% of all African American students enrolled in degree-granting institutions attended HBCUs, down from 18% in 1976 (Snyder & Dillow, 2012; NCES, 2016a). Similarly, there were declines in the percentages of degrees awarded by HBCUs, with 35% of undergraduate degrees awarded to African Americans in 1976–1977, compared to 15% in 2013–2014 (NCES, 2016a).

Students describe a compelling portrait of the support they can experience at an HBCU. In one study at a mid-Atlantic HBCU, 11 African American male juniors and seniors who had participated in a pre-college preparatory program for students with limitations were interviewed (Palmer & Gasman, 2008). Participants reported the accessibility, support, encouragement and caring of faculty and administrators. For example, one respondent indicated that "you sit there for an extra hour and it's just amazing. I never knew people [could] be that generous" (p. 59). Students also described the availability of peer support for motivation. One student described the importance of "having friends that have the same common goals as I do, that inspires me to push myself even farther, 'cause they all have personal achievements, and it's not a competition things. It's all about uplifting one another" (p. 61). These students noted the broader supportive nature of the campus community and the availability of peer and other mentoring relationships.

CULTURE AND NONCOGNITIVE FACTORS IN EDUCATION

As we note throughout this book, African Americans are not a monolithic group, and African American parents vary in their ethnic identity, socialization beliefs, and cultural and child-rearing practices. As African American children transition from their homes and communities to school, they may encounter schools that are not culturally congruent with their prior socialization experiences, or they may face some level of cultural transition. Prior to desegregation and declines of infrastructure in some African American communities, schools were more frequently an integral part of the community infrastructure and largely shared the culture of the children. Parents may now choose to educate their children in schools that emphasize culture and ethnicity. Students may choose to go to a predominantly White school or to an HBCU. The diversity of these potential educational settings raises questions as to the role culture and ethnicity play in the educational experiences of African Americans.

Several conceptual and critical perspectives have been used to support our understanding of the role and relevance of culture in the educational experiences and needs of African Americans. In *The Mis-Education of the Negro*, Carter G. Woodson (1933/1972) argues that neither practical (e.g., industrial) nor classical (e.g., liberal arts education) training was especially successful among Blacks during the late-19th and early 20th centuries. He strongly criticizes the lack of focus on the history, development, and experience of the Negro in the curricula and proposes that education for the Negro should support an understanding of self, history, literature, and religion. Education should serve to uplift others of the same race who have not had access to resources or opportunities. Others such as Freire (1970/1989) and R. G. Potts (2003) similarly argue that the goals of education can be to transform, empower, and uplift those who are being educated.

African-Centered Approaches to Education

Kunjufu (1984) and Akbar (1983) criticize mainstream educational curricula as those that "train" children, as opposed to educating them. Training individuals, Kunjufu suggests, builds on skills of rote memorization and prepares young people for the role of employee in a job. In contrast, education supports students in learning to think in preparation for careers in which they serve as employers. In *Countering the Conspiracy to Destroy Black Boys*, Kunjufu (1985) presents the Fourth-Grade Failure Syndrome, suggesting that this age/grade represents a pivotal point in the educational experiences of African American males. Kunjufu suggests that the academic performance of African American males drops off at this point, as Black boys see schools and their curricula as culturally and personally irrelevant. Kunjufu (1985) points to multiple contributors to the early disengagement of many Black males from educational settings. These include lack of relevant role models for youth in their early educational experiences, the transition from social-relational to competitive-individualistic classroom environments, parental apathy, and the increasing negative influence of peers and media.

Other cultural factors relevant to learning may be important to the educational experience of African American children. Considering communalism among African Americans (see Chapter 2), the role of relationships may be particularly relevant. Wimberly (2002) emphasizes the importance of school relationships between teachers and students. He notes that African American high school youth frequently do not have the types of social connections with teachers (e.g., contact in and out of classroom time) that may support their access to higher education. Shade (1982) suggests that in American schools, the cognitive style that supports academic achievement is sequential, analytical, and object oriented. Her review of the literature describes the learning styles of African Americans, in contrast to the learning styles of Whites, as universalistic, intuitive, and relational. Boykin (1983, 1994) suggests that Black children prefer educational environments that are congruent with their cultural preferences for verve. Hale-Benson (1990) suggests that Black children prefer relational learning settings and experiences. Research by Neblett et al. (2009) has also indicated that parental socialization of African American adolescent males is related to their academic persistence. One additional area in education where cultural factors have been particularly apparent revolves around the use of Black English. African American Vernacular English (AAVE) (also known as Black English or Ebonics) has been described as a rule-governed linguistic system with its own syntactic structure, lexicon, and phonology. (For further discussion of Ebonics and related aspects of African-centered perspectives on cognitive style, see Chapter 9.)

Identity and Group Membership in Education

Stereotype Threat

Research by several scholars supports our understanding of the linkage between group membership, self-identification, and academic achievement. Based on a series of studies and related theoretical work (e.g., Steele, 1992, 1997; Steele & Aronson, 1995), Claude Steele and his colleagues suggest that Blacks and members of other groups classified as numerical minorities may be subject to *stereotype threat* or *stereotype vulnerability*. This vulnerability refers to the pressure experienced by a member of a stereotyped group in a performance situation where he or she is at risk of confirming a negative or pejorative stereotype. For African Americans, academic performance situations may increase concerns about confirming or being judged based on beliefs regarding the intellectual abilities of their racial group. Impairments in performance associated with these concerns are reflected in what Steele describes as the overprediction phenomenon. In these situations, even when African Americans are academically capable, as reflected in aptitude scores (e.g., SAT or ACT scores) that are comparable to their White peers, they demonstrate lower academic performance. Steele argues that this lower performance may be due to processes associated with the priming of racial stereotypes about academic performance.

In an earlier study, Steele and Aronson (1995) gave both African American and White college students an academic performance measure. In one condition, respondents were asked to complete a questionnaire that asked general questions about their background (e.g., age, gender, major) prior to undertaking the performance measure. In the second condition, participants completed a similar questionnaire that ended with a question asking their race (race prime condition). African American students in the race prime condition showed lower performance than both African American students in the control condition and White students in either condition.

Beyond these internal processes, Steele (1992) also raises questions as to whether subtle clues in the social environment (e.g., the manner in which instructors ask or respond to different students in their classes) communicate performance expectations and membership or inclusion within the specific learning community. In addition to Steele's perspective, Crocker and Major (1989) propose that membership in a stigmatized group may lead individuals to devalue the self domains in which they demonstrate lower performance. For example, research on African American adolescents indicates that academic competence is less central to their overall self-esteem than is their social competence with peers; in contrast, academic competence was of greater centrality or importance to the self-concept of White adolescents.

Disidentification With Education

Ogbu and colleagues (e.g., Fordham & Ogbu, 1986) proposed that some African Americans may reject education because it is identified with an economic and status attainment system linked to their oppression by Whites. To identify with and pursue achievement within this status system is to identify with and buy into a system that is established and controlled by a group that has historically oppressed African Americans. Consequently, African Americans may adopt an "oppositional cultural frame of reference" and perceive educational attainment as "acting White." Within their conceptualization, Fordham and Ogbu suggest that there are three different types of American minorities: Immigrant minorities are cultural or ethnic groups who chose to come to the United States because of political or economic opportunities. Autonomous minorities are social groups with voluntary membership based on personal and individual preference, which, relative to the majority American context, are a numerical minority (e.g., Mormons). Autonomous minority groups are more frequently assimilated or integrated into mainstream middle-class American social culture. In contrast, subordinate or "caste-like" minorities have come to the United States either through slave trade or political or economic duress and most often have physical markers (such as skin color or physical morphology) that signal their membership in these stigmatized groups. Within the status attainment system, these groups experience blocked opportunities for advancement (e.g., a glass ceiling) and perceive bias in their efforts for full and equal participation in the status attainment system. It is these subordinate minorities that are more likely to experience the conflict between their cultural identities and participation in the American educational system. This disidentification with the educational arena is implicated in the lower educational performance of African American students. The disidentification process may characterize the developmental experiences of some African Americans but not all. For example, Lundy (2003) suggests that the oppositional framework may be more relevant to the beliefs and attitudes of African American men than women.

Racial identity differences might also be related to differences in disidentification. Chavous et al. (2003) examined the associations between racial group identity and academic indicators. The research group examined data on 606 African American youth in the 12th grade who were followed for 2 years. Racial identity was measured using a brief version of Seller's MIBI. From this scale, Centrality (i.e., the extent to which an individual's ethnicity is important to him or her), Public Regard (i.e., the respondents' perception of others' positive or negative values and attitudes toward African Americans), and Private Regard (i.e., the individual's own feelings toward African Americans) were measured. Analyses resulted in four clusters or groups based on profiles of youths' ethnic identity attitudes and beliefs. (a) The Buffering/Defensive group was high in Centrality and had high Private Regard but felt Blacks were seen negatively by others. (b) The Low Connectedness/High Affinity group was high in Private Regard and thought others viewed African Americans negatively but was low in the Centrality of its ethnicity. (c) The Idealized group was high along all three dimensions. (d) In contrast, the Alienated group was low across all three dimensions. Although there were no GPA differences across the four groups, the Alienated group had the highest percentage of individuals not in school in 12th grade and the lowest percentage of individuals in a 2- or 4-year institution of higher education 2 years later. This group also demonstrated lower interest in school than the Idealized or Buffering/Defensive group, and they were also lowest in self-efficacy. Youth in the Buffering/Defensive group had the highest percentage of individuals in higher education. In contrast to the work of Ogbu or others that implicate high levels of group identity with lower academic performance, Chavous et al. suggest that high Private Regard as a component of ethnic identity is associated with more positive academic outcomes.

Grit

Recently, there has been considerable interest in the role of noncognitive variables, notably *grit*, in the academic achievement of African American students. Grit is a concept that reflects an individual's consistency in perseverance and persistence toward her or his goals, even in the face of challenges (Duckworth, Peterson, Matthews, & Kelly, 2007). Some educational programming, such as the Knowledge Is Power Program (KIPP; n.d.) has integrated the concept of grit into their program and curricula. Research by Strayhorn (2014) examined the contributions of grit to the academic performance of 140 African American male college students at 4-year, predominately White institutions. Grit was associated with college grades and high school academic performance and predicted college academic performance after controlling for a range of variables, including prior academic achievement (e.g., ACT scores, HS GPA).

PERSPECTIVES ON WORK, CAREER, VOCATIONS, AND EMPLOYMENT

Historical Perspectives on Work

History has shaped the experience of work, employment, and career concerns of individuals of African descent in America. Traced back from the initial capture of slaves by the Portuguese in the mid-1400s, the transatlantic slave trade came to Jamestown, in the colony of Virginia, in 1619 with the arrival of approximately 20 Angolans who had been taken from a Spanish slaver by a privateer. Although the early North American experiences of Africans were structured as indentured servitude, the 17th and 18th centuries marked a history of the social and legal curtailment of the rights and social status of individuals of African descent by local, state, and federal statute. Over this period, "a person held to service or labor" (Fugitive Slave Law, 1850, 9 Stat. 462) was rendered to the status of lifelong, intergenerational chattel slavery. By the first U.S. Census in 1790, there were 757,363 Blacks, of which 697,897 were enslaved and 59,466 (approximately 8.5%) were free. By 1860, the population of Blacks in the United States totaled approximately 4 million, of which 488,070 (or approximately 11%) were free (Steckel, 1998). In 1808, the United States ceased the importation of enslaved individuals, but the domestic slave trade continued.

The economic and political relevance of the "peculiar institution," with the economic growth of the Northern industrial economy of the 19th century, and the economic expediency of slavery in a Southern tobacco- and cotton-based agricultural economy, served as critical to the secession of the Confederacy. Following the Civil War and the emancipation of Southern slaves, the establishment of Black Codes in many Southern states allowed newly freed Blacks to enter into employment contracts but curtailed personal freedoms and economic opportunities. The establishment of the Freedmen's Bureau offered some educational opportunities and resources for employment advocacy. The Reconstruction period (1867–1877) offered a brief period of economic hope that was largely unfulfilled. Many Blacks had access only to tenant farming and sharecropping, and with the increasing imposition of Jim Crow laws, political and economic opportunities for African Americans were again curtailed. For the vast majority of formerly enslaved Blacks, there was no "40 acres and a mule." Economic and employment issues played significant roles in the migration of African Americans to Northern industrial centers for employment opportunities during the early to mid-20th century. With the suburbanization of job opportunities and the transition from a manufacturing to a service economy, employment had declined among African Americans.

African-Centered Perspective on Employment

The broader American cultural context places strong emphasis on the role and importance of work and employment. These include values involving a strong Puritan work ethic, the emphasis of cultural roles of breadwinners, perceptions of the United States as the "land of opportunity," and associated beliefs that it is a meritocracy where individuals can "pull themselves up by their bootstraps." This American context involves a cultural model of upward social mobility where each generation is expected to surpass the social status and access to financial resources of the prior generation. In contrast, from an African-centered perspective, the concepts of Ujima and Ujamaa are relevant. Ujima—that is, collective work and responsibility—is one of the Nguzo Saba, articulated as part of the core of Africentric principles and values. Here, rather than an individualistic model of economic achievement and progress, work is described within a communal framework and is linked explicitly to a sense of interdependence and responsibility for members of the group. A related construct is Ujamaa, or cooperative economics. Here, members of the group are called to support collaborative economic efforts through their initiation, maintenance, and support of businesses that profit the group and members of the community. These principles present a significantly different cultural perspective on work from the mainstream American model. Whereas issues of competition and individual profit characterize the American capitalistic economy and many workplace settings, Africentric perspectives, in contrast, emphasize cooperation, group benefit, and economic success of the collective.

Measuring Employment

Data on work and employment come from the Bureau of Labor Statistics (BLS). Monthly, beginning in 1940, the BLS has conducted the Current Population Survey (CPS), which is based on a sample of approximately 60,000 households in a nationally representative sample. According to the BLS,

- People with jobs are employed.
- People who are jobless, looking for jobs, and available for work are unemployed.
- People who are neither employed nor unemployed are not in the labor force. (BLS, 2001)

Data from BLS are based on individuals age 16 or over who are not in a mental health or penal institution or in active service within the armed forces. Persons within this population are identified as being within the *civilian labor force*. Individuals not in the labor force are those under age 16 or individuals who are institutionalized, going to school or retired, or in active military duty. Those classified as employed work for pay or in family-operated work for at least 15 hours per week or are temporarily out of their work positions due to illness, vacation, weather, or other personal reasons. Individuals classified as unemployed are in the labor force but are currently without a job, have actively looked for work within the past 4 weeks, and are available for work or waiting to be called back from a layoff. Among individuals not in the labor force, further distinctions are made among those who are marginally attached and those defined as discouraged workers. Individuals are identified as marginally attached to the workforce if they currently desire employment and have pursued work during the last 12 months and are available to work. Discouraged workers are a subset of the marginally attached. Discouraged workers are individuals not currently seeking employment because

- they believe no job is available to them in their line of work or area,
- they had previously been unable to find work,

TABLE 6.2 ■ Unemployment Rate of Civilian Population 20 Years and Older by Race and Sex		
	Male	**Female**
White	3.4	3.3
African American	5.9	6.2

Source: Bureau of Labor Statistics (n.d.).

- they lack the necessary schooling, training, skills or experience, or

- employers think they are too young or too old or they face some other type of discrimination. (BLS, 2001)

While unemployment rates have declined for all racial and ethnic groups, data from the Bureau of Labor Statistics show that the seasonally adjusted unemployment rate among African Americans in February 2018 was substantively higher than that of White males. Substantial differences were also seen for females (see Table 6.2). Unemployment disparities among those 16 to 19 years of age are especially notable with unemployment rates of 11.5 for White youth and 24.8 for African American youth (BLS, n.d.)

Psychological Perspectives on Work, Career, and Employment

Within psychology, several areas of study are relevant to consideration of work and employment. Vocational psychology has been defined by Savickas (2002) as "the study of vocational behavior and development," where "vocational refers to the responses an individual makes in choosing and adapting to an occupation" (p. 382). Richardson, Constantine, and Washburn (2005) proposed an expansion of the definition of vocational psychology. They suggested that it be defined "as a field, comprised of theory, research, and intervention practices, that is committed to the importance of work and relationships in people's lives, to helping people live healthy and productive lives, and to social justice, especially with respect to providing access to opportunity for those marginalized or disadvantaged due to social locations such as gender, race, and class" (p. 59). This proposed definition is inclusive of those who might work at home and play central roles as caretakers for children, the elderly, or individuals requiring more extensive care at home.

The concepts of career and vocation often involve a sense of personal choice or "calling" and an emphasis on these work choices and experiences over the life course. Savickas (2002) also underlines the importance of being specific in the use of terms. For example, career development indicates a specific reference to change within a developmental or life course perspective, as opposed to occupational or vocational behavior, which is an interaction with the environment that does not necessarily involve a temporal, sequential, or developmental perspective. An additional area of psychology that informs perspectives on the psychological experiences of African Americans in the work world involves industrial-organizational (IO) psychology. IO psychology involves "the scientific study of the workplace. Rigor and methods of psychology are applied to issues of critical relevance to business, including talent management, coaching, assessment, selection, training, organizational development, performance, and work–life balance" (http://www.siop.org).

Work, Career, and Vocational Experiences of African Americans

Some research (e.g., Aries & Moorehead, 1989) suggests that career and work issues may not be as central to the identity of African American adolescents as it is to White youth. For example, Lease (2006) found that racial identity was not associated with the number of careers that African American high school students considered. Research has also suggested that African American youth and adults who have more limited access to middle-class pathways to the "American Dream" may develop and access a "Modified American Dream" (Burton, Allison, & Obeidallah, 1995). Here, the expression of adult social status may be reflected through spirituality, independence and parenting, creativity, or the possession and display of accessible consumer indicators of success (e.g., cars, jewelry, sneakers) rather than employment.

African Americans have faced bias in hiring, as well as in promotion and salary increases. Research by Bussey and Trasvina (2003) used "undercover tests" in which Black and White candidates applied for jobs in temporary employment agencies in California and found that White employees were hired at a rate of 4 to 1 in Los Angeles and 2 to 1 in San Francisco. "Tester" pairs were hired by the researchers for similarity in personal characteristics (e.g., appearance, interpersonal style) and for similarity in skills and qualifications. Both received training, and the African American candidate presented a profile to potential employers that was slightly stronger. The African American candidate also initiated contact in advance of the White counterpart. The authors report,

> White testers were offered a position 77% of the time, while the African American testers were offered a position 67% of the time. Additionally, White testers were offered long-term and permanent positions twice as often as were their African American counterparts. In a number of cases, the testers were treated differently even when one of them was never seen by the employer. Since the White tester experienced a more favorable outcome than her African American counterpart in 92% of these cases, it is possible that the employers inferred the racial identity of the testers on the basis of name (e.g., Shawnette vs. Julia, Tamara vs. Emma) or accent. In nine cases, the African American tester was never interviewed, while her White partner was interviewed and offered a position. (p. 11)

Once on the job, African Americans may be less likely to be promoted, may receive lower levels of compensation, and may be more likely to be terminated (Castilla, 2008; Wilson, 2005). In addition, as broader employment opportunity has opened for African Americans in the post–civil rights era, concerns have continued with respect to the glass ceiling. Cotter, Hermsen, Ovadia, and Vanneman (2001) characterize the glass ceiling as gender or ethnic disparity in promotion or salary increase at upper levels of occupational status that occurs during the latter course of an individual's career and is not explained by other factors (e.g., education, years of experience). Their findings using data from the Panel Study of Income Dynamics (waves between 1976 and 1993) support the presence of a glass ceiling for African American women; however, the salary and disparities for African American men were consistent across all job status groups, not just at upper levels. Although historical factors may affect these findings, few subsequent analyses have been undertaken.

METHODOLOGICAL AND RESEARCH ISSUES

In considering methodological issues relevant to education and work among African Americans, it is important to distinguish between various educational indicators and measures. Some research focuses on learning and cognition using tests or assessments such as intelligence tests, other cognitive assessments (e.g., SAT scores), or achievement tests. These indicators are most often norm referenced—that is, measures that compare individuals to the average performance of others in their age group. Other studies assess educational achievement, employing indicators such as school grades. In addition, educational attainment—that is, how far a student continues in school (e.g., high school, college, postgraduate degree completion)—is used as an educational indicator. Educational attainment tends to show higher correlations with life outcomes (e.g., adult employment, income) than do grades or cognitive assessments. Which index is important depends largely on what specific question is being asked; specificity in the use, review, and analysis of educational issues is important. For example, is educational persistence more important than scoring high on an index of cognitive functioning with regard to successful life outcomes?

As noted earlier in our discussion of special and GT education (and as will be noted in Chapter 9), issues relevant to the measurement and conceptualization of cognitive abilities and intelligence require careful attention and consideration. For example, assessment of youth for GT education placement often does not include indicators of intelligence such as creativity, improvisation, and attributes in which African American children may be socialized to excel. Overall, research on African Americans has been plagued by problems in the narrow conceptualization and operationalization of intelligence and cognitive performance. This has included heavy reliance on single indicators and significant limitations in disentangling the influence of culture and ethnicity, race as a biological factor, and socioeconomic disadvantage.

In examining indices relevant to education, there have been difficulties in computing rates of graduation and high school completion. Greene and Forster (2003) note three primary methods—(a) survey (e.g., CPS), (b) use of school administrative data, and (c) use of enrollment and graduation counts. Survey methods may count both traditional graduates and individuals who complete their GEDs, although there is no evidence that these two groups have similar outcomes. School data are often hampered by students' residential moves and lack of adequate tracking mechanisms. In addition, schools may have inadequate resources; also, there are individual variations in state definitions of *dropout*. Additional methods involve comparisons of enrollment and graduation data. For example, some methods (e.g., Greene & Winters, 2002) are based on estimating the size of the 12th-grade cohort of possible graduates (e.g., based on estimates of the size of the ninth-grade cohort and the percentage of population change over time) and then examining the percentage of those students that receive diplomas by the end of their senior year.

EVIDENCE-BASED PRACTICES FOR IMPROVING EDUCATIONAL OUTCOMES

What works? Several interventions and programs targeting educational experiences across different developmental periods have shown effectiveness and promise in supporting strong educational outcomes among African Americans. For example, work by the Rameys in the Abecedarian and related studies has supported the importance of quality preschool education (Ramey et al., 1992; Ramey & Ramey, 2004). The original study included a random assignment of 111 children to intervention and control groups. All children were from socially at-risk families, reflected in factors such as low family income (50% below federal poverty level) and low maternal education (averaging about 10 years of schooling). The majority of participants (98%) were African American. Both control and intervention groups also received access to nutrition support, medical care, and family social services. In addition, if participants in either control or intervention groups performed below developmental cutoffs on two successive assessments, they were referred to developmental clinics.

The intervention group participated in full-day center-based care and educational programs starting at 6 months of age for 50 weeks of each year. Intervention group children showed developmental and cognitive scores in the normative range through age 4.5. Children in the control group showed developmental performance declines by 18 months. The Rameys note that the resulting differences between the intervention and control groups are generally equal to the size of cited differences between African Americans and Whites in population studies of cognitive performance. They underline that these findings support the important role of early experience in understanding between-racial-group differences. The Abecedarian intervention has been replicated in several studies, including with groups of children who were low-birthweight babies (Ramey et al., 1992). Longer-term follow-up studies indicate that positive effects persist through school age as reflected in higher reading and math test scores, lower retention in grade, and lower rates of special education placement. In addition, positive effects continue among young adults (e.g., 70% of intervention participants at age 21 were engaged in employment or higher education compared with 40% of the control group). These findings and other analyses of the costs and clear benefits of early childhood interventions have led several economists (e.g., Rolnick & Grunewald, 2003) and states to urge and undertake policy for substantial investments in children's early childhood development.

It is especially important to note that several factors (e.g., teacher training, program intensity and "dosage," a focus on prevention versus remediation, and interventions targeting children's development) may be important to early intervention success (Ramey & Ramey, 2004). Quality factors may be important to consider in the educational experiences of African American children, as data suggest that although African American preschool-age children may spend more time in center-based care, their care appears to be of somewhat lower quality than that experienced by their same-age White peers (Magnuson & Waldfogel, 2005).

Educational experiences supporting excellence and focusing on the specific educational needs of African American youth have shown promise in supporting positive educational outcomes for African Americans. Schools such as Westside Preparatory School, founded by Marva Collins in 1975 in Chicago, and the Marva Collins Preparatory School are examples of the rich educational opportunities available to African American students. Another school discussed in the opening story is Urban Prep in Chicago. Schools that promote strong connections between parents and the schools have also shown great promise in supporting the educational outcomes of African American students.

Some school districts that have enacted the Comer School Development Program (SDP) model also show great promise in providing effective educational experiences for African American students, especially in low-resource communities (Comer, 2004). The SDP model focuses on supporting six developmental pathways: physical, psychological, language, social, ethical, and cognitive. The program provides school structures to support

- school planning teams involving administrators, teachers, and parents;
- student and staff support teams that work to facilitate relationships and communication; and

- parent teams that are based on no-fault problem solving, consensus decision making, and collaboration.

Operational processes that support schools in the SDP model are

- comprehensive planning based on an understanding of child development;
- staff development based on the comprehensive plan; and
- assessment and modification.

According to Millsap et al. (2000), students in schools that more effectively implement the Comer model and who remain in those schools for longer periods of time show higher educational gains.

African American students are disproportionally suspended and expelled. Restorative justice practices are evidence-based practices that have been used to reduce the percentage of racial and ethnic minority students who are expelled and suspended (González, 2012). Restorative justice is a movement away from zero-tolerance policies that mandate suspensions and expulsions, which disproportionately affect African American and other ethnic minority children (Teasley, 2014). Restorative justice is based on developing values such as relationships, respect, and responsibility. A goal of restorative justice programs is to address and restore damage from problematic behaviors and wrongdoing and to improve discipline by strengthening relationships and reducing violence and disruptive behaviors (Teasley et al., 2017). These programs seek to integrate the student back into the school community rather than to isolate the student from the school community (González, 2012). The practice relies on students, parents, local community members, administrators, teachers, and staff working together. Restorative dialogue is a key component of some restorative justice programs. It involves holding a victim–offender mediation panel where offending students face the consequences of their actions with the victim (González, 2012). Juries of peers are another restorative justice practice whereby student peers determine the penalty of infractions. Family and group conferences, another practice, involve bringing together members of the school community and involved family members (González, 2012). Restorative justice programs have been implemented in schools across the United States, including Oakland, San Francisco, Baltimore, St. Louis, Santa Fe, Philadelphia, and Denver, among other cities. Evaluation of these programs has shown significant decreases in suspensions and expulsions for African American and other students of color (Teasley et al., 2017).

Considering the overrepresentation of African American students in special education settings, Irvine (2012) discussed a culturally responsive pedagogy and presented four key recommendations for training of special education teachers. These included (a) developing caring relationships with students while maintaining high expectations, (b) engaging and motivating students, (c) selecting and effectively using learning resources, and (d) promoting and learning from family and community engagement.

There are a number of emerging and promising educational resources that are leveraging the use of technology and social media. Khan Academy (n.d.), a nonprofit, free online educational resource, provides a range of educational experiences for a broad range of learners. The website offers "practice exercises, instructional videos, and a personalized learning dashboard that empower learners to study at their own pace in and outside of the classroom." It also offers free SAT prep, and has partnered with the College Board to support advanced placement teachers and students with AP test prep. Zhang (2015) examined Internet search patterns at the state level, and found that in states where there were more searches for Kahn Academy, eighth-grade students performed better on reading and math performance on the National Assessment of Educational Progress (NAEP). The author also found that lower rates of searches for Kahn Academy by Internet users occurred in states with lower proportions of college graduates and higher proportions of Black students and students served by the Individuals with Educational Disabilities Act (IDEA). In contrast, in states with higher percentages of Hispanic and African American public school students, there were more Internet searches for Cartoon Network. The research raises concerns and possibilities around the use of the Internet as a resource for education, as opposed to entertainment. With the emergence of new technologies, we may see expansion of digital learning beyond massive open online courses (MOOCs), to the incorporation of 3-D and immersive technologies, which raises important questions as to the potential future of educational access and opportunity for African Americans.

CRITICAL ANALYSIS

Education plays a central role in American culture. Within the mainstream American context, education serves as a marker of social status and status attainment. Although there are high values placed on education within the African American community, for many children, particularly those in low-resource urban communities, there are significant disconnects between these values and available opportunities. Although segregation within educational settings has decreased in some settings, educational segregation remains significant. Educational funding policies at the state and federal levels continue to significantly disadvantage students in many urban school districts. Despite striking down the concept of "separate but equal," more recent court decisions have basically admitted failure and largely backed away from supporting or upholding ideals of equal access and essentially uphold de facto segregation. These failures of leadership, vision, and relevance are reflected in the lower rates of school completion by many African American students. The question of who has failed—students, parents, schools, or policy makers—is important for us to consider.

The structural linkage of educational systems to jurisdiction of residence and the associated tax base raises questions as to the importance of housing policy in supporting educational outcomes. The concentration of urban poverty, often supported through failed housing policy, leaves poor urban minority youth triply disadvantaged—by limited family economic resources and models of educational attainment, by lower-resourced schools, and by more limited community infrastructure. These youth are often further disadvantaged by more limited access to employment opportunities.

Just as focus on educational policy is critical, so is attention to current shifts in educational leadership structures. In some urban school settings, public schools are moving from governance by independently elected school boards to leadership by city officials and appointed bodies, frequently with significant corporate leadership. These changes may result in more limited community voice in public education. It is equally reasonable to question whether community voice has been effective in advocating for the educational needs of African American children. Interests in the development of charter schools and the privatization of education raise concerns among some community and educational leaders. However, educational priorities for African American children cannot be secondary to employment concerns of teachers' unions or the prerogatives of corporate America.

Schools used to be critical resources in the structure of African American communities, and teachers and principals were significant in the fabric of African American children's lives. Teachers and principals often lived in the same community as the children who attended their school. The disconnection of schools and teachers from roles within the community and the broader development of African American children is a substantial loss.

Assumptions that college is the singular educational goal for many African American youth and the apparent discontinuity between high school and vocational opportunities warrant attention and consideration. Although some research suggests that employment during middle and high school, especially employment of over 20 hours a week, can diminish educational outcomes, not all research has found employment to consistently be a detriment to developmental outcomes. Leventhal, Leventhal, and Cameron (2001) found that employment for African American male youth ages 16 to 17 was positively associated with high school graduation and with greater likelihood of attending college. Linnehan (2001) found that participation in a work-based mentoring program involving 202 African American urban high school students resulted in positive effects on GPA and attendance. Employment and opportunities to access economic resources may be a relevant concern to African American youth who, in some settings, may play significant roles as economic contributors to households.

The significant educational challenges faced by African American males raise continuing concern and warrant ongoing attention. Multiple intervention strategies have targeted this population, including vocal support for single-sex educational opportunities. Recently released federal regulations have made such educational opportunities more available, but existing research has not found consistent evidence supporting positive outcomes associated with single-sex educational settings. There are ongoing studies designed to further our understanding of the potential effectiveness of single-sex education for African American males and females. Examinations of data from 184 studies found modest advantages for single-sex school in math performance in uncontrolled studies but only minor differences using more rigorous examinations (Pahilke, Hyde, & Allison, 2014). However, because of the limited number of high-quality studies focusing on African Americans, the specific effectiveness of single-sex schools could not be examined in this study.

A 2007 Brookings study by Isaacs suggests that there is an increasing divide in the African American community—a tale of two increasingly separated communities—one with access and a second experiencing increasing isolation and challenge. From a developmental perspective on social roles, one of the key developmental outcomes would be adult economic viability and self-sufficiency; however, for many African American children and youth, the minimum assets, resources, and pathways to support this core developmental outcome are limited and constrained.

Conceptual models of "getting by" as opposed to "getting ahead" (Marjoribanks, 1995) may be appropriate to our analysis, where African American individuals and families may be traveling different pathways. Some may strive to achieve the American middle-class model of upward mobility, and in this pursuit, they may face additional burdens in their struggle for advancement. Others may be working simply to survive or get by in the face of limited opportunities for economic progress, discouragement, few models of upward mobility, or low motivation. This is a troubling prospect, especially for African American children, whether from lower- or middle-income families.

Although household income of African Americans has increased over the past 40 years, the persistence of the racial income gap is concerning, and it is alarming that middle-class African Americans do not appear to be very successful in passing on the benefits of their income and social status to their children. It may be difficult to pull oneself up from the bootstraps when either the boot or the strap is missing. In addition, one can consider whether certain sectors of the American capitalistic system have increasingly defined economic roles for some African American males as the generators of prison jobs and construction contracts. Again, failures of policy, vision, understanding, and leadership appear relevant. Historically, we can see that many African

Americans have made significant educational and career achievements, even when their facilities were separate and far from equal. Efforts to connect and bridge individuals and communities to educational and job opportunities warrant attention, as do early interventions to introduce youth to careers and to increase career efficacy and choices. Notwithstanding the talents and abilities of many African American teens, youth in disadvantaged communities need exposure and access to wider pathways of success beyond popular media images of low-base-rate and high-payoff trajectories involving sports and music. Youth in lower-resource communities need alternatives to early parenthood and involvement in drug sales as career trajectories.

Summary

Educational opportunities are important resources for individual development, as well as individual economic and career achievement, with clear implications for the broader economic development and financial resources within the African American community. With both positive attitudinal values toward and significant historical investments in education, a long-term, historical perspective shows that African Americans have made notable educational strides over the past 150 years despite considerable barriers. Many of these barriers persist, and African American students, especially students in low-income urban communities, continue to face significant disparities in access to equitable educational resources. African American children are more likely to be placed in special education and less likely to be identified for GT education. The courts have played—and continue to play—a significant role in arbitrating access to equitable educational opportunities. Recent court decisions have circumscribed voluntary strategies for communities to provide desegregated educational opportunities.

Beyond access to equal structural resources, theoretical perspectives underline the important role that culture plays in the educational experience, through inter- and intrapersonal processes that influence performance and students' view of academic achievement as relevant and related to their cultural sense of self. A range of traditional and culturally based academic opportunities are available to African American learners. Educational policy and related structural factors shape and constrain the educational opportunities available to many African American children. Family support and neighborhood context support positive educational outcomes for African Americans, especially African American males. Research makes it clear that many African American students face processes and social interactions in the school context that may affect their school experience. The African American community and psychologists working on educational issues will continue to face important questions about the education of African Americans. What structures are most effective in supporting positive educational and employment outcomes for African Americans? To what extent do current curricular content and educational processes "train," as opposed to "educate," African American students? What does it mean to effectively educate an African American at the start of the 21st century? How do these perspectives inform our understanding of the link between work and involvement in the labor force?

The role of education and work have and will continue to play a crucial role in the African American community. The African proverb indicating that "He who learns, teaches" is consistent with Woodson's and Freire's perspectives on education, implicating both the important role of cultural education for African Americans and the collaborative communal dynamics of education. It also may underline that an important part of the community's work is education. African Americans may have important roles in shaping the educational and work experiences of their community and may not be able to rely on mainstream American culture and educational structures to understand, acknowledge, or address these educational and employment needs.

7

NEIGHBORHOODS AND COMMUNITIES

Sticks in a bundle are unbreakable.

—**Bondei proverb**

LEARNING OBJECTIVES

- To understand definitions of neighborhood and community

- To consider the importance of neighborhood and community to African Americans from both traditional and Africentric perspectives

- To understand the processes through which neighborhoods influence African Americans

- To consider how the communities in which African Americans live have changed over time

- To become familiar with the ways in which history and public policy have shaped where African Americans live

- To consider how interventions at the community or neighborhood level support well-being for African Americans

SEGREGATED LIVING LINKED TO HIGHER BLOOD PRESSURE AMONG BLACKS

BY CARMEN HEREDIA RODRIGUEZ

For African-Americans, the isolation of living in a racially segregated neighborhood may lead to an important health issue: higher blood pressure.

A study published Monday in JAMA Internal Medicine suggested blacks living in such areas experienced higher blood pressure than those

(Continued)

(Continued)

living in more diverse communities. Moving to integrated areas was associated with a decrease in blood pressure, and those who permanently stayed in localities with low segregation saw their pressure fall on average nearly 6 points.

Kiarri Kershaw, assistant professor of preventive medicine at Northwestern University in Chicago and lead author of the study, said the findings reinforce the close relationship between social policy and community health outcomes.

"It lends credence to the notion that we should bring public health practitioners and health policy officials to the table to make these decisions," she said. Researchers used data from a long-term study that has followed 2,280 African-Americans over the course of 25 years, checking in every three to seven years to track blood pressure.

Heart disease is the leading cause of death in the United States, and African-Americans are disproportionately affected by the condition. According to the American Heart Association, 46 percent of non-Hispanic black men and nearly 48 percent of non-Hispanic black women live with a form of heart disease, while about 36 percent of non-Hispanic white men and 32 percent of non-Hispanic white women do.

Georges Benjamin, executive director of the American Public Health Association, said the burden to address such disparities falls on society at large.

"It doesn't just hurt African-Americans or people of color. This hurts everybody," he said. "Because everyone pays not just in terms of humanity, but in terms of dollars."

Doctors generally record two numbers for blood pressure: the diastolic pressure—the blood's force inside the veins when the heart is at rest—and the systolic pressure, which gauges the blood's force when the heart beats. Blood pressure is measured in millimeters of mercury, or mmHg (using mercury's chemical element symbol), with systolic pressure reported first, such as 115 mmHg over 75 mmHg.

Researchers found residential segregation was associated with changes in systolic blood pressure, which is tied to adverse cardiovascular events, such as a heart attack. The findings did not show any changes in diastolic blood pressure.

The scientists also collected data on a variety of other social indicators including level of education, poverty and marriage status. They ranked the level of segregation in participants' neighborhoods as "low," "medium" and "high" based on the number of African-Americans in the larger area.

When compared to African-Americans living in highly segregated locations, participants living in medium-segregation neighborhoods recorded blood pressure that was on average 1.33 mmHg lower. Those residing in low-segregation areas were an average 1.19 mmHg lower.

Blood pressure for black residents who permanently moved into medium segregation locations decreased on average 3.94 mmHg. African-Americans who stayed in low-segregation locales saw an average decrease of 5.71 mmHg.

Although single-digit changes do not appear impressive, a separate study published in 2015 found a 1 mmHg decline in blood pressure led to 20 fewer heart failures and 10 fewer cases of coronary heart disease and stroke per 100,000 black individuals.

"At the population level, a 1 mmHg reduction can result in substantial reduction in poor cardiovascular events," Kershaw said.

The research is part of the Coronary Artery Risk Development in Young Adults (CARDIA) study, partially funded by the federal government, which has tracked participants since 1985. The four CARDIA sites are Chicago, Birmingham, Ala., Minneapolis and Oakland, Calif.

For several decades, researchers have been looking into the effects of residential segregation on health disparities. A 2001 article by David R. Williams and Chiquita Collins identified segregation as a "fundamental cause of racial differences in health" because of its role in dictating access to other determinants of health like education and employment.

Mark Huffman, a practicing cardiologist and assistant professor of preventive medicine and medicine-cardiology at Northwestern

University, said this study's findings reinforce the importance of his patients' environments. Medicine alone cannot address the disparities created by segregation, he said, and practitioners must be cognizant of how well their patients can adhere to the recommendations given to them in the doctor's office.

"I need to get to know my patients—about where they live and what it's like—to be able to understand how they can implement my recommendations . . . that are easy to say and hard to implement," said Huffman. "And certainly harder to implement if doctors don't understand where their patients live, work and play."

Source: Rodriguez (2017).

INTRODUCTION AND OVERVIEW

When marchers crossed the Edmund Pettus Bridge in 1965, was this an act of individuals or of a community? How do we think about the collective actions of the Black Panthers, the Student Nonviolent Coordinating Committee, the Southern Christian Leadership Council, the NAACP, the National Council of Negro Women, or 100 Black Men? When riots erupted in Washington, D.C., after the assassination of Martin Luther King Jr., in Los Angeles after the televised beating of Rodney King, and in Ferguson, Missouri, following the shooting death of Michael Brown, were these actions grounded in a sense of community, shared identity, and connectedness among people of African descent? Does this same sense of social connection underlie the development of benevolent societies by northern free Blacks during the late 1700s and early 1800s? What does the term *Black community* mean when Darren Wilson says, "I like the Black community," or when Donald Trump says, "We're going to rebuild our inner cities because our African-American communities are absolutely in the worst shape that they've ever been in before. Ever. Ever. Ever." As Northern migration during the early 20th century and desegregation during the 1960s changed urban African American neighborhoods, how do we understand whether these changes benefited the lives of African Americans or changed their sense of connection to one another?

In considering our ideas about the African American community, we face an important conceptual challenge. What is the *Black community*? Are we talking about the predominately and historically African American neighborhoods and geographic areas in southeast Washington, D.C., Harlem, Compton and Watts, and the South Side of Chicago? Or are we speaking instead of a national community of Americans of African descent who are joined by a shared sense of connection to one another—a common peoplehood, history, heritage, and sociopolitical experience and challenge? How does community make a difference to African Americans? Does it really matter where Blacks live?

Whether in a high-rise apartment building in a bustling urban neighborhood, a farmhouse in a small rural community, or a house in a suburban development, African Americans live, grow, and die in the context of a geographical, physical, and social community. Historical forces and social policy have significantly shaped the racial composition of American neighborhoods. In turn, the availability of resources, such as type and quality of housing stock, schools, and libraries, as well as things that may, for some, seem as mundane as access to stores and groceries that sell fresh fruits and vegetables, are linked to place. Cities and communities continue to struggle with the legacy of policies and issues of race that shape where people live. For example, our opening cover story sheds light on the deleterious effect of living in a segregated community on the blood pressure of African Americans. But a community is more than the houses or apartments in which people live. In this chapter, we examine how the places we live are important to the psychology of African Americans.

In this chapter, we address these questions. We begin with definitions of community and neighborhood. Then, we provide a description of African American communities, including historical perspectives on the communities within which African Americans live and to which they move. We examine theories that help us understand how physical neighborhoods are relevant to the psychology of African Americans, and we present lessons learned about the role that both neighborhood and community play in the lives of African Americans. We provide an overview of strategies that have been used to study neighborhoods and community, as well as a discussion of interventions that have targeted the communities in which African Americans reside. We close with a chapter summary.

Definitions

German sociologist Ferdinand Tonnies (1855–1936) provides an early perspective on defining the concept of community. He uses the two terms, *Gemeinschaft* and *Gesellschaft*, to describe the development of modern communities. For Tonnies, Gemeinschaft reflects our traditional, preindustrial sense of community that is defined as association based on family and kinship relationships, neighborhood, and friendship. These social ties are linked through loyalty, affection, love, and closeness and are reflected in the proximal social structures of family households, villages, and small towns. In these settings, we think of individuals who know and care about one another and depend on each other not only for shelter, food, and clothing but also for relationships and support. Current manifestations of Gemeinschaft would include close-knit neighborhoods and areas that have retained their small-town qualities. As industrialization began to change our sense of social connection, communities were organized and linked based on the structures of a civil society. The term Gesellschaft reflects the sense of community based on social interaction for the structured exchange of resources. This type of community is more typical of a modern industrial society and the development of cities and urbanization. Modern cities and professional associations would be reflections of Gesellschaft. Within these social structures, the roles that individuals play are specialized, and there may be a greater risk of social isolation.

Chaskin and Richman (1992) offered a definition of community as

> the local context in which people live. It is referred to by its geographic identity, but its place on the map is only one of its attributes. It is a place of reference and belonging, and the community includes dimensions of space, place, and sentiment as well as of action. It is defined by a dynamic network of associations that binds (albeit loosely) individuals, families, institutions, and organizations into a web of interconnections and interaction. (p. 113)

The local community is "a functional unit in which goods and services are provided and consumed, interpersonal relationships are created and maintained, participation in activities is shared" (Chaskin & Richman, 1992, p. 8). This definition of community is not necessarily dependent on clear geographic boundaries (e.g., different residents may have slightly different conceptions of where the neighborhood begins and ends). It assumes that the community's residents hold in common a range of mutual experiences and circumstances and share access to an array of organizations, institutions, services, resources, and activities.

These definitions emphasize that when we speak of community, we are not simply talking about a geographical location but a sense of social connection and belonging. McMillan and Chavis (1986) describe this perception as one's "psychological sense of community . . . a feeling that members have of belonging, a feeling that members matter to one another and to the group, and a shared faith that members' needs will be met through their commitment to be together" (p. 9). This conceptualization of community also involves a sense of membership, influence, integration, needs fulfillment, and emotional connection. In this circumstance then, when we speak of the African American community, we may be speaking of both a broader sense of linked social identity and shared experience, as well as a community defined by proximity in a physical and geographic sense.

Definitions of Neighborhood

Similar to definitions of community, definitions of neighborhood vary across different academic disciplines. Chaskin (1998) notes that neighborhoods have been defined "as a social unit, neighborhoods as a spatial unit and the neighborhood as networks of relationships, associations and patterns of use" (p. 1). Boundary designations of these areas have included politically defined neighborhoods, based in the community or residents' civic organizations designed for the legitimate representation of residents and their goals within the local political sphere; social neighborhoods, which reflect external boundary assessments for marketing, analytic, or programmatic efforts; and physical neighborhoods, which are based on designated, bounded geographical areas for government administrative use (Chaskin, 1998). African Americans are more likely to define neighborhood based on social relationships than on location (Lee & Campbell, 1990).

Although Tonnies (1925) considers ethnic communities to be reflections of Gesellschaft (society), not Gemeinschaft (community), we can consider whether and how the African American experience is reflected within both concepts. Historical experiences and ongoing structural supports of residential segregation in the United States have led to the residential concentration of many African Americans in circumscribed neighborhoods and geographic areas that vary widely in their resources and infrastructure. However, for many African Americans, their personal sense of identity includes a strong sense of membership in "the African American community," regardless of the racial composition of the neighborhood within which they currently reside.

Communalism

Beyond definitions of community and neighborhood, conceptually, the idea of *communalism* is also important to our discussion of African Americans and community. As we saw earlier within Chapter 3 in discussions of self-concept, African Americans have a more socially embedded and connected sense of self. Venter (2004) posits that, "In African culture the community always comes first. . . . The individual is born out of and into the African community and will always be part of the community." The importance of social interdependence and belonging, as well as one's sense of being, is grounded within the context of membership in the collective and is conceived as a fundamental component of African philosophy, worldview, and the African personality

(Boykin et al., 1997). The idea that "I am because we are" reflects this idea that a person of African descent's sense of membership in the community fundamentally shapes sense of self. Ubuntu, discussed in Chapter 8, also describes this concept; relationships are essential to one's own well-being (Hoffmann & Metz, 2017).

Research has highlighted the importance of this sense of connection and membership to well-being for African Americans. In a sample of 67 African American and 230 White women, communalism was a better predictor of maternal stress and negative affect than ethnicity or socioeconomic status during childhood or adulthood (Abdou et al., 2010). Although the White women scored higher on the measures of communalism overall, among African American women, higher communalism was predictive of lower blood pressure. This research highlights how fundamental social connections are among African Americans.

Community Psychology and Africentric Psychology

Community psychology is an area of specialization in psychology that focuses explicitly on the role of psychology in the community. This area of psychology considers community as the principal unit of analysis. It emphasizes the systemic interaction of individuals and groups within their physical and social environments. Brookins (1999) provides a useful comparison of community psychology to African psychology, noting both similarities and unique features of each paradigm. Brookins's analysis notes that both community and African psychologies emphasize an ecological perspective that sees the individual within his or her broader social context. However, the conceptual foundations of an African psychology also emphasize African philosophy, spirituality, and a liberation ideology. Both perspectives also operate from a humanitarian values orientation; however, the African perspective underlines the importance of integrating theory and research and the "lived experience" of African Americans. Social change strategies within community psychology include prevention, empowerment, advocacy, and self-help. African perspectives also view empowerment as an important change strategy but emphasize empowerment as a vehicle for the development of "race consciousness and self-actualization" (Brookins, 1999, p. 40).

Brookins criticizes community psychology for its traditional focus on supporting an individual's skills in coping with a challenging community as opposed to attempting to reduce the risk and challenge that African Americans experience within their communities. In general, research within African psychology more strongly emphasizes community experience, participation, and dissemination. Brookins's analysis underlines the need for ongoing community change and the development of long-term perspectives on change for African Americans and their communities.

One area of research focus within community psychology is the examination of the relation of individuals to their social and community networks, as well as the ways in which these social settings impact the individual. Research on social support, for example, using data from the National Survey of American Life demonstrated the importance of community. Taylor et al. (2016) found that African American women and African Americans with higher incomes were more likely to indicate that they received support from and provided support to members of their social networks. African Americans were connected and involved in exchanges with extended family, friends, and Church members. Research by Taylor, Chatters, Woodward, and Brown (2013) suggests that African Americans are more involved with kin networks when compared with White respondents, but African Americans are somewhat less involved with friendship networks. Kin and Church social networks have been found to serve as protective factors to reduce depression and to improve mental health (Chatters et al., 2015).

Community "Capacity" and Why Neighborhoods Are Important to Study

One of the reasons that it is important to better understand neighborhoods and community is because of the important and significant impact that neighborhood and community factors have on the well-being of African Americans. LaVeist (2003) matched data from the National Survey of Black Americans, a national multistage probability sample of 2,107 African Americans, with the National Death Index. The author found that racial segregation predicted mortality even after controlling for age, health status, sex, marital status, and level of educational attainment. Earlier research (LaVeist, 1993) found racial segregation to predict differences in Black and White infant mortality rates. That neighborhood racial composition predicts these health outcomes is reflected in the opening article and underlines the importance of examining neighborhood context in understanding the psychology of African Americans. This article implicates segregated neighborhoods as a factor in hypertension for African Americans.

Neighborhoods and communities are important to study because they impact the behavior, emotional experience, cognitions, and well-being of African Americans. In a study following a sample of 48,359 women between 1995 and 2005, researchers analyzed data from the Black Women's Health Study (BWHS; Coogan et al., 2010). They found that neighborhood disadvantage plays a significant role in weight gain. This was especially true among African American women at higher levels of education, even after adjusting for factors including age, exercise routine, and family income.

Research has also indicated that neighborhood disadvantage may account for differences in rearrest rates among African American female juvenile offenders. Chauhan, Reppucci, Burnette, and Reiner (2010) found that African American adolescent female offenders and White offenders reported similar levels of antisocial behavior following incarceration but that African American females were more likely to be rearrested, especially for nonviolent crimes. However, once neighborhood disadvantage was controlled, there were no racial differences in rearrest rates. In other words, what appeared to be race-based effects were accounted for by neighborhood differences between African American and White adolescent female offenders.

Other research has considered the link between neighborhood factors and academic achievement. In a sample of third- to fifth-grade students from a predominantly African American (87.8%) urban public school system, student perceptions of school and neighborhood safety and objective ratings of neighborhood safety were associated with lower academic performance. School-level poverty appeared to account for a part of these relationships (Milam, Furr-Holden, & Leaf, 2010). Whitaker, Graham, Severtson, Furr-Holden, and Latimer (2012) found learning motivation to be negatively affected by both family dysfunction and neighborhood disorder (e.g., perceived crime, public substance use, safety, excess filth and noise in the neighborhood) in a sample of 216 African American middle school students living in urban neighborhoods.

Research has also suggested that neighborhood and racial identity may combine to predict the academic performance of African American youth. In a study of 564 African American eighth graders, Byrd and Chavous (2009) found both neighborhood opportunity and ethnic pride to be positively associated with grade point average (GPA). Neighborhood opportunity was measured by assessing the availability of upwardly mobile adults within the local census tract (i.e., percentage of college graduates and those in professional or managerial positions), parents' reports of economic opportunities for youth (e.g., ratings of likelihood of finding a well-paying job), and institutional resources such as after-school programs. In neighborhoods characterized by limited economic opportunity, high ethnic pride was associated with higher GPA. In contrast, in areas with greater economic opportunity, higher ethnic pride was associated with lower GPA. What might this counterintuitive result suggest? Could there be greater resistance against more positive and explicit racial expressions in higher-income areas that influence academic performance? Could youth in these areas be more likely to adopt an "oppositional cultural framework" that may be more rejecting of traditional views of education as a means of economic advancement? We next turn to a discussion of demographic and historical perspectives on the African American community.

DEMOGRAPHIC AND HISTORICAL PERSPECTIVES ON THE AFRICAN AMERICAN COMMUNITY

In understanding the role of community and neighborhood in the experience of the African American community, it is useful to consider the geographical areas within which African Americans reside. Historical perspectives on African American neighborhoods and communities also provide a foundation for understanding contemporary issues.

Communities During and After Slavery

Several factors in the American enslavement experience challenged a sense of community and social connection among Americans of African descent. The history of the transatlantic slave trade was built, in part, on the selling of prisoners engaged in intertribal conflict and warfare into enslavement. Historical descriptions characterize West African experiences of community as being based on proximal family and tribal networks that excluded other African tribal groups. Enslaved Africans were separated from their families and tribes, and members of different tribal groups were mixed so frequently there was no common language. Breakup and dispersion of families and of biologically based kinship networks through commerce were practices that further disrupted social connections. Despite these efforts and forces, historical narratives describe rich and complex social connections among members of many slave communities. Separations from blood kin supported the construction of social networks not bound by biological relationship. Aunts, relatives, and unrelated enslaved Africans cared for children when parents were sold away. We see such connections today among fictive kin (see Chapter 5 for further discussion). In addition, communities of free Blacks engaged in building neighborhood capacity through the development of community infrastructures, frequently organized around religious institutions (Horton & Horton, 1997).

Migration Patterns

After the Civil War, a trend toward northern migration began, based, in part, on southern hostility, Jim Crow laws, economic crises in the South, and perceived employment opportunities in the North. Northern migration slowed with the Great Depression but expanded between the 1940s and the 1950s and continued through the 1970s. Overall, these residential transitions resulted in greater geographic dispersion of Blacks in the Northeast and Southwest and in greater urbanization.

For example, in 1860, when 85% of American Blacks were enslaved, 90% lived in the rural South. In contrast, U.S. Census estimates from 2010 showed that 55% of African Americans reside in the South (Rastogi, Johnson, Hoeffel, & Drewery, 2011). Beginning in the 1970s, the migration of Blacks out of the South began to reverse, with population growth occurring in both southern metropolitan and nonmetropolitan areas and Black population declines from Northeast and West (Frey, 2014). These changes are taking place in the broader context of the browning of America (Johnson & Kasadra, 2011). For example, the White population was 75% of U.S. population in 1995, was 67% in 2005, and by 2050 is projected to be less than 50%.

The patterns of racial residential mobility and government policies that have supported a legacy of ethnic variations and segregation in residence continue to play an important role in the experience of community by African Americans.

Contemporary Residential Patterns: Where African Americans Live

Historical forces and policy continue to shape the communities within which African Americans reside today. Although there had been a general trend toward suburbanization in postwar large urban areas, the availability of this residential option for African Americans had been considerably restricted because of biases and discrimination in housing policies and practices. For example, Powell (1999) argued that racism and federal housing and transportation policies historically supported urban sprawl and subsidized White flight while simultaneously reducing investments in increasingly poor urban neighborhoods. Government and banking policies, including redlining (i.e., refusing to lend in an area because of race), were central in supporting the residential isolation of African Americans in poor urban communities; this picture is changing, however.

Recent data indicate many major urban areas, such as Chicago, Dallas, Detroit, and even Atlanta, have lost African American population over the past decade (Frey, 2011). These trends reflect the greater geographic presence and lower racial concentration or isolation of African Americans across residential communities. For example, while approximately 20% of urban neighborhoods had no Black residents 50 years ago, in the most recent Census, 199 out of 200 neighborhoods had Black residents (Glaeser & Vigdor, 2012). Based on data from the 2010 Census, outside the South, non-Hispanic African Americans were more likely to live in the largest urban cities; however, between 2000 and 2010, there were declines in the proportion of African Americans living in these large cities. Within metropolitan areas, by 2010, half of African Americans were residing in suburban areas (Frey, 2014). Racial residential segregation peaked between 1960 and 1970 and has reflected a steady but slow decline since then (Logan & Stults, 2011).

Despite these overall changes, it is notable that in metropolitan areas, particularly those with higher relative presence of African Africans, decreases in racial isolation appear to be occurring. This is because of the higher presence of Asians and individuals of Hispanic origin, as opposed to the presence of Whites (Logan & Stults, 2011). These residential changes suggest that many African American children may grow up in neighborhoods very different from those of their parents and grandparents.

Using national averages within metropolitan areas, the typical Black lives in a neighborhood that is 45% Black, 35% White, 15% Hispanic, and 4% Asian. In contrast, the typical White lives in a metropolitan neighborhood that is 75% White, 8% Black, 11% Hispanic, and 5% Asian (Logan & Stults, 2011). Black isolation has declined in great part due to the increase in Latino and Asian residents in neighborhoods where Blacks reside.

These changes may also further emphasize the importance of considering Wilson's (1987) suggestion that the sense of social connection and community within many predominantly African American urban neighborhoods has declined significantly since the mid-20th century. The loss of these social connections results in many individual- and community-level challenges. In addition, despite many of the historical problems of the residential segregation of African Americans, many political gains have been based on the concentration of African Americans within specific voting districts. Redistricting and gerrymandering of political boundaries represent ongoing struggles to achieve and maintain voting districts that allow fair representation of African American communities.

Table 7.1 shows urban areas with the lowest and the highest levels of segregation. The segregation index can range from "0" (complete integration) to "100" (complete segregation). Urban areas with the lowest levels of segregation grew fastest in comparison to areas highest in segregation, which are experiencing declines in population.

Poverty and African American Communities

Census data also suggest that the concentration of poverty in many urban, predominately African American communities is declining. Data from the 2014 American Community Survey (ACS) indicate that 26% of African Americans live in poverty, compared with 14% for the total population. Higher percentages (38%) of Black children live in poverty than other children in the U.S. (22% overall). Blacks and Hispanics continue to reside in neighborhoods characterized by higher levels of poverty than Asians and Whites. Using 2005–2009 ACS data, affluent Blacks, on average, lived in a neighborhood that was 13.9% poor, slightly higher than the 12.9% poverty rate where the average poor White household resided. Approximately a quarter of poor Blacks live in high-poverty neighborhoods, compared with 7.5% of poor Whites. In addition, 28% to 45% of poor Black children (versus 6.2% of White children) and 24.2% of poor Black adults (versus 8.2% of White adults) are estimated to live in poor neighborhoods. The average level of neighborhood poverty for Blacks was 19%, compared with a neighborhood poverty rate of 10.7% for Whites in metropolitan areas.

Research indicates that neighborhood poverty declines for Blacks are occurring faster than declines in segregation (Firebaugh & Acciai, 2016). Comparing data from 1980 through 2010, Whites are increasingly living in poorer neighborhoods, and Blacks are increasingly living in neighborhoods with lower levels of poverty, but disparities remain despite these declines (Firebaugh & Farrell, 2016).

Environmental Health Risks

There are environmental health risks to which African Americans are disproportionately exposed because of their places of residence. African Americans in low-income communities are more likely to reside near transportation routes, industrial sites, and toxic waste sites that increase their exposure to airborne and other toxins (United Church of Christ Commission for Racial Justice, 1987). These toxins and other environmental pollutants may play a role in the high rates of asthma experienced by African Americans. Due to the aging housing stock and limitations in the comprehensive implementation of lead abatement programs, African American children have disproportionately higher rates of lead exposure, which can lead to a range of negative cognitive and behavioral effects and even death (Schnur & John, 2014). These types of risks continue as tragically reflected in the recent Flint, Michigan, experience (Sampson & Winter, 2016). Here, state and federal officials have been implicated in knowing that the city's aging water system was producing elevated lead levels in the water but did not

TABLE 7.1 ■ Ten Least and Most Segregated Metropolitan Areas With Population Change, 2000 to 2010

Least Black–White Segregated Metros	Segregation Index, 2010	Percent Population Change, 2000–2010
Tucson, Ariz.	36.9	16.2
Las Vegas–Paradise, Nev.	37.6	41.8
Colorado Springs, Colo.	39.3	20.1
Charleston–North Charleston–Summerville, S.C.	41.5	21.1
Raleigh–Cary, N.C.	42.1	41.8
Greenville–Mauldin–Easley, S.C.	43.6	13.8
Phoenix–Mesa–Glendale, Ariz.	43.6	28.9
Lakeland–Winter Haven, Fla.	43.9	24.4
Augusta–Richmond County, Ga.–S.C.	45.2	11.5
Riverside–San Bernardino–Ontario, Calif.	45.7	29.8
Most Black–White Segregated Metros	**Segregation Index, 2010**	**Percent Population Change, 2000–2010**
Milwaukee–Waukesha–West Allis, Wisc.	81.5	3.7
New York–Northern New Jersey–Long Island, N.Y.–N.J.–Pa.	78.0	3.1
Chicago–Joliet–Naperville, Ill.–Ind.–Wisc.	76.4	4.0
Detroit–Warren–Livonia, Mich.	75.3	–3.5
Cleveland–Elyria–Mentor, Ohio	74.1	–3.3
Buffalo–Niagara Falls, N.Y.	73.2	–3.0
St. Louis, Mo.–Ill.	72.3	4.3
Cincinnati–Middletown, Ohio–Ky.–Ind.	69.4	6.0
Philadelphia–Camden–Wilmington, Pa.–N.J.–Del.–Md.	68.4	4.9
Los Angeles–Long Beach–Santa Ana, Calif.	67.8	3.7

Note: Metro areas with fewer than 500,000 total residents or where non-Hispanic Blacks made up fewer than 3% of the population were not included when ranking Black–White segregation indices.

Sources: Segregation Indices: William H. Frey, Brookings Institution, and University of Michigan Social Science Data Analysis Network, Analysis of 1990, 2000, and 2010 Decennial Census tract data, accessed at www.psc.isr.umich.edu/dis/census/segregation2010.html, on Aug. 29, 2011. Population Data: Population Reference Bureau, analysis of 2000 and 2010 Decennial Census data.

intervene to mitigate lead exposure to community residents. Research has also indicated that African American and Latino students in Michigan attended schools in geographic areas with higher levels of airborne toxins (Mohai, Kweon, Lee, & Ard, 2011).

Factors Shaping Residential Patterns

Powell (1999) argues that racism and federal housing and transportation policies have supported urban sprawl and subsidized White flight while simultaneously reducing investments in poor urban neighborhoods. Work by Pietila (2010) includes historic analysis of the operation of federal policy through the Home Owners' Loan Corporation (HOLC). The HOLC produced "color-coded" maps that were used from the 1930s to recommend or deny mortgage approvals in neighborhoods. Often, these maps, based on criteria that were biased, did not support approvals in neighborhoods where African Americans resided. Government and banking policies, including redlining (i.e., refusing to lend in an area because of race), have persisted. Some believe redlining grew worse during the 1980s because the federal government decreased enforcement of fair-lending laws and the Fair Housing Act of 1968. These redlining practices can be examined by looking at available digital resources such as "Mapping Inequality" (see https://dsl.richmond.edu/panorama/redlining). This resource provides the opportunity to examine these historic documents and consider how they have shaped the housing and neighborhood experiences, as well as the wealth accumulation, of African Americans today.

Several factors continue to support the concentration of poverty in low-income neighborhoods within which African Americans are overrepresented. These include (1) rising urban housing costs and displacement of lower-income residents by the gentrification of many urban neighborhoods, (2) the development of new rings of poverty in many older suburban neighborhoods, and (3) the lack of effective regional cooperation in most large metropolitan areas. Despite many of the problems of residential segregation of African Americans, many of their political gains have been based on the concentration of African Americans within specific voting districts. There are ongoing struggles to achieve and maintain voting districts that allow fair representation of African American communities.

Housing and Urban Development (HUD) research using "paired test" methods show racial and ethnic bias in housing. In a paired test, two people, one White and the other minority, present as equally qualified home seekers and ask about available homes or apartments. The paired test methodology systematically measures how often discrimination occurs across housing markets (Turner et al., 2013). Well-qualified African Americans were told about 11.4% and shown 4.2% fewer rental units when compared with Whites. When buying, African Americans were told about 17% and shown 17.7% fewer available homes than White counterparts.

In a review of HUD's paired test studies over time, there were declines in discriminatory behaviors toward Blacks in being informed about available rental and sale units between 1977 and 2012. However discrimination reflected in being shown fewer sales units has not shown any notable change. Housing discrimination based on race is discussed also in Chapter 4 on "Race and Racism."

Discriminatory practices related to housing have also had significant impact on African Americans not only through its impact on where Blacks live but also on asset and wealth accumulation. Home ownership has been an important strategy in wealth accumulation for American families. Sullivan, Meschede, Dietrich, and Shapiro (2015) report that 45% of African Americans are homeowners compared with 73% of Whites. In addition, the median home equity of a Black homeowner is $50,000, compared with $85,800 for White homeowners. In research using the Panel Study of Income Dynamics, Burd-Sharps and Rasch (2015) found that during the recovery (2009 to 2011) from the Great Recession, the typical African American household lost 40% of assets not including home equity and 53% of wealth when home equity was included. In contrast, changes in household wealth for White families during this same period, both including and excluding home equity, approached zero. African Americans were disproportionately represented within the subprime market, which was associated with foreclosure. In response to more constrained wealth accumulation, African Americans have been more frequently required to get funds from retirement accounts to cover loan costs.

The places where African Americans reside are also shaped by their patterns of moves between neighborhoods or households. African Americans experienced decreases in their rates of residential mobility over the second half of the 20th century. However, African Americans tend to have relatively high 5-year mobility rates (42.9%, compared with 33.7% for non-Hispanic Whites) (Ihrke & Faber, 2012). When African Americans move, they are more likely to occur generally within the same general geographic area (around 66% of moves). This higher rate of residential mobility may be due, in part, to lower overall rates of homeownership among African Americans.

Using data from the Project on Human Development in Chicago Neighborhoods (PHDCN), Riina, Lippert, and Brooks-Gunn (2016) found that Black and Hispanic respondents lived in neighborhoods characterized by greater residential instability (turnover in residents) and experienced stronger links between neighborhood instability and parent–child conflict. This may suggest that neighborhoods play a more significant role in the parenting and development of minority children than of White children in the study.

Residential mobility presents challenges to communities: Neighbors may not develop strong social connections or neighborhood-based support, and children may move from school to school. These disruptions undermine access to resources that are built on the foundation of well-established social relationships.

The 2008 economic crisis had a disproportionate negative effect on African Americans, who accounted for 7.9% of foreclosures among first-time homeowners who purchased homes between 2005 and 2008, compared with a rate of 4.5% among non-Hispanic White borrowers (Bocian, Li, & Ernst, 2010). Related research suggests that foreclosures may further differentially impact the families of African American school-age children and expose them to higher levels of residential change.

Impact of Neighborhood on Psychosocial and Health Outcomes

Residential location may be an important factor in psychosocial and adaptive outcomes for African Americans. Where one lives shapes the types of activities in which one engages, the level of risk one faces, and the types of assets and resources available (e.g., housing stock, libraries, walking trails). For example, older African Americans who live in neighborhoods with higher levels of home occupancy engaged in higher levels of physical activity (Hannon, Sawyer, & Allman, 2012). The residence of African Americans closer to major roadways was associated with left ventricular end systolic disorder, which is a marker and structural risk for heart failure, suggesting that exposure to traffic pollution increases health risks (Weaver et al., 2017). In an examination of racial concentration and segregation, those living in areas with a higher concentration of African Americans had higher levels of proximity to psychiatrists but greater likelihood of treatment by general doctors and nonpsychiatrists (Dinwiddie, Gaskin, Chan, Norrington, & McCleary, 2013).

Among African American cocaine users, those who lived in rural settings perceived less need for, effectiveness, availability, access to, and affordability of treatment (Borders, Booth, Stewart, Cheney, & Curran, 2015). Based on data from the U.S. National Survey of American Life, African American women residing in rural settings were less likely to meet criteria for a major depressive disorder (MDD) during their lifetime or over the past 12 months compared with women residing in urban settings. In contrast, rural White women were more likely to meet criteria for lifetime MDD or MDD over the past 12 months compared with rural African American women (Weaver, Himle, Taylor, Matusuko, & Abelson, 2015).

THEORETICAL PERSPECTIVES ON COMMUNITIES

Several theories and research support our understanding of the role of neighborhood and community. We consider these in our examination of trends in neighborhood composition and the effects of neighborhood on African Americans.

Africentric perspectives suggest that community, social connections, and relationships may be particularly important for African Americans. Some Western theoretical perspectives have also emphasized the importance of a sense of connection to the psychological functioning of individuals. These include Bronfenbrenner's (1979) ecological theory underlining the role of context in development (described in Chapter 11) and Émile Durkheim's (1897/1951) sociological analyses of anomie and suicide, which were seen as consequences of the lack of community, among others. Some other well-known perspectives on communities are discussed next.

Social Disorganization Theory

Much of the recent theoretical work examining the effects of neighborhood contexts on psychological outcomes traces its origins to the work of the Chicago School of Sociology's social disorganization theory (Shaw & McKay, 1969). Social disorganization theory links criminality to limitations in a community's social resources and capacity to meet the needs of its residents. This results in an erosion of social controls. Factors such as limited community-level economic resources, ethnic heterogeneity, and high rates of residential mobility reflect community social disorganization. Sampson, Raudenbush, and Earls (1997), working on the Project on Human Development in Chicago Neighborhoods (PHDCN), found a negative relationship between community violence and residents' sense of collective efficacy—that is, neighborhood residents' beliefs that they can effectively have an impact on behavior within their communities. The PHDCN has provided a rich source of information on neighborhood factors that affect children and families (for additional information, see https://www.icpsr.umich.edu/icpsrweb/PHDCN/about.jsp).

Neighborhood organization or disorganization affects outcomes across a variety of domains (Tendulkar, Koenen, Dunn, Buka, & Subramanian, 2012). Exposure to an incident of neighborhood violence (a homicide within the block group during the week prior) predicts lower performance on reading and vocabulary assessments among African American children ages 5 to 17 (Sharkey, 2010). Neighborhood disadvantage experienced during childhood (age 6 to 12) is predictive of lower verbal ability scores (Sampson, Sharkey, & Raudenbush, 2008). Community violence exposure at moderate or high levels was found to be associated with asthma risk among African American children ages 0 to 9 after individual-level variables (e.g., maternal education and asthma, child age, gender, family violence) were taken into consideration. The effect of community violence on asthma risk appears to be mediated by collective efficacy (Sternthal, Jun, Earls, & Wright, 2010).

Related work has identified the physical environment as a potential focus for interventions. The "broken windows" theory suggests that crime is more likely to occur in areas where the physical environment is disorganized and unkempt (Wilson & Kelling, 1982). The theory suggests that the disorganization of the physical space in a neighborhood sends a message to potential criminals that residents do not care about their neighborhood. Although healthy and safe housing and neighborhoods are important to our physical, emotional, and social well-being, community interventions that address only "broken windows" may not adequately address the full range of supports and resources needed by community residents. Research by Sampson and Raudenbush (1999) suggests that the community's sense of collective efficacy may be a more important indicator of neighborhood crime than the upkeep of the physical environment. Public policy and police practice that have evolved out of the "broken window" theory have resulted in police intervening with people in the community for small and minor infractions. Some would link these practices to zero-tolerance policies, stop-and-frisk policing, and the tragic escalation of encounters such as those resulting in the deaths of Alton Sterling and Eric Garner. Research on the effectiveness of practice linked to broken windows theory has been mixed (Braga, Welsh, & Schnell, 2015), but overall, research suggests that "aggressive order maintenance" does not produce safer communities.

Social Capital

Social capital (Coleman, 1988; Putnam, 1993) is an additional theoretical perspective that can assist in understanding the contribution of social relationships within neighborhood and community contexts. According to Coleman (1988), social capital involves three primary components: (a) obligation and expectations involving reciprocity, (b) information channels based on relationships, and (3) shared norms and values with effective sanctions.

In contrast to Coleman's emphasis on social capital as the relations among people, other conceptualizations of social capital have emphasized more civic and community structural perspectives that link social capital to organized community infrastructure and processes, such as civic engagement and democratic participation (Putnam, 1993). This civic-democratic construction of community social capital is argued to facilitate "coordinated actions" and "enable participants to act together more effectively to pursue shared objectives" (Putnam, 1995, pp. 664–665).

Alternative Conceptualization of Neighborhood

Another conceptual perspective on neighborhood effects comes from Jencks and Mayer's (1990) analysis of conceptual pathways through which neighborhoods may affect individual-level outcomes. The five models articulated by Jencks and Mayer include contagion (epidemic) models, which suggest that community residents influence the behavior of their peers based on the level of residents' susceptibility to risk. Collective socialization models suggest that neighborhood adults serve as role models who monitor and socialize children and youth in the community. Institutional models emphasize the role of community-level infrastructure and institutional resources (e.g., quality schools, libraries, recreational facilities, police), whereas social competition models suggest that community residents may compete for limited environmental resources. In contrast, relative deprivation models suggest that individuals engage in social comparison and evaluate their status relative to peers within the community.

Based on their analysis, Leventhal and Brooks-Gunn (2000) offer the following explanations for the effects neighborhoods have on their residents:

Institutional resources: The availability, accessibility, affordability, and quality of learning, social, and recreational activities; child care; schools; medical facilities; and employment opportunities present in the community

Relationships: Parental characteristics (mental health, irritability, coping skills, efficacy, and physical health), support networks available to parents, parental behavior (responsivity/warmth, harshness/control, and supervision/monitoring), and the quality and structure of the home environment

Norms/collective efficacy: The extent to which community-level formal and informal institutions exist to supervise and monitor the behavior of residents, particularly youth's activities (deviant and antisocial peer-group behavior) and the presence of physical risk (violence and victimization and harmful substances) to residents, especially children and youth. (p. 322)

Leventhal and Brooks-Gunn (2000) also note that there are racial and ethnic differences in neighborhood effects on Black and White children. For example, characteristics such as high socioeconomic status may have less impact on the well-being of African American children than on that of White children (Leventhal & Brooks-Gunn).

RESEARCH ON AFRICAN AMERICAN COMMUNITIES

Research examining the role of neighborhood contexts in the lives of African Americans has expanded over the past 20 years. In the following section, we first discuss W. J. Wilson's work, and then we present research on the link between neighborhood characteristics and indicators of well-being among African Americans, especially children.

Disadvantaged Neighborhoods

In *The Truly Disadvantaged* and *When Work Disappears*, Wilson (1987, 1997) argues that the concentration of poverty in poor urban neighborhoods and the range of negative factors associated with urban poverty (e.g., out-of-wedlock births, murder rates) result from the loss of resources from urban cores. Critical among these resources are higher socioeconomic status groups—that is, working- and middle-class African Americans—who migrated out of inner cities during the second half of the 20th century. Wilson proposes that these historical transitions in urban poor communities are linked to neighborhood structures and processes that support limited access to employment, social resources, and infrastructure.

Wilson rejects the "culture of poverty" hypothesis that focuses on individual-level dysfunction. Wilson describes the increasing inaccessibility of jobs in many inner-city neighborhoods. The loss of jobs near urban cores has been linked historically to the suburbanization of manufacturing, increased educational requirements for jobs because of technological advances, and automation that has reduced the number of industrial jobs. With working- and middle-class African American families moving to suburban neighborhoods, the resulting depletion of community infrastructure and resources resulted in social isolation and concentration of poverty in these urban neighborhoods. Wilson notes that more recent census data suggest that urban poverty is being dispersed over larger geographic areas with lower population density, resulting in more abandoned housing and greater opportunities for neighborhood drug trafficking, drug use, and related crime.

Narratives from community residents illustrate the impact of historical community changes on the depletion of community resources and infrastructure. One resident described changes in her urban neighborhood in Chicago:

> I've been here since March 21, 1953. When I moved in, the neighborhood was intact. It was intact with homes, beautiful homes, mini mansions, with stores, Laundromats, with cleaners, with Chinese [cleaners]. We had drug stores. We had hotels. We had doctors over on Thirty-ninths Street [sic]. . . . We had the middle and upper class. It has gone from affluent to where it is today. And I would like to see it come back, that we can have some of the things we had. (Wilson, 1997, p. 3)

This conceptual analysis emphasizes that limited access to employment and increased neighborhood-level risk helps explain the complex interplay of neighborhood-level changes in murder rates, out-of-wedlock births, and unemployment. In contrast to the oft-quoted proverb "It takes a village to raise a child," the decline of these urban neighborhoods reflects the loss or destruction of "the village" and its social connections and supports.

Research illustrates negative psychological outcomes associated with neighborhood disadvantage. Cutrona et al. (2005) examined the relationship of depression with neighborhood factors using data from a study of African Americans living in rural communities, small towns, and midsized cities (Cutrona, Russell, Hessling, Brown, & Murry, 2000). Participants were female primary caregivers of children (ages 10 to 12). The adult sample ranged in age from 24 to 80 (mean = 37.0). Neighborhood disadvantage was computed based on census economic data (i.e., per capita income, the proportions of female-headed households, persons receiving public assistance, households living below the poverty level, and men who were unemployed) and participant rating of physical disorder and social deviance within their neighborhoods. Neighborhood context was associated with the experience of clinical depression among African American women. In addition, neighborhood disadvantage interacted with negative life events to predict future depression. Women who lived in disadvantaged neighborhoods and who experienced a higher number of negative life experiences were more likely to be depressed.

Neighborhood and Child Developmental Outcomes

A considerable body of literature indicates that many aspects of the physical environment (e.g., exposure to toxic substances, crowding, poor housing quality) affect child development (Evans, 2006). These differences in neighborhood and residential context vary by race. A variety of policy processes disadvantage African Americans and other racial and ethnic minorities through more limited access to infrastructure (e.g., quality water and sewage systems) and limited voice in decision-making processes that shape their neighborhood environments (Frumkin, 2005; Wilson, Heaney, Cooper, & Wilson, 2008).

The Fragile Families and Child Wellbeing Study found in a sample of 2,865 participants from 20 metropolitan U.S. cities that Black and Hispanic unmarried mothers reported higher levels of parenting stress than White mothers (Franco, Pottick, & Huang, 2010). However when factors such as social support, maternal education, and maternal health were controlled, neighborhood disorder played a more negative role in the parenting stress of White single mothers than of Black single mothers. The authors raise the possibility that social support, resilience, and the presence of other similar ethnic community residents may play a role in these more adaptive outcomes for Black mothers.

Leventhal and Brooks-Gunn (2000) conducted an extensive literature review examining neighborhood effects on child development. Their analysis suggests that neighborhood may affect young children and adolescents across a range of specific developmental outcomes, but these effects may vary by race. For example, there were fewer cognitive benefits (measured using IQ scores) for young African American children (aged 0–6) of having higher-income neighbors, as compared with White children (Brooks-Gunn, Duncan, Klebanov, & Sealand, 1993; Chase-Lansdale & Gordon, 1996; Chase-Lansdale, Gordon, Brooks-Gunn, & Klebanov, 1997; Duncan, Brooks-Gunn, & Klebanov, 1994). However, several academic performance indicators suggest that affluent neighbors and ethnically diverse neighborhoods benefit African American males (Duncan, 1994; Ensminger et al., 1996; Halpern-Felsher et al., 1997). Affluent neighbors and ethnically diverse neighborhoods are correlated with higher academic achievement among African American males.

In a study on the relationship of neighborhood poverty to cognitive performance, Caughy and O'Campo (2006) found neighborhood poverty to be associated with the problem-solving skills of young children beyond the contributions of family poverty. In this study, 200 African American families from 39 Baltimore neighborhoods with a child between the ages of 3 and 4 participated. Examining academic performance, Plybon et al. (2003) found that positive perceptions of neighborhood cohesion were related to school self-efficacy and self-reported grades among a sample of 84 urban African American adolescent females.

Winslow and Shaw (2007) conducted a longitudinal study examining the potential role of neighborhood factors in understanding child behavior problems in a sample 218 African and European American families with young boys. Participants were recruited in a mid-Atlantic metropolitan area from families accessing the Women, Infant and Children (WIC) Nutritional Supplement Program. Participating families completed initial measures when the male child was age 1.5 and completed additional assessments at ages 2, 3.5, and 6. Neighborhood disadvantage was measured based on census block group variables, including family income, poverty, unemployment, educational attainment, public assistance, and single-mother households. Ethnicity was strongly associated with neighborhood disadvantage, with African American families residing in more disadvantaged communities. In addition, African American ethnicity was associated with the parent more likely remaining single across the study time frame. Child behavior problems at age 6 (measured using the Child Behavior Checklist) were more likely to occur in neighborhoods characterized by high levels of disadvantage, as opposed to low or moderate disadvantage, suggesting a "threshold" effect.

According to Leventhal and Brooks-Gunn (2000), the benefit of high socioeconomic status neighborhoods may be more important for White than for African American youth. Citing the work of Sampson, Morenoff, and Earls (1999), Leventhal and Brook-Gunn (2000) attribute this "to the fact that African American children who reside in affluent neighborhoods are more likely to be living in closer geographic proximity to less affluent neighborhoods (i.e., larger environments that are more disadvantaged). In contrast their White peers, who, although residing in similarly affluent neighborhoods, are in closer geographic proximity to other affluent neighborhoods" (p. 328).

Riina, Martin, Gardner and Brooks Gunn (2013), in a study of 461 African American adolescents (mean age = 15.24), found that perceived racial discrimination when both inside and outside of their own neighborhood was associated with higher levels of internalizing behaviors (e.g., anxiety, depression). In addition, experiencing racial discrimination within one's own neighborhood predicted externalizing (e.g., aggression) behavior. When youth lived in neighborhoods perceived as high in cohesion—that is, where neighbors are trusted and seen as helpful and supportive—the effects of neighborhood discrimination were buffered. Youth living in these neighborhoods did not show a link between externalizing behaviors and neighborhood experiences of discrimination.

Child Development, Parenting, and Neighborhood Risk

Despite the challenges presented by higher-risk neighborhoods, several researchers have explored the potential role that parenting has on buffering or countering these risks. For example, some parents are effective in using a "community bridging" parenting style. This style encompasses three types of strategies: (a) youth monitoring, (b) resource seeking, and (c) in-home learning (Jarrett, 1999).

Youth monitoring works to protect teens from neighborhood risks through the close parental supervision of the youth's whereabouts and the management of peer relationships. Monitoring may also involve chaperonage. When more extreme measures are deemed necessary to protect a child, the child may be removed from the neighborhood and sent to live with relatives. Resource-seeking strategies involve parents promoting their children's development by identifying and accessing available institutional supports both within and outside of their residential neighborhoods, sometimes through the utilization of extended kinship ties. In-home learning strategies involve the social reinforcement of desired behaviors and promotion of academic skills and competence. "Inner city neighborhoods with limited social, economic, and institutional resources demand that parents be 'super-parents' to ensure conventional development for their adolescents" (Jarrett, 1999, p. 49).

Dorsey and Forehand (2003) examined the relationships among neighborhood social capital, parenting, and child adjustment in a study of 130 African American children and mothers from New Orleans. The index of social capital was based on perceived and available support, information, social control, and parents' reports of neighborhood cohesion and trust. Measures of positive parenting included relationship quality, disciplinary consistency and appropriateness, and parental monitoring. Neighborhood dangerousness was based on parents' perceptions and indication of the presence of nine risks identified by community leaders. Child adjustment was measured based on reports of children's internalizing and externalizing behavior. Social capital was positively associated with positive parenting, which, in turn, was associated with better child adjustment. In addition, social capital was associated with lower reports of neighborhood dangerousness, which was associated with better children's psychosocial adjustment.

Research by Caughy, Nettles, O'Campo, and Lohrfink (2006) suggests that parental racial socialization practices may interact with neighborhood factors to predict cognitive and behavioral outcomes for African American children. This study involved 241 African American first-grade students and their families. As the negative social climate (e.g., social and physical disorder, fear of retaliation and victimization) in a neighborhood increased, parental attitudes and socialization that emphasized racial discrimination increased. Socialization emphasizing racial pride was associated with perceptions of higher neighborhood social capital. Compared with those residing in predominately White neighborhoods, parents in predominantly African American or mixed-ethnic neighborhoods were more likely to report communicating racial socialization messages involving mistrust.

One study examined the potential roles of neighborhood risk (operationalized as hassles that may occur in urban contexts), racial socialization, bicultural competence, parental support, and parental criminal involvement among 131 African American adolescents. Study participants were between the ages of 14 and 19 with a mean age of 15.89. The author found only neighborhood risk and racial socialization were significantly predictive of youth's ethnic identity development. Low neighborhood risk and high racial socialization were associated with higher ethnic identity (Bennett, 2006). Neighborhood disadvantage has also been associated with lower aspirations for college in a sample of urban African American adolescents (Stewart, Stewart, & Simons, 2007). In summary, research indicates that neighborhoods and communities affect the health and well-being of African American adults and children.

Research on Factors Reflecting a Positive Community Orientation Among African Americans

Research provides insight into the ways in which African Americans' sense of connection to other members of the African American community operate. Orientation to the African American community is seen in studies on organ donation and in other helping activities (see also chapter on "Prosocial and Antisocial Behavior"). For example, although African Americans donate organs at rates similar to their representation in the U.S. population, African Americans have higher levels of representation on transplant waiting lists (Bratton, Chavin, & Baglia, 2015). In a study of 736 participants recruited from historically African American sororities and fraternities, measures of cultural attitudes toward organ donation were found to be associated with being registered as an organ donor (Andrews et al., 2016). Lower mean scores on the General Barriers subscale (e.g., "If I signed up to donate my organs, my family members would not approve"), but lower mean scores on the Racial Benefits scale (e.g., "Organ donation is part of my responsibility to the black community") and Disparity Barriers scale (e.g., "In general, doctors give preference to white people over black people when deciding who will receive an organ") may reflect the role of cultural mistrust in decisions to donate organs.

Bennett, Sheridan, and Richardson (2014), in a qualitative study of African Americans who provided home-based care of older family members or close friends, note the construction of this care as ministry linked to the caregiver's spirituality and sense of identity. This raises the possibility that a sense of communalism or connection to one's community may be associated with and tied to spirituality and identity factors among African Americans. Research by Grayman-Simpson and Mattis (2012) is consistent with this perspective, finding that informal community helping and the satisfaction reported from helping were both associated with self-reports of religiosity in a sample of African Americans.

It is also notable that African Americans' sense of well-being and life satisfaction may be associated with positive perspectives or experiences of group solidarity and economic achievement. For example, the life satisfaction of individual Whites declines as the average income for Whites in a particular state increases, suggesting a social status or comparison effect. In contrast, among African Americans, life satisfaction increases as state-level average income for Blacks increases (Davis & Wu, 2013). Income effects on happiness were not seen for Hispanic or Asian participants.

Other research has examined behaviors that might reflect communalism or the opportunities provided by belonging to the social networks of members of the African American community. For example, using data from the General Social Survey, a nationally representative random sample of households, Hamm and McDonald (2015) found that African Americans are 61% more likely to extend job-finding assistance over the past year to someone they know compared with Whites. However, when Census tract poverty rate and racial composition are added to the analytic model, Blacks have no greater likelihood of extending assistance than Whites. This result suggests that in high-poverty and more racially segregated areas, African Americans may engage in lower levels of offering job assistance. Prior theory and research have found that African Americans may not benefit from job finding because their networks may be more limited in access to high-quality employment opportunities.

METHODOLOGICAL AND RESEARCH ISSUES

Methodological and research issues discussed include measures of community and neighborhood and ways in which to study community effects. When conducting research on context, researchers have several options in operationalizing community and neighborhood. From an Africentric perspective, researchers can utilize the communalism scale developed by Boykin et al. (1997). This 31-item scale was developed using four samples of college students and assesses interdependence and individuals' sense of social obligation with items such as, "I believe that a person has to work cooperatively with family and friends." The measure has good reliability and validity. Another available measure that includes collective efficacy and neighborhood cohesion was used by Sampson and Earls in the PHDCN studies (Sampson et al., 1997). Neighborhood cohesion assesses the perceptions of community residents with respect to trust (e.g., "People around here are willing to help their neighbors"). Collective efficacy is an index of residents' sense of control and influence reflected in their ratings of items such as whether they would intervene if children were engaging in behavior such as showing disrespect to an adult. These measures are reliable and valid.

Leventhal and Brooks-Gunn (2000) note that researchers use a variety of strategies to study neighborhood effects, including national databases, city and regional studies, neighborhood-level studies, and experimental designs. Units of analysis vary, and data are taken from the U.S. Census, boundaries and administrative districts set by local governments, government administration (e.g., police, local housing), and participant ratings of their perceptions of neighborhood characteristics. Windshield surveys are also used as objective assessments of neighborhoods. For example, the Neighborhood Assessment of Community Characteristics (Burton, Price-Spratlen, & Spencer, 1997; Spencer, Cole, Jones, & Swanson, 1997a; Spencer, McDermott, Burton, & Kochman, 1997b) is a windshield survey of social (e.g., presence of children playing, visibility of police, gender and ages of community members) and physical (e.g., housing stock, playgrounds and parks, Churches) characteristics of neighborhoods. The survey was developed by Margaret Spencer (Spencer et al., 1997a, 1997b). Different versions of the measure allow trained evaluators or trained community residents to drive or walk through discrete neighborhood sectors and rate them.

Researchers have also noted that the effects of neighborhood interventions and broad-scale community change efforts are often difficult to detect (e.g., Auspos & Kubisch, 2004). There has been some attention to the use of forecast evaluation and other strategies to measure broader community change initiatives and to assess community capacity (e.g., Goodman et al., 1998). The Forecast model (Goodman, Wandersman, Chinman, Imm, & Morrissey, 1996) involves articulating models of a project's processes and outcomes, identifying markers and milestones of the implementation of the project's model, implementing measures that assess whether program milestones have been achieved, and using the data collected to make meaning and create understanding of the project, its process, and outcomes.

Strategies used to assess community capacity include the examination of resident and leader participation, community leadership factors, relevant community-building skills, the ability to access or acquire resources, and the strength of social and organizational networks. Other strategies include the psychological sense of community, knowledge of the community's history, the community's ability to use power and influence, the presence of a clear sense of values, and the ability of the community to reflect critically on issues relevant to change (Goodman et al., 1998). It is also important to note that earlier conceptions of socioeconomic status considered residence along with factors such as income, education, and employment (Hollingshead & Redlich, 1958). Over time, these contextual factors have been less frequently included in indices of socioeconomic status. However, research clearly indicates that these factors, beyond family-level income or educational status, play a significant role in understanding the psychology of African Americans. Perhaps most importantly, in considering the broad body of research on African Americans, there may be an attribution of effects and outcomes to an individual, family, culture or membership in a racial or ethnic group, without considering the potential contribution of contextual or neighborhood effects.

EMPIRICALLY SUPPORTED PRACTICES AND POLICY FOR COMMUNITY AND NEIGHBORHOOD IMPROVEMENT

Research on the effects of neighborhood has a wide range of intervention and policy implications. Strategies such as community empowerment and community organization can be used to build on community assets (e.g., Kretzmann & McKnight, 1993). Young-Laing's (2003) analysis of community development and organizing strategies provides a historical analysis of community-building efforts within the African American community. She discusses the roles of the Universal Negro Improvement Association, the Southern Christian Leadership Conference, and the Black Panther Party in community change. In her analysis, Young-Laing points to three primary strategies currently used by African Americans to promote community change. These include political and social action (with the focus being on changing social policy through protest, political effort, and media), resource and capacity development (where individuals work to build local community resource access and capacity), and cultural empowerment (emphasizing cultural education and raising cultural consciousness). This work is consistent with the earlier Progressive Era strategies of figures such as Ida B. Wells-Barnett and Lugenia Burns Hope, who organized and provided services and resources to individuals and families within challenged African American communities during the late 1800s and early 1900s (O'Donnell, 1996).

Neighborhood interventions, such as the Annie E. Casey Foundation's Plain Talk strategies (http://www.aecf.org/m/resourcedoc/aecf-walkingtheplaintalkAdvocacy Reprint-2000.pdf) similarly work with community residents or community health workers to provide door-to-door outreach, bringing resource information to their neighbors. The Plain Talk intervention has been used to address adolescent pregnancy. The program works to create a shared view of community prevention needs, and increase community skills to intervene, and improve youth access to adult and other resources. Resources such as the Community Tool Box (http://ctb.ku.edu/en) and programs such as Communities That Care (http://www.communitiesthatcare .net) provide guidance and a process to support communities in using research-based strategies to address community challenges.

Interventions have focused on work with individuals and groups at the community level to increase individual-level coping, reduce neighborhood risk, and increase community capacity. Several capacity-building efforts have begun to emphasize the role that the community plays in shaping its own destiny. For example, the Urban Institute's National Neighborhood Indicators Partnership involves several groups that work to "democratize data" (i.e., make data about the community easily accessible) so that communities can more effectively plan and advocate for the change they want in their communities. Groups can monitor where crimes occur and work with police to address their concerns, or they can examine the availability of public resources and advocate for new initiatives. These efforts provide hope that many neighborhoods can more effectively address the challenges that result in neighborhood-level risk.

The potential to use housing policy to address challenges facing urban community residents has been informed by the Gautreaux Project, a quasi-experimental study where families moved to other residential areas in the city or to suburban areas following a federal court decision finding discriminatory practices in the Chicago Housing Authority. Adolescents within families who moved to the suburbs had higher rates of employment than peers who remained in the city (Kaufman & Rosenbaum, 1992; Popkin, Rosenbaum, & Meaden, 1993; Rosenbaum, Kulieke, & Rubinowitz, 1988; Rosenbaum & Popkin, 1991). A 15-year follow-up found that residents continued to reside in neighborhoods characterized by lower crime rates, higher income, and greater racial diversity than their neighborhoods of origin (Keels, Duncan, Deluca, Mendenhall, & Rosenbaum, 2005). Residents who were initially placed in more segregated neighborhoods tended to move to more integrated and racially balanced neighborhoods over time.

Sharkey (2012), using analysis and data from a series of studies, raises questions as to whether family moves in largest part result in the "reproduction of unequal neighborhoods." Building on data from the PHDCN across a 7-year period, family moves within neighborhoods and within Chicago result in minimal changes in the median income unless families move outside Chicago; however, African American families are only 40% as likely as White families to make such moves. For example, African American families living in poor neighborhoods who move are most likely to move either to another African American poor neighborhood or to a non–African American poor neighborhood. In comparison, families living in a poor mixed-race neighborhood who moved were most likely to move to a mixed nonpoor neighborhood within Chicago or to a White nonpoor neighborhood outside Chicago.

CONTEMPORARY ISSUES
BUILDING NEIGHBORHOODS OF OPPORTUNITY?

In December of 2012, the U.S. Department of Housing and Urban Development (HUD) announced the award of $108.9 million in funding to revitalize four distressed communities in Cincinnati, San Antonio, Seattle, and Tampa through its Choice Neighborhoods Initiative (HUD, n.d.).

The program, initiated in 2010, pursues the following outcomes:

- Transform distressed public and/or assisted-housing units into physically and financially viable housing for the long-term;

- Support positive health, safety, employment, mobility, and education outcomes for residents in the target development(s) and the surrounding neighborhoods; and

- Create viable, mixed-income neighborhoods that have access to well-functioning services, high quality public schools and education programs, public assets, public transportation, and improved access to jobs. (HUD, 2013)

Based on prior study, HUD argues that the program has the potential to reduce crime and increase community access to services and improved community infrastructure, reduce demand for public housing dollars, and increase community resident quality of life. The administration requested $150 million for the 2013 budget year, but the future of the program and funding levels going forward, with federal budget fights continuing, remain in question.

The program is discussed as a complement to the Promise Neighborhoods Initiative that announced funding of $60 million to 17 communities that target "local-led efforts to improve educational opportunities and provide comprehensive health, safety, and support services in high-poverty neighborhoods" (U.S. Department of Education, 2012). The program was designed to transform neighborhoods by

1. Identifying and increasing the capacity of eligible entities that are focused on achieving results for children and youth throughout an entire neighborhood;

2. Building a complete continuum of cradle-to-career solutions of both educational programs and family and community supports, with great schools at the center;

3. Integrating programs and breaking down agency "silos" so that solutions are implemented effectively and efficiently across agencies;

4. Developing the local infrastructure of systems and resources needed to sustain and scale up proven, effective solutions across the broader region beyond the initial neighborhood; and

5. Learning about the overall impact of the Promise Neighborhoods program and about the relationship between particular strategies in Promise Neighborhoods and student outcomes, including through a rigorous evaluation of the program. (U.S. Department of Education, n.d.)

These policy initiatives present hopeful opportunities to address challenges in high-poverty neighborhoods. Here, it may be important to consider the link between types of neighborhood change and specific outcomes of interest. For example, Dobbie and Fryer (2009) underline the importance of the charter school experience of youth as it relates to their academic progress. This raises questions as to whether physical and structural changes in neighborhoods, without attention to the opportunity infrastructure of the neighborhood, are adequate. It is important to consider whether the redevelopment of physical structures or resources supporting economic mobility (e.g., access to high-quality schools and supports, such as transportation infrastructure that allows access to employment) are more important. Other neighborhood interventions have also raised important questions about the potential negative impact of residential displacement and the disruption of social networks. Considering the importance of communalism, these disruptions may be especially important to consider for African Americans.

CRITICAL ANALYSIS

Where you are from and where you live are central factors in access to educational and employment opportunities. Communities vary greatly in resources, neighborhood amenities, housing quality and in the presence of stressors and environmental toxins. The lack of community transportation infrastructure can work to further isolate and establish barriers to resources and opportunity. Many of the decisions that established the current infrastructure of urban communities were made 50 or more years ago, and race and racism were implicit or explicit drivers of these decisions in many communities, especially in urban communities. This poses a series of important questions for psychology. Do we continue to focus on individual strategies that increase the competencies and capacity of individuals to live in resource-poor communities, or would greater benefit come from focusing on strategies that change communities? Should housing policy be the primary intervention that supports positive development and reduces psychological risk for African Americans?

We are experiencing slow but notable changes in residential segregation and in suburbanization for African Americans. Efforts to revitalize urban neighborhoods and redevelop public housing communities (e.g., HOPE VI and Choice Neighborhood) could inform potential avenues to reduce neighborhood disadvantage. In our current political, cultural, and social climate, the likelihood of these interventions is unclear. The use of these interventions must be considered in relation to potential effects on the social resources within communities and neighborhoods. This raises important questions. Does neighborhood revitalization displace families or lead to the disruption of social networks? Does the desire of public housing residents to return to Ward IX in New Orleans primarily reflect their desire to reconnect with their social and neighborhood networks? Can housing interventions be organized to maintain and potentially strengthen neighborhood networks?

Within an American context that emphasizes "rugged individualism," our focus within mainstream psychology on the experience of the individual is often made independent of context. Studies frequently do not describe with any depth the settings from which participants are drawn, and studies even more rarely consider the ways in which these contexts may change over time. The chapter considers the linkages between one's sense of connection to the group—that is, a "psychological sense of Black community"—to issues of well-being, attitudes, and behavior. Notably, the growing body of work suggests the potential importance of this sense of connection to positive attitudes and actions directed at others and linked to one's sense of spirituality. These connections underline the need to consider the ways in which we consider integration within African American psychology. The literature on positive psychology, identity, development, and mental health are relevant to our current considerations of community membership and residence. Research reviewed within this chapter clearly underlines the significant role that neighborhood and community play in the psychology of African Americans. These contextual factors must increasingly play a role in our development of research, our conceptual and theoretical models, and in interpreting research findings.

Summary

African Americans have membership in multiple communities, including those defined by being Americans of African descent, as well as being members of diverse sets of neighborhoods. Important sociopolitical and historical factors, including structural racism, have shaped—and continue to shape—the places where African Americans live. These settings, in turn, frequently define the sets of social and infrastructural resources available to individuals living within those communities. Historical factors have included the impact of the northern migration of Blacks during the late 1800s and early 1900s; the positive but time-limited economic benefits of migration; the concentration of urban poverty linked to changes in job access; and the impact of suburban development, job relocation, and housing and banking policies. Several theories help us to understand the role of community in the psychology of African Americans, including the important role of communalism from an Africentric perspective. The sense of connection among African Americans is theorized to be an important component of our cultural heritage, and initial research suggests that this communalism functions to protect individuals and communities. African American parents may develop specific strategies to support the adaptive development of their children when they grow up in challenged communities. Some educational achievement outcomes may be linked to neighborhood characteristics for African American males.

There are several ways of measuring community, including windshield surveys and the use of Census data. Other disciplines have a lot to offer in support of our understanding of ways to build community. Efforts at "rebuilding the village" will require a long-term perspective and a shift from individual-level interventions that support African Americans in coping with challenges to interventions that work to reduce the risk in these neighborhoods. Building on the assets and strengths of African American communities is crucial to the availability of resources within these communities.

The Bondei proverb "Sticks in a bundle are unbreakable," illustrates the importance of the community and connections in the strength and development of African Americans. Whether in neighborhoods, in social or political groups, or from one's sense of self, the African American community is core. This sense is reflected in an excerpt from Martin Luther King Jr.'s "Letter From a Birmingham Jail": "We are caught in an inescapable network of mutuality, tied in a single garment of destiny. Whatever affects one directly, affects all indirectly" (King, 1963, p. 290).

INDIVIDUAL AND DEVELOPMENTAL PROCESSES

8

INTERPERSONAL AND CLOSE RELATIONSHIPS

One finger cannot lift up a thing.

—African proverb

LEARNING OBJECTIVES

- To understand the nature of relationships

- To become familiar with friendships and peer relationships among African American adolescents

- To become more knowledgeable about relationships and love in Africa

- To identify factors that affect the selection of romantic partners among African Americans

- To become more knowledgeable about factors that contribute to interpersonal attraction among African Americans

- To become familiar with interracial attitudes, friendships, and relationships

- To become familiar with some of the issues in lesbian, gay, bisexual, and transgender relationships

- To identify some of the methodological challenges to studying African American relationships

- To identify some practices for promoting positive interpersonal relationships among African American adolescents

HOW RAP MUSIC INFLUENCES AFRICAN AMERICAN GIRLS' PERCEPTIONS OF SKIN COLOR

BY TOMMEKA SEMIEN

Do you know a young, African-American female who listens to hip-hop and rap music? Chances are that her self-image is being influenced by the lyrics. Interviews with young African-American girls revealed they believed that today's hip-hop and rap artists placed more value on the beauty of "redbones" and "yellowbones" than that of dark-skinned African-American girls and women.

Morgan L. Maxwell, Jasmine A. Abrams and Faye Z. Belgrave published their study about rap music and skin color in the *Psychology of Music*. The study included both focus groups and individual interviews with teenage African-American girls. The purpose of the study was to determine if rap music served as a conduit for messages about skin color to African American adolescents. The research indicated that rap music influenced messages about skin color such as a preference for "light-skinned females".

Previous research has indicated that hip-hop and rap music influence many aspects of African American "development and behavior". However, little research is available in reference to colorism or discrimination based on physical traits. Researchers believed it was important to acquire more information on this topic since many associate rap music with negative social behaviors including lowered self-worth and substance abuse (Wilder, 2010; Wilder & Cain, 2011).

Researchers utilized the help of non-profit organizations serving youth in the target population. Participants were solicited from the organizations. Prior to the start of the study, participants were required to obtain written parental consent and were made fully aware of the purpose of the study. All participants were compensated at a rate of $10 and received a small gift bag. The final group of subjects comprised a total of 30 African-American girls between the ages of twelve and sixteen. Only female participants were selected since the researchers believed that colorism messages were more targeted to females.

All participants engaged in interviews individually or with a focus group at the site where they were recruited. The choice for the type of interview was made based solely on the number of anticipated participants per site—four or more became a focus group. Participants were asked four questions pertaining to their perception of light-skinned Black girls; dark-skinned Black girls; messages about skin tone from rap music; and how those messages should be used.

Additional questions were asked to clarify responses as needed. To help participants feel comfortable with the discussion, the interviewer was an African-American female.

The data collected during interviews was based on a systematic review of responses. All interviews were recorded and transcribed; reviewed by a second transcriber; and finally by the lead researcher.

The final transcript was analyzed for words found frequently such as "pretty," "music videos," and "light skin." Another analysis was conducted to identify longer strings of related code or words such as "rappers like Lil Wayne prefer light skin." Final review of all data indicated three recurring themes: 1) rap music sends messages showing preference to light-skinned females; 2) messages about dark-skinned females were either missing in music or negative; and 3) music used specific nicknames to describe females based on skin tone.

"Findings indicated participants consistently identified rap music and rappers as primary sources of skin color related messages. From this genre of music and affiliated artists, girls are made aware that lighter-skinned women are more desired than those with darker skin," the researchers said.

The volunteer participants in this research study indicated that their self-image was affected by messages in rap music that approved colorism. Though not evaluated, it might be assumed that these messages also played a role in influencing males to choose a mate based on the suggested, desirable physical traits. The Maxwell et al. study may serve as the foundation for future research that evaluates how rap music and culture influence young adults from multiple populations including diverse ethnic and socioeconomic populations.

"Given the popularity of rap music, and the potential impact of skin color dissatisfaction on girls' body image perceptions and psychological wellbeing, understanding rap music as a medium through which skin color related messages are transmitted is important," the researchers concluded.

Source: Semien (2016).

INTRODUCTION, DEFINITIONS, AND HISTORICAL PERSPECTIVES

All humans have a need to belong, to affiliate, and to be in relationships with others. Friendships and meaningful relationships with others are essential (Berscheid, 1985). We form relationships to have fun, to share intimacies, and to get our needs and goals met. In this chapter, we examine interpersonal and close relationships from the perspective of African Americans. We also discuss attraction, noting some racial and ethnic differences. For example, as seen in the cover story, skin color is a factor in attraction and interpersonal relationships for African Americans. We return to this subject later in this chapter.

We begin this chapter with an overview of the nature of relationships and follow it with a discussion of relationships among Africans. Friendships and peer relationships are discussed next, followed by a discussion of romantic relationships including the conceptualization of love. We also review factors that affect mate selection among African Americans. We then discuss interpersonal attraction and review influences on our choice of friends and partners. Along with proximity and similarity, physical attraction is a factor in our relationship choices. We review skin color, hair texture, and other physical attributes as they relate to African American attraction and relationships. Interracial relationships, including friendships and intimate relationships (e.g., dating, marriage), and also gay and lesbian relationships are discussed next. Some research and methodological issues are identified, followed by a discussion of best practices for improving positive interpersonal relationships. The chapter concludes with a critique and summary.

The Nature of Relationships

A relationship is "a state of affairs existing between those having relations or dealings" (Merriam-Webster, n.d.). Relationships exist for varying reasons and operate in many ways. Relationships are voluntary and involuntary. Relationships with one's family are involuntary. A relationship with a romantic partner is voluntary. Some relationships are oriented toward getting one's needs and goals met. Other relationships exist because they are fulfilling for partners involved. Still other relationships exist because one person feels responsible for the other, as in a parent–child relationship. One useful distinction in understanding relationships is the distinction between communal and exchange relationships (see discussion in section "Exchange and Communal Relationships").

Equitable Relationships

One norm-governing relationship is equity (Deutsch, 1985). In general, people want their relationships to be equitable. This means that we want out of a relationship as much as we put into it. An assumption of equity theory is that people want to maximize their outcomes in a relationship. When we perceive that a relationship is inequitable, we feel distressed. The greater the inequity there is, the greater the distress we feel. We feel this distress even if we are on the receiving end of the relationship. In other words, we want to get out of a relationship as much as we put in, but we do not want the benefits from a relationship to greatly exceed our inputs. When people are in an inequitable relationship, they will try to restore equity, or they will leave the relationship. However, all relationships do not operate based on equity theory. Some research suggests that relationships among people of African descent are not based on equity. Exchange and communal relationships help to explain these relationships.

Exchange and Communal Relationships

In both exchange and communal relationships, there are exchanges, but the rules that govern them differ (Clark & Mills, 2012). In exchange relationships, people give benefits with the expectation that they will soon receive comparable benefits. This is akin to what we think of as an equitable relationship. Communal relationships are those in which one person feels responsible for the well-being of another person. Communal relationships usually occur between family members, friends, and romantic partners. Exchange relationships may be between employees and employers, coworkers, neighbors, and, in some cases, friends.

In communal relationships, one person benefits his or her partner without an expectation of benefits in return. People are more attentive to the needs of a partner in a communal than in an exchange relationship. People in communal relationships prefer to talk about emotional and intimate topics, such as likes and dislikes. People in an exchange relationship prefer to talk about nonemotional topics, such as an activity or a hobby. Because of values that are oriented toward relationships, most people of African descent have communal relationships.

Relationships Among Africans

As discussed in Chapter 2, an attribute among people of African descent is a value for interpersonal relationships. Other terms used to describe this value include communalism, relationship orientation, collective orientation, and relational. This relationship orientation includes sensitivity to the emotional state of others and an orientation that considers others in one's thoughts and activities (see Chapter 2). Relationships among Africans may be less hierarchical than those found in Western cultures. On the nature of relationships as an African core value, the scholar Gyekye (1996) writes,

> The communal structure of African society has created a sense of community that characterizes social relationships among individual members of the African society. Communal values consider the importance of the community and include mutual aid, caring for others, interdependence, solidarity,

reciprocal obligation, and social harmony. Interpersonal relations are what make up a community. (p. 35)

A community is a group of persons tied together by interpersonal relationships, which are not necessarily biological; these people share common values, interests, and goals. Community exists for the benefit of the individual member. The communalistic orientation is also seen among contemporary African Americans. The extended family is one such example of communalistic relationships. Another example is involvement with and practices of the Church and other places of worship. Relationships among African American family members are discussed in Chapter 5, and faith-based institutions are discussed in Chapter 10.

Ubuntu

The African concept of *Ubuntu* can be used to describe relationships from an African-centered perspective (Ramose, 2003). Ubuntu is a kind of affinity and kinship among and between indigenous people of Africa. The *Ubuntu* philosophy is found from the Nubian Desert to the Cape of Good Hope and from Senegal to Zanzibar. Ubuntu means humanity to others and "I am what I am because of who we all are" (Dreyer, 2015). An Ubuntu ethic is the tendency to pursue communal relations with other individuals. Relationships, or people's capacities for relationships, are viewed as essential to one's own well-being (Hoffmann & Metz, 2017).

An example of Ubuntu helps us understand how the notion of freedom is conceptualized from an African-centered perspective. In Western society, an individual's freedom is seen as the ability to function well regardless of the conditions of others. Ubuntu philosophy conceives of freedom as an individual's ability to care for others. From this orientation, freedom is a form of interdependence with others (Hoffmann & Metz, 2017). As another example, poverty from an Ubuntu perspective is viewed as a disruption of relationships in three ways. One, poverty interferes with an individual's ability to care for others. Two, poverty is an indicator of the lack of responsibility and care on the part of state (or governing institutions) for individuals they are supposed to care for. Three, an individual cannot attain well-being by depriving others or benefiting from their deprivation. Ubuntu would consider that this individual has failed in relationships with others. Practically, this means when wealthy individuals do not speak out against or work to alleviate poverty, they are not practicing Ubuntu. We next turn to a discussion of friendships and peer relationships among African Americans.

FRIENDSHIPS AND PEER RELATIONSHIPS

Peer relationships and friendships are important to the social and psychological well-being of humans. Close friendships can be very rewarding. Friends provide support, intimacy, a confidant, and an activity partner. Some differences in male and female friendships will be discussed next. This will be followed by a discussion of African American adolescent, adolescent male, and adolescent female friendships.

Gender Differences in Friendships

Close friendships can occur with opposite-sex members, but generally, close friends are of the same gender. The nature of close friendships differs for men and women (Baumgarte & Nelson, 2009). Women rate their friendships more positively than men do, and their friendships are more intimate. Male friends bond by participating in common activities, whereas female friends bond by sharing feelings and emotions. Both men and women are more likely to self-disclose to women friends. And men are more likely to name their wives as friends than vice versa. Women's relationships are more spontaneous and personal than men's. Differences between African American male and female friendships are similar to those of other ethnic groups. Some exceptions will be discussed.

Gender differences in friendship are universal. David-Barrett et al. (2015) conducted a cross-cultural study of gender differences in friendships using a sample of approximately 112,000 individuals from nine regions of the world. Facebook profile pictures were reviewed based on the assumption that profile pictures relate to the user's desire to project a certain impression. The authors used random search terms to select users who shared their friends publicly and located the profile pictures of all of the friends of each user. Each photograph was coded as to the type of picture (including the number of persons in the picture) and gender of user. Males had a higher number of friendships than females and were more likely to present themselves as part of large all-male groups. Women posted pictures of themselves with fewer friends and had more dense social networks. The findings suggest that females tend to focus on intimate relations with a few other females, while males' friendship networks are larger and more spread out. Gender differences between male and female friendships exist for African Americans as with other ethnic groups. Some exceptions will be noted next.

Racial and Ethnic Differences in Friendship Networks

Friendship networks vary by ethnicity (Belgrave & Brevard, 2015). Research suggests that Whites are more involved in friendship networks than African Americans. However, African Americans tend to rely on both biological and fictive kin more so than Whites and to have more kin in their networks. Data from the National Survey of American Life were used to explore friendship and kin networks among different racial and ethnic groups (Taylor et al., 2013). The sample consisted of African Americans (N = 3,570), Caribbean Blacks (N = 1,621) and Whites (N = 891). The findings showed that Whites interacted with and provided support to friends in their network more frequently than African Americans. Whites were also the recipients of support from friends more frequently than African Americans and Black Caribbeans. African Americans (11%) were more than 2 times as likely as Whites (4.7%) to indicate that they hardly ever or never interact with friends. African Americans and Black Caribbeans had more fictive kin in their network than Whites. This study's findings suggest that kin are a large part of the network of African American and Caribbean Blacks and support the significance of family and kin in African Americans lives (see Chapter 5).

African American Adolescent Friendships

Friendships are important for adolescents, and there are several benefits of friendships, including psychological and social well-being. A study of friendships among various racial and ethnic sophomore high school students showed differences in friendships patterns (Cherng, Turney, & Kao, 2014). A nationally representative sample of over 12,300 students was used. Findings showed that racial and ethnic minority groups reported fewer friendships than Whites. For example, 95% of

Whites reported at least one friend, whereas 91% of Blacks, 93% of Latinos, and 93% of Asians reported at least one friend. There were also small but notable differences with regard to socializing with friends; 98% of Whites reported that they socialized with friends versus 97% of Blacks, 95% of Latino, and 94% of Asians. The finding of fewer friends for ethnic minority adolescents compared with White adolescents are consistent with those for adults; however, these ethnic differences are very small.

Friendships tend to occur within one's own racial or ethnic group, with individuals seeking out peers who are similar to them (Byrne, Clore, & Smeaton, 1986). In contrast, African American adolescents may be less likely to have friends in similar networks than other racial and ethnic groups (Belgrave, 2009). For example, African American adolescents are less likely to have friends who attend the same school as they. They also choose friends who are less similar academically and with regard to drug use but who are more similar in ethnic identity (Hamm, 2000). Also, some research supports that some African American adolescent males who excel academically are not accepted by their African American peers (Tyson, Darity, & Castellino, 2005).

Dolcini et al. (2004) examined the content and quality of adolescent friendships in an urban African American neighborhood. The study looked at cliques. Cliques were defined as small, close-knit groups ranging in size from 3 to 10 and composed of peers who were similar with respect to age, gender, and race. The researchers conducted interviews with 113 friends whose ages ranged from 13 to 21. The study found that half of the respondents were in cliques, and about one-fifth were in dyads only; the others were not linked with friends. The average clique consisted of four youth of the same gender and ethnicity. The friendships were relatively long term, with a mean friendship length of over 5 years. The trust levels of the friendships were high, and friends provided each other with instrumental support (e.g., lending money). Levels of emotional support and intimacy were not as high as instrumental support. The findings from the study by Dolcini et al. (2004) illustrate the function that friendships serve for African American adolescents. Feelings of trust, intimacy, and instrumental support were available from friends. It is likely that these benefits of friendships cross all ethnic and racial groups.

African American Adolescent Male Relationships

African American adolescent male friendships affect psychological, social, and academic well-being, yet there has been limited research on close friendships among African American adolescent males (Belgrave & Brevard, 2015; Way, 2013).

In the literature, representation of friendships among adolescent boys, especially African American and other ethnic minority males, often frame them as being more interested in playing, competing, and boasting than in talking together and sharing personal aspects of their lives. However, longitudinal studies of friendships among boys from early to late adolescence dispute this story (Way, 2013).

Way describes the friendship of Black, Latino and Asian American boys based on interviews conducted with 135 boys enrolled in a longitudinal study of friendship. Three themes emerged from these interviews. One was the importance of and the desire they have for sharing secrets in their close relationships. Sharing secrets was what defined a best friend, and violations of secrets were a primary reason for terminating close friendships. The second theme was that close friendships were important for mental health. Boys reported that without their close friends, they would be depressed, unhappy, and all alone. The third theme was that friendships were lost and or trust violated as the adolescents transitioned from middle to late adolescence, although there was a continued desire for friendships. As the boys grew older, close friendships changed.

Reasons were that boys sometimes connected having close friendships to being feminine, and others reported that they did not have time for male friends. Overall, intimacy in friendships diminished as boys grow into manhood.

In a study of peer friendships among African American adolescent males, Cunningham and Meunier (2004) examined how relationships with peers influence the bravado attitudes that are sometimes seen among African American youth, especially those from high-risk neighborhoods. Bravado is a hypermasculine or macho identity that individuals who live in high-risk environments develop as a reactive style (Cunningham & Meunier, 2004). Peer relationships and bravado were examined in a sample of 356 adolescent African American boys in an urban southeastern U.S. city. The authors found that poor attitudes toward and relationships with peers, including alienation from peers, discomfort speaking to peers, and the experience of neighborhood gang or turf problems were related to bravado attitudes. It appears that bravado attitudes may, in part, be related to the lack of positive peer experiences among some African American adolescent males.

Thus, programs that help males to develop positive peer relationships should be useful in enhancing overall well-being and in deterring boys from gangs and peers who are engaged in problem behaviors. To address ways to increase positive adolescent male relationships, Belgrave, Allison, Wilson, and Tademy (2012) developed a curriculum for African American adolescent males. One of the objectives of this curriculum is for boys to increase positive interactions and relationships with each other. Activities and discussions in the curriculum build on interdependent activities and cooperative problem-solving skills. The curriculum is discussed in more detail later in this chapter.

African American Adolescent Female Relationships

Positive peer relationships are important for self-worth and success across many life domains for girls also. Relationships are central to females and to people of African descent, so positive and fulfilling relationships are especially critical to African American girls' identity and self-worth. Relationships are important across the life span, but during the adolescent years, relationships become more salient and important to girls' growth and development.

There are many transitions during early adolescence. Some of these include puberty, transitioning from elementary to middle school, and growing independence in selecting own peers and friends. It is also during this period that we see an increase in negative interpersonal relationships among girls. Relational aggression is a negative aspect of an interpersonal relationship. Relational aggression involves behaviors such as gossiping, withdrawing affection to get what you want, and socially excluding others (Crick & Grotpeter, 1995). Girls are more likely to engage in relational aggression than boys, who are more likely to engage in physical aggression (Crick & Grotpeter, 1995).

We have implemented several programs that focus on decreasing relational aggression and strengthening positive relationships among African American adolescent females (Belgrave, 2002; Belgrave et al., 2004, 2008). In these programs, we have emphasized the importance of peer relationships. Our programs involve creating an environment whereby positive sister relationships can be facilitated among girls in early adolescence. This program is described in a curriculum called Sisters of Nia (Sisters of Purpose); it is discussed in the best practices section of this chapter.

A very different kind of relationship is a romantic relationship, and this is discussed next.

ROMANTIC RELATIONSHIPS

A romantic partner is that one person in the world to whom you feel closest (Berscheid, Snyder, & Omoto, 1989). An intense close relationship may be described as love. There are different types of love, and there are cultural differences in how love is conceptualized. We begin this section with a discussion of love, the emotion found in most romantic relationships, followed by a discussion of mate selection for romantic relationships in general and among African Americans more specifically.

What Is Love?

Love is difficult to define, as it is a subjective experience. It differs from liking and is not limited to intimate relationships. Most scholars agree that there are two types of love, companionate love and passionate love. Companionate love is the feeling of intimacy and affection that does not include physiological arousal, passion, and desire (Hatfield & Walster, 1978). Passionate love involves intense feelings and physiological arousal for another. Companionate love is seen in close friendships. Companionate love may also be present in passionate love relationships. A relationship in Western culture typically starts with passionate love and then is replaced with companionate love. Passionate love develops quickly, whereas companionate love develops gradually. Passionate love is more intense and includes both positive and negative emotions. Other forms of love include parental love and altruistic love. More recent conceptualizations of love include the investment in the well-being of the other for his or her own sake (Heigi & Bergner, 2010).

Romantic love seems to be a universal life experience. In a study of romantic relationships, Regan, Durvasula, Howell, Ureño, and Rea (2004) examined when first love occurred among African American, Latino, and White adolescents. The authors found that first romantic love experiences did not differ by ethnic group. Most of the males and females had fallen in love at least once, around the age of 17. This was true for all ethnic groups. This suggests that romantic love most likely occurs during the period of late adolescence to early adulthood.

Love in African Cultures

Research on passionate and companionate love, specifically among Africans, is scarce. When one hears the term *love* in the United States, one thinks of romantic love. This is very different from a traditional African approach to love in which love is expected to develop after marriage, as couples share their lives along with their families (Dixon, 2014). In traditional African culture, partners were selected based on values, health, and family background. Parents assumed responsibility for selecting partners for their children, marriages were arranged, and a dowry or bride price might be paid. While this practice is waning in Africa and throughout the world, the family continues to play a large role in mate selection in Africa.

Love is conceptualized and experienced differently in African than in Western countries. The notion of love seems to be linked to "caring for" in some African cultures. Ghanaians' conceptualization of love was explored by interviewing 61 participants (39 men, 22 women) who ranged in age from 20 to 70 years (Opare-Henaku, 2017). Participants were asked their definitions and experiences of love. Over 96% of the participants believed that love is expressed by meeting one's relational obligations to children, spouse, parents, and other relatives. This type of love involves financial support; providing food, clothing, shelter, and emergency support; being physically present (e.g. visiting the sick); and providing advice and social support. More than half the participants in Opare-Henaku's study reported that love is helping people, including friends and strangers in need. This type of love would involve, for example, helping an elderly person cross the street or giving financial and verbal support to a friend when needed. Almost half of the participants felt that love was expressed by caring actions for others (e.g., visiting an ill person). A few participants believed that love was a public display of affection, such as kissing (children) and hugging (husband). While this study's findings are limited to one West African sample, interviews suggest that an important feature of love in African culture is caring for others. This is akin to Ubuntu discussed previously.

African American Romantic Relationships

Research suggests that young African American adults may experience some challenges in forming and sustaining romantic relationships. As discussed in the "Family and Kin" chapter, there is a lower marriage rate and higher divorce rate for African Americans than other racial or ethnic groups (Kogan et al., 2013). Several factors may account for these challenges, including contextual factors, such as lower levels of employment, racial discrimination and resulting stress, and multiple responsibilities assumed by both partners. See "Contemporary Issues" box for a discussion of some of the challenges African American women face in finding a mate.

Family and community factors affect relationship quality among African Americans. Kogan et al. (2013) studied the influence of family and community factors along with individual-level factors, such as negative relationship schemas, and how these factors affected romantic relationships. Negative relationship schemas are cynical or negative views of relationships. Data were collected from African American youth at four time periods when they ranged in age from 10 to 21. Of the 689 participants at the fourth data collection time period, 318 (46.2%) were in a committed romantic relationship (dating, cohabitating, or married). Measures were obtained of parenting (relationship warmth and parental monitoring), community stressors (e.g., interpersonal discrimination, crime, victimization), negative relational schemas, and romantic relationship health (e.g., relationship satisfaction, lack of verbal abuse). The study found that parenting and community-related stressors at ages 10 and 12 predicted negative relational schemas at age 18. Youth who lived in families with poor parenting practices and who lived in communities with stressors had more negative relational schemas, whereas youth from families with positive parenting practices and who lived in stress-free communities had more positive relational schemas. Relational schemas, in turn, predicted romantic relationship health at age 22. Exposure to community stressors influenced the development of relational schemas as youth develop expectations of poor interpersonal relationships early in life. Negative relationship schemas led to poor romantic relationship quality. In a second study, Kogan, Yu, and Brown (2016) also found that harsh parenting practices, along with racial discrimination, led to poor relationship commitment-related behaviors.

Mate Availability

Finding a desirable dating partner and mate depends on many factors. Males and females with similar lifestyles and characteristics are not distributed proportionally. We next discuss mate availability in the general population and for African Americans.

Mate availability is dependent on two concepts: (a) marriage squeeze and (b) sex ratio imbalance (Tucker & Mitchell-Kernan, 1999). Marriage squeeze is the decrease in the availability of marriage partners among female baby boomers. This shortage of partners is because of an increase in the number of women born relative to men.

Sex ratio imbalance is defined as the imbalance of the ratio of men to women. Sex ratio is expressed as the number of males to females. This ratio varies by geographic region, urbanicity, socioeconomic level, and age. In 2010, overall, there were about 96.7 men for every 100 women (Howden & Meyer, 2011). The sex ratio was 90.1 for African Americans, 96.3 for Whites, 92.8 for Asian/Pacific Islanders, 98.7 for American Indian/Alaska Native, and 105.4 for Latinos/Hispanics (Spraggins & U.S. Census Bureau, 2005). The data show that the sex ratio is imbalanced more for African American women than for other ethnic groups.

Sex ratio imbalance is particularly high among African American college students. This is important to note as college is a context in which suitable mates are met. In 2013, 64% of Black students enrolled in undergraduate institutions were women, compared with 36% who were men (Snyder & Dillon, 2015). On historically Black college and university (HBCU) campuses, Black women account for 62% to 76% of the student body.

Economic Feasibility

The relationship between economic stability and marriage has been examined among African Americans. There is a decline in marriage among African Americans. Compared with Whites, more African Americans end up not married. One perspective on the decline in African American marriage is that it is due to the decline in economic viability (low employment and unemployment) among African American men, as well as higher levels of incarceration of African American men (Raley & Sweeney, 2009; Tucker & Mitchell-Kernan, 1999). Over the past several decades, the increasing economic marginality of African American males has made them less desirable as potential husbands. Also, some African American males may not be as interested in becoming husbands because they are constrained in their ability to perform the provider role in marriage. A long-term view of economic instability is an important factor in decisions to marry rather than to cohabit. When there are perceptions of lower long-term economic stability for the male partner, marriage is less likely. While economic disadvantage appears to play a role in Black–White marriage disparities, it does not account for all of the disparities. Other factors that are cultural also account for these differences.

Some research suggests that African Americans may hold attitudes and cultural values about marriage that differ from other racial and ethnic groups. For example, African American families may be structurally different from families in other racial and ethnic groups and may place more emphasis on family ties and kin than on affiliations based on marriage (Raley & Sweeney, 2009). Other researchers suggest that norms that accept nonmarital childbirth are more prevalent in the African American community than in other communities.

Mate Selection

Socialization and cultural influences affect the process of mate selection. In the United States, we tend to marry someone who is similar in age, race, education, religion, and other demographic characteristics. This norm is known as homogamy (Fu & Heaton, 2008). Another norm for marriage is known as the marriage gradient. This is the informal norm for women to marry men who are of higher socioeconomic status and older than they and for men to marry women who are of lower socioeconomic status and age than they (Knox & Schacht, 2010). This norm affects partner choice by limiting the number of potential mates for women, especially as women get older. On the other hand, this norm provides more options to men. However, it also

CONTEMPORARY ISSUE

WHY ARE PROFESSIONAL AFRICAN AMERICAN WOMEN NOT FINDING PARTNERS?

One of my colleagues, Dr. Sonia Banks, once said to me, "It is easier for a Black woman to get a PhD than a husband." Dr. Banks, a clinical psychologist, subsequently established a support group to help African American women find partners. She also developed a program to strengthen relationship quality among couples already in relationships.

Ann Brown (2017) explores the lack of mate availability for African American women in a posting on "Why Black Boss Women (Still) Find It Hard to Find Equal Mates." According to Brown, African American women who are looking for mates with the same educational and professional background may have few choices (especially when compared with women of other racial and ethnic groups). For example, 49% of college-educated Black women marry a male with similar levels of educations versus 84% of White women who marry men with equal levels of education. On the other hand, educated professional African American men have more choices; they tend to choose a partner comparable in status or education or one with less education and professional status. Complicating mate availability is that African American women are less likely to date outside of their race than African American men and women from other racial and ethnic groups.

There are several websites devoted to African American relationships and dating, and relationship experts offer suggestions. Kelli Fisher and Tana Gilmore, matchmaking experts and columnists, note that African American women are often socialized regarding the importance of getting their education, choosing a well-paying and successful career, and being able to take care of themselves (Fisher & Gilmore, 2017). Single-minded devotion to education and career, especially during the period in which stable partnerships are established, may limit the time and effort African American women devote to finding a good partner. Fisher and Gilmore suggest that women be intentional about finding a mate and to not let potential good mates pass by while gaining education and career success. African American women who desire a mate will also need to be more flexible with regard to mates having equal educational and career status. Here, other qualities, both extrinsic (e.g., job stability, income, work flexibility, especially if there are children) and intrinsic (e.g., kindness, similar values and beliefs, humor), may carry more weight. Finally, flexibility in dating men who are not African American is important to consider.

Of note, most of the discussion surrounding the lack of mate availability is limited to heterosexual relationships. It is not clear if this is the case for same-gender relationships, and more research is needed on this topic.

affects men if they cannot find women of lower status or women of the same or higher status who would want to marry them. As will be discussed, these norms may not be as applicable to African Americans.

Another norm in the United States is that men are more likely to prefer and marry mates who are more physically attractive than themselves, whereas women are more likely to prefer and marry men with higher levels of education and income potential than themselves. This norm is grounded in social exchange theory. According to social exchange theory, a relationship will exist if it benefits both partners. One attribute is exchanged for another. In this case, social status from the male partner is exchanged for physical attractiveness from the female partner.

Homogamy and social exchange norms may not operate in the same way for African Americans as for other ethnic groups. Africentric beliefs among some African Americans may emphasize relationships and character over attributes such as material wealth and education. There are other reasons why African Americans may not subscribe to social exchange norms. Partner choice is more limited for African American women. African American females tend to be better educated and more upwardly mobile than African American males. See the "Contemporary Issue" box for further discussion of this topic. Also, a substantial percentage of African American males in the marriageable age category (20s to 30s) are involved in some way in the criminal justice system. Finally, African American women have a longer life expectancy than African American men. Therefore, many African American females will either have to marry down, postpone marriage, marry someone from another race, or marry someone who is much older or younger.

Mate Selection Among African Americans

What are some of the characteristics affecting mate selection for African Americans? And are these characteristics the same as for other racial and ethnic groups? Never-married men and women in the general population were asked about characteristics of a desired mate for marriage. Seventy-eight percent of women placed importance on finding a husband with a steady job. Steady employment was more important than same moral values such as religious beliefs, education, or racial and ethnic background (Wang & Parker, 2014). On the other hand, 62% of never-married men reported that it was very important to choose a woman for marriage who held similar ideas about having and raising children.

Murty, and Roebuck (2016) investigated preferred characteristics for choosing marriage partners among African American college students. The study also examined undesirable characteristics in a marriage partner. Participants were asked to list, in order of their importance, up to eight positive characteristics that were important in selecting a mate. They were then asked to also list up to eight negative characteristics or the most undesirable qualities in selecting a mate. Females listed as of highest importance character attributes (e.g., honest) (47.9%), followed by career attributes (e.g., goal-driven) (27.4%) and relationship attributes (e.g., faithful) (15.7%) for potential marriage mates. Physical attraction was not among the top-10 qualities that females preferred in a marriage partner. In fact, only about 9% of women listed physical attraction as an important attribute. Males, on the other hand, listed physical attributes (e.g., good-looking) as the highest attribute singularly and/or in combination with another attribute. The highest second preference for men went to relationship attributes (e.g., loving, caring), and the third attribute was character (e.g., honest).

In terms of dislike, females were most likely to mention character limitations, and these were mentioned by 72.4% of participants. Undesirable characteristic mentioned by men were more diverse. Men reported they would not want a partner who was unattractive (33.2%) and a partner with character limitations (33.6%). The findings that women desire mates who have a good career and good character while men desire attractiveness is consistent with findings of studies conducted with other racial and ethnic groups on gender differences in mate selection.

In another study, King and Allen (2009) administered surveys to 344 African Americans across a variety of settings and locations, including colleges and universities, sorority and fraternity meetings, social service agencies, bowling alleys, and nightclubs. Participants were mostly in their 30s, well educated, and with income levels higher than the median per capita income for African Americans. Participants were asked about characteristics of an ideal marriage partner, including social economic status, race, spirituality and religion, reliability, self-confidence, priority given to sex in the relationship, willingness to be affectionate, and commitment to monogamy. Honesty and sensitivity were seen as the most important characteristics in an ideal marital partner. The majority of respondents indicated that their ideal marriage partners would be reliable, monogamous, affectionate, financially stable, confident, religious, and spiritual. While a majority of respondents preferred African American marital partners, 45% believed that race should not matter when choosing a partner (King & Allen, 2009).

There were some gender differences in ideal marital partner characteristics. Women valued financial stability and completion of formal education more than men. Interestingly, the authors found a large discrepancy in the respondents' income and the income of their ideal marriage partners such that all respondents saw as ideal a partner who earned considerably more than they did. This was true of both males and females. Participants in this study were relatively well educated with higher-than-median incomes and perhaps wanted to maintain and/or move up in terms of social mobility. However, the author noted if men and women are seeking partners who earn more than they, there will be fewer partner choices available. Another factor that influences mate selection is physical attractiveness.

Physical Appearance and Mate Selection

One of the physical characteristics that affects mate selection is skin color. Historically, being light skinned has been a favored status in mate selection. Studies conducted during the 1940s through the 1960s indicated that skin tone was a predictor of socioeconomic status, employment, and mate selection among Blacks. Persons with lighter complexions had better employment opportunities, higher income, and higher occupational status. Blacks who were light-skinned were favored more than dark-complexioned Blacks by Whites because they were closer in appearance to Whites (Hill, 2002; Hughes & Hertel, 1990). Skin color was a source of status among African Americans and became a factor in mate selection (Goode, 1982). A premium was placed on an African American woman who was light-skinned, and skin color was considered an asset for marriage. Hunter (2002) determined, in an analysis of skin color and economic ascension, that African American women who were lighter-skinned not only earned higher wages but also were more likely to marry men with higher education levels than darker-skinned women.

Today, there is less but still some evidence that mate selection preferences are influenced by skin color. Hamilton, Goldsmith, and Darity (2009) examined the influence of skin color on marriageability and found that young Black women with light complexions had a 15% greater probability of marriage than Black women with darker complexions. In a study using a national sample of racial and ethnic groups, darker skin was negatively associated with expectations to marry and the belief that marriage is important (Landor & Halpern, 2016). These more recent findings corroborate the results of earlier studies on skin color and mate selection.

On the other hand, some research suggests disadvantages for both very light and very dark skin African Americans, especially from African Americans. While dark-skin African Americans may be stigmatized, light-skin African Americans may also be stigmatized due to the perceived privilege of looking White (and not Black enough) (Adams, Kurtz-Costes, & Hoffman, 2016).

INTERPERSONAL ATTRACTION

Interpersonal attraction is generally a prerequisite to the formation of a relationship. One of the most influential determinants of whether we are attracted to others is proximity. The people we are most attracted to tend to be people we live close to. In a classic study conducted in 1950, Festinger, Schachter, and Back (1950) investigated friendship formation among couples who lived in different apartment buildings. Residents were assigned to apartments at random as vacancies occurred. However, when they were asked to name their three closest friends in the entire housing project, 65% of the friends they named lived in the same building, although the other buildings were close by.

Patterns of friendships within a building also demonstrated the influence of proximity. Residents tended to like those who lived closest to them within the building: 41% of next-door neighbors said they were close friends, 22% of those who lived two doors apart said they were close friends, and 10% of those who lived on opposite ends of the hall said they were close friends. Proximity increases attraction because of familiarity and exposure. The more exposed we are to something, the more we come to like it (Aronson, Wilson, & Akert, 2002). Interracial attitudes are improved by proximity. Research suggests that the ethnicity of one's roommate, the degree of interracial contact in residence halls, and participation in various types of extracurricular activities are strongly related to the development of interracial friendships (Martin, Tobin, & Spenner, 2014a; Stearns, Buchmann, & Bonneau, 2009).

Another antecedent of interpersonal attraction is similarity. We tend to like and to be attracted to people who are demographically similar to us in terms of socioeconomic status, education, and religion. We also are attracted to those who have values and opinions that are similar to ours (Berscheid, 1985). Similarity increases interpersonal attraction in three ways. First, we think that people who are similar to us will like us. Second, people who are similar to us provide us with some validation of our beliefs and values. Third, we tend to be more negative toward people who are not similar to us in values and beliefs and ascribe more negative values to these people. We also like those who like us. When a person communicates either verbal or nonverbal liking for us, we are more likely to return the affection than when they do not communicate liking for us. This is, in part, because of the self-fulfilling prophecy. When we think another person likes us, our behavior will be consistent with the expectation we feel the person has of us.

Finally, we tend to like persons who are more physically attractive. Physical attraction is especially a factor in initial attraction. This is true for both men and women. Men tend to value physical attractiveness more than women do (Feingold, 1990; Li et al., 2013). However, this may be changing; as women's economic power increases, they also may favor physical attractiveness more so than previously (Fiske, 2014). The importance of physical attractiveness is not limited to heterosexual relationships; it is also seen in lesbian, bisexual, gay, and transgender (LBGT) relationships.

What Is Attractive?

There are some universal opinions of what is beautiful. A meta-analysis (a comparison of many studies) found agreement across many cultures as to what constitutes an attractive face (Cunningham, Barbee, & Pike, 1990; Little, 2014). In the study by Cunningham, Barbee, and Pike, students from different ethnic groups, including Asian, Latino, Black, and White, rated the appearance of women from all of these ethnic groups. Overall, the ratings were consistent in sharing agreement as to what was attractive. In general, faces that are symmetrical are considered more attractive than faces that are not symmetrical. Other features that are considered attractive include youthfulness, averageness of face to others in the population, masculinity or femininity, and faces that look healthy.

Other dimensions used in the evaluation of physical attractiveness are body type, hair, and skin color. Skin color, hair texture, and body weight are attributes in which

African Americans physically differ from other ethnic groups and racial and ethnic differences in how these physical attributes are valued. There is also a great deal of variability among African Americans in these physical characteristics.

Skin Color

Skin color bias has a pervasive impact on life outcomes affecting self-concept, mate choice, and social mobility (Breland-Noble, 2013). As discussed previously, historically, African Americans with light skin have been considered more attractive than those who are darker skinned. Light-skinned African Americans were the offspring of slave masters and enslaved women and were treated better than those who were dark skinned. They were given more household duties as opposed to field duties and had better living conditions. Free Blacks were more likely to be light than dark (Wade, 1996; Wade & Bielitz, 2005). Skin color became a criterion for success and prestige in the African American community. African Americans, along with Whites, considered light skin, White facial features, and straight hair to be more attractive than dark skin, Black features, and kinky hair. In a comprehensive review of studies on skin color bias across the lifespan, Adams et al. (2016) conclude that overall research indicates that darker skin color has negative consequences, including more discrimination, worse health outcomes, lower socioeconomic status, and harsher penalties within the legal system.

It is not surprising that skin color is a factor in attraction. Skin color affects the basic process of categorization. Categorization, in turn, activates stereotypes leading to discrimination and prejudice (Adams et al., 2016) Using a computer categorization task, Maddox and Gray (2002) found that African Americans were categorized based on skin color by both African American and White respondents. Also, in this study, the authors found that African Americans with dark skin were described using more negative and stereotypic traits than were African Americans with light skin. African Americans with light skin were described using more positive and nonstereotypical traits. This study is important because it demonstrates how skin color operating as a basic process for categorization can lead to stereotyping and more negative judgments and decisions about dark-skinned African Americans relative to light-skinned African Americans by African Americans, as well as other racial and ethnic groups.

Watson, Thorton, and Engelland (2010) conducted an experiment to evaluate African Americans' attitudes and perceptions of American female models with light and dark skin in advertisements. In this experiment, 299 African American male students from three universities were presented a photograph of models with medium skin color whose appearance had been digitally manipulated as either light or dark skin. The men were randomly assigned to view one of the manipulated photos and then to rate the model's attractiveness, attitude toward the advertisement, and attitude toward the brand. Findings revealed that African American men rated the model, the brand, and the advertisement significantly higher in the photo with the light-skin manipulation than the photo with the dark-skin manipulation, indicating a continued preference for lighter-skinned females.

In an examination of skin color and its perception among African American females, Wilder and Cain (2011) found participants learned to associate blackness with negativity and lightness with ideal beauty from maternal figures, such as grandmothers, aunts, and mothers. Moreover, these familial figures confirmed, negated, or countered colorist beliefs. Hunter (2005) also revealed the contrasting evaluations of skin color among African American women to be divisive, such that dark skin women resented fair-skinned women and found them to be in competition for the attention of African American men.

There are gender differences in skin color bias. Compared with Black males, Black females have been affected more by their skin color, hair texture, and facial features (Breland-Noble, 2013; Adams et al., 2016). Skin color does not typically advantage (or disadvantage) African American males as much as it does females. According to Wade and Bielitz (2005), many prominent African American male athletes and entertainers are dark skinned with a dominant physical stature. These traits may be used for assessing African American males' attractiveness. Informing this conclusion was Wade's earlier work (1996) in which he surveyed African American men and women and found males with dark skin self-ratings to have higher ratings of sexual attractiveness than males with fair skin (1996).

Hill (2002) used data from the NSBA to determine gender differences in skin color bias with respect to attractiveness. Interviewers were asked for their subjective opinion as to the attractiveness of the person they interviewed. They found that skin color influenced the attractiveness ratings assigned to African American women in a compelling way. The association between skin color and rating of attractiveness was significantly weaker for men.

Preference for females who are light skinned is evident when we see that successful Black males often marry women of lighter skin tone. Movies and television often cast women who are light skinned in the leading love role, whereas women who are dark skinned play the mammy or the comedian. A disproportionate number of television programs and advertisements and popular music (particularly rap) videos feature light-skinned and light-eyed women (Maxwell, Abrams, & Belgrave, 2016; Perkins, 1996). See cover story about how these messages affect the self-image of African American girls and adolescents. These women are presented as desirable and beautiful. In contrast, when darker-skinned women with more African features are presented, they are often portrayed as maternal, belligerent, and lacking sensuality. As noted in the cover story, lyrics of "redbones" and yellowbones" have an effect on the self-image of African American girls and adolescents. Of note, this is changing as there are now more darker-skinned African Americans in contemporary media (e.g., Viola Davis, Tika Sumpter, Gabourey Sidibe, Danielle Brooks).

Hair Texture

Historically, curly and nappy hair has been considered "bad" hair, and long, straight hair has been considered "good" hair. However, this trend is changing somewhat, as reflected in the title of a popular children's book, *Happy to Be Nappy* (hooks, 1999). Today, there are considerably more natural hair care salons, products, and advertisements than in the past. Also, there is more acceptance of the diversity of hairstyles that include straight, curly, twists, braids, locs, Afros, extensions, and weaves. At the same time, many in the business and corporate world believe ethnic hairstyles like braids and locs are unprofessional. On Hampton University's campus, an HBCU, students in the school of business were told not to wear their hair in braids or locs (Hamilton, 2006) or they would risk being kicked out of the MBA program. In a more personal example, a fundraising effort for the first author's son's sports team encouraged parents to donate time working at a large amusement park in return for a contribution to the team. A flyer from this amusement park contained the instructions that locs were not allowed.

Unfortunately, African American women continue to be admonished and to face some bias for wearing natural hairstyles. For example, a Black waitress in training in a restaurant in Toronto, Canada, was sent home because of the way in which she wore her natural locks (Friedman, 2016). In a high school in Louisville, Kentucky, a policy was put in place to ban some types of natural hairstyle (Roberts, Torres, & Brown, 2016). These are just two of many other examples that have surfaced in the media recently about hair texture bias.

Bias against natural or textured hair is implicit as well as explicit. The Perception Institute conducted a study called "The Good Hair Study" with a national sample of 3,475 men and women and 688 women from an online natural hair community (Johnson, Godsil, MacFarlane, Tropp, & Goff, 2016). Findings showed both explicit and implicit bias. The Hair Implicit Association Test (IAT) showed implicit bias toward Black women's textured hair (versus smooth hair). Textured hair is kinky hair. The findings also showed that the majority of participants regardless of race had an implicit bias against Black women's textured hair. However, Black women who were part of an online natural hair community showed a preference for Black women's textured hair. The authors noted a "hair paradox" among Black women. Their explicit attitudes toward textured hair were positive, but the majority still held an implicit bias against textured hair. This study also found that Black women felt pressure to have straight hair for professional reasons.

A good hairdo is important to the self-presentation of many African American women, and African American women spend the necessary time and money on their hair. This includes long hours at the beauty salon, purchase of hair care products, and purchase of synthetic and human hair. Black women spend more money and time on their hair than women in other racial and ethnic groups (Johnson et al., 2016). The versatility of African American hair and the availability of diverse styles and products allow African American women an opportunity to be creative in hairstyle. A good hairstyle is essential to looking good. African American men also appreciate a good haircut and style, and there is wide diversity in their hairstyles also.

Body Weight

In the United States, thinness is considered attractive. Being thin demonstrates access to high-protein and low-fat foods. However, in areas of the world where there is famine and disease, body fat indicates health and attractiveness. In a study of the preference for female body size in 26 countries from 10 world regions, heavy women were judged to be more attractive than slender women in places where food is in short supply (Swami et al., 2010). Also, in 9 of the 10 world regions (the exception was East Asia), males were more likely than females to select a heavier figure as attractive. The same may be true in some cultural groups in the United States, as African American culture differs from White culture in standards of attractiveness regarding body weight.

Research suggests more variability among African Americans in terms of importance of body weight as a standard for attractiveness. African American males, in particular, have demonstrated more flexibility in what is considered an attractive weight. Other research has shown that adolescent and young adult African American women who are high normal weight and overweight are not disadvantaged in terms of dating compared with low normal-weight women, suggesting that very thin African American women may be at a disadvantage with regard to dating (Granberg, Simons, & Simons, 2015). Ali, Rizzo, and Heiland (2013) found that obese White teen girls were less likely to have been in a romantic relationship compared to their nonobese peers. This was not the case with Black obese teens whose relationship experiences did not differ from nonobese Black teens

Reactions to overweight and obese persons also differ between African Americans and Whites. In a national study of adolescents, interviewers rated White and Black girls on physical attractiveness (Ali, Rizzo, & Heiland, 2013). Overweight and obese White girls were less likely to be perceived as physically attractive when compared with normal-weight White girls. Among African American girls, being overweight or obese also lowered attractiveness ratings but not to the extent that it did for White girls. Overall, research suggests that weight is not as important in determining physical attractiveness for African Americans as for other racial and ethnic groups.

There are some ethnic differences in perception of body image and feelings about the body. Breitkopf, Littleton, and Berenson (2007) examined body image among 1,217 low-income White, African American, and Latina women who attended a medical clinic. Participants completed a body image questionnaire, and body mass index (BMI) was obtained from reviewing medical charts. Among African Americans, almost all normal-weight and a number of overweight and obese participants indicated their weight to be normal. In contrast, nearly all overweight and obese Whites and Latinas believed themselves to be overweight. Also, more than 30% of normal-weight Whites and Latinas believed that they were overweight. The authors also found that Whites and Latinas with higher BMIs were more ashamed of their appearance than their lower-BMI peers. This pattern was not observed among African Americans.

Cultural norms among African Americans are that larger body sizes are not considered obese or overweight. In one study, African American women were presented with a Body Image Scale with figures of different body sizes (Lynch & Kane, 2014). They were asked to classify figures as overweight, obese, or too fat and then to select their own body size. Fifty-six percent of overweight women (BMI > 25) and 40% of obese women (BMI > 30) did not classify their body size as overweight, obese, or too fat. In another study, African American men and women whose BMI placed them in the obese category indicated a desire for weight loss; however, almost half of the men and women who were overweight indicated that they would like to maintain their weight (Parham-Payne, 2013).

Research also suggest that weight is not as relevant to body image among African Americans as other physical attributes such as skin tone and hair, discussed previously. Focus groups were held with African American female college students who were asked about unique issues related to African American women's body image and beauty (Awad et al., 2015). The importance of hair to body image was emphasized repeatedly by participants and emerged as the most frequent body image domain for women, with participants reporting a large amount of money and time devoted to their hair. Skin color was another theme echoed by participants, who reported that a preference for light skin still exists and affects the way they think about themselves and others. Another theme was that a thick/toned/curvy body type was ideal for African Americans, and being thin was ideal for White women. Overall, research suggests that body image for African American women is viewed differently than for other racial and ethnic groups.

INTERRACIAL ATTITUDES, FRIENDSHIPS, AND RELATIONSHIPS

The United States is a diverse society. But how often do people of different ethnic and cultural groups interact in friendships and intimate relationships? How do African Americans and other racial and ethnic groups feel about interracial dating and marriage? We address these and related questions next.

Interracial Friendships

Interracial friendships are affected by where people live, work, and go to school. However, even with increased opportunity to live and work in mixed-race settings, the friendships and social networks of Americans remain racially homogenous. For example, among Whites, 91% of the people in their social network are White; 83% of the people in African Americans' social network are African American, and 64% of the people in Hispanics' social network are also Hispanic (Cox, Navarro-Rivera, & Jones, 2016).

What are some of the factors that are associated with interracial friendships among children and adolescents? School environment is one factor. Children attending ethnically diverse schools have more ethnically and racially diverse friends than students attending racially and ethnically homogeneous schools (Killen, Kelly, Richardson, Crystal, & Ruck, 2010; McGlothlin & Killen, 2005). Killen et al. found that European American children attending ethnically diverse public elementary schools were more likely to view racial exclusion as wrong and more likely to estimate that racial segregation occurs than were students enrolled in low-diversity schools (Killen et al., 2010).

Cooperative learning teams in schools in which students are rewarded for group success and not for individual success also seem to encourage cross-race friendships. Studies of cooperative learning teams among schoolchildren show increases in both the quantity and quality of students' interracial friendships.

Similarly to children, adults who participate in cooperative learning teams and work ventures tend to have more interracial friends. Business environments that reward team and group achievement instead of individual achievement foster more interaction and more interracial friendships. The contact hypothesis may explain this relationship.

The contact hypothesis has been used to explain social relationships among different ethnic and racial groups (Emerson et al., 2002). According to contact theory, more interracial contact will lead to greater liking and contact between different ethnic and racial groups. A national sample of 2,561 ethnically and racially diverse Americans was surveyed. The authors found that adults who had earlier interracial contact in schools and neighborhoods were more likely to have more racially and ethnically diverse friends than those who did not have earlier interracial contact in schools and neighborhoods. Also, adults with prior interracial contact were more likely to attend religious congregations that were multiracial, as opposed to uniracial religious congregations, and to be interracially married. These findings held true for Whites, African Americans, and Hispanics but not for Asians. The authors note that even limited prior contact in multiracial settings contribute to contemporary interracial relationships and appear to have important effects on contemporary social ties. The contact hypothesis only leads to increased favorable intergroup relations when contact is positive. Negative contact decreases interracial friendships by increasing anxiety and prejudice (Hayward, Tropp, Hornsey, & Barlow, 2017; Techakesari et al., 2015).

Among college students, those attending schools that are more racially diverse report more interracial friendships (Bowman, 2012). Other factors that support interracial friendship among college students include structural diversity (i.e., number of students of color at the institution), being in diverse friendship groups prior to college, having a roommate who is racially/ethnically different, and diversity education (Goldstein, 2013; Kim, Park, & Koo, 2015). Factors that are negative for interracial friendship include participation in Greek life, especially for White students, and participation in religious student organizations (Kim, Park, & Koo, 2015).

Interracial Romance

Favorable attitudes toward interracial dating and marriage have increased steadily over the past few decades, although there are still some negative attitudes. Interracial dating and marriage vary demographically and geographically. People who live in

California and other states on the West Coast are more likely than persons who live in other parts of the United States to date and marry interracially.

Interracial Dating

In general, studies show fairly high levels of acceptance of interracial dating, with approval of interracial dating higher for others than for self (Lewis & Ford-Robertson, 2010). Acceptance of interracial dating and marriage is especially high among those 18–29 years of age; about 90% of individuals in this age group are accepting of marriage to someone who is not in their racial or ethnic group. African Americans are much more likely to interracially date than to interracially marry (J. Lewis & Ford-Robertson, 2010). Gender is a factor in interracial attitudes and behavior. Men are more likely than women to date interracially (Thomas, Barrie, & Tynes, 2009).

Participation in interracial dating is affected by several factors. One study included ethnically diverse students (N = 1,174) attending five universities that were both historically Black colleges or universities (HBCUs) and predominately White institutions (PWIs) (Field, Kimuna, & Straus, 2013). Participants were asked whether they approved of interracial dating and whether their parents would approve. Approval of interracial dating and marriage for African American/White unions were lower than for Asian American/White unions. Approval of interracial relationships was also lower for African American women than African American men. Finally, approval of interracial relationships was lower at HBCUs than PWIs.

In another study of college students, Stackman, Reviere, and Medley (2016) examined attitudes toward interracial dating among African American male and female college students (N = 387) attending (HBCUs) and (PWIs). A majority (72.6%) of the students reported favorable attitudes toward interracial dating; 11.3% were opposed; 16.1% were undecided. At both HBCUs and PWIs, males reported more favorable attitudes toward interracial dating than females. Females at PWIs had more favorable interracial dating attitudes than those at HBCUs.

Parenting roles and expectations influence whether interracial dating is a choice for children. In many African American families, it is the mother who plays the key role in accepting or not accepting an interracial relationship. In White families, the father is the key parent and sets expectations and norms about relationships, including interracial dating. Women may be more open than men to the relationship choices of their sons and daughters. Because the primary African American parent is more likely to be the mother, this could account for more acceptance of interracial dating among African Americans.

Internet dating sites offer other information about preferences for interracial dating (Sweeney & Borden, 2009). Most Internet daters limit dating to those within their own racial groups. Yancey (2007) found in a national sample of Internet personal advertisements that political conservatism is inversely related to willingness to date regardless of race. Religiosity is inversely related to willingness to interracially date at all, suggesting that political ideology and religiosity both affect interracial dating. Endorsement of multicultural ideological beliefs is associated with increased interracial attraction (Brooks & Neville, 2016).

Interracial Marriages

Until as recently as 1967, interracial marriage in the United States was a felony (Porterfield, 1982). The rate of interracial marriages has increased dramatically over the past 35 years. In 2015, about 1 in 6 (17%) newlyweds were married to a person of a different racial or ethnic group and 1 in 10 married people had a spouse of a different race or ethnicity (Livingston & Brown, 2017). The largest increase in interracial marriages has been for African Americans. In 1980, 5% of African Americans married someone of a different race or ethnicity; in 2015, this had increased to 17%. Asians and Hispanics are most likely to intermarry, with about 29% of Asian newlyweds and 27% of Hispanic newlyweds intermarrying. African American women are much less likely to marry interracially than are African American males.

In 2015, 24% of African American men married outside their race or ethnicity, compared with 12% of African American women (Livingston & Brown, 2017). White male–Black female marriages have traditionally been one of the least common of all possible interracial combinations and were almost nonexistent prior to the 1970s. However, this is changing, and more African American women are beginning to view interracial marriage as an option (Thomas et al., 2009). African Americans are more likely to marry Whites than they are to marry members of other ethnic groups.

In overview, interracial and interethnic marriages among African Americans have become more common than in the past; however, these marriages are fewer than interracial marriages among other ethnic minority groups.

LESBIAN, GAY, BISEXUAL, TRANSGENDER, AND QUEER (LGBTQ) RELATIONSHIPS

On June 26, 2015, same-sex marriage became legal in the United States, and marriage equality was possible for all couples. Research and literature on African American LGBTQ relationships within psychology have been fairly limited. Even more limited has been writings on transgender relationships.

Research on same-sex couples suggests that same-sex couples have long-term and fulfilling relationships and that there are few differences in the relationship outcomes of same-sex and heterosexual couples. Peplau and Fingerhut (2007) summarized research on same-sex relationships and made the following observations: (a) Research has shown that contemporary lesbians and gay men establish enduring intimate relationships and have negated the stereotype that these relationships are inferior to the relationships of heterosexual couples. On assessments of love, satisfaction, and relationship adjustment, same-sex and heterosexual couples are very similar. (b) Research has discredited the myth that same-sex relationships mimic heterosexual marriages by forming "husband" and "wife" roles. Most gay and lesbian couples in the United States share homemaking activities and financial responsibilities rather than dividing them into roles where one partner is the "wife" and the other partner is the "husband." (c) Research on same-sex relationships has contributed a new approach to examining social influence in relationships. For example, studies of heterosexual relationships have shown that men and women use different strategies in relationships. Studies of same-sex relationships show that regardless of gender or sexual orientation, partners with less power in the relationship tend to use strategies such as withdrawal or supplication. Relationship satisfaction and investment influence relationship commitment among same sex couples, as is the case with heterosexual couples (Barrantes, Eaton, Veldhuis, & Hughes, 2017).

Macapagal, Greene, Rivera, and Mustanski (2015) studied relationship development in young LGBTQ couples noting that while there are some similarities, there are also some differences for sexual minority couples. Sexual minority women report that the progression of relationships may be slowed by different levels of being out, along with relationship stress (e.g., pretending to be friends and not partners in public) (Patterson, Ward, & Brown, 2013). Patterson et al. interviewed 36 same-sex couples about their relationship history and progression. They found that while relationship stages and progression were similar to that of heterosexual adults, relationship experiences were shaped by factors such as sexual identity, developmental stage, and gender. For example, similar to heterosexual relationship development, same-sex couples described movement toward more serious phases of their relationship that involved overt symbols of commitment such as engagement. However, same-sex couples' experiences at different stages were impacted by their sexual or gender minority identity. Couples often met during LGBTQ social networks that made known their LGBTQ status, unlike heterosexual cisgender young adults, who do not have to seek out a heterosexual-identified social network. Also compared with heterosexual couples, young same-sex couples may cohabitate for different reasons. Among heterosexual emerging adults, cohabitation tends to come about because of necessity. However, for LGBTQ couples, lack of family support of one's sexual or gender identity affected cohabitation choices. The desire to have children was similar for same-sex and heterosexual couples. However, the options available for having children differed. Participants described plans for family though adoption and medically assisted reproductive technology. These strategies are generally considered optional or alternative for heterosexual couples.

African American Same-Sex Couples

U.S. Census data on African American same-sex couples was compiled at the Williams Institute at the University of California, Los Angeles (Williams Institute, 2013). Some statistics are as follows:

1. Approximately 3.7% of African Americans consider themselves LGBTQ.

2. Nationally 1 in 250 (0.4%) African American households are led by a same-sex couple.

3. Fifty-eight percent of same-sex couples are female.

4. About 34% of African American same-sex couples are raising children.

5. African-American same-sex couples tend to live in areas that have a higher percentage of African Americans.

6. The top-five states with the highest percentages of LGBTQ individuals among the African American adult population include the District of Columbia where 9.7% of African American adults are LGBTQ, New Jersey (6.7%), Michigan (5.6%), New York (5.1%), and North Carolina (4.5%).

African American LGBTQ couples have similar relationships and face similar issues as do non-Black and White LGBTQ couples. However, there are some issues that are unique because of race and sometimes class. Homophobia, double and triple minority status, and fear of disclosure are issues that affect African American LGBTQ couples.

An example of an issue that affects African American same-sex male couples is stereotypes of African American male sexuality. Stereotypes of African American males may carry over to stereotypes of men who have sex with men (MSM). While research has stereotyped Black men as sexually dominant and aggressive in relationships, research on MSMs show these men demonstrate pleasure, affection, and love for their sexual partners (Calabrese, Rosenberger, Schnick, & Novak, 2015).

An online survey was conducted among a racially diverse group of men who indicated that their last sexual encounter was with a male partner (N = 21,905). Participants were asked whether they experienced pleasure, whether they displayed affection, and whether they felt love for their partner. A large majority of Black MSMs who experienced their last sexual event with a male partner felt love for, perceived love from, and verbalized love to that partner. Contrary to Black male stereotypes, Black MSMs did not show a meaningful pattern of difference from other-race MSMs in their likelihood of experiencing pleasure, affection, and love.

LGBTQ relationships have been affected by the Black Church, as the Black Church has been identified as a contributor to homophobia in the African American community (Schulte & Battle, 2004). African Americans were less likely than other racial and ethnic groups to support gay marriage in 2015, notably because of religious beliefs against gay unions (See Table 8.1). Although these beliefs are changing, there is some continued resistance to marriage equality among some religious African Americans. On other topics of gay equality, there are fewer differences between African Americans and other racial and ethnic groups. This is especially so among younger African Americans (see Table 8.1) (Cooper, Cox, Lieneesch, & Jones, 2016).

African American Gay and Lesbian Disclosure

African Americans who are LBGT are less likely than Whites who are LGBTQ to disclose their sexual orientation. Kennamer, Honnold, Bradford, and Hendricks (2000) conducted a study on disclosure among African American and White men. They found that White men were more likely to disclose their sexuality, to have associated with gay and bisexual groups, and to have gay and bisexual friends. The authors also found that as education increased, White men were more likely and African American men were less likely to disclose sexual orientation and association with LGBTQ groups. According to the authors, the difference in disclosure may be due to higher social stigma of being gay in the African American community, which may be exacerbated for men with more education. African American LGBTQ individuals have the added challenge of having to juggle racial and sexual identity during the process of coming out. Sexual orientation may not be discussed even when African American families and communities support racial identity, and racial issues may not be discussed by the LGBTQ community (Trahan & Goodrich, 2015). When families are supportive, that support may be dependent on the relationship being invisible (Greene, 2000). However, most individuals who are LGBTQ do eventually disclose their sexual orientation to close members of their family networks.

TABLE 8.1 ■ Percentage of Respondents Who Report Favoring Gay and Lesbian Couples to Marry Legally	
All Americans	55
All Black Americans	43
Black Americans 18–29	63
Black Protestants	38

Source: Williams Institute (2013).

METHODOLOGICAL AND RESEARCH ISSUES

We discuss two research and methodological issues to consider when studying interpersonal relationships among African Americans. These revolve around (a) the lack of research conducted with African Americans on this topic and (b) conceptualizing and measuring relationship constructs that may not be universally meaningful. Constructs such as communalism may be particularly applicable when conducting research on interpersonal topics with African American populations.

Lack of Research

There has been a voluminous amount of literature and research on interpersonal relations, especially in the field of social psychology. Interpersonal relationships are central to well-being across many domains. Yet there has been fairly limited research on this topic conducted with African American samples. The research that has been done has been sporadic and not integrative. In reviewing literature and research for this book, it was often the case that only limited research could be identified for any given topic. In searching for research on African American or Black love, there were few published empirical studies, although there are voluminous writings in the popular literature on this topic. On the topic of African American LGBTQ relationships, there was scarce research in psychology and the social sciences. The limited research that there was tended to focus on White gay and lesbian couples. Like many studies of heterogeneous couples, studies of same-sex couples have typically recruited younger, well-educated, middle-class, White volunteers. Similarly, the literature on friendship patterns among African American youth revealed only a few studies on this topic. Given the importance of friendships and relationships, there is a need for more systematic study of African American friendships and interpersonal relationships. This research should consider both historical and contemporary factors that affect family, intimate, and other types of relationships.

Conceptualization and Measurement

Like so many other topics in psychology, methods and measures used to assess relationship quality and outcomes may not be as relevant to African Americans. As we have seen in this chapter, variables that are correlated with mate selection, attractiveness, and other aspects of interpersonal relationships vary across racial and ethnic groups. These variables are important when considering theories of interpersonal attraction. For example, as noted previously, partner selection among African Americans is influenced by contextual factors (e.g., community, employment) and institutional policies (e.g., higher incarceration of African American men), as well as personal preferences (e.g., preference for lighter skin color).

Given communal and interpersonal orientations among African Americans, more research on how these values might contribute to meaningful interpersonal relationships is needed. For example, does higher communalism correlate with more relationship satisfaction and quality of relationships? The communalism scale was developed by Boykin et al. (1997) to assess communalism. The scale is described in Chapter 2 but is relevant here as this scale captures the interpersonal orientation style found among people of African descent. Some of the interpersonal relationship–oriented items in this scale include, "I am constantly aware of my responsibility to my family and friends," "I like to help other students learn," and "I place great value on social relations among people." High scores on the scale generally suggest better psychosocial functioning for African Americans, and it would be interesting to see if this extended to relationship quality.

There are also other cultural concepts that might affect interpersonal relationships among African Americans. For example would ethnic identity and spirituality affect relationship choice and satisfaction? And what do African Americans want and look for in friend and partner relationships? We might also consider the concept of loneliness, which is an unfamiliar concept among Africans on the continent. Is loneliness experienced qualitatively differently by African Americans from how it is experienced by other ethnic and racial groups? Finally, we see that the conceptualization of love is different among Africans, at least Ghanaians, than for those living in the United States. These are just a few of the topics where additional research would shed some light on key aspects of interpersonal relationships among African Americans.

BEST PRACTICES FOR IMPROVING RELATIONSHIPS

Positive and healthy relationships are important to social and psychological well-being. We next discuss two culturally enhanced programs for increasing positive interpersonal relationships among African American adolescent girls and boys. These curriculums were developed by the authors of this text and are based on several years of working with African American adolescents.

The 16-session curriculum called Sisters of Nia was designed to increase cultural attributes such as ethnic identity and pride and, while doing so, to increase positive and mutually fulfilling relationships among girls in early adolescence. Positive interpersonal relationships are desired and fulfill many important needs of girls during this age period. At the same time, during this period, girls began to engage in relationally aggressive acts, such as exclusion, gossiping, and taunting. The curriculum developed by the first author and colleagues (Belgrave, Cherry, Butler, & Townsend, 2008) aimed to reduce this relational aggression and to promote positive relationships among girls through activities that bonded girls to each other and to young adult female facilitators. Girls met in small groups designed to facilitate interaction and interdependence. Each session engaged the girls in team-building activities, including activities in which they had to cooperate and work together to solve problems. Two of the sessions were devoted to relationships. In these sessions, girls discussed the meaning of relationships and what it meant to be a sister friend. Girls were rewarded for being cooperative and kind to each other.

To extend the benefits of the lessons learned outside the group, girls were also given homework assignments in which they were to practice being a sister friend. The findings from an evaluation of this curriculum showed increased cultural attributes such as racial identity and more positive relationships, as seen in decreased relational aggression (Belgrave et al., 2004). Anecdotally, our discussion with teachers and staff at the school where the programs have been implemented confirm positive changes in interpersonal relationships among the girls. Teachers have reported that those who participated in the program were more likely to be kind to and to look out for one another. Other areas in which interpersonal relationships might be important are with regard to increased interracial attitudes and increased tolerance for different groups. Findings on some of these strategies are discussed in Chapter 4.

A companion curriculum to Sisters of Nia, Brothers of Ujima, was developed to increase positive relationships and prosocial behavior among African American boys (Belgrave et al., 2012). This curriculum for preadolescent and adolescent boys uses culturally grounded methods to bring African American boys together to promote appropriate interpersonal skills and prosocial behaviors. The aim is to have the program not only increase positive and prosocial behavior within the peer group but also to have these behaviors extend to the family and community. The curriculum used the Principles of Nguzo Saba (Seven Principles of Kwanza), African proverbs, and supportive adult males as the means with which to inculcate cultural values. Older males model and provide opportunities for the boys to practice positive prosocial behavior and resist problem behaviors.

CRITICAL ANALYSIS

One of the challenges in writing this chapter was to decide on what to cover, given the large array of subtopics under the broad topic of interpersonal relationships. Interpersonal relationships cover diverse topics, ranging from mate selection to interracial dating to friendships among African American adolescents. At the same time, there was limited research and literature (at least in the psychological literature) on several aspects of interpersonal relationships among African Americans. Many of the studies cited were conducted on smaller subpopulations, and the results cannot be generalized to the broader population of African Americans. For example, most of the studies on interracial attitudes and dating have been conducted on the West Coast, where interracial dating is more common. Also, most studies regarding attitudes toward interracial dating have been conducted using college student samples.

There was very little information on African American LGBTQ relationships in the psychology literature, as few papers could be identified. Although there has been more support of marriage equality and rights of LGBTQ individuals, same-sex marriage remains somewhat of a divisive topic among African Americans, especially older and religious African Americans. Just as it is important to consider cultural aspects of interpersonal relationships among African Americans, it is also important to recognize that cultural aspects of relationships differ for same-sex and straight couples. The limited research there is on this topic has been conducted with White couples; much more research is needed given the intersectionality of being both a sexual and an ethnic minority.

One area for future research and discussion is the use of the Internet for initiating and maintaining relationships. Chat rooms and sites such as Facebook are frequently used by all Americans. We need to find out how this technology may be changing the fundamental way in which friendships and other types of relationships are initiated and maintained. It would be interesting to understand more about the use of the Internet for connecting with others and how it affects quality of life. An additional question would be how the benefits (and possible adverse consequences) of relationships and contacts initiated over the Internet differ from the more traditional relationships. Similarly, online dating among African Americans has only received limited attention in the scholarly literature, and more research is needed. Anecdotal evidence suggests that there may be some differences in online dating for different ethnic and racial groups. Research on these topics would enable us to explore and understand the development of relationships and friendships among African Americans in a more comprehensive fashion.

Due to space limitations we did not cover close and intimate relationships such as marriage in detail. Some statistics were provided in Chapter 5. But the dynamics of African American male and female relationships is an important topic, especially considering the low marriage and high divorce rate among African Americans. Similarly, we did not cover the negative side of intimate relationships, such as partner and dating violence and rape. Some of the literature and research on this topic is covered in Chapter 15.

Finally, more research and prevention programming are needed to promote positive friendships and interpersonal relationships. If communal and interpersonal relationship orientations are core attributes found among people of African descent, then programs that foster these relationships should be beneficial. The curricula developed by the authors for improving interpersonal relationships among African American adolescent boys and girls would seem to be a step in the right direction.

Summary

The proverb "One finger cannot lift up a thing" illustrates the need for others in our lives. Relationships with others, including friendships and romantic relationships, have been the focus of this chapter. All humans have a need to belong, to affiliate, and to be in relationships with others. Relationships can be exchange or communal. In exchange relationships, people give benefits with the expectation that they will receive comparable benefits in return. Communal relationships are those in which the person feels responsible for the well-being of the other person. Relationships among Africans may be described as communal. Communal relationships consider the importance of the community and include mutual aid, caring for others, interdependence, solidarity, reciprocal obligation, and social harmony. Ubuntu also describes African relationships.

Close friendships are rewarding, with many benefits. Friendships are important to African American youth just as they are to members of other ethnic groups. Friendships offer feelings of trust, intimacy, and instrumental support. There are gender differences in friendships with women having fewer and more intimate friends than men. The social networks of African Americans tend to have more family and kin and fewer friends relative to other racial and ethnic groups. African American adolescent boys who are not involved in interpersonally rewarding friendships may show bravado attitudes, and girls may engage in relational aggression.

A romantic partner is that one person in the world to whom you feel closest. An intense close relationship may be described as love. There are two main types of love: passionate and companionate. There are cultural differences in how love is conceptualized, with the Western conceptualization of love being more passionate than companionate. Africans' view of love is that it means caring for others. African American women have fewer potential mates from which to select than do African American men or women from other ethnic groups. Therefore, African Americans do not always subscribe to the same norms as other ethnic groups for mate selection.

We are attracted to individuals who are in close proximity to us, who are similar to us demographically, and who have similar values and beliefs. We also like people who are physically attractive. There is agreement across cultural groups as to what constitutes an attractive face. Historically, African Americans with light skin have been considered more attractive than those with darker skin. There is also implicit and explicit bias against coarse or textured hair. Ethnic differences in perception of ideal body weight also exist. African Americans are more likely to endorse a heavier ideal body weight and less likely to stigmatize overweight persons.

Most Americans approve of interracial dating, with fewer approving of interracial marriage. African American women are less likely than African American men to date and marry outside their racial and ethnic group. Research has shown that the relationship quality of same-sex and heterosexual couples does not differ, for the most part. Marriage equality was achieved in 2015; however, some African Americans continue to oppose marriage equality, especially older and more religious African Americans. More research is needed on the topic of interpersonal relationships among African Americans, and more programs to improve relationships, including friendships and romantic and intimate relationships, are needed.

9

COGNITION, LEARNING, AND LANGUAGE

Knowledge kept to oneself is as useless as a candle burning in a pot.

—Oromo proverb

LEARNING OBJECTIVES

- To be able to define learning, cognition, language, and related terms

- To understand knowledge acquisition from an African-centered perspective

- To become familiar with some features of cognition and learning styles of African Americans

- To become more knowledgeable of Ebonics and Black English and how it differs from Standard American English

- To become more knowledgeable of how to improve cognitive skills among African Americans

- To learn how Black English can be used to increase reading and writing skills of African American children

DO YOU SPEAK D.C.? GEORGETOWN LINGUISTS STUDY WASHINGTON-AREA LANGUAGE

BY REBECCA SHEIR

WAMU 88.5, November 30, 2012

Washington, D.C. area residents share a number of things: a special appreciation for a good half-smoke, knowledge of walking on the left/standing on the right, and a love/hate relationship with the Beltway. But do Washingtonians share a particular way of speaking? Is there such thing as a specifically D.C. accent, dialect or language?

(Continued)

(Continued)

Researchers at Georgetown University's Linguistics Department are trying to answer that very question, through The Language and Communication in the D.C., Metropolitan Area Project (LCDC).

Project members have interviewed nearly 150 Washingtonians, and listened to recorded interviews from the 1960s, to get a clearer idea of how people in the D.C. area talk. And not just how people talk, says PhD student Anastasia Nylund, but "how people tell stories, what people tell stories about, and how people use language to sort of situate themselves in the social life of the city."

Let's start with that first one: "how people talk." Nylund says she's found that when you ask folks in D.C. if they speak with an accent, "A lot of people will say, 'Well, I don't really have an accent.'"

But, Nylund adds, they also say they're often perceived as having one.

"I've got people telling me, 'some people think I'm from the south, and other people think that I'm from the north. And I'm wondering where they get that from, because I'm a Washingtonian.' Or 'People hear a southern drawl, and maybe it's there. But I don't hear it. I'm not southern; I'm a Washingtonian.'"

And that, Nylund says, shows how closely language is connected with identity. And ever since D.C. became the nation's capital in 1791, its language and identity have been richly influenced by African American culture.

"Some people would say that Washington speech is African American speech," she says. "And the most probably distinctive is some of the local words. Like 'bama,' for [an] uncool person. 'Jont,' for pretty much anything; any noun can be replaced with 'jont.' 'Cised'—to be cised about something: psyched."

But as Anastasia Nylund's colleague, Patrick Callier attests, the study of African American English in D.C., goes beyond words, since he's been studying how sound systems in African American English in D.C. have been changing over time, particularly, certain vowels. "I looked at the pronunciation of the vowel in 'glide' or 'pry' or 'price,'" Callier explains. "And in traditional southern vernacular, be it white or African American, that would be pronounced like 'glahd' or 'prah.'"

But as he and his team have analyzed LCDC's archival recordings from the 1960s, "basically what we've seen over time is a slight decrease in overall use of this 'prah' pronunciation among African Americans, particularly among African American women."

Patrick Callier may have the vowels covered, but Jessi Grieser another sociolinguist PhD at Georgetown, is all about the consonants. In particular: TH.

"So, saying 'dat' instead of 'that,'" she explains, "and how much that comes out." Grieser says a number of factors seem to affect how much it comes out among speakers, such as "who they're talking to, what they're talking about, whether the person they're talking to is also white or black, all these sorts of things." Grieser recalls interviewing this one woman about her traditionally African American neighborhood, and how she thinks it's changing. "As she was talking about her neighborhood becoming integrated, she started using the more standard English as opposed to African American English variants. So she was using 'dat' and 'de' and all these things as the neighborhood was black. And as the neighborhood became whiter, so did her speech." Examples like these, Anastasia Nylund says, demonstrate how fluid language can be, as it reflects the ever-changing social, cultural, political and economic landscapes of Washington, D.C. "Language isn't something that just happens," Nylund says. "It's not just something that we're born with. It's something that we use creatively as we go through our lives." And the beauty of something like The Language and Communication in the D.C., Metropolitan Area Project, she says, is how it can capture some of that language, and . . . she and her colleagues hope . . . bring about a greater understanding of this dynamic and complex place we call home.

Source: Sheir (2012).

INTRODUCTION, DEFINITIONS, AND HISTORICAL FRAMEWORK

The news story describes unique aspects of language among African Americans in the predominately African American city of Washington, D.C. Black English and Ebonics are discussed in this chapter, along with cognition and language. Learning, cognition, and language are products of one's socialization. The socialization experiences of African Americans are influenced by both African and American cultures. The process of acculturating enslaved Africans left its indelible mark on current language structures—as in the case of Black English and its modern-day counterpart, Ebonics, both of which are based on English and African language structures. Common patterns of learning, cognition, and language among African Americans are not genetically predetermined, but they are influenced by culture and the socialization process.

Differences between African Americans and other ethnic groups in learning, cognitive patterns, and language should not be interpreted as deficits in either group. For example, African American English, African American Vernacular English, Black English, and Ebonics are often negatively contrasted with Standard American English (SAE). Ebonics may be associated with low socioeconomic status or lack of education. Some consider it a "ghetto" language. In fact, many African Americans believe Ebonics or Black English to be inferior; the debate about whether Ebonics should be recognized as an acceptable language is as prevalent among African Americans as it is among non–African Americans. Yet the unique features of Ebonics have evolved from legitimate language structures used by speakers from both Africa and the United States (Rickford & King, 2016). According to Kretzschmar (2008), the struggle over the legitimacy of Ebonics is, in part, due to contrasting opinions between linguists and the lay public about what constitutes a language because the lay public is not aware of what constitutes a language.

Ebonics is the language of communication among many African Americans in the United States. In this chapter, we review the unique features of African American language, cognition, and learning and examine how they interact. Cognitive patterns and language begin at an early age. Therefore, much of the research on cognition and language has been conducted with children; consequently, most of the studies referenced in this chapter focus on children. First, we analyze the relevant terms and historical perspectives on the study of cognition and learning among African Americans. Next, we discuss unique aspects of African American cognition and learning, beginning with historical perspectives. Then, features of African American language are discussed. This is followed by a discussion of methodological and research issues and best practices. The chapter ends with a critical analysis and a summary.

Definitions

Cognition is the process of thinking or mentally processing information. Information may take the form of images, concepts, words, rules, or symbols (Coon, 1997). Cognitive functions include attention, perception, thinking, judging, decision making, problem solving, memory, and linguistic ability (Gall, Beins, & Feldman, 1996). Learning is the process through which experience causes permanent change in knowledge or behavior (Woolfolk, 1998). Simply put, learning is the cognitive process of acquiring knowledge (Colman, 1994). Language is a fundamental learning tool. Language is a collection of words and/or symbols and rules of use that support thinking and communication (Coon, 1997).

African American Cognition: Historical Perspectives

Historically, within psychology, the study of cognition among African Americans has examined cognitive and intellectual differences between African Americans and Whites. Many of the studies conducted in psychology in the 19th and 20th centuries focused on these differences. For the most part, studies found that African Americans were inferior to Whites in their performance of many cognitive tasks, including performance associated with general intelligence and perceptual fluency, as well as in analysis and synthesis of information. A study discussed in Chapter 1 is representative of the type of research done during this early period. Peterson (1923) tested White and Negro children using group intelligence and individual learning tests. He found significant race differences: White 8-year-old children scored higher than Negro 10-year-old children on both group and individual tests. Peterson concluded that these differences pointed to inferior intellect rather than low socioeconomic status among the Negro children because 60% of the White 8-year-olds came from poor sections of the city, while 97% of the Negro 10-year-olds came from one of the best Negro schools in the city.

He reported that about 83% of the Whites were smarter than the Negroes and that only 15% to 18% of the Negroes were as smart as the Whites. According to Peterson, differences between the two groups were most notable on tasks that required abstract and logical thinking. Based on the finding that Negroes did not possess abstract and logical thinking, he recommended that there be less of this type of education for Negro children. Peterson did not consider that although the Negro children may have been at one of the best Negro schools in town, there were still substantially fewer resources at these Black schools than there were at the poor White schools.

In psychology, a voluminous amount of research has been written on differences in intelligence and other cognitive tests between African Americans and Whites. Some of this research is reviewed in Chapter 6. This research show that African Americans score lower than Whites on intelligence tests. In this chapter, we discuss some of the differences in cognitive and learning styles that might account for these differences, considering that the methods of instruction in the United States favor learning styles that might be less conducive to the learning styles of African American students (Carter, Hawkins, & Natesan, 2008; Durodoye & Hildreth, 1995; Rouland, Matthews, Byrd, Meyer, & Rowley, 2014).

Also, although most work continues to exclude comparisons with or considerations of African Americans and other ethnic and cultural groups in the United States (e.g., Asian Americans, Latinos, Middle Eastern Americans), some progress has been made in methods used for studying differences between Blacks and Whites. This work has also focused on evaluating the unique features of African American language and cognition and what the implications of these differences are within academic environments, including institutions of higher learning. The unique features of cognition among African Americans affect how knowledge is acquired and used and thus affect the group's learning styles. These unique features are discussed next.

The Acquisition of Knowledge

The acquisition of knowledge and how knowledge is used varies according to culture. Myers (1988, 2009) contrasts a Eurocentric view with an Africentric view of knowledge acquisition. According to Myers, the Eurocentric view of knowledge assumes that external, or objective, understanding is the basis of all knowledge. From this perspective, knowledge is acquired by observing the external environment. Counting and measuring are ways of acquiring this type of knowledge. The process by which learning goals are met focuses on that which is measurable, repeatable, and reproducible. Knowledge acquisition from a Eurocentric perspective would be considered as valid and true if that knowledge is derived from measuring, counting, and quantifying information. Knowledge derived this way is considered valid if it is considered objective. From this perspective, learning goals rely heavily on some form of technology or established social or scientific system of evaluation. The cultural system that supports this type of knowledge acquisition is more likely to link self-worth and value to extrinsic criteria that are measurable, such as the amount of money one makes, the level of education one has attained, and the affluence of the neighborhood in which one lives.

In contrast to a Eurocentric approach to knowledge acquisition, an Africentric framework places the origins of knowledge within an intrapersonal and social context (see Chapter 2). From an Africentric view, Myers (2009) posits that self-knowledge is the basis of all knowledge: "The Afrocentric epistemology starts out assuming the interrelatedness of all things and that whatever you believe is, is for you, given [*sic*] your conceptual system" (Myers, 1985, p. 36). Recognition of one's own perceptions, values, and feelings is necessary for knowledge acquisition. Knowledge is subjective and is based on each person's perspective.

Within an Africentric framework, knowledge that is derived from individuals with whom one has positive interpersonal relationships has value over and beyond knowledge that is generated by experts or published in established media. On this point, Myers writes, "The highest value lies in the interpersonal relationship between man/woman. . . . Self knowledge being the basis of all knowledge, the unconditional positive regard for the natural order must begin within and be generated outwardly, manifesting at a critical point in terms of interpersonal relations among people" (Myers, 1985, pp. 36–37). Making meaning of the world clearly means two different things from Eurocentric and Africentric frameworks.

More than 35 years ago, Kochman discussed how differences in perceptions of knowledge acquisition can create conflict between African Americans and Whites. In his book *Black and White Styles in Conflict*, Kochman (1981) discusses differences in how Black and White students view the truth and authority of an idea. As a college professor, Kochman had observed that White students were likely to regard information as true or authoritative if it had been published or put forth by an expert. Furthermore, White students were likely to present their ideas in an impersonal way. For these students, the merits of the idea and the credibility of its original source established its authenticity. White students did not see themselves as personally responsible for the idea, and their obligations were limited to the presentation of the idea. The merits of the ideas were independent of who was presenting the idea. On the other hand, among Black students, attention was focused on who in the classroom presented the idea. Kochman's Black students considered it important to have a personal opinion on an issue; they believed that the value and truth of the idea presented was linked to the presenter. Black students wanted to know that the presenter cared about the idea enough to have a personal opinion. Thus, if the presenter was passionate about the idea, more weight was given to its validity than if the presenter was neutral. Along the same lines, if the presenter had positive interpersonal relationships with class members, more weight was given to the idea.

Kochman (1981) further observed that differences in establishing the authority of information often produced conflict between Black and White students. For example, White students would make statements they believed to be true because of who said them and where they were published. Black students would view these statements in light of their own personal opinions and would challenge White students to either agree or disagree with the statements. Because White students did not feel that they had to agree or disagree, they were seen by Black students as copping out and not being willing to give their own opinions. White students, on the other hand, saw Black students as being too personally involved and not able to give an objective opinion of the idea. Although Kochman's work was published some time ago, similar patterns may still be seen today.

Bell (1994) identifies two features of a cultural model of knowledge acquisition among African Americans. Her cultural model assumes that attention is paid to both affect and symbolism. The affect dimension captures the preference for social, personal, and spiritual aspects of knowledge acquisition. Consistent with Kochman's observation, knowledge is acquired within the context of social and personal relationships. One's spiritual beliefs also play a role in knowledge acquisition. Here, learning is linked to one's belief that there is spiritual significance to acquiring knowledge. Similarly, Obasi and Smith (2009) acknowledge the role of spirituality in knowledge acquisition. They describe key features of African epistemology (e.g., how knowledge is acquired) and note that knowledge acquisition is not limited to space, time, and the five senses but that spiritual mediums in the forms of prophecy, telepathy, and dreams are all ways in which knowledge can be obtained about the past, present, and future. Knowledge is arrived at from active participation and experiences in the universe.

The other dimension of knowledge acquisition described by Bell involves the symbolic dimension. This dimension captures the conceptual organization of information for the learner. This dimension is rational. It recognizes that the analytical approach to knowledge acquisition co-occurs with the affective approach.

The early work of Kochman, Myers, and Bell suggests that there are variations among African Americans and other ethnic groups in how knowledge is acquired. These variations are assumed to be due to socialization practices and are believed to affect learning.

COGNITIVE STYLES

Cultural variations in cognitive style assume that individuals attend to and process information from the environment in ways consistent with their cultural group (Hilliard, 1992; Watkins, 2002). The majority of the research conducted on cognitive styles has been done in the field of cross-cultural psychology. This work has shown that the cognitive style of individuals from collective cultures, such as those found in Asia and Africa, differ from the cognitive style of individuals from individualistic cultures, such as the United States and Great Britain (Nisbett & Miyamoto, 2005; Varnum, Grossmann, Kitayama, & Nisbett, 2010). Research on cognitive styles also suggests that the cognitive style of African Americans and other ethnic minorities differs from that of Whites. However, it is important to note that some research has found few differences in cognitive style by ethnicity (Tomes, 2008).

Barbara Shade (1991, 1997) has written about the unique ways in which African Americans process and analyze information in their environment. Her analyses of the cognitive style of African Americans share similarities with analyses of cognitive style patterns found among individuals from collective cultures (Varnum et al., 2010). Shade's analyses of cognitive patterns among African American youth address the type of stimuli that are attended to, the sensory channels that are used, and how information is integrated and applied. Given the voluminous amount of stimuli within our environment, it is not possible to attend to all or most of it, so we select the information most relevant to us. Culture and socialization determine what is relevant. Studies show that African Americans and Whites attend to dissimilar types of stimulus information. Some of the work of Shade and colleagues is reviewed next.

Attention to Social and Interpersonal Stimuli

African American children's perception of their environment shows that they usually attend more to social and interpersonal aspects than to physical aspects of their environment. In a classroom setting, African American children are more likely to attend to the teacher or to each other than to aspects of the physical environment, such as desks, blackboard, and chairs (Hale-Benson, 1986). A preference for the social over the physical environment may be socioculturally determined. This preference may be due, in part, to living in an urban environment, home to a large percentage of African Americans (Shade & Edwards, 1987).

Stimuli are abundant in urban environments, so one must choose that to which one will attend. Social stimuli, in contrast to physical stimuli, are more likely to be personally relevant. Rewards and punishments can be received from others, who can either help us to achieve or prevent us from achieving our goals. Another reason for the preference among African Americans for social stimuli over physical stimuli is that people of African descent tend to place value on communalism and relationships (see Chapter 2).

People who are more in tune with their social environment are more likely to be sensitive to facial expressions and the emotions they convey. Being in tune with emotions of others is linked to social competence (Glanville & Nowicki, 2002). Sensitivity to emotions expressed nonverbally has a functional origin for African Americans in the United States and Blacks around the world. Under oppressive and discriminatory conditions, the ability to detect emotional states was beneficial. During slavery, in particular, sensitivity to nonverbal cues was helpful to slaves who could not communicate verbally with Whites. Some research suggests that African Americans are better than European Americans in reading facial emotions (Shade & Edwards, 1987). However, other research has found no ethnic differences and has shown that there is a preference for better understanding of own-race emotions rather than emotions from other races (Yankouskaya, Humphreys, & Rotshtein, 2014).

Sensory Preference

African Americans differ from Whites not only in what is attended to in the physical environment but also in their preference for certain sensory channels. Within the United States, most information is transmitted via the visual channel. However, the visual channel may not be the only preferred modality for African Americans (Shade, 1991, 1997). Studies suggest that African Americans may prefer auditory (hearing) and tactile (touching) channels when receiving information. We will return to this when we discuss the concept of verve as a preference for multiple stimuli in learning styles (Cunningham & Boykin, 2004). Consequently, presenting information in auditory as well as other sensory modes may lead to more effective learning for African Americans (Grace, 2004).

African American children may prefer to use kinesics or movement in learning contexts (Carter et al., 2008). Later in the chapter, we discuss studies of movement and rhythm among African American children and the implications of movement and rhythm on learning.

Holistic Approach to Information Organization and Analysis

There are also preferences among different cultural groups for the manner in which information is organized and analyzed. To better understand these preferences, a distinction is made between a holistic approach and an elemental (or analytical) approach to how information is organized and analyzed.

A holistic approach organizes information relationally—that is, by how bits of information belong together or by the connection that stimuli have to each other. An elemental approach to organizing information considers the commonality of stimuli. For example, consider the following social stimuli in which a decision has to be made as to which two of the three stimuli belong together: a student, a teacher, and a principal. An elemental approach to organizing this information might pair the teacher with the principal because they are both adults and school staff. A holistic approach to organizing this information might link the student with the teacher since the teacher is responsible for teaching the student. Some African Americans demonstrate a preference for integrating information using a holistic approach rather than an elemental, piecemeal approach. In the next section, we discuss analytical and relational learning styles, which parallel the contrasts between the elemental and holistic approaches.

In summary, African American children likely attend to multistimuli and especially social stimuli. They also may prefer receiving information via auditory and tactile channels, along with visual channels. Some may be likely to organize information more holistically rather than in a piecemeal fashion. These preferences are socioculturally and not biologically determined.

LEARNING STYLES

As noted previously, the process by which information is acquired is culturally determined. Self and relational considerations influence the ways in which African Americans learn most effectively. African American learning styles are likely influenced by the learning styles transposed from communities in Africa, along with the influence of the African American family and Church (Durodoye & Hildreth, 1995). Most of the research on learning styles have been conducted with children and in the field of education

Unfortunately, there has not been significant contributions of research on learning styles of African American children over the past 30 years. Dr. Janice Hale (2016), who wrote the seminal book (*Black Children: Their Roots, Culture, and Learning Styles*) on learning styles of African American children in 1982, commented,

> Most of the scholarship that is produced by African American scholars is in the form of dissertations. . . . The most glaring omission as I review the scholarship that has been produced is that the scientific foundation has not been created in 30 years to support this area of inquiry. The science is not there. (p. 445)

Bell (1994) contrasts two learning styles—the analytical learning style and the relational learning style (see Table 9.1). The analytical learning style is similar to the elemental way of organizing information, and the relational learning style is akin to the holistic style for integrating information. Although there is variability within all ethnic groups, some African Americans may have learning styles that are more relational, and European Americans may have learning styles that are more analytical. Because analytical learning is more Western and reflects the learning style of the majority, some may view relational learning as inferior to analytical learning. Differences in learning styles have implications for how students are taught, how they perform, and whether they are successful in educational settings. However, these different styles should not be considered better or worse but simply different.

TABLE 9.1 ■ Definitions and Classroom Applications of Learning Styles	
Relational	**Analytical**
Field Self-Centeredness Learning by orienting self toward social and personal cues in learning situations and a greater interest in people than nonpeople.	**Stimulus Centeredness** Learning by focusing on features of stimuli and emotional distancing or objectivity from the stimulus object.
Field Dependence Learning by attending to the whole environment and focusing on integrating all stimulus material.	**Field Independence** Learning by rule-based categorization with a preference for individualistic problem solving and tendency to attend to one aspect of the environment.
Spontaneity Learning by responding more immediately to stimulus material rather than responding in a systematic way.	**Reflectivity** Learning by spending time reflecting on stimuli and processing information in a systematic way.
Examples of application in classroom	*Example of application in classroom*
• Students working in a group to solve a problem. • Asking students to focus on every aspect of the situation or problem. • Giving students the opportunity to provide their immediate responses to a problem. • Discussing events that directly affect students.	• Students working independently to solve a problem. • Asking students to focus on the major issue or problem. • Giving students time to reflect upon and systematically approach and solve problem. • Discussing events devoid of students' personal experiences.

Analytical Learning Style

In Western culture, knowledge is acquired through rational and analytical methods. A set of rules by which information is attended to and organized is used. Stimulus centeredness, field independence, and reflectivity are chief components of the analytical learning style. Table 9.1 provides definitions, examples, and applications of components of the analytical learning style and the relational learning style.

Stimulus Centeredness

Stimulus centeredness means that the attributes of a stimulus object, rather than personal social features, determine how knowledge is acquired about that object. For example, a child might learn that a cat is an animal by looking at a picture of a cat while repeating a number of times that the cat is an animal.

The focus on stimulus features over personal or social features is associated with an emotional or affective distancing or objectivity from the stimulus object. A person using an analytical learning style can acquire knowledge without attending to the social context. This kind of learning separates or inhibits feelings when information is processed. Technologies like distance and Internet learning, which do not include an interpersonal aspect, would be appropriate for those with this learning preference. Learning void of an interpersonal context might not be preferred by some African Americans. For example, in one study, 174 African American students (age ranged from 7 to 16) showed negative attitudes toward online learning reporting anxiety and lack of confidence, although these same students had positive attitudes toward use of computers (Okwumabua, Walker, Hu, & Watson, 2011).

Another study on preferences for distance education was conducted at HBCUs (General Accounting Office [GAO], 2003; cited in Rovai, Gallien, & Wighting, 2005). Distance learning involves no face-to-face contact between student and teacher. The study found that only about half of HBCUs offer distance education to undergraduates. The reason HBCUs reported that they did not use distance learning was teachers' preference for teaching face to face. Another study (Smith, 2011) reported a reluctance on the part of some HBCU leaders to embrace online education, noting that 78% of respondents at HBCUs believed that students need more discipline to succeed in an online course. Furthermore, 70% of faculty members at HBCUs believe that there are higher costs to develop online courses, and 60% do not accept online instruction by faculty. However, given that HBCUs have historically provided an education to students who otherwise would not have had it, Smith urges these institutions to be responsive to the need to offer online courses. More recent online technology has created possibilities for teachers and students to engage with each other in more personal ways. Additional research relevant to African Americans' preferences or lack of for online learning is warranted.

In terms of student preferences for e-learning, some research suggests that field-independent learners (discussed next) who also learn through focusing on stimulus centeredness show a greater preference for e-learning than field-dependent learners. Sözcü, İpek, and Kınay (2016) examined differences between field-dependent and field-independent university students in Turkey and found that field-independent learners preferred e-learning and distance education courses more than field-dependent learners.

Field Independence

Field independence is another aspect of the analytical learning style. Field independence is a cognitive style that includes rule-based categorization of objects; preferences for individualistic problem solving; formal, rule-based, logical reasoning; and individual responsibility (Nisbett, Peng, Choi, & Norenzayan, 2001). Learners who are field independent focus on the parts rather than the whole when information is processed. For example, a classroom is seen as individual components (e.g., students, teacher, books, desks) rather than globally as a classroom. When this learning style is used, attention to any one aspect of the environment is facilitated. Individuals who are field independent are able to impose organization and structure to relatively unstructured environments, whereas people with a field-dependent cognitive style tend to have a lesser ability to distinguish figures from the background. While variations within cultures exist, people from a given culture typically share the tendency to be either high or low in field independence (Gibson, 2003). People from cultures that are more individualistic (e.g., United States, Western Europe) tend to be more field independent (Triandis, 1989; Witkin & Goodenough, 1977).

Cultural differences in learning styles also include variations in family and child-rearing practices that are associated with differences in field independence (Berry, 1992; Engelbrecht & Natzel, 1997). Cultures and families that encourage autonomy, personal responsibility, and individual achievement tend to have a more field-independent cognitive style. These practices focus on the autonomy of the individual and personal agency. Attention to specific objects in the environment is discrete; objects are viewed as having a starting and ending point (Nisbett et al., 2001). People in these cultures are viewed as independent agents, and an object is viewed as separate from its context. Although there is variability, in general, the learning styles of African Americans may be less field independent than those of Whites (Bell, 1994; Shade, 1997; Rouland et al., 2014). However, more recent research on field independence among African Americans is needed given the context in which African Americans are socialized.

Reflectivity

Another aspect of the analytical learning style is reflectivity. Those with a reflective learning style spend more time and energy reflecting and processing information; they do this in a sustained and systematic way. People with a reflective learning style think about a concept, experience, or activity and then evaluate it (Jordi, 2011). Only after a process of reflection and evaluation will these learners make a decision or integrate information. One study found that reflective students used independent study more, listened more actively and carefully to others, and used previously acquired information more frequently (Alghasham, 2012). Analytical learners who are reflective may make fewer mistakes when problem solving because of the cautious manner in which they process information.

There may also be a higher tolerance of stimulus repetitiveness among analytical learners. For example, a point could be repeated several times for an analytical learner without the message disinteresting the learner. Much of the learning that takes place within educational institutions in this country assumes an analytical learning style. Students are encouraged to be independent learners, and a goal of education is to have students learn how to access and use information on their own. Students are taught to be objective processors of information and not to let their personal feelings influence what they learn. Furthermore, they are taught to process information reflectively by carefully considering all information prior to making a decision. For some African American students, this environment may not always be conducive to learning.

Relational Learning Style

The relational learning style is characterized as holistic processing of information. There is a preference for field self-centeredness (rather than stimulus centeredness), field dependence (rather than field independence), and spontaneity (rather than reflectivity) (Bell, 1994; Ibarra, 2001). See Table 9.1.

Field Self-Centeredness

Self-centeredness is an orientation toward social and personal cues in learning situations in which social features of the environment are used to process information (Bell, 1994; Shade, 1997). To put it another way, the relational learner who relies on self-centeredness is more interested in people than nonpeople. Here, the relationship that a person (e.g., a student) has with the information provider (e.g., a teacher) may influence whether the individual listens and learns. This is akin to what Kochman (1981) observed decades ago among his Black students: The credibility of information presented was linked to the presenter.

A self-centered learner is more motivated to acquire knowledge that can be applied to addressing or solving social problems rather than to learn simply for the sake of knowledge. For example, if a self-centered learner is learning about theories of poverty, information on ways in which poverty might be alleviated will help these learners to master the materials.

Field Dependence

Field dependence is characterized by the tendency to perceive and process stimulus material holistically. Field-dependent learners may be described as less analytical, less attentive to detail, more socially oriented, and more sensitive to criticism and feedback from others (Berry, 2004; Miyamoto, Nisbett, & Masuda, 2006). Stimulus material and problems are processed by attending to features of the stimulus materials in an integrated way. Using the previous example, a discussion of theories of poverty, devoid of attention to the cultural, historical, policy, experiential, and personal context of poverty, would not be as useful for the field-dependent learner as the field-independent learner.

Field-dependent learners are aware of what is going on in the social context in which they acquire knowledge (Engelbrecht & Natzel, 1997). People from more collectivist cultures (African, Asian, and Hispanic/Latino) tend to be more field dependent. As with field independence, field-dependent cognitive styles affect family and child-rearing practices. Cultures that value conformity, social obligation, reverence, and respect for elders tend to have a more field-dependent learning style because these practices focus on harmony, interdependence, and collective agency. Among field-dependent learners, attention is directed toward all attributes of the environment, and objects in the environment are continuous, overlapping, and interrelated (Nisbett et al., 2001). While there are variations, overall, African Americans and other ethnic minority groups in the United States may be more field dependent than Whites.

Spontaneity

Spontaneity is a preference for responding to the obvious and prominent aspects of stimulus material. This response style compared with the reflective response style is more immediate and not constrained by an in-depth evaluation of the stimulus material. In a problem-solving situation, a spontaneous learner might more quickly make a decision about a course of action. In one study, spontaneity was associated with a learning style that emphasized active experimentation over reflective observation (Bozionelos, 1996). Learners high in spontaneity might be advantaged in learning situations where they have to be quick on their feet and respond instinctively and immediately but disadvantaged in situations that require a systematic analysis of a problem or issue.

Learning Style and Academic Achievement

African American children with a relational learning style may not be as successful in school as those with an analytical learning style. Some research suggests that students with a relational learning style may be disadvantaged. This is likely to occur when underestimating a child's learning potential results in lower expectations for these children (Berry, 2004).

Berry (2004) discusses the importance of recognizing the learning style of African American students when teaching mathematics, emphasizing that it is important to help students understand the connections between mathematics and their contextual and cultural ways of knowing. One way of doing this is by using the National Council of Teachers of Mathematics (NCTM) recommendations and standards (Berry, 2004). These standards include *Problem Solving, Reasoning and Proof, Communicating, Connections,* and *Representation* (NCTM, 2000). Students can gain mathematical knowledge through *Problem Solving* which encourages African

American children to use creativity, improvisation, and experimentation to solve math problems. When teaching math, the *Reasoning and Proof* standard can be used by supporting expressive individualism and encouraging students to cultivate a distinctive personality. Also, students can be encouraged to use their preference toward divergent thinking when developing mathematical arguments. The *Communication* standard can be achieved by using orality and by providing opportunities for students to share their thoughts and problem-solving strategies with other students. The *Connection* standard refers to the ability to interconnect mathematical ideas to understand how these ideas build on one another to produce a sound whole. It also emphasizes the interdependence of thoughts, ideas, and experiences. One way to achieve the *Connection* standard is for teachers to provide students with experiences that are personal for them and that consider their unique cultural context. Another way teachers can meet the *Connection* standard is by interweaving mathematics with patterns, rhythm, music, and movement. The *Representation* standard encourages students to use representations (e.g., symbols, images, pictures) to organize and communicate mathematical ideas. The *Representation* standard also encourages the application of mathematical representation to solving real-world problems. According to Berry, the *Representation* standard is akin to African American learners' preference for concrete imagery, creativity, verve, and divergent thinking. Accordingly, mathematics teaching should be stimulating and provide opportunities for hands-on experiences that promote interactive engagement among students and among teachers and students. African American students in classrooms that use these five standards based on practices of the NCTM have positive mathematical outcomes. Students in these classrooms outperform students who are taught using traditional mathematical curricula (Berry, 2004).

In summary, African American students with a relational learning style prefer learning within a social environment, through affective means, and have a higher tolerance for stimulus variety and change. Relational learners are also more likely to value learning for its social and practical value. In the United States, a learning style that is self-centered, field dependent, and spontaneous may disadvantage African Americans who attend school and work in environments that reward stimulus centeredness, field independence, and reflectivity.

However, recent research suggests that the cognitive and learning style of African Americans may be shifting and that there may be variability in their cognitive styles. Tomes (2008) investigated the learning style of 159 White and ethnic minority students (most of whom were African Americans). Tomes hypothesized that ethnic minority students—and African Americans students, in particular—would score lower on the concrete learning style of learning and higher on the abstract learning style. Concrete learning style is similar to the field-independent learning style in which objects are seen as separate and individualized. The abstract learning style is similar to the field-dependent learning style in which objects are seen as integrated and overlapped. The study found that ethnic minority students were more likely than White students to have a concrete style, although these differences were not statistically significant. Given the lack of differences, these findings suggest that there may be more variability in learning and cognitive styles among African Americans than previously thought.

Communal Learning Style

Some research suggests that African Americans learn better in settings in which there is harmony, cooperation, affect, and a sense of community (Seiler & Elmesky, 2007). Consequently, African Americans do not learn as well in environments that are highly stratified and competitive (Rovai et al., 2005). A learning style that recognizes the interconnections among people describes the communal approach. Sharing information is encouraged because it emphasizes the importance of social interconnectedness (Cunningham & Boykin, 2004). Communal learning is contrasted with independent learning, where each individual is responsible for his or her own learning. A few studies have examined the effects of communal learning contexts on the cognitive performance of children.

Albury (1998) conducted a study with low-income African American and European American children in the fourth grade. The purpose of the study was to examine the effects of group versus individual learning contexts on vocabulary. Students were given a pretest to determine initial vocabulary skills. They were then assigned to one of four learning conditions. (a) The first condition was the individual condition: Three children worked at the same table and were given separate study materials. They were told that any one of them achieving 18 out of 25 on a posttest would receive a reward. (b) The second condition was the interpersonal competition condition: Three children sitting at a table were given separate materials and told that the one receiving the highest score would receive a reward. (c) In the group competition condition, three participants at a table were given one set of materials and were told that they were competing against other groups to receive a reward. (d) In the communal condition, three students were at a table and were told the importance of sharing information. Participants in all groups were given 20 minutes to study the material. The learning groups were ethnically homogeneous; Black children composed four of the learning groups, and White children composed four of the learning groups.

Results showed that European American children learned most in the individual study condition and least in the communal condition. African American children learned most in the communal condition and the next highest amount in the group competition condition. They gained the fewest points in the individual condition. African American children in the communal condition not only scored higher at posttest but also had the highest learning gains of all groups in the study. African American children reported that they liked the group study condition best, whereas European American children liked the individual study condition best.

The findings from a qualitative study of African American children are consistent with this finding. Wilson-Jones and Caston (2004) conducted a qualitative study of academic achievement and cooperative learning among rural African American boys in third grade to sixth grade. They interviewed 16 students about their preferences for learning materials. They found that students expressed a preference for learning by working in groups with other students more than by working alone.

In summary, some studies have shown some benefits of a communal learning style among African American children (Coleman, 1998; Cunningham & Boykin, 2004; Rovai et al., 2005). These studies have found that when African American children are in communal learning contexts (in contrast to individualistic learning contexts), the quality and quantity of their learning are enhanced.

Verve, Rhythm, and Learning

Other cultural dimensions seen among African Americans are the orientation toward verve and rhythm. These orientations affect learning style. *Verve* is a term coined by Boykin and colleagues to describe an improvisational style expressed as rhythmic and creative. This can be seen in movement, posture, speech patterns, and behavior (Boykin, 1983; Cunningham & Boykin, 2004). Verve arises out of the contextual environment in which many African Americans live. When the home and neighborhood environments of African Americans are examined, much physical intensity and variation are seen. The immediate sensory environment of African Americans lends itself to receptiveness to heightened variability and intensity of stimulation. Accordingly, incorporating this heightened level of sensory stimulation can lead to enhanced performance for African American children.

Within the learning environment, the presence of verve would suggest a preference for several stimuli rather than one repetitive stimulus. There is also a preference for stimulus change, a higher energy level, and faster pace. According to Boykin, verve is important in terms of how children learn. The didactic "teacher talks and students listen" mode of learning may not work as well with African American children who have a verve orientation.

African American children who are taught in a traditional middle-class school culture that is absent of "vervistic" learning opportunities might be disadvantaged (Carter et al., 2008). Carter et al. examined verve and academic achievement among African American and European American eighth graders who attended an urban school in Texas (N = 211, 104 European Americans and 107 African Americans). The authors found that African American children had significantly higher verve levels than European American children. Verve was measured by the Child Activity Questionnaire (CAQ), an 18-item survey developed by Boykin and Mungai (1997). The authors also found that students with high levels of verve scored lower on the mathematics section of a test than students with lower verve scores. Carter et al. reported that one of the reasons for this is that mathematics can be abstract and nonstimulating, and mathematics tend to be taught using routine paper and pencil. Accordingly, students with lower verve levels or students who need less stimulation may perform higher on mathematical tasks than students with high verve levels. One recommendation arising from this research is to train teachers to be culturally responsive in recognizing learning styles such as verve that might be preferred by some African American students.

Rhythm is the regular repetition of weak and strong elements, often silence and sound, in speech, music, art, and everyday life. Rhythm is expressed in one's movement and other activities of daily living. The cultural orientation by which the environment is experienced through rhythm may affect cognitive and learning processes. Jones (2003), in his analysis of resiliency and coping among African Americans, noted that rhythm is a recurring pattern of behavior that gives energy and meaning to experiencing the external environment. Boykin and colleagues have shown that learning among African American children is enhanced under conditions of rhythm and verve (Cunningham & Boykin, 2004; Tuck & Boykin, 1989). The study described in the next section on movement illustrates this research.

Movement

Movement is another dimension that is salient in the lives of African Americans. Learning contexts that provide opportunities for movement expression facilitate the learning performance of some African American children (Allen & Butler, 1996; Cunningham, 1997; Cunningham & Boykin, 2004). African American students may perform better under conditions where there is movement and music than where there is not. Findings from a study conducted by Allen and Butler illustrate the role of movement and music in performance.

Allen and Butler (1996) investigated whether music and the opportunity to move facilitated cognitive processing in African American and White third graders. Children's performance on reasoning tasks was measured under two conditions: high-movement expressive (HME) and low-movement expressive (LME). In the

HME condition, the children could move around while a rhythmic tune was playing. They were told that they could dance or clap if they wanted as they listened to a story being read. In the LME condition, children were told to sit or stand but not to move in front of the person who was reading the story.

A reasoning task was used to assess three types of processes: encoding, inferring, and mapping. Encoding tasks required children to identify names, events, and actions in the story. Inferring tasks required children to understand the relationship between characters and events. Mapping tasks required children to understand the relationship between separate events.

The findings showed that African American children's performance was slightly better under the HME condition than the LME condition, and White children's performance was significantly better under the LME condition. In the HME condition, African American children performed at the same level as the White children despite the fact that the White children were from middle-class backgrounds and the African American children were from low-income backgrounds. The performance of the African American children defied expectations and the norm. This finding is important and suggests that African American children can perform at levels comparable to other academically successful ethnic groups when they are taught under culturally congruent conditions.

In a replication and update to this study, Cole and Boykin (2008) found that African American fourth graders had the highest performance under a condition in which there was polyrhythmic (occurrence of different rhythms) music and HME opportunity (compared with a condition in which there was no polyrhythmic music or low movement opportunity). They also found that both fourth and sixth graders had the lowest performance (story recall) in conditions in which there was no music or movement. Cole and Boykin write, "It is interesting that our results contradict a great deal of the psychological research asserting the distractibility of syncopated and percussive music" (p. 348).

The results of studies by Boykin and colleagues suggest that movement is a culturally socialized attribute among African Americans. However, clearly more work is needed to understand how this information might be used in programs targeting increased academic achievement.

Learning Preferences and Misdiagnoses

As discussed, spontaneous behaviors, use of body language, movement, and the like might indicate verve and rhythm and movement preferences. However, sometimes, these forms of self-expression and receptivity to the social environment are seen as an indicator of attention deficit disorder (Trotman & Moss-Bouldin, 2014). The child with high levels of verve and movement may be viewed as acting out and not paying attention to the teacher. An incorrect diagnosis of a child may lead to inappropriate placement in special education classes. In addition, these labels may create a negative self-fulfilling expectation. Diagnostic assessment of a child should consider culturally specific ways of learning.

In summary, the homes of African American children are filled with higher levels of sensory stimulation, leading to an orientation labeled *verve*. Learning environments that capture the preference of African American children's propensity for verve, rhythm, and movement may be culturally conducive to learning.

Cultural Factors in Learning
Among African American College Students

Although the vast majority of research on learning has been conducted on students in Grades K–12, there has been some more (albeit limited) research that

CONTEMPORARY ISSUES
CAN AFRICAN-CENTERED EDUCATION IMPROVE LEARNING OUTCOMES AMONG AFRICAN AMERICAN STUDENTS?

Over the past two decades, more and more African-centered schools have been started. These schools, both independent and public, are mostly in urban areas such as Washington, D.C., Philadelphia, New York City, Detroit, Atlanta, and Chicago. According to Newman (2012), African-centered schooling emphasizes holistic development of students, and students are taught in ways consistent with their learning styles. Teachers are aware that African American children are highly visual, auditory, and fashion-oriented. Consequently, students are exposed to a high degree of stimuli at an early age, which involves music, dance, rhythm, and other creative expression.

African-centered schools assume that African American children will do better in an environment that considers their learning style and that incorporates African values and rituals in education. These schools provide instruction that focuses on communal and relational learning and students being part of a collective. Another emphasis of African-centered schools is family involvement and the involvement of students in the local and global communities. Some of the schools' curriculums use the Principles of Nguzo Saba (discussed in Chapter 2) as the foundation for students' academic, social, and moral development. Other curriculums may involve the teachings of ma'at and Kiswahili.

Newman (2012) summarizes and then addresses some of the criticism of African-centered schools. One criticism is that

these schools may threaten the present educational system's status quo. However, these schools should not threaten the status quo because they were developed specifically to address the concern of the miseducation of African American youth in traditional schools. Another criticism of African-centered schools is that these schools single out Black children and, by doing so, implicitly support segregation. In response to this criticism, Newman notes that there are many other cultural groups that focus on a specific target group (e.g., Catholics engage in Catholic-centered education, all-girls schools engage in female-centered education). A final criticism Newman counters is that African-centered education may teach myths as facts and instill in students a sense of false pride. This criticism is refuted by the fact that the true history of Africans has been intentionally excluded from the standard curriculum, resulting in mainstream education that does not cover all of Africa's history. Therefore, African-centered education can help to restore facts and truths about Africa and African people.

We are not aware of any large-scale evaluation that has included African-centered schools and assessed whether youth attending these schools perform better on social, academic, and moral achievement than African American youth attending traditional schools. But given the dismal level of academic achievement and the large educational disparities, these schools warrant serious consideration.

suggests that academic achievement of African American college students is also mediated by learning style. Consistent with research on children, this research suggests that African American college students also learn best under conditions where learning takes place in a culturally congruent environment.

One aspect of culture is communication styles. Rovai et al. (2005) discuss college classroom communication, noting that African American students learn best when teachers use specific strategies and skills. One such skill is teacher immediacy (Gorham, 1988; Neuliep, 2002). Teaching immediacy is defined as teacher indicators that show increased sensory stimulation, attentiveness, liking, psychological closeness, and active engagement and interaction. Nonverbal indicators of teacher immediacy include smiles, eye contact with students, and movement around the classroom during teaching. Verbal signs include things such as addressing students by name, using humor, and talking to students before and after class. Note, some of the indicators of immediacy are similar to those features of relational learning. Insofar as African American instructors may display these signs of teacher immediacy, HBCU classrooms may increase cultural congruency for students and enhance student learning (Rovai et al., 2005)

In summary, the work of Rovai and colleagues suggests that attention to the learning styles of African American college students might also increase performance.

LANGUAGE

What Is Black English?

Coon (1997) defines language as a collection of words or symbols and rules for combining them that facilitates thinking and communication. Language spoken by African Americans has been referred to as African American English, African American Vernacular English, Black language, Black English, and Ebonics. African American English is a systematic, rule-governed linguistic system that is spoken *by many* but not all African Americans in the United States (Washington, 1996). It is estimated that at least 80% of African Americans speak some form of African American English (Hollie, 2001).

Robert Williams coined the term Ebonics in 1973. The term came from the words *ebony*, which means black, and *phonics*, which refers to speech sounds (Williams, 1997). Williams defined Ebonics as "the linguistic and paralinguistic features that represent the communicative competence of West Africa, the Caribbean and the United States" (Williams, 1997). When the term Ebonics is used, many people associate slang words such as bling-bling (meaning "glittery or expensive jewelry"). However, there are other words that represent Ebonics such as *kitchen*, "the especially kinky hair at the nape of one's neck," that are unique to the Black culture. Unlike slang terms, these "Black" words have been around generationally and are well known among Blacks from all regions and age groups and are unknown (in their "Black" meanings) outside the African American community (Rickford, n.d.).

According to the Linguist Society of America, most linguists refer to the distinguishing speech of African Americans as Black English, African American English (AAE), or African American Vernacular English (AAVE) (Rickford, n.d.). However, some scholars prefer the term Ebonics (or African American language), which highlights the African roots of African American speech and the linkages to languages spoken elsewhere in the Black Diaspora. These are all the same. In this chapter, we use the term African American English.

Both the academic and lay communities have discussed Black language extensively, and there have been divergent opinions on the validity and usefulness of Black language among African Americans. Two landmark cases spoke directly to the consideration of Black language (Smitherman, 2004). The first case, *King v. Ann Arbor* (1979), was filed on behalf of 15 Black children who attended school in Ann Arbor, Michigan. The children lived in a low-income community. The judge ruled that the Ann Arbor school district had to consider Black English in its educational process. It also acknowledged the responsibility of schools to teach Black children Standard American English (SAE). This case was significant because it recognized the legitimacy of Black English and laid the foundation for Black English to be recognized in the educational process.

Almost 20 years later, in December 1996, the Oakland, California, school board adopted the position that in order to achieve SAE proficiency, the unique language of African Americans must be recognized. This position generated a lot of controversy. Opponents of this position felt that it encouraged inferior education for Blacks. Some thought that by recognizing as legitimate a language that was not SAE, African Americans would not be able to compete in the real world where SAE is the norm. Supporters of the new policy argued that the recognition of Black English as a language would help develop language strengths in students by building on Black English in the classroom. For example, SAE could be reinforced if teachers were familiar with the language students used. Rather than always correcting students for using Black English, teachers could allow students to communicate using this language while teaching them SAE. Opponents felt that using Ebonics would promote another educational handicap for African Americans.

Others have advocated the use of code-switching teaching methods that allow students' home language to facilitate appropriate nonstandard and standard contexts for writing and speaking (Hill, 2009). Rather than view Black English as incorrect, code-switching teaching methods require that teachers make a transition from the paradigm of correction to helping students use language patterns in appropriate setting. In order to do this, teachers must be knowledgeable of Black English features.

Dialect or Language?

Whether Black English is a language or a dialect has been heavily debated. According to Smitherman (2004), whether a language is defined as such depends on who has the power to define. Because Blacks have less power than the majority Whites in this country, they alone cannot define Black English as a language. Validation and recognition from the majority culture is necessary for Black English to be recognized as a language. Smitherman further notes that the language of Blacks has been considered inferior and consequently has been used to justify the discrimination and exclusion of Black people from major social, political, and economic institutions. Because Black English has been stigmatized, many middle-class African Americans have rejected it, feeling that those most likely to speak it belong to a lower class. Middle-class African Americans would rather not risk being stigmatized, though some do speak Black English at home. Among the general population, the conventional wisdom is that dialects are bad and SAE is good. Sociolinguists do not see things this way, however. According to sociolinguists, dialect means a variety of a language—like Appalachian English or Boston English or any other variety of English. Among sociolinguists, all dialects are created equal (Hamilton, 2005). Hamilton quotes Orlando Taylor (linguist and speech-language specialist):

> If a group is considered to be ignorant, primitive, backward, ill-informed, then their language is given similar attributes. The problem is that African American people and Black people around the world are perceived by dominant societies to be inferior, and so their language is perceived in a similar way. (p. 35)

Williams (1997) also rejects the notion that Black English is not a language. He discusses two theories on the origins of Ebonics: (a) the pidgin/creole theory and (b) the African retention theory. According to the pidgin/creole theory, Africans who were brought to the United States from Africa spoke many languages. Pidgin is a simplified version of the language of different slave groups. The children of slaves acquired as their language the pidgin their parents spoke, and the new language that the slaves' children spoke was called creole. Eventually, a process referred to as "Englishization" began. The speaker maintained the original communication style, some lexical items, and the ability to code-switch. During the Englishization process, enslaved Africans and their descendants began to speak some SAE.

The second theory on the origin of Ebonics is that it is the retention of features of African languages that represents the deep structure of Ebonics. Some West African languages such as Ibo, Twi, Ful, Yoruba, and Wolof are relatives of Ebonics.

A third theory on the origin of Ebonics is that it has an English origin. Scholars advocating this view point to the fact that most of the vocabulary of Ebonics is from English and that much of its pronunciation could have come from the nonstandard dialects of English indentured servants and other workers with whom enslaved Africans interacted (Rickford, n.d.).

Siegel (2006) analyzes why, in spite of the fact that sociolinguists consider varieties of languages such as Black English, Appalachian English, and creole languages to be legitimate languages, those languages continue to be considered incorrect. The lack of recognition of these as legitimate languages accounts for the fact that different teaching approaches used to help nonstandard-English-speaking children to read and write SAE have not been successful. Siegel discusses four ideological myths that account for the continued lack of recognition of Black English. (a) One is the myth of egalitarian pluralism. This is the notion that there is basic equality among different ethnic and cultural groups. This position, however, ignores differentials in advantage and privilege between different cultural groups, including the privilege of language that may be equal in linguistic terms but not in social or practical terms. (b) Related to egalitarian pluralism is the myth of equal opportunity in which schools are supposed to offer a level playing field so that anyone can be successful if she works hard and applies herself. The fallacy of this ideology is that anyone who learns SAE will have the same opportunities for academic and vocational success, and this is, of course, questionable. (c) A third ideology is the pervasive belief in the superiority of the standard language. Here, the notion is that in order for dominant groups to continue to dominate, those groups need to convince subordinate groups that the status quo is the natural order of things. Language then becomes a primary medium of social control and power. (d) The final ideology is that of monolingualism as the normal condition—and in this case, SAE would be the normal condition.

Features of Black English

Black English has many unique features. It is derived from European American English (called Standard English), West African languages, and African American pidgin and creole languages spoken at different times and in different regions of the United States. Some of the unique features of Black English, as summarized by Smitherman (2004), Washington (1996), Wheeler (2008), Rickford (1999), and Rickford and King (2016), are described next.

Use of the Verb Be to Express Habitual Action

The use of *be* is derived from a verb structure that is found in many African languages, in the Caribbean, and in West African Pidgin English. The verb *be* in this context is used to convey a qualitative nature and consistency of an action over time. "He be playing" is qualitatively different from, "He is playing." The SAE version would be, "He is playing all the time" or "He is constantly playing."

Zero Copula

A unique feature of African American English is the absence of the copula. The complete sentence can be a noun or pronoun followed by an adjective, adverb, verb, or noun (e.g., "He fast," or "She my sister"). SAE, on the other hand, requires a form of *to be* to complete a sentence (e.g., "He is fast," or "She is my sister"). Zero copula is more likely to follow pronouns than full noun subjects (Wyatt, 1995; e.g., "He strong," as opposed to, "He is strong"). This aspect of Black English is found in West African languages.

Use of the Word Been With Stress to Convey the Remote Past

This language pattern gives weight to events and actions that occurred in the distant past by stressing the word *been* in conversation. For example, "She had been finished cleaning the room," or "We had been home." The stress on the word *been* indicates that this action occurred some time ago. The SAE equivalent to the first example would be, "She had finished cleaning her room a long time ago."

Turning a Word Into Its Opposite

Words that are traditionally thought of as negative may be given a positive connotation. This is especially seen in Black slang. For example, the word *bomb* is used to denote something that is really good. "I loved that video. It was the bomb," may be used to denote liking something a lot rather than something dangerous, such as an explosion.

Using a Pronoun to Repeat the Subject for Emphasis

Subjects are repeated in a pronoun form when the speaker wants to emphasize a point about the subject. For example, "John, he left two hours ago," or "The baby, she is learning to walk." The SAE usage. "The baby is finally learning to walk." This feature of speech is seen in some West African languages.

Showing Possession by Context and/or Juxtaposition

In Black English, there is no standard rule for how possession is shown. For example, "My sister name is Shanita," or "He live near my cousin house," rather than, "He lives near my cousin's house." In SAE, possession is shown by the letter "s" preceded by an apostrophe.

Lack of Subject–Verb Agreement

In African American English, subject and verb may differ in number or person—for example, "What do this mean?" instead of, "What does this mean?" Another example. "The toys is broken rather than, "The toys are broken."

Multiple Negation

Two or more negative markers in one sentence may be used in African American English. This may be used to emphasize a point: "I don't got no money," may be used instead of, "I don't have money." Or "Shana can't buy no car," instead of, "Shana cannot buy a car."

Zero Past Tense

In African American English, *-ed* is not always used to convey regular past constructions, or the present tense form is used in place of the irregular past form, for example, "Her dress was stain," instead of, "Her dress was stained." Another example: "The bicycle was damage," instead of, "The bicycle was damaged."

Omission of the Final Consonant in Some Words

In African American Vencular English (AAVE), scome words are pronounced with the final consonant omitted. For example, words like *past* are pronounced "pas," *desk* as "des," and *build* is "buil." According to Rickford (n.d), this feature also occurs in some White English, especially in the South, but, in general, occurs more frequently in Ebonics.

Usage of Words Whose Meaning Are Unique to African Americans

African American English or Ebonics also consists of the usage of words that are primarily known to or used by African Americans and not known or used in the general population. For example, John Rickford reported after 35 years of teaching at Stanford and asking hundreds of students about their familiarity with words such as *ashy* and *kitchen* that almost all African Americans students knew a different use of these terms but very few students from other ethnic groups knew the culturally nuanced meaning of these terms (Rickford & King, 2016). *Ashy* in AAVE means dry skin in the winter, and *kitchen* means the kinky hair at the nape of the neck (Rickford, 1996).

African American Vernacular English has distinctive words. However, many of these words are often slang and used mostly by youth. And these words, while shared by many African Americans, also are sometimes used by other ethnic groups. The core of African American Vernacular English across most age groups is those words that most strongly adhere to the language's origins in the creole speech of enslavement (Rickford, 1996). Some common African American or Ebonics words used are shown in Table 9.2. Many of these words are used mostly by youth.

Meaning of Speech for African Americans

One's social and cultural meaning is conveyed in how one talks. Ogbu (1999) studied the patterns of African Americans in a speech community (i.e., a population that shares the same language and a common theory of speaking) to understand the social meaning and context of their speech. Ogbu observed and interviewed students, parents, grandparents, and other adults in a Black speech community in Oakland, California. The study revealed the following findings:

1. Participants knew that there were two English dialects in the community, slang English and proper English.

2. The community perceived that White people spoke correct or proper English and that Black people spoke slang English. Black and White people's English differed in vocabulary, accent, and attitude. The same statements could be interpreted differently when spoken by a Black or a White person.

3. Black English was regarded as more appropriate for speaking in the community, and proper English was regarded as more appropriate for school.

TABLE 9.2 ■ Some Common Words Spoken in African American English/Ebonics

40: 40 oz. malt liquor beverage

Baller: one who spends huge amounts of money

Bangin: impressive, enjoyable

Benjamins: $100 bills

Boo: one's lover or boyfriend/girlfriend

Bounce: to exit a location or situation

Chips: money

Crib: house

Dawg: close friend

Def: really good

Flava: a person's style

Flow: skills

Homie: friend

Jacks: steal

Kicks: sneakers

Off da hook: excellent, cool

Peace out: goodbye

Peeps: one's friends

Po po: the police

Pop: shoot

Shady: acting unlike a friend

Shortie: a woman or sometimes girlfriend

Straight: fine, ok

Threads: clothes

Trippin: crazy

Whack: sorry, sad, pathetic, not cool

4. Students switched between slang and proper English in the school, speaking slang in the hallways and proper English in the classroom.

5. Children learned slang before they learned proper English. Because slang was learned within the family and community, children felt more comfortable with it.

6. Parents and children recognized that a slang dialect might cause problems at school.

Participants in Ogbu's study believed that proper English was necessary for school and employment success. On the other hand, they felt that proper English could threaten their identity within their community. Speaking proper English was regarded by some as trying to be White and thinking that you are superior to other Black people. Some residents felt that speaking proper English was "putting on airs" by not talking in what was assumed to be one's natural way of speaking. Furthermore, they felt that White people forced proper English on Black people, resulting in a loss of slang language and, thus, the loss of an element of Black culture.

Perceptions of Black English

Language is not only a means of communication but also is used to form initial impressions of others (Koch & Gross, 1997). Findings from studies suggest that among African Americans in mainstream society, SAE may be seen as more desirable, and speakers of Black English may be seen as not competent (Billings, 2005; Doss & Gross, 1992).

Billings (2005) examined whether assessments of competence, trustworthiness, and social distance vary as a function of whether the speaker uses Black English or SAE. A total of nine video clips were used and presented to participants: Three of the nine clips had a White person speaking SAE, and three had an African American speaking SAE. The final three had an African American speaking Black English. The sample consisted of 261 participants, males and females and African Americans and Whites. The results indicated that African American speakers of SAE were preferred to White speakers of SAE. Billings speculated that this may have been due to a novelty effect in that they expected African American speakers to use Black English. However, speaking Black English led to lower ratings in seven dimensions, including intelligence, articulation, aggression, education, and qualifications. These are all measures of competence. There were no differences across the groups in terms of the scales measuring trustworthiness (e.g., honesty, likability, attractiveness). The author speculates that perhaps the competence aspects of person perception affect Black English speakers more than the trust aspects.

African American English and Stigma

The study by Billings suggests that African Americans who speak Black English are likely to be perceived as less competent than those who do not. Similarly, there has been a negative response to African American English voiced by many notable and famous African Americans (e.g., Maya Angelou) and educators, as well as the general public (Rickford & King, 2016).

In an interesting analysis of the stigma attached to African American English, Rickford and King (2016) discussed how the African American Vernacular English of the prosecution's star witness in the Zimmerman case was discredited because of her language. In a paper titled "Language and Linguistics on Trial: Hearing Rachel Jeantel (and Other Vernacular Speakers) in the Courtroom and Beyond," Rickford and King identify linguistic elements in Jeantel's speech that contributed to the lack of credibility of this key witness whose testimony directly contradicted Zimmerman about Trayvon Martin. She reported, for example, that Trayvon Martin was running away from Zimmerman instead of running toward him, as reported by Zimmerman. Rickford & King write:

> She was the prosecution's star witness, testifying for nearly six hours, longer than any other single witness at the trial. However, her vernacular speech was pilloried on social media, and one of the six jurors (B37) said, in a TV interview with CNN's Anderson Cooper after the trial (July 15, 2013), that she found Jeantel both 'hard to understand' and 'not credible'. In the end, despite her centrality to the case, 'no one mentioned Jeantel in [16+ hour] jury deliberations. Her testimony played no role whatsoever in their decision. In a sense, Jeantel's dialect was found guilty as a prelude to and contributing element in Zimmerman's acquittal. (p. 950)

Rickford and King carefully analyzed Jeantel's speech in almost 15 hours of trial-related events that were recorded and found that her speech was "neither 'inarticulate' nor 'incoherent', but a systematic exemplification of the grammar of AAVE" (p. 957). Rickford and King discuss several other court cases in which English vernaculars (dialect) from the United States, Australia, Africa, and the United Kingdom were either mistranscribed or misunderstood, noting that interpreters in court and related circumstances are not usually provided for dialects of a language, only for foreign languages. The implications of jurors and others not understanding and stigmatizing the testimony of witnesses and defendants who speak African American English has enormous implications for fairness in court and related proceedings.

Recognizing the necessity of accurate translation of African American English, the DEA (Drug Enforcement Agency) advertised for fluent Ebonics speakers to serve as a translator for wiretapping (Page, 2010). Much media attention followed, including stories by CNN (Cratty, Hayes, & Gast, 2010) and ABC news (Netter, 2010). Linguists and scholars on this topic contributed that Ebonics is a legitimate language with its own unique features, and speakers of this language could be of value to the DEA in translating the communication of African Americans involved in drug trafficking.

In spite of some stigma, many notable writers have used African American speech in their work and have praised it (Rickman, n.d.). These include writers such as Paul Laurence Dunbar, James Baldwin, Zora Neale Hurston, August Wilson, and Toni Morrison. Others, including African American preachers, comedians, and especially rappers, use African American English to convey realism or a dramatic effect to their message.

METHODOLOGICAL AND RESEARCH ISSUES

Methodological challenges include potential variables that might confound ethnic and racial differences in learning styles and how differences in learning styles might lead to lower performance on cognitive assessments for African American children and youth.

One methodological limitation of studies that have investigated learning, cognition, and language is that these studies have not typically used the types of design and controls that could account for other potential influences on language and cognitive style. For example, differences in learning styles could be influenced by factors other than ethnic and cultural differences; these differences are not always controlled in studies. School climate is one such factor and may differ for those students who attend and do not attend predominantly African American schools (Rovai et al., 2005). Also, African Americans and other ethnic minority groups are more likely to attend schools in urban areas than are Whites, who are more likely to attend suburban and rural schools. Differences in school climate may vary between urban, rural, and suburban schools. These differences are not generally controlled for in studies of African American children's learning styles (Rovai et al., 2005). A controlled study with African Americans, Latinos, Asians, and Whites who are represented in rural, urban, and suburban school systems might tease out whether these differences are unique to African Americans overall or African Americans attending urban schools (Rovai et al., 2005).

A related issue is that socioeconomic status or class is generally not considered in this research. African American children, relative to White children, are more often reared in households of lower socioeconomic status, and they are more likely to live in communities that reflect this status. One study addressed this limitation somewhat, in that students in this study came from households more varied in socioeconomic status (Rouland et al., 2014). It would be interesting to observe the cognitive and language styles of different ethnic groups across a range of socioeconomic conditions to determine the role of socioeconomic class. Clearly, more research is needed to tease out the effects of variables such as school climate, socioeconomic class, and type of geographic community on learning and cognitive styles.

Another methodological issue with more serious consequences is that knowledge acquisition and differences in learning styles might, in part, account for the lower performance of African Americans compared with other ethnic groups on standardized tests. Although recent research suggests variability in learning style among African Americans, we can still expect a fair number of African American students to have more relational and holistic learning styles. If one group is disadvantaged by the way tests are designed and administered, the question arises as to whether the test is valid for that group. According to scholars (Bell, 1994; Durodoye & Hildreth, 1995) people who have more analytical problem-solving strategies tend to do better on intelligence tests. These tests are designed such that when a rational and analytical method is used to solve a problem, the answer tends to be intended, or "correct." On the other hand, the attributes that characterize African Americans' way of learning and problem solving may not be reflected on the intelligence test. When the test taker uses relational methods to solve the problem, he or she may choose the unintended, or "wrong," answer. According to Bell, learning environments that facilitate self-centeredness, field dependence, and holistic orientations should facilitate more effective learning and problem-solving skills among African Americans. African Americans should perform best when these aspects are reflected on tests and in other assessment situations. These considerations have implications for the way in which intelligence and other related attributes are assessed. African Americans will most likely achieve lower test scores given these differences in learning styles. (See Chapter 6 for a more detailed discussion of intelligence testing among African American students.)

PROMISING PRACTICES FOR INCREASING COGNITIVE AND LANGUAGE SKILLS

Understanding learning and language styles of African American children could contribute to their educational success. Most educational systems do not support alternative learning styles. Learners who are analytical and elemental in their approach tend to do better on individually administered cognitive and achievement assessments than those who are relational and holistic. This may, in part, account for lower test scores for African American children. Attending to cultural differences, specifically in learning activities, should improve learning and, subsequently, test scores for African Americans. On this topic, Asa Hilliard (1992), one of the country's foremost experts on cultural issues in education, wrote, "All students have an incredible capacity for developing the ability to use multiple learning styles, in much the same way that multiple language competency can be accomplished" (p. 373). On the other hand, African Americans have to function and compete in many environments that are not supportive of their unique learning style. Learning when and how to modulate one's learning preferences might be another strategy when the environment is not responsive to the African American learner.

Improvements in Student Learning

There has been limited research in psychology that has examined whether learning environments that are consistent with African American culture result in higher achievement than those that are not. The research conducted by Wade Boykin and colleagues, discussed earlier, has shown some promise. This research demonstrated that African American children performed better under learning conditions involving music and movement than under conditions when these elements were not present (Cole & Boykin, 2008). A study by Boykin and Cunningham (2001) is illustrative of how this work can be used in teaching environments. The purpose of this study was to determine the effects on performance when integrating cultural factors in the presentation and content of task materials. Sixty-four African American children participated in this study. They were low-income and ages 7–8 years. The children listened to stories read under two contextual conditions. In one condition, children were allowed high-movement expressive (HME), and in the other condition, they were not. This second condition was called the low-movement expressive (LME) condition. Also, the content of the story contained either high-movement examples, such as dancing and jumping, or low-movement themes, such as standing and walking. Boykin and Cunningham found that children had better story knowledge under the HME condition than under the LME condition. Children also had better story knowledge when high-movement themes were used in stories than when low-movement themes were used. The highest performance was seen in the conditions with both HME and high-movement themes. The study has implication for how classrooms might be structured to facilitate learning, and additional studies to attenuate or confirm these findings are warranted.

A more recent study shows support for improved achievement using both cultural and mainstream approaches to learning. Rouland et al. (2014) investigated classroom culture and achievement among 74 African American fifth graders. Trained research assistants rated classrooms as embodying mainstream cultural styles (defined as bureaucracy, individualism, and competitive) or Afrocultural cultural styles (verve, affect, orality, and communalism). Students attended 1 of 40 elementary schools in a Southeastern city in the United States. While most studies have included mostly low-income African American children, the parents of these children were of diverse socioeconomic statuses. The researchers obtained students' achievement test scores and ratings of students' social skills from teachers. The findings were mixed with regard to the influence of Afrocultural versus mainstream classroom cultural style on student achievement showing an interaction. Students in classrooms high in both Afrocultural and mainstream cultural values had higher reading and math achievement scores. Children in classrooms with high mainstream cultural values that did not also have high Afrocultural values, or classrooms low in both tended to have lower achievement scores. Afrocultural styles were positively associated with teachers reporting higher social skills and negatively related to teachers reporting problem behaviors. Mainstream cultural values were not related to achievement. The study findings suggest that classrooms that embody both a mainstream and an Afrocultural style may improve African American student achievement.

Strategies When Working With African American Children

Most of the work on learning and cognitive styles has been conducted in the field of education and has specifically focused on classroom environment and curriculum development in multicultural classrooms (Lanson-Billings, 1999). This work has been primarily done in educational settings and with younger children rather than older children and adults. Several educators have discussed ways in which African American children may benefit from instruction that captures their learning and cognitive preferences. For example, Barbara Shade (1997) identified strategies for creating culturally responsive classrooms by recognizing preferences of different cultural groups. Shade, citing the work of Janice Hale (1982) and Joyce E. King (1994) along with her own, offers these suggestions for those who are working with African American children. Shade also believes that although these suggestions are designed for younger students, they may also work for older students. These recommendations include the following:

1. Provide affective or emotional support. This might include small-group learning, peer tutoring, and grouping of different students in a manner that resembles a family.

2. Provide tasks that will give students a sense of combined responsibility for their learning and the learning of their peers.

3. Provide opportunities for students to explore their community, and encourage them to use their knowledge for the benefit of their community.

4. Provide opportunities in academic tasks in which students can develop or enhance their self-concept and identity, and provide opportunities for creative expression. These activities should be structured so that students can successfully accomplish them along a gradation of increasing difficulty.

5. Expose students to African and African American culture and traditions. Include meaningful curriculum and symbolism from the African and African American cultural traditions, such as the use of proverbs, an emphasis on African orality, public performance, and artistic expression in music, dance, and other art forms.

6. Provide sufficient opportunity in which children can talk and express themselves, and give them the opportunity to hear music while they work.

See Chapter 6 for a further discussion of strategies for enhancing learning and cognition among African American children.

Culturally Responsive Classrooms

Other educational scholars have discussed the advantages of culturally responsive teaching environments, classrooms, and practices as a mechanism for addressing the unique learning needs of African American children (Brown, 2004; Madsen & Mabokela, 2002; Mayfield & Garrison-Wade, 2015). Culturally responsive teaching is defined by Gay (2000) as "using the cultural characteristics, experiences, and perspectives of ethnically diverse students as conduits for teaching them more effectively." Based on a review of literature on success factors for the education of students of color, Mayfield and Garrison-Wade identified several culturally responsive practices. One factor was shared power and leadership with students, parents, and teaching and administrative personnel. Some examples of shared power include having empowerment counseling groups, familiar support structures, shared decision making, and collaborative building of knowledge among teachers. When power is shared, educators and administrators must ensure that the entire school culture is empowering so that policies and procedure do not disadvantage some students. Another culturally responsive practice focuses on the educational environment where students can interact with and learn from each other. Here communal values can be encouraged by interdependent and cooperative methods of learning. Similarly, culturally responsive environments might allow students to move about and express themselves with rhythm and verve. Carter et al. (2008) recommend that African American students with high levels of verve be assigned to teachers who engage in culturally responsive teaching and those that are not proficient in culturally responsive teaching be supported to develop skills in this area.

A culturally responsive environment would also promote positive identity development by integration of diversity and information about people of African descent in curriculum materials, as well as having African American teachers engaged in instruction (see Chapter 3 for further information on increasing racial and ethnic identity). This practice would help students understand the historical and contemporary context of African Americans in this country and across the Diaspora. Professional development might be required for some teachers. Culturally responsive environments require bringing into the school systems the culture of the community through active parental involvement, hiring and promotion of African American educators and staff, and in-service training for all school personnel (Cazden & Leggett, 1981).

Khalifa, Gooden, and Davis (2016) highlight the importance of culturally responsive leadership, emphasizing that this leadership must be responsive. Culturally responsive leadership includes school leaders who are action oriented and who have the ability to create school contexts and curriculum that is effective with the educational, social, political, and cultural needs of students.

Improving Language Skills

A related question is, What is the best language to use when educating African American children? According to Smitherman (2004), educational and institutional policies should recognize the legitimacy of Black English. Black English could be a language of coinstruction, especially among children who live in environments where it is spoken. The distinctive language patterns and other aspects of Black English should not be viewed as dysfunctional and inferior but as a unique style that can aid in instruction inside and outside the school system. Black English is functional for most Black people and is a valid means of communication.

At the same time, language policy must also emphasize the need for SAE competency among African Americans. SAE is often rejected or not fully accepted by African Americans because it is associated with White English. Rejection of SAE may be linked to ethnic pride, especially among African Americans. However, when one's native language is accepted and respected, there may be less reluctance to accept SAE. The acceptance of both languages may greatly benefit African American children and adults.

Hill (2009) made the following recommendations to teachers who have students who are Black English speakers: (a) Never tell students that the language they speak in the home is wrong and that SAE is correct. (b) Inform students that everyone speaks nonstandard English, and explore additional forms of English to compare. For example, teachers could identify characters from different cultural groups on television. (c) Help motivate students by exploring how they express common ideas before emphasizing grammar rules. (d) Provide students with written feedback when they are using SAE features. (e) Model corresponding grammatical features used in Black English and in SAE.

Wheeler (2008) suggests that teachers put away the red pen and provide structured instruction in code-switching to help urban African American students use language more effectively. Given the relationship between teachers' negative attitudes about stigmatized dialects and lower academic achievement, teachers need to be cognizant of how to teach students who do not speak SAE. Students who do not speak SAE are not making errors, but are speaking and writing consistent with the communication patterns in their community. A linguistically knowledgeable teacher understands the use of Black English and grammar patterns and helps students to recognize the patterns of both by comparing and contrasting both patterns of English. Wheeler also recommends that teachers train students to learn how to code-switch using a form of metacognition. Metacognition is knowledge about one's own thinking processes. Here, students can consider the setting they are in and intentionally choose the appropriate language style for that setting.

Using the Oral Tradition to Improve Learning

A consideration of the African American oral tradition could be used in literacy activities that would be engaging for youth. According to Grace (2004), effective teaching strategies could consider aspects of the African American oral tradition that facilitate engagement with literacy practices. One form of hip-hop that may be included in the curriculum with less risk is culturally conscious hip-hop. Culturally conscious hip-hop is oral text with lyrics and messages that enlighten with social consciousness, engage with politicized messages, and empower by instilling cultural and self-awareness (Grace, 2004). Culturally conscious hip-hop artists include India.Arie, Erykah Badu, Jill Scott, and Musiq Soulchild, among others. Their lyrics may be used to enhance the literacy engagement of African American youth.

The infusion of African American oral tradition requires a teacher who is willing to be a colearner with students. It also requires a teacher who is unfamiliar with specific cultural practices of his or her students to be willing to learn about them. And finally, it requires the establishment of a safe and trusting learning environment by encouraging the acquisition of knowledge through cooperative learning (Grace, 2004).

In summary, a consideration of how to best facilitate learning among African American children provides some suggestions of how understanding unique features of African American cognitive and language styles is likely to enhance children's overall performance outcomes.

CRITICAL ANALYSIS

A discussion of whether African Americans have unique cognitive and language styles is subject to divergent opinions. An argument against identifying differences is that cognitive differences may imply that African American children are not only different but also not likely to benefit from educational experiences that ensure the success needed to function in this society. When the discussion is on AAE, even more controversy arises. Most of the research and resulting discussions have been on children, and the conversation has centered on whether it is adaptive for educational and learning environments to consider African American learning style and cognition. An example of controversial comments were those made in a speech by the Reverend Wright (former pastor of President Barack Obama) to the National

Association for the Advancement of Colored People (NAACP) in Detroit on April 27, 2008. Many (including many African Americans) objected to Reverend Wright's statements where he quoted the work of Dr. Janice Hale and Dr. Geneva Smitherman; these scholars have said that Black children learn differently from Whites and that their learning and language are not deficient but simply different. In blogs posted after these comments were made, several people expressed outrage, saying that emphasizing racial differences was not in the best interests of society at this point. Others posed questions about whether teachers should be required to teach students of different ethnic groups using different methods. Still others questioned the practicality of teaching children while considering their culture and language, noting that African Americans have to compete in the same real world as other ethnic and racial groups. What was missing in many of the reactions to Reverend Wright's statements was an understanding of historical and contemporary socialization practices that have contributed to differences and the functionality of the unique aspects of African American language and cognition. As noted by Jones (2003), African American practices and values have been adapted by African Americans in this country and have been instrumental in helping African Americans not only to survive but also to thrive.

Most of the research and literature on cognition and learning style has been done in education, particularly among students in elementary schools. However, we are beginning to see more work, albeit limited, on learning styles and their impact on academic achievement among students in college. If learning styles of African Americans differ, then this also has implications for students in higher education. One could also see the implications for employment and job productivity. Interactive and communal environments and tasks that encourage movement and creative expression might result in better performance than those environments and tasks that do not.

There has been limited work in psychology on African American cognitive and learning styles and how attending to these styles might facilitate learning goals. Furthermore, much of the work was conducted more than 20 to 30 years ago, and recent work is not evident, at least not within the psychological literature. As Dr. Janice Hale, an eminent scholar of Black children's learning style noted, science on this topic has been stagnant. We might also consider the potential losses to a society that builds its knowledge on a subset of cognitive strategies. There may be learning benefits to both field dependence and field independence. If we only value one, we might miss the societal benefits of utilizing and applying these cognitive skills in a variety of educational, work, and societal domains. Clearly, we need to continue to conduct work in this area to better understand if and how differences in learning, cognition, and language manifest themselves and what the implications of these differences are.

We were able to identity a good amount of literature on Black English. Despite the position of sociolinguists over the past 40 years that Black English is a language, some continue to believe that Black English is an incorrect or a degenerate form of SAE. These views are held by African Americans, as well as by members of society in general (Siegel, 2006). Siegel compares the negative views about AAE with other languages, such as Appalachian English—as well as creole languages that are spoken in Jamaica and Hawaii. He notes that it is no coincidence that social groups who speak marginalized varieties of languages are themselves often marginalized.

Summary

The proverb at the beginning of the chapter states, "Knowledge kept to oneself is as useless as a candle burning in a pot." One feature of learning for African Americans is the utility or practicality of knowledge. Learning will be facilitated to the extent that knowledge gained can be used to solve problems. This and other culturally congruent aspects of cognition, learning, and language have been discussed in this chapter.

African American culture influences learning, cognition, and language. Cognition is the process of thinking or mentally processing information. Learning is the acquisition of knowledge and is a cognitive process. Language is the collection of words and/or symbols and rules of use that allow for thinking and communication. The acquisition of knowledge and how knowledge is used vary across cultural groups. According to Myers (1988), the Eurocentric view of knowledge acquisition assumes that external, or objective, knowledge is the basis of all knowledge. From an Africentric perspective, knowledge acquisition occurs within social and interpersonal contexts.

Cognitive patterns also differ among cultural groups. African American children's perception of their environment shows that they many attend more to social and interpersonal aspects than to physical aspects of their environment. Many also prefer to receive information from multiple channels, including auditory, tactile, and visual channels. Some African American learners are likely to process information using a holistic rather than an elemental approach.

Although there is variability, African American children are likely to use a relational learning style. The relational learning style focuses on social rather than nonsocial aspects of the learning environment, uses a gestalt or relational approach to learning, and uses spontaneity when processing information.

African American children tend to perform better and prefer a communal learning environment over an independent learning environment. Achievement and performance are also enhanced in learning environments that include verve, rhythm, and movement. Understanding the learning style of African American children should facilitate their performance on intelligence and other tests.

AAE has several unique features. It is derived from SAE, West African languages, and African American pidgins and creoles spoken at different times and in different regions of the United States. It is a legitimate language with consistent structure and rules of use. A consideration of the cognitive styles and language of African Americans should facilitate learning and achievement. At the same time, speakers of AAE are more likely to be seen as less competent than speakers of SAE, as there is some stigma attached to speaking AAE or Ebonics.

Several educators and researchers have identified ways in which academic performance and achievement among African American children can be improved by attending to learning styles and languages.

10

RELIGION AND SPIRITUALITY

He who leaves truth behind, returns to it.

—African proverb

LEARNING OBJECTIVES

- To be able to define religion and spirituality

- To become aware of spiritual and religious practices and beliefs among African Americans

- To become more knowledgeable about historical perspectives on African American religion

- To become familiar with Traditional African religion

- To be able to describe the African American Church and other religious institutions

- To understand how religious and spiritual beliefs and practices affect health and well-being

- To become knowledgeable about methodological and research issues associated with studying religion and spirituality among African Americans

- To become familiar with programs that use religiosity and spirituality to improve well-being of African Americans

HOW BLACK AND WHITE CHRISTIANS DO DISCIPLESHIP DIFFERENTLY

BY KATE SHELLNUTT

When it comes to spiritual formation and discipleship, African American Christians are in it together. Black believers are more likely to position their growth in Christ in the context of community and fellowship, while white Christians take a more individualized

(Continued)

(Continued)

approach, according to a study released this week from Barna Research.

The survey found that twice as many black Christians as whites were currently being mentored or discipled by a fellow believer (38% vs. 19%). Over a quarter of black Christians also served as mentors themselves, compared to 17 percent of white Christians.

The prevalence of such relationships relates to traditional models of leadership and lineage in African American churches. In an interview with CT about his book *Reviving the Black Church*, pastor Thabiti Anyabwile described how "most of our pastors were in some kind of apprenticeship in preparation for the ministry. They would sit under another pastor or have a 'spiritual father' who would pour himself into them."

Black Christians also preferred group-based discipleship to one-on-one (32% vs. 22%), while white Christians favored being discipled on their own (39% vs. 31%), according to Barna. They are four times more likely than white Christians to list study groups as "very important" to their spiritual development.

Natasha Sistrunk Robinson, a mentoring coach and author of *Mentor for Life*, numbers among the churchgoing African Americans who see group mentoring as essential.

"In a mentoring small group, your learning is going to be enhanced because you're not just hearing the philosophy of one person; rather you are drawing near to God by sharing in the diverse experiences of the group," she wrote. "When we mentor people and intentionally make disciples in this way, we also create safe places for people to learn and grow, to love and be loved well."

Barna researchers pointed out that fellowship was a particularly strong component of mentorship for African Americans. "There are plenty of similarities in how both groups define

the primary goals of discipleship," the report stated, "but black Christian leaders are more likely to say 'deepening one's faith through education and fellowship' is a goal of discipleship (85% compared to 71%)."

The group mindset among African Americans also stems from church history and current racial tensions. Black churches and denominations formed when their members were excluded from white fellowship. Given that Martin Luther King Jr.'s observation on Sunday morning segregation mostly still holds true, believers continue to view these congregations as "a necessary place of refuge and resistance" in the aftermath of racially motivated violence and systemic injustice, CT columnist Christena Cleveland wrote.

About a third of black Christians and more than a quarter of white Christians say getting through tough times motivates them to pursue spiritual growth.

These realities add significance to fellowship found in churches and small groups. While white Christians are more likely to label their spiritual lives as "entirely private," African Americans see their spiritual lives as intertwined with the social and political situations they face. Almost half of black Christians (46%) believe their spiritual lives impact society at large, compared to 27 percent of white Christians.

"There's something powerful about being together. It reminds me of a Henri Nouwen quote about the ministry of presence that suggests we underestimate just what being together means," said Cleveland, discussing a retreat held for Christian women of color last year. "Often we want to preach eloquent sermons or produce some sort of amazing artistic expression to touch people's hearts, and that's great . . . but a lot of it is laughing and knowing that we're not alone."

Source: Shellnutt (2017).

INTRODUCTION, DEFINITIONS, AND BACKGROUND

Religious practice and spiritual beliefs are significant to the lives of most African Americans. Spiritual and religious beliefs and behaviors influence family and social relationships, choice of romantic partners, alcohol and drug use decisions, and community involvement. As seen in the cover story, religion is an integral part of African American lives. Within the same religious denomination, practices differ for African Americans than other racial and ethnic groups. Religious practices from Africa followed enslaved Africans in the New World and were integrated with Christianity to produce unique beliefs and expressions that continues today (Wilford, 2016). Physical and psychological well-being and coping mechanisms are also notably affected by religious and spiritual beliefs (Mattis, 2000).

In the first section of this chapter, we provide definitions and information on religious groups, practices, and activities among African Americans. We discuss historical influences, particularly religion in West African culture and historical perspectives on African American religion; then, we examine some unique features of the African American Church including the Black MegaChurch. We then review research on the links between spirituality, religion, and well-being. We also examine contemporary topics. Methodological issues related to conceptualizing and measuring spirituality and religion are considered, followed by a discussion of best practices, a critical discussion, and a chapter summary.

African Americans are of diverse faiths, but the majority of African Americans are Christian. Although our discussions of the religious experiences and activities of contemporary African Americans will focus significantly on Christian perspectives, we will also discuss the role of Islam and African religions in the experience of African Americans.

Definitions

Religion differs from spirituality, although the terms have been used interchangeably. People generally report themselves to be more spiritual than religious. Spirituality comes from the Latin word *spiritus* (spirit). Spirituality has been defined as the belief in a sacred force that exists in all things (Potts, 1991). Spirituality is not dependent on any doctrine, organization, or culture but rather on individual beliefs. To be spiritual implies the construction of existential meaning and values based on factors other than the physical body, material world, or science. Meraviglia (1999) defines spirituality as "experiences and expressions of one's spirit in a unique and dynamic process reflecting faith in God or a supreme being; connectedness with oneself, others, nature, or God; and an integration of the dimensions of mind, body, and spirit" (p. 29).

Religion comes from the Latin word *religio* (good faith ritual). Religion is a "system of beliefs and practices that nurture the relationship with the Supreme Being" (Meraviglia, 1999, p. 25). Religion involves universal life experiences and the meaning that is attached to these experiences. The universal experiences include all the ways in which humans make sense of the world, including making sense of birth, death, joy, sorrow, knowledge, ignorance, success, failure, love, hate, suffering, relief, body, and spirit (Musser & Price, 1992). Although religiosity and spirituality differ, much of the research reviewed in this chapter references both, and the terms used in this chapter will correspond to usage cited by authors.

Mattis (2000) studied the differences in the meaning of spirituality and religion in an African American sample. Respondents defined spirituality as a connection to a higher power. They considered spirituality to be the internalization and expression of key values, such as goodness in daily life. Spirituality was conceptualized as one's relationship with a higher power or with transcendent forces, including nature. Religion was seen as the mechanism for achieving spirituality. Both African Americans and Caribbean Americans tend to identify as both religious and spiritual (Mattis & Grayman-Simpson, 2013).

Religious Activity

Chatters, Taylor, Bullard, and Jackson (2009) analyzed data from the National Survey of American Life (NSAL) and found high levels of religious activity among African Americans. More than two-thirds of African Americans indicated that they were members of places of worship. Participants also reported high levels of involvement in nonorganizational religious behaviors, such as prayer and reading religious material (Chatters et al., 2009).

High levels of religious activities are found across various Black populations. Using data from the NSAL, Chatters et al. (2009) assessed differences between African Americans, Black Caribbeans, and non-Hispanic Whites on 12 measures of religious participation (e.g., listening to religious television and radio programs, praying and asking someone to pray for self, and self-rating of religiosity). African Americans reported higher levels of religious behaviors than did non-Hispanic Whites on all 12 measures. Caribbean Blacks also had higher levels of religious participation than non-Hispanic Whites on 10 of the 12 measures. African Americans and Caribbean Blacks reported similar levels of religious participation, with the exception of Church membership rates, participation in Church activities, reading religious materials, and requesting prayer from others, with Caribbean Blacks scoring lower on these measures than African Americans. Church participation may be lower among Caribbean Blacks due to time in this country, immigrant status, and not having found a regular place to attend Church.

Findings in the Chatters et al. (2009) study are also seen in research published by the Barna Group (2011), which conducts research on religion, spirituality, and faith in the United States. The Barna Group reported on major shifts in beliefs in faith and religious practice over the past 20 years for African Americans, Whites, and Hispanics, noting overall significant declines in religious activities, such as weekly Church attendance, Bible reading, and volunteering in Church. However, African Americans religious beliefs and behaviors were fairly stable, with fewer changes than the other ethnic groups. For example, a 20-year decline in being un-Churched (e.g., not attended any Church during previous six months other than for special occasions, such as a wedding) declined from 25% to 40% for Whites and from 20% to 40% for Hispanics, but there was no decline for African Americans. Similarly, the Pew Religious Landscape Survey also reported racial and ethnic differences in religious affiliation. This survey found that 18% of African Americans reported themselves as religiously unaffiliated, compared with 20% of Hispanics and 24% of Whites (Pew, 2015). As noted in the cover story, African American Christians tend to view Church participation as community fellowship.

A survey of the Barna Group found that Blacks were more likely than Hispanics and Whites to engage in Church activities, including Sunday school class and volunteering at their Church, and to read the Bible other than at Church. African Americans were only half as likely as Whites or Hispanics to not have a Church; to have the belief that their commitment to Jesus Christ was important in their daily life; to believe that God is the "all-knowing and all-powerful" Creator of the universe who rules the world; and to believe they have a personal responsibility to share their religious beliefs with others. See Table 10.1 for additional information on differences in religious practices and beliefs among African Americans and other ethnic groups (Barna Group, 2005).

Church attendance is an important Sunday ritual in many African American households. The typical Sunday service for African Americans is 70% longer than that attended by Whites. The typical Black Church has more people in attendance than the typical White Church, with attendance about 50% greater in Black Churches than in White Churches (Barna Group, 2005). The pastor is an influential person, and 65% of African Americans report that pastors of Black Churches are important

TABLE 10.1 ■ Religious Beliefs and Practices, by Race and Ethnicity

	White	Black	Hispanic	Asian
Read the Bible in past week	36%	59%	39%	20%
Attended religious service in past week	41%	48%	38%	23%
Prayed to God in past week	81%	91%	86%	46%
Participated in a small group past week	16%	31%	27%	13%
"Bible is totally accurate" (strongly agree)	36%	57%	40%	24%
"Satan is not a living being" (strongly disagree)	30%	27%	30%	14%
"Jesus Christ sinned while on earth" (strongly disagree)	37%	49%	35%	22%
Born-again Christian	41%	47%	29%	12%
Atheist or agnostic	12%	5%	7%	20%
Aligned with a non-Christian faith	11%	12%	10%	45%

Source: Barna Group (2005).

leaders in the African American community. Black Churches are informal and safe places where many African Americans go for help. Black clergy play a pivotal role in providing different types of help, including addressing mental and physical health issues (Allen, Davey, & Davey, 2010).

Religious Groups

African Americans belong to many different denominations, including Baptist, African Methodist Episcopal, Jehovah's Witnesses, Church of God in Christ, Seventh-day Adventist, Nation of Islam, Presbyterian, Lutheran, Episcopal, Roman Catholic, and many others. According to the Pew Forum on Religion and Public Life (2008), African Americans are more likely than members of other racial and ethnic groups to report affiliation or formal membership with a religious denomination. The report adds that "even among black adults who are unaffiliated (12%), more than two-thirds (70%) say that religion is somewhat or very important in their lives" (pp. 40–41). In contrast, among the overall unaffiliated population, only one-third report that religion is somewhat or very important in their lives. Data for the Pew U.S. Religious Landscape Survey were collected in 2007 and were based on interviews with more than 35,000 Americans, ages 18 and older (Pew Forum, 2008).

Most Blacks in the Pew survey reported belonging to Protestant denominations (see Figure 10.1). Baptists account for the vast majority of the historically Black Protestant Church members. The National Baptist convention is the largest of the

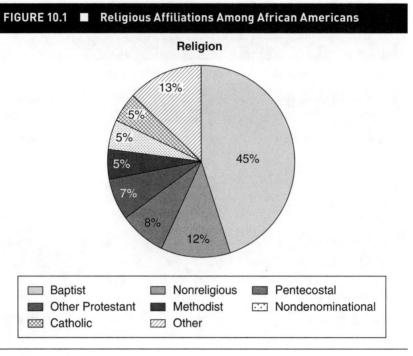

FIGURE 10.1 ■ Religious Affiliations Among African Americans

Religion

Legend:
- Baptist
- Other Protestant
- Catholic
- Nonreligious
- Methodist
- Other
- Pentecostal
- Nondenominational

Source: Pew Research Center's Forum on Religion & Public Life, U.S. Religious Landscape Survey (2008).

historically Black Baptist denominations and is the fourth-largest Protestant denomination. Black members of historically Black Churches are more likely to have been raised in their denomination (69% compared with 54% for all Protestants) and are less likely to have come from faiths outside the Protestant Church in comparison with Protestants as a whole (10% vs. 16%). Whites (45%) and Blacks (42%) are more likely to change denominations than non-Latino Asians (37%) or Latinos (35%). Blacks also represent a significant percentage of other religious denominations. African Americans account for 22% of Jehovah's Witnesses and 24% of Muslims in the United States (Pew Forum, 2008).

Demographic Factors
Associated With Religious Activity

African American religious participation varies by demographic factors. Women are more religious and attend religious services more frequently than men, and older persons attend more frequently than younger ones (Flannelly, Galek, Kytle, & Silton, 2010). Married persons attend religious services more frequently than persons who are not married. Those with more years of education attend services on a more frequent basis than those with fewer years of education.

There are also regional differences in religious attendance. Southerners have higher rates of religious service attendance than persons in other regions of the United States. Residence in an urban, rural, or suburban area does not affect religious service attendance.

Demographic differences are also seen in prayer. Older individuals pray more than younger individuals. In a study of four age cohorts (18–30, 31–40, 41–60, and 61 and higher), Levin and Taylor (1997) found that prayer is more frequent in successively older cohorts. The findings from this study also show that African Americans pray more frequently than Whites and females more frequently than males. Finally, there are differences among African Americans and Black Caribbeans on some religious practices, with having a Church home and Church attendance lower for Black Caribbeans than for African Americans (Chatters et al., 2009).

HISTORICAL INFLUENCES

There are many religious practices used by people of African descent. These include Ifá (Yoruba faith), Akan, and other African-derived or adapted religions such as Vodou or Santería, which are practiced especially in countries with large populations of people of African descent (e.g., Brazil, Haiti, Cuba). Our discussion here, however, centers on African religion and spirituality experiences in West Africa.

African religions have played a significant role in the historical and contemporary lives of African Americans. African religious traditions are frequently discussed from a pan-African perspective that underlines their notable similarities. Specific traditions are also linked to practices derived from African religions from specific nations in Africa and to unique sets of religious practice in the United States. For example, the Yoruban religion, also known as Ifá, involves a monotheistic belief system with a god Olorun or Olodumare. This tradition originates from the West Africa Yoruban and Bantu peoples in Nigeria and Benin. The cosmology of Ifá involves a pantheon of *orishas* (smaller deities). These include deities such as Shango, the god of thunder, and Yemalla, the goddess of the sea and the moon. The religion involves the practice of *babalawo* (diviners), who assist practitioners in identifying their personal *orisha*. *Tambor* (celebrations) involve trance possessions by priests or initiates during a liturgy that involves singing, drumming, and dance. As with many African religions, Ifá is syncretic—that is, the belief system is nondogmatic, permeable, and tolerant of other belief traditions. The varied belief systems of different sects or different religions are not seen as mutually exclusive or in conflict but are seen as part of a whole. Consequently, these belief systems have historically tended to evolve by the addition of new beliefs to existing ones.

Christianity—and more specifically, Catholicism—influenced areas of West Africa and the enslaved individuals who were settled in Cuba and Brazil. Yoruban religion incorporated many Catholic structures, and Regla de Osha evolved. (Regla de Osha is also known as Lukumi, Macumba, or Santería, an originally pejorative name given by the Spanish that has become increasingly used by practitioners.) Within Santería, many of the original *orishas* are identified with individual Catholic saints. The practice is found in areas of Florida, Puerto Rico, New Jersey New York City, and Los Angeles. Followers are also in Venezuela, the Dominican Republic, Cuba, and Mexico. Estimates of the number of practitioners in the continental United States are wide ranging, but the American Religious Identification Survey (ARIS) estimates 22,000 American practitioners based on their random telephone survey of 50,281 households conducted in 2001.

Beyond Santería, other adaptations of the traditional Yoruban religion include Candomble, practiced in Brazil; the Shango Baptist or *orisha* religion, found in Trinidad and Tobago; and Voudoo (or Voudoun), practiced in Jamaica, Haiti, and New Orleans. Spiritual practices within traditional African religions involve drumming, dance, sacrifice, and possession by gods. Organizations such as the National African Religion Congress (NARC) operate to represent and support the rights of all African-based religions in the Diaspora (NARC, 2013). The NARC serves as an accrediting body for priests and priestesses of traditional African religions.

Religion and Spirituality in Traditional African Culture

Jaco Beyers, a South African scholar, wrote that the majority of our definitions and understanding of religion have come from a Western background, with the dominant religion of the West being Christianity (Beyers, 2012). In trying to understand African religions, scholars have tended to Westernize African religions, taking them out of their cultural and historical context. An African understanding of religion emphasizes (a) a holistic approach to understanding unity; (b) the importance of the meaning that religion creates; (c) the use of religion as the framework for understanding rituals; and (d) an understanding that religion is the background against which social values should be understood. Furthermore, according to Beyers, African religion does not tend to differentiate the transcendental from the earthly and does not attempt to present one unified understanding of religions.

Spirituality and religion permeate every aspect of the African's life, from birth to death, regardless of life circumstances. Within traditional African society, the person is immersed in religious experiences that start before birth and continue after death. In fact, African religion may be better thought of as a philosophy of life. Names of people have religious meaning; rocks and streams are not just objects but are objects with religious significance; the sound of the drum operates at a spiritual level (Mbiti, 1970). Within social, economic, and political systems, the influence of religion is evident. In politics, people believe that the king is divine. In economics, many traditional Africans believe that malevolent forces, spirits, or juju (magic) cause crop failure. In the social world, there is the belief that supernatural forces cause success. In the moral arena, many Africans fear instant retribution by divinities.

Africans explain the world around them in religious terms. In all that is undertaken, whether it is cultivating, sowing, harvesting, eating, or traveling, religion and the spiritual world are at work. Individuals cannot separate themselves from the community's religion. This implies that in traditional African society, there are no atheists or agnostics.

Although many Africans are Christians or Muslims, Traditional African Religion is the basis for religious activities for many Africans in past and contemporary times. According to the Ghanaian scholar Gyekye (1996), there is no religion that has been misunderstood or misrepresented more than Traditional African Religion. Traditional African Religion has been referred to as primitivism, animism, paganism, and fetishism. When the European missionaries came to Africa, they did not need to convince Africans to believe in God or life after death. In fact, Traditional African Religion shares three basic beliefs with other religions: (a) belief in a Creator who is in control of the universe, (b) belief that man's bond to his Creator and his later separation from the Creator is due to his own fault, and (c) belief that man will attempt to reconcile himself with his Creator and that this reconciliation will lead to his salvation.

Features of Traditional African Religion

Each community in Africa has its own system of religious beliefs and practices. However, despite the different religious systems, there are many practices, beliefs, and rituals that are common to all. None of these religions is revealed, like those of Christianity, Islam, or Buddhism.[1] Because Traditional African Religion is not a revealed religion, it is difficult to point to a specific time in history when it was founded. Traditional African Religion operates beyond any such notion.

One feature common to all traditional African religious communities is the belief in mystical power, and a belief in the existence of mystical forces or powers in the universe that can be tapped by those human beings who have the knowledge to do so for good or ill. Because these experiences cannot be given scientific explanations, some scholars have associated African religion with the practice of magic. In Traditional African Religion, God (though not the Christian God) is the Supreme Being but not the object of direct worship. Worship is directed at nature—trees, rivers, mountains, and rocks. This does not mean that African religion is nature worship but rather that objects of nature are inhabited by spiritual beings who exist as intermediaries between God and humans but who cannot be seen by the human eye. Worship is directed toward these spiritual beings and not toward the object itself. Consequently, objects of nature take on spiritual meaning and respect.

The major beliefs of Traditional African Religion are described below (Gyekye, 1996; Quarcoopome, 1987):

Belief in a Supreme Being. There is a supreme being who is a God who created all things. Through one's experience in the world, one comes to know that God exists. Africans refer to God as Creator, the Great One, Omnipotent, Omnipresent, and the Great Spirit. God is everywhere, but God is also believed to be far away, beyond the reach of humans. There is nothing greater than God, and humans should humble themselves before God. "If you want to say something to God, say it to the wind. The wind is everywhere and blows in all directions; and even though it is intangible, its effects are felt everywhere. In the same way, God is everywhere. Thus, daily acts of worship such as prayer, offering, and sacrifices are presented to God. One is completely dependent on God" (Gyeke, 1996, p. 9).

God Is Good. God is identified with goodness. The goodness of God is seen in the satisfaction of human needs, including supplying rain, averting disasters, and healing diseases. God is compassionate, generous, and kind. God is fair and rewards those who are good and punishes those who are evil. Humans are expected to exercise free will for good rather than evil, and so the human being, not God, is held responsible for all acts of good or evil.

Belief in Divinities. The divinities stand next to God and are God's children. They are ministers of God who have derived powers and act as intermediaries between God and man. They are nature spirits and dwell in objects in nature, such as rivers, lakes, trees, mountains, and so forth. God is worshipped indirectly through them. The divinities are therefore worshiped daily, weekly, and annually.

Belief in Spirit Beings. After God and the divinities come the spirit beings. These spirits may be good or bad, but they are usually good. Spirits are immaterial but can assume dimensions when they wish to be seen. Ghost spirits are spirits of those who die a cursed or bad death—that is, by hanging, drowning, or disease. Sometimes, these spirits may enter into animals or birds to destroy or harm people. These spirits are bad spirits.

Beliefs in Ancestors. The ancestors are the heroes and heroines from various tribes. Ancestors are believed to have special powers in the afterlife and, through these powers, to intervene in the lives of the living. They also act as intermediaries between God and the divinities and men. Ancestors are the unseen members at family or tribal meetings and serve as guardians. The ancestors are respected and honored and are remembered, especially at annual festivals.

Belief in the Practice of Magic and Medicine. Magic is the attempt to influence people and events by supernatural means. Magical objects, like charms, talismans, and amulets, are used as protection against evil forces, such as witchcraft and sorcery, and to achieve success. Some may use magic to harm others or to gain an advantage. Medicine is the art of restoring and preserving health. An African belief is that medicine is closely associated with religion. The Divine Healer (i.e., God) dispenses medicine through the divinities and to spirits who, in turn, provide the knowledge to priests, medicine men, and traditional healers.

The Soul Is Immortal. Traditional African religious views on death and immortality are complex. There is the common view that the soul is an immortal part of the human being that survives death, and in an afterlife, this soul will give an account of its physical life to God. Because the soul returns to God when the person dies, the soul is immortal. This immortal soul enters the world of the spirits, that which is beyond this world. This belief implies that a person is immortal.

Little Concern With Afterlife. While there is belief in an afterlife, traditional African religions do not concern themselves with what kind of life will be led by the immortal soul. For example, there are no beliefs about heaven or hell, a better life, or resurrection. In contrast to an emphasis on a better life after death, as in many Christian religions, more focus is placed on the attainment of human fulfillment in this world. Religion is considered essential to attain the needs and happiness of human beings in this life. Prayers often request that God provide comforts and the things necessary for a happy, satisfying life. This belief emphasizes that religion must have a social value. Religious faith is perceived as useful and practical, rather than as a means for salvation.

Communalism. Traditional African Religion is communal and supports the values of social solidarity, harmony, and cooperation. Traditional African Religion is not primarily useful for the individual but for the community to which the individual belongs. Community celebrations and rites, with public drumming, dancing, and singing, have religious meanings. They are important occasions for the collective affirmation of communal values and strengths, bonding members of the community together.

Provides a Moral Code. Traditional African Religion provides sanctions for the moral obligations and responsibilities of community members. The enforcement of these sanctions is often done by the traditional religious leader. Misfortunes that befall individuals or communities are often interpreted as punishment for bad behavior or failure to fulfill moral obligations to kinsfolk and the community. Good fortunes are seen as rewards for meeting the community's moral obligations.

Traditional African Religion in Contemporary Africa

Although the primary religions in Africa are Christianity and Islam, Africans practice components of Traditional African Religion alongside these two religions. In sub-Saharan African, there are approximately 234 million Muslims (about 15% of the Muslim population) and 470 million Christians (about 20% of Christians worldwide) (Pew Research Center, 2011). The Pew Research Forum conducted a survey in 19 African countries about traditional religious practices. Respondents had strong belief in the protective power of sacrificial offerings and sacred objects. One in five persons in every country reported believing in the evil eye (the ability of certain people to cast malicious curses or spells). In 5 of the 19 countries (Tanzania, Cameroon, Democratic Republic of the Congo, Senegal, and Mali), the majority of the people held this belief.

African traditional religious beliefs and practices also informed day-to-day living. In 14 of the 19 countries, about a third of respondents indicated that they sometimes consulted traditional healers when someone in their household is sick. In five of the countries (Cameroon, Chad, Guinea Bissau, Mali, and Senegal), over half of the respondents reported using traditional healers. In three countries (Tanzania, Senegal, and Mali), more than half of the respondents had high levels of traditional African religious beliefs. In eight other countries, between 25% and 50% endorsed high levels of traditional religious beliefs (Cameroon, South Africa, Guinea Bissau, Chad, Botswana, Ghana, DR Congo, and Liberia) (Pew Research Center, 2011).

Traditional African Religion in the United States

Several religious practices (discussed previously) among Blacks in the United States and the Caribbean share some features of Traditional African Religion. For example, Santería, which is a combination of Yoruba spirituality and elements of Catholicism, is practiced throughout the United States in cities such as New York, New Orleans, and Los Angeles.

Religions such as Christianity and Islam experienced by contemporary African Americans share some commonalities with Traditional African Religion. Like Traditional African Religion, these religions provide a mechanism to support the political, educational, health, and social needs of community members. These influences are especially apparent in many traditional African American Churches but are also evident in Islam. The religious institution in the African American community has historically provided the moral dictates of how members should behave. The head of the Church, temple, or mosque is a leader not only within the religious organization but also within the community.

Historical Perspectives on African American Religion

Enslaved Africans came to the United States carrying with them a variety of religious beliefs and traditions. Practicing traditional African religions or a combination of Christian practices and traditional African practices, these individuals did not arrive in the Americas as blank religious slates.

During the colonial period, the spirituality of Blacks appeared to be of limited interest to White settlers (Gomez, 1998). In the mid to late 1700s and during the 1800s, slave owners most frequently used Christianity as a means of social control to keep enslaved Africans compliant and docile. Slave owners and clergy taught enslaved Africans that Christianity would save their souls and provide them with a good afterlife if they were obedient to their masters. This emphasis on afterlife was one difference seen in religious beliefs among Africans in Africa and enslaved Africans in America. In addition, Christian doctrine was shaped to support social and political rhetoric that provided a rationale for sustaining the "peculiar institution." However, Churches and spirituality also served as opportunities for enslaved Africans to communicate through hidden messages embedded in the lyrics of spirituals. Spirituals spoke of freedom and sometimes communicated maps or signals related to escape plans or directions relevant to the Underground Railroad.

Blum (2011) describes the symbolic importance of Jesus for enslaved Africans. Prior to the Civil War, Jesus was both a unifying force and a divisive symbol. Jesus provided an example of a different approach to enslavement and was a medium in which to discuss spiritual and legal bonding, violence and escape, individual liberty, and collective revolutions. Christ also represented an authority symbol that, on some occasions, surpassed national laws. Nat Turner, an enslaved African from Southampton County, Virginia, best exemplified this point. Nat Turner was a slave and a preacher who, in 1831, at the age of 30, led a rebellion that resulted in 60 White deaths. Deeply religious, Turner had received what he believed was a sign from God to lead the rebellion. Over 200 Blacks were killed by angry Whites in the days after the rebellion was put down.

Although many enslaved Africans adopted Christian beliefs, those beliefs and religious practices were notably shaped by their native spirituality. Enslaved Africans began organizing their own worship services and met at prearranged times in secret places for singing, preaching, and praying. Jesus Christ became a figure of liberation for enslaved Africans as they identified with his persecution, were strengthened by his perseverance, and found hope in his resurrection (Lincoln & Mamiya, 1990). Enslaved Africans found hope and comfort in the presence of God, in meetings to support each other, and in music and dance. Within the Church, they felt respected and in control of their destiny. The Church remains today a place where African Americans can achieve respect and influence regardless of life circumstance.

In the latter part of the 18th century, independent congregations and Churches for African Americans were formed. Due to segregation, African Americans could not worship with Whites, so they formed their own congregations (Phelps, 1990). These independent Churches allowed African Americans to emphasize aspects of Christianity that spoke to their unique experiences in America. For example, emphasis was placed on the humanity of enslaved Blacks as "children of God" rather than as "three-fifths of all other Persons."

The theme of liberation and control continues to echo in contemporary Black Churches. Theologians such as James Hal Cone, one of the early Black liberation theologians, supported independence from White Churches that had failed to support the struggles of Blacks against racism and oppression. Cone and other Black liberation theologians incorporated African American cultural resources and traditions within their perspectives on spirituality. This perspective also emphasized Jesus's identification and alignment with the poor and support of the dignity and worth of the downtrodden. The freedom to be all that God intended has been a key theme in civil rights and equality messages, including those of the civil rights leader Martin Luther King. The message of liberation and freedom is consistent with messages that preach against the negative self-images of African Americans brought about by internalized racism. Conceptually, from a Black liberation perspective, God is Black, in the image of Black people.

Along with messages of liberation and empowerment have been messages about the responsibility of the African American Church to provide social, economic, psychological, and educational support to its people. The African American Church has been described as the only institution within the African American community that is owned and controlled solely by African Americans (Cook, 1993). Consequently, no other institution in the United States has the level of loyalty and attention to and by African Americans as does the Church (Allen et al., 2010).

Islam

The history of Islam among Americans of African descent traces its beginnings to early enslavement. Scholars estimate that 15% to 30% of Africans who were brought to the United States as slaves were Muslim. The majority of the remaining practiced indigenous forms of worship. Most were converted to Christianity. Most became Baptist, although slaves from Louisiana became Catholic because of the French settlers in that area (Black Demographics, n.d.). Analysis of historical accounts and documents estimates that of the more than 400,000 enslaved Africans who came to British North America during the slave trade, more than 200,000 came from areas where there was a significant Muslim presence and influence (Gomez, 1998). The documentation of this presence includes the history of Spanish settlement in northern Florida predating the arrival of the British and public notices of runaway slaves bearing Islamic names. With limited access to support the intergenerational transmission of Islamic practice (e.g., access to copies of the Quran and education in Arabic) and the promotion of Christianity among enslaved Africans, the practice of Islam among Blacks diminished significantly.

During the 20th century, many African Americans converted to the Islamic faith as a result of the perceived view that White Christianity was oppressive. The physical images of a White Jesus made many African Americans turn to the teachings of the Honorable Elijah Muhammad and the Black Muslim faith. The renewal of Islamic practice among African Americans is traced to the 1913 establishment of the Moorish Science Temple Divine and National Movement of North America by Noble Drew Ali in Newark, New Jersey. One of Ali's disciples, Wali D. Fard (believed to be of Turkish ancestry), established the Temple of Islam and named himself the head of the Nation of Islam (NOI). Fard taught that Blacks could succeed only through separation from Whites. It was there in Detroit, Michigan, that Robert Poole became a minister within the Temple and later became known as Elijah Mohammad, subsequently establishing the NOI in Chicago.

Membership in the NOI increased notably during the lifetime of Malcolm X. The NOI was seen as especially attractive to men because it addressed the economic needs of the community and the social roles of men within the African American community. Warith Muhammad succeeded his father as the leader of the NOI and eventually changed the racial separation doctrine. Under his leadership, the NOI became the Muslim Society of America and practiced orthodox Sunni Islam, which teaches the acceptance of people of all races. The history of Islamic practice traced to the NOI involves the formation of several different splinter groups, including the Bililliam Community and World Community Al-Islam in the West, the Lost Found Nation of Islam, and the Five Percenters. In 1977, Minister Louis Farrakhan split with Warith and established the Original Nation of Islam, now known as the NOI.

According to data from the Pew Research Center on U.S. Politics & Policy (2011), Muslims are currently the most racially diverse religious group in America. Individuals of African descent account for 23%, Whites account for 30%, Asians account for 21%, other mixed ethnicity account for 19%, and Hispanics account for 6%. Among Muslims age 18 and older, 63% were born abroad. Among Muslim immigrants to the United States, 41% are North African or Middle Eastern immigrants, 26% are from the South Asian region, and the rest are from sub-Saharan Africa, Europe, or elsewhere. The Muslim Society of America contains the largest number of African American Muslims and is estimated to number approximately 2.5 million. The NOI is estimated to have between 30,000 and 1 million adherents.

CONTEMPORARY AFRICAN AMERICAN CHURCHES

As noted, African Americans belong to diverse religious denominations and worship in diverse places (i.e., mosque, hall, temple, and Church). Religious scholars have commented on the lack of attention to non-Christians in psychological research on African Americans and religiosity (Mattis & Grayman-Simpson, 2013). In this Chapter we have discussed some non-Christian forms of religiosity.

The majority of African Americans worship within the Church, and so the Church is the primary focus of the following discussion. Among African Americans, the Church, as an institution, is second in importance only to the family. Following enslavement, the Church became the community's central institution for civic, art, economic, business, education, and political activities (Allen et al., 2010; Calhoun-Brown, 1998). This role continues today. The Church serves several purposes for its members: It is the place to receive spiritual renewal, religious education, family and community connections, and reinforcements and rewards for positive behaviors and service to the community.

Features of African American Churches

Although there is a great deal of diversity within and between African American Churches, there are some features common to most African American (Christian) Churches. These features, as described by Cook and Wiley (2000) and others, are discussed next.

Community Fellowship

Churches provide an opportunity for people in a community to belong. Many individuals are born into a Church and remain within the Church until they die (Cook & Wiley, 2000). The Church becomes part of the extended family, and Church life is often intermixed with family life. The concept of the Church family is relevant to many African Americans and describes the overarching involvement of the Church in its members' lives. The Church provides stability, affirmation, connection to others, recreational activity, and opportunities for educational and learning experiences. Finding a Church home becomes important when African American families move (Boyd-Franklin, 2010). Some continue as members of their previous Church; others seek out a new Church, usually with a similar ministry, closer to their new residence. Most African Americans participate in activities and services outside of routine Sunday worship services. Children participate in activities such as Sunday school and Vacation Bible School. Adults participate in Sunday school, Bible study, choir, and special interest groups (i.e., women's ministry, couples ministry, prison ministry, and so on).

Sometimes, resources available to Church members are extended to those outside the congregation. Support groups, educational and tutoring programs, and health programs are some examples of such resources. Larger Churches may offer programs to support community residents, including school and childcare facilities, clothing and housing, support for incarcerated individuals, and counseling and support for individuals affected by substance abuse and HIV/AIDS.

There are many leadership and service positions and ministries in African American Churches. Civil rights and political action activities are undertaken by many Churches. Many of the civil rights activities of the 1950s and 1960s began in the Church. Some contemporary Churches and religious leaders explicitly support political positions and candidates, and this support has raised legal concerns regarding the nonprofit IRS status of these organizations and the associated prohibition of political endorsements.

Often, the values, attitudes, and behavior of a Church stem from its members. Although the Church is a positive force in most people's lives, it may also be a source of conflict, as when the Church's values are in conflict with individual values and beliefs. This may be especially the case with adolescents, who may be influenced more by peers than by the Church. Also, some members, such as LGBTQs, are not always embraced by the Church (see discussion of lesbian, gay, bisexual, transgender, and queer issues later in this chapter).

Women Are Followers

Traditionally, African American Churches have been led by men, with congregations composed largely of women and children (Cook & Wiley, 2000; Lowen, 2016). This is not because African American women are not available and trained in Church leadership, as African American women are in seminary schools at rates only slightly less than African American men. In 2015, 4,183 Black women entered the Association of Theological School (ATS) recognized seminaries compared to 4,809 Black men (ATS). However, a 2015 survey of 4,436 congregations found that only 8.6% had a female as their sole or senior leader (Faith Communities Today, 2015). The leadership structure usually involves men in the pulpit and majority women in the pew—men in power and women following their edicts. The extensive and significant contributions of African American women are made as lay leaders, not as religious heads of Churches (Lowen, 2016). Women usually conduct most of the Church activities, from organizing fellowship dinners to laying out the clothes for a baptism.

Some Christian Churches hold to the biblical writing that the man is the head of the household and thus has to be the head of the Church. Research on Church leadership is mostly from the male perspective and even seen in televised reality shows such as *The Preachers of Atlanta*, where the role of women is traditionally to be a pastor's wife or "first lady" (Hervet, 2014).

With the increase in seminary training for women, we expect to see more women gaining influence in leadership positions and becoming Church senior pastors. The "Contemporary Issues" box provides an interesting analysis of the role of the Church in the lives of African American women and raises the question as to whether this would be the case if more Church leaders were women.

CONTEMPORARY ISSUES
ARE BLACK CHURCHES KEEPING BLACK WOMEN SINGLE?

African American women report the highest level of religious engagement and spiritual beliefs than any other ethnic group. Also, African American women are least likely to be married than any other ethnic group (see Chapter 5). Furthermore, African American women are more likely than African American men to attend Church, volunteer at Church, and support the mission and activities of the Church. At the same time, African American women are most often in the pews and not the pulpit, maintaining social harmony and goodwill and not delivering sermons and making decisions within the Black Church. Author and blogger Deborah Cooper details in a controversial paper that it is the Black Church that is keeping Black women single. Cooper questions whether the inordinate amount of blind and unwavering faith that Black women have in the Church is misplaced. She maintains that the Black Church is responsible for the conservative and antiquated attitudes put forth by spiritual leaders that encourage women to serve the Church instead of taking care of themselves. According to Cooper, Black Churches espouse the traditional gender roles for women to be submissive and wait for a "good man" who is sent from God. These messages keep women in a position where they are sitting and waiting for a man to magically come to them. It is the spiritual leader of the Church, most often a man that is delivering these messages. These and other pitfalls of the Black Church are discussed in Cooper's book, *The Black Church: Where Women Pray and Men Prey* (2012). The book, while controversial, is interesting and provides another perspective on issues, including the role of the Church, that affect Black women.

Worship Practice Is Based on the Holy Trinity

As noted, the majority of African Americans are members of the Christian faith, including Baptist or other Protestant denominations. Therefore, many of the practices described next are rooted in these traditions. Worship practices in Christian African American Churches are based on belief in a Holy Trinity that includes God the Father, Jesus Christ the Son, and the Holy Spirit. African American Christians consider Jesus the One who liberates, reconciles, heals, and guides (Cook & Wiley, 2000).

Music, an important part of the Church service, provides an opportunity for people to relate to lyrics of joy, peace, and thoughts of a better time in the future or the pain and sorrow of life. Clapping, dancing, testifying, and shouting provide other ways for African Americans to express themselves spiritually and are linked to cultural forms and styles of expression found in traditional African religions.

The music in worship services has become more diverse with hip-hop Christian music a part of many workshop services, especially services in urban neighborhoods with younger congregants (Huyser-Honig, n.d.; Watkins, Barr, Bryand, Curtis, & Moss, 2007). These Churches are responding to the need to reach and include young people in Church activities, and hip-hop music and culture is way of connecting with youth.

Congregations regularly engage in prayer, a crucial aspect of the worship service. In many services, members share testimonials, or stories, that tell how God is working in their lives. Biblical scripture informs Church members how God is available through the written word. The preacher's sermon can be comforting, educational, and practical in that it may address what should and should not be done. There is the expectation that attending the service will change the people's lives in some way—that is, when they leave, they will be different from who they were when they arrived.

The Pastor Is Influential

The pastor typically has great influence both in the African American Church and in the larger community. As in African cultures, religious leaders are the link and the intermediaries between individuals and God. The values and beliefs of the pastor influence the beliefs, values, and behaviors of Church members. Pastors provide counseling to members, and they are called on in good times (weddings and house blessings) and bad times (funerals and sickness) (Allen et al., 2010). The African American pastor is influential in setting the agenda for programs and activities that are implemented in the Church (Rowland & Isaac-Savage, 2014).

Funerals Support Grief

Funerals in African American Churches involve members of the Church coming together to grieve and celebrate the life of the one who has died. Funerals support the grief process and are viewed as "homegoing" celebrations. The deceased has passed from this life to a better life and has returned home to join God and previously departed loved ones (Cook & Wiley, 2000). Celebrations for the deceased came from the period of enslavement where death was seen as freedom and a reason to celebrate with many believing that the deceased's soul returned to his or her native African homeland—hence, the term *homegoing* service (FuneralWise, n.d.).

The funeral service provides support for the deceased's family and loved ones. Testimonials from friends and family speak of the good actions of the deceased while living and what that person may be doing in heaven. The pastor who delivers the eulogy may assure family and friends that the deceased will have a good and eternal life in heaven and that he or she will be reunited with loved ones who have gone on.

When there is a notice of death, Church members are supportive to the family of the deceased. They may reach out with cards and gifts and help those in grief with their daily routines by preparing meals and doing other household chores.

Religious Practice: Linking the Past, Present, and Future

Transitions in contemporary Christian religious practice among many African Americans reflect historical changes in social structures and contemporary adaptations to technology but continue to reflect their cultural connection to traditional African religious practices. With the emergence of television and social media, the Black Church has assimilated, adopted, incorporated, and taken advantage of these cultural transitions. Televangelism reaches into African American homes, bringing a mix of theological perspectives, incorporating African cultural communication styles and structures, and increasingly reflecting and articulating the values and messages of a prosperity theology.

Throughout these historical transitions and changes, there is the consistent presence of elements of traditional African religions. Religious structures adapt and incorporate religious experience and spiritual practice to fit the changing lives of the community. The expressive, emotional, communal, and musical elements of traditional African religious practice are incorporated and integrated into each new social and historical shift or technological innovation.

The Black MegaChurch

The Black MegaChurch is a relatively new institution in the African American community, with the majority of MegaChurches formed after 1980. The Black MegaChurch seats several thousand people, with 2,000 to up to 17,000 persons attending an average worship service. There are about 149 MegaChurches in the United States. Tamelyn Tucker-Worgs (2011) conducted a comprehensive study of the Black MegaChurch and described several features. The majority are located in predominantly Black neighborhoods and tend to exist in areas where there is a large African American suburban population. In terms of denomination, the majority are Baptist (57%), followed by nondenominational (21%), and Sanctified (e.g., Church of God in Christ, Pentecostal) (10%) (Tucker-Worgs, 2011). The denominational Churches appear to function more like nondenominational Churches.

Tucker-Worgs (2011) identified several characteristics of the Black MegaChurch. These Churches have a variety of programs and ministries that offer a wide range of activities for congregants. Activities and programs include educational ministries (e.g., Sunday school, Bible study), teen ministries, singles ministries, couples ministries, and health and wellness ministries. MegaChurches use technology and media more so than the average Church in outreach and worship services. This might include streaming videos with televised Church services in local markets. MegaChurches tend to have sophisticated and interactive websites where books, CDs, and other religious materials can be purchased. Some have recording studios.

In terms of leadership, MegaChurches tend to be led by a charismatic male leader who is educated with a doctoral or graduate degree. His average age is 49. Like more traditional Black Churches, women make up the majority of congregants and often serve as organizers of Church activities and ministries. While women are copastors, assistant pastors, and associate pastors, less than 1% of Black MegaChurches have a woman as a senior pastor (Tucker-Worgs, 2011).

According to Tucker-Worgs (2011), the Black MegaChurches of today fulfill similar needs for the suburban middle class as the storefront Churches fulfilled for the early 20th century Black migrants from the South. These Churches offer religious experiences that are accessible and relevant to the lived experiences of the African American middle class. Black MegaChurches engage in civic involvement more so than the average Church, including political engagement and community development. They also provide social services, especially health and food distribution activities.

Black MegaChurches have been viewed both positively and negatively. For example, there has been declining religious experiences overall for African Americans, but the Black MegaChurch has seen growth. These Churches also offer community outreach and programs that help people in the local community. However, the high-profile and wealth lifestyle of some of the Church leaders have been pointed out as a concern.

SPIRITUALITY, RELIGION, AND WELL-BEING

The findings from several studies show that various dimensions of spirituality and religiosity increase subjective well-being, lower depression and mental distress, reduce mortality and illness, and improve relationship quality (Davis-Smith, 2007; Ellison, Burdette, & Wilcox, 2010; Kuentzel, Arble, Boutros, Chugani, & Barnett, 2012; Marks, Nesteruk, Swanson, Garrison, & Davis, 2005). Religious institutions are settings in which informal social support is obtained and given, and religious institutions are also sites of health promotion and wellness activities and programs (Taylor, Chatters, Lincoln, & Woodward, 2017).

Spirituality and Coping With Stressful Events

Studies have shown spirituality to be an influential factor in helping African Americans cope with problems and stressful life events (Lynn, Yoo, & Levine, 2014). Spirituality gives meaning to one's life and provides an alternative way of constructing an understanding for life's outcomes. A belief that one's final destiny is in God's hands provides hope and inspiration. These beliefs are especially adaptive for individuals who may have lived under harsh circumstances.

Several studies have shown that among diverse African American populations, spiritual and religious beliefs are an integral part of coping with adverse situations. Spiritual beliefs are linked to positive and adaptive coping strategies, such as planning and organization. Hayward and Krause (2015) found in a national sample of African Americans that religious practices were associated with using positive coping strategies such as prayer, working harder, and talking to others about the problem. The absence of spiritual beliefs is associated with maladaptive coping strategies, such as denial and use of alcohol and drugs (Fife, McCreary, Brewer, & Adegoke, 2011; Mattis & Watson, 2009).

Spirituality and religiosity can buffer against stress when providing caregiving for infirm family members. Although providing care to an infirm family member can be very stressful, African American caregivers have typically appraised caregiving situations as being more favorable and less burdensome than have White caregivers (Sun, Kosberg, Leeper, Kaufman, & Burgio, 2010). Sun et al. examined the role of religiosity in coping with stress among caregivers of family members with dementia. The sample involved both African American and non-Hispanic White caregivers. They found that African Americans reported less caregiver burden than White caregivers. The lower perceived burden among African Americans was explained by religious activity (e.g., "How often do you attend Church?") and religious coping (e.g., "I try to find comfort in my religion"). Religious involvement might provide additional support to caregivers and reduce isolation. Consistent with the support provided by religious involvement are studies that have shown that African American parents with children with chronic conditions and disabilities use spirituality as a coping mechanism (Allen & Marshall, 2010; Belgrave, 1998). Allen and Marshall examined spirituality as a coping resource for African American parents of chronically ill children. Parents reported several positive religious coping patterns such as "having faith in God," "showing that we are strong," and "believing in God."

Spirituality has also been linked to better coping outcomes among children who live in neighborhoods with increased violence and crime. Children who live in high-crime neighborhoods often display post-traumatic stress symptoms similar to those found among children who live in countries at war. Saunders (2000) examined post-traumatic stress disorder among 71 African American children between the ages of 9 and 11, selected from neighborhoods in high-crime, high-poverty communities in Houston, Texas. Those children who held high spiritual beliefs were protected from the effects of violence and showed fewer symptoms of posttraumatic stress than those without such beliefs. Among young African Americans living in a public housing community, religiosity was associated with less antisocial behavior. More religious participants were less likely to be involved in property damage, theft, and automobile theft (Salas-Wright, Tirmazi, Lombe, & Nebbitt, 2015).

Spirituality is also a factor in how individuals cope with HIV/AIDS (Dalmida, Holstad, Dilorio, & Laderman, 2012). A study of 118 African American women living with HIV/AIDS showed associations between different components of spirituality and measures of quality of life (George, Holstad, Diloria, & Laderman, 2011). Existential well-being (e.g., purpose of life, interconnections with others) was significantly and positively associated with quality of life and accounted for life quality above and beyond factors such as sociodemographic status, HIV medication adherence, CD cell count, and so on. Existential well-being was also inversely related to depression, with higher existential well-being associated with less negative mental health. Religious rituals and practices are one mechanism for achieving spirituality. For Christians, religious practices provide a relationship with God through prayers and reading the Bible.

Spirituality and Psychosocial Functioning

Spirituality affects mental health both directly and indirectly. Indirectly, spirituality promotes better mental health by reducing stress through the adaptive coping strategies, mentioned previously. Religious practices and spiritual beliefs, in and of themselves, are coping strategies that are linked to other positive coping strategies (i.e., better health care and less drug and alcohol use) (Mattis & Watson, 2009; Whitley, 2012). Spirituality also has a direct connection to mental health outcomes.

Religious beliefs and practices have been shown to help lower depression. In a national study of 607 African American adults, Ellison and Flannelly (2009) assessed how religious practices at Time 1 predicted depression 3 to 4 years later. Respondents who reported receiving a great deal of guidance from religion in their day-to-day lives at Time 1 were about half as likely to have major depression at Time 2, while controlling for other factors that affect depression.

Religious beliefs and practices are also related to couple and marital happiness (Furdyna, Tucker, & James, 2008). Data from the National Survey of Religion and Family Life was used to investigate the association between religious involvement and relationship satisfaction among different ethnic groups, including African Americans, Hispanics, and non-Hispanic Whites (Ellison et al., 2010). The authors found that couples in same-faith relationships and those in relationships in which both partners attended religious services regularly had higher relationship satisfaction than those who did not. In this study, African American respondents with and without partners reported significantly higher levels of Church attendance, in comparison with non-Hispanic White respondents. Approximately 40% of African American participants reported that their partners regularly attended Church, compared with 29% of non-Hispanic White participants.

Fincham, Ajayi, and Beach (2011) examined the relationship between spiritual experiences of 487 African American couples and their marital quality and satisfaction. The religiosity of the husband was related not only to his own marital satisfaction but also to his wife's marital satisfaction. Spirituality was related to both own and partner satisfaction for husband and wife. Commenting on these significant associations, Fincham et al. (2011) speculate that spirituality might have a positive effect on communication within a relationship and allow for discussion when there is conflict. Spirituality also likely facilitates opportunities for cooperation.

Religiosity and spirituality are inversely related to risky behaviors, such as drug use and risky sexual behaviors among youth (Mattis & Grayman-Simpson, 2013). Boyd-Starke, Hill, Fife, and Whittington (2011) examined how religious beliefs affected HIV risk among college students. They found that higher levels of spirituality were linked to less risky sexual behaviors but that measures of religiosity, such as Church attendance, were not. In other studies, relationships between religious beliefs and practices of parents have been linked to less risky sexual attitudes and behavior among their adolescent children (Landor, Gordon, Simons, Brody, & Gibbons, 2011). This may, in part, be due to moral values that guide children not to have sex before marriage. These values may be transmitted by parents, especially by those who are religious. Landor and colleagues assessed the impact of religiosity of African American adolescents and their parents on sexual behaviors and attitudes. They found that religion was a protective factor for risky sexual behaviors, such as early sexual initiation, multiple sexual partners, and inconsistent condom use. They also found that religious commitment of parents was positively related to the adolescent's religiosity, such that adolescents with more religious parents were more religious themselves.

Spirituality and religiosity have been linked to less tobacco and other drug use (Montgomery, Stewart, Bryant, & Ounpraseuth, 2014). In a national sample of African American and Black Caribbean men, Bowie et al. (2017) found, after controlling for factors such as income, education, and stress, men who reported attending religious services almost daily or weekly had lower odds of smoking than men who never attended religious activities. Religiosity may serve as a buffer between discrimination and substance use (Henderson, 2017). Under conditions of discrimination, more substance use is likely but less so for those with strong religious beliefs.

The correlation between religiosity and substance use is especially strong among African American Muslims (Mattis & Grayman-Simpson, 2013). A central ideology of Islam is that the body is God's gift to humans. Because the body is seen as a heavenly gift, Islam explicitly forbids the consumption of alcohol or of any food or substance that is intoxicating or that harms the body (Rajaram & Rashidi, 2003).

Spirituality and Health

Many studies have examined the role of spirituality and religiosity on health and illness among African Americans. Spirituality and religiosity help to protect individuals from the effects of stress on physical health. Those with high religiosity and spirituality have better physical health and recover from illnesses more quickly than those with low spiritual beliefs (Powell-Young, 2012). Religious practices and spirituality are also linked to less pain and better medical and rehabilitation outcomes (Bediako et al., 2011; Harvey & Cook, 2010; Waldron-Perrine et al., 2011). African Americans are more likely to use prayer for health reasons than are other ethnic groups, both praying themselves and asking others to pray for them (Gillum & Griffith, 2010).

Black religious institutions and Church membership provide a type of support that expands one's social support network. Church membership provides care, concern, and resources that may facilitate healthy behaviors. Debnam, Holt, Clark, Roth, and Southward (2012) examined religious social support and health behaviors among African Americans. The national sample consisted of 2,370 African American men and women who were asked questions about fruit and vegetable consumption, physical activity, alcohol use, and cigarette use. The authors found that several dimensions of religious social support predicted fruit and vegetable consumption, moderate physical activity, and reduced alcohol consumption.

Spiritual practices are beneficial for those who have chronic conditions and those who may be recovering from traumatic injury. Bediako et al. (2011) found that positive religious coping explained unique variance in hospital admissions for persons with sickle cell disease after accounting for other demographic and illness variables. Higher levels of positive religious coping were associated with fewer hospital admissions.

Waldron-Perrine et al. (2011) studied African Americans with traumatic brain injury. Respondents reported on their religious and spiritual beliefs, and rehabilitation professionals reported on their rehabilitation outcomes. The authors found that religious well-being, as measured by a sense of connection to a higher power, was a unique predictor of life satisfaction, distress, and functional ability; higher levels of religious well-being led to higher levels of life satisfaction, less distress, and greater functional ability. However, public religious practices were not associated with quality-of-life measures.

The study by Waldron-Perrine et al. (2011) suggests that certain dimensions of religious beliefs may be more important than others when considering health. And while most research has shown a significant positive relationship between religious practices and favorable health, there are some exceptions. Dodor (2012) used data from the National Longitudinal Study of Adolescent Health to examine the relationship between religiosity and health behaviors and obesity among African Americans ages 28–34. They found that high levels of Church attendance combined with religious practice were associated with healthy eating habits. At the same time, they found that higher levels of time spent in prayer while making religion more important in life were associated with poor eating habits. This study suggests that the relationship between religiosity and health outcomes is dependent on the specific component or dimension of religiosity. Here, the protective benefits of religiosity on health behaviors must be considered in light of which dimension might be beneficial and which one might not be beneficial.

The link between religious beliefs and health may differ for African Americans and Whites. In one study, Steffen, McNeilly, Anderson, and Sherwood (2003) studied religious coping and blood pressure in a sample of African Americans and Whites. Religious coping involved praying and turning to God for support. They found that higher levels of religious coping were significantly related to lower blood pressure among African Americans but not among Whites. In the African American sample, higher levels of religious coping strategies were correlated with less depression, more social support, and less alcohol use. Similarly, another study found among Black and White participants undergoing treatment for alcoholism, that as purpose in life increased, sobriety also increased, for Blacks more so than for Whites (Krentzman, Farkas, & Townsend, 2010).

CONTEMPORARY TOPICS

There are several contemporary issues that come to mind when discussing spirituality, religion, and African Americans. One issue is the role of African American Churches when considering psychological and social issues, such as depression and LGBTQ members. A second topic is the role of the African American Church in salvation and liberation. These contemporary issues are discussed next.

African American Churches and Psychological and Social Issues

The Church is important in the lives of African Americans and provides religious and spiritual affirmation, as well as support in areas of psychosocial needs. Religion and religious institutions also influence well-being and emotional health through shaping other social identities, particularly racial, political, and sexual identities (Mattis & Grayman-Simpson, 2013). For example, strong racial and ethnic identity are associated with higher Church attendance (Mattis & Grayman-Simpson, 2013).

However, some African American Churches, especially Christian ones, have traditionally held the view that counseling and mental health services are not needed and that all one needs is God. Fortunately, this view is changing, and many Churches have added mental health and counseling components to their ministry (Allen et al., 2010). Mainline Protestant and Catholic denominations tend to be more open to counseling than Pentecostal and Holiness Churches, which may be more traditional. Cook and Wiley (2000) and others discuss ways in which some African American Churches handle psychological and social issues; these are reviewed next.

Depression and Other Mental Illnesses

Depression is an issue that must be considered in light of the client's spirituality. Some African Americans, especially those who are deeply religious, may see therapy as antispiritual (Boyd-Franklin, 2010). One of the symptoms of depression may be a cessation of spiritual activities that could be helpful in treatment. Individuals may stop praying, reading the Bible, attending Church, or seeking out other Church members. They may feel embarrassed to ask the Church for help. Some may be reluctant to take medication, especially if they feel that the Church's view is that taking medication reflects doubt in God's ability to heal. Hence, depressed persons may view symptoms not as depression but as lacking spiritual connection to God and a lack of faith (Plunkett, 2014). Depressed clients may need support and education to help them benefit from therapy. In addition, they may need to be supported and reminded of the benefits of engaging in routine spiritual activities (Cook & Wiley, 2000).

Many African Americans may seek help from clergy when experiencing emotional distress, and sometimes, clergy are the first and only professionals from whom individuals seek help (Allen et al., 2010; Chatters et al., 2011). In a national study of African Americans, Chatters et al. found that respondents were more likely to seek help for a personal problem from ministers than from family doctors, psychiatrists, and other mental health professionals. Women were more likely than men to seek help from a minister, as were more educated respondents and those with higher incomes. Also, Pentecostals were more likely to seek help from a minister for personal problems than other denominations (Chatters et al., 2011). Unfortunately, some clergy continue to struggle with their congregants' mental health needs because they may not have the necessary clinical skills to diagnose and treat mental health problems.

Barriers for receiving mental health services that exist in the larger African American community are also seen in the African American Church. These barriers include stigma, the view that professional help is a sign of spiritual flaws, and lack of access to professional and culturally competent services. Dempsey, Butler, and Gaither (2016) identified several factors that account for why African Americans may seek out mental health support from the African American Church, as opposed to mental health agencies. These include the fact that (a) mental health services provided by the Church are likely to be free, accessible, and to have an informal referral and intake process; (b) there is familiarity with the provider of the mental health services, and a positive relationship may already exist with the provider; (c) ethnic matching and cultural congruence is more likely making the relationship culturally congruent; and (d) rituals and other familiar therapeutic experiences are provided by the Black Church (e.g., fellowship, verbal prayer, singing).

While African American Churches engage in many physical health initiatives (e.g., cancer screening, HIV prevention, blood pressure checks) in collaboration with local agencies, mental health collaborations are less likely and should be encouraged. Dempsey et al. identified best practices for successful collaboration between Churches and mental health agencies: (a) mental health professionals must assess and understand the Church culture, etiquette, and protocol (e.g., not addressing a Church official by his or her first name); (b) mental health professionals should seek approval from and discussion with the leader of the Church—the discussion should include mutual benefits of the partnership; (c) the mental health professional should participate in ongoing Church health fairs and similar activities that promote healthy living; (d) mental health training to Church leadership about mental health issues and local community resources could be provided; and (e) mental health professionals may be more effective if they join the Church community by providing services in Church settings rather than mental health agencies.

HIV Prevention

As discussed in Chapter 14, HIV is disproportionally high in the African American community and accounts for a large degree of mortality and morbidity. There have been several programs and activities in the African American Church that address HIV prevention.

The leader or pastor of African American Churches plays a pivotal role in HIV prevention activities (Aholou et al., 2016). Aholou et al. conducted focus group and identified three themes regarding the role of the Church in HIV prevention. These were as follows: (1) The pastor's endorsement and authority as the leader was important in HIV prevention; (2) the Church's stand on sexual health should be a part of a holistic ministry in order to facilitate engagement; and (3) HIV prevention efforts require financial and human resources.

A large national multidenominational sample of African American faith leaders was interviewed to explore barriers and best practices for HIV prevention in African American Churches (Bryant-Davis et al., 2016). All participants were involved in HIV prevention activities at their Church. The faith leaders identified several best practices to consider when implementing HIV prevention programs. These included (1) forming HIV-specific ministries with personnel devoted specifically to HIV prevention; (2) community outreach by working with local community residents and community agencies currently providing HIV prevention services; (3) the need for grant funding and resources outside of the Church to provide prevention; and (4) integrating HIV prevention and awareness within Church services. Additionally, as found in the Aholou et al. study, the commitment from faith leaders was essential to HIV prevention, and this commitment should include messages from the pulpit. Some of the barriers identified in the study included the minister's theological concerns as they relate to sexuality, lack of information about HIV, and stigma associated with HIV, along with negative views on homosexuality.

One recommendation for HIV prevention is for Churches to address HIV prevention as a part of sexual health in a manner that is inclusive to all and not just subgroups (Powell, Herbert, Ritchwood, & Latkin, 2016).

Addiction

Addiction is another issue that should be considered in light of spiritual beliefs. There is diverse opinion within African American Churches on how individuals with addictions should be treated. Some Churches prohibit the use of alcohol and drugs, thereby discouraging individuals from admitting that they have a problem and seeking help. Other Churches recognize the extent of addictive diseases in the African American community and offer support groups like Alcoholics Anonymous. Church members (and sometimes pastors) may offer testimonies of how God delivered them from their addictions and imply that this is all that is needed for treatment. While these testimonials are encouraging for some, they may be discouraging to others if they do not feel similarly healed (Cook & Wiley, 2000).

While there are varying opinions on how the African American Church should respond to addictions, for many African Americans, addiction is seen as being in misalignment with one's spiritual purpose. African Americans in recovery from addiction report that ongoing recovery is a process that is dependent on a relationship with God. Engagement in religious activities, including prayer and reading the scripture, is critical to recovery (Whitley, 2012).

For some individuals, religion may be another type of addiction. These individuals may move from being addicted to drugs to becoming overly involved in Church activities or by becoming inflexible about spiritual doctrines. Therapists may want to explore clients' positive and negative addictive behaviors and how the Church's practices support these behaviors.

Lesbian, Gay, Bisexual, Transgender, and Queer (LGBTQ) Issues

While there has been some positive movement in Churches becoming more welcoming spaces for LGBTQ individuals, LGBTQ issues are, in general, admonished, neglected, or avoided in African American Churches. Conservative Churches may speak out about the evils of homosexuality and see homosexuality as a choice that an individual makes to be immoral. In extreme doctrine, Churches have claimed HIV/AIDS to be God's punishment for homosexuality. LGBTQ persons who attend religious institutions that are intolerant of LGBTQ identities may be exposed to homophobic messages that adversely affect their well-being. Homophobia in the Church may also limit LGBTQ individuals' from seeking support from leaders and others in the Church. Finally, homophobia may reduce individuals' ability to integrate their sexual, racial, and spiritual identities (Mattis & Grayman-Simpson, 2013). Some cultural beliefs in the African American Church also support views that negatively affect LGBTQ persons (Barnes, 2013b). For example, traditional ideology or the tendency to elevate the nuclear family may encourage heterosexism.

Churches with more liberal views are more accepting of LGBTQ individuals. However, there is often no open discussion of LGBTQ as an alternative lifestyle, nor are Church services and practices geared for LGBTQ members. For example, few Churches perform union ceremonies for same-sex couples. And many LGBTQ members of African American Churches are closeted about their lifestyles despite their consistent participation in Church services and communities. Barnes (2013b) explored sexual orientation, along with other issues, in a qualitative study of 35 clergy attending seminary in a large metropolitan Southern city. The findings were that clergy supported a "hierarchy of tolerance" (p. 1424) in which there was support of inclusivity in Church membership but not leadership. Barnes noted that ironically these beliefs are similar to the historic views of African American female clergy. Churches such as the Metropolitan Community Church that focus specifically on LGBTQ members are frequently located in metropolitan areas. In addition, a number of Unity Fellowship Churches have been developed to serve the African American LGBTQ community.

In spite of the stigma from some African American Churches with regard to homosexuality, African American LGBTQ individuals continue to have strong religious attitudes and practices. Foster, Arnold, Rebchook, and Kegeles (2011) conducted interviews to explore the roles of religion and spirituality in the lives of 31 young Black men who have sex with men. Six themes emerged from these interviews: (a) They participated in formal religious institutions during childhood; (b) spirituality continued to be important to these men; (c) there was homophobia and stigma in traditional Black Churches; (d) there was tension between being a man who has sex with men and being a Christian; (e) religious beliefs impacted men's personal empowerment and coping strategies; and (f) they were compassionate about how others are treated.

Quinn, Dickson-Gomez, and Kelly (2015) found similar themes in interviews with pastors of Black Churches (N = 21) and young men who have sex with men (N = 30). Although homonegativity was reported in Black Churches, involvement was still important to the young men, and many stayed in Black Churches that were not affirming of their sexuality.

The Role of the Black Church in Salvation and Liberation

Many clergy and laypersons have debated whether the Church should seek to liberate or save people. Religious practices within the Church can promote a sense of well-being that contributes to pride, self-worth, and independence. Furthermore, many Christians believe that God must be present to strengthen the Black race. On the other hand, salvation is a basic doctrine of Christianity, and many consider that the primary responsibility of the Church is to serve as a vehicle for salvation. Churches that focus on salvation concentrate their efforts on saving souls and guiding people toward a life that will be rewarded in the afterlife. These Churches typically have a strict interpretation of biblical doctrine. Churches that focus on liberation strive to help individuals achieve what is necessary to attain the best possible quality of life on this Earth. These Churches may have active programs that support civic, economic, and educational activities. Most Churches attempt to promote both salvation and liberation.

Africentric Thought and a Theology of Liberation

According to liberation theology, contemporary Christian faith must be like the Black Power movement and address freedom and other issues addressed by the Black Power movement and other movements of oppressed groups (Clark, 2013). Liberation theory argues that the life of Jesus is best interpreted through contemporary freedom movements. Africentricity should appeal to Christians of African descent because it addresses two main issues: the need for self-revelation and social justice. Africentric Christian religious leaders such as Jeremiah Wright (leader of Faith Temple in Chicago, Church of President Obama) believes that the goal of theology is to relate "the essence of the Gospel" to "the forces of liberation" in the communities of the oppressed (Cone, 1970, p. 1, as cited in Clark, 2013).

Liberation, for Africentric persons, means transforming Black consciousness and reforming Black culture, including understanding Black history. Black clergy who are Africentric endorse a culturally grounded and politically relevant faith (Clark, 2013). Clark refers to congregations that use Africentric frameworks as Nia-driven Churches (purpose-driven), with the ultimate goal of transforming self-understanding of Black people in light of God's purposes.

METHODOLOGICAL AND RESEARCH ISSUES

For people of African descent, there are many methodological questions relevant to issues of religion and spirituality. Central questions include, "What is spirituality and how is it related to culture?" and, "What does it means to be spiritual and African American?" A related question is, "What is the best way to measure religion and spirituality among African Americans?"

Spirituality From an African-Centered Perspective

From an African-centered perspective, spirituality is intricately linked to all aspects of one's life and cannot be viewed as a separate dimension. It would be difficult, if not impossible, to isolate spiritual beliefs and practices from other life domains. For example, one's physical health is linked to one's higher power, as is one's economic success (or lack thereof). Although African Americans' spiritual beliefs differ from those found in traditional Africa, there are some parallels. The labeling of an event or practice as spiritual may depend on the spiritual interpretation of its meaning. For example, success at a job could be viewed as an act of God. The birth of a child may be seen as a spiritual event. One's recovery from an illness can be seen as a result of faith and God's will. These interpretations are not unique to people of African descent but may be found among other spiritual believers.

Measuring Religiosity and Spirituality

There are several measures of religion, spirituality, and related constructs (i.e., purpose in life, values, belief in God, and so on; Hill & Hood, 1999; Lewis, 2008). Because the development of these measures has included only a small number of African American participants, it is not clear how valid they are when used with African American populations (Lewis, 2008). Measures of religion include measures of religious beliefs and practices, religious attitudes, religious orientation, religious morals and values, religious coping and problem solving, and relationship-with-God scales. These measures may not consider the meaning of spirituality and religion from an African-centered perspective.

While religion and spirituality are not unique to African Americans, their expressions are culturally determined (Utsey, Lee, Bolden, & Lanzier, 2005). African Americans may view spirituality as a force that is integrative and essentially active and meaningful in day-to-day life. This conceptualization of spirituality may not be captured by a scale.

More recent attention has been devoted to measures that assess religious and spiritual beliefs and practices among African Americans (Holt et al., 2010, 2012; Roth et al., 2012). One measure that was developed specifically for African American Christians is the Attitudes toward Religious Help-Seeking Scale (Hardy, 2015). This measure addressed the need for a culturally specific and validated measure of religiosity and spirituality. The measure was developed to address the intersectionality of race, religion, and stigma associated with help seeking among African American Christians. The measure has three parts that include demographic variables, preferred source of help during times of crisis, and religious help-seeking behaviors. The Religious Help Seeking Behaviors subscale uses a Likert-type format that ranges from "1" Strongly Disagree to "4" Strongly Agree, with higher scores indicating a stronger preference for religious help-seeing from one's pastor. Validation of the measure included two samples of socioeconomically diverse African American Christians. There are two subscales: "Pastoral Disapproval" and "Significance of Faith." Items from the Pastoral Disapproval subscale include "I would not use pastoral counseling because [pastor] would think I don't trust God to handle my problems" and "Some issues are too personal to discuss in pastoral counseling." Items from the Significance of Faith subscale include "A primary reason I would use pastoral counseling is because the pastor would understand how my faith/religion impacts my issues" and "I have considered using pastoral counseling for a serious personal problem rather than a therapist" (p. 392). Psychometric properties of the scale were found to be acceptable.

Other measures have focused on religiosity or religious practices. One good measure of religious practices used with African American populations comes from the National Survey of American Life. This survey asks about several aspects of religiosity, such as prayer frequency, watching religious television, listening to religious radio, reading religious books and materials, and forging connections with people from Church (Institute for Social Research, n.d.).

The connection between religion and health is salient, especially for those with high levels of religious activity (Holt et al., 2010). This connection may be due to several factors, including the fact that religiously active people tend to have healthier lifestyles and engage in fewer unhealthy behaviors, such as tobacco, alcohol, or drug use. Religious people may also be more likely to believe that illness is a punishment for sin. Holt et al. (2012) developed a scale that measures these two religious health mechanisms, perceived religious influences on health behavior, and illness as a punishment for sin using a sample of African Americans. The Perceived Religious Influence on Health Behavior Scale consists of 10 items with items such as, "God helps me to maintain a healthy lifestyle" and, "Because of my religious/spiritual beliefs, I abstain from smoking." The Illness as Punishment for Sin Scale contains items such as, "Illness is the result of one's negative thoughts" and, "Illness is caused by a sinful lifestyle." The scale has acceptable reliability and validity. Measures such as these might be useful in assessing how religiosity affects health and also useful when developing programs that attend to religious beliefs and practices for persons who may have serious health problems.

EMPIRICALLY BASED PRACTICES USING RELIGION AND SPIRITUALITY

Most of the work examining science-based practices associated with religion or spirituality has focused on using belief systems as the underlying structure for behavioral change programs. Consequently, the focus of these programs has not been on strengthening religious or spiritual beliefs per se. A second way in which spirituality and religion have been used is in the involvement of African American religious organizations as institutions from which to recruit participants or in which to implement programs and interventions (Lumpkins, Greiner, Daley, Mabachi, & Neuhaus, 2013).

Empirically supported interventions have targeted behavioral changes in a number of domains and with diverse populations, including African American women, children and youth, and the elderly. Intervention programs have targeted behaviors that prevent and/or reduce or eliminate the negative consequences of an existing health problem. In addition, programs have been implemented to increase positive healthy behaviors. Examples of spiritual and religious institution–based interventions include (a) programs for women with breast cancer (Boyd & Wilmoth, 2006); (b) breast and cancer screenings for women (Haynes, Escoffery, Wilkerson, Bell, & Flowers, 2014; Matthews, Berrios, Darnell, & Calhoun, 2006); (c) programs for women who are homeless and women who use cocaine (Stahler et al., 2005); (d) programs to improve dietary behaviors and exercise (Campbell, Resnicow, Carr, Wang, & Williams, 2007; Resnicow et al., 2005; Timmons, 2015); (e) diabetes prevention interventions (Davis-Smith, 2007; Duru, Sarkisian, Leng, & Mangione, 2010); (f) programs for addressing mental health issues (Gum et al., 2012; Hankerson & Weissman, 2012); (g) programs targeted at preventing substance abuse and HIV prevention (Francis & Liverpool, 2009; Wingood et al., 2013b); and (h) programs targeting suicide prevention (Molock, Matlin, Barksdale, Puri, & Lyles, 2008). The majority of these interventions have targeted improvements in physical and wellness outcomes, as opposed to psychological and mental health outcomes. Two programs described next provide examples of how religion and spirituality can be used in programs for African Americans.

Boyd and Wilmoth (2006) describe how spirituality and religion were used in an innovative project called the Witness Project. The Witness Project was grounded in the spiritual roots of African American women and used affirmation to increase women's belief in their ability to take action to save their lives. The practice of witnessing was used as an intervention strategy to reduce the high mortality rate of African American women with breast cancer living in Arkansas. The project used breast cancer survivors, referred to as witness role models, to tell their breast cancer stories, from detection through treatment.

The Witness Project began in 1991 and was designed to reach out to low-income and rural African American women. Witness role models shared their stories with their congregations as personal religious experiences and testified by explaining how this experience changed their lives. Survivors were paired with a lay health advisor who taught breast self-exams and discussed mammography and the role it plays in early detection. The program was effective in increasing mammography and breast self-examinations (Erwin, Spatz, Stotts, Hollenberg, & Deloney, 1996). The Witness Project currently has programs in several sites across the country. It is implemented in community organizations as well as Churches and in urban as well as rural areas (National Cancer Institute, 2013).

Francis and Liverpool (2009) reviewed several faith-based HIV prevention programs for African American populations, noting that Churches and faith-based organizations provided opportune environments in which to implement HIV prevention programs. One program reviewed was Teens for AIDs Prevention (TAP). This program was developed by the AIDS Ministries Program of Connecticut. This Church-based program trains youth as peer HIV/AIDS educators who then present HIV/AIDS prevention programs to other teens in their communities. The program has a 17-module curriculum that includes generic material for teens on HIV/AIDS prevention along with religious-specific materials, such as clarification of values. The program is mostly implemented within Churches but can also be done in other settings (Merz, 1997).

Boyd-Franklin (2010) provided examples of how spirituality and religion can be incorporated when treating African American clients with mental health problems. Boyd-Franklin discussed the treatment of one young African American female college student dealing with separation from her home and family. This young lady was referred because of academic failure and depression. In working with this client, Boyd-Franklin identified family and community changes that the college student had experienced. She had been close to her family and very involved in her Church, going there often after school and participating in the choir and other activities. The White therapist was able to connect her client to a Black administrator who took her to a Black Church that provided her with watch care. The therapist recognized that a major problem was a sense of isolation and loneliness that came from loss of family and spiritual connectedness from being on a predominantly White campus. According to Boyd-Franklin, isolation is not the norm within the collectivistic African American culture and can lead to mental health problems, such as depression.

These are a few examples of the many programs and interventions that have demonstrated successful outcomes when based on spiritual and religious cultural values and when they are implemented in religious settings.

CRITICAL ANALYSIS

Religion and spirituality have historically played and continue to play a complex set of roles within the lives of African Americans. Religion and spirituality serve as coping resources, support access to resources and connection to sources of social status, and provide opportunities for the development of leadership capacities. Understanding the intersection of social, political, spiritual, and economic roles that the Church plays within the community requires both conceptual and methodological clarity and precision. Hunt and Hunt (1999), for example, examine the voluntary nature of participation within the African American Church as a social institution. Their examination of the semi-involuntary thesis indicates that

> segregation has shaped two major forces that traditionally mobilized involvement in the African American Church, especially in the segregated Churches of the historic, mainline denominations: (1) the structural absence of secular outlets for achievement that indirectly made the African American Church the community context in which status, leadership, and respectability could be achieved, and (2) the cultural presence of powerful community moral pressures to support the institution that provided material and spiritual nourishment to the African-American community. (p. 780)

This conceptual model raises questions as to what the primary role of the Church is. Does the Church primarily provide culturally relevant opportunities to access social and political networks, or is it a source of spiritual, coping, and moral support?

We have noted repeatedly the significant African cultural base within which many aspects of the contemporary religious experience are grounded. We believe that it is important to consider the role of Traditional African Religions and practice and the historical and cultural influence and role of Christianity and Islam in the colonial experience on the African continent and the enslavement experience in the Western hemisphere. It is relevant to note the cultural tensions between the more syncretic and open religious traditions of Africa and the more dogmatic and prescriptive Christian and Islamic traditions. These contrasts raise questions as to the ways in which culture and values affect the spiritual and religious experiences of African Americans. How is the growth of the recent theology of prosperity relevant to doctrines of prosperity, as opposed to secular American values on consumption and external manifestations of self-worth? How do we resolve the tensions between values of a Black liberation theology and prosperity theology? If "I am because we are," then who does the Church serve? In a tradition that sees the complementarities of different religious beliefs, how do we understand our connections to members of different faiths and different cultural groups? How tolerant are we of members of other religious traditions or who disagree with our beliefs around sexual behaviors and identities? How consistent are we in our application of the "Golden Rule"? In face of descriptions as the "most segregated place in America on a Sunday morning," researchers have recently turned their attention to factors that are relevant to increased racial diversity within congregations. Dougherty and Huyser (2008) found that racially diverse Church leadership, charismatic workshop practices, and opportunities to connect in small groups support integration within religious organizations.

In our ongoing efforts to strengthen and enhance our knowledge and understanding of the religious experience of African Americans, it is notable that statistics and data on religious membership are not systematically collected, and sources of data have often excluded African Americans within their sampling. The federal government, since the 1950s, has ceased systematic collection of information on religious affiliation. Although this clearly supports greater protection against religious discrimination, which is especially important with the increases in religious intolerance post-9/11, we must acknowledge the related difficulty in supporting a deeper understanding of our religious practice. Given the significance of spirituality and religiosity in the lives of African Americans, more research is needed on the conceptualization and measurement of these constructs.

The continuing significance of the role of religion in the political experience of African Americans is clear but raises a range of critical questions. How much are or should Churches be separated from the state? What role should the Black Church play in the political arena, how far should religious institutions go in endorsing specific candidates and social issues, and how should these roles shape their status as nonprofit organizations? Should the business and financial practices of prosperity and other televangelists come under the scrutiny of the federal government? Whether concerns over the fiery rhetoric from the pulpit of Pastor Jeremiah Wright or the decision of Keith Ellison, the first Muslim and first Black from Minnesota to serve in the U.S. Congress, to be sworn in using the Quran, religion continues to be a significant factor in the political experience of Black Americans.

Summary

The proverb at the beginning of this chapter, "He who leaves truth behind, returns to it," symbolizes the ongoing and unending connection of peoples of African descent to spiritual truths, apparent or not. Beliefs about God, religious practices, and spiritual beliefs influence all aspects of life among African Americans.

Religion and spirituality are interwoven into many aspects of life for the majority of African Americans. Religion differs from spirituality in that religion composes practices and rituals, and spirituality is one's relationship with a higher being. African Americans attend Church more often, engage in more religious practices, and hold stronger religious and spiritual beliefs than do other ethnic groups. There is diversity among African Americans in religious affiliation, but most are Christian and members of a Baptist denomination. Older persons, females, and Southerners attend Church and pray more often than younger persons, males, and people who live outside the South. The Black MegaChurch is a recent institution in the African American community and is defined as a Church that seats more than 2,000 persons in a typical worship service.

Spirituality and religion often provide the moral code for a community. Traditional African Religion shares some similarities with Christian religions but also differs in many respects. Several features of Traditional African Religion remain in contemporary Africa and are also seen in the religious and spiritual experiences of American Americans.

Research has shown that religious and spiritual beliefs are associated with better coping and better mental and physical health. Religion has been used to both oppress and liberate African Americans. During enslavement, Christian doctrine was used to justify slavery and oppression. However, enslaved Africans could relate to Christian messages by identifying with the liberation of Jesus Christ, who was a persecuted and oppressed figure.

Some contemporary topics include the role of the Church in addressing psychological issues, such as addictions and depression, and LGBTQ issues. African American Churches are institutions of both liberation and salvation. Most measures of religion and spirituality have not been developed with African American samples and should be used cautiously. The religious measure from the National Survey of American Life is an exception, as is the Attitudes toward Religious Help-Seeking Scale. There are several empirically supported interventions that have been developed with consideration of religious doctrines and spiritual beliefs. These interventions are often implemented within Churches and other faith-based institutions.

Note

1. A revealed religion is one in which divine truth is believed to be revealed to one person who becomes the founder (i.e., Jesus Christ, Muhammad, or the Buddha).

11

LIFE SPAN DEVELOPMENT

One is born, one dies; the land increases.

—Ethiopian proverb

LEARNING OBJECTIVES

- To understand theoretical perspectives on the development of African Americans

- To understand demographic indicators, developmental processes, and developmental outcomes relevant to African Americans

- To appreciate research on the main periods of human development, including infancy and childhood, adolescence, adult years, and older age

- To understand the relative strengths and weaknesses of different research approaches to understanding the development of African Americans

- To appreciate approaches used in intervention programs designed to support positive development among African Americans

AFRICAN-AMERICAN DEATH RATE DROPS 25 PERCENT

Press Release, Centers for Disease Control Newsroom, May 2, 2017

The death rate for African-Americans (blacks) declined 25 percent from 1999 to 2015, according to a new CDC *Vital Signs* report released today. But disparities still persist between blacks and whites. Although blacks as a group are living longer, their life expectancy is still 4 years less than that of whites.

Disparities in all age groups are narrowing because death rates are declining faster among

(Continued)

(Continued)

blacks than among whites. The overall disparity in death rates between these two races for all causes of death in all age groups was 33 percent in 1999 but fell to 16 percent in 2015. The racial death rate gap closed completely for deaths from heart disease and for all causes of death among those 65 years and older.

Of concern, the study also found that blacks in their 20s, 30s, and 40s are more likely to live with or die from conditions that typically occur at older ages in whites, including heart disease, stroke, and diabetes. Risk factors for some diseases, such as high blood pressure, may go unnoticed and untreated during these early years. Notably, the death rates for homicide among blacks did not change over the 17 years of the study.

The report also describes improvements in other causes of death, such as a dramatic decrease of about 80 percent in HIV deaths among 18- to 49-year-olds from 1999–2015. Dramatic drops in HIV deaths were also seen among whites. Still, a wide disparity remains with blacks seven to nine times more likely to die from HIV.

"We have seen some remarkable improvements in death rates for the black population in these past 17 years. Important gaps are narrowing due to improvements in the health of the black population overall. However, we still have a long way to go," said Leandris Liburd, Ph.D., M.P.H., M.A., associate director, CDC's Office of Minority Health and Health Equity. "Early health interventions can lead to longer, healthier lives. In particular, diagnosing and treating the leading diseases that cause death at earlier stages is an important step for saving lives."

Social and economic conditions, such as poverty, contribute to gaps in health differences between blacks and whites, according to the report. In all age groups, the analysis showed that blacks had lower educational attainment and home ownership and nearly twice the rate of poverty and unemployment as whites. These risk factors may limit blacks' access to prevention and treatment of disease. Other risk factors that affect health outcomes for blacks include obesity and less physical activity.

CDC researchers analyzed data from the U.S. Census Bureau, National Vital Statistics System, and CDC's Behavioral Risk Factor Surveillance System (BRFSS) to examine factors that may influence disparities across the life span.

Among the key findings from the report:

- Blacks ages 18 to 64 are at higher risk of early death than whites.

- Disparities in the leading causes of death for blacks compared with whites are pronounced by early and middle adulthood, including homicide and chronic diseases such as heart disease and diabetes.

- Blacks ages 18–34 years and 35–49 years are nine times and five times, respectively, as likely to die from homicide as whites in the same age groups.

- Blacks ages 35–64 are 50 percent more likely to have high blood pressure than whites.

- Blacks ages 18–49 years, are two times as likely to die from heart disease than whites.

- Blacks have the highest death rate for all cancers combined compared with whites.

"It is important that we continue to create opportunities for all Americans to pursue a healthy lifestyle," said Timothy Cunningham, Sc.D., lead author and epidemiologist with the Division of Population Health, CDC. "Public health professionals must work across all sectors to promote health at early ages." Public health agencies and community organizations should continue to implement programs proven to reduce health disparities, and partner with other sectors, including education, business, transportation, and housing, to create social and economic conditions that promote health starting in childhood to continue to close the gap in health outcomes. Proven prevention measures such as healthy eating, physical activity, tobacco cessation, disease screenings, and medication adherence remain important to reduce disease and early death.

The Federal government collects data on prevention measures and risk factors that impact health through programs such as Healthy People 2020. For more information on CDC efforts to reduce disparities through prevention and removing barriers to health equity, visit www.cdc.gov/healthequity.

Source: Centers for Disease Control (2017).

INTRODUCTION AND DEFINITIONS

When we look at newborns, hear their first cries, count their fingers and toes, and check the color of their ears, we imagine with hope and wonder who these little people will become. All too soon, they will crawl, stand, talk, walk, and then run, ride a bike, and learn to read. They will go to school and be asked, "What do you want to be when you grow up?" Their world will grow from that of their families to neighborhood and peers, and with access to books, travel, or technology and social media, they may gain a sense of their place in the global community. They will grow larger, learn who they are, and decide who they want to be. They may rely less and less on parents and form increasingly important friendships. They will face many choices. Should I go to college? What kind of career should I have? Should I get married? Have kids? Where will I live? As adults, who have these little people become, and as they enter their maturity and look back across their lives, how will they assess their choices? How will the community use and respect their knowledge and wisdom as elders and care and support them as they age?

Developmental psychology is the study of the physical, emotional, cognitive, and behavioral changes in humans, beginning at conception and continuing through death. This field of study describes and explains the processes and phenomena that shape our behavior and experience across the course of our lives. Over the past several decades, developmental psychology has moved from a primary focus on development that takes place during childhood and adolescence, to include a life span perspective—that is, to examine developmental changes that occur across the entire life course, ranging from prenatal influences through older age.

In considering the development of African Americans, we seek to understand the unique features of this developmental experience. How do culture, history, and social forces shape the contexts in which African Americans live, grow, and develop? What roles do family, school, peers, and neighborhood play in the development of African Americans? What challenges are faced, and how do we define positive developmental outcomes? Developmental psychology is concerned with how well African American infants, children, adults, and seniors fare across each period of development.

In this chapter, we first define key concepts in life span development and then describe the demographic population of African Americans. Next, we discuss theories that can help us to understand the development of Americans of African descent, and we provide a research-based snapshot of African Americans at different developmental periods. We raise methodological issues to consider in reviewing or conducting research with African Americans. Then, we consider empirically supported interventions designed to support the positive development of African Americans and end the chapter with a critical analysis and a summary.

On some level, we might consider a significant portion of the entire book to be an examination of the development of African Americans. When we examine development, we often look at the contexts within which an individual develops. Many of these settings, such as family, schools, peer relationships, and religious institutions, are addressed in detail within other chapters in this book.

Developmental psychology is also interested in the processes important in understanding change, stability, and growth. These processes may include learning and cognitive development, gaining a sense of self and identity, developing the capacity for intimacy and entering relationships, and achieving success at school or in the workplace. We can also expand our understanding of development by considering a range of positive and negative developmental outcomes, such as well-being or compromises in health or engagement in destructive behavior such as violence or drug use. We cover many of these issues—including education, cognition, identity development, and adjustment—in other chapters. We will not duplicate coverage of these materials but will focus on specific developmental processes and issues relevant to African Americans at different age periods. In this chapter, we provide a select overview of important developmental issues for African Americans in infancy, middle childhood, adolescence, adulthood, and older age.

Definitions and Key Concepts

Within a developmental perspective, several processes are central. For example, *maturation* is the biologically directed set of genetically sequenced changes that shape our physical and behavioral development and our movement from embryo to mature adult. *Ontogeny* refers to the development and unfolding of an individual's life. Developmental psychology has struggled with nature-versus-nurture questions and has focused considerable attention on understanding both genetic and environmental contributions to individual development. This work attempts to understand how much our genetic makeup (i.e., genotype) contributes to our actual phenotype, which is the unique expression of this genetic makeup, shaped by the context in which we develop to manifest in the person we actually become. There has been increased consideration of the interaction of genetic and environmental factors. For example, Bradley et al. (2011) found that childhood maltreatment among low-income, urban African Americans was associated with both disorganized attachment styles and challenges in emotion regulation, but differences in regulating emotions and attachment depended on a specific genetic variation found in the nervous system.

The study of developmental psychology involves our attempt to understand humans' physical development and the impact of social contexts (such as families, peers, and communities) on that development. It includes studies of how our emotional, cognitive, and social capacities develop and shape the direction of our lives. This direction can be toward positive outcomes (e.g., good physical health, school achievement, successful employment), or it can be toward more challenges (e.g., problems with drugs and alcohol, school failure, mental health challenges).

Some developmental perspectives and theories focus on models or conceptions of stages or phases. Stages refer to sequential developmental periods that are characterized by specific developmental phenomena that are qualitatively different from factors that characterize prior or subsequent stages. Often, these stages have a prescribed invariant sequence and are conceived to build on the achievements of the prior stages of development. The Freudian theory of psychosexual development, Piagetian perspectives on cognitive development, and Erikson's ideas on psychosocial development are examples of stage theories. In contrast to stage perspectives, some developmental theories emphasize the continuity in development. Behavioral developmental perspectives are more continuous in nature.

Another important concept in our understanding of development across historical time is the idea of a *cohort*. A cohort is a group of people who were born and grew up within a particular period. When we talk about Baby Boomers (those born after World War II until the mid-1960s), Generation X (those born between the mid-1960s through the early 1980s), Millennials (those born between the early 1980s to around 2000), or Generation Z (those born since the early 2000s), we are discussing age groups or cohorts of individuals within the United States who are thought to share similar developmental experiences and settings.

African Americans are an incredibly diverse group. Male, female. Young, old. Baptist, Muslim, atheist, and Buddhist. Rich, middle class, and of lower income. The study of the development of African Americans can assist us in understanding the development of subgroups. However, much of the available literature is based on between-group comparisons that help us see, on average, how African Americans compare in developmental processes and outcomes with members of other racial and ethnic groups. We must take care to understand that taking an average for more than 40 million people does not capture the diversity within the African American community, but it allows us to make broad comparisons between ethnic groups. In addition, different studies may take varied approaches relative to the inclusion of recent African immigrants and multiracial individuals.

DEMOGRAPHICS

To assist us in understanding the development of African Americans, we provide a brief demographic portrait of African Americans in different age groups. *Demography* is the descriptive study of human populations, including change over time and distribution across different descriptive categories and characteristics. It uses a range of indicators (e.g., income, educational achievement, health data) to allow us to understand how various groups compare on these various indicators. Differences across groups can help us to understand where there may be particular challenges, the need for intervention, or the need for additional study to further our understanding of these differences. Changes in these indicators can reflect changes in social conditions and structures.

Life Expectancy and Age of the African American Population

For an African American male infant born in 2015, his life expectancy would be 72.2 years, compared with a life expectancy of 76.6 years for a White male infant born at the same time. For an African American female infant born in 2015, her life expectancy would be 78.5 years, compared with a life expectancy of 81.3 years for a White female infant (National Center on Health Statistics, 2017). Cunningham et al. (2017) examined trends in life expectancies between 1999 and 2015 across gender and ethnic groups. As noted in the opening article, data reflect a closing of the life expectancy gap between African Americans and Whites. Although death rates declined for both African Americans and Whites across this time period, the declines were larger for African Americans. For all age groups below age 65, racial disparities in mortality persisted. It is notable that the death rates for African Americans 65 and older have been lower than those for Whites since 2010.

The African American population tends to be younger than Whites, although somewhat older than members of other racial groups (e.g., Asians, Hispanics, Native

Americans). For example, as illustrated in Table 11.1, whereas approximately one-third of Black males and females are 19 years old or younger, only one-fourth or fewer of White males and females are in this age group. In contrast, although more than 40% of White males and females are 45 or older, approximately one-third of Black males and females are in this age group. The aging cohort of baby boomers is increasing the percentages of older adults for both ethnic groups since the last census.

In later sections of this chapter, we consider issues such as reproductive, birth, and mortality rates among different age groups that can help us better understand these ethnic variations in age group composition. These variations are also important in considering the developmental function of different age groups within a community. What are the advantages and disadvantages of having an overall younger population? What are the implications for the survival of the group? What are the implications for the demands placed on adults raising a relatively large cohort of youth? What are the losses from having fewer seniors available to support and provide wisdom and guidance to the community?

Childbirths

Demographic data can help us understand reproductive trends among African Americans. We can consider a range of questions: Are Blacks having more or fewer children? How old do Blacks tend to be when they become parents? Are there changes in the number of African American births?

Demographic data indicate that the fertility rate among African American women (births per 1,000 women age 15–44) declined from 25.3 per 1,000 in 1970 to 20.4 per 1,000 in 1985. There was a slight increase in the fertility rate during the late 1980s and early 1990s (with a peak rate of 22.4 per 1,000 in 1990) and a reduction continuing through 2015 (14.3 births per 1,000 in 2015 compared with a rate of 12.4 for all races in that year; Martin, Hamilton, Ostermam, Driscoll, & Matthews, 2017).

Nonmarital births for African American women 15–44 across this same period showed an increase from 81.1 per 1,000 in 1980 to 90.7 per 1,000 by 1989. This was followed by a general decline through 2003 (65.9 per 1,000), modest increases during the mid-2000s (e.g., 71.4 in 2007) and declines through 2015 (59.6 per 1000

TABLE 11.1 ■ Percentages of the Population by Age and Ethnic Group				
Age	% Black Males	% White Males	% Black Females	% White Females
Under 5	7.9	6.0	7.0	5.5
5–9	7.9	6.2	7.0	5.7
10–19	17.7	13.2	15.6	12.2
20–29	15.5	13.3	14.8	12.5
30–44	20.1	19.5	20.5	18.6
45–64	23.5	28.4	24.8	28.4
65 and up	7.3	13.5	10.3	17.0

Source: U.S. Census Bureau (2010a).

in 2015). Teen fertility rates increased among 15- to 19-year-old African American women from 97.8 per 1,000 in 1980 to 114.8 in 1991, subsequently dropping to 32.0 in 2015. This 2015 rate remains notably higher than that of non-Hispanic Whites (21.3 per 1,000) but slightly lower than that of adolescents 15 to 19 years old of any Hispanic origin (34.9 per 1,000).

The higher rate of births among unmarried parents and earlier timing of births among African Americans have been of concern because of the research indicating negative effects on both the educational outcomes for the mother (Klepinger, Lundberg, & Plotnick, 1995) and developmental outcomes for the infant (Levine, Pollack, & Comfort, 2001; Mathews, Curtin, & MacDorman, 2000; Moore, Morrison, & Greene, 1997). These earlier births and the higher rates of single-parent families among African Americans can also have important implications for the extended family and result in higher rates of intergenerational caregiving and child-rearing. Various reasons for the earlier timing of childbearing have been offered, including young women's concerns about their health and capacity to reproduce if they delay childbearing (Geronimus, 1991, 1996).

Notable and of particular concern for African American women is the increase in pregnancy-related deaths over the past two decades. In 1987 there were 7.2 recorded pregnancy-related deaths per 100,000 births in the United States, compared with 17.3 in 2013 (CDC, 2017). During the period 2011–2013, there were 40.4 deaths per 100,000 live births for African American women, compared with 12.1 such deaths for White women. Cardiovascular disease, other noncardiovascular diseases, infections, hemorrhage, cardiomiopathy, embolisms, and hypertensive disorders are among the top causes of pregnancy-related deaths for all women.

Infant Mortality

Infant mortality rates have declined for African Americans over the past several decades (from 22.2 per 1,000 pregnancies in 1980 to 14.0 per 1,000 pregnancies in 2000 and to 11.1 in 2013). However, rates of infant mortality for African Americans remain over twice that for non-Hispanic White American infants (5.1 per 1,000; CDC, 2015; Matthews & MacDorman, 2015). The leading causes for infant deaths among African Americans are low birth weight (at a rate of 260.7 per 100,000 live births, 3.5 times the rate for White infants), congenital malformations (141.6 per 100,000; 1.2 times the rate for White infants), maternal complications (at 86.5 per 100,000 live births, 2.9 times the rate for White infants) and sudden infant death syndrome (SIDS, at a rate of 73.3 per 100,000 a rate 1.8 times that found among White infants). To place these numbers in context, among the 225 countries ranked, the United States was estimated to have an infant death rate of 5.8 in 2016, with lower rates in Hungary, (5.0), Canada (4.6), Cuba (4.5), Portugal (4.4), Lithuania (3.8), Iceland (2.1), and Japan (2.0) (CIA, 2017).

Poverty

Understanding African Americans' access to income and resources is important, as socioeconomic status is associated with a range of positive or negative developmental outcomes. In contrast to a national poverty rate of 13.5% in 2015, African Americans had a poverty rate of 24.1%, down from 27.4% in 2010. The effect of the economic downturn resulted in increases in the percentage of individuals living in poverty overall, and African Americans were especially hard hit by the 2008 economic crisis. The federal poverty threshold for a family of four (with two children under age 18) in 2015 was $24,036 (U.S. Census, 2016i). Using data from the 2015 American Community Survey (Kids Count, n.d.), 12% of non-Hispanic White children and 36% of African American children lived in poverty. Because of their larger representation in the American population, however, 31% of all poor children were White while 24.8% of children living in poverty were African American.

Notably, poor Black children living in nonmetropolitan areas have higher rates of poverty (46.7%) than those residing in urban areas (35.5%). This is consistent with metro/nonmetro differences for non-Hispanic White (15.9 versus 20.7) and Hispanic children (30.0 versus 33.3%; USDA, 2017).

Early Deaths, Incarceration, and Suicide

Child and teen death rates are on the decline. In 2005, there were 43 deaths per 100,000 African American children ages 1 to 19. This decreased to 36 by 2015 (Annie E. Casey Foundation, n.d.). In comparison, rates for 2005 and 2015 among White children were 30 and 24 per 100,000, respectively. African American males have a disproportionately high death rate in the 12- to 19-year-old age category, with rates of 94.1 deaths per 100,000 for Black males versus 62 for White males, 34 for Black females, and 31 for White females (Minino, 2010). Among African American males ages 15 to 19, the leading cause of death (2014) was homicide (48.6% of deaths), followed by unintentional injuries (24.1%) and suicide (7.1%) (Office of Minority Health and Health Equity, n.d.). This compares with unintentional injuries being the leading cause of death for White males (44.5%), with suicide (24.9%) and homicide (7.6%) falling as the second and third causes of death for the 15- to 19-year-old age group (OMHHE, n.d., b). These data underline the particularly precarious developmental risks and challenges faced by African American males. Although we must be careful not to ignore the positive developmental outcomes achieved by the majority of African American males, these data clearly point to the need to attend to and address developmental challenges that negatively affect outcomes for African American males.

African Americans have a higher rate of incarceration than White Americans. According to 2017 data from the Federal Bureau of Prisons, African Americans represent 37.7% of inmates. while Whites are 58.7% of the federal inmate population (FBOP, n.d.).

Suicide rates are lower for African Americans than other racial and ethnic groups. Data from 2015 indicate that rates (per 100,000) were 5.7 for African Americans compared with 13.8 for Americans overall, 6.2 for Asian/Pacific Islanders, and 11.0 for Native Americans (American Association of Suicidology, 2017).

Employment and Education

Employment and educational attainment are lower for African Americans than Whites. The seasonally adjusted unemployment rate among African Americans age 20 or older for February 2018 was 5.9% for men and 6.2% for women, compared with 3.4% and 3.3% for White men and women, respectively (BLS, 2017). This follows a significant increase in the unemployment rate, which increased notably after the 2008 economic downturn and peaked at 16.8% for African Americans during 2010 (Federal Reserve Bank of St. Louis, 2014). In 2015, 84.7% of African Americans age 25 or older had graduated high school (U.S. Census, n.d.), up from 79.9% in 2005. Twenty-two percent of African Americans over age 25 had a bachelor's degree or higher, and 8.2% of African Americans had advanced graduate or professional degrees (Ryan & Bauman, 2016).

Seniors

With the aging of the baby boomers, the percentage of seniors in the American population is projected to grow. By 2030, there will be about 70 million older persons, more than twice their number in 2000. People 65 years and older represented 12.4% of the population in the year 2000 but are expected to grow to be 20% of the population by 2030. Minority populations are projected to represent 24% of the elderly population in 2020, up from 16.3% in 2000 (AOA, 2011, p. 3). African Americans who were 9% of the 55- to 79-year-old population in 2004 are projected to be 14% of this age group by 2050 (American Council on Education, 2007).

Between 1999 and 2030, the African American population over age 65 is projected to increase by 131%, compared with 81% for Whites. Compared with White seniors, African American seniors have more limited access to economic resources. In 2010, whereas 18.0% of elderly African Americans had incomes below the poverty level, only 6.8% of older Whites lived below the poverty level (AOA, 2011).

Among American seniors, there are ethnic variations in educational achievement levels, with 87% of African Americans over age 65 having completed high school in 2015, compared with approximately 93.3% of non-Hispanic Whites and 66.7% of Hispanics (Ryan and Bauman, 2016). Historical factors (e.g., segregation, lack of educational access, lack of family economic resources) underlie these ethnic differences.

Challenges and Strengths

This demographic portrait presents a picture that is both positive and challenging. Many poor African American infants are clearly at higher developmental risk than their White counterparts, and overall, African Americans are at greater risk for several negative health outcomes. However, it is promising to see improvements in the trends for African Americans across a range of life and health indicators. To the extent that development is linked to access to economic resources, African Americans (especially African American children and elders) have more limited access to economic and related health resources. This comparative analysis, however, focuses only on traditional indicators of outcomes, uses middle-class Whites as the normative comparison group, and may not capture many developmental outcomes that are important from the cultural perspective of many African Americans.

For example, Burton et al. (1995) note adaptations among African American adolescents in inner cities with limited access to resources and opportunities to support middle-class outcomes. These include adaptation of traditional developmental goals (e.g., revising the American Dream) to focus on accessing short-term, attainable symbols of middle-class success and achieving adult status through varied pathways to economic independence. Among these are a sense of spiritual well-being (often accompanied by engagement with a religious organization), expression of creative talents and abilities, and serving as a community and family resource. In describing the success of a 19-year-old man who had dropped out of school, one community leader said,

> Anthony may not have finished high school and he may not have a job, but he is the treasure of our community. He helps the young mothers around the neighborhood with their kids. He does the grocery shopping for some of the old folks around here who can't get out. And he keeps the peace between rival street gangs in the community. (Burton et al., 1995, p. 133)

It is important for research to clarify culturally and contextually relevant indicators of developmental "success." Having a high-status job and achieving possessions reflective of upper-middle-class or upper-class social status does not always mean happiness. These issues may be particularly important to consider as developmental outcomes. In addition, as there are changes in the contexts within which African Americans live and develop, such as the increasing suburbanization of urban African American populations (see Chapter 7), we may need to attend to potential changes in associated life course outcomes.

THEORETICAL PERSPECTIVES ON THE DEVELOPMENT OF AFRICAN AMERICANS

Several theoretical perspectives have been used to shape and further our understanding of developmental phenomena. Sigmund Freud and Anna Freud's stage model emphasized stages in the description of psychosexual development (Muus, 1988). These theoretical perspectives focused on the sequential resolution of a stage-based developmental progression hypothesized to shape subsequent development. In contrast, the behavioral, learning, or social learning theories of B. F. Skinner, Watson, and Bandura have also been used in supporting our understanding of development. These perspectives emphasize the individual learning episodes that shape an individual's ongoing development and articulate no specific sequence of developmental tasks or stages (Muus, 1988).

Whether considering more stage, dynamic, or learning perspectives on development, these theories tend to emphasize a universal perspective on human development. That is, regardless of the context or population, developmental processes or progression are believed to occur in a similar fashion for all humans regardless of context or culture. Anthropologist Franz Boas and his students, Ruth Benedict and Margaret Mead, challenged these universal perspectives and proposed that development may be shaped by more proximal cultural and contextual forces. This perspective is called cultural relativism. Several more recent developmental perspectives emphasize the role of culture and context in development. These include Vygotsky's social cognitive theory and Bronfenbrenner's ecological model.

Vygotsky Social Cognitive Theory

Vygotsky's (1934/1978) work in social cognition and learning emphasized the role of culture in development and posited that

> every function in the child's cultural development appears twice: first, on the social level, and later, on the individual level; first, between people (interpsychological) and then inside the child (intrapsychological). This applies equally to voluntary attention, to logical memory, and to the formation of concepts. All the higher functions originate as actual relationships between individuals. (p. 57)

Vygotsky suggested that culture not only shapes the content of a child's cognitions (i.e., what a child thinks) but also shapes the process of cognition (i.e., how a child thinks). Several researchers and theorists have suggested that the cultural and developmental contexts of African American children support the development of cognitive preferences and related learning styles that emphasize (a) relationships, social interactions, and emotional expressiveness; (b) verve, rhythm, movement, and kinesthetic; and (c) oral, verbal, and auditory modes (Boykin, 1978; Hale-Benson, 1986; Shade, 1991; Townsend, 2000; see also Chapter 6). A strong oral tradition that uses social interactions and that integrates physical movement into everyday activities, from jump rope and patty-cake to walking and dancing, are among factors that characterize the rich cultural environment experienced by many African American children. These factors may be important when considering the cultural implications for teaching and education (Townsend, 2000). Vygotsky's analysis also notes that culture supports the content of our learning and cognitions. As an illustration, consider hip-hop and rap, music forms that are grounded in a Black history of oral tradition

CONTEMPORARY ISSUES
RESEARCH IN AFRICA INFORMS ROLE OF CULTURE IN UNDERSTANDING HUMAN DEVELOPMENT

In a 2011 article, Super, Harkness, Barry, and Zeitlin provide a compelling perspective on the ways in which research focusing on African children has informed and shaped our understanding of child development. These authors note that beyond research in the United States and Europe, research on the African continent was among the earliest to be conducted on child development. Similar to Boas's, Benedict's, and Mead's perspectives on cultural relativity, developmental studies conducted in Africa have served as a resource to address the challenges of cultural assumptions and generalizations and sometimes engaged local "researchers" to assist. In effect, the research provided the opportunity to observe and examine culturally different child-rearing practices and ecological niches in rural African communities that provided important new perspectives on child development. This included learning about African infant care practices that involved intentional motor instruction, exercise, movement, infant stimulation, and massage. Other child-rearing practices (such as the importance of sibling care) refined our understanding of constructs such as secure attachment. In addition, research in Africa was used to examine and make distinctions about developmental constructs such as operational thinking. This aspect of cognitive development was considered within the context of specific developmentally and culturally based experiences.

This research also examined the presence of universal cognitive developmental sequences that appeared to be grounded in normative biological maturation and development.

Super et al. (2011) note the developmental significance of social responsibility as a form of intelligence in Africa. Their review of the literature suggests the intentionality of African child-rearing practices to desired developmental outcomes and child socialization for future social roles.

This analysis of cross-cultural research raises a series of critical questions and issues for the development of African Americans today. Considering the diversity of developmental settings and ecological niches within which African Americans live, which set of cultural goals and developmental outcomes should parents and communities pursue? Are all mainstream American cultural norms worthy of pursuit? Rugged individualism and individual personal achievement or standing on the shoulders of others? Crossing the finish line alone or together? As opportunities continue to open for African Americans and developmental contexts for African Americans continue to change, how will communities provide relevant socialization to support preparation for future social roles? And should we consider what might be lost in translation?

with an emphasis on rhythm and a highly varied content of messages. However, some hip-hop and rap include blatant misogyny and negative messages strongly reminiscent of Azibo's (1996) perspective on mentacide (i.e., the imposition and destruction of a group's cultural resources through their experience of oppression; see Chapter 13 for further discussion). From Vygotsky's perspective, the content of these negative messages may shape developing cognitions and understandings of the social world and illustrate the tension between African-centered perspectives on culture and the sequelae of racism.

Bronfenbrenner and Ecological Theory

An additional model that emphasizes the role of context is Bronfenbrenner's (1977) ecological theory. Ecological theory suggests that development is shaped by the interaction between the person, the contexts within which the person develops, and the types of exchanges that take place in the interaction between the individual and his or her context. Person factors include characteristics of the individual (e.g., age, gender, ethnicity or race, temperament, personality) or the individual's specific competencies (e.g., social skills, academic ability). Context includes factors such as residence in an urban or rural community, family structure, and neighborhood characteristics. Processes involve exchanges such as parental monitoring, teaching style, and dating behaviors. Bronfenbrenner believed that developmental outcomes are a function of the specific individual, his or her unique developmental context, and the specific developmental processes involving the individual.

Bronfenbrenner described a series of contexts that may affect development. These include the microsystem—that is, the social relationships in which the individual is directly involved (e.g., peers, family, teachers); the mesosystem—that is, the next level of context that encompasses the connections between different microsystems (e.g., linkages between home and school or between family and peers); the exosystem—that is, the social settings that may indirectly affect development but where the individual does not have direct contact (e.g., school boards that set educational and school policy, the supervisors at a parent's place of employment); and the macrosystem—that is, the broader context that involves the social structure, including media, culture, and government. To these systems, Bronfenbrenner (1986) added the need to consider the chronosystem, or the set of temporal and historical changes that may affect development and alter the settings, contexts, and characteristics of the individual.

We can consider Bronfenbrenner's ecological theory of development for African Americans. Questions at the person level might ask whether there are specific group characteristics inherent to African Americans that play a role in shaping developmental outcomes. In the process domain, questions might focus on whether developmental processes (e.g., socialization processes) are similar or different for African Americans and other cultural groups and how these shape development. In the contextual domain, we might examine how the settings in which African Americans develop shape their emotions, thinking, and behavior. Finally, we can also consider how changes in contexts, processes, and people, over time, shape developmental outcomes for African Americans.

Taking the intersection of the last two dimensions of Bronfenbrenner's ecological model (i.e., context and chronosystems), we can briefly illustrate how developmental contexts for African Americans have seen an amazing transition over the past 75 years. Most recent demographic data indicate that African Americans more frequently live in the South and in urban areas in the Northeast, Midwest, and

West (see Chapter 7 for a fuller description of neighborhoods and communities). Historians note that Northern migration based on the combination of Jim Crow laws in the South and employment opportunities in the North and Midwest resulted in a large movement of African Americans between the end of the Civil War and 1970. In addition, the move of industries to the suburbs with limited access to transportation, and the concurrent movement of middle-class African Americans to the suburbs, resulted in the concentration of poor African Americans in many urban cores (Wilson, 1987, 1997). Poor families had support from Aid to Families with Dependent Children, established in 1935, but families were eligible only if one parent was absent or incapacitated. It was not until 1968 that the "man-in-the-house" rules were struck down by the Supreme Court (*King v. Smith*, 1968). Many suggest that these policies limited child and family access to male parents and role models for cohorts of poor urban youth.

Currently, media and technology, increasing cultural diversity and globalization, and hip-hop culture are critically important factors in the developmental contexts of African Americans as reflected in Bronfenbrenner's ideas about the macrosystem. When we consider developmental outcomes, such as educational attainment, personal adjustment, and family creation, it is important to set our understanding within the dramatic historical changes in the social contexts within which African Americans develop. For example, how are variations in the family formation strategies of African Americans linked to the changes in historical opportunities? And how are historical changes in the community contexts of urban African American communities linked to changes in suicide and adolescent incarceration rates?

Phenomenological Variant of Ecological Systems Theory

Spencer, Dupree, and Hartmann (1997) offer an expansion of ecological theory that explicitly considers the experience of African Americans. In their phenomenological variant of ecological systems theory (PVEST), Spencer et al. suggest that the processes and outcomes linked to any specific phenomenon are shaped by the individual's meaning making and the developmental, sociocultural, and contextual influences that shape that meaning making. The PVEST model is reciprocal and suggests that for African Americans, contributions to risk and adaptation include social-cognitively based social and self-appraisals linked to race, gender, socioeconomic status, physical status, and biological characteristics.

For example, it is possible that social and cultural meaning attributed to being a large, dark-skinned female adolescent as opposed to a small, light-skinned male adolescent may shape both interpersonal and intrapersonal perceptions and result in variation in risk linked to self-cognitions (also see Chapter 8 for a discussion of interpersonal relations). These risks, protections, and possibilities, in turn, influence and are influenced by an individual's immediate experience of stress and adaptation. These experiences are shaped by factors such as neighborhood dangers and resources, access and utilization of social support, and daily hassles. Stress and adaptation experiences are linked to coping methods involving either adaptive (e.g., self-acceptance) or maladaptive (e.g., male bravado) problem-solving strategies. These more event-dependent coping reactions are also reciprocally tied to more stable coping styles and identities (e.g., personal and cultural goals and perceptions related to personally and contextually available means to achieve these goals). These identities influence and are influenced by developmentally specific productive (e.g., competence) and adverse (e.g., deviance) life stage outcomes, which, in turn, are linked back to risk contributions.

RESEARCH ON THE DEVELOPMENT OF AFRICAN AMERICANS

Within the scope of this chapter, it is impossible to provide a complete review of the developmental literature on infants, toddlers, preschoolers, children in middle childhood, adolescents, young adults, middle-age adults, and the elderly. In addition, as noted in the introduction, several other chapters in this book address important core issues in development in detail (e.g., family, identity, education, community, adjustment). In this section, we provide an overview of some key findings relevant to African Americans in four specific developmental periods: prenatal period, infancy, and early childhood; adolescence; adulthood; and older adulthood.

Prenatal Period, Infancy, and Early Childhood

Research data suggest that, as a broad demographic group, African American infants may begin their lives at a higher level of risk. As noted previously, African American infants are at a higher risk of preterm birth (Matthews, MacDorman, & Thoma, 2015). An emerging body of work is beginning to uncover potential contributors to this risk. Stout et al. (2017) note that preterm births were associated with the decreased richness and variability of the vaginal microbiome in a predominately African American sample. A microbiome is the bacteria or other microorganisms that live within our bodies. There is a growing body of work suggesting that the microbiome has a notable influence on aspects of our health and well-being. Additional work has also raised the possibility that genetic factors associated with the strength of the amniotic sac may account for some portion of the racial difference in premature births (Wang et al., 2006).

Research has indicated a potential link between African American women's higher risk for depression and preterm births. This work indicated that African American women who experience depression had higher levels of stress and anger and were at risk for earlier births and having babies with lower birth weights compared to non-depressed African American mothers (Field et al., 2009). Research has also found self-reported prior experiences of depression in African American mothers to be associated with physiological regulation (resting heart rate and heart rate variability) in African American neonates (newborn infants) (Jacob, Byrne, & Keenan, 2009).

Stress may play a role in birth outcomes for African American women. Zhao et al. (2015) found that financial stressors—but not other types of stressors—were associated with low birth weight (LBW) among African American but not White mothers who participated in the Los Angeles Mommy and Baby Study (N = 4,970). In related research, Braveman et al. (2015) found no differences in preterm births among African American and White women at the lowest levels of economic resources; however, infants born to African American mothers were at greater risk of LBW at higher income levels when compared with their White peers.

African American mothers may make different infant care choices compared with mothers from other cultural groups. For example, African American infants are less likely to be breast fed compared with other American infants. Using data from the 2011–2015 National Immunization Survey, Anstey, Chen, Elam-Evans, and Perrine (2016) note that African American mothers were least likely to have initiated breast-feeding (64.3%), breastfed their children through 6 months (14%) and continued through the first year of life (17.1%), compared with White non-Hispanic mothers (81.5%, 22.5% and 30.8%, respectively). This suggests that fewer African American infants may accrue the reported benefits associated with breast-feeding (e.g., lower risk of SIDS, asthma, and obesity; United States Breastfeeding Committee, 2002).

Research also suggests that there are significant benefits of breast-feeding for mothers (e.g., lower risk of obesity, lower rates of ovarian and premenopausal breast cancer) (Moreno, Furtner, & Rivara, 2011).

DeVane-Johnson, Woods-Giscombé, Thoyre, Fogel, and Williams's (2017) review of the literature suggests that several factors are relevant to disparities breastfeeding. These include social characteristics, such as being single and of low socioeconomic status, perceptions of breastfeeding (e.g., concerns around physical or social discomfort, perceptions of the quality, and benefits or risk of breast milk) and limited or poor information on relevant information provided by health care providers.

Research has questioned the assumption that single-parent family structures result in poorer parenting by African Americans. Using data from the Comprehensive Child Development Project, a study of 4,410 low-income families followed over 5 years, Foster and Kalil (2007) examined the effects of living arrangements on child developmental outcomes. Overall, family structure appeared to have a limited influence on children's well-being and development. Family structure was a significant predictor of internalizing behavior problems (e.g., anxiety, depression) but only before maternal educational expectations for her child and maternal depression were taken into account. African American children living in a blended family were found to have higher levels of externalizing behavior problems (e.g., aggression), as opposed to those living with the mother alone, with biological parents, or within multigenerational families.

Beyond family structure, research has suggested that African American parents may be more likely to use corporal punishment. For example, Berlin et al. (2009) found higher rates of spanking among low-income African American parents of toddlers compared with low-income White and Latino families. Westbrook, Harden, Holmes, Meisch, and Whittaker (2013) also examined physical discipline among low-income, high-risk African American families. Slightly over half (54%) of the 69 African American low-income mothers reported using physical discipline with their children (mean age = 15.8 months; ranging from 3.5 to 25 months)

Research by Mitchell et al. (2014) suggests that the disadvantaged environments in which some Black children grow up may result in biological indicators (e.g., telomeres), which reflect the effects of stress and aging. Telomeres are the repetitive sequence of genetic material at the end of each chromosome that, in effect, serve as protective ends of chromosomes to prevent fusion with other genetic material or the degradation of important genetic information. As we age, with the replication of each genetic sequence as cells divide, a bit of the telomere is lost or not replicated. Stress has been found to result in shorter length of telomeres. Mitchell et al. found that in a sample of African American boys (age 9), those whose environments were characterized by disadvantage (lower family economic assets, lower maternal education, harsh parenting and parental instability/structure) had shorter telomeres. These differences were especially notable among boys who possessed a genetic variant for neurotransmitters (dopamine and serotonin) suggesting a greater sensitivity to environmental (i.e., experiential or "nurture") conditions.

Early Childhood Care Arrangements and Experiences

One important question relevant to the development of African American children is how the settings and environments in which they grow up affect their development. Using data from the Survey of Income and Program Participation, Linda Laughlin (2013) examined the childcare arrangements of American children, ages 5 and under and between the ages of 5 and 14, during the spring of 2011. For both preschoolers and school-aged children, sibling care was used more frequently among African Americans as compared with Whites and Hispanics, whether mothers worked or not.

Grandparents were engaged to provide care at relatively similar levels across all racial and ethnic groups for preschool children and for African American school-aged children, whether mothers worked or not. African American and Hispanic children had higher rates of participation in Head Start and African American children were more likely to be in some type of regular care. Data are presented in Table 11.2.

TABLE 11.2 ■ Childcare Arrangements by Mother's Employment Status and Race/Ethnicity

	Grandparental Care	Sibling Care	Day Care	Nursery/ Preschool	Head Start	No Regular Care
Preschoolers						
Mother Not Employed						
White alone	12.7	7	2.4	3.3	4.6	75.3
Black alone	14.9	13.7	14.1	B	7.6	56.8
Hispanic (any race)	10.1	7.6		2.3	5.5	78.1
Mother Employed						
White alone	32.3	9.8	21.8	7.8	5.1	12.4
Black alone	31.7	18.1	22.5	8.2	9.9	9.7
Hispanic (any race)	34.1	15.8	10.9	4.5	8.9	10.8

	Grandparental Care	Sibling Care		Enrichment	Self- Care	No Regular Care
School-Aged (5–14)						
Mother Not Employed						
White alone	6.1	6.8		9.5	6.7	77.3
Black alone	11.8	15.8		9.6	5.3	68.1
Hispanic (any race)	4.9	7.4		3.9	4	82.4
Mother Employed						
White alone	18	13.8		19.4	14.9	36.2
Black alone	18.5	22.2		16.2	10.1	31.9
Hispanic (any race)	23.2	20.5		16	9.6	32.5

Note: "B" indicates the base is less than 75,000.

Source: Linda Laughlin (2013).

Adolescence

Adolescence follows childhood and spans the period of development characterized by the physical changes of puberty, reflecting the biological transition to physical and sexual maturity. Adolescence is also defined based on the social transitions reflected in the move to middle and high school, as well as the entry into dating and social relationships that anticipate pair bonding, cohabitation, and marriage. This period of development precedes adulthood, where youth are expected to take on adult social roles in their communities, including entry into work and the possibility of family formation. Often, this period of development is characterized by chronological age, beginning with early adolescence around age 11 to about age 14, middle adolescence which spans from around age 15 to 16 or 17, and late adolescence, which usually is considered the range from around age 17 or 18 to the early 20s. African American adolescents, especially those youth growing up in resource-poor communities, face a range of challenges in the transition to adulthood. In the words of Chestang (1972), these youth face "character development in a hostile environment," have limited access to employment opportunities, and sometimes show early expectations of and transitions to markers of adult role attainment.

Physical Development

Research has suggested that African American female adolescents show earlier physical development compared with their White female counterparts, with average age at menarche at 150 months for White girls and 144 months for African American adolescent girls (Reagan, Salsberry, Fang, Gardner, & Pajer, 2012). Based on data from the National Health and Nutrition Examination Survey (Sun et al., 2002), African American female participants displayed initial breast development at 9.5 years of age compared to 10.4 years for their same-age White peers. Earlier research and reviews by Tanner (Eveleth & Tanner, 1976) noted that African American children and youth show markers of faster physical maturity and larger size than their White peers. Researchers have questioned whether this earlier physical development among American youth is in general linked to exposure to specific hormones and chemicals or to the higher rates of obesity among American children, especially African American and poor children.

The increasing rates of obesity among African American children and adolescents are another significant area of developmental concern. Considering the years between 1999 and 2012, 28.5% of White children were obese compared with 35.1% of African American children between ages 2 and 19 (Skinner & Skelton, 2014). Obesity is associated with higher risk of type 2 diabetes, high blood pressure, and early sexual development, each of which is associated with a range of negative outcomes. These increases in obesity have been linked to several factors. Some of these include more sedentary behaviors among African American children, concerns over safety in higher-risk communities, more limited access to sports in lower-resource communities, consumption, targeted marketing and poor access to healthy and affordable food, as well as cultural patterns of eating.

Summer vacation may be an important time to consider in understanding weight increases among African American children (von Hippel, Powell, Downey, & Rowland, 2007). In this study of 5,380 children in kindergarten and first grade, weight gains were higher during summer months. Racial and ethnic differences indicated that African American and Latino children entered school with higher body mass indexes (BMIs) and demonstrated faster increases in BMI than their White

TABLE 11.3 ■ 2015 Youth Risk Behavior Study: Sexual Risk Behaviors (percentages of high school students)			
	Black+	Hispanic	White+
Ever had sexual intercourse	48.5	42.5	39.9
Had sexual intercourse for the first time before age 13 years	8.3	5.0	2.5

+ Non-Hispanic

Source: CDC, Morbidity and Mortality Weekly Report (2016).

peers during the summer vacation period. Less structured activities and lower supervision of sedentary and snacking behavior may be implicated.

Roles, Developmental Tasks, and Identity

Adolescence is a period of development when teens enter new social roles, take on new responsibilities, and engage in behaviors reflecting their transition to adulthood. One area of particular concern for this period of development focuses on the transitions involving sexual activity. Using findings from the 2015 National Youth Risk Behavior Survey, data on students in ninth through 12th grade indicate that more Black youth have engaged in sexual intercourse, and more Black youth have had intercourse at a younger age than their Hispanic and White peers (see Table 11.3).

As described previously in the chapter, African American youth also experience higher rates of adolescent childbearing than their White peers but lower rates in comparison to their Latino peers. In urban, low-resource communities, researchers have discussed issues of age condensation in African American families where adolescents and parents (particularly when these parents were young parents themselves) may be engaging in similar developmental life tasks (e.g., completing or continuing education, dating, seeking employment; Burton et al., 1995).

African American youth in families with limited economic resources may face a discrepancy in the role expectations they face. At school, they may be expected to act as children and respond to the authority of the adult, whereas in their homes and communities, they may take on important adult financial and childcare roles. The challenges many African American youth face, particularly in low-resource communities and in the face of higher risk of experiencing violence and death, may lead to individual- and community-based socialization that pushes youth to transition earlier into adult roles. They thus miss the opportunity of an idealized protected childhood. Alternatively, some have proposed that for middle- and upper-class teenagers and young adults, the developmental period of adolescence is being extended.

With physical and sociocognitive development and changes in developmental social contexts and social roles, adolescence is considered a developmental period when issues of identity become focal. "Who am I?" and "What will I become?" are central developmental concerns. Research suggests that ethnic identity may be an especially important component of identity development for African American youth (Aries & Moorehead, 1989). In examining changes in and correlates of ethnic identity development during adolescence, Altschul, Oyserman, and Bybee (2006) found that racial connectedness and beliefs that academic performance is important to one's ethnic group was associated with higher grade point averages. Awareness of racism and connectedness in eighth grade predicted higher GPA in the ninth grade. For a broader discussion of issues of identity development, see Chapter 3.

Adolescence is also a period characterized by the increased importance of the peer group. Peers have increasing influence, especially regarding issues and behaviors relevant to the peer social domain. Parental behaviors shift in response to their child's development but remain important in shaping the lives of their children. Parents' socioeconomic resources and decisions select the environmental contexts in which their children develop. Parental behaviors such as monitoring influence the types of peers with whom their children are engaged. For example, research by Nebbitt, Lombe, and Lindsey (2007) indicates that male and older African American youth living in public housing are more likely to associate with negative peers. However, parental monitoring and support are associated with lower levels of negative peer affiliation.

Work by Hurd and Zimmerman (2010) has also underlined the importance of adults in adolescent transitions to adulthood. In a longitudinal study of 615 African American adolescents followed 5 years after high school, having a natural or informal mentor (who was not a parent or stepparent) was associated with greater declines in depressive symptoms. Greater declines in depression were seen for males with natural mentors than for females with natural mentors. In addition, those with natural mentors engaged in lower levels of sexual risk behavior.

African American Racial Parenting and Socialization

Among developmental processes, of particular interest with regard to African American children and adolescents are the processes of parenting and racial socialization. In examining parenting, researchers frequently consider dimensions defined by levels of parental control and levels of parental warmth and responsiveness. Parenting low in warmth and high in control is categorized as authoritarian, and parenting high in warmth and responsiveness and high in control is considered authoritative or democratic. Parenting described as being high in warmth and low in control is described as permissive, and parenting low in warmth and low in control is considered disengaged or neglectful. Research has raised the question as to whether parenting styles may differentially affect African Americans, as opposed to children from other ethnic groups.

Radziszewska, Richardson, Dent, and Flay (1996) and Attaway and Bry (2004) used samples of African American adolescents and found relationships between parenting style and educational outcomes. Attaway and Bry found stronger parental beliefs about control to be associated with lower GPAs. There are varied perspectives on the stricter parenting found among some African American parents. Some see this more controlling style as culturally adaptive, both linked to a history of enslavement and oppression and appropriate in supporting child safety in high-risk settings. Watkins-Lewis and Hamre (2012) found "traditional beliefs" (i.e., stronger authoritarian beliefs about parenting) among mothers to predict lower math scores and first-grade school performance, as rated by teachers in a sample of African American families with young children. Maternal warmth and confidence predicted higher scores in math, reading, and phoneme knowledge. Pezzella, Thornberry, and Smith (2016) did not find mean differences between African American and White youths' experiences. Parenting style and authoritative parenting was negatively associated with delinquency for both White and African American youth. In addition, authoritarian parenting was important for African American youth at higher levels of risk but not low risk levels. Risk was measured as a cumulative risk index, which included gang membership, unsupervised time with friends, delinquent beliefs, neighborhood drug use, and negative life events. Findings were based on analyses of data including 414 African American and 114 White teens from the Rochester Youth Development Study.

In another study, parenting factors were related to mental health among African American teens. Examining data from the Birmingham Youth Violence Study involving 594 adolescents (mean age = 13.2), Mrug, King, and Windle (2016) found elevated rates of depression among African American teens were explained in large part by poor parenting (harsh or inconsistent discipline). Other factors included parent's lower level of educational attainment, greater exposure to violence, and lower school connectedness, as well as youths' higher levels of aggression and delinquency.

Wang, Hill, and Hofkens (2014) examined the relationship between parenting variables and youth educational, behavioral and emotional functioning using data from the Maryland Adolescent in Context Study. This study involved a sample of 1,452 families across three waves of data collection in seventh, ninth, and 11th grades. The sample was about 56% African American, 39% White, and the remainder belonging to other or biracial groups. The sample crossed a representative range of family incomes. African American parents and parents with more limited financial resources reported lower levels of preventive communication from schools when youth were in the seventh grade. African American parents reported more structure at home and greater linking of education to the future than did White parents of seventh graders. The provision of structure at home was more important for the academic performance of African American youth than their White counterparts. Parental involvement was associated with lower levels of adolescent problem behavior and depressive effects, but there were no racial-ethnic differences in these effects.

Research by Varner and Mandara (2013) suggests that there may be some truth in the popular saying in the Black community that "Mothers love their sons but raise their daughters." Participants in the study came from 796 families who were part of the economically diverse Maryland Adolescent Development in Context Study sample. The research examined the role of gender in parental monitoring and expectations. Overall, mothers had lower expectations for boys as compared with girls, and girls had less autonomy in their decision making and higher levels of monitoring.

One specific aspect of parenting behavior of interest to the development of African American children and adolescents is racial socialization. McHale et al. (2006) examined parenting and racial socialization in 162 two-parent African American families with children. Mothers more frequently reported engaging in racial socialization, although the mean rating suggested that both parents engaged in racial socialization sometimes. Maternal and paternal warmth were associated with cultural socialization and preparing their children to deal with racial bias. Maternal socialization was more frequently directed at adolescents as compared with younger children, and fathers were more significantly involved in the socialization of their sons. Maternal cultural socialization was associated with youth ethnic identity, and paternal racial socialization was linked to lower levels of depressive symptoms.

In a sample of 150 parents of African American adolescents living in low-resource circumstances (Elmore and Gaylord-Harden, 2013), supportive parenting and parents' use of messages communicating racial pride were associated with lower levels of perceived externalizing and internalizing behaviors. Derlan and Umana-Taylor (2015) found that youth who experienced greater racial socialization from family members and a higher percentage of same-ethnicity peers reported a greater sense of belonging to their racial-ethnic group. This sense of racial belonging, in turn, was predictive of youth reporting that they were better able to resist peer pressure to engage in negative or problem behaviors. Study participants were 250 African American teens (mean age = 15.57 years).

Smith, Reynolds, Fincham, and Beach (2016) examined the relationship between parental experiences of racial discrimination (i.e., parent's rating of how often they or their partner had experienced different types of racial discrimination) and parent's racial socialization practices (e.g., teaching about culture, preparing youth to handle bias, promoting mistrust) across 3,222 families. Mothers reporting higher levels of racial discrimination were more likely to engage in all three aspects of racial socialization. Fathers who reported higher levels of experienced bias for themselves or their partner were more likely to promote mistrust and prepare their sons for bias. However, only when their female partners (i.e., daughter's mother) reported higher levels of bias did fathers increase preparing their daughters for bias.

Thomas and Blackmon (2015) examined the effect of the shooting of Trayvon Martin on parenting practices through analysis of open-ended questions. Responses were obtained from 104 parents of African American children ranging in age from 6 to 18. Parents expressed concerns for the safety of their children, as well as over the continued experience of racism. Respondents noted their belief in the greater targeting of racism and risk for male children, and many respondents indicated that Black children need to be prepared by their parents and families to face racism. One respondent noted,

> I am worried about living in a country with a history of regarding young Black men as a threat. Thinking about the reason why I am constantly reminding them to stand up straight, dress the part, keep your hands in sight at all times and never, ever let your anger get the best of you. I am worried about the risks he runs as a Black teenager or young Black man just by walking down the street with a snack, the racism and history that lie behind that "talk" are a part of my own story. (pp. 80–81)

Another parent noted in response to the death that "It has reiterated for me that I need to continue to be vigilant about preparing them for the inequities of life and about their appearance and other people's perception. That they should always be themselves, but be conscious of how others see you" (pp. 82–83).

Adulthood

So what have you become now that you're all grown up? What's your job? Married? Got kids? The lives of adults are not just the developmental time between becoming an adult and growing old. Much of our understanding of adult development is linked to our cultural ideas as to the social roles that adults fulfill within their communities. Our development during childhood and adolescence prepares us to make successful transitions into work, relationship, and community roles.

Compared to other developmental age periods, there has been more limited theoretical and empirical attention to adult development. Some perspectives on adult development include employment and career development, religious involvement, family roles, and the strain of balancing these varied adult social roles. These perspectives are presented in other chapters. In the following section, we provide theoretical and empirical work that has focused specifically on the developmental experiences of African American men and women.

African American Women's Development

Building on Levinson's (1978) model of adult development, Ruffin (1989) proposes that African American women may experience variations in their developmental experiences and that these variations may be shaped, in part, by the timing of marriage, parenthood, and career. Levinson's original model suggests that after adolescence, we go through a transition period (around age 17 to 18) to early adulthood that lasts from our early 20s until our early 40s. Next, we begin a transition to middle adulthood, which lasts from our mid-40s until our early 60s. We then transition into late adulthood during our mid-60s. This work was based on a study of women between ages 35 and 45. In Ruffin's qualitative study of eight working African American women, she divided her sample into three groups. (a) The first group married early and began child-rearing during their early to mid-20s. (b) The second group had never married or had divorced by their early 30s. (c) The third group either remained unmarried or married late. Findings from her study underlined the importance of the historical context in which the women grew up and developed. These historical and developmental contexts shape resources, opportunities, available social support, and conceptions of female social roles. For example, few of the women in Ruffin's study had access to mentors to support career development and transitions; for those who had mentors, the mentors were also African American. Racial identity and related coping styles were a central theme in Ruffin's analysis, and life events linked to subjects' social networks also shaped life course decisions and trajectories.

Reflecting on the demographic data presented earlier, we can note that biologically, African American women may reach physical maturity somewhat earlier than their White peers. African American women may also transition to behaviors and social roles associated with adult roles and status (e.g., sexual activity, parenting) at a somewhat earlier age than their White female peers. Recent data note that Black women are somewhat less likely to marry and are more likely to marry at a later age than White women. For example, the median age for first marriage in 2010 was 26 years of age for a White woman and 30 years of age for an African American woman (Martin, Astone, & Peters, 2014b). In addition, historically, African American women have more consistently been part of the labor market, a role that White women also have increasingly assumed. These data and conceptual perspectives raise critical questions about the development of African American women and the potential monocultural view on development and adults' social roles, norms, and expectations projected onto them. African American women's roles in nuclear and extended families, connections in extended networks, and their economic roles may be shaped not just by the potential constraints and challenges of an American context but by culturally shaped choices. These choices may not prioritize stereotypic views of white picket fences over equally fulfilling relational and pragmatic realities.

African American Men's Development

Similar to our considerations for African American women, we can examine the developmental course and "status" of African American men, which is shaped by middle class, mainstream expectations. Herein, adult men in an American context are viewed stereotypically as breadwinners and traditional heads of households. Focusing on the early adulthood of African American males, Gooden (1989) also built on Levinson's work and interviewed a sample of 10 African American men, half of whom were employed as teachers or administrators in the public school system and half of whom he identified as "street men" because of their participation "in street corner society" (p. 64). The experiences of the school sample reflected a developmental course that reflected the limited availability of adult male support but the presence of support from female family members. These men had stable occupational transitions but generally did not achieve their highest career aspirations, due, in part, to resource constraints, challenging life events, and social network demands. These men were also involved in the life of the broader community. The majority had married and experienced some level of marital conflict but relatively low levels of marital disruption.

The street group also reported a lack of support from older males as mentors and had work lives marked by instability, with few opportunities for advancement. They tended to start families early, and they experienced high levels of disruption of intimate relationships. These relationship challenges were linked to fear of intimacy, extramarital relationships, and inability to handle conflicts within their relationships. Some men in this group had established stable long-term employment, but many experienced difficulty in making a successful transition to well-paying, long-term jobs. Both groups reported financial concerns as part of marital conflict, but street men reported economic resources that were more limited, and thus, their relationships may have suffered more from this additional financial strain.

Recent data suggest that the findings of this historical analysis persist today. Demographic data reflect the more limited access to and lower likelihood of African American men having educational and employment opportunities that support roles as breadwinners and heads of households. Efforts to obtain economic resources, income, and social status through illegal means places some Black men at higher risk of incarceration and involvement in the criminal justice system.

A significant body of research has also questioned and examined assumptions regarding the role of African American fathers in the lives and development of their children. Although fewer African American children are raised in married or two-parent households, research has also suggested that nonresident African American fathers are involved in the lives of their children. For example, Leavell et al. (2012) found in a sample of White, Black, and Latino fathers with preschool-age children that African American fathers had more engagement with their children than White fathers; the highest levels of engagement occurred between African American fathers and sons.

Other recent research has focused on further exploring the role, experiences, and impact of African American fathers. Threlfall, Seay, and Kohl (2013) used qualitative data from interviews with 36 fathers raising children in low-resourced urban neighborhoods to explore participants' conceptions of being a father. Providing for children was seen as a primary and fundamental role and included emotional and educational support beyond care for needs. Limited economic resources shaped fathers' engagement and acted as a burden that sometimes limited their connection with their children. Poor employment opportunities, the demands of child support with limited financial resources, and the combination of increased neighborhood risk were important concerns raised by these fathers. Fathers also voiced concern around the need for their children to be taught how to survive, both within and outside their neighborhoods. Some spoke to their hope and aspiration for their children to leave their current neighborhoods but also recognized the need for preparation for success despite having come from challenging circumstances.

Perry and Lewis (2016) similarly found in interviews with 25 African American fathers that they (1) desired to be a positive role model in their child's life; (2) they wanted to raise and take care of their children financially; (3) they provided their children with lessons on how to live a good life (e.g., how to treat women, how to recognize a good man); and (4) they wanted to provide emotional support to their children.

Older Adulthood

Our earlier demographic portrait noted that African Americans have a shorter life expectancy and that once they reach this level of maturity, many African American elders face both economic and health challenges. The cohorts of African American elders over age 65 were born before or in the 1950s. Some were children during the northern migration and the Great Depression, and many had experienced the rigid segregation and overt discrimination of the pre–civil rights era. Data from a random sample of 531 lower-income African Americans with a mean age of 73 indicated that 11.9% of participants were employed and 20% engaged in volunteer activities. Well-being was associated with younger age, greater perceived social support, better health, higher neighborhood satisfaction, and greater participation in leisure and religious activities (Moon, 2012). For support and coping, some research has suggested that African American elders rely on spirituality as a means of coping (Krause, 2003).

Despite these challenges, many African American elders continue to play crucial roles in their communities. Research has documented the important role of African American grandparents as primary care providers for their grandchildren, especially when parents have challenges with drug dependency (Burton, 1992; see also Chapter 5). Murphy, Hunter, and Johnson (2008) note that recent shifts in policy emphasizing kinship care have further challenged grandparents who provide parenting support to their grandchildren and children

The enactment of the Adoption and Safe Families Act (ASFA) in 1997 has included care options that seek termination of parental rights for children who have been in and out of home care for 15 of their last 22 months. This research was based on focus groups with 22 African American caregiving grandparents in North Carolina (Murphy et al., 2008). The grandmothers in the study seemed caught between the traditions of African American families and the intersection of these traditions with the public policy of the child welfare system. Participants described a sense of obligation and family legacy that supported their choices to take on parental roles for their grandchildren. However, they also perceived a lack of support and appreciation of the significant sacrifice of taking on the parental caretaking role from the child welfare system. Significant concerns were also voiced around the intrusiveness of regulatory practices and the tension between external conceptions of appropriate roles with those the grandparents felt to be appropriate. The authors noted the significant anger experienced by many of these caretakers and suggested consideration of a more intergenerational conception of policy that appreciates the family unit, as opposed to the individual children and adults involved. Additional discussion of the role of African American grandparents is presented in Chapter 5.

In considering the normative developmental experiences of African American seniors, researchers analyzed focus group results from an examination of the everyday conflicts and stressors experienced by older African American women (Weitzman, Dunigan, Hawkins, Weitzman, & Levkoff, 2002). This work points to everyday stressors involving concerns about current or future functional disability and transportation to accomplish tasks such as shopping and accessing medical care. Two areas of social conflicts emerged—those with family members and those with same-age peers, including neighbors and other senior center attendees. With family members, conflicts with grandchildren sometimes focused on the perceived lack of respect, and with their children, on child-rearing issues. With peers, issues of rudeness or longstanding grudges were noted as sources of conflict. Responses to these difficult situations appear to be characterized largely by avoidance.

Research by Baldwin, Jackson, Okoh, and Cannon (2011) found regional differences in well-being and underlined the importance of resiliency and optimism during older age for African Americans. In a sample of 52 older African Americans (mean age = 74), those living in the North reported lower levels of psychological distress than their Southern counterparts. Reported experiences of individual racism were associated with lower resiliency, whereas reports of cultural racism were positively associated with resiliency. Individuals who worked as professionals reported higher levels of race-related stressors but also higher levels of resiliency when compared with blue-collar workers.

As generations age, many African Americans note the importance of capturing the oral history and wisdom of older groups of African American seniors, as reflected in efforts such as Camille Cosby and Renee Poussaint's (2004) book, *A Wealth of Wisdom: Legendary African American Elders Speak*. From an African perspective, elders are respected and revered members of the community, and even beyond their life span; as ancestors, they remain ongoing members of the community.

METHODOLOGICAL AND RESEARCH ISSUES

Reviews and analyses of research on the study of African American children notes a range of historical and ongoing concerns regarding the methods used in studies of child development (McLoyd, 1991; Rowley & Camacho, 2015). These concerns include representativeness of sample, the utilization of measures developed for and normed on Whites, and the emphasis on race-comparative versus race-homogeneous studies. We discuss these and related issues next.

Race-Comparative Studies

Race-comparative studies examine and contrast children of different racial groups on a set of measures or indicators, whereas race-homogeneous studies descriptively examine factors within a single racial group to describe how members of a specific racial group behave and develop.

Sue (1983) suggests that historically, the literature examining ethnic minority groups has moved away from inferiority models, which hypothesize that African Americans and other non-European ethnic groups are inherently inferior to Whites. Subsequent to the use of inferiority models was the use of deficit models, which did not lay blame on ethnic minority groups for lower performance on specific indicators but which used comparative analyses to document the effects of external factors on performance. Researchers relying on the deficit perspective often ignored the strengths of ethnic communities and did not seek to understand cultural factors relevant to the psychology of the group. Cross-cultural models utilize more "value-free" analyses of cross-cultural differences, and bicultural models consider the dual status of ethnic groups. These models are often used by researchers who are members of the focal ethnic group to support the use of appropriate methodologies and interpretations. A report produced by the APA (2008) on resiliency among African American children highlights several models that focus on factors that contribute to the healthy development of African American children and adolescents. Also, recent work on positive youth development offers perspectives that are important alternatives to a "deficit paradigm" when examining developmental contexts and processes during adolescence (Leman, Smith, & Petersen, 2017).

Inclusion and Representativeness of Sample

Another crucial consideration in research is inclusion and representativeness of African Americans in research samples. Many studies lack specificity in the description of the sample of African Americans involved in the study, their residence, and their access to economic resources. Given the cultural, residential, educational, and economic diversity among African Americans, it is important to locate the sample used in any study. Then, the reader can critically examine whether research that is used to describe African Americans as a whole (i.e., as an entire population of people) is actually representative of the entire range of experiences and performance of all African Americans. For example, a considerable proportion of the developmental literature on African Americans focuses on lower-income and urban samples as opposed to rural or middle-class African American samples. This raises the question of the generalizability of the findings to different groups of African Americans.

Longitudinal and Cross-Sectional Designs

Developmental researchers sometimes use a longitudinal research design, in which the same research participants are followed across time and changes and continuities in their development are examined. Cross-sectional studies take a "snapshot" approach and are based on data collected at a single point in time. A cross-sectional study might compare different age groups at the same point in time. In contrast to longitudinal studies, cross-sectional studies do not allow researchers to make statements about change. For example, they cannot say whether differences between the younger and older members of the sample are due to normative developmental changes that occur for an individual across time or due to historical effects. When longitudinal designs are used, issues of attrition—that is, the extent to which research participants are retained in the study across time—become very important. Factors that impact the lives of many lower-income African Americans (e.g., residential mobility, lack of financial and other social resources) may make it difficult for researchers to keep research participants retained in the study over time. Investigators have developed strategies to support African American and other ethnic research participant engagement over time (e.g., Dilworth-Anderson & Williams, 2004). Useful strategies have included interviewer consistency across time, training project staff in issues relevant to African American families, access to project staff through toll-free phone numbers, and employing social media tools and other technology, as well as flexibility in the scheduling and rescheduling of research tasks and contacts.

Measures

There are also cultural assumptions in some research that may reflect an ethnocentric and often Eurocentric bias. In some developmental research, standardized measures are used that examine age norms for performance on a specific measure or the presence, absence, or level of a descriptive indicator.

Many measures have historically been normed on middle-class White samples. When African Americans or other ethnic groups are included, they are only included in a stratified sample based on their representation within the broader American demographic context. Although this inclusion allows comparisons to be made between individuals and the overall American norms, considering the diversity within and between cultural groups, it is often difficult to fully understand the implications of comparisons of individual African Americans with overall national norms.

For example, what does it mean if an African American child scores lower than the American norm on a particular index? What support does the index provide in understanding the contributions of the individual's experience with similar test situations or stimuli, the contribution of the individual's abilities, and the individual's access to environments, social resources, and opportunities relevant to the specific index? How does the use and interpretation of the index inform our understanding of what work is needed for knowledge development, intervention or prevention, and policy?

Research has suggested that race may play a significant role in some of the classic measurement strategies that are utilized within developmental research.

For example, in developmental research, peer nominations or peer ratings are well-established measure strategies. These sociometric strategies are generally based on asking children or teachers, most often within a school class, to rate their peers (or students) on certain characteristics or to nominate them as fitting within groups defined by specific criteria (e.g., most fun to hang out with, most popular, most likely to start a fight). Jackson, Barth, Powell, and Lochman (2006) examined peer nominations across 59 fifth-grade classrooms in eight schools, which ranged from 3% to 95% African American. Results indicated that overall, African American children fared less favorably on ratings of Leader and Fights, but their ratings improved as the percentage of African American students in the classroom increased. In examining the role of teacher race, African American and White students were marginally rated more favorably when their race matched that of the teacher for the peer "Like Most" rating. For the rating of Leader, White children were rated more favorably overall, but the differences in ratings were larger in classrooms led by White teachers.

One resource for developmental research in childhood and adolescence is the Black Caucus of the Society for Research on Child Development (SRCD). SRCD has a significant history in supporting access to rigorous research on the development of children of color and in supporting scientists to foster the growth of this body of knowledge.

BEST PRACTICES AND PROMISING INTERVENTIONS FOR IMPROVING DEVELOPMENTAL OUTCOMES

Our review has underlined that because of the overrepresentation of African American children and youth growing up in contexts that have limited resources and high levels of risk, they may face high levels of developmental challenge. Broad policy investments have shown effectiveness in reducing risk relative to basic developmental supports (e.g., WIC). Beyond basic community and policy interventions to support healthy development, prevention and intervention services have targeted a range of positive developmental outcomes (e.g., high school completion, employment).

Interventions to Improve Prenatal Health and Birth Outcomes

Several interventions have targeted prenatal risk factors. In a randomized control intervention study, El-Mohandes et al. (2008) sought to address known prenatal risks in a sample of low-income African American women. Risk behavior and status within the sample involved smoking (21.7%), exposure to smoke environmentally (82.7%), depression (50.7%), and intimate partner violence (36.8%). Participants were randomly assigned to usual care (control) or intervention targeting the specific risk behavior (e.g., social cognitive intervention for smoking and smoke exposure, cognitive behavioral therapy for depression, behavioral counseling for intimate partner violence). On average, mothers participated in 3.9 prenatal sessions and 0.8 postpartum sessions. During the postpartum period, 32.1% of the intervention group reported no risk, compared with 24.0% of the usual care group. Members of the intervention group reflected greater complete or partial resolution of the risk (63%) compared with the usual care group (54%).

Considering the higher risk of LBW for African American infants, a three-component intervention was developed for use with premature African American infants. Teti et al. (2009) found that providing a video on the developmental needs of premature infants, repeated infant assessments, updates with parents on the child's developmental progress, and infant massage resulted in increases in maternal self-efficacy beliefs for all intervention parents. In addition, this combination supported mental and physical development increases for extremely low birth weight (<1000 g) infants in the intervention condition.

Some interventions have focused on supporting healthy birth outcomes. Norbeck, Dejoseph, and Smith (1996) examined the provision of social support on LBW pregnancy outcomes among African American mothers. A sample of low-income pregnant African American women who were low in social support was randomly assigned to intervention and control conditions. The intervention involved four in-home social support sessions and phone calls between sessions. The intervention was provided by nurses. The rate of LBW was 9.1% in the intervention group and was significantly lower compared with 22.4% in the control group.

Based on a review of research on breastfeeding norms, cultural supports, and deterrents, Reeves and Woods-Giscombe (2015) recommend the development of culturally relevant programs to encourage breastfeeding among African American women. This might include engaging fathers, networking and peer support to enhance breastfeeding, and support for health care providers around the benefits of breastfeeding for African American infants.

Interventions to Improve Child and Adolescent Outcomes

Youth advocates, researchers, and policy makers have identified resources needed to support positive youth development. These efforts identify three focal developmental outcomes: the ability to financially support and care for oneself and one's family, the ability to develop and sustain healthy relationships, and the ability to contribute to one's community. After-school programs and involvement in the Boys and Girls Clubs, Boy Scouts and Girls Scouts, and the YMCA or YWCA youth programs are examples of youth development resources. Organizations such as the Forum for Youth Development (http://www.forumforyouthinvestment.org) and the Search Institute (http://www.search-institute.org) have focused on work emphasizing the sets of resources and assets that support positive developmental outcomes for children and adolescents. Recent work has begun to focus on the sets of resources and supports that support successful transitions to adulthood (e.g., the Ready by 21 program within the Forum for Youth Investment). These resources include guidelines that can support communities, including their elected and other leaders, in working collaboratively to implement policy and programming to support adaptive outcomes.

Formal and informal mentoring relations and programs have also been identified as important developmental interventions. Whether through a formal relationship established through Big Brothers and Big Sisters or informal support, research has identified several important components of effective mentoring relationships. A meta-analysis by DuBois, Holloway, Valentine, and Cooper (2002) identified several important factors that predicted positive outcomes for mentoring youth: systematic monitoring procedures for program implementation, mentors' backgrounds in help-related professions or roles, clear expectations for the frequency of contacts between youth and mentors, ongoing mentor training, provision of structured activities for the youth–mentor dyad, and support of parental involvement. Within these relationships, especially relationships that cross racial and ethnic groups, training and attention relevant to issues of culture are suggested (Spencer, 2006).

Over the past 20 years, there has been growing interest in programs and interventions to explicitly socialize African American youth to better understand what has been lost from cultural practices that support their racial identity and African ancestry. This involves the explicit cultural socialization of youth into the values, practices, beliefs, and behaviors needed to function in adult social roles. A range of rites-of-passage programs based on African cultural traditions have supported the transition of youth from childhood by officially marking their entrance into adult status within the community. Research indicates that participation in these cultural programs may provide access to cultural knowledge and support the development of beliefs that counter drug use and other negative behaviors (Belgrave et al., 2008, 2012).

Interventions for Seniors

There are several interventions designed to support seniors and those providing care for African American elders. Qualitative research has been conducted on the benefits of participation in multipurpose facilities for older African Americans. Taylor-Harris and Zhan (2011) found African American seniors participating in a multipurpose senior facility described physical benefits (such as access to water exercise programs and better regulation of food intake), greater social connectedness, and reductions in loneliness. They also reported opportunities to transition from work roles to greater freedom in activity and role choice.

African American religious leaders also note the important role of Churches in supporting elders (Stansbury, Beecher, & Clute, 2011). These clergy present a holistic picture of the physical and mental health needs of older African Americans. However, individual institutions and ministries varied, particularly smaller or more rural Churches, in their capacity to provide a wide range of health or other human services. Notably, faith-based organizations have been considered as important resources in promoting physical activity among older African Americans adults (King, 2001).

In summary, a number of promising intervention and prevention programs have shown success in facilitating positive developmental outcomes among African Americans from the prenatal period to old age.

CRITICAL ANALYSIS

Developmental psychology is very important in supporting our understanding of the development of African Americans; however, there are many limitations and gaps in the research and theoretical literature. As we noted before, African Americans are a very diverse group, and attempting to describe a normative or average experience of development serves to minimize the important and informative variations experienced by African Americans. Studies that focus on the developmental experiences of children growing up in low-resource inner cities do not characterize the developmental experiences of all African American children.

The United States is largely organized as an "age-graded" society—that is, we tend to organize our social institutions and processes by clustering or grouping individuals within the same age group. For example, we organize schools into grades and most often develop separate childcare and senior care centers. Developmental research most often reflects this structure and focuses on individuals within age groups as the unit of analysis. The developmental experiences of African Americans, however, often appear to be organized by intergenerational family units. Children are frequently cared for by grandparents and siblings; seniors are important resources within the family and household unit. Children participate in household work and directly experience the adult social roles within the family. The assumptions of age-graded social structures may not as easily fit the developmental experiences of many African Americans. The benefits of these cross-age processes may be important and relevant to both cultural and economic factors within African American families.

Another set of developmental disconnects appears between the varied contexts and settings in which individuals grow and develop. Historical changes in urban communities suggest growing separations between institutions such as family, school, and neighborhood, which historically have combined to form a rich set of connected developmental resources. These disconnects may serve to limit access to social capital that can be an important developmental resource for African Americans.

As a developmental context, the United States is a very challenging setting for children growing up in low-resource families and communities. In international comparisons, child policy investments within the United States are woefully lagging. The United States has a highly problematic political history that has far too often used issues of race to undermine domestic social policy with far too limited consideration of the impacts on children and families. We may not fully appreciate how such politically expedient rhetoric reinforces stereotypes and racism and undermines developmental opportunities for children. Child policy sometimes acts to pit one developmental period against another, with limited consideration of the needs for life span developmental supports.

Psychology's programmatic focus on intervention and prevention and efforts to strengthen the skills and competence of individuals may not fully appreciate the depletion of resources within certain developmental contexts for individuals living in urban, poor communities. Similarly, calls for personal responsibility and for African Americans to pull themselves up by their bootstraps may not fully appreciate that development takes place in context. Those who succeed despite developmental odds and challenges may do so with the support of others.

The dramatic historical changes that have occurred over the past 100 years, including rapid technological changes and globalization, are significant chronosystem changes with important implications for the development of African Americans. These changes and their impact on the developmental contexts, resources, and opportunities are critically important considerations for the African American community.

Summary

In this chapter, we provided a demographic portrait examining the lives of African Americans. Although individually diverse, African Americans as a group have a younger mean age and tend to have children when they are younger. African Americans also have shorter life expectancies than other ethnic groups. Although we see positive trends in the health and life course trajectories of African Americans, disparities still remain.

Several theoretical perspectives, including Vygotsky's theory, Bronfenbrenner's ecological theory, and M. Spencer and colleagues' phenomenological variant of ecological systems theory help us understand the role of context and culture and support our understanding of the development of African Americans.

Because of fewer resources and higher levels of environmental risk, some young children and adolescents (especially those living in areas of concentrated poverty) may be at risk for poor developmental outcomes.

Adults rise to the developmental challenges of work, family, and community shaped by their historical and sociocultural context. Elders continue to play important support functions within the community, especially as a resource for children; their wisdom and contributions are important to acknowledge.

Overall, research and theory suggest that understanding the ways in which African Americans grow and develop requires the consideration of a range of historical and cultural factors that have influenced the development of individuals and historical cohorts of African Americans.

In conducting developmental research, careful identification and specification of the target population and care with generalizations are warranted because of the overrepresentation of lower-income urban African Americans in the existing research literature. From an African perspective, life is cyclical. The Ethiopian proverb, "One is born, one dies; the land increases," acknowledges the contributions of all members of the community, the cyclical nature of life, and the forward progression of individuals along the paths of their development. Despite challenges, African Americans continue to make progress from generation to generation.

ADJUSTMENT AND ADAPTATION

HEALTH, ILLNESS, AND DISABILITY

He who conceals his disease cannot expect to be cured.

—Ethiopian proverb

HALF OF BLACK GAY MEN AND A QUARTER OF LATINO GAY MEN PROJECTED TO BE DIAGNOSED WITHIN THEIR LIFETIME

If current HIV diagnoses rates persist, about 1 in 2 black men who have sex with men (MSM) and 1 in 4 Latino MSM in the United States will be diagnosed with HIV during their lifetime, according to a new analysis by researchers at the Centers for Disease Control and Prevention (CDC). The study, presented today at the Conference on Retroviruses and Opportunistic Infections in Boston, provides the first-ever comprehensive national estimates of the lifetime risk of an HIV diagnosis for several key populations at risk and in every state.

"As alarming as these lifetime risk estimates are, they are not a foregone conclusion. They are a call to action," said Jonathan Mermin, M.D., director of CDC's National Center for HIV/AIDS, Viral Hepatitis, STD, and Tuberculosis Prevention. "The prevention and care strategies we have at our disposal today provide a promising outlook for future reductions of HIV infections and disparities in the U.S., but hundreds of thousands of people will be diagnosed in their lifetime if we don't scale up efforts now."

CDC researchers used diagnoses and death rates from 2009–2013 to project the lifetime risk of HIV diagnosis in the United States by sex, race and ethnicity, state, and HIV risk group, assuming diagnoses rates remain constant. Overall, the lifetime risk of HIV diagnosis in the U.S. is now 1 in 99, an improvement from a previous analysis using 2004–2005 data that reported overall risk at 1 in 78.

However, this overall progress masks large disparities:

- Gay and bisexual men continue to be most affected by the HIV epidemic in the U.S. At current rates, 1 in 6 MSM will be diagnosed with HIV in their lifetime, including 1 in 2 black MSM, 1 in 4 Latino MSM, and 1 in 11 white MSM.

- African Americans are by far the most affected racial or ethnic group with a lifetime HIV risk of 1 in 20 for men (compared to 1 in 132 for whites) and 1 in 48 for women (compared to 1 in 880 for whites).

- People who inject drugs are at much higher lifetime risk than the general population, and women who inject drugs have a higher risk than men (1 in 23 compared with 1 in 36).

- People living in the South are more likely to be diagnosed with HIV over the course of their lifetime than other Americans, with the highest risk in Washington, DC (1 in 13), Maryland (1 in 49), Georgia (1 in 51), Florida (1 in 54), and Louisiana (1 in 56).

Detailed findings, including data for all states and racial/ethnic and risk groups, are available on the 2016 CROI resources page.

"These estimates are a sobering reminder that gay and bisexual men face an unacceptably high risk for HIV—and of the urgent need for action," said Eugene McCray, M.D., director of CDC's Division of HIV/AIDS Prevention. "If we work to ensure that every American has access to the prevention tools we know work, we can avoid the outcomes projected in this study."

CDC's High Impact Prevention approach focuses on delivering the most effective prevention strategies—including HIV testing, ongoing care and treatment for people living with HIV, pre-exposure prophylaxis (PReP, a daily anti-HIV pill for high-risk uninfected people) and condoms—to the populations that are most heavily affected by the epidemic. CDC devotes more HIV prevention resources to MSM, especially MSM of color, than to any other risk group. And since 2010, CDC has greatly increased HIV prevention funding to Southern health departments and community-based organizations, to reflect the burden of HIV in the region.

Source: Centers for Disease Control (2016).

INTRODUCTION, DEFINITIONS, AND BACKGROUND

As reported in the cover story, the high rate of HIV is alarming among African Americans. Yet as noted by the Centers for Disease Control, there is action that can be taken to reduce disparities in HIV and other health conditions. In this chapter, we discuss reasons for and consequences of disparities in health outcomes and care for African Americans. We also discuss factors that promote good health and well-being for African Americans. Cultural values and beliefs have a pervasive impact on health, illness, and disability outcomes among African Americans. Socioeconomic status, racism, and oppression also contribute to health outcomes. In this chapter, we review factors that contribute to the physical health of African Americans. Mental health is discussed in Chapter 13.

Physical health is a function of biological, psychological, social, and environmental factors. We begin with an overview of relevant definitions and a discussion of the health status of African Americans. Health promotion, disease prevention, and health care utilization are discussed next. Psychological models of health and illness behavior and culturally based health and illness models for African Americans follow. We next review four health conditions that disproportionately affect African Americans, hypertension, HIV/AIDS, sickle cell disease, and diabetes. This is followed by discussions of methodological and research issues, empirically supported practices for improving health, a critique, and a chapter summary.

Definitions

Health psychology is the field of psychology that studies psychological influences on how people stay healthy, why they become ill, and how they respond to illness (Taylor, 2014). Health psychologists are concerned with health promotion and illness prevention behaviors, as well as with how people experience illnesses and disabilities. Although this chapter focuses on physical health, the definition of health is broad. WHO defines health as "a state of complete physical, mental and social well-being and not merely the absence of disease or infirmity" (WHO, n.d.).

Illness is the condition of being in poor health (Neufeldt & Guralnik, 1996). A chronic illness is a disease that persists over a long period that typically cannot be cured but managed (Taylor, 2014). A disability is a limitation in performing certain functions and tasks that society expects of an individual (Institute of Medicine [IOM], 1991).

Factors Affecting the Health of African Americans

African Americans have poorer health outcomes than most other major racial or ethnic groups in the United States. The disparities are especially noteworthy when comparisons are made with Whites. Socioeconomic factors such as employment, income, and education affect access to health and medical services, and lack of access to such services contributes to poor health outcomes. With the passage of the Patient Protection and Affordable Care Act (ACA) (also known as Obamacare) in March 2010, access to health care increased for African Americans, as it did for all Americans. The ACA was especially beneficial to Americans who could not obtain health insurance through employment, and one barrier to health care was eliminated. However, this may change with the Trump administration, as the Republican Party has been opposed to the ACA since its passage. The reason for the opposition from the Republican Party is the rising insurance cost to citizens covered by the ACA. Recent attempts (July 2017) to repeal and replace the ACA failed (July 2017). However, a new tax bill passed December 2017, included a provision to repeal the individual mandate part of the ACA. The individual mandate requires Americans to purchase health insurance (unless they qualify for a hardship exemption).

Poor health outcomes among African Americans are attributed to many factors other than socioeconomic factors and availability of affordable health insurance. We should also not assume that all African Americans face poor health outcomes, as there is a great deal of diversity among African Americans. Differences in health outcomes among African Americans may be due to how well one copes with discrimination, lifestyle risk factors (e.g., cigarette smoking), geographical residence (urban, rural, and suburban), and whether one is U.S or foreign born.

The U.S. Census defines as Black any persons with ancestry from Africa. Within the United States, there are differences in health outcomes among U.S.-born African Americans, Black immigrants, and first-generation U.S.-born immigrants, including immigrants from the Caribbean, Latin America, and Africa. Studies that have examined the health of these ethnic groups have confirmed differences (Griffith, Johnson, Zhang, Neighbors, & Jackson, 2011; Jackson & Antonucci, 2005). For example, health scores are highest among first-generation Caribbean immigrants, followed by African Americans, and then second- and third-generation Caribbean immigrants. Interestingly, Caribbean Blacks born in the United States resemble African Americans in health status more than they resemble native-born Caribbean Blacks. The better health among first-generation Caribbeans is attributed to immigration selectivity bias, as these immigrants are likely to have higher levels of education and income. First-generation Caribbean Blacks may also have had healthier lifestyles in their countries of origin, stronger support systems, and may have experienced less racism and discrimination.

One indicator of health status is allostatic load. Allostatic load is the physiological wear and tear on the body that results from chronic stress. Higher allostatic load is associated with poorer health (e.g., heart disease, type 2 diabetes, depression). Using data from the National Health and Nutrition Examination Survey, allostatic load scores were compared for U.S.-born and foreign-born Blacks. Foreign-born Blacks had lower allostatic loads than U.S.-born Blacks (Doamekpor & Dinwiddle, 2015).

Lower socioeconomic status of African Americans has been viewed as a primary reason for poor health outcomes; however, socioeconomic factors do not account for all of the health disparities between African Americans and Whites (Belgrave, 1998; Woolf & Braveman, 2011). Cultural beliefs, along with institutional policies within health care institutions, also contribute to poorer health outcomes for African Americans. In addition, health care provider bias and lack of knowledge about and sensitivity to African American culture may contribute to the underutilization of health care systems by African Americans.

Health Disparities

Healthy People 2020 is the U.S. Department of Health and Human Services 10 year goals for health promotion and disease prevention in the United States. Healthy People 2020 identified the achievement of health equity and the elimination of health disparities as an overriding goal of the nation's public health agenda for this decade. Health disparities for African Americans exist across almost all indicators, including morbidity, mortality, disability, treatment, and health promotion and disease prevention. Health disparities do not begin in adulthood but originate at earlier stages, beginning in the prenatal period (Lhila & Long, 2012). Throughout childhood and beyond, African Americans confront cumulative environmental stressors that damage the body's ability to regulate and respond to stress.

As is discussed throughout this chapter, much has been written on health disparities and health equity, including the root causes and what to do about them. Research on health disparities has ranged from examining sociocontextual and environmental factors such as residential segregation, to daily experienced racism and discrimination.

CONTEMPORARY ISSUES
IS LOOKING GOOD KILLING AFRICAN AMERICAN WOMEN?

African American women spend much more time, care, and money on their hair than women from other ethnic and racial groups. Could chemicals that are used in hair care products contribute to their health disparities? Hair products containing estrogen- and endocrine-disrupting chemicals have been found to be associated with several adverse health outcomes (Collins, 2004), including increased breast cancer risk (Llanos et al., 2017), infertility (Wise, Palmer, Reich, Cozier, & Rosenberg, 2012), and premature sexual development in African American girls (Tiwary, 1998). Hair products, including perms, hair oils, leave-in conditioner, root stimulator, and others, are more likely to be used among African American women than women in other racial and ethnic groups. James-Todd, Senie, and Terry (2011) conducted a study of 301 African American, African Caribbean, Hispanic, and White women from the New York metropolitan area. Women were asked about the frequency and duration of hair products used. They found that more African American (49.4%) and African Caribbean (26.4%) women used

products containing estrogen-disrupting chemicals than Hispanic (16.5%) and White women (7.7%). According to the authors, frequent and chronic exposure to hormonally active chemicals in hair products can increase the risk of negative health outcomes associated with this exposure. A study that received a large amount of media exposure linked hair relaxer to fibroids (Wise et al., 2012). Wise et al. used data collected from more than 23,000 African American women to examine the link between hair relaxer and fibroids. They found a statistically significant link between frequency of hair relaxer and fibroids.

In a review of scientific studies on hair products used by African American women and breast cancer, Stiel, Adkins-Jackson, Clark, Mitchell, and Montgomery (2016) noted that there was a growing body of evidence of a link between use of certain hair products and potential breast cancer risk for African American women. Hair care products used by African American women may have endocrine-disrupting chemicals (EDCs) that have been linked to cancer.

Recent research has also explored the link between hair products used by African American women and health disparities (see "Contemporary Issues" text box).

Health care disparities also exist for Blacks in other countries. The Canadian Community Health Survey assessed disparities in health outcomes for Black and White Canadian men and women (Veenstra & Patterson, 2016). This study found that Blacks were more likely than Whites to report chronic conditions, such as diabetes and hypertension, after controlling for household income, smoking, and other factors linked to hypertension and diabetes.

Mortality and Morbidity

Morbidity is the rate of disease or proportion of disease in a given locality or nation, whereas mortality is the incidence of death (Neufeldt & Guralnik, 1996). Several conditions account for morbidity disparities between African Americans and other ethnic groups. These conditions also contribute to excess deaths among African Americans. Excess deaths are the number or incidence of deaths from a certain risk factor in a population that is over and above the number in the unexposed group (DHHS, 1985). Excess deaths represent the leading causes of deaths among African Americans. These include heart disease, malignant neoplasms (cancer), cerebrovascular diseases (strokes), unintentional injuries, diabetes mellitus, homicide, chronic lower respiratory diseases, nephritis, nephritic syndrome and nephrosis (kidney disease), septicemia, and human immunodeficiency virus (HIV) (NCHS, 2015b).

Infant mortality, a major indicator of the health and well-being of a country, is defined as the death of a baby before his or her first birthday. Infant and neonatal (prior to birth) mortality is a major health disparity for African Americans. The infant mortality rate per 1,000 for African Americans is 11.1 and more than twice the infant mortality for Whites, Hispanics, and Asian/Pacific Islanders. In fact, infant mortality is higher for African Americans in the U.S. than it is in many developing and third-world countries (CIA, 2014). Unfortunately, racial disparities in infant mortality will likely persist as White educated women are the only group predicted to meet the Healthy People 2020 objective to reduce infant mortality to 6.0 infant deaths per 1,000 live births (Loggins & Andrade, 2014).

Cardiovascular disease is a leading cause of death in the United States. Large racial disparities exist for heart disease, which is 68% higher for African Americans than for Whites (NCHS, 2011). Disparities for African American men are also notable. For example, African American men are 30% more likely to die from heart disease and 60% more likely to die from stroke than are White men (Graham & Gracia, 2012). While breast cancer rates are similar for African American and White women, 5-year survival rates are much higher for White than African American women (92.0% versus 80.5%).

Although there have been some improvements in health outcomes for African Americans, mortality disparities have remained fairly consistent over the past four decades. In fact, fewer than 20% of health disparities faced by African Americans show evidence of decreasing (AHRQ, 2014).

Differentials in Life Expectancy

Life expectancy discrepancy between African Americans and Whites has decreased since 1990 but remains notably higher, especially for males. Table 12.1 shows that African American males born in 2014 have a life expectancy of 72.5 years, and White males born in the same year have a life expectancy of 76.7 years. Similarly, White females have a higher life expectancy (81.4 years) than African American females (78.4 years). Table 12.1 also shows the expected number of years

Specified Age and Year	White Males	Black Males	White Females	Black Females
At birth	76.7	72.5	81.4	78.4
At 65 years	18.0	16.3	20.5	19.6
At 75 years	11.2	10.5	12.9	12.7

TABLE 12.1 ■ Life Expectancy by Race and Sex in the United States, 2014

Source: National Center for Health Statistics (NCHS) (2015b).

before death for each racial group at ages 65 and 75. Note that the racial discrepancy between African Americans and Whites decreases with age. Table 12.1 also shows that the life expectancy discrepancy between African American and White women is not as high as it is between African American and White men.

Prevalence of Health Conditions Causing Deaths

Death causes for selected health conditions among African Americans and other ethnic groups are shown in Table 12.2. African Americans have higher mortality than Whites and most other racial and ethnic groups across all selected conditions. For example, mortality from diabetes mellitus is almost twice as high for African Americans as it is for Whites. Mortality from HIV/AIDS is about 8 times higher for all ethnic groups other than Hispanics, and mortality from homicide is 3 to 9 times higher for African Americans than for other ethnic groups (NCHS, 2015b).

Chronic conditions also disproportionally affect African American children. Asthma is especially a concern for African American children, who are more likely to die from asthma than other racial and ethnic groups (CDCa, 2011).

Disability Among African Americans

About 1 in 7 African Americans reports a limitation of activity caused by a chronic condition. In 2012, limitations were reported on each ethnic group as follows: 19.2% of American Indians/Alaska Natives, 15.7% of African Americans, 12.4% of Whites, 11.3% of Hispanics, and 7.5% of Asians (NCHS, 2013, p. 14). Limitations in activities of daily living affect one's ability to carry out routine tasks and to function within the home, community, and workplace. It is not surprising that activity limitation is higher for African Americans compared with most other ethnic groups because of higher levels of morbidity. With the exception of American Indian/Alaska Natives, African Americans are more likely to report their health as fair or poor, with 13.6% of African Americans, 14.1% of American Indians/Alaska Natives, 12.2% of Hispanics, 8.3% of Whites, and 7.3% of Asians reporting their health as fair or poor (NCHS, 2015b).

Stroke is a major cause of disability and contributor to limitation in activities of daily living in the United States. African Americans have the highest prevalence of stroke among any ethnic group (3.8% for African American, 2.5% Hispanic/Latino, 2.3% for Whites, 2.8% for American Indian/Alaskan Native, and 1.6%

TABLE 12.2 ■ **Age-Adjusted Death Rates by Cause and Race and Ethnic Group in the United States, 2014**

Cause of Death	Deaths per 100,000				
	Black	White	Hispanic	Asian/ Pacific Islander	American Indian/ Alaska Native
All causes	849.3	725.4	523.3	388.3	594.1
Diseases of the heart	206.3	165.9	116.0	86.1	119.1
Ischemic heart disease	112.8	99.3	75.3	55.1	76.4
Cerebrovascular diseases	49.7	35.2	30.2	28.3	25.4
Malignant neoplasm	185.6	161.9	112.4	98.9	106.7
Colorectal, rectum, and anus cancer	18.6	14.0	11.1	9.5	10.9
Trachea, bronchus, and lung cancer	44.5	42.9	18.3	22.7	27.8
Chronic lower respiratory diseases	28.4	43.1	17.5	12.5	29.9
Pneumonia and influenza	16.1	15.1	12.8	12.9	15.1
Chronic liver disease and cirrhosis	7.2	11.2	14.5	3.5	24.2
Diabetes mellitus	37.3	19.3	25.1	15.0	31.3
HIV/AIDS	8.3	1.1	2.0	.3	1.2
Infant mortality (per 1,000)	11.11	5.06	5.0	3.9	7.7
Unintentional injuries	33.8	43.1	26.8	15.1	49.5
Motor vehicle–related injuries	11.1	11.1	9.6	4.6	16.6
Suicide	5.5	14.7	6.3	6.0	10.9
Homicide	17.2	3.0	4.5	1.5	5.8

Source: National Center for Health Statistics (2014).

for Asian) (NCHS, 2015b). In summary, statistics show many health disparities for African Americans manifested in lower life expectancy and higher mortality, disease prevalence, and functional limitations.

HEALTH PROMOTION, DISEASE PREVENTION, AND HEALTH CARE UTILIZATION

Health Promotion and Disease Prevention

African Americans are less likely than most other ethnic groups to engage in health promotion and disease prevention activities, such as regular preventive checkups, physical activity and exercise, and consuming recommended amounts of fruits and vegetables. Regular preventive checkups and visits to health care providers could decrease the amount and severity of long-term and chronic health and disability problems.

In terms of physical activity, 43.6% of African Americans 18 and over met the guidelines for aerobic physical activity in 2014 (compared with 41.3% for Hispanics, 47.5% for Asians, and 51.3% for Whites) (NCHS, 2015a, Table 57). Living in neighborhoods without safe spaces to walk and exercise and neighborhood crime are some reasons African Americans engage in less physical activity (Shuval, 2013). Some African American women do not engage in exercise that causes perspiration because it may "sweat out the hair" (Huebschmann, Campbell, Brown, & Dunn, 2016). Having hairstyles not affected by perspiration is one strategy to reduce this barrier.

Eating at least three servings a day of fruits and vegetables is associated with reductions in obesity and chronic illnesses such as diabetes and hypertension. Yet studies have shown poorer nutritional intake among African Americans and Hispanics than Whites. For example, African American children are more likely to consume sweets and sugar-sweetened drinks than other ethnic groups, which increases the likelihood of obesity (Urrutia-Rojas et al., 2008). African Americans also spend less on fruits and vegetables than Whites (Ryabov, 2016). However, these differentials disappear when socioeconomic status and residential segregation are controlled for. There are fewer outlets in which to purchase healthy food options in segregated African American neighborhoods.

Being overweight and/or obese is a major risk problem among many African Americans because it is a precursor for several chronic conditions, such as diabetes, hypertension, stroke, heart disease, and cancer. About 82% of African American females over the age of 20 are overweight or obese, compared with 63.5% of White females. Over 56% of African American women are obese, compared with 35% for White women. African American men are less likely to be overweight or obese than White men, 69.6%, compared with 73.7% for White men (NCHS, 2015b). Being overweight and obese begins in childhood for African Americans, especially African American girls. Currently, 35.2% of Black youths ages 2 to 19 are overweight or obese, compared with 31.8% of all children and adolescents (Ogden, 2014). African American children live in neighborhoods with more fast-food restaurants than other types, and they are more likely to see fast-food advertisements than children in other ethnic groups. African Americans are also more likely to visit the emergency room compared with other ethnic groups, suggesting less preventive behaviors (NCHS, 2015b, Table 73); 21.3% of African American children under the age of 18 visited the emergency department within the past 12 months, compared with a rate of 16.7% for all children.

Stress resulting from perceived and actual discrimination adversely impacts health promotion behaviors. Sims et al. (2016) examined how discrimination affected several health behaviors using national health data. After controlling for socioeconomic status and age, discrimination was associated with more smoking, a greater percentage of dietary fat, and fewer hours of sleep (Sims et al., 2016).

Health Care Utilization Patterns

Morbidity, mortality, disability, and activity limitations are affected by health care utilization patterns. The extent to which African Americans receive regular and routine preventive medical care affects long-term health status. African Americans are less likely than Whites to have primary-care physician contacts and more likely to have emergency room visits and longer periods of hospitalizations (CDC, 2011a; NCHS, 2015a). Longer hospitalizations suggest that African Americans who are hospitalized are sicker when admitted to the hospital. When health and medical care is not routinely accessed when needed, later disease and outcomes are more severe.

Access Factors

Access factors include whether health and medical care and rehabilitation services are affordable and available when needed. Other access factors are whether facilities are convenient to the consumer, whether the health facility's hours are feasible for the consumer, and whether there is accessible transportation to the treatment facility.

One reason for disparities in health care access for African Americans has been the lack of health insurance. This barrier was reduced for some with the Affordable Care Act (ACA). The ACA has resulted in decreased disparities in health access for African Americans. Chen, Vargas-Bustamante, Mortensen, and Ortega (2016) found that the ACA resulted in significant reductions in being uninsured, delay in necessary care, lack of access to primary care and medications, and poor health outcomes for African Americans.

One access problem is the location of medical treatment facilities. Clinics, hospitals, social service agencies, rehabilitation agencies, and other facilities are often not located within urban communities or in close proximity to where African Americans live. Consequently, travel to and from facilities may require time, economic resources, and public transportation infrastructure that may not be available (Kimmel et al., 2017).

Other Barriers Affecting Health Care Utilization

There are nonsocioeconomic access factors that contribute to lower utilization of health and medical services by African Americans. In 2002, the IOM issued a report titled "Unequal Treatment: Confronting Racial and Ethnic Disparities in Health Care" (Smedley et al., 2003). The report committee reviewed over 100 studies that assessed the quality of health care for various racial and ethnic minority groups while considering or holding constant insurance status, patient income, and access factors. The review identified several sources of health care disparities while acknowledging that some racial groups may respond differently to treatment.

Factors that were considered were those related to the operation of the health care systems and the regulatory climate in which those systems operate. These include factors such as cultural barriers, the fact that African Americans may be disproportionately enrolled in lower-cost health plans, the types of incentives in place to contain cost, and where minorities tend to receive care. For example, ethnic minorities are less likely to access care in a private physician's office, even when insured at the same level as Whites.

The second source of health care treatment disparities was related to uncertainty that a physician may have about the condition of a patient. In this case, physicians and other health care providers may hold prior beliefs about patients based on factors such as race, age, and gender. Racism and stereotyping may play a subtle but influential role in keeping African Americans from needed medical services. The IOM report noted, "There is considerable empirical evidence that even well-intentioned Whites who are not overtly biased and who do not believe that they are prejudiced typically demonstrate unconscious implicit negative racial attitudes and stereotypes" (p. 4).

Moskowitz, Stone, and Childs (2012) conducted two studies that addressed the question of unconscious physician bias. They investigated whether stereotypes unconsciously influenced the thoughts and behaviors of physicians. In Study 1, physicians were asked what cultural stereotypical diseases were associated with African Americans within the medical community. Hypertension was most often mentioned, followed by sickle cell anemia, stroke, HIV, coronary artery disease, obesity, and drug use. In Study 2, White physicians were primed through subliminal exposure to faces of African American or White men via computer. When primed by African American men, the participants reacted more quickly to stereotypical diseases. This pattern of results suggested an implicit association of certain diseases with African Americans. These were diseases that African Americans were genetically predisposed to (e.g., sickle cell disease) but also conditions with no biological association (e.g., drug use) to African Americans. The authors conclude that implicit stereotyping occurs among health care providers that these providers are not aware of. These stereotypes may unduly influence diagnoses and treatment.

Another indicator of physician bias is seen in ethnic differences in pain medication. Researchers have noted that African Americans and other racial and ethnic minorities are less likely to receive pain medication, to receive lower doses of pain medication, and to have longer wait times in the emergency room compared with Whites (Campbell & Edwards, 2012).

Still another reason for disparities in treatment is that African Americans may not trust the health care system. Such mistrust largely stems from historical accounts of unethical medical procedures conducted on African American patients, with one of the most graphic examples being that of the Tuskegee study.

Distrust of the Medical System and Medical Providers

Lack of trust among health care providers and the medical system also account for underutilization of health care by African Americans (Tucker, Moradi, Wall, & Nghiem, 2014). In a book titled *Medical Apartheid*, Harriet Washington (2006) describes how the exploitation of African Americans in the name of science has contributed to African Americans' distrust of the medical establishment. *Medical Apartheid* tracks the exploitation of Blacks from colonial time to present. Although the Tuskegee syphilis experiment is well known, other less well-known scientific studies were equally horrifying, as reported by Washington. For example, one study was conducted by Dr. James Marion Sims, who was a founder in gynecological medicine.

Washington reported that Dr. Sims experimented on the genitalia of unanesthetized slave women as part of his research.

The Tuskegee study has been cited as one of the major studies that promoted distrust of the medical establishment (Byrd & Clayton, 2001). Between 1932 and 1972, the U.S. Public Health Service conducted an experiment on 399 Black men in the late stages of syphilis. These men were, for the most part, uneducated and poor. They were not told they had syphilis but were informed that they were being treated for "bad blood." With the disease untreated, these men were left to degenerate and acquire many of the effects of advanced syphilis, including heart disease, paralysis, blindness, insanity, and death.

Even when, by 1943, penicillin was known and was being used to treat syphilis, these men were denied access to treatment. By the end of the experiment, 28 of the men had died directly of syphilis, 100 were dead of related complications, 40 of their wives had been infected, and 19 of their children had been born with congenital syphilis. These men and their families were sacrificed in the name of science. In spite of the Henderson Act of 1943, a public health law that required testing and treatment for venereal disease and despite the WHO's specification that informed consent was needed for experiments involving human beings, the Tuskegee experiment continued. The suspicion and fear generated by the Tuskegee study remain among some African Americans today.

Mistrust of the medical establishment has contributed to conspiracy theory beliefs. The results of a 1999 survey showed that 27% of African Americans believed that the U.S. government created HIV/AIDS as a plot to exterminate Blacks, and another 23% of African Americans could not rule out the possibility that this might be true (Landrine & Klonoff, 1999). While we know more about the origin and transmission of HIV, some African Americans still believe in conspiracy theories.

In a study of ethnic differences about conspiracy theories, Ross, Essien, and Torres (2006) examined the prevalence of the belief that HIV was created by the U.S. government among a community sample of four racial and ethnic groups: African Americans, Latinos, non-Hispanic Whites, and Asians. The authors found that 27.3% of African American men reported believing that HIV was created by the U.S. government; another 16.6% reported that they did not know. The researchers found that among Black women, 31.2% believed HIV was created by the government, and 18.2% reported not knowing. The Hispanic sample had the next highest percentage of conspiracy beliefs about HIV, with about 22% of this group agreeing with the statement. The implication of these conspiracy theories is that they can affect behaviors such as not seeking needed medical care and risky sexual behaviors. Researchers found a correlation between conspiracy theories and risky sexual behaviors. Bogart, Galvan, Wagner, and Klein (2011) found that greater belief in HIV conspiracies was associated with a higher likelihood of unprotected sex.

Mistrust of the medical provider has been linked to less patient satisfaction. Patient satisfaction influences utilization of health care services (Moore et al., 2013). Moore et al. investigated several factors (religiosity, access to care, mistrust, and racism) and patient satisfaction among men with prostate cancer. The authors found that mistrust and racism were the factors most negatively associated with participant dissatisfaction. Other factors related to patient satisfaction and utilization included perceived discrimination and poor communication from providers (Cuevas, O'Brien, & Saha, 2016).

Stereotype Threat

Stereotype threat, used to explain the underperformance of African Americans within academic and educational environments, may also account for disparities in health care utilization. Stereotype threat is a maladaptive psychological state that people experience when they feel that they may confirm a negative stereotype associated with their cultural group (Steele & Aronson, 1995). This negative psychological state creates stress and anxiety, which leads to underperformance in math and other areas of achievement. Aronson, Burgess, Phelan, and Juarez (2013) discuss how stereotype threat can also explain why African Americans are less likely to access health care, to adhere to recommended medical treatment, and to have poorer health outcomes than Whites. African Americans have negative health interactions in the health care environment, and stereotype threat continues this process. Negative health interactions include provider bias, as seen in differentials in diagnoses, referrals, and treatment, along with abbreviated communication and impaired interactions from health providers. Stereotype threat occurs when African Americans believe that they are being negatively stereotyped, which leads to vigilance around stereotype-relevant cues. In this situation, it is important to note that stereotype threat does not require actual bias but only the perception of bias. Once the health care environment is perceived as biased, stereotype threat affects physiological, psychological, and self-regulatory behaviors that contribute to health disparities. Stereotype threat elevates blood pressure, induces anxiety, and increases aggressive behavior and other self-regulation problems. Stereotype threat also leads to patient behaviors that compromise treatment, such as avoidance of health care systems, compromised communication with health care providers, and nonadherence to treatment plans.

In an experimental test of stereotype threat, Black and White women were engaged in a virtual health care situation. Participants were asked to imagine that they were in a virtual waiting room that had pictures of Blacks portrayed in stereotypical ways. Stereotype threat was manipulated by priming women to think about their ethnicity. Negative stereotypes of Black females were also displayed (Abdou & Fingerhut, 2014). Participants then imagined themselves entering the examination room to see a middle-age White male physician. Women then completed measures of anxiety and racial identity. Findings were that Black women with high ethnic identity reported significantly greater anxiety while waiting to see the physician than other women (e.g., White women or Black women with low ethnic identity). In a real-life encounter, anxiety from stereotype threat would lead to poorer communication with the provider and less compliance to follow-up visits and treatment.

Divergent Values and Communication

When the health care provider is not familiar with or does not acknowledge differences in cultural values, attitudes, and communication patterns, the exchange between the professional and the consumer may be negative, nonproductive, or counterproductive. Under these conditions, the consumer may not return for needed health and medical services.

To illustrate a cultural difference between African Americans and Whites, a colleague who works in a hospital recounts the communication exchange between African American consumers and White health care specialists (e.g., physical therapists, occupational therapists, nurses). These health care professionals refer to African American consumers informally by their first names instead of more formally as, for example, Mr. Turner or Mrs. Jones. Although this may be how the White health care professional communicates with White consumers (using informality to promote an interpersonal relationship), the African American consumer may, in fact, view this lack of formality as being talked down to and may find such language offensive. African Americans may perceive being called by one's first name as disrespectful, especially older men who were historically addressed by White persons using their first names as a way to keep them in their place (Belgrave, 1998).

Another example of how cultural values affect communication and subsequently health care utilization is derived from an understanding of the communal and relationship orientation of African Americans. The communal orientation stresses and places a positive value on the person's ability to connect with and to establish a harmonious interpersonal relationship with others. From this perspective, the ability of the health care provider to establish an interpersonal relationship with the consumer should facilitate health care utilization. If the African American consumer likes or connects with the health care professional, health and medical utilization patterns should be facilitated. It is important for the provider to convey sincerity and genuineness when dealing with the consumer. This orientation may be contrasted with a more Eurocentric orientation, whereby perceived expertise and competency, rather than interpersonal relationship, may be more valued. For African American consumers, the health provider's expertise and skill may not be enough, and compliance to recommendations is likely to be influenced by how well the consumer likes, trusts, and respects the professional.

Another potential conflict is when health and medical professionals speak in professional or technical jargon—minimizing the consumer's ability to understand the message. Twenty-three percent of African Americans reported difficulty with communication with health care providers (Alliance for Health Reform, 2004). Unanswered questions may remain unanswered, and the opportunity to inform and educate is lost. Similarly, health care providers may not communicate all information needed to make an informed decision (Griffith, Allen, & Gunter, 2011). Griffith et al. interviewed older African American men and found that many did not go to the doctor and, in some instances, were afraid to go. When they did go, they were uncomfortable with the tone used by doctors and reported that the doctors offered them little useful information on how to make lifestyle and behavioral changes. They also reported that doctors often told them what to do rather than how to do it.

Hood, Hart, Belgrave, Tademy, and Jones (2012) found that trust of the doctor was an important factor in African American males' health decisions. They interviewed 40 African American men recruited from barbershops about the role of the health care provider and health decisions. Trust in the health care provider was listed as the primary reason the participant assumed an active role in making health decisions. These African American men reported that trust was built on mutual respect, which allowed them to feel at ease with their provider and more apt to ask questions and voice their opinions. Those men who were involved in the decision-making process did so when they trusted the expertise of their health care provider, when the provider shared information and was an active listener, and when the patient–provider relationship had been in effect for a long period.

Patients are more likely to adhere to recommended guidelines when health care providers are perceived as culturally sensitive (Tucker, Rice, Marsiske, Nielson, & Herman, 2011). Tucker et al. conducted a study of 229 African American and White patients recruited from two community-based primary care clinics. Patients completed measures of perceived cultural sensitivity of their providers' behaviors and attitudes, trust in physicians, and other measures assessing health-promoting lifestyle, medication adherence, and dietary adherence. The authors found that among both ethnic groups, perceived provider cultural sensitivity directly affected trust and satisfaction with care. For African American patients, provider cultural sensitivity also had a positive influence on dietary adherence.

African Americans are more likely to access and engage in health care when (1) providers use person-centered care (i.e., recognize patients' contribution for their own health care); (2) show genuine interest in the patient and his or her family;

(3) take time to establish trust and mutual respect; and (4) become aware of and work on their own biases (Hansen, Hodgson, & Gitlin, 2016).

Health care utilization among African Americans also improves when services and programs are delivered in a culturally congruent way. One culturally congruent method may be to encourage access to health care through faith-based institutions and messages. A program that integrated biblical scriptures representing various aspects of health behaviors in health messages proved to be successful (Tetey, Duran, Andersen, Washington, & Boutin-Foster, 2016). One message used in this campaign was "Your Body Is a Temple: Know Your Risk for Heart Disease."

We next turn to models that help us to understand health and illness behaviors.

MODELS OF HEALTH AND ILLNESS BEHAVIORS

Social and Psychological Models

Several social and psychological models have been developed to help explain and predict health behaviors. In this section, we give an overview of three widely used models—(a) the health belief model, (b) the theory of planned behavior, and (c) self-efficacy theory—and provide a critique of the usefulness and the limitations of these models for understanding health and illness behaviors in African Americans.

Health Belief Model

The health belief model is one of the oldest health models (Wallston & Wallston, 1984). The health belief model was developed to explain public participation in screening programs and has been used to predict a variety of health and illness behaviors (e.g., exercise, diet, getting breast exams, taking medication, keeping appointments, HIV/AIDS protective behaviors).

According to the model, people who perceive a severe health threat or feel susceptible to a particular disease are motivated to make behavioral changes if they perceive that the benefits of risk reduction behaviors outweigh the costs of performing the behaviors (see Figure 12.1). Readiness to take a health action is determined by a person's perceived likelihood of susceptibility to the illness and by personal perception of the severity of the consequences of getting the disease. Together, these make up the person's vulnerability. The potential benefits of a given behavior are weighed against the potential barriers to or costs of action. A cue to action, whether an internal cue, such as a symptom, or an external cue, such as a prevention message, is necessary to trigger a health behavior. The health belief model is depicted in Figure 12.1.

An example will show how components of the health belief model can be used to explain whether an individual engages in HIV/AIDS protective behavior such as condom use. First, a person must perceive that she or he is susceptible to acquiring HIV/AIDS and, second, that HIV/AIDS is a severe disease. Assuming this is the case, then the benefits of wearing or having a partner wear a condom (e.g., less worry about contracting HIV/AIDS) are weighed against the barriers and costs of condom use (e.g., less pleasure, embarrassment, partner may not want to use condom). The four beliefs shown in Figure 12.1 determine whether a condom is used.

Several studies have shown that components of the health belief model predict or explain a variety of health behaviors among African Americans, including cancer-screening behaviors (Oliver, Grindel, DeCoster, Ford, & Martin, 2011), sexual risk behaviors (Kennedy et al., 2007), vaccinations (Chen, Fox, Cantrell, Stockdale, & Kagawa-Singer, 2007), hypertension self-management (Long, Ponder, & Bernard, 2016), and physical activity (Juniper, Oman, Hamm, & Kerby, 2004). Juniper et al. found that perceived barriers, perceived severity, cues to action, and self-efficacy were significantly lower among physically inactive versus physically active African Americans.

Other studies have found that the health beliefs of African Americans may differ from those of Whites and/or that the health belief model does not predict health outcomes (Davis, Buchanan, & Green, 2013; Steele et al., 2001). African Americans may have lower risk perception of disease (Akinleye et al., 2011). In one study of genetic susceptibility testing for Alzheimer's disease, African American participants were less concerned about developing Alzheimer's disease and had lower levels of perceived disease risk than did White participants (Akinleye et al.). Calvin et al. (2011) examined the perception of risk for diabetes complications among 143 African American adults with type 2 diabetes. They found there was a low perception of risk for diabetic complications, which was inconsistent with physiological indices of risk. Fewer than 33% of the participants saw themselves as being at high risk to develop any complications. Aycock and Clark (2016) found among mostly African American females that their perception of stroke risk was lower than actual risk, with most participants (66%) believing they were of no or low risk while 59% of the sample were at moderate and high risk. Perception of HIV risk among African Americans also tends to be underestimated by African Americans (Nunn et al., 2011).

Theory of Planned Behavior

The theory of planned behavior was developed by Fishbein and Ajzen (1975) to study predictive behaviors across several domains, including physical health (Fisher, Fisher, & Rye, 1995). See Figure 12.2 for components of this model. According to the theory, one's intentions to perform a certain behavior are the best predictor of that behavior. Behavioral intentions are determined by attitudes toward the behavior and beliefs about subjective norms (e.g., expectations and values of significant others). Attitudes toward performing a certain behavior are a function of individuals' beliefs about the consequences of performing the behavior, multiplied by their evaluations of these consequences. Individuals' subjective norms are a function of their perception of social support from important others for performance of a preventive behavior, multiplied by their motivation to do what they believe the

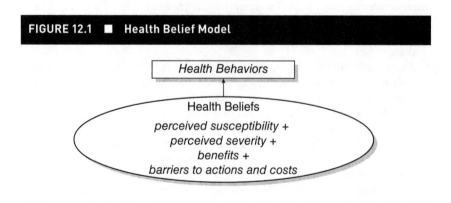

FIGURE 12.1 ■ Health Belief Model

Health Behaviors

Health Beliefs

perceived susceptibility +
perceived severity +
benefits +
barriers to actions and costs

Source: Wallston & Wallston (1984).

significant other wants them to do. The components of the model are shown in Figure 12.2.

An example will illustrate how variables in the theory of planned behavior affect behavior. One's intention to engage in HIV/AIDS preventive behavior, such as condom use, is determined by one's intention to wear a condom during a specific sexual encounter. Intentions are shaped by attitudes toward condom use and whether significant others also have favorable attitudes toward condom use. Attitudes are influenced by positive or negative beliefs about the effectiveness of condoms. If one believes that condoms are effective, resulting condom use is likely to occur.

The theory of planned behavior has been used to explain several health behaviors among African Americans, including blood pressure self-care (Peters & Templin, 2010), HIV/AIDS prevention behaviors (Jemmott & Jemmott, 2007; Mausbach, Semple, Patterson, & Strathdee, 2009), physical activity (Martin et al., 2005), cigarette smoking (Nehl et al., 2009), and eating behaviors (O'Neal et al., 2012). The theory of planned behavior has been used to predict HIV-related behaviors with several Black populations within and outside the United States, including Ghanaians (Asare & Sharma, 2009), Namibians (Smith & Nguyen, 2008), South Africans (Saal & Kagee, 2012), Tanzanians (Schaalma et al., 2009), and persons from Benin, Guinea, and Senegal (Godin et al., 2008). Asare and Sharma studied components of the theory of planned behavior and condom use among Ghanaian immigrants living in the Midwest. Participants completed a questionnaire that contained the constructs found in the theory of planned behavior. Perceived behavioral control and subjective norms predicted intention to use condoms; behavioral intention for condom use was a significant predictor of actual condom use.

FIGURE 12.2 ■ Theory of Planned Behavior

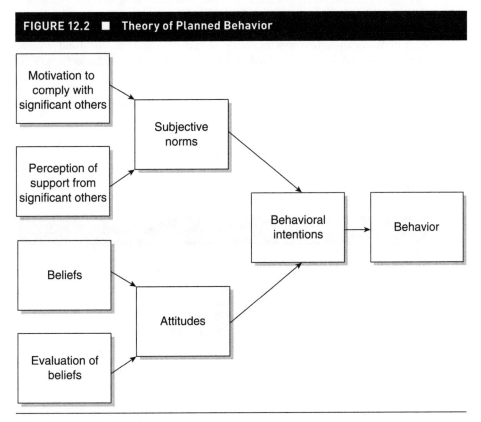

Source: Fishbein & Aizen (1975).

Self-Efficacy Theory

Self-efficacy theory is concerned with whether people can exert control over their motivation, behavior, and social environment (Bandura, 1977). Self-efficacy theory, like the theory of planned behavior, was not developed exclusively as a theory of health behavior but has been used extensively to understand and predict health behaviors. The theory predicts that one's beliefs about one's capability to perform a desired task will predict one's success at completing that task. Self-efficacy beliefs are usually specific; that is, one has efficacy with regard to a specific task or effort (e.g., Jean has high self-efficacy regarding her academic performance). Self-efficacy affects behavior by increasing the goals one sets. Persons with high self-efficacy will set higher goals and show persistence when goals are not met. High self-efficacy influences the strategies one uses to achieve goals and favorably influences the effectiveness of problem solving. Persons with low self-efficacy beliefs doubt their abilities and may be inefficient and ineffective problem solvers. Self-efficacy affects emotional responses. Low self-efficacy beliefs lead to anxiety and less successful coping efforts. High self-efficacy beliefs are developed through knowledge, skills, practice, and the support of significant others (Bandura, 1977; Maddux & Lewis, 1995). Competency in desired behavior contributes to strong self-efficacy beliefs. A model of self-efficacy theory is depicted in Figure 12.3.

Self-efficacy is associated with favorable health behaviors. Increased self-efficacy has been linked to increased HIV protective behaviors among African Americans from disadvantaged neighborhoods (Nehl, Elifson, DePadilla, & Sterk, 2016), less substance use among women (Taylor & Williams-Salisbury, 2015), increased fruit and vegetable intake and physical activity (Halbert et al., 2014), and increased adherence to HIV medication (Brown, Littlewood, & Vanable, 2013), among other health behaviors. Health interventions that have targeted changes in self-efficacy among African Americans have shown improvement in diets (Shin et al., 2015) and physical activity (Mama et al., 2015) and reductions in sexually transmitted infections (STI) (Wingood et al., 2013a).

Critique of Models

These three models of health behavior have several similarities: (a) All assume that health is a valued priority of individuals. (b) They assume that individuals have the potential to engage in actions on their own behalf. (c) They are cognitively based, with an emphasis on beliefs. (d) They all have a vast amount of health literature

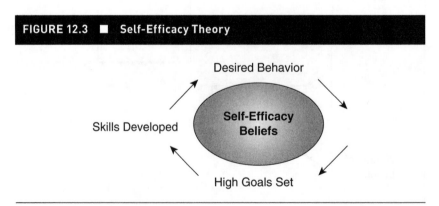

FIGURE 12.3 ■ Self-Efficacy Theory

Desired Behavior

Self-Efficacy Beliefs

Skills Developed

High Goals Set

Source: Bandura (1977).

devoted to them. In general, the models are useful for predicting health-related behavioral changes (and have been able to predict health promotion behaviors such as exercise and diet) (Komar-Samardzija, Braun, Keithley, & Quinn, 2012; Maddux & Lewis, 1995), as well as health care activities, including adherence to medication and self-care activities (Warren-Findlow, Seymour, & Huber, 2012). These models have also been useful in explaining illness-related behaviors, such as coping with chronic illness and disabilities (Belgrave, 1998). Finally, all three models have been used to account for drug prevention (Hahn & Rado, 1996) and the prevention of sexually transmitted infections (Wingood et al., 2013a).

Yet despite their widespread use, some scholars have questioned whether these models are useful for understanding and explaining health behaviors of African Americans (Belgrave, 1998; Cochran & Mays, 1993; Marin et al., 1995). In a critique of the usefulness of these models for understanding HIV/AIDS prevention behavior among African Americans, Cochran and Mays note that the models rely on the assumption that behavior is individualistic and rational. However, African Americans may engage in behavior because of social, family, and community obligations, not just for self (Simon, 2006). The second limitation noted by these authors is the minimization of the importance of economic factors in health behaviors. For example, access to regular physical examinations may not be possible for people even with health insurance if they do not have reliable transportation and reasonable travel time to a health care facility. Kimmel et al. (under review) found that geographical distance and travel time to a health facility affected whether people living with HIV received comprehensive HIV care. In the Kimmel et al. study, African Americans had longer travel time to comprehensive HIV care facilities than Whites.

Other limitations of social cognitive models are that they do not account for structural factors (poverty and living in segregated neighborhoods), implicit bias of health care providers, and institutional racism in the health care system—all known to affect health promotion, disease prevention, and treatment adherence behaviors. As such, these models may not be as useful for explaining the health behaviors of African Americans as they are for Whites. Townsend et al. (2007) found that the theory of planned behavior may be more useful in explaining preventive behaviors when cultural factors such as ethnic identity and Africentric values are included. The study by Townsend et al. will be discussed later in this chapter.

CULTURAL MODELS OF HEALTH AND ILLNESS

A culturally congruent model of health for African Americans recognizes core values and ways of behaving among people of African descent (Simon, 2006). The role of spirituality and religious practice in addressing health concerns within traditional African religions is clear and explicit, and some of these practices are adhered to by African Americans. African Americans are likely to use spirituality in health promotion efforts and as a framework for coping with stressful circumstances (Bediako & Neblett, 2011; Debnam et al., 2012; Tait, Laditka, Laditka, Nies, & Racine, 2011). Consequently, spirituality should be integrated into treatment practices and health promotion efforts when appropriate.

African American Churches contribute to positive health outcomes within the African American community. African American Churches provide the mechanism for health screenings (e.g., for high blood pressure, sickle cell disease), prevention activities (e.g., exercise classes) and communicating and disseminating health information. African American Churches have also been used as recruitment sites for HIV prevention and other health promotion activities (Coleman, Lindley, Annang, Saunders, & Gaddist, 2012; Peterson & Cheng, 2011; Sbrocco et al., 2012).

The role of the family—including the extended family—must also be considered in understanding health and illness outcomes among African Americans. The Black extended family has been considered a source of emotional, material, and social support for African Americans with medical and health care needs (Belgrave, 1998). Compared with Whites, African Americans are more likely to care for an elderly or infirm family member in the home (Dilworth-Anderson & Goodwin, 2005).

Racism and Physical Health

Racism affects the health status of African Americans in several ways (Hickson et al., 2012; Kwate, Meyer, Eniola, & Dennis, 2010; Mwendwa et al., 2011). First, racial discrimination can negatively impact the quality and quantity of medical care, as well as treatment compliance. Perceived discrimination is associated with poor medication adherence among African Americans with hypertension (Forsyth, Schoenthaler, Chaplin, Ogedegbe, & Ravennell, 2014). Other research shows implicit bias held against African Americans by White providers, which is linked to biased treatment recommendations (Williams & Wyatt, 2015).

Second, the experience of specific racial incidents and discrimination may adversely affect health by causing psychological distress and other changes in physiological processes (this explanation is discussed more thoroughly in the section on hypertension) (Brody et al., 2014). Hill et al. (2017) examined the relationship between perceived discrimination and heart rate variability among healthy African American young adults (N = 103). Heart rate variability is a measure of parasympathetic cardio influence and is generally a protective factor for cardiovascular health. The authors found that high perceived discrimination was associated with low heart rate variability; this relationship was especially strong for African Americans reporting frequent experiences of discrimination involving threats and physical harassment.

Third, at an institutional level, racism operates through many institutional structures, such as residential segregation, to impact the health of African Americans. Many racial and ethnic minorities live in communities where there is a disproportionate number of health-compromising conditions, such as environmental pollutants, high availability of tobacco and alcohol products, unhealthy food sources, and a lack of health-promoting resources, such as full-service grocery stores and parks and recreation facilities (Smedley, 2012). Corral et al. (2012) studied the impact of residential segregation (e.g., whether participants resided in a totally integrated or totally segregated neighborhood) on health behaviors in a national sample of African American adults. They found that after controlling for individual-level variables, such as gender, education, and age, residential segregation contributed to being overweight or obese. African Americans living in more rather than less segregated neighborhoods were more likely to be overweight or obese. The impact of racism on physical health is also addressed in Chapter 4.

When health and other social outcomes of the poorest and the richest counties in the United States are considered, race/ethnicity is a factor (Egen, Beatty, Blackley, Brown, & Wykoff, 2017). Using socioeconomic status as an indicator of income, Egan and colleagues examined data from 3,141 counties and found that the percentage of the population that is African American in the poorest state was 4.5 times that in the wealthiest state. Thirty-seven percent of people in the poorest states were African American, compared with 7.9% of African Americans in the wealthiest state. Males living in the poorest state had a life expectancy of almost 10 years less than males living in the wealthiest state. Individuals living in the poorest state (compared with the wealthiest states) had double the smoking prevalence, were 50% more likely to be obese, and had twice as many persons per primary care physicians.

Fourth, discrimination contributes to poor health outcomes because some of the negative coping strategies (e.g., alcohol and drug use) used by members of oppressed groups also impair physical and mental functioning (see Chapter 14).

SELECTED HEALTH AND ILLNESS CONDITIONS AMONG AFRICAN AMERICANS

In this section, we review four health conditions common among African Americans. These conditions were selected because their prevalence is substantially higher among African Americans than among other ethnic groups. They are also reviewed because (with the exception of sickle cell disease) they contribute to leading causes of death among African Americans.

Hypertension

Hypertension or high blood pressure is defined by either having elevated blood pressure (systolic pressure of at least 140 mmHg or diastolic pressure of at least 90 mmHg) or taking antihypertensive medication. Hypertension occurs when blood pressure, the force of the blood flowing through blood vessels, is consistently too high (American Heart Association, 2017).

Hypertension is a risk factor for heart disease, stroke, kidney disease, diabetes, and other chronic conditions. Hypertension is substantially higher among African Americans than among other ethnic groups. For example, among African Americans over 20, 42.4% of African American men and 44% of African American women have hypertension, compared with 30.2% for White men and 28.6% for White women (NCHS, 2015b).

Income and education are factors in hypertension prevalence and control among African Americans. The prevalence of hypertension is higher among African Americans who are poor and less educated. The etiology of hypertension is complex. Genetic and physiological differences have historically been thought to account for some of the ethnic differences in hypertension prevalence. However, Non, Gravlee, and Mulligan (2012) refuted this fact by assessing the relative contribution of education and genetic ancestry in blood pressure. Genetic ancestry was estimated using a genome-wide set of autosomal markers. The authors found that education, not genetic ancestry, significantly predicted blood pressure variability among African Americans. Each year of education was associated with a .51 mmHg (millimeters of mercury) decrease in hypertension. Also, the higher prevalence of hypertension in Blacks living in the United States than in Africa suggests that environmental and behavioral factors account for the higher prevalence for Blacks living in the United States (Fuchs, 2011).

Research has shown that African Americans who have darker skin color have higher levels of blood pressure than those who have lighter skin color. The effects of skin color on elevated blood pressure seem to be mediated by socioeconomic status. One study found an association between skin color and blood pressure only in African Americans who were of low socioeconomic status (Klag, Whelton, Coresh, Grim, & Kuller, 1991). This may be due to fewer resources among those of low socioeconomic status and lesser ability to deal with the psychosocial stressors associated with darker skin color, such as discrimination (Hall, 2007; Klonoff and Landrine, 2000).

In a study of 196 African American female college students, Armstead, Hebert, Griffin, and Prince (2014) examined skin color, chronic stress, and family history of hypertension. They found that skin color was a significant predictor of both systolic and diastolic blood pressure, along with body mass index (BMI). Skin color ratings were assessed by three laboratory assistants trained in skin color rating. Darker skin tone was associated with a larger BMI, a contributor to hypertension. Stress exposure may be greater for darker women and trigger corticosteroid release associated with the development of body mass and central adiposity. Darker skin tone, along with chronic life stress, were associated with higher resting systolic and diastolic blood pressure; and likely, chronic stress accounts for this increase in blood pressure for darker African Americans.

Dietary habits of African Americans also contribute to higher rates of hypertension. Processed foods, fried foods, and foods high in saturated fat, total fat, and sodium content contribute to increased prevalence of diabetes. Obesity, which is higher among African Americans, is a contributor to hypertension (Swinburn, Caterson, Seidell, & James, 2004). Food deserts also account for increased hypertension among African Americans. Food deserts, characterized by poor access to healthy and nutritious food, often occur in urban and poor neighborhoods. Neighborhoods with high proportions of African Americans and Latinos have fewer supermarkets or chain stores and the distance to supermarkets is also further in predominantly African American neighborhoods (Beaulac, Kristjansson, & Cummins, 2009).

Increased hypertension among African Americans is also attributed to exposure to discrimination and more chronic social stressors (e.g., racism, unemployment, economic problems) (Hicken, Lee, Morenoff, House, & Williams, 2014; Sims et al., 2012; Steffen et al., 2003). In a large national study of over 4,900 African Americans, Sims et al. found that lifetime discrimination was associated with higher levels of hypertension. Dolezsar et al. (2014) conducted a meta-analysis of the relationship between perceived racial discrimination and hypertension using 44 articles with a sample size of 32,651. The sample was 62.2% Black, 13.6% White, 11.8% Hispanic, and 12.4% other. The authors found a significant relationship between perceived discrimination and hypertensive status and a stronger relationship for Blacks than other ethnic groups.

In a multiethnic study, using a representative sample, Hicken et al. (2014) found that Blacks reported the highest race-related vigilant stress of all racial or ethnic groups. Among Blacks, each unit increase in vigilance-related racism stress was associated with a 4% increase in odds of hypertension.

Implicit racial bias held by African Americans also affects the relationship between racial discrimination and hypertension. Using the Implicit Association Test (IAT) (discussed in Chapter 4), Chae, Nuru-Jeter, and Adler (2012) found among African American men that held an anti-Black bias, more frequent reports of discrimination were associated with a higher probability of hypertension. Among men with a pro-Black implicit bias, more frequent reports of discrimination were associated with lower hypertension risk, suggesting that pro-Blackness or racial identity was protective under conditions of discrimination.

Racial discrimination also affects whether a person takes his or her prescribed medication (Cuffee et al., 2013). In a sample of approximately 800 African American adults, racial discrimination was associated with medication adherence. Trust in the physician explained this relationship such that racial discrimination led to mistrust, and it was this mistrust that decreased adherence to hypertensive medication.

Several social and environmental factors contribute to hypertension, including social support (Coulon & Wilson, 2015). Changing health habits result in substantially reduced hypertension. These habits include sodium reduction, reduction in weight and obesity, and exercise. Also, the negative effects of discrimination on blood pressure can be reduced by cultural variables, such as racial identity and Africentric values (Neblett & Carter, 2012).

AIDS/HIV

As discussed in the opening story, no ethnic or racial group has been more affected by HIV than African Americans. African Americans are more likely to be infected with HIV and to die from HIV-related consequences than any other ethnic group (CDC, 2015). African Americans make up approximately 12% of the population of the United States but accounted for 45% of the new HIV/AIDS diagnoses and 40% of the persons living with HIV in 2015 (CDC, 2016). African American males make up almost one-third of all HIV diagnoses, with rates more than 8 times that of White men. While rates of HIV infection among African American women decreased by 42% from 2005 to 2014, African American women still have high rates of HIV infection. African American women currently represent 62% or nearly 2 out of every 3 HIV diagnoses among women (CDC, 2016). African American women's rate of HIV diagnoses is 16 times that of White women.

HIV/AIDS is one of the five leading causes of death among African American women and men ages 25–44 years old. Among African American men, the primary route of transmission is sexual contact with other men. Among African American women, the primary route of transmission is high-risk heterosexual contact. In 2013, African Americans who died of HIV or AIDS accounted for 54% of total deaths attributed to HIV or AIDS in the U.S.

According to the CDC, ethnicity and race, in and of itself, is not a risk factor, but African Americans are more likely to have challenges associated with risk factors (CDC, 2011b). Some of these include the following: (a) African American women are more likely to be at risk because of sex with African American males who are injection drug users and who have sex with men. (b) Injection drug use is the second-most-prevalent cause of HIV infection among African American men and women. (c) African Americans have the highest rates of sexually transmitted infections, which is a risk factor for HIV. (d) Concealment of homosexual behavior among African American males because of stigma and other factors creates additional risk. (e) The incarceration of African American men also increases HIV risk because incarceration is often linked to involvement with drugs and high-risk sex. (f) Socioeconomic and structural factors such as poverty, lack of health care, and lack of preventive health care also contribute to HIV risk. Racially segregated neighborhoods are one structural factor accounting for higher HIV rates among African Americans. African Americans who live in racially segregated and concentrated urban neighborhoods engage in more sexual risk behaviors (e.g., more partners, lack of consistent condom use) than those living in neighborhoods that are less racially segregated (Lutfi, Trepka, Fennie, Ibanez, & Gladwin, 2015).

Many treatment and prevention efforts have used psychological theories to understand, prevent, and treat HIV. For example, Townsend et al. (2007) used the theory of planned behavior, along with ethnic identity, and Africentric values to explain HIV risk (e.g., sexual intent, number of partners) among 148 African

American adolescents. Components of the theory of planned behavior included attitudes, peer norms, and perceived behavioral control. The findings showed significant relationships between components of the theory of planned behavior and sexual intent and number of partners. Ethnic identity was significantly related to perceived behavioral control and peer norms, such that a strong ethnic identity was associated with higher perceived behavioral control and having fewer friends with risky behavior. Africentric values predicted attitudes about sexual risk, with higher Africentric values related to higher awareness of sexual risk. Townsend et al. noted the importance of including cultural constructs in models of HIV risk. There have been several initiatives to address the HIV epidemic among African Americans. Some of these will be reviewed under the Empirically Supported Practices section of this chapter.

HIV can be managed with antiretroviral drugs. While medication adherence is important for maintaining viral suppression, African Americans living with HIV have poorer medication adherence and subsequent outcomes than their White counterparts. For example, fewer than half (49%) of African Americans living with HIV have achieved viral suppression. Mistrust is one factor that might account for differences in medication adherence (Dale, Bogart, Wagner, Galvan, & Klein, 2016). Dale and colleagues investigated the role of medical mistrust on electronically monitored antiretroviral medication adherence over a 6-month period among African American men living with HIV. They found that general medical mistrust (e.g., suspicion toward providers) was associated with lower continuous medication adherence over time.

Dale et al. (2016) looked at exposure to HIV conspiracy beliefs (discussed earlier) of HIV positive individual and medication compliance. The authors found that the expression of HIV conspiracy theories by members of HIV positive networks was associated with less medication adherence. The findings of this study suggest mistrust must be addressed to improve HIV prevention and medication adherence among African Americans living with HIV. Other factors that can prevent HIV and improve treatment include individual-level variables (e.g., social support, safe-sex), community variables (e.g., accessible HIV testing, treatment), and structural factors (employment and housing).

Sickle Cell Disease

Sickle cell disease is a group of genetic blood disorders that affect 1 out of every 400 to 500 African Americans (Desforges, Milner, Wethers, & Whitten, 1978). The sickle cell gene is more common among those whose ancestry can be traced to a geographical region where malaria was a significant threat. The sickle cell gene provided protection against malaria for people of African and Mediterranean descent. The symptoms of sickle cell disease are variable and can range from mild to severe. One of the complications of sickle cell disease is vasco-occlusion. This is a process whereby blood flow is affected due to the involved red blood cells that are sticky and rigid and flow poorly throughout the body. These vasco-occlusions are painful and can result in destructive changes in the body's organs, involving the eyes (blindness), brain (stroke), heart (failure), lungs (scarring), liver/spleen (failure), kidneys (loss of function), or sex organs (impotence; Holbrook & Phillips, 1994).

New medication and treatment regimens have made the complications of sickle cell disease less severe today than in the past. Nevertheless, individuals with sickle cell disease will have to cope with many health challenges throughout their lives. Since pain is the most common symptom, learning to cope with pain is important.

Schatz et al. (2015) showed reduction in pain among children who received cognitive behavioral therapy (CBT) coping skills training for pain management. The intervention consisted of one session of CBT training and practice at home using smartphones over a period of 8 weeks. Children (N = 46, age ranged from 8–21) completed daily dairies with measures of coping strategies and pain intensity. At post-test, children who used the CBT skills training showed reductions in next-day pain intensity.

Poor sleep quality has been implicated in increased pain for individuals with sickle cell disease. In a study of 75 African American adults with sickle disease, nights of shorter sleep duration, less efficient sleep, and increased fragmented sleep were followed by days of greater pain severity (Moscou-Jackson, Finan, Campbell, Smyth, & Haythornthwaite, 2015).

In terms of psychological well-being, people with sickle cell disease have a higher incidence of social and psychological problems (including anxiety and depression) than people without sickle cell disease (Lemanek & Ranalli, 2009; Matthie, Hamilton, Wells, & Jenerette, 2015). Matthie and colleagues interviewed 29 young adults with sickle cell disease (ages 18–35) about their experiences. Participants reported challenges with maintaining a good quality of life and taking care of themselves; interruptions to their family, work, and social roles; and sometimes difficulties accessing needed health care.

Problems with sickle cell disease are attributed to chronic pain and increased anxiety that may be associated with concerns about body deterioration or mortality (Barrett et al., 1988). Among children, the disease may disrupt patterns of normal functioning, such as going to school, developing independence from adults, playing with peers, and dating (among adolescents). However, more recent studies focusing on resiliency have shown that most children and adolescents show resilience in response to stressors associated with sickle cell disease. Resilience occurs when there are adaptive coping processes, a supportive family and social support network, and intrapersonal responses the child can draw on (Ziadni, Patterson, Pulgarón, Robinson, & Barakat, 2011). Positive communications with a medical provider, as well as religious support, also help patients cope with sickle cell disease (Derlega et al., 2014). Finally, use of positive religious coping was associated with significantly fewer hospital admissions for persons with sickle cell disease (Bediako et al., 2011).

Historically, there has been stigma attached to having sickle cell disease, in part because it is a disease that primarily affects African Americans in this country (Bediako & Moffitt, 2011). People with sickle cell disease have been concerned that the diagnosis will lead to more stereotyping and discrimination in the work environment. For example, a famous singer, Tionne (T-Boz) Watkins, did not disclose that she had sickle cell disease until she became ill on tour. She later became a spokesperson for persons with sickle cell disease.

It is possible for people with sickle cell disease to have a good quality of life. Management of the psychological as well as the medical aspects of the disease is important. Good psychological adjustment among persons with sickle cell disease can be enhanced by an optimistic and hopeful outlook, family and other support, consistent adherence to health recommendations, and good communication with health providers (Ziadni et al., 2011).

Diabetes

Diabetes mellitus is a group of diseases characterized by high levels of blood glucose. It results from defects in insulin secretions, action, or both (Diabetes Prevention

Program Research Group, 2002a). African Americans are much more likely to have diabetes than other racial and ethnic groups; 18.0% of all African Americans ages 20 years or older have diabetes compared with 11.9% for all other racial and ethnic groups (NCHS, 2015b). One in four African American women over the age of 55 have diabetes. Diabetes is a leading cause of death and disability among African Americans. Approximately 90% to 95% of African Americans with diabetes have type 2 (rather than type 1) diabetes. Type 2 diabetes occurs later in life and is caused by the body's resistance to the action of insulin and to impaired insulin secretions. Type 2 diabetes can be treated with diet, exercise, pills, or injections. A much smaller percentage of African Americans have type 1 diabetes, which usually develops before age 20. It is always treated with insulin.

Several factors contribute to the higher incidence of diabetes among African Americans. Genetics may play a role. For example, some researchers speculate that for type 2 diabetes, there is a gene that came from Africa. Years ago this gene was functional and enabled Africans, during feast and famine cycles, to conserve food energy more efficiently when food was scarce. The gene that developed to help survival in Africa may instead make a person more susceptible to developing type 2 diabetes now (Harris et al., 1998).

A second risk factor for diabetes is prediabetes, also known as impaired glucose tolerance. This occurs in people whose blood glucose levels are higher than normal but not high enough for them to be diagnosed with diabetes (American Diabetes Association, 2008).

Being overweight is a third risk factor for diabetes (Crespo, Keteyian, Heath, & Sempos, 1996; Troiano, Flegal, Kuczmarski, Campbell, & Johnson, 1995). In addition to being overweight, the location in which the excess weight is carried contributes to the risk. African Americans are more likely to have upper-body fat. Related to this factor is another: physical activity. Researchers speculate that lower levels of physical activity may be one of the major contributors to increased diabetes among African Americans.

African Americans with diabetes experience more complications and have greater disability, functional limitations, and deaths due to diabetes than do Whites (American Diabetes Association, 2012). Among African Americans with diabetes, poor glycemic control is seen in almost 25% (NCHS, 2015b). African Americans are also much more likely to develop serious complications from diabetes than Whites. These include blindness, end-stage renal disease, and amputations (Chow, Foster, Gonzalex, & McIver, 2012).

As with hypertension, the prevalence of diabetes varies among Blacks based on their region of birth. Using data from a national sample of Blacks, Ford, Narayan, and Mehta (2016) analyzed data on diabetic prevalence by region of birth. Foreign-born Blacks had significantly lower reported diabetes prevalence (8.94% vs. 11.84%) than U.S.-born Blacks when controlling for education and income. These differences did not remain when body mass index was controlled for, implicating obesity as a significant factor in diabetes. This study's findings point to the important role of reductions in obesity in diabetic prevention.

Individuals can lower their risk for diabetes. The Diabetes Prevention Program Research Group conducted a study that looked at how type 2 diabetes could be prevented or delayed among people with impaired glucose tolerance, a risk factor for diabetes (National Diabetes Information Clearinghouse, 2002). The findings of this study show that people at high risk for type 2 diabetes can lower their chances of developing diabetes with lifestyle modifications, such as diet and exercise. The Diabetes Prevention Program and a cultural adaptation of this intervention are discussed in more detail later in this chapter.

METHODOLOGICAL AND RESEARCH ISSUES

When conducting health and medical research among African Americans, researchers must address several methodological issues. We next discuss (a) lack of participation in research and clinical trials, (b) inadequate data collection protocols and measures, and (c) the cultural context of participants.

Lack of Participation in Research and Clinical Trials

An often-cited problem in conducting research on African American samples is gaining access to communities and participants within these communities. As discussed previously, some African Americans may be distrustful of health and medical research and programs, especially those that do not originate from within the African American community. Suspicion may also be elevated for any research that involves biological samples. African Americans have been used as "subjects" in programs of research to gain insight into a medical problem or health issue without the knowledge gained coming back to benefit the African American community. This was seen in the Tuskegee study discussed previously. In focus group discussions with African Americans who both agreed and declined to participate in cancer research, Somayaji and Cloyes (2015) found mistrust contributed to lack of participation. Along with mistrust, participants reported fears of the unknown, death, conspiracy, and discrimination.

African Americans are also less likely than other racial and ethnic groups to participate in clinical trials. Clinical trials are intervention research studies necessary to evaluate the efficacy of treatment for a particular condition. Only by participating in clinical trials can one know whether a specific treatment is efficacious for a particular cultural group. The lack of participation of African Americans in clinical trials results in not being able to identify factors related to disease prevalence and treatment that may be unique to African Americans (Luebbert & Perez, 2016).

African Americans are not as likely as Whites to be referred for clinical trials, and when they are referred, they are less likely to participate. Eggly, Barton, Winckles, Penner, and Albrecht (2015) investigated racial differences in patient communication with an oncologist by viewing video-recorded oncology visits. They found that visits with African American patients, compared with visits with White patients, were shorter overall and included less discussion of clinical trials.

Even when referred for participation in clinical trials, African Americans are less likely to participate. Luebbert and Perez (2016) conducted a literature review and identified 20 articles on barriers to participating in clinical trials for African Americans. Several barriers were identified. Trust issues were one. Several studies showed that African Americans were less likely to trust their physician and other health care providers (than Whites) and to have overall distrust against clinical research. A second barrier was experimental issues. African Americans were more willing to participate in low-risk studies, such as completing surveys and giving blood and urine samples, as opposed to studies considered at higher risk (e.g., injections, new medications). A third barrier was communication issues (discussed previously). Communication issues involved lack of awareness of clinical research opportunities and lack of understanding of terminology, including language used in the consent form. A fourth barrier was logical issues, such as time commitment, travel distance, transportation, and general inconveniences. When potential participants evaluated the cost against the benefit (generally a financial incentive), decisions were often made to avoid participation in clinical trials.

To gain support for conducting research and planning appropriate programs that may ultimately benefit African Americans, it is necessary to develop positive relationships with both formal and informal community stakeholders. These may include leaders of religious and civic groups, local citizen groups, sororities, fraternities, and faith-based organizations. Community-based participatory research is especially useful when conducting health-related research with African Americans. Research by Fouad, Johnson, Nagy, Person, and Partridge (2014) showed that when members of the local community were hired and trained to work on the research team, recruitment and retention of African Americans in clinical trials increased. Use of the African American Church has also aided in recruitment for research and clinical trials (Langford, Resnicow, & Beasley, 2015). The endorsement of the Church leader is helpful in this regard (Odulana et al., 2014). Addressing issues of mistrust and historical reasons for mistrust, along with involvement of community and faith-based institutions, should increase African Americans' participation in research and clinical trials.

Inadequate Data Collection Protocols and Measures

A second methodological consideration is that measures and data collection protocols that have been developed for White participants may not be appropriate for African Americans. In our research, we have found it necessary to be flexible when collecting data with African American families, especially parents. Often research participants have other priorities than being a "subject" in a research study. We have collected data in homes, at public places such as libraries and recreational centers, and at fast-food restaurants. Another problem in conducting health and medical research is that often health and medical status measures and instruments have not been developed with consideration given to the health problems and diseases that affect African Americans. Consider research on health and psychological outcomes among persons with sickle cell disease. The health status measures that have been developed for other types of chronic illnesses may not be appropriate for sickle cell disease. For example, pain and accompanying physical and psychological symptoms from a sickle cell crisis may differ from the pain and/or discomfort from other types of medical conditions (e.g., asthma).

Cultural Context of Participants

The cultural context in which individuals experience a chronic illness must also be considered. Researchers should be aware of other social and economic issues that the individual has to deal with in addition to the disease. Treatment recommendations are not likely to be taken seriously if the clients or research participants are concerned with basic shelter, food, and safety needs. In addition, there may be concerns of confidentiality among participants with stigmatizing conditions. HIV is one such condition. Issues of stigma and confidentiality may be especially salient to an HIV-positive African American male research participant because of higher levels of stigma associated with being gay in the African American community. These issues may interfere with recruitment of participants in research protocols.

EMPIRICALLY SUPPORTED PRACTICES FOR REDUCING MORBIDITY AND MORTALITY

Ways of reducing health disparities must consider changes at the individual behavioral level, as well as broader changes in systems, including how health care is delivered in this country. We next discuss system-level changes, followed by empirically supported programs that have reduced the risk of HIV and diabetes.

System-Level Changes

Satcher et al. (2005) discuss several system-level changes for reducing health disparities among African Americans. One suggested change at the national level is universal health care for all Americans. Having a primary health care home would ensure that integrated and comprehensive care could be provided when needed. The Patient Protection and Affordable Care Act mitigated some of the problem of lack of access to routine health care. However, at this writing, it is not clear that it will remain. Proportionate representation of African Americans in the health care professions might also reduce some of the biases in diagnoses and treatment. Further biases in diagnoses and treatment can also be reduced by making health care providers aware of racial and ethnic disparities and providing cross-cultural education and training to health care providers (Smedley et al., 2003).

Change at the community level is also critical to reducing disparities. Programs that promote the health of communities might include more exercise-friendly neighborhood features, such as walking trails and low- or no-cost recreational facilities. Grocery and food stores with healthy and nutritious food items would also help reduce health disparities (Satcher et al., 2005).

Programs to promote better health are more likely to be achieved when researchers and health professionals work collaboratively with key community stakeholders. Collaboration should occur in the planning stages and when trusting relationships and secure commitments have been developed. Some effective programs and interventions that have involved community partnerships include interventions that reduce cardio-metabolic risk among high-risk African American women (Villablanca, Warford, & Wheeler, 2016); increase recommended vegetable and fruit consumption among rural African Americans (Barnidge et al. 2015); and address multiple health problems in the community (Ferre, Jones, Norris, & Rowley, 2010). We next discuss empirically supported interventions for the prevention of two major causes of morbidity and mortality among African Americans: HIV and diabetes.

Preventing HIV

Although advances in treatment for AIDS have dramatically slowed the progression of HIV to AIDS, a cure for AIDS has not been found. Efforts to address the HIV epidemic in African American communities have been instituted at the national, community, and individual levels. Through the Minority HIV/AIDS Initiative, funds have been provided through several governmental (e.g., CDC) and nongovernmental (e.g., Ryan White) agencies to provide HIV prevention, testing, and treatment services to minorities in communities with high HIV incidence. Some of the cities with high incidence of HIV include Atlanta, Baltimore, Chicago, Los Angeles, Miami, New York, and Washington, D.C.

HIV prevention efforts instituted by psychologists have generally targeted behavioral change at the individual level. However, risk reduction efforts targeted at the individual level are limited, as these interventions typically are costly with regard to facilitator training and program implementation. Intervention sessions can only be carried out by a trained facilitator and to a limited number of participants. These program can be inconvenient to participants as well because participants can attend sessions only at scheduled times. Web-based interventions require less training time and are more flexible for participants.

Billings et al. (2015) conducted a randomized trial to evaluate the efficacy of a web-based HIV behavioral intervention for African American women. This intervention, called Safe Sistah, did not require any on-site support or technical assistance. High-risk African American women (ages 18–50) were recruited from a community health center located in a low-resource neighborhood. High-risk was defined as either multiple male sexual partners in the past 2 months or inconsistent condom use.

The goal of Safe Sistah was to increase condom negotiations particularly in steady relationships because most African American women are infected by their primary male partner. Based on an initial assessment of user-specific risk, the woman may receive training in areas related to (a) increasing condom use; (b) enhancing safer sexual communication; (c) reducing sexual risks associated with alcohol and other drugs; (d) enhancing partner selection and reducing the number of partners; and (e) increasing the probability of refusing sex safely. The intervention is audio-narrated with diverse elements, including video and interactive exercises and quizzes. Safe Sistah is culturally congruent and includes videos of African Americans and messages of gender empowerment and positive racial identity. Women receive training in how to implement a specific skill via models who use vignettes and through practice by using interactive exercises. Most women completed the video in 88 minutes during one sitting.

Women completed several measures of condom use and HIV risk and protective behaviors 1 month and 4 months after the Safe Sistah intervention. Findings showed significant reduction in HIV risk for women in the intervention group compared with the control group. Condom frequency was increased by 63% after the completion of the study among intervention participants. Participants in the intervention group also increased sexual communication and sexual refusal and were more likely to use condoms after alcohol use than those in the control condition.

There have been a few attempts to use an Africentric framework in reducing HIV risk. One program described in Chapter 2 was the Healer Women Fighting Disease Integrating Substance Abuse and HIV Prevention Program for Black Women Project (Nobles et al., 2009). Preliminary findings evaluating this project show positive results for changes in positive feelings about the self and HIV-protective behaviors. Given the toll HIV has had in the African American community, there is still much to do regarding HIV, and more effective interventions are needed for different subgroups (e.g., older populations, teen populations). More research on best practices for promoting HIV testing among African Americans is also needed. HIV testing reduces the rate of new transmissions and links HIV positive individuals to health care. Undiagnosed infections of HIV are responsible for over 50% of new HIV infections, as persons unaware of their HIV infection are significantly more likely to transmit the virus than those who know their positive status (Marks, Crepaz, & Janssen, 2006).

Reducing Diabetes

Behavioral change techniques have also proven useful for decreasing diabetes risk. The Diabetes Prevention Program (DPP) was a large study funded by the National Institute of Diabetes and Digestive and Kidney Diseases (Diabetes Prevention Program

Research Group, 2002b). The multisite study investigated whether small to moderate amounts of weight loss and increased physical activity or treatment with an oral diabetes drug medication could prevent or delay the onset of type 2 diabetes. Participants in the study were all overweight and prediabetic. There were three groups of participants: (a) the lifestyle intervention group, (b) the drug group, and (c) a placebo control. The study involved 3,234 participants across 27 sites. Forty-five percent of the participants were from ethnic minority groups. The lifestyle intervention group received counseling about diet, physical activity, and behavioral modification. The goals for this group were for participants to change their diet to include less fat and fewer calories and to get 150 minutes of exercise per week. The drug group took 850 mg of metformin (a drug that treats diabetes) twice a day. The third group received placebo pills instead of metformin. The drug group and the placebo group received written information about diet and exercise, but they did not have the intensive counseling regarding diet and exercise.

Participants were followed for almost 3 years. The DPP found that participants who lost a modest amount of weight through dietary changes and increased physical activity sharply reduced their chances of developing diabetes. Statistics showed that the incidence of diabetes was 11.0, 7.8, and 4.8 cases per 100 person-years in the placebo, metformin, and lifestyle groups, respectively. The DPP has become a well-known and often-used resource for reducing diabetes incidence. More information, including materials, can be obtained at DPP (n.d.).

The DPP has been translated and culturally adapted for use within ethnic minority communities (Hall, Lattie, McCalla, & Saab, 2016). Boltri et al. (2008) conducted a faith-based adaptation of the DPP for African Americans at risk of type 2 diabetes. The intervention was delivered in African American Churches and modified for group delivery. A Church leader led the group in a prayer at the start of each session. There were significant reductions in weight, blood pressure, and fasting glucose levels at 6 and 12 months postintervention.

CRITICAL ANALYSIS

Most of the leading causes of death among African Americans (i.e., cardiovascular disease, stroke, hypertension, diabetes, HIV/AIDS, and homicide) are influenced by lifestyle and behavioral factors. Interventions to change risk behaviors could dramatically reduce morbidity and mortality. For example, the DPP resulted in decreases in the onset of diabetes with small to moderate modifications in diet and exercise. Psychologists have knowledge of the models of behavioral change (some were reviewed in this chapter) and how to change behaviors. Yet enormous health disparities remain across almost every health indicator for African Americans. Thus, a critical question is, how are information and skills for behavioral change transmitted to African American populations who are most in need of health promotion and disease prevention messages? How is information shared and accessed? What structures within communities and schools could best be used to support these behavioral changes?

Two institutions that could serve as conduits for health promotion and disease prevention messages and interventions are schools and Churches. Since all children have to attend school, this should be a good place in which to develop good nutritional and fitness habits from preschool through high school. At the same time, emphasis on achievement test scores have reduced and/or cut out unstructured playground time and physical education activities within many schools. Churches and other religious institutions could also play a larger role in health interventions. For example, framing health messages within a religious or spiritual framework (i.e., the body is God's temple) may also contribute to good health practices.

At the same time, focusing exclusively on individual-level change or even family and community change will not eliminate health disparities. There have been literally thousands of published papers on successful behavioral interventions, and yet, while health outcomes have improved, disparities have not changed for African Americans in the past 50 years. Changes in structural systems and national policy may be the only solution to equality in health care. Universal health care and accessible health care that rewards health care providers for prevention rather than treatment should reduce health disparities and improve the health and well-being of African Americans. This has been the goal of the Affordable Care Act, but it may be repealed under the current administration. It is also important to recognize the role of poverty in health disparities. About one-third of African Americans live at or below the poverty level; employment, food, and housing are priorities over health care, especially preventive health care.

Internet and smartphone usage is high among African Americans, which means that African Americans can be reached and engaged in ways not previously seen. E-health (electronic health) is a promising new technology for improving health outcomes of African Americans and likely to be used more in the future. More research is needed on the best way to use this technology to reach African Americans across many health domains and in various environments (e.g., rural and urban communities)

Summary

The proverb at the beginning of this chapter, "He who conceals his disease cannot expect to be cured," conveys the importance of acknowledging one's health condition and engaging in corrective actions and behavior. As we have noted throughout this chapter, many of these behaviors are influenced by culture.

There are disparities between African Americans and other racial and ethnic groups in morbidity, mortality, and health and in medical and rehabilitation utilization patterns. Several factors contribute to these disparities, including access factors, attitudinal barriers, cultural differences, and various forms of racism, and race-related stress. Factors that affect access to health care and treatment include poverty, lack of medical insurance, where people live, mistrust of the medical system, and divergent values and beliefs about wellness and illness. Strategies for improving utilization patterns and adherence can be implemented at the individual, family, community, and institutional levels.

Models of health, particularly, the health belief model, the theory of planned behavior, and self-efficacy theory, have been used to understand and predict health-related outcomes. But these models have limited use for predicting health outcomes among African Americans. Theories that consider culture, race, ethnicity, and class could be used to augment these models. For example, cultural models of health might involve the family and attend to spirituality in treatment efforts. Stress stemming from racism and discrimination also play a larger role in health disparities for African Americans.

Hypertension, HIV/AIDS, sickle cell disease, and diabetes are found among African Americans at rates much higher than those of other ethnic groups. Although the symptoms and consequences of these diseases can lead to serious health problems, these diseases can also be managed with appropriate medical and psychological treatment delivered in a culturally appropriate manner.

There are several methodological problems to consider when conducting health-related research and interventions with African Americans. These include (a) lack of participation in research and clinical trials, (b) inadequacy of data collection and measures, (c) and cultural context of participants. Much effort has been directed toward reducing health disparities and improving the health of African Americans. These include both system-level interventions and individual-level interventions. Programs targeting individuals have been effective in preventing HIV and diabetes. However, health care disparities remain after 50 years; structural and national policy changes are needed.

13

PSYCHOSOCIAL ADAPTATION AND MENTAL HEALTH

The wind does not break a tree that bends.

—Sukuma proverb

LEARNING OBJECTIVES

- To understand traditional and African-centered definitions and conceptualizations of mental disorder

- To understand how mental illness is viewed in African cultures

- To become aware of the prevalence of mental disorders among African Americans

- To review the role of culture in psychotherapeutic interventions

- To identify challenges in identifying mental illness among African Americans

- To identify efforts to improve mental health of African Americans

RACIAL TRAUMA IS REAL: THE IMPACT OF POLICE SHOOTINGS ON AFRICAN AMERICANS

BY ERLANGER A. TURNER AND JASMINE RICHARDSON

There have been many changes within the criminal justice system as a means to deter crime and to keep citizens safe. However, research demonstrates that often times men of color are treated harshly which leads to negative perceptions of police officers. The recent shootings in Baton Rouge, Falcon Heights, and Dallas have exposed many individuals and their families to

(Continued)

(Continued)

incidents of police brutality that reminds us that as a society work needs to be done to improve police and community relations.

In light of these recent events, many people have witnessed these traumatic incidents through social media or participation in marches in their cities. The violence witnessed toward people of color from police continues to damage perceptions of law enforcement and further stereotype people of color negatively. In a study published in the American Journal of Public Health (Geller et al., 2014), the authors reported that 85% of the participants reported being stopped at least once in their lifetime and 78% had no history of criminal activity. What is more concerning is that the study also found that those who reported more intrusive police contact experienced increased trauma and anxiety symptoms. Furthermore, those who reported fair treatment during encounters with law enforcement had fewer symptoms of PTSD and anxiety.

What Is Racial Trauma?

In addition to the mental health symptoms of individuals who have encounters with law enforcement, those who witness these events directly or indirectly may also be impacted negatively. In an attempt to capture how racism and discrimination negatively impacts the physical and mental health of people of color, many scholars have coined the term "racial trauma" or race-based traumatic stress. Racial trauma may result from racial harassment, witnessing racial violence, or experiencing institutional racism (Bryant-Davis & Ocampo, 2006; Comas-Díaz, 2016). The trauma may result in experiencing symptoms of depression, anxiety, low self-esteem, feelings of humiliation, poor concentration, or irritability.

Effects of Racial Trauma on Communities of Color

Decades of research have noted the impact of discrimination and racism on the psychological health of communities of color (e.g., Bryant-Davis & Ocampo, 2006; Carter & Forsyth, 2009; Comas-Díaz, 2016). Although

not everyone who experiences racism and discrimination will develop symptoms of race-based trauma, repeated exposure may lead to the following. According to a report on *The Impact of Racial Trauma on African Americans*, Dr. Walter Smith notes the following effects of racial trauma:

Increased vigilance and suspicion – Suspicion of social institutions (schools, agencies, government), avoiding eye contact, only trusting persons within our social and family relationship networks

Increased sensitivity to threat – Defensive postures, avoiding new situations, heightened sensitivity to being disrespected and shamed, and avoid taking risks

Increased psychological and physiological symptoms – Unresolved traumas increase chronic stress and decrease immune system functioning, shift brains to limbic system dominance, increase risks for depression and anxiety disorders, and disrupt child development and quality of emotional attachment in family and social relationships

Increased alcohol and drug usage – Drugs and alcohol are initially useful (real and perceived) in managing the pain and danger of unresolved traumas but become their own disease processes when dependency occurs

Increased aggression – Street gangs, domestic violence, defiant behavior, and appearing tough and impenetrable are ways of coping with danger by attempting to control our physical and social environment

Narrowing sense of time – Persons living in a chronic state of danger do not develop a sense of future, do not have long-term goals, and frequently view dying as an expected outcome

Coping With Racial Trauma

Racial trauma or race-based trauma often goes unnoticed. These hidden wounds that adults and youth of color experience are worn like invisible weights. Hardy (2013) provides the following eight steps to heal after experiencing racial injustices in our community.

1. **Affirmation and Acknowledgement:** This involves professionals helping the individual to develop a sense of understanding acceptance of racial issues. This step is important because it opens the door for us to dialogue about issues related to race.

2. **Create Space for Race:** Creating space allows an open dialogue with our communities about race. Hardy notes that we must take a proactive role to identify race as a significant variable and talk openly about experiences related to race.

3. **Racial Storytelling:** Gives individuals an outlet to share personal experiences and think critically about events in their lives. This provides an opportunity to hear others voice how they have been treated differently due to their race and it helps expose hidden wounds through storytelling.

4. **Validation:** Can be seen as a personalized tool used to counter devaluation. This provides confirmation of the individuals' worth and their redeemable qualities.

5. **The Process of Naming:** With the scarcity of research on the effects of racial trauma on mental health, there is of course no name as of yet making it a nameless condition. This in turn increases the doubt and uncertainty. By naming these experiences we give individuals a voice to speak on them and also recognize how they impact them. If we apply a mental health condition, individuals may experience symptoms similar to post-traumatic stress disorder (PTSD).

6. **Externalize Devaluation:** The aim for this step is to have people focus on increasing respect and recognizing that racial events do not lower their self-worth.

7. **Counteract Devaluation:** This step uses a combination of psychological, emotional, and behavioral resources to build self-esteem and counter racial attacks. This helps prevent future loss of dignity and sense of self.

8. **Rechanneling Rage:** By rechanneling rage, individuals can learn to gain control of their emotions and not let emotions consume them. This is an important step because it empowers people to keep pushing forward after adversity. This may include taking steps to engage in activism or self-care strategies such as spending time with family.

Source: Erlanger & Richardson (2016).

INTRODUCTION AND DEFINITIONS

When we are able to work, play, love, and handle the challenges that life throws our way, we enjoy a sense of well-being, contentment, competence, peace, and perhaps even happiness. Although most of us experience times when we feel down, overwhelmed, upset, or disappointed, the extent to which difficult emotions, thoughts, or behaviors interfere with our ability to function may reflect difficulties and problems in adaptation and mental health. In this chapter, we consider issues of well-being and health for African Americans. The opening story highlights how events such as police shootings interrupt and interfere with the well-being of African Americans.

In this chapter, we examine the psychosocial adaptation of African Americans. This includes an overview of definitions and conceptual perspectives on well-being, as well as conceptual and theoretical models of adjustment and maladaptation. We then examine empirical perspectives on the mental health of African Americans and methodological issues relevant to adjustment, including assessment. We also consider ways in which African Americans respond to problems in adaptation, including their use of mental health services and the ways in which these services can be provided most effectively. The chapter then reviews some evidence-based interventions and ends with a critical analysis and chapter summary.

Definitions, Perspectives, and Historical Context

Mental health is defined by the World Health Organization (WHO) as a state of well-being in which every person realizes his or her own potential, can cope with the normal stresses of life, can work productively, and is able to make a contribution in his or her community (WHO, n.d.). The *Diagnostic and Statistical Manual of Mental Disorders, Fifth Edition* (DSM-V, 2013) defines a mental disorder as a clinically significant behavioral or psychological syndrome or pattern that occurs in an individual and that is associated with present distress (e.g., a painful symptom) or disability (i.e., impairment in one or more important areas of functioning) or with a significantly increased risk of suffering death, pain, disability, or an important loss of freedom (American Psychiatric Association, 2013). In the United States, the DSM-V is the primary classification system used by professionals to understand mental illness and psychological maladaptation This system, grounded in the medical model, is based on illness concepts and defines psychological dysfunctions as deviations from a state of health.

Other theoreticians have articulated African-centered perspectives on mental health and adaptation. For example, Azibo (1989) writes,

> Mental health is the achievement in the psychological and behavioral spheres of life of a functioning that (a) is in harmony with and (b) embraces the natural order . . . [and is] that psychological and behavioral functioning that is in accord with the basic nature of the original human nature and its attendant cosmology and survival thrust. (pp. 176–177)

Rather than a focus emphasizing mental "illness" (from a health or medical model perspective), the focus, from an African-centered perspective, is on mental "order" and "disorder." Azibo criticizes the Eurocentric perspective for its lack of a conceptually and theoretically grounded articulation of the concepts of mental health. Grounded in the African cosmological principle of *Anokwalei Enyo* ("two relative truths"; Wobogo, as cited in Azibo, 1989), Azibo writes that mental order and disorder must be seen in relation to one another. Azibo further emphasizes the importance of the self and survival; one's sense of communal self and the acknowledgment of the role of cultural values are important in understanding mental health and personal adjustment. Mental order is considered "correct psychological and behavioral functioning" (Azibo, 1989, p. 179) that is congruent with the natural order, universal forces, and God. Another important concept in Azibo's model is mentacide, the process by which individuals lose their psychological Blackness.

Mentacide has been defined as the intentional destruction of an ethnic group's collective mind or the oppressive imposition of another culture as a means of dominating the oppressed group. Mentacide includes forms that affect peripheral aspects of the self (i.e., major depression, generalized anxiety, or eating disorders) or that are alienating in nature (i.e., that undermine an individual's psychological sense of his or her ethnicity).

Based on results from a qualitative study of 117 college-age, adult, and older adult African Americans, Edwards (1999) provides a hierarchy of dimensions that define the "essential characteristics of a psychologically healthy African American/Black person" (p. 306). Starting with the most important one, the dimensions of African American psychological health are the following:

Ideological/Beliefs: Possessing a sense of spirituality, including the need for a belief in God and being in touch with a greater power or Supreme Being; having a strong cultural identity, and being proud of one's cultural heritage; being practical and having common sense

Moral Worth: Showing self-respect, positive self-esteem, demonstrating a sense of honesty, and responsibility and being true to oneself and others; expressing true respect and compassion for others

Interpersonal Style: Communicating and interacting well with others to develop, maintain and strengthen healthy relationships; being assertive and able to demonstrate respect for others while still expressing oneself and one's true feelings

Competence: Having capacities such as intelligence, being flexible and resilient, pursuing educational growth, and possessing skills to survive

Determination: Being determined and demonstrating the capacity for will power and self-control, including being goal oriented

Unity: Maintaining or possessing a sense of inner peace; having good self-knowledge and understanding; striving to be one's best

Health/Physical: Being in good physical health, including having a healthy diet, taking care of one's appearance and appreciating one's own sense of beauty (pp. 292–293)

This list is congruent with many of the core African-centered values of spirituality, communalism, a relational orientation, and interdependence. (See Chapter 2 for a more detailed discussion of these core values). We next turn to a brief review of mental illness in Africa.

Mental Illness in Africa

While there is a great deal of diversity on the continent, mental health is often not discussed in African cultures nor is treatment for mental illness sought. A shortage of mental health professionals also contributes to the lack of treatment. Even individuals experiencing high levels of trauma, such as those affected by Ebola and HIV, may not receive necessary mental health treatment (Reardon, 2015). The majority of published studies on mental illness has been conducted in South Africa, with a modest number of studies carried out in Nigeria and Ghana. Many of these studies have examined mental health prevalence and outcomes of persons living with HIV, especially those conducted in southern Africa.

Lay Persons' Beliefs About the Causes of Mental Illness

Many people in Africa believe that the cause of mental illness is supernatural and characterized by having evil spirits and being a victim of witchcraft (Abbo, Okello, Ekblad, Waako, & Musisi, 2008; Makanjuola et al., 2016). These beliefs are not only indigenous to African cultures but also seen in many other countries. Knettel (2016) surveyed English-speaking scholars in psychology from 65 different countries, asking the question, "What beliefs do people from this country hold about the causes of mental illness?" He found large differences between regions. Countries in the Latin America/Caribbean, sub-Saharan Africa, North Africa/Middle East, and South Asia regions all rated high on people believing in supernatural causes of mental illness. Canada and the United States and countries in regions such as Europe and Central Asia, as well as Russia, Australia, and New Zealand, rated supernatural causes much lower and were more likely to believe that the causes of mental illness were related to heredity and social stress.

An example of a study on beliefs about supernatural causation of mental illness is one conducted by Campbell et al. (2017). Two hundred South African Xhosa people with schizophrenia were interviewed using a structured clinical interview protocol (Campbell et al., 2017). The authors found that the majority of participants (N = 125) believed that their mental illness was brought about by being bewitched by others because of jealousy. The authors note that this explanation is consistent with the understanding of jealousy-induced witchcraft in some southern African communities.

Africans who have higher levels of self-stigma regarding mental illness are more likely to believe it is caused by supernatural forces. Makanjuola et al. (2016) explored stigma beliefs and supernatural causes of mental illness in three African countries, Nigeria, Ghana, and Kenya. Participants were diagnosed with psychosis and were judged to be well enough to participate in the study. Individuals who held high stigma about their mental illness were more likely to ascribe a supernatural cause to their illness (e.g., evil spirits, witchcraft).

Stigma

Research shows that in most African countries, there is widespread stigma against persons with mental illness. In a study of over 2,400 community participants in the Yoruba-speaking parts of Nigeria, a survey found that 96.5% believed that people with mental illness were dangerous and violent (Gureje, O., Lasebikan V., Ephraim-Oluwanuga, O., Olley, B., & Kola, L. 2005). Most community members did not want to even have basic social interaction with a mentally ill person. Another study conducted in Nigeria also found that 61% of respondents desired a high level of social distance from a person with a mental illness (Adewuya & Makanjuola, 2008). Barke, Nyarko, and Klecha (2011) interviewed 203 participants from urban regions in Ghana about stigma. They also interviewed 105 patients who were recruited from psychiatric hospitals. High levels of stigma existed in the general population, and patients also reported experiencing high levels of stigma. Higher levels of education were correlated with less stigma.

Treatment

There are many barriers to mental health treatment in Africa. At the same time, many African organizations are working to identify culturally appropriate ways to treat individuals with mental illnesses. As discussed, one barrier to treatment is stigma. Musyimi et al. (2017) convened focus groups of community health workers and traditional and faith healers in Kenya to discuss mental health and illness. Challenges identified included mistrust of health providers, cultural misunderstandings, and stigma related to mental illness. Other barriers included the lack of infrastructure for mental health programs and other resource barriers.

National programs to address mental illness require leadership and coordination at the national, regional, and district level for routine monitoring of mental health care, ways to increase mental health service utilization, ways in which to address sigma (Hanlon et al., 2017), and training of community health workers (Tilahun et al., 2017). Deinstitutionalization of persons with mental illness and integration into the community are strategies considered in South Africa (Sunkel, 2014).

While mental illness is not as stigmatized by African Americans to the extent it is by Africans, stigma toward mental illness exists and remains an ongoing concern with respect to access to mental health care for African Americans (Hunter et al., 2017). Ward, Wiltshire, Detry, and Brown (2013) conducted a study using a community-based sample of 272 African Americans ages 25–72. Respondents believed that having mental illness results in negative consequences, with women being more likely to hold this belief than men. Respondents reported major concern about stigma but some level of openness to seeking help.

Stigma is a barrier to seeking mental health services in the United States as in Africa. Clement et al. (2015) conducted a systematic review of 144 qualitative and quantitative studies, which had 90,189 participants. The authors found that stigma had a higher effect on mental health-seeking behaviors for African Americans and other racial and ethnic minorities than Whites. Stigma was associated with feelings of shame and embarrassment. The qualitative studies with African American participants indicated that they were more likely to include themes such as "weak," "keeping it within the family," and "nondisclosure."

Finally, stigma is related to parental willingness or intention to seek care. African American parents reported higher stigma-related beliefs about seeking mental health care for their children and less positive attitudes about mental health care (Turner, Jensen-Doss, & Heffer, 2015).

THEORETICAL PERSPECTIVES ON PSYCHOLOGICAL ADAPTATION AND DYSFUNCTION AMONG AFRICAN AMERICANS

Several schools of thought have been utilized within American psychology to understand and intervene with behavior that is viewed as maladaptive. More recently, more integrative models of psychology have evolved that underline the interaction of human systems in understanding adaptation and maladaptation.

In the psychological traditions of western Europe, psychological maladjustment has been viewed from multiple theoretical frameworks. In the Western tradition, there are developmental models that emphasize deviations from a "normal" sequence of maturation or skill development. These perspectives consider maladaptation as a lag in or arrest from acquiring the abilities or skills that an individual is expected to achieve during a specific developmental period. For example, Freud viewed psychological dysfunction as an arrested development in an individual's expected progression through normal stages of psychosexual development. These problems in development most often result in the use of maladaptive strategies (e.g., defense mechanisms) in response to the distress or anxiety generated because of competing internal and external stressors.

Other views of maladaptive psychological functioning include behavioral perspectives from the early work of Skinner, Pavlov, and Watson. Behavioral perspectives define psychological dysfunction as the set of undesirable (to the individual in his or her social context) behaviors. Dysfunction is based on the learning and maintenance of maladaptive behavioral responses through reinforcement, association (e.g., classical conditioning), or modeling. Behavioral perspectives utilize comparisons of individuals' behaviors to age norms or averages. For example, the Child Behavior Checklist (Achenbach & Edelbrock, 1984) is an instrument used to examine behavioral problems in children and adolescents and is based on comparing reports made by parents, teachers, or children/adolescents of how frequently a young person engages in a specific behavior (e.g., lying) with how often other children of that individual's similar age and gender engage in that behavior.

Those who hold a humanistic perspective (e.g., Rogers and Maslow) view maladaptation as rising from the conflicts individuals experience in trying to meet their needs and the conflicts they might experience between their view of themselves (i.e., their actual or "real" self) and the person that they believe they should be (i.e., their "ideal" self). In contrast, family system theories view individuals as part of a system (i.e., the family) and see psychological problems in an individual as stemming from ineffective strategies and problems in the ways that the family functions and interacts.

In conceptualizing psychological dysfunction among African Americans, several authors have used European models as a point of departure. Building on the psychodynamic tradition, Welsing (1991) emphasizes the role and importance of symbolism. For example, Welsing suggests that the shape, color, and size of balls used in American sports, as well as weapons (e.g., guns, missiles) and historical monuments, reflect psychodynamic and symbolic issues that have deeper racial and sexual implications. (For a broader discussion of Black–White issues incorporating a psychodynamic perspective, also see Fanon, 1967.)

Hayes (1982), building on behavioral perspectives, describes Radical Black Behaviorism, which proposes that the American context acts as a Skinnerian box within which many African Americans do not emit behaviors that elicit rewards from those who control resources. Consequently, many African Americans experience deprivation in the form of barriers and are denied access to food, education, and employment, or they receive minimal reinforcement. This is because those controlling positive consequences do not value and appreciate behaviors relevant to African American culture, and African Americans are not socialized or enculturated to engage in behaviors valued by Whites.

Biopsychosocial Perspective on Adaptation

Biopsychosocial perspectives emphasize the interaction of biological, psychological, and social systems in our understanding of an individual's behavioral, emotional, and cognitive functioning. A behavioral problem (i.e., a psychological symptom) may be rooted in a genetic vulnerability (i.e., a biological factor), which may or may not be exacerbated by an environmental condition (e.g., higher levels of stressful experiences because of social stratification, limited access to resources).

An example of this work can be found in the literature on African Americans and stress and coping. Lazarus and Folkman (1984) define stress as the experience of threat, loss, or challenge by individuals when they perceive that they do not have the personal resources to respond to the demands they are facing. Coping is defined as the emotional, behavioral, and cognitive strategies and responses used by a person in response to these demands. One's experience of stress is related to both one's cognitive perception of an event or circumstance as causing threat, loss, or challenge (i.e., primary appraisal) and one's sense of whether one has enough resources with which to respond to the demand (secondary appraisal).

Research has shown the importance of biological factors in understanding the mental health of African Americans. Odgerel, Talati, Hamilton, Levinson, and Weissman's (2013) considered serotonin-related genetic variations that might underlie ethnic differences in the diagnosis of depression between African Americans and Whites. Analyses were based on data from a community sample including 954 African Americans and 2,622 European Americans participating in the National Institute of Mental Health Molecular Genetics of Schizophrenia Study. African Americans had lower frequencies of the S allele and SS genotype at 5-HTTLPR and higher rates of the G allele at rs25531 than Whites. The S allele has been associated with a smaller amygdala, which is theorized to be related to more limited or weaker signaling to moderate or lessen fear responses.

Brody et al. (2014) examined a sample of 331 rural African American adolescents from the South to look at allostatic load, a concept reflecting the demand on an individual's biological system. Allostatic load was measured using a composite score based on indicators including overnight cortisol, epinephrine and norepinephrine, resting blood pressure, and a measure of system inflammation. Youth were followed from age 16 to 18. Youth who had high stable perceptions of discrimination had higher levels of allostatic load at age 20. This effect was buffered by the availability of emotional support.

Stress Among African Americans

Research using the stress and coping model has found that as a group, African Americans experience higher levels of stress than Whites (e.g., Askenasy, Dohrenwend, & Dohrenwend, 1977; Bennett et al., 2004; Utsey & Hook, 2007) and that both race and socioeconomic status contribute to stress experiences. In addition, race and socioeconomic status may interact such that African Americans at lower levels of socioeconomic status are at higher risk of negative stress-related outcomes (Ulbrich, Warheit, & Zimmerman, 1989).

African Americans may also have high levels of stressful life experiences linked directly to individual and specific experiences of overt racism. Landrine and Klonoff (1996b) developed the Schedule of Racist Events to measure an individual's exposure to such experiences. This 18-item inventory assesses how often respondents have experienced racist events (e.g., "How many times have you been treated unfairly by people in service jobs [store clerks, waiters, bartenders, bank tellers, and others] because you are Black?") over the past year and in their lifetime. The authors found that African American adults who reported greater exposure to racist events were more likely to report higher levels of smoking, health problems, and stress-related symptoms (e.g., depression, anxiety, interpersonal sensitivity). A meta-analysis by Pascoe and Smart Richman (2009) found perceived discrimination to predict poorer health and mental health outcomes across all ethnic and gender groups.

In addition to overt experiences of racism, African Americans may also experience what is referred to as *mundane extreme stress* (Peters & Massey, 1983). This is stress that is attributed to the chronic and often subtle daily experiences of bias, discrimination, and racism. Using data from the National Survey of American Life, Keith, Lincoln, Taylor, and Jackson (2010) found experiences of discrimination to predict depressive symptoms among African American women. Schwartz and Meyer's (2010) review of stress and mental health notes that although among African Americans elevated levels of stress predict higher levels of mental disorder and African Americans tend to experience higher levels of stress, there are limited differences in mental disorders between racial groups.

In conceptualizing work with diverse ethnic groups, including African Americans, Slavin et al. (1991) proposed an adaptation of Lazarus and Folkman's model that considers the explicit role of culture in the experience of stress. These authors suggest that culture may be important in shaping the experience of stress at each step of the stress and coping process. This may involve cultural variations in the ways that events are perceived. For example, someone who is African American may believe an event is occurring because of his or her race and ethnicity. Culture may also shape the types of coping resources to which an individual has access or that an individual decides to use. For example, African Americans may be more likely than members of other cultural groups to use fictive kin as coping resources (Stack, 1974). Culture may also shape the specific types of outcomes that are linked to stress exposure. For example, African Americans are overrepresented among individuals suffering from a range of stress-related diseases (e.g., heart disease and stroke; see Chapter 12).

Research has examined the role of microaggressions and their relationship to the mental health of African Americans. Sue and Constantine (2007) define microaggressions as brief, commonplace, and subtle insults and indignities that convey negative or denigrating messages to people of color. Nadal, Griffin, Wong, Hamit, and Rasmus (2014) examined the experience of microaggressions in a racially diverse sample of 506 people ranging in age from 18 to 66; 15.8% were African Americans, 12% were White, 25.9% were Latino/a, and 31% were Asian. Participants were recruited from an undergraduate psychology class or via community websites and online e-mail groups. African Americans, Latinos, and Asians reported higher levels of microaggressions than White respondents. African Americans reported experiencing greater assumptions of inferiority and school and workplace microaggressions and microinvalidations (messages that exclude or negate the reality of racial/ethnic minorities; Sue & Constantine, 2007) than Asians or Whites. African Americans also reported experiencing more second-class citizenship and assumptions of criminality than Asians, Whites, or Latinos. Microaggressions were inversely related to positive emotions.

Homes, schools, and communities may be stressful environments for African American youth, leading to mental health problems, including anger, aggression, and depression (Brady, Winston III, & Gockley, 2014). Brady et al. identified several stressors within the home, school, and community that impact the well-being of African American youth. Financial strain and stressors and inadequate support for parents in the home, especially in the case of single-parent-headed households, affects well-being of children in the home. Community stressors include the lack of social and economic resources that undermine community cohesion and collective efficacy, while generating neighborhood disorder and mistrust between residents. School stressors include safety threats and systematic discrimination and bias that lowers academic expectations and achievement and increases disciplinary actions. While noting these stressors, Brady et al. also discussed protective factors that can attenuate the impact of negative stressful family, school, and community factors on well-being of youth. These include factors such as community stability, high ethnic identity, and positive parenting practices.

African-Centered Perspectives on Adaptation

In addition to the Africentric perspective presented earlier in Azibo's definition of mental order and disorder, several Africentric theorists have provided conceptualizations of psychological adaptation and maladaptation. For example, Myers (1991,

1992) writes that an African worldview is an optimal worldview that not only promotes an individual's well-being but also provides a scientific and therapeutic perspective on psychological adjustment that supports optimal human functioning at both individual and societal levels. (See Chapter 2 for additional information on the optimal worldview).

Azibo's Model of Mental Health and Disorder

Azibo's (1989) model of mental health and disorder takes *"the Black perspective* (cultural, historical, and conceptual analysis that employs and affirms principles deriving from the African social reality) *as the conceptual base for addressing the psychology of African people"* (emphasis in original). His definition assumes that "personality has a biogenetic basis" (p. 175) and that there is a natural order to all things. Azibo operates from a "meta-personality" perspective that articulates three levels or components of a racially (i.e., genetically) based human personality. The "inner core" includes physical or biological factors, such as spirituality, melanin, and rhythm. The "outer core" consists of cognitive components, such as attitudes, values, and beliefs, as well as the behavioral manifestations of these components. Azibo also identifies a third core of "nonracial" aspects of personality. These are peripheral individual differences, such as shyness and assertiveness.

Azibo (1989) provides an alternative conceptual model of maladaptation for African Americans that includes "psychological misorientation," a basic Black personality disorder that results from an individual operating without an African belief system. Azibo (2014) defines misorientation as

(a) interpreting and negotiating reality or proceeding in the world with that part of one's individual consciousness that determines his or her psychological Africanity (racial identity) being bereft of cognitions and lacking ideation that would orient him or her toward prioritizing own-race maintenance and, most importantly, (b) the person's cognitive structure/ideational mechanism, i.e., constellation of beliefs, values, attitudes, and so forth is composed of concepts opposed to or incongruous with African-centricity in thinking and behaving. (p. 48)

When misorientation is present, there is incongruence between a person's biological-genetic base and that person's behavior and cognition.

According to Azibo (2013), misorientation is a precursor to another African American personality disorder—materialism depression. Materialism depression is a sense of relative deprivation and need for possessions to support one's sense of self. Materialistic depression is defined as "An orientation that values and emphasizes money, being fashionable, good looks, and being personally connected to all that . . . . Because of the sheer prevalence in Euro-American social reality of materialism and individualism orientations, it is plausible that the acquisition by U.S. Africans of materialism and individualism orientations is likely, perhaps even inescapable" (Azibo, 2006, pp. 19, 24). Azibo identifies several symptoms of materialist depression: wanting a lifestyle that one cannot afford, engaging in crime to obtain money to buy material things, desiring status symbols and items of conspicuous consumption, and feeling ashamed of oneself, family, or community because of poverty.

Azibo writes that misorientation and mentacide may play a role in a range of personal identity conflicts (e.g., individualism and anxiety over one's collective identity); reactionary disorders (e.g., psychological brainwashing, burnout, oppression violence reactions), as described by Fanon (1963); self-destructive disorders (e.g., suicide, prostitution, drug and alcohol abuse, Black-on-Black crime), as described by Akbar (1981); and theological (i.e., religious) misorientation (e.g., adherence to a religious system in conflict with one's culture and ethnicity), as described by Azibo (1989). It is important to note that mentacide may occur without misorientation. For example, persons may suffer problems in psychological adaptation from the process of mentacide (e.g., developing a generalized anxiety disorder associated with life stress) without being misoriented (i.e., the individual would still have a "correct" Black cognitive orientation). Discussions of this system for describing adaptive and nonadaptive mental health among African Americans are consistent with this earlier work (Azibo, 2008, 2014).

Extending this perspective, Abdullah (1998) discusses disorders such as "mammyism" as a subcategory of psychological misorientation. Mammyism involves the dysfunctional assumption of caretaking behaviors and roles by African American women to the detriment of themselves and their own families and social networks.

Akbar's Perspectives on Mental Disorder

Akbar (1981) articulated a classic nosology of mental disorders based on the premise that a pathological society (i.e., a social system that incorporates racism, oppression, and unnaturalness) leads to four types of disorders: (a) self-destructive (described earlier), (b) alien-self, (c) anti-self, and (d) organic. Within the alien-self disorder, individuals behave in ways that do not support their survival. Akbar indicates that individuals may manifest this disorder through neurotic anxiety and identity disturbances, such as low self-esteem. A person with an anti-self disorder identifies with and has internalized the majority culture's negative stereotypes and pejorative attitudes regarding Blacks. Anti-self individuals express overt and covert hostility toward their own group. Akbar argues that organic disorders (e.g., hypertension, schizophrenia) may also be related to pathological social processes and linked to anti- and alien-self disturbances.

Race and Culture in Psychotherapy

Several psychotherapists have conceptualized models for understanding, and improving mental health interventions provided to African Americans. There are several treatment options and factors involving race, culture, and ethnicity that may play a role in African Americans' experience of psychotherapy.

Early work by Kardiner and Ovesey (1951) and Grier and Cobbs (1968) emphasized the negative impact of racism on the adaptation and functioning of African Americans. Advocates have called for improved mental health services for African Americans and members of other racial and ethnic groups because of the perceived "cultural encapsulation" of available mental health services. Cultural encapsulation involves the chauvinistic and inflexible use of a worldview or set of cultural values incongruent with the client group being served. These incompatible values are used to interpret behavior and enact treatment without the awareness, appreciation, or skill sets in the therapist to consider the role that culture may play in the therapeutic process. These perspectives are based on etic (i.e., universal) assumptions that everyone is similar in their display of behaviors related to psychosocial functioning and that therapeutic change processes are identical and equally effective across different cultural groups.

Boyd-Franklin's work with African American clients emphasizes the culturally shaped social contexts of Blacks and is based on a multisystem model of psychotherapy. Boyd-Franklin (1989) proposes that therapeutic work with African Americans should focus on the family. Therapy with African American families should involve work across multiple systems, including the individual; the "real" (i.e., the functional as opposed to nuclear or biological) family and household; the extended and nonblood family; and Church, community, and social service organizations. Boyd-Franklin suggests that the treatment process is circular, involving (a) joining and engaging the family, (b) initial assessment of the family, (c) problem solving, (d) family prescriptions and assignments, (e) information gathering through completing a family genogram (i.e., a family tree), and (f) work to "restructure" the family.

Barrera, Castro, Strycker, and Toobert (2013) note that there can be cultural adaptations of mental health interventions to make the interventions more relevant for African Americans. These adaptations involve five stages: information gathering (e.g., literature reviews, qualitative research with key informants), preliminary design (e.g., gathering input from key informants on draft materials), preliminary testing (e.g., involving staff training, pilot studies), refinement (integrating feedback from pilots), and conducting final trials (which may involve tests for mediation or interaction with respect to participant characteristics). Results from Barrera and colleagues' review also indicate that in more cases, culturally enhanced interventions demonstrate better outcomes than usual care or controls.

Therapeutic Interventions With African American Children

Research also supports the importance of identity and cultural factors to adjustment during childhood and adolescence. Yasui, Dorham, and Dishion (2004) found that ethnic identity is important to the adjustment of African American adolescents. Mandara, Gaylord-Harden, Richards, and Ragsdale (2009) found ethnic identity to be associated with lower levels of depressive symptoms in African American adolescents. The role of culture and identity may consequently be important in psychotherapeutic interventions.

Forehand and Kotchick (2016) note the importance of considering cultural factors in parent training, which has been demonstrated to be effective in reducing child behavior problems. For African Americans, these authors state that parent training should consider the communal nature of parenting; strict discipline; transmission of cultural values involving perseverance, independence, positive racial identity, and respect for authority. Parents should also address the role of religion.

Other groups have developed and evaluated parenting programs specifically geared toward African American parents and families. For example, the Center for the Improvement of Child Caring (CICC) has developed the Effective Black Parenting Program (n.d.), which focuses on enhancing the parenting dimension of warmth and positive control for parents of children ages 2 to 18. Evaluations have reported reductions in parents' subtle forms of rejection and in children's delinquent behavior. In addition, the Black Parenting Strengths and Strategies Program–Child (BPSS-C) is a parenting intervention that incorporates African American culture and racial socialization practices (Coard, Foy-Watson, Zimmer, & Wallace, 2007). In a randomized control trial, intervention parents showed increases in positive parenting and reductions in harsh discipline, as well as declines in parent-reported externalizing behaviors.

Bratton et al. (2013) describe the use of child-centered play therapy (CCPT) in a sample of 54 low-income preschool children with disruptive behaviors participating in early Head Start. The sample was 42% African Americans, 39% Hispanic, and 18% White. As an intervention, CCPT allows children the "freedom to direct their play and fully express their inner world within the limits of a safe and predictable therapeutic relationship characterized by empathy, genuineness and unconditional positive regard" (p. 30). Intervention participants received on average 20 sessions (two times a week for 30 minutes). Within the intervention group, 21 of 27 improved from clinical to nonclinical levels and normal levels of disruptive behavior compared with 5 of 27 in the control group.

Ethnicity and Psychopharmacology

Medication therapy for psychiatric disorders is another treatment option; information on this treatment option is useful in examining ethnic and racial factors in mental health treatment and outcomes. Moore and Mattison (2017) examined percentages of the adult population aged 18 to 85 who took psychiatric drugs, including (1) antidepressants; (2) anxiolytics, sedatives, and hypnotics; and (3) antipsychotics. Over 16.7% of adults in the United States filled one or more prescriptions for psychiatric drugs in the United States. Large differences in psychiatric drug use were found among racial and ethnic groups. The authors found that 20.8% of White adults, 9.7% of Black adults, 8.7% of Hispanic adults, and 4.8% of Asian adults used a psychiatric drug. These differences in medication use raise questions as to why these ethnic differences exist. Are members of some cultural groups more wary of psychopharmacological treatments? Are physicians less likely to provide access to medication for certain ethnic group clients?

Research has also suggested that there may be race-related biogenetic factors that underlie specific differential responses to medication (Rothe, Pumariega, & Rogers, 2008). Cultural factors, including diet and behavior, also play roles in the metabolism and effect of certain psychotropic medications. In a naturalistic study of adolescents receiving care for treatment of schizophrenia, Patel et al. (2006) found African American youth to demonstrate a significant decline in total, internalizing, and externalizing scores on the Child Behavior Checklist at the 90-day follow-up in response to risperidone, an antipsychotic medication. Improvements in internalizing persisted at 1- and 2-year follow-ups. In contrast, for Whites, there were no significant differences at follow up.

Grossman et al. (2008) examined genetic variations in metabolism relative to effectiveness, dosing, and side effects of five antipsychotic medications in a sample of clients with chronic schizophrenia, including Whites and African Americans. For one of the five medications, African Americans with a lower activity variant of a drug-metabolizing enzyme (the FMO3 gene) experienced a significant elevation of adverse drug reactions, but largely, the research found no or minimal effects of genetic variations in drug effects.

Acculturation Model and Mental Health Treatment

Berry and colleagues (Berry, 1980; Berry & Kim, 1988) suggest that a client's level of acculturation can play an important role in his or her experience of mental health services. Berry argues that acculturation can be viewed as a series of stages with multiple outcomes. The first phase is that of precontact, when each culture is independent and has its own unique characteristics. In the contact phase, different cultural groups begin to interact with one another. This is followed by a conflict stage, during which pressure is exerted on the minority group to accommodate to the majority group behaviors and values. In the crisis phase, this conflict comes to a head. The final phase, adaptation, involves the two groups stabilizing their interactions (or lack thereof) into one of several modes of acculturation.

These resolutions may involve assimilation, a status where one group gives up its cultural practices and assumes the cultural practices of the majority group, or integration, where the minority group retains its own cultural practices but also participates in the cultural practices and social world of the majority group. Other modes of acculturation include separation, a status where groups choose not to interact with one another, and segregation, a status where the minority group is forcibly separated from social interaction with the majority group. There may also be accommodation, such that there are changes in the cultural practice of the majority group to include some of the practices of the minority group. When this occurs and there is some sense of merging and balance in the integration of the cultures, this is considered a fusion of the cultures. Finally, in a status of marginalization, an individual or group does not engage in the cultural practices of either the majority or minority group and is effectively excluded from these social worlds.

Berry (Berry, 1980; Berry & Kim, 1988) suggests that the stages of intercultural contact and modes of acculturation have an important impact on cultural group functioning and use of services and are reflected in assumptions of both the client and the therapist. A therapist can use the acculturation framework to better understand how an individual has organized the role of ethnicity in his or her life, how acculturation may have played a role in the individual's dysfunction, and how acculturation can play a role in interventions to improve functioning. For example, a therapist might work to understand the level and experience of engagement and support an African American client has with networks in the community, at work, and with family and peers to gain a sense of the individual's possible marginalization or his or her loss of culturally based coping strategies.

Ethnic Validity Model and Mental Health Treatment

The ethnic validity model of Tyler, Brome, and Williams (1991) has also been used as a framework to understand therapeutic encounters. This model suggests that therapeutic encounters can involve the interaction between culture-defining group members and non-culture-defining group members. Different types of pairings (e.g., a culture-defining group therapist with a non-culture-defining group client, a non-culture-defining group therapist with a non-culture-defining group client) have the potential to result in different types of gains and losses, advantages and disadvantages. For example, when an African American therapist works with an African American client (i.e., a non-culture-defining group therapist with a non-culture-defining group client), either could assume that they are operating from a shared cultural perspective or worldview, but this may not be true. Consider the pairing of a therapist working from an African-centered perspective with a client who views his or her ethnic group membership negatively or sees this group membership as unimportant. Tyler et al. (1991) suggest that this type of pairing illustrates that race (i.e., the physical characteristics associated with racial group membership) may tell us very little about more proximal factors (e.g., similarity in values, respect for differences in cultural values) that may be more important in effective therapy. Use of this model can assist therapists in avoiding assumptions about clients.

Related work by Helms and colleagues further suggests that client racial identity attitudes are related to preference for race of therapist (Parham & Helms, 1981) and emotional reactions to therapeutic experiences (Richardson & Helms, 1994). An individual who is at the pre-encounter stage may not have a preference or may prefer a different race clinician, while a client in the immersion stage may have a strong preference for a same-race therapist. (For discussion of pre-encounter and immersion stages, see Chapter 3). Given ethnic and racial differences in response to race of therapist, there is a need for more African American psychologists and mental health professionals (see Chapter 1).

African Therapeutic Practices

In contrast to American service delivery models, Maiello (1999), a White, Western psychotherapist, describes the work of a South African healer, a *sangoma*. This description involves the successful traditional healing of a young man who had experienced confusion, hallucination, stereotypic movement, and loss of reality contact. The *sangoma*'s treatment involved the young man coming to live with the healer, day and night, for two-and-a-half weeks, so the *sangoma* could observe him, to understand what was "not right" with him. The *sangoma* then prepared an appropriate *muthi* (medicine) for the patient to drink. Another *muthi* was applied to the patient's legs "to prevent the patient from running away from the therapy," and a third *muthi* was placed in the patient's nose and ears during sleep to stop the patient from hearing "his own stuff" and to bring him back to hearing and listening to his fellow human beings (Maiello, 1999, p. 245).

> One day . . . he gets up and recognizes you. This is the beginning of the last phase of treatment, which is given during daytime. From the moment when the patient can hear and recognize another person again, he must go back to work. The therapy becomes verbal, but the words remain closely related to concrete external reality. . . . [The *sangoma*] worked with him, day by day, until he was "right" again, that is, until objects and names, words and actions matched as they had done before the illness. (pp. 221–222)

Research on African-centered perspectives on mental health and adaptation underline the role of culture and the importance of indigenous healers in psychotherapeutic interventions. Tsa-Tsala (1997) suggests that conceptions of health and disease from an African perspective reflect a holistic perspective, encompassing an understanding of a world where wellness is a matter of harmony. In contrast, disharmony has ancestral, intergenerational, and spiritual genesis, as well as social and communal implications. As noted earlier, there are also lay beliefs of supernatural causation of mental illness, which prompt alternative treatment.

Research has noted the complementarity and similarity between professional and traditional healing practices, and these examinations stress the importance of including traditional and religious healing practices, which may often involve herbal remedies (Madu, Baguma, & Pritz, 2000). For example, Ojelade, McCray, Ashby, and Meyers (2011) describe the therapeutic use of Ifá.

As a worldview and practice, Ifá is grounded in the Yoruba cosmology and views mental health, physical health, and spirituality holistically. Treatment may include spiritual baths, the use of talismans, chanting, and sacrifice, as directed by a priest or priestess. The authors provide a case example involving the treatment of an 8-year-old male with attention difficulties. Working with a counselor with access to local Ifá priests, the intervention involved a spiritual bath, activities with father and son to promote weekly remembrances of the child's mother who had died, as well as support from the counselor to support monitoring of schoolwork, softening of interpersonal style, and implementing of clear limits.

Ojelade, McCray, Meyers, and Ashby's (2014) study of African healing practices in the United States show that Western mental health problems were conceptualized as spiritual issues. In addition, mental challenges were seen as originating from Westernization or supernatural forces. The study also noted the use of personal resources, the services of the priest or priestess, or referrals to Western therapy as means of addressing these mental health problems. Edwards's (2011) analysis of indigenous healing in southern Africa suggests a "perennial psychology" that reflects the continuity of an understanding of humanity and healing that traces its roots to ancestral Africa. This psychology is holistic and presents an integrated view of humans involving their physical being, their spirituality, their ancestral connections, and their interconnectedness to their environment. Concepts of illness prevention and health promotion are linked to the promotion of holistic and spiritual wellness and healthy relationships. Illness is conceived through the disruption or injury to these relationships or balances; healers may use various strategies to restore holistic harmony and balance or to address spiritual discord.

DATA ON MENTAL HEALTH OF AFRICAN AMERICANS

Epidemiological Studies

Epidemiological studies are used to understand rates of psychopathology in a group and variations between groups. Epidemiology is the study of the rates of the incidence and prevalence of a health or mental health condition in a population (i.e., an entire group of people, e.g., Americans) or a representative sample of those people. The *incidence* of a disorder is the number of new cases that occur within a particular period (e.g., within a year), whereas *prevalence* involves the total number of people within a population or a representative sample of a population that has a specific disorder at a particular point or period (e.g., over a lifetime). To better understand the incidence and prevalence of mental disorders within the United States, several epidemiological studies have been conducted. These studies help us to understand similarities and differences between ethnic and racial groups in types and rates of psychopathology.

Data from the National Epidemiological Study on Alcohol and Related Conditions provide data on disorders among racial and ethnic groups. The sample included 7,529 African Americans and 24,502 non-Hispanic Whites (Gibbs et al., 2013). Results indicated that African Americans had lower 12-month and lifetime rates of psychiatric diagnoses, any substance abuse disorders, mood disorders, or anxiety disorders. African Americans were more likely to meet the criteria for personality disorders, including paranoid histrionic and schizoid disorders, than non-Hispanic Whites.

National Survey of Black Americans (NSBA) and the National Survey of American Life (NSAL)

The NSBA and the more recent NSAL provide information about the mental health of African Americans (NSAL, n.d.). The original NSBA sample included 2,107 African Americans 18 years of age or older. The study used a national probability sample, selecting participants so that they were representative of the broader population of African Americans in the United States. Wave I data was collected in 1979–1980. Three subsequent waves of data were collected (Wave II, a 1987–1988 telephone survey follow-up of 951 adults; Wave III, a 1988–1989 telephone survey follow-up of 793 adults; and Wave IV, a 1992 telephone survey follow-up of 659 adults interviewed in the 1987–1988 and the 1988–1989 surveys). In contrast to many research questions that focus on between-group comparisons—in most cases, between African Americans and Whites—the NSBA provides an important opportunity to examine the variability (i.e., within-group differences) of mental health issues among African Americans.

With the NSAL, interviews were conducted with 3,570 African Americans 18 years of age or older, in addition to 891 non-Hispanic Whites and 1,621 individuals of Caribbean descent between 2001 and 2003. In addition, 1,170 African American adolescents ages 13 to 17 were interviewed. Results from the study indicate that the lifetime prevalence of major depressive disorder (MDD) is lower among African Americans (10.4%) than Whites (17.9%) or Caribbean Blacks (12.9%). Both African and Caribbean Americans are more likely to rate their MDD as more severe and disabling than Whites; however, they are less likely to receive MDD treatment (Williams et al., 2007). In contrast to Whites who were at greater risk for generalized anxiety disorder, panic disorder, and social anxiety, African Americans and Caribbean Blacks were at greater risk for experiencing post-traumatic stress disorders (Himle, Baser, Taylor, Campbell, & Jackson, 2009).

Approximately half of Blacks with serious disorders use intervention services to address their distress (48.5%), and about 40% of African Americans or Caribbean Blacks with serious disorders specifically use mental health services (Neighbors et al., 2007). Females, individuals with more years of education, those with insurance, and those between the ages 30 and 59 were higher service users.

NSAL data have been used to examine depression among older adults (Woodward, Taylor, Abelson, & Matusko, 2013), as well as to examine the role of social support in social anxiety disorder (Levine, Taylor, Nguyen, Chatters, & Himle, 2015).

CONTEMPORARY ISSUES

STIGMA VS. SUPPORT

In January 2013, rookie Royce White of the Houston Rockets was suspended for "Refusing to Provide Services" because he declined to report to practice as he reportedly worked to address his generalized anxiety disorder (GAD). With this condition, an individual may

- Worry very much about everyday things
- Have trouble controlling their constant worries
- Know that they worry much more than they should
- Not be able to relax
- Have a hard time concentrating
- Be easily startled
- Have trouble falling asleep or staying asleep
- Feel tired all the time
- Have headaches, muscle aches, stomach aches, or unexplained pains
- Have a hard time swallowing
- Tremble or twitch
- Be irritable, sweat a lot, and feel light-headed or out of breath
- Have to go to the bathroom a lot. (NIMH, n.d.)

The same month, Michelle Williams of Destiny's Child indicated that she has struggled with depression. Speaking out to encourage others to seek assistance, Williams notes, "We're taught, 'Just go to Church and pray about it. The Lord is going to heal you.' Well, in the meantime, I believe God-gifted people, physicians, doctors, therapists—that's your healing. Take advantage of it." "Go see a professional so that they can assess you. It's OK if you're going through something. Depression is not OK, but it is OK to go get help."

These popular figures and their experiences support efforts to make emotional challenges more visible and to reduce the related stigma. Churches and other cultural resources within the African American community have also become increasingly available to provide intervention supports. The Patient Protection and Affordable Care Act, if left intact, also has the potential to expand mental health service access for many African Americans. However, it may take some time to build adequate and culturally relevant capacity to meet the mental health service needs of African Americans.

Other Findings on Prevalence of Psychological Dysfunction Among African Americans

There are other indicators that provide insight into the psychosocial functioning and adaptation of different cultural groups. Data from the National Health Interview Survey provide the percentage of adults aged 18 and over who experienced serious psychological distress during the past 30 days (Clarke, Norris, & Schiller, 2017). Serious psychological distress was assessed by asking respondents how often they experienced each of six symptoms of psychological distress (e.g., nervousness, hopelessness, worthlessness). As seen in Figure 13.1, there were few differences among racial and ethnic groups in experience of psychological distress. Prevalence for each of the three racial and ethnic groups is slightly under 4%.

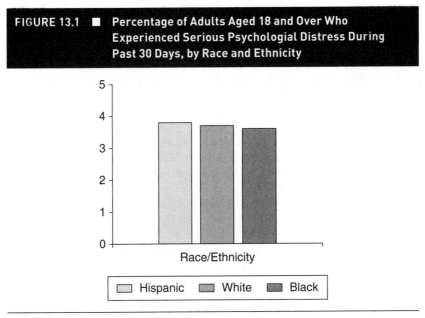

FIGURE 13.1 ■ Percentage of Adults Aged 18 and Over Who Experienced Serious Psychologial Distress During Past 30 Days, by Race and Ethnicity

Source: Clarke, Norris, & Schiller (2017).

Suicide rates vary by race and ethnicity. In 2015, the highest suicide rate per 100,000 was 15.1% among Whites, and the second highest rate (12.6%) was among American Indians and Alaska Natives. Lower rates per 100,000 were found among Asians/Pacific Islanders (6.4%) and African Americans (5.6%) (American Foundation for Suicide Prevention, n.d.). The rate for Black females was 2.1 compared to 9.4 for Black males. These data may not reflect the actual number of deaths by suicide among African American males because the data do not take into account phenomena such as "suicide by police," high rates of homicide, and other related forms of self-endangerment. Individuals who are members of both sexual minority and racial or ethnic minority groups have more suicides because of increased exposure to stress and discrimination (Meyer, Frost, & Nezhad, 2014).

While overall suicide rates are higher among males than females; suicidal ideations and experiences and feelings of sadness are higher among female than male youth.

TABLE 13.1 ■ Percentage of High School Students Who Felt Sad or Hopeless,* by Sex and Race/Ethnicity

Race/Ethnicity	Female	Male
White	37.9	19.2
Black	33.9	17.6
Hispanic	46.7	24.3

*Almost every day for 2 or more weeks in a row so that they stopped doing some usual activities during the 12 months before the survey.

Source: Kann, McManus, Harris, Shanklin, Flint, Hawkins, et al. (2016).

Data from the Youth Risk Behavioral Surveillance Survey (YRBSS) show some racial and ethnic and gender differences on these indicators (Kann et al., 2016). The YRBSS survey is a national school-based survey of students in Grades 9–12. The survey assesses several health problems. One question asks students whether they had felt so sad or hopeless almost every day for 2 or more weeks in a row that they stopped doing some usual activities. The prevalence of having felt sad or hopeless was higher among females than males in all racial and ethnic groups (see Table 13.1). The percentage of students who felt sad or hopeless was highest for Hispanic females and lowest for African American males. Other questions asked students whether they had seriously considered attempting suicide during the 12 months before the survey or made plans to attempt suicide (see Tables 13.2 and 13.3). Seriously attempting suicide was higher for females than males across all racial and ethnic groups and slightly lower for Blacks compared with Whites and Hispanics. Similar findings were found for the question about making a suicide plan, with females more likely to report they had made a plan than males. Female students were also more likely to attempt suicide than male students. White males were less likely to report attempting suicide. These statistics suggest that suicidal

TABLE 13.2 ■ Percentage of High School Students Who Seriously Considered Attempting Suicide and Who Made a Plan About How They Would Attempt Suicide During the 12 Months Before the Survey

Race/Ethnicity	Seriously Considered Attempting Suicide		Made a Suicide Plan	
	Female	Male	Female	Male
White	22.8	11.5	18.4	9.3
Black	18.7	11.0	17.3	10.6
Hispanic	25.6	12.4	20.7	10.9

Source: Kann, McManus, Harris, Shanklin, Flint, Hawkins, et al. (2016).

TABLE 13.3 ■ Percentage of High School Students Who Attempted Suicide*		
Race/Ethnicity	**Female**	**Male**
White	9.8	3.7
Black	10.2	7.2
Hispanic	15.1	7.6

*One or more times during the 12 months before the survey

Source: Kann, McManus, Harris, Shanklin, Flint, Hawkins, et al. (2016).

thoughts and ideations of youth are of concern across all racial and ethnic groups, and comprehensive suicide prevention is needed within schools and communities.

While African Americans have lower lifetime prevalence of suicide, lesbian, gay, and bisexual (LGB) ethnic minorities are at increased risk for suicide relative to White LGB youths. Among self-identified LGB participants, O'Donnell, Meyer, and Schwartz (2011) found that the risk of a suicide attempt was significantly higher among African Americans and Latinos than Whites in their study; the lifetime suicide attempt was 19.5 for Blacks, 22.7 for Latinos, and 9.1 for Whites.

Mental Health Service Utilization

Studies have shown racial and ethnic differences in mental health service utilization. These findings are seen across different age groups. Costello, He, Sampson, Kessler, and Merikangas (2014), using data from the National Comorbidity Survey Adolescent Supplement, examined mental health services among adolescents over the past 12 months. The sample contained 10,148 youth ages 13 to 17; African Americans represented 15.1% of the sample. Males were more likely to receive school or juvenile-justice-based services. Parents with college education were more likely to seek services for their children. African Americans were less likely to receive mental health care than other ethnic groups.

Racial and ethnic differences in mental health service utilization are also seen among young adults. In a systematic review of 18 studies with 96,297 participants (focused on ages 18 to 24), members of racial groups reported lower use of mental health services (Li, Dorstyn, & Denson, 2016). Among college students, African American, Asian, and Hispanic students in a multicampus study involving 13,028 respondents were less likely to use mental health services than White students (Hunt, Eisenberg, Lu, & Garthright, 2015).

Jimenez, Cook, Bartels, and Algeria (2013) examined data from the Medical Expenditure Panel Surveys (MEPS) from 2004 to 2009. The study focused on older adults who were aged 60 or older and included 1,658 respondents of whom 303 were African American, 981 were White, and 374 were Latino/a. There were no differences in need or severity of illness across Whites, African Americans, or Latinos. African Americans and Latinos had lower income and levels of education and were more likely to be from urban areas and to have public insurance or HMO participation than Whites. Both Latinos and African Americans were less likely to initiate mental health treatment. Older African Americans, as well as Latinos, were more likely to receive outpatient care, without psychotropic medication.

Involuntary Commitment

African Americans tend to be overrepresented among individuals involuntarily committed to public mental hospitals in the United States (Lindsey & Paul, 1989). Based on principles of dangerousness (associated with the risk of injury to self or others) or grave disability (i.e., inability to function in independent self-care) due to mental illness, the majority of states allow individuals to be legally hospitalized without their consent. Rates of involuntary commitment have declined since the 1960s because of legal protections for individuals, patient rights, and increased utilization of psychotropic medications; however, African Americans have continued to be at greater risk of involuntary commitment. Early arguments linked higher rates of involuntary commitment for African Americans with several factors. Using 2003 data from New York State, African Americans continued to experience higher rates of outpatient involuntary commitment. However, once factors such as poverty, local mental health prevalence rates, and local rates of mental health services were controlled, race did not appear to account for these differences in commitment (Swanson et al., 2009).

RESEARCH ON THE ROLE OF CULTURE, IDENTITY, AND DISCRIMINATION IN WELL-BEING

Several cultural and racial constructs promote psychosocial functioning and mental health well-being. Discrimination, on the other hand, is linked to poor psychosocial functioning.

Racial Identity

Recent research presents a complex picture of the role of culture in the experiences of emotional and behavioral functioning among African Americans. Data from 3,570 respondents collected between 2001 and 2003 as part of the National Survey of American Life were analyzed (Hughes, Kiecolt, Keith, & Demo, 2015). African Americans who strongly identified with their social group and evaluated it positively had higher self-esteem and reported greater levels of mastery and fewer depressive symptoms. However, when African Americans rated their group more negatively but were strongly identified with or closer to the group, they reported lower mastery and high depressive symptoms. This is consistent with an internalized racism perspective. In this situation, African Americans feel close to African Americans but rate African Americans as a group negatively.

Research by Chae et al. (2014) suggests that a pro-Black bias may serve as a buffer against experiences of racism, even at the biological level. These findings were based on analyses of data from a community sample of 92 African American men, recruited from the San Francisco Bay area, born in the U.S. and aged between 30 and 50. Slightly over the majority of the sample (54.3%) were unemployed, and 29.2% were living below the poverty threshold. The study examined experiences of discrimination, the implicit bias of respondents (i.e., the tendency to exhibit unconscious bias that is pro- or anti-Black), and telomere length. Telomeres are sequences, or "caps," at the end of a chromosome that function to protect the ends of the chromosome and prevent them from fraying or fusing. These caps tend to shorten as we age and in response to stress and are an indication of aging. The racial discrimination reported by participants included interactions with the police or courts (85.9%), obtaining employment (72.7%), and at work (70.7%). Within the sample, racial discrimination interacted with respondents' implicit racial bias to predict telomere length, after controlling for sociodemographic variables. Individuals with a pro-Black bias who reported greater racial discrimination had longer telomeres. In contrast, men with an anti-Black bias who reported racism had shorter telomeres, suggesting that there is a physiological cost to the internalization of negative racial bias and attitudes

Racial Discrimination

Many studies have shown that racial discrimination leads to poor mental health outcomes. Mouzon, Taylor, Keith, Nicklett, and Chatters (2017) found among older African Americans (N = 773) that everyday racial discrimination was associated with worse mental health (e.g., anxiety, depression, serious psychological distress). Myers et al. (2015) examined trauma and adversity in a sample of 500 low-income African American and Latino adults in south central Los Angeles. Greater exposure to trauma or adversity was associated with greater mental health challenges. African Americans reported higher levels of discriminatory experiences than Latinos, with African American women reporting the highest levels overall. African American women reported the highest adult trauma scores and the highest levels of psychological distress.

Calbabrese, Meyer, Overstreet, Haile, and Hansen (2015) examined the association between discrimination and mental health considering the Minority Stress framework, which suggests that minority status across membership in multiple groups that experience oppression may result in cumulative disadvantage. The study compared the discrimination experiences and mental health status of LGBQ or other sexual minority or nonheterosexual African American women, White women, and African American men. African American sexual minority women reported more discrimination, as well as lower levels of psychological and social well-being, than White sexual minority women. In comparison to African American sexual minority men, African American sexual minority women reported more depressive symptoms and lower social well-being. The analyses suggest that African American sexual minority women face the triple effects of marginalization, experiencing discrimination based on race, gender, and sexual orientation and that these multiple dimensions of oppression may compromise their well-being.

Discrimination is associated with poorer mental health among African American children, as well as adults. Priest, Paradies, Trenerry, Truong, Karlsen, & Kelly (2013) reviewed 121 studies examining the relationship between experiences of racism and adaptation for African American, Latino, and Asian youth ages 12 to 18. The authors found relatively consistent associations between discrimination and a negative impact on mental health in 76% of the outcomes. Racial discrimination compromised adaptive adjustment indicators (e.g., self-esteem, self-worth, resilience) in 62% of outcomes examined. Racial discrimination affected behavior problems (e.g., externalizing, delinquency) in 69% of outcomes examined. The review further suggested these negative mental health outcomes were less likely to be significant among younger children (e.g., preschoolers) as compared with older youth.

Cooke, Bowie, and Carr'ere (2014) administered measures of perceived ethnic discrimination and anxiety and depression to an ethnically diverse sample of African

American, European American, and multiracial children (N = 88; ages ranged from 8 to 14). Cook et al. found that African American children perceived greater discrimination at school than European American children. There were no differences between the multiracial students and the European American students on perceived discrimination. The relationship between social discrimination and feelings of exclusion and rejection was stronger for the African American children than the other two groups.

Smith-Bynum, Lambert, English, and Ialongo (2014) similarly found relationships between racial discrimination and psychological symptoms in African American adolescents. Smith-Bynum and colleagues examined longitudinal patterns of racial discrimination in a sample of urban African American youth (N = 504) and how patterns of racial discrimination related to changes in depression, anxiety, and aggressive behaviors over a 4-year period. Three groups of discrimination were identified. The increasing discrimination group (10% of sample) consisted of youth who reported increased discrimination from Grades 7 to 10. The decreasing discrimination group (16% of sample) was composed of youth whose perception of racial discrimination began at a moderate level and decreased from Grades 7 to 10. The stable low group (74% of group) consisted of adolescents who perceived relatively low levels of discrimination in Grades 7 to 10. The authors found that adolescents who reported increasing racial discrimination over time displayed poorer mental health outcomes (e.g., depressive symptoms, aggressive behaviors) compared with the other two groups. While the majority of the sample reported some experiences with racial discrimination during middle and high school, most were in the low racial discrimination group. This may reflect the fact that most youth resided in predominantly African American communities.

Research shows that discrimination is linked to biological markers for stress. Discriminatory experiences predict increases in neuroendrocrine risk markers, proinflammatory cytokines, cortisol, and cardiovascular reactivity and telomere length, a biomarker for aging. Telomere length is shorter in African Americans and leads to several physical and mental compromising health conditions (Lee, Kim, & Neblett, 2017).

Racial Cultural Socialization

Racial socialization (see Chapters 3 and 5) affects child and youth mental health. Reynolds and Gonzales-Backen (2017) conducted a meta-analysis on racial and ethnic socialization and mental health of African American youth. They identified 21 published studies that had examined the relationship between racial and ethnic identity and mental health of African American children, youth, and young adults. Mental health outcomes included self-esteem, depression, psychological stress and distress, anxiety, anger, psychological well-being, and resiliency. The authors found that the abundance of the studies supported a positive effect of racial socialization on mental health outcomes. For example, one study found that racial socialization messages were related to lower levels of aggression among children (Banerjee, Rowley, & Johnson, 2015). Another study found that cultural pride reinforcement messages were related to lower anxiety among children and among young adults (Bannon, McKay, Chacko, Rodriguez, & Cavaleri, 2009). The findings suggest that racial socialization practices by parents can be important in preventing depression and anxiety, in fostering self-esteem and resiliency, and in buffering the effects of discrimination. Given the strong findings regarding the beneficial effects of ethnic identity, Reynolds et al. suggest that programs and activities that promote racial socialization be incorporated into psychotherapy with African American clients.

METHODOLOGICAL AND RESEARCH ISSUES

As suggested throughout this chapter, there are important methodological issues that are central to examining mental health problems among African Americans. We have discussed rates and types of psychopathology among African Americans and approaches to treating African American clients. An additional issue is what assessment measures and strategies are most appropriate for use with African Americans. We discuss assessment issues next.

Assessment

Assessment is the process that mental health professionals use to understand what type of problem(s) an individual is experiencing. Assessments may involve unstructured or structured interviewing of the identified client or other important people (e.g., parents, spouse, teacher) to better understand the presenting problem. The client or other informants may also be asked to complete questionnaires, checklists, or other measures that assist the mental health professional in making a diagnosis that classifies the individual according to a set of established criteria or symptoms associated with a specific type of problem. As noted earlier in this chapter, the DSM-V (American Psychiatric Association, 2013) is the diagnostic framework most frequently used by American psychologists, psychiatrists, hospitals, and insurance providers.

Butcher, Nezami, and Exner (1998) identify a number of challenges in psychological assessment across different cultural groups, including language limitations, exposure to and experience with assessment processes, and variations in the manifestation of the same disorder. The definition of what is considered "normal" varies from culture to culture, and individuals undergoing an assessment may be influenced by cultural differences in motivation and differences in expectations for how they should interact with other people. Psychologists must consider whether a specific assessment task is culturally appropriate and whether it has the same psychological meaning (or equivalence) across different ethnic and racial cultural groups.

Assessment With Adults: The Minnesota Multiphasic Personality Inventory

The MMPI (Hathaway & McKinley, 1940) was created as an adult assessment tool for use by mental health professionals and researchers. The MMPI-2 (Butcher, Dahlstrom, Graham, Tellegen, & Kaemmer, 1989) is a revision of the original measure and is the current version in use. The MMPI-2 contains 567 true–false items and takes approximately 60 to 90 minutes to complete. Ten clinical scales—Hypochondriasis [Hs], Depression [D], Conversion Hysteria [Hy], Psychopathic Deviate [Pd], Masculinity–Femininity [Mf], Paranoia [Pa], Psychasthenia [Pt], Schizophrenia [Sc], Hypomania [Ma], and Social Introversion [Si]—and validity scales (e.g., F, L Lie, K Correction) are the options used most frequently by clinicians and researchers.

Because the standardization samples for the original MMPI contained no African Americans, there were concerns that the measure might be biased for use with African Americans. Despite inclusion of African Americans in the standardization sample of the MMPI-2, concerns of bias remained (e.g., Dana & Whatley, 1991). Numerous studies were conducted on the MMPI, and questions were raised as to whether there were differences in psychopathology between African Americans and Whites. Reviews of this work, with a range of study samples (e.g., normal, substance abuse, psychiatric), have found no consistent pattern of racial differences (e.g., Greene, 1987). Studies controlling for other demographic factors (e.g., sex, age, socioeconomic status, education, urban vs. rural residence, marital status, hospital status, timing of testing) report few differences in MMPI scores due to ethnicity (Bertelson, Marks, & May, 1982).

Additional Issues in Assessments With Adults

Even when clinical assessment tools are valid and reliable in research settings, we cannot be sure that they are reliable and valid in actual clinical practice. For example, Garb's (1997) review of studies on bias in clinical judgment (e.g., in diagnosis, ratings of adjustment) reports that African Americans are more likely to be diagnosed as having schizophrenia and less likely to be diagnosed as having a psychotic affective disorder than are Whites. Data from mental health service settings similarly suggests a discrepancy, such that African Americans are more likely to be overdiagnosed with schizophrenia and underdiagnosed with depression (Adebimpe & Cohen, 1989; Neighbors, Jackson, Campbell, & Williams, 1989). The overdiagnosis of schizophrenia may be related to African Americans' greater likelihood of presenting in clinical settings with Schneiderian first-rank symptoms (i.e., auditory hallucinations, delusions, and loss of agency; Carter & Neufeld, 1998). Whaley's (1998) work also suggests that issues of mistrust may play a role in the overdiagnosis of schizophrenia and underdiagnosis of depression among African Americans. Whaley argues that the concept of "paranoia" represents a dimension ranging from low or relatively minor levels of mistrust to extreme paranoia, including severe delusions and hallucinations. He presents data suggesting that African Americans demonstrate higher levels of general distrust than Whites and that when socioeconomic status is controlled, this ethnic difference is no longer significant. Whaley also notes a stronger association between mistrust and depression among African Americans than among Whites. This difference in levels of association raises questions as to whether assessment strategies may confuse mistrust and paranoia and contribute to problems in accurately diagnosing both depression and schizophrenia among African Americans. The issue of mistrust may also be reflected in nondisclosure by African American clients, which is sometimes interpreted as resistance. Related to this, Ridley (1984) suggests that some tendencies by African Americans to initially mistrust a therapist may be healthy or adaptive.

Assessment and Treatment of Hyperactivity Among African American Children

There has been considerable interest in the assessment and diagnosis of attention deficit hyperactivity disorder (ADHD) among African American children. In their review, Gingerich, Turnock, Litfin, and Rosen (1998) suggest that although ADHD is believed to be biological in nature, cultural factors also may play an important role in the manifestation of the disorder and its diagnosis. Findings from comparative studies conducted in the 1970s show African American children are rated higher than White children on symptoms of ADHD on parent and teacher rating scales (e.g., Anderson, Williamson, & Lundy, 1977; Blunden, Spring, & Greenberg, 1974; Goyette, Conners, & Ulrich, 1978). Multiple perspectives have been offered to explain these differences. Boykin (1978) raised the possibility that symptoms of hyperactivity among African American children are sometimes confused with verve, a cultural preference for high levels of stimulation and activity in the environment.

More recent findings on racial and ethnic differences in ADHD diagnosis are mixed. In an examination of 133,091 children receiving services in the New York State public mental health service system, African American and Hispanic children ages 3 to 17 were more likely to receive a diagnosis of ADHD (Siegel, Laska, Wanderling, Hernandez, & Leverson, 2016). However, using a population-based sample of 4,297 children followed from fifth through 10th grades, African American and Latino children were less likely to have a diagnosis of ADHD once socioeconomic factors and ADHD symptoms were controlled (Coker et al., 2016). Among children in the sample diagnosed with ADHD, parents of African American children were less likely to report medication use. Similarly, African American children in the nationally representative Early Longitudinal Study Kindergarten Class 1998–1999 (N = 17,100, of whom 15.73% to 14.74% were African American) were less likely to have received a diagnosis of ADHD and, if diagnosed, less likely to be taking prescription medication related to ADHD.

Using data from the NIMH Multimodal Treatment Study of Children with ADHD (MTA), teachers rated African Americans as higher on ADHD and oppositional defiant disorder symptoms than they rated their White peers (Arnold et al., 2003). The research found that African American and Latino children benefited from the combination of medication and behavioral treatments more than their White peers. Diagnosis of ADHD is very important, as African American youth who received a diagnosis of AADH before age 13 are at greater risk of juvenile arrest, suspension or expulsion, and educational attainment at age 18 to 23 (Behnken et al., 2014).

Assessment From an African-Centered or Cross-Cultural Perspective

When considering assessment from an Africentric perspective, clinicians and therapists have several scales to choose from that can assist them in understanding a client's correct orientation, including Baldwin's African Self-Consciousness (ASC) Scale (Baldwin, 1984; Baldwin & Bell, 1985; see also Chapter 2). The ASC Scale is based on "a theoretical construct that attempts to explain the psychological functioning and behavior of persons of African descent from their own cultural perspective" (Baldwin et al., 1992, p. 284). Baldwin (1981, 1984) proposes a model of Black personality consisting of two core components: (a) the African Self-Extension Orientation (ASEO) and African Self-Consciousness (ASC). ASEO is based in spirituality and allows for self-extension—that is, the self, consciously and unconsciously, is defined in group or corporate terms (in contrast to the Eurocentric conceptualization of the self emphasizing individual identity). The ASC Scale measures African Americans' assessments about African and African American culture, cultural awareness, and perspectives on societal issues, such as liberation and survival related to racism (described in greater detail in Chapter 2).

Research by Kohrt et al. (2014) raises important questions in considering the role of culture in the experience of culture-specific syndromes and cultural concepts of distress. In this research, the Systematic Assessment of Quality in Observational Research Cultural Psychiatry Epidemiology ranking system was adapted to create a Cultural Psychiatry Epidemiology version. Analyses were conducted on 45 studies with 18,782 participants examining "culture bound" or "idioms of distress" (including culture bound syndromes listed in the DSM-V). Such syndromes are specific or unique to individual cultures. For example, Brain fag syndrome is a condition experienced in Western Africa "characterized by distress from thinking too much . . . includes headaches and an experience of a worm crawling in the head" and Kufungisia is a condition "associated with general psychological distress and common mental disorders in Zimbabwe" (p. 367).

Mental Health and Social Status:
The Confounding of Race and Socioeconomic Status

One important issue in trying to understand data on the mental health status of African Americans is the confounding of socioeconomic status and ethnic group membership within the United States. For example, census data clearly indicate that African Americans have overall lower levels of income and educational attainment than do Whites and that they are more likely to live below the poverty level. Research also indicates that socioeconomic status is related to mental health. Individuals with lower levels of resources are more likely to have a psychiatric diagnosis. Two models have been proposed to explain the link between socioeconomic status and psychopathology. (a) The social causation hypothesis suggests that the greater experience of stress and more limited access to resources and supports lead to problems in adaptive functioning. (b) In contrast, the social selection hypothesis suggests that vulnerabilities, potentially biological in nature, lead to problems in adaptation, which, in turn, lead to individuals entering (or being selected into) a lower socioeconomic level. There is reasonable support for the social causation hypothesis, and data suggest that social selection also may occur—not such that individuals drift downward within their lifetime or cohort but that they may fail to progress economically or replicate their parents' socioeconomic status level (Hudson, 1988).

Research by Kessler and Neighbors (1986) found that ethnicity and socioeconomic status interact such that members of ethnic minority groups low in socioeconomic status are at higher risk of mental disorder. This association does not appear to hold for all disorders, however. Gavin et al. (2010) found that while household income was associated with higher risk for major depressive disorders among Whites, this association did not hold for African Americans, Asians, or Latinos. Similarly, educational attainment, while predictive for White men and women, was not associated with decreased risk for major depressive disorders among African American, Latino, or Asian men or women. There was a significant relationship between major depressive disorders and education for foreign-born Blacks, however. Being out of the labor force or unemployed was associated with major depression disorders for African American as well as White, Asian, and Latino men.

Research by Scott et al. (2014), using the World Mental Health Surveys, suggests that subjective social status—that is, the relative sense of social position or status—within one's social setting may be important beyond objective measures of social status, such as education or income. Scott and colleagues found subjective social status to contribute to mental disturbance after objective social status was controlled. Such results may be important to understanding the role of social status in the mental health of African Americans.

PROMISING AND EVIDENCE-BASED PRACTICES FOR IMPROVING MENTAL HEALTH OUTCOMES

Evidenced-based care has become an increasingly important priority within the medical and mental health service professions. Evidence-based practice (EBP) emphasizes the importance of treatment outcomes and the use of intervention and treatment strategies and clinical practice that have demonstrated efficacy and effectiveness. Efficacy research examines whether a specific intervention has the intended effects in a controlled setting, underlining the internal validity of an intervention. Effectiveness studies examine whether interventions work in traditional, real-world practice settings, emphasizing the external validity of the intervention. EBP also builds on clinical decision making that is informed by research, client preferences, and clinical expertise. Some people narrowly define EBP and emphasize only empirical evidence (Aisenberg, 2008). This may present a challenge for African Americans and members of other ethnic groups, as there have been significant critiques that ethnic minorities, including African Americans, are largely missing from efficacy studies for mental health interventions (DHHS, 2001).

In an extensive review of scientific evidence on the use of psychosocial mental health treatment interventions, Miranda et al. (2005) describe a growing body of literature on the use of evidence-based treatments on African Americans. These authors conclude that available research lends support to the effectiveness of evidence-based care in the treatment of depression, parent management, and interventions for ADHD among African Americans. The review notes that although there is appreciation that issues of culture and context are relevant to the provision of mental health services, questions remain regarding cultural adaptations of evidence-based therapies.

Research examples suggest the promise of cultural adaptations and efforts to develop evidence-based interventions for African Americans. Kohn, Oden, Munoz, Robinson, and Leavitt (2002) report on the adaptation of cognitive behavioral therapy for African American women. The cultural adaptations involved structural adaptations (e.g., changing language, structuring the group to promote cohesion, adding a closing ritual) and the addition of culturally relevant therapy modules (e.g., healthy relationships, spirituality, religion, African American family issues, and African American female identity). Outcome evaluations of the women who completed the culturally adapted therapy and the women who completed traditional cognitive behavioral therapy reflected decreases in symptoms for both groups. The cultural group had higher depression scores at baseline and experienced a larger decrease in scores at posttest.

The Department of Health and Human Services (HHS) Substance Abuse Mental Health Services Administration (SAMHSA) has developed a web-based National Registry of Evidence-Based Programs and Practices (NREPP, www.nrepp.samhsa .gov) that presents selected interventions that are effective or promising. Of the 40 newly reviewed and effective mental health interventions in the NREPP database, 30 interventions have been assessed in samples that included African Americans. These included interventions such as Problem Solving Therapy, Psychoeducational Multifamily Group Therapy, and Trauma Focused Cognitive Behavioral Therapy.

A growing body of work continues to explore evidence-based and empirically supported interventions for African Americans (e.g., see the work of Breland-Noble, Bell, & Nicolas, 2006). These interventions have examined both specific interventions and efforts to improve the quality of traditional mental health care and access. For example, Partners in Care (Halpern, Johnson, Miranda, & Wells, 2004) is a care quality improvement program targeting depressed clients in primary health care settings. In this work, two quality improvement interventions were implemented and evaluated, both focusing on providing information on accessing appropriate treatment for depression to clients in seven managed primary care organizations. Primary care clinics within these organizations were randomly assigned to usual treatment or to one of the two quality improvement conditions: one focusing on information regarding care involving medication and the second focusing on therapy. The quality improvement efforts included in-kind clinic resources to support improvements, the development of trained clinician teams, access to a toolkit of relevant education resources and materials, and nurse specialists who had training to support and facilitate access to appropriate care. At 6 and 12 months, the quality improvement interventions reduced the percentage of African American and Latino clients identified with a probable disorder to a greater extent than it reduced the percentage of Whites.

Guidelines and Practices for Improving Mental Health

In 2001, the surgeon general published a report, "Mental Health: Culture, Race, and Ethnicity." This report underlined the lack of an adequate scientific base and professional workforce prepared to effectively respond to the mental health needs of American ethnic group populations, including African Americans (DHHS, 2001). Beyond investments in research and training, the report also called for steps to address system-level barriers to mental health care.

Multiple professional groups have also called for efforts to strengthen mental health service delivery to African Americans and other ethnic minority populations. Within the American Psychological Association, there are several groups and programs that support these efforts. The Office of Ethnic Minority Affairs of the APA exists to promote an understanding of the influence of culture and ethnicity on behavior. This office encourages increased public knowledge of the special psychological resources and mental health needs of communities of color. The Society for the Psychological Study of Ethnic Minority Issues, Division 45, is the professional group within the APA whose members' work focuses on ethnic minority issues and concerns. The Association of Black Psychologists (ABPsi) has within its mission the improvement of mental health of all people of African descent.

Several programs have worked to increase the number of ethnic group psychotherapists, including African Americans. Within the ABPsi, the Student Circle (originally the Student Division) was organized in 1993 to respond to student members' needs within ABPsi. The American Psychological Association has also worked to increase the number of ethnic group psychologists who provide services to ethnic group members. APA also promotes the development of a knowledge base that supports better understanding of psychological issues relevant to persons of color through funding of the APA Minority Fellowship program.

American Psychological Association (APA) Guidelines

In 1990, the APA published "Guidelines for the Provision of Services to Cultural and Linguistic Minority Groups." These core guidelines support the following:

- Psychologists educate their clients to the processes of psychological intervention, such as goals and expectations; the scope and, where appropriate, legal limits of confidentiality; and the psychologists' orientations.

- Psychologists are cognizant of relevant research and practice issues as related to the population being served.

- Psychologists recognize ethnicity and culture as significant parameters in understanding psychological processes.

- Psychologists respect the roles of family members and community structures, hierarchies, values, and beliefs within the client's culture.

- Psychologists respect clients' religious and/or spiritual beliefs and values, including attributions and taboos, since they affect worldview, psycho-social functioning, and expressions of distress.

- Psychologists interact in the language requested by the client and, if this is not feasible, make an appropriate referral.

- Psychologists consider the impact of adverse social, environmental, and political factors in assessing problems and designing interventions.

- Psychologists attend to as well as work to eliminate biases, prejudices, and discriminatory practices.

- Psychologists working with culturally diverse populations should document culturally and sociopolitically relevant factors in the records. (APA, 2002)

In 2002, APA published "Guidelines on Multicultural Education, Training, Research, Practice, and Organizational Change for Psychologists." Guideline 5 focuses on issues relevant to the provision of psychological services, indicating that "Psychologists strive to apply culturally-appropriate skills in clinical and other applied psychological practices" (APA, 2002).

National Center on Minority Health and Health Disparities

In addition to the efforts of professional associations, Congress has supported work to address mental health issues in ethnic minority populations. P.L. 106-525, the Minority Health and Health Disparities Research and Education Act of 2000, was enacted by Congress and created the National Center on Minority Health and Health Disparities, with the mission to "lead scientific research to improve minority health and eliminate health disparities" including mental health (National Institute on Minority Health and Health Disparities [NIMHD], n.d.). This goal is pursued with the work of the National Center on Minority Health and Health Disparities (NCMHHD) that

- Plans, reviews, coordinates, and evaluates all minority health and health disparities research and activities of the National Institutes of Health

- Conducts and supports research in minority health and health disparities

- Promotes and supports the training of a diverse research workforce

- Translates and disseminates research information

- Fosters innovative collaborations and partnerships. (NIMHD, n.d.)

Progress in achieving these goals and tracking of efforts to reduce health disparities is monitored through the work of the Agency for Healthcare Research and Quality (Snowden, 2012).

Training Cultural Competence

Culturally compatible interventions may positively affect the mental health service experience of clients. Keyser, Gamst, Meyer, Der-Karabetian, and Morrow (2014) found therapists' own ethnic identity to predict their self-rated cultural competence in a sample of 371 child therapists. African American clients were also more likely to return to see African American counselors than White counselors.

Resources have been developed to assist those providing culturally appropriate psychological services to African American clients. These would include books, such as *The First Session With African Americans: A Step by Step Guide* by Janet Sanchez-Hughley (2000), *Black Women's Mental Health* by Evans, Bell, and Burton (2017), *Black Families in Therapy* (Boyd-Franklin, 2013), and professional training videotapes on psychotherapy with African Americans, such as *Working With African American Clients* (Parham, 2005).

Not all therapeutic interventions are traditional psychotherapy encounters. Gregory and Phillips (1997) describe NTU (a Bantu word that means "essence") therapy, an Africentric approach to therapy that integrates concepts of harmony, balance, interconnectedness, and authenticity. NTU is spiritually based and uses the principles of Nguzo Saba (see Chapter 2 for principles) as guidelines for living in harmony. NTU has been used with several treatment and prevention services, including in-home family therapy, case management, crisis intervention, parenting skills, and other cultural programming including rites-of-passage programs (Cherry et al., 1998; Foster, Phillips, Belgrave, Randolph, & Braithwaite, 1993).

CRITICAL ANALYSIS

A range of significant historical factors have shaped the current landscape of mental health services and care. The development of psychotropic medications and rise of patient rights supported increased deinstitutionalization during the middle of the 20th century. Proposed changes in mental health policy to develop community-based infrastructure were undercut by the implementation of federal block grants to states during the 1980s. Variable state investments in mental health care, along with limitations in the coverage of mental health care by private and public insurers, have supported a highly variable and often fragmented mental health care system.

Issues raised within this chapter have articulated several factors that may disadvantage African Americans in seeking high-quality, effective, culturally relevant, and competent mental health services. There are multiple and significant barriers, including reluctance to pursue care due to stigma, limited availability of therapists from cultural groups that match client preferences, and limited funding for mental health care. There are also potential issues associated with therapists' cultural competence and access to relevant training, as well as limited research on culturally relevant, evidence-based interventions for African Americans. Federal, state, and local policy makers have considerable work to do in reducing the burden of suffering among African Americans and other ethnic group individuals.

Several factors continue to challenge our ability to build our empirical literature on mental health issues and treatment with African Americans. Issues of mistrust associated with the history of unethical behavior among researchers (see Chapter 12) challenge efforts to build our literature on EBP for African Americans. Resources such as the *Outreach Notebook for the NIH Guidelines on Inclusion of Women and Minorities as Subjects in Clinical Research* (2001) are available to provide support and guidance in addressing issues relevant to the involvement of specific populations in mental health research (e.g., Meinert, Blehar, Peindl, Neal-Barnett, & Wisner, 2003).

Our reliance on professional models shaped by traditional medical service delivery models can also result in a narrow range of service options appropriate for African Americans. Outreach models and peer, community-based, and paraprofessional models may provide useful service alternatives. Interventions and policy initiatives that address a range of critical risk factors, such as socioeconomic status and educational access, may serve as relevant intervention options, especially considering the role of oppression and related sociocultural factors in the mental health of African Americans. Appreciation of the life constraints and role demands experienced by African Americans may shape service delivery to make mental health services more accessible in settings and at times reasonable for the work and family lives of African Americans. Investment in prevention and integrated service system models that link mental health and other health and human services may work to address the multiple set of interrelated factors that place some African Americans at risk of a host of negative health, mental health, and sociocultural outcomes.

Even when African Americans access services, there may be challenges associated with race and discrimination in the service setting. Holley, Tavassoli, and Stromwall (2016) conducted a qualitative study of 20 persons with mental illness (N = 13) or their family members (7) who were of color (N = 15) and/or LGB (N = 12). Although there were positive aspects of treatment, respondents indicated that they experienced discrimination within mental health treatment programs. These included being ignored or not listened to, experiencing condescension or disrespect, including being perceived as less intelligent, or not being seen as complex individuals with unique needs.

There may also be tensions between therapeutic models and the traditional values within the African Americans community. Using work from the VA/Clergy Partnership Project, Sullivan et al. (2014) described such tensions between traditional religious approaches and traditional mental health services. For example, African Americans in the South may seek spiritual solutions for substance use to be addressed and resolved through one's relationship with God (Cheney, Booth, Borders, & Curran, 2016). Notably, research with African American clergy describes the importance of pastoral care in "shepherding the flock."

Several organizations are continuing to spearhead efforts to reduce and eliminate disparities in mental health care, status, and outcomes. For example, SAMHSA and the National Alliance of Multi-Ethnic Behavioral Health Associations (NAMBHA; www.nambha.org), a nonprofit association of behavioral health associations, have worked to establish resources. These include the National Network to Eliminate Disparities in Behavioral Health and the Eliminating Mental Health Disparities. In addition, the National Alliance on Mental Illness (NAMI) makes available resources to support effective services and access for African Americans' illness. These efforts will continue to be important in reducing mental health disparities and reducing the burden of suffering experienced by African Americans and other communities of color.

Summary

In this chapter, we presented an overview of issues supporting our understanding of the psychosocial adjustment of African Americans. Mental illness is stigmatized in Africa and within some African American communities. Stigma affects treatment access and utilization.

There are multiple theoretical perspectives on psychosocial adaptation, including medical, psychodynamic, behavioral, and African-centered models.

Epidemiological data estimate psychopathology rates among African Americans. Additional estimates have come from studies such as the NSBA and the NSAL. Data indicate relatively few significant differences in rates of mental illness between African American and White adults. However, there are notable differences in mental health service utilization by African Americans and members of other ethnic groups.

There is a growing consideration of biological and genetic factors that may contribute to our understanding of the mental health of African Americans. There have also been both mainstream (e.g., MMPI) and African-centered (e.g., ASC Scale) measures of well-being and maladaptation.

Mental health professionals have called for improved access to culturally appropriate services for African Americans, and research has suggested that training can be important in improving the service experience of African Americans. Resources to support effective psychotherapy with specific subgroups of African Americans are available.

In closing this chapter, it is important to acknowledge that there is a large literature encompassing a broad range of issues related to psychological adaptation of African Americans. This chapter has presented only a select overview of issues representing both classic questions and new directions. The Sukuma proverb, "The wind does not break a tree that bends," suggests that individuals' ability to cope with the challenges they face supports their adaptation and adjustment. Having the capacity to bend, to be flexible, but to remain firmly rooted reflects a sense of maintaining the connection to one's footing but being able to handle and effectively respond to life's stresses.

DRUG USE AND ABUSE

When the cock is drunk, he forgets about the hawk.

—Tshi proverb

LEARNING OBJECTIVES

- To become familiar with drug use prevalence among African Americans

- To understand ethnic and racial differences in drug use consequences and disparities

- To become familiar with historical patterns of drug use

- To understand risk and protective factors for drug use among African Americans

- To understand the role of cultural and institutional factors in drug use

- To be able to identify culturally congruent programs for preventing and treating substance use

- To become familiar with methodological and research issues when studying substance use

SAN FRANCISCO SEEKS TO BAN SALE OF MENTHOL CIGARETTES, FLAVORED TOBACCO PRODUCTS

BY ELAINE KORRY (2017, APRIL 20)

San Francisco has unveiled a tough anti-tobacco proposal that would ban the retail sale of menthol cigarettes and other flavored tobacco or tobacco-related products that are often the first choice of minority group members and teenagers who smoke.

Supervisor Malia Cohen, sponsor of the proposed ordinance, joined Tuesday with public health

(Continued)

409

(Continued)

experts and community advocates to announce the measure, which she said goes beyond more narrow laws on flavored tobacco in cities such as Chicago, Berkeley and New York.

"The legislation I've authored is a full restriction on the sale of all flavored tobacco products, and that does include menthol. There are no exemptions," Cohen said. This includes cigarettes, cigars, smokeless tobacco and e-cigarettes. San Francisco Supervisor Malia Cohen sponsored the ordinance that would ban the retail sale of menthol cigarettes and other flavored tobacco products.

The proposed ordinance is designed to address two major groups, youth and minorities, who have been targeted in successful, well-financed advertising campaigns that promote menthol cigarettes and flavored noncigarette tobacco products. The products often attract African-Americans, Asian-Americans and Latinos, as well as teenagers.

San Francisco Mayor Ed Lee endorsed the proposal. "We know from research and studies that tobacco-related diseases continue to be the No. 1 cause of preventable deaths, especially among low-income and minority communities," he said.

A similar measure is being considered in Oakland.

Cohen, who represents the predominantly African-American Bayview-Hunters Point district of San Francisco, said the ordinance grew out of her personal experience with family members who smoked menthol cigarettes and died of cancer, and her desire to spare San Franciscans a similar fate. "This is an evidence-based tobacco prevention strategy that will save lives and cut costs for taxpayers who are collectively shouldering the health care costs of tobacco-related illnesses," she said.

Nearly 9 in 10 African-Americans who smoke prefer menthol cigarettes, according to the federal Centers for Disease Control and Prevention. Menthol is believed to make the harmful chemicals contained in cigarettes more easily absorbed by the body, and some research shows that menthol cigarettes are more addictive than regular ones, according to the CDC.

"African-Americans don't have a genetic disposition that makes them smoke menthol cigarettes," said Dr. Valerie Yerger, an associate professor of health policy at the University of California–San Francisco. "It's the result of a very conscious advertising campaign by the tobacco industry." Menthol cigarettes are also preferred by a majority of Latinos and Asian-Americans who smoke, according to Randy Uang, director of tobacco prevention and control services at Breathe California, a Golden Gate Public Health Partnership.

Public health experts say restricting menthol and other flavored tobacco would improve health outcomes not only for the minority populations but also for teens. "Because flavors play such a key role in youth starting to smoke, restricting access to these products means that fewer youth will start smoking," said Uang.

Flavors are popular with inexperienced smokers, he said, because they mask the taste of tobacco and decrease the irritating effects of nicotine.

E-cigarettes are now the tobacco-related product most commonly used by young people in the U.S., according to the CDC. It found that more than 8 in 10 youths ages 12–17 who vape said they use flavored e-cigarettes that taste like mint, candy or other sweets.

The San Francisco ordinance, if approved, would fill a gap in federal legislation that authorized the U.S. Food and Drug Administration to regulate tobacco. In 2009, the FDA banned "characterizing flavors," such as candy, fruit and chocolate, in cigarettes. But, faced with tobacco industry lobbying, it stopped short of prohibiting menthol in cigarettes or flavorings in other tobacco-related products such as e-cigarettes, little cigars and smokeless tobacco.

Tobacco-control advocates, such as Yerger, have been pushing the FDA to ban menthol and other flavorings for years. "This ordinance didn't happen overnight," she said. "It's been a very long process and part of that has been gathering evidence about the role of menthol in hooking kids at a very early age and the tobacco industry knowing that it has the ability to do that by manipulating the levels of menthol in their products."

Cohen noted the tobacco lobby is strong in Sacramento and she's expecting pushback from the industry. "I would imagine they will be fighting this legislation every step of the way," she said.

If enacted, the tobacco ordinance would become effective Jan. 1. Enforcement would be the job of the Department of Public Health, which also would be responsible for educating retailers about the new restrictions.

Source: Korry (2017).

INTRODUCTIONS, DEFINITIONS, AND HISTORICAL PERSPECTIVES

Although we often hear about illicit drugs in the African American community, legal drugs (e.g., tobacco, alcohol) account for the majority of the health and social problems among African Americans. The news story tells the harmful effects of menthol cigarettes and flavored tobacco products consumed by the vast majority of African American smokers. As will be discussed, the long-term effects of tobacco use are severe with regard to mortality, illness, and disease, more so than any other drug. Although African Americans do not consume drugs more than members of other ethnic groups, they are more likely to suffer negative social, health, and legal consequences from their use (Babb, Stewart, & Bachman, 2012).

We begin this chapter with definitions relevant to drug use and involvement and then provide a historical overview of drug use in Africa, drug use among enslaved Africans, and current drug use among African Americans. Next, we discuss the causes and consequences of drug use for African Americans, covering the topics of drug initiation, co-occurring behaviors, risk and protective factors, and the role of cultural factors as protection against drug use. We then examine institutional and societal influences, including the role of poverty, and racism and discrimination, and differences in drug-related incarceration rates for African Americans and members of other racial and ethnic groups. Next, we provide an overview of methodological and research issues that are relevant to research on drug use and abuse among African Americans. We follow this with an examination of best practices for addressing problems associated with drug use. Finally, we provide a critical analysis and a chapter summary.

Definitions

The National Institute on Drug Abuse (NIDA) defines a drug as a chemical compound or substance that can alter the structure and function of the body. Drug abuse is the use of illegal drugs or the inappropriate use of legal drugs (NIDA, 2000). Illicit drugs are illegal. Illicit drugs, as identified by the National Survey on Drug Use and Health (SAMHSA, 2005b) include marijuana or hashish, cocaine or crack cocaine, inhalants, hallucinogens, heroin, or prescription-type drugs used nonmedically. Marijuana is the illicit drug that is used most frequently. Drug addiction is a chronic disease that is characterized by drug seeking and use that is compulsive or difficult to control, despite harmful consequences. Drug addiction is considered a brain disease and not a matter of lack of willpower or personality flaws (National Institute of Drug Abuse, 2016).

Historical Patterns of Drug Use in Africa and the United States

Historical perspectives provide insight into current patterns of drug and alcohol use among African Americans by examining drinking patterns of indigenous Africans. In their book, *Doing Drugs: Patterns of African American Addiction*, James and Johnson (1996) write that enslaved Africans arriving in America often came from ethnic groups that used fermented maize (corn) or millet as a food and a trade product, in social interactions, and as a sacred drink. Beer was used as an offering to gods and as a reward to those who had worked the land (Gordon, 2003). From the 16th to the 18th centuries, West, East, and Central Africans brewed beer and wine, and southern Africans engaged in some use of cannabis (marijuana; Ambler, 2003). Among specific African ethnic groups, alcohol was drunk in a group context—in religious and sacred events—rather than individually. For example, when the Asante (of Ghana) celebrated the harvest festival, *odwira*, it was commonplace to have liquor as an integral part of the festivities:

> The . . . King ordered a large quantity of rum to be poured into brass pans in various parts of the town: the crowd pressing around. . . . All wore their handsomest cloths, which they trailed after them in a length, in a drunken emulation of extravagance. (Ambler, 2003)

Although alcohol was consumed at these special occasions, other drugs were not commonly seen in West African society.

Role of Drugs in the Slave Trade

By the 1700s, alcohol had acquired an economic function and was used as currency in slave trading. It is estimated that alcohol purchased from 5% to 10% of all slaves in West Africa (Ambler, 2003). The connection between alcohol and the slave trade was circular, and it involved New England, Africa, and the West Indies (James & Johnson, 1996). Sugar and molasses from the British and Spanish West Indies were shipped to New England, where they were distilled into rum. The rum was then sent to Africa, where it was exchanged for slaves. These slaves were shipped to the West Indies to work in the cane fields.

Drug Use During Enslavement

Drinking during the period of enslavement was limited. The social drinking patterns of African Americans living in slavery included weekend and holiday use and drinking at celebrations. This drinking pattern was shaped, in part, because of the dawn-to-dusk work demands on slaves. Slave masters permitted and encouraged the use of alcohol as a reward during harvest times (Suggs & Lewis, 2003).

Drug Use Following the Civil War

Immediately after the Civil War, many Blacks became more involved in the Protestant Church. Church doctrine forbade alcohol consumption, and this prohibition restricted drug use. Black Churches of all denominations grew dramatically after the Emancipation Proclamation, and they promoted either abstinence or moderation in drinking. However, following the Civil War, many African Americans migrated North, frequently to urban areas, in search of employment. Greater exposure to urban life contributed to heavier drinking patterns and to high levels of addiction among African Americans. Rather than restricting alcohol use to celebratory occasions, many African Americans began to use alcohol to cope with problems of daily living brought on by poverty and racism. Around this time, opium use also increased in the United States. Chinese workers, brought to the western United States to build railroads, are largely credited with introducing opium into the United States (James & Johnson, 1996).

Drug Use From 1900 to 1930

Illegal drug use in the early 1900s was mostly limited to ex-convicts and criminals. However, by the 1930s, African Americans were disproportionately represented in the known addict populations of major urban areas. There was an expansion of clubs and bars in African American cities and communities during the 1930s; with this expansion came increased opportunity for alcohol and other drug use (James & Johnson, 1996).

Drug Use in the 1940s and 1950s

During the late 1940s and 1950s, heroin use increased in urban African American communities. Marijuana, which had previously been used only by specific subgroups of African Americans, such as prisoners, was also beginning to be used by more diverse groups of African Americans. However, the overall impact of heroin addiction, which was concentrated in urban areas, was relatively small compared with the broader impact of alcohol on both rural and urban Black communities (James & Johnson, 1996). During this period, African American communities tolerated high levels of alcohol use because of the oppressive circumstances and high levels of stress under which many African Americans lived. Options for those who wanted alcoholism treatment were very limited in the 1950s and 1960s. Hospital treatment programs were designed for middle-class Americans, and self-help programs such as Alcoholics Anonymous were not available in African American communities. Many African Americans who were addicted to alcohol could not get treatment.

During the 1950s and 1960s, organized drug syndicates gained control of drug production and distribution. With limited employment options available to them, many younger African Americans in urban communities became involved with drug preparation, packaging, and sales. This involvement of some younger African Americans in the drug trade continues today, as does control by organized drug syndicates.

Drug Use From the 1970s to 2000

The 1970s, 1980s, and 1990s saw the rise of the use of powdered cocaine, which led to the appearance of crack cocaine. Perhaps more than any other drug, crack cocaine has had a devastating impact on African American families and communities. Although cocaine has been used since 1890 in medicines and drinks, it was not introduced to the African American community until the 1980s. Its introduction had a detrimental effect on the people of the community: As addiction emerged, the social problems of crime, family disruptions, and disease drastically increased. Another distressing effect of cocaine was the staggering number of African American men who were prosecuted for its distribution. The Anti-Drug Abuse Act of 1986 created a disparity in sentencing for those arrested for crack cocaine, as opposed to those arrested for powdered cocaine. This was particularly debilitating for the African American community, where crack cocaine was the drug most likely to be used. In December 2007, the U.S. Supreme Court ruled that differences in the sentencing of crack cocaine and powdered cocaine offenders were unjust by a 7–2 vote. With these new guidelines, judges have discretion over sentencing offenders for crack cocaine violations.

In 2010, President Obama signed into legislation the Fair Sentencing Act, which decreased harsh penalties associated with small amounts of cocaine possession.

CURRENT DRUG USE AMONG AFRICAN AMERICANS

The National Survey on Drug Use and Health provides data on patterns of drug use among different age, gender, and ethnic groups (SAMHSA). The National Survey utilizes a sample of the civilian noninstitutionalized population age 12 and older in the United States. Table 14.1 provides the percentage of drugs consumed by African Americans and other racial and ethnic groups by age group over a 30-day period (SAMHSA, 2014a). Within the 12- to 17-year-old age category, White youth have the highest prevalence of most drugs and Asian youth have the lowest prevalence, with drug use among African American and Hispanic youth in between. In the 18- to 25-year-old age group, Asians consume the least amount of drugs. Within this age group, the prevalence of drug use for other racial and ethnic groups varies by the specific drug used. For example, Whites and American Indians/Alaskan Natives have the highest prevalence for cigarettes and alcohol while Whites and African Americans have the highest prevalence for illicit drugs and marijuana. In the 26 and older age group, American Indians/Alaskan Natives have the highest prevalence of most drugs.

Although overall, drug use is less common among African Americans and other ethnic groups than among Whites, it is important to note that there are disproportionately higher rates of drug-related problems among ethnic minority groups. African American and Hispanic youth show higher prevalence for drug-related social problems than do White youth (Wallace & Muroff, 2002; Zapolski, Pedersen, McCarthy, & Smith, 2014). Drug use among African Americans disproportionately contributes to incarceration, HIV, and other social and health problems. This may be due to fewer resources available to assist African Americans with drug-related problems. For example, African American men are 47% more likely to develop lung cancer than are White men (Lung Cancer Fact Sheet, n.d.). African American smokers have more difficulty than members of other ethnic groups in quitting (Stahre, Okuyemi, Joseph, & Fu, 2010). Difficulty in quitting may be related to African Americans being more likely than Whites and other ethnic and racial groups to smoke mentholated cigarettes (see cover story). Among African Americans who are current smokers, about 85% report smoking mentholated cigarettes compared with about 29% for White and Hispanic smokers (Villanti et al., 2016). Smokers of mentholated cigarettes have higher nicotine dependence, which makes it more difficult to quit and increases adverse health effects. We next discuss diversity in substance use among Blacks followed by a review of the use and effects of select drugs: alcohol, cigarettes, marijuana, cocaine, and illicit drugs.

DIVERSITY IN SUBSTANCE USE AND ABUSE AMONG BLACKS

Patterns of drug use and abuse vary among Blacks living within the United States, as well as Blacks living in other countries. Data from a large national study of Blacks living in the United States found Caribbean Blacks had lower lifetime prevalence of alcohol dependence and drug abuse than African Americans (Gibbs et al., 2013).

TABLE 14.1 ■ Prevalence of Selected Substance Use in the Past Month by Age and Ethnicity in 2014

	Ages 12–17					Ages 18–25					Ages 26 and Older				
	Black	White	Hispanic	Asian	American Indian or Alaskan Native	Black	White	Hispanic	Asian	American Indian or Alaskan Native	Black	White	Hispanic	Asian	American Indian or Alaskan Native
Cigarettes	2.2	6.3	3.8	1.3	8.6	23.8	33.3	22.2	15.3	38.7	25.2	22.3	17.7	8.9	35.0
Alcohol	8.6	13.2	11.2	4.5	*	48.7	66.0	52.9	49.2	53.1	48.5	60.9	48.6	40.7	44.5
Binge drinking[a]	0.2	1.3	1.1	0.0	*	5.5	13.7	8.6	4.6	11.2	5.0	6.7	5.0	1.7	9.7
Illicit drugs[b]	9.8	9.3	10.5	3.5	10.6	24.0	23.6	18.2	11.8	20.7	10.3	8.6	6.3	2.7	14.5
Marijuana	6.9	7.7	7.9	2.5	9.4	22.9	21.0	15.6	9.1	16.3	8.1	7.1	4.2	1.6	11.4

Source: SAMHSA (2014).

*Low precision; no estimate reported.

a. Five or more drinks on the same occasion at least once in the past month.

b. Illicit drugs include marijuana or hashish, cocaine (including crack cocaine), heroin, hallucinogens, inhalants, or any prescription-type psychotherapeutic drug used nonmedically.

National prevalence of substance abuse was examined in three countries, United States, Guyana, and Jamaica (Lacey et al., 2016). The U.S. sample included U.S. African Americans and Caribbean-born Blacks. Overall, rates of substance abuse were highest among U.S. African Americans (11.5%), followed by Caribbean Blacks (9.6%) living in the United States who were foreign-born. Prevalence of substance abuse was much lower among Blacks in Guyana (2.7%) and Jamaica (2.6%). The lower percentage of drug use for Blacks in Guyana and Jamaica might also be due to how drugs are defined in these countries, as there may be some cultural norms to view drugs such as marijuana as medicinal. These differences in drug abuse suggest that drugs are used to cope with structural and discriminatory factors in the United States not present in other countries.

Alcohol

Although alcohol is a legal drug for those of drinking age, alcohol consumption and abuse is a major cause of morbidity, mortality, disability, and property destruction in this country. Among African American youth ages 12 to 17 in 2014, (8.6%) reported past-month alcohol use and less than 1% reported binge drinking. In the 18- to 25-year-old and the 26 and older age groups, almost half of African Americans reported consuming alcohol over the past 30 days (see Table 14.1).

Precursors to alcohol use differ for African American than White youth. For example, research has shown that alcohol expectancies are linked to alcohol use such that beliefs about positive alcohol expectancies predict alcohol use for youth. However, expectations of more positive experience drinking alcohol did not predict alcohol use among African American youth as it did for White youth (Banks & Zapolski, 2017). This research suggests that divergent factors may lead to alcohol use for different ethnic groups.

Cigarettes and Related Products

Tobacco use is a leading contributor to disability, illness, and death in the United States. Table 14.1 shows the rate of smoking for African Americans across three age groups. As shown in Table 14.1, cigarette smoking at 2.2% was substantially less common among African Americans than most other racial and ethnic groups (except Asians) from ages 12 to 17. However, the percentage of African Americans smoking cigarettes increases at ages 18–25 to 23.8%, and the prevalence continues at a slightly higher rate among those 26 and older at 25.2% and is comparable to other racial and ethnic groups.

Table 14.2 provides the percentage of specific tobacco products by race and ethnicity among high school students. Prevalence of tobacco use for most products is lower among African Americans than other racial groups, with the exception of cigars, where African Americans consume an amount comparable with Whites and Hispanics. This is likely due to use of little cigars and cigarillos among African American youth (discussed later).

As indicated in the cover story, African Americans are more likely than other ethnic groups to smoke mentholated cigarettes, which may be more harmful and carcinogenic (Hooper et al., 2011; Stahre et al., 2010). Furthermore, the quit rate for smokers of mentholated cigarettes is less than that for smokers of nonmentholated cigarettes (Smith, Fiore, & Baker, 2014; Stahre et al., 2010).

Why are African Americans more likely to smoke mentholated cigarettes than any other ethnic group? A study by Lisa Henriksen and colleagues account for part of this reason (Henriksen et al., 2011). The authors found that tobacco

CONTEMPORARY ISSUES

AFRICAN AMERICANS AND MENTHOLATED CIGARETTES

When I (Belgrave) ask students which drug is responsible for the most morbidity and mortality among African Americans, most of them answer crack cocaine first and alcohol second. However, tobacco accounts for more excess deaths and health disparities than all of the other drugs combined. Cigarette use, specifically mentholated cigarettes, among African Americans is of interest to me because of the adverse effects cigarettes have had on mortality in my family. Both of my parents smoked mentholated cigarettes, as did all five of my brothers at some point in their lives. Cigarettes contributed to excess

morbidity for my father in the form of lung cancer and for my mother in the form of pulmonary disease. Although I have studied tobacco use among African Americans for many years, I had little influence on the tobacco use of family members. Why? Because tobacco is psychologically and physiologically very addictive. While African Americans report similar rates of cigarette use as other racial and ethnic groups, the consequences of such use is notably worse. Once African Americans start to smoke, it is incredibly difficult for them to stop. Mentholated cigarettes account for some of the difficulty in stopping.

companies increased the advertising and lowered the sale price of mentholated cigarettes in stores near California high schools with larger populations of African American students. The authors noted that these marketing practices are predatory and geared toward enticing young African Americans into becoming smokers. The researchers found that for every 10 percentage point increase in the proportion of African American students at a school, the per pack price of Newport (the leading brand of mentholated cigarettes) was 12 cents lower. At the same time, prices for the leading nonmentholated brand were not related to school demographics. Since lower prices tend to increase cigarette use, this is an important finding. Because of findings such as this, several antitobacco advocates have called for the U.S. Food and Drug Administration to ban mentholated cigarettes. Cities such as San Francisco (as indicated in the cover story) have

TABLE 14.2 ■ Estimated Percentage of Tobacco Use in the Preceding 30 Days by Product and Race/Ethnicity Among High School Students – National Youth Tobacco Survey				
	African American	Whites	Hispanic	Non-Hispanic/ Other Races
Any tobacco use	17.2	26.5	26.7	15.3
Electronic cigarettes	5.6	15.3	15.3	9.4
Cigarettes	4.5	10.8	8.8	5.3
Cigars	8.8	8.3	8.0	2.6

Source: Arrazola et al. (2015).

already done so. Cigarettes are clearly a lethal drug that has contributed vastly to health disparities among African Americans.

e-Cigarettes

Electronic cigarettes (e-cigarettes) were introduced into the United States around 2007. E-cigarettes are battery-operated devices that deliver nicotine with flavorings and other chemicals to users in vapor instead of smoke (National Institute on Drug Use, 2016b). The health risk of e-cigarettes remain unknown, although they have been promoted as a safer than traditional cigarettes because they do not deliver nicotine by burning.

E-cigarettes are the most commonly used tobacco product among youth with 3.9% of middle school youth and 13.4% of high school students reporting use (Arrazola et al., 2015). E-cigarettes are likely to be used along with other tobacco products, and many youth believe e-cigarettes have minimal health risk. White youth are more likely to use e-cigarettes than African American youth (Anand et al., 2015). However, African American youth are less knowledgeable about e-cigarettes than other racial and ethnic groups and are also less likely to perceive e-cigarettes as having health risks or to be addictive (Webb & Kolar, 2016).

E-cigarettes seem to serve as a gateway to traditional cigarettes. Recent research suggests that adolescents who begin to use e-cigarettes at a young age are more likely to progress to using traditional cigarettes than youth who do not consume e-cigarettes (Unger, Soto, & Leventhal, 2016).

Little Cigars and Cigarillos

Over the past 10 years, little cigars and cigarillos (LCCs) have risen in popularity, and cigar sales have increased due to these products whereby traditional cigarette sales have decreased. Little cigars and cigarillos are popular among African Americans adolescents and young adults (Nasim et al., 2015). Several factors make these products desirable (Cantrell et al., 2013). One, LCCs do not have the same regulations as cigarettes regarding flavors, sales, and marketing. Two, LCCs may be sold individually or in small packs of five and thus can be purchased cheaply. Three, LCCs often come in flavors appealing to youth and young adult populations, including candy and alcohol flavors. And four, federal and state taxing of LCCs make these products less expensive than cigarettes.

Little cigars and cigarillos are more likely to be advertised in African American neighborhoods than non–African American neighborhoods (Roberts et al., 2015). LCCs were surveyed in 750 licensed tobacco retail outlets that sold tobacco products in Washington, D.C. (Cantrell et al., 2013). The study found that LCCs were more available in African American communities. LCCs were also lower in price, and more advertising of these products was outside the store when compared with non-African American neighborhoods. The marketing and sale of LLCs is an example of how the tobacco industry has systematically targeted certain tobacco products in African American neighborhoods.

Illicit Drugs

Illicit drugs include illegal drugs (e.g., heroin, amphetamine, LSD, marijuana) and/or the misuse of prescription medications and drugs for household uses. Illicit drug use among African Americans is shown in Table 14.1. African Americans in the 18- to 25-year-old range have the highest prevalence of illicit drug use when compared with African Americans in other age groups, with 24% of African Americans in this age range reporting past-30-day illicit drug use. About 10% of African Americans 26 and older and ages 12–17 reported illicit drug use. Although marijuana is legal for recreational use in some states, it is still considered an illegal drug in most states and accounts for much of the illicit drug use. Overall, the prevalence of illicit drug use among African Americans is comparable to Whites and higher than that of other racial and ethnic groups.

Marijuana

Marijuana use in the United States is increasing. Marijuana is the most commonly used illicit drug among adolescents. Use sometimes involves the replacement of tobacco in cigars or cigarettes with marijuana, resulting in what is referred to as "blunts." Twenty-six states and the District of Columbia currently have laws legalizing marijuana in some form, and in eight states and the District of Columbia, marijuana is legal for recreational use (Governing, 2016). The states where marijuana is legal for recreational use are Maine, Massachusetts, Colorado, Alaska, Nevada, California, Oregon, Washington, and the District of Columbia. About 23% of African Americans in the 18- to 25-year-old group report marijuana use over the previous 30 days, and African Americans in this age group are more likely to report marijuana use than other racial and ethnic groups. Among African Americans, marijuana use drops off substantially in the 26 and older group, with 8.1% reporting past-month use.

More than half (54.9%) of African American youth age 12 to 17 reported that marijuana is fairly or very easy to obtain (SAMHSA, 2005c). African American and Hispanic youth are less likely to believe that there are serious consequences associated with marijuana use compared with other ethnic groups.

Marijuana is often used with other substances. In a study of the co-occurrence of marijuana and other substances by ethnicity, Pacek, Malcolm, and Martins (2012) found that marijuana disorder was greater among African Americans than Whites and Hispanics. Marijuana use was also more likely to co-occur with alcohol use disorders among African Americans when compared with other ethnic or racial groups. Marijuana use among African Americans also tends to co-occur with tobacco use (Montgomery, 2015).

Cocaine

Cocaine is an illicit drug whose use has been associated with many severe consequences. Use of cocaine, especially crack cocaine, has been incredibly destructive within African American communities. Health, social services, medical, and judicial systems are burdened with the consequences of cocaine addiction. The distribution of crack cocaine within many low-income African American communities accounted in large part for elevated criminal activity, high incarceration rates, and other social problems especially during the 1970s and 1980s. The most common drug for which African Americans are charged with drug-related crime offenses is crack cocaine. Eighty-three percent of all federal crack cocaine cases in 2011 involved African Americans (U.S. Sentencing Commission, 2011). While incarceration of African Americans is high for cocaine sales and distribution, overall, cocaine use is relatively rare compared with other drugs. In 2013, the rate of current cocaine use among young adults aged 18 to 25 was 1.1%, and the rate in other age groups (> 26) was even lower (SAMHSA, 2014a).

Cocaine is powerfully addictive and is characterized by a high frequency of relapse following treatment (NIDA, 2002). The nature of cocaine addiction makes it very difficult to treat. One indicator of a community's cocaine problems is emergency room visits arising out of cocaine use. The prevalence of emergency room episodes is substantially higher for African Americans than for Whites, as is treatment for cocaine use (SAMHSA, 2011). Several explanations exist for the cocaine treatment disparity. African Americans are more likely to use the cheaper but more potent and addictive form of cocaine (crack), which may be more dangerous. African Americans may have less access to powdered and crack cocaine that is pure. In addition, African Americans who are addicted may have less access to treatment than Whites. However, it is worth noting that total past-year and -month use of crack cocaine has continued to decline (SAMHSA, 2011).

Substance Abuse and Dependence

Substance abuse and dependence varies among racial and ethnic groups. In 2013, among persons ages 12 or older, the rate of substance dependence or abuse was 4.6% among Asians, 7.4% among African Americans, 8.4% among Whites, 8.6% among Hispanics, 10.9% among persons reporting two or more races, 11.3% among Native Hawaiians or Other Pacific Islanders, and 14.9% among American Indians or Alaska Natives (SAMHSA, 2014a).

African Americans were more likely to report needing substance abuse treatment in the past year for illicit drug use (4.1%) versus other ethnic and racial groups (3.0%). African Americans were less likely to report needing treatment for alcohol abuse (6.8% for African Americans and 7.8% for other groups) (SAMHSA, 2013).

There are ethnic and racial differences in completion of treatment for substance abuse disorders. African Americans and Hispanics are less likely to complete treatment than Whites, especially for alcohol and methamphetamine disorders, substances for which African Americans have lower rates of disorder use (Mennis & Stahler, 2016).

CAUSES AND CONSEQUENCES OF DRUG USE

The etiology of drug use focuses on why people start using drugs. Experimentation with drug use most often begins during adolescence. We focus on the etiology of drug use among youth, as opposed to drug use among adults. Factors that contribute to initial drug use are different from factors that contribute to continuing drug use and addiction. Once use turns to abuse and addiction, psychological and physiological mechanisms strongly support continued use. Consequently, we devote more attention to understanding initial drug use than to understanding why people continue to use drugs.

Drug Use Initiation

Drug use is often initiated in early to mid-adolescence. During adolescence, one explores new activities, and drug experimentation may be one such activity. Initiation often begins with cigarettes and alcohol, which are considered gateway drugs to other drugs, such as marijuana.

However, contrary to cigarettes being a gateway drug for marijuana, marijuana appears to be a gateway drug for cigarette use among African American youth. Vaughn, Wallace, Perron, Copeland, and Howard (2008) examined whether marijuana was a gateway drug for African American and other ethnic minority youth (mean age = 15.5). African American youth were significantly more likely to initiate marijuana use before cigarette use. Over one-third of African Americans reported initiating marijuana before cigarettes (37.9%), compared with less than one-quarter of youth in the other ethnic groups (Caucasian = 17.3%, Latino/Latina = 21.7%, biracial/other = 20.8%).

Drug initiation starts around the age of 11 to 12 for youth of all ethnic groups. The seventh and eighth grades (when most youth are 13–14) are the peak years for the initiation of alcohol use (SAMHSA, 2005a). Regarding marijuana use, about 53% of youth reported first marijuana use between the ages of 12 and 17 (SAMHSA, 2006). Youth who do not use these substances during the adolescent period are less likely to use drugs as adults and to have adverse effects from such use. Among adults who reported that they used marijuana at the age of 14 or younger, 13.2% were classified as drug dependent or a drug abuser, a percentage that was 6 times higher than for youth who initiated marijuana at the age of 18 or older.

In terms of tobacco addiction, nearly 9 out of 10 cigarette smokers first tried smoking by age 18 (U.S. HHS, 2014). When considering all substances, African American youth tend to start drug use at a later age than youth from other ethnic groups (Duncan, Lessov-Schlagger, Sartor, & Bucholz, 2012; Gutman, Eccles, Peck, & Malanchuk, 2011). Also, the progression of substance experimentation, or light use to heavy use, tends to be slower for African Americans than for other groups (Finlay, White, Mun, Cronley, & Lee, 2012).

African Americans are provided their first drugs from extended family members and friends. African American males are likely to be provided their first substances from extended family members while African American females are likely to be provided their first substances from male peers (Gilliard-Matthews, Stevens, Nilsen & Dunaev, 2015).

Co-Occurring Behaviors

Drug use among adolescents is often associated with other problem behaviors, such as low academic achievement; delinquency; and early, risky sexual activity. According to problem behavior theory, drug use is part of a syndrome of other problems including juvenile delinquency, low interest in school, and aggressive and violent behavior (Jessor & Jessor, 1977). Problem behaviors may also co-occur because of an interaction of environmental factors and personal tendencies toward psychopathology. Understanding the co-occurrence of problem behaviors has implications for preventing drug use and associated problem behaviors. Interventions that focus on a common set of risk factors may be better than those that focus on a singular risk factor (Busseri, Willoughby, & Chalmers, 2007; Elkington, Bauemeister, & Zimmerman, 2010).

There is a strong association between youth delinquency, violence, and drug use. There may be common etiological factors for all of those problem behaviors, as they are all influenced by executive functions that develop as youth transition toward adult roles (Botvin & Scheier, 1997; Mobley & Chun, 2013). Research on drug abuse and violence suggests that drug use does not precede or follow violence but tends to co-occur at similar levels of frequency and severity. The underlying cause of violence may be the same as the underlying cause of drug use. Adolescents who reported juvenile justice system involvement versus no involvement were more than 2 times as likely to report substance abuse, mental health problems, and delinquent behaviors (Voisin, Kim, Takahashi, Morotta, & Bocanegra, 2017).

There is also a strong association between problem behaviors in school and drug use. Some school-related problems that are linked to drug use include failing a class, being held back a year, and being suspended or expelled (Trenz, Dunne, Zur, & Latimer, 2015).

Consequences

Early use of drugs has been associated with serious consequences of drug use and problems in later life. Youth who begin using drugs early are at increased risk for drug abuse in later adolescence and adulthood. As noted earlier, adolescent drug use has been linked to higher risk of other negative behaviors, such as school failure, poor school performance, and delinquency (Brook, Brook, & Pahl, 2006; Trenz et al., 2015). While African Americans consume less alcohol and other drugs than Whites, they have more drug- and alcohol-related problems, including legal, health, and financial problems from consuming (Babb et al., 2012; Zapolski et al., 2014).

Other serious consequences of drug use are accidental overdose, motor vehicle accidents, injury, disability, and morbidity. Early drug use is also correlated with victimization, including dating violence (Doherty, Robertson, Green, Fothergill, & Ensminger, 2012; Temple & Freeman, 2011), especially among African American girls and women. In one study, a large sample of African Americans were followed longitudinally from age 6 to age 42. The authors found a pathway from adolescent substance use to violent victimization for females (Doherty et al., 2012).

Whereas youth who initiate cigarette and other drug use in late adolescence are less likely to develop drug dependence into adulthood than those who have an earlier age of onset, the trend for African Americans is just the opposite. In fact, late onset is associated with greater cigarette use persistence into adulthood among African Americans than for Whites (Kandel, 2006). This phenomenon has been described as the crossover effect (Geronimus, Neidert, & Bound, 1993). The crossover effect refers to the fact that while African American youth have lower levels of drug use than White youth, they cross over or catch up during adulthood.

Risk and Protective Factors

There are both risk and protective factors for drug use. Risk factors are those characteristics or circumstances that predispose youth to drug use. These could include individual attributes, situational conditions, or environmental contexts. Research shows that not one but several risk factors contribute to drug use among youth. In general, the greater the number of risk factors, the greater the probability of drug use (Hawkins, Catalano, & Miller, 1992; Sloboda, Glantz, & Tarter, 2012). Research also suggests that individuals may be predisposed to substance abuse disorders and that actual use and misuse of substances is contingent on micro- and macro-environmental influences. Risk factors can be categorized under the individual, family, peer, school, and community domains.

Research has also examined protective factors against substance abuse. These factors are hypothesized to buffer individuals against stressors that might occur in the midst of risk factors, such as neighborhood and family disorganization (Grover, 1998; Jones & Neblett, 2016). Protective factors may interact with risk factors and prevent, moderate, or lessen the effects of risk factors. Protective factors can prevent drug use by providing the youth with a strong sense of self-competence that results in drug refusal efficacy.

Protective factors can be categorized in the same domains as risk factors and include the individual, family, peer, school, and community. The following protective factors have been found to be associated with less drug use and antidrug attitudes: (a) having a range of adaptive social coping skills; (b) self-efficacy and the ability to adapt to changing circumstances; (c) positive social interaction; (d) family cohesion, attachment, and bonding; (e) parental supervision and monitoring; (f) school and community norms and standards against substance use; and (g) school achievement and commitment. The concept of resilience has also been used to explain why some youth with multiple risk factors do not use drugs. Masten and Coatsworth (1998) defined resilience as "manifested competence in the context of significant challenges to adaptation or development" (p. 206).

Individual Factors

Individual factors are those that characterize individual-level susceptibility to drug use. These include dispositional and psychological factors, demographic factors, and biological factors. Several dispositional factors are associated with drug use. These include sensation seeking and rebelliousness (Malmberg et al., 2012; Stanton, Li, Cottrell, & Kaljee, 2001) and lower achievement needs (Bachman, Staff, O'Malley, Schulenberg, & Freedman-Doan, 2011; Finn, 2012). Low self-worth, aggression, alienation, and delinquency (Botvin & Scheier, 1997; Doran, Luczak, Bekman, Koutsenok, & Brown, 2012) are also associated with drug use in general. However, alienation and rebelliousness seem to be more strongly related to drug use for White than African American youth (Wallace & Muroff, 2002). Individual-level protective factors against drug use include social skills, problem-solving skills, social responsiveness, cooperativeness, emotional stability, and a positive self-concept (Grover, 1998; Stone, Becker, Huber, & Catalano, 2012).

Genetic or biological factors may also play a role in drug use. Studies of twins show that there may be a genetic predisposition for drug abuse and addiction. Other researchers have also found moderate to high genetic influences on addiction (Agrawal & Lynskey, 2008). However, limited research has been conducted on genetic factors that contribute to substance use and abuse among African Americans, and there is a need for more genetic research (Dick, Barr, Guy, Nasim, & Scott, 2017).

Regarding smoking, studies suggest that African Americans absorb more nicotine from smoking than do White or Hispanic smokers (Carabello et al., 1998; Pérez-Stable & Benowitz, 2011). Cotinine is nicotine that has been metabolized by the body and is a marker for nicotine levels. Studies have shown that African Americans metabolize and eliminate nicotine more slowly and inhale higher doses of nicotine per cigarette than White smokers. The level of serum cotinine is higher among African American smokers than among White smokers consuming the same number of cigarettes (Pérez-Stable & Benowitz). The higher levels of cotinine could account, in part, for why African Americans have a higher incidence of smoking-related diseases and have a more difficult time quitting than their White and Hispanic counterparts. Researchers speculate that if higher cotinine levels are linked to higher absorption of other health-compromising ingredients in cigarette smoke, it may help explain the higher rates of lung cancer deaths among Black smokers than among White smokers (Langreth, 1998; Schwartz, 1998).

Family Factors

Parental and family variables affect youth drug use. Family conflict, poor communication, and negative interactions with parents have been associated with adolescent drug use (Brook, Pahl, & Ning, 2004; Clark, Belgrave, & Abell, 2012). Positive family interactions, attachment, communication, and support have been associated with reductions in drug use (Bahr, Hoffman, & Yang, 2005; Brook et al., 2004).

Parental monitoring and supervision of adolescents' behavior have been linked to lower levels of substance use (Clark et al., 2012). Monitoring by adults is especially beneficial during middle school, when children may be most susceptible to peer influence (Wallace & Fisher, 2007). Clark et al. recruited 567 African American adolescents and examined both parental and peer influence on drug use. The authors found parental monitoring to be a significant factor in frequency of drug use. Parental monitoring of a child's peers and peer group activity was also important because peers are especially influential with regard to drug use. In another study, Clark and colleagues identified several other parenting factors that affected alcohol use. These included parental monitoring and control, parental disapproval of use, and parent–child relationships (Clark, Nguyen, Belgrave, & Tademy, 2011). In a related study, high parental knowledge (defined as parental awareness and information about a child's activities, whereabouts, and association) was linked to less use of all substances among African American adolescents in Grades 6–11 (Clark et al., 2012).

Family structure has also been associated with adolescent drug use (Miller & Volk, 2002). Among the general population, youth in single-parent homes are somewhat more likely to use drugs than youth who reside with both parents. African American youth are more likely than White youth to reside with one biological parent. The assumption is that two parents can provide more supervision and serve as a buffer for problems and stressors youth may face. However, the impact of family structure on drug use is mixed for African American youth. While some research has shown that African American youth who live with residential fathers use less drugs than those without (Montgomery & Marinos, 2016), other research suggests that drug use among African American youth is not greater in one- versus two-parent households (Belgrave et al., 1997; Paxton, Valois, & Drane, 2007). In terms of ethnic differences in the impact of family structure, research has shown that family structure has a stronger relationship with substance use for White than for African American adolescents (Paxton et al., 2007). Research with African American youth suggests that it is the quality or type of family relationship that makes a difference in substance use more so than the structure of the family relationship (Belgrave et al., 1997).

Siblings, especially older siblings, influence drug use. Older siblings model drug-using behaviors, provide access to drugs, and help conceal drug use from parents. In a study of African American adolescents, Pomery et al. (2005) found that older siblings' willingness to use drugs predicted drug use among younger siblings two years later. The influence of older siblings seemed to be greater for African Americans living in high-risk neighborhoods.

Peers

Peer influence is a strong predictor of drug use during adolescence (Bahr et al., 2005; Clark et al., 2012; Elkington et al., 2010). Youth who have peers who use drugs are more likely to use drugs than those whose peers do not use drugs. Peer cluster theory assumes that peers influence drug use both directly and indirectly (Oetting & Beauvais, 1986). Youth try their first drugs with peers, and peers provide drugs, model drug-using behaviors, and influence attitudes toward drugs. Both peer pressure and peer drug use have been shown to be related to the frequency of drug use (Epstein, Williams, & Botvin, 2002; Jaccard, Blanton, & Dodge, 2005). African American youth who associate with peers who engage in risky behaviors have less drug refusal efficacy and more alcohol and marijuana use (Clark et al., 2012).

Given the strong influence of peers, many drug prevention programs have been designed to increase skills to resist peer pressure for drug use. These programs teach children to identify negative drug influences, to develop the skills needed to resist peer persuasion, and to cope with peers who may be critical of non-drug-using youth (Botvin & Kantor, 2000; Georgie, Sean, Matthew, & Rona, 2016).

School Factors

In general, school problems are markers for a number of risk factors, including drug use. Lack of attachment with, commitment to, and interest in school have been associated with drug use among youth (McCluskey, Krohn, Lizotte, & Rodriguez, 2002; Piko & Kovács, 2010). School absenteeism is one of the most consistent predictors of student substance use (Hill & Mrug, 2015). School-related problems, such as school failure, truancy, and special placements, are higher among drug users (McCluskey et al., 2002). Behavioral problems in school as early as first grade are linked to drug use later in high school (Reboussin, Ialongo, & Green, 2015). Reboussin and colleagues found that African American youth who had behavioral problems (e.g., attention concentration, externalizing behavior) in first grade were more likely to transition to marijuana use in early high school than youth without behavioral problems. These findings are important to consider in early substance use prevention. High academic performance and interest is a protective factor against drug use.

However, school problems seem to be more related to drug use among White than African American youth. Wallace and Muroff (2002) found that although African American seniors in high school have lower academic performance than White seniors, they have higher levels of school involvement. When these researchers examined school risk factors and academic achievement, they found school risk factors to more strongly predict White seniors' cigarette and alcohol use than Black seniors' use. This is not to say that academic achievement is not linked to drug use among African American youth, but the association may not be as strong as it is for other ethnic groups. In fact, in a large sample of over 1,000 African American youth, Corona, Turf, Corneille, Belgrave, and Nasim (2009) found academic achievement to be the strongest predictor of substance use among African American eighth and tenth graders. Academic achievement was a stronger predictor than other variables that have been known to predict drug use, such as family conflict, neighborhood disorganization, and peer problem behavior.

Poor school management, characterized by disorganization and poor school morale, has been linked to increased drug use (Mayberry, Espelage, & Koenig, 2009). School policy also contributes to drug use. Schools that do not enforce drug policies tend to have higher levels of drug use among students than those schools where there are strictly enforced policies against drug use (Evans-Whipp, Beyers, & Lloyd, 2004).

Community Factors

There are several community-level influences on drug use for youth. Access and availability of drugs are predictors of drug use. Youth who live in communities where drugs are more easily accessible use more drugs than those who do not have such access. For example, liquor stores are more common in low-income communities than in middle-income communities. Stores selling liquor are often small convenience stores where community residents go to purchase food and other household items because of the absence of large supermarket chains in their neighborhoods. These liquor stores make alcohol much more accessible than in middle-income neighborhoods.

Violence and violence exposure are community risk factors for substance use (Wallace, Neilands, & Sanders-Phillips, 2017). Wallace and colleagues examined the link among youth between neighborhood risk, as measured by community violence and substance use, by considering the role of psychological outlook, along with neighborhood risk. Psychological outlook was conceptualized as hopelessness, future orientation, and self-efficacy. In a study of 592 African American youth (mean age = 15.58), the authors found that neighborhood risk, along with having a negative psychological outlook, was linked to drug use. One plausible reason for the link between violence exposure and substance use is that young people's outlook on life may be affected by experiencing violence, subsequently leading youth to turn to substance use as a way of coping.

Drug use is also prevalent in communities that have high levels of physical and social disorganization. Communities with densely packed low-income housing developments, high crime rates, youth gangs, low surveillance of youth, and adult illicit behavior show higher rates of youth drug use. Like their adult counterparts, youth may turn to drugs to deal with the stress of their environment. One study of 398 African American young adults assessed the physical disorder of the neighborhood residential block where the youth lived. Neighborhoods with high levels of physical disorder had higher levels of marijuana use (Furr-Holden et al., 2015).

Economic and employment opportunities within a community play a role in drug use and associated negative behaviors. The availability of jobs, recreational activities, and community resources are dependent on the economy of a community. Distressed communities provide few alternative activities in which youth can engage. In fact, when African Americans relocate to a neighborhood with better economic and employment conditions, they report fewer alcohol- and drug-using members in their social networks (Linton et al., 2016). Under-resourced communities provide little employment and few legitimate opportunities for youth to earn money. Among some youth, drug use and drug selling are distinct and separate activities, and drug selling may not be seen as a negative activity. Lambert, Brown, Phillips, and Ialongo (2004) conducted a longitudinal study of urban African American adolescents on community perceptions and drug use. The authors found that the students' perceptions of neighborhood disorganization (i.e., violence/safety and drug activity) in Grade 7 were associated with increased tobacco, alcohol, and marijuana use in Grade 9.

Neighborhood collective efficacy is a community factor that protects African American youth from the harmful effects of witnessing and experiencing violence. Collective efficacy is the presence of shared trust and cohesion among residents, along with the desire of the neighborhood to help regulate youth behavior (Sampson et al., 1997). Adults in communities with high collective efficacy help monitor youth and intervene when they see youth misbehaving. Under conditions of youth victimization, substance use is less for those living in neighborhoods with high versus low levels of collective efficacy (Fagan, Wright, & Pinchevsky, 2014).

Marketing of Tobacco Products in African American Neighborhoods

African American and White neighborhoods vary greatly in terms of the marketing of tobacco products. African Americans are exposed to tobacco marketing more so than other racial and ethnic groups (Roberts et al., 2015). In the United States, point-of-sale (POS) marketing (i.e., marketing where tobacco products are sold) is the primary avenue for marketing tobacco products. Lee, Henriksen, Rose, Moreland-Russell, and Ribisl (2015) conducted a systematic review of neighborhood sociodemographic factors that affected the marketing of cigarettes and other tobacco products. This systematic review contained published studies that examined presence and quantity of marketing of tobacco products at POS to determine whether disparities existed by neighborhood demographic factors in the United States and in other countries. The majority of the studies were published in the United States (N = 33). Findings relevant to marketing of tobacco products in African American communities were (1) strong evidence of targeted marketing in more disadvantaged neighborhoods; (2) higher prevalence of marketing at the POS in neighborhoods with more Black residents; (3) greater marketing of menthol tobacco products in Black neighborhoods; (4) a disproportionate amount of marketing of little cigar and cigarillos in neighborhoods with more Black residents; and (5) neighborhoods where Black children resided had significantly more marketing of menthol cigarettes near where candy was sold.

The Lee et al. (2015) study shows that both mentholated cigarettes and little cigars and cigarillos are more likely to be marketed in African American communities than other racial and ethnic communities. This finding was also seen in a study by Cantrell et al. (2013). In a study of 750 licensed tobacco retail outlets in Washington, D.C., researchers found that the likelihood of the store having little cigars and cigarillos were higher in African American neighborhoods than others. The price of these products was also lower in African American neighborhoods, and there was greater marketing at the store exterior. Lower pricing may serve as a cue for initiation and use of these products. This is an illustration of how the tobacco industry targets African American youth for drug use initiation.

Cultural Factors

There has been recent research on the positive role of cultural variables in preventing drug use and abuse among African American youth. The findings from this research assume that spirituality, positive ethnic identity, and strong cultural values serve as protective factors for African American youth. These findings have resulted in a call for the development of culturally specific drug prevention and treatment programs (Gilbert & Goddard, 2007; Webb, Francis, Hines, & Quarles, 2007). The assumption is that drug prevention information presented in culturally meaningful and relevant formats can be effective in inoculating youth from those personal attributes and ecological factors that are associated with initiation of drug use. Culturally specific values and beliefs about self and about how to relate to others—especially to one's community—can be protective for African American youth. African American youth who have internalized spirituality, Africentric values, and a positive racial identity are better able to resist and/or delay drug initiation (Belgrave et al., 1997, 2000).

Spirituality

One dimension of an Africentric worldview, spirituality (and religiosity), is linked to less drug use (Stevens-Watkins & Rostosky 2010). In a study of over 1,000 students from two HBCUs, Bowen-Reid and Rhodes (2003) found that students who use marijuana are less spiritual than those who either stopped using or who have never used marijuana. Belgrave et al. (1997) found that African American youth who attend Church and who discuss religious and spiritual topics within the home are less likely to use drugs (cigarettes, beer, wine, etc.) than those with fewer religious practices. Belgrave et al. note that the religiosity of youth in their relatively young sample (i.e., ages 9 and 10) probably reflects the religiosity of parents and other adults in the home. In households where experiences are organized around spiritual and religious activities, there may be fewer opportunities for youth to experiment with drugs. In addition, in households where parents and other adults do not use drugs, there is less access to drugs. Religious activity likely shapes exposure to other risk factors, including high-risk peers and poor friendship choices.

Religious activity sometimes provides a monitoring function. Steinman and Zimmerman (2004) examined how religious activity was associated with risk behaviors concurrently and developmentally among urban African American adolescents. In their study, 705 African American adolescents were interviewed during their high school years. The authors found that declining religious activity was associated with increases in alcohol among males and increases in sexual activity among females. They also found that the more frequently African American males attended Church in ninth grade, the less of an increase they had in marijuana use throughout high school. For females, religious activity in ninth grade was associated with less cigarette use throughout high school.

Spirituality provides both direct and indirect benefits against drug use especially under conditions of trauma and stressful life conditions. One study examined the role of spirituality as a moderator of the relationship between traumatic life experiences and drug use in a sample of African American women (N = 206) (Staton-Tindall, Duvall, Stevens-Watkins, & Oser, 2013). Spirituality was directly related to alcohol use. In addition spirituality moderated the relationship between traumatic life events and cocaine use. Specifically, as the number of reported traumatic life events increased among participants, women with higher levels of spirituality (compared with lower levels) consumed less cocaine.

Other studies have shown that religiosity is an important factor in substance abuse recovery (Fife et al., 2011). African American women who engaged in higher Church attendance with their family had better recovery from substance abuse.

Ethnic Identity

Ethnic identity has been defined as feelings of belongingness, attachment, and behavioral dispositions toward one's own ethnic group (Phinney, 1992). Several studies have shown a relationship between ethnic identity and reduced problem behaviors among youth. Ethnic identity is associated with increased academic achievement (Wong et al., 2003), better coping (Greig, 2003), and lower sexual risk (Beadnell et al., 2003) among African American youth. In general, ethnic minority youth with strong ethnic identity are less likely to use drugs (Brook, Zhang, Finch, & Brook, 2010; Kong et al., 2012; Nasim, Utsey, Corona, & Belgrave, 2006; Townsend & Belgrave, 2000).

A study by Zapolski et al. (2017) confirmed that ethnic identity was protective for ethnic minority youth. A national diverse sample of 34,708 students who were African American, Asian, Hispanic, multiracial, Native American, and White was included in this study. Higher ethnic identity correlated with less past-month drug use for African Americans, Hispanic, and multiracial youth but not for White youth. Ethnic identity was not associated with lower drug use for White youth. The path linking ethnic identity to less drug use for African American and other ethnic minority students was through drug attitudes. Higher ethnic identity was associated with more negative drug attitudes, and more negative drug attitudes led to less drug use.

Africentric Values

Ethnic identity has to do with one's personal and individual sense of affiliation with one's ethnic and cultural group. Africentric values, on the other hand, have to do with the beliefs, values, and cultural dispositions of people of African descent. Like ethnic identity, Africentric values have been associated with prosocial behavior and positive coping strategies (Thompson & Chambers, 2000). The limited research that has been conducted has shown that Africentric values are related to less drug use among African American youth (Belgrave et al., 1997; Nasim, Corona, Belgrave, Utsey, & Fallah, 2007b).

Nasim, Belgrave, et al. (2007) found that Africentric values had both a direct and protective effect on alcohol use among African American youth. Africentric values protected youth from alcohol initiation and use when these youth had peers with high-risk behaviors. Spirituality and ethnic identity were also negatively associated with drug use in the same study. In another study, Belgrave, Brome, and Hampton (2000) examined the relative contribution of culturally specific variables to drug use. The authors investigated the incremental contribution of culturally specific factors in predicting drug outcomes, when controlling for other variables that have traditionally been identified as correlates and/or predictors of drug use among adolescents. These other variables included individual variables (e.g., self-esteem), family variables (e.g., family cohesion), and peer variables (e.g., peer drug attitudes). The results of this study indicated that cultural variables, such as Africentric values, along with racial identity, contributed significantly to understanding drug knowledge, drug use, and drug attitudes among African American youth. Cultural variables were as strongly associated with drug variables, as were more traditional variables.

There are several reasons why Africentric values may be related to drug attitudes and use. Africentric values may, in general, promote positive behaviors and a healthy, drug-free lifestyle. Families who adhere to strong Africentric values may be less affected by stressors and may be more protected under adverse or stressful conditions that could lead to drug use. In essence, drug use is probably antithetical to Africentric values and beliefs.

Institutional and Societal Factors

In addition to cultural and identity factors that operate on an individual level, there are several institutional and societal influences on drug use among African Americans. About 26% of African Americans live below the poverty level, and many more are considered poor or near poverty (Macartney, Bishaw, & Fontenot, 2013). Poverty is almost always associated with living in neighborhoods with low economic viability and other social problems. We now review how poverty and racism and discrimination contribute to drug use. Then, we review cocaine as an example of how institutional discrimination affects sentencing differentials between African Americans and Whites.

Poverty

Poverty is a risk factor for drug use (Williams & Latkin, 2007). C. Williams and Latkin conducted a study of 249 neighborhoods in Baltimore, Maryland, and found neighborhood poverty to be significantly associated with cocaine and heroin use. On the other hand, social support and ties to employed people were protective factors against drug use. The lack of employment seems to be a primary reason for the link between poverty and drug use. Individuals who are not in the labor force and those with low levels of education are more likely to live in communities with a high degree of poverty and subsequently engage in more drug use and abuse (Valdez, Kaplan, & Curtis, 2007).

Racism and Discrimination

Racism and discrimination have been shown to influence substance use and abuse in several studies (Brody, Kogan, & Chen, 2012b; Clark, 2014; Gerrard et al., 2012; Thompson, Goodman, & Kwate, 2016). Drugs may be used as a coping strategy for racism and discrimination. Gerrard et al. found that African American adolescents and young adults who endorsed substance use as a coping strategy were more willing to use substances after experiencing discrimination. Similarly, Brody, Kogan, and Chen (2012b) found in a sample of African American male adolescents that high levels of perceived discrimination were significantly associated with increases in substance use. Perceived discrimination was linked to substance use through lower levels of school engagement and increases in affiliation with substance-using peers. The causal pathway of this relationship was such that discrimination influenced substance use rather than vice versa. Another pathway between racism and discrimination and substance use is anger and reduced self-control: These variables have been shown to increase susceptibility to substance use. Discrimination leads to anger, and anger can lead to substance use (Gibbons et al., 2012). Discrimination seems to be a more influential factor in substance use among males than females.

Sanders-Phillips et al. identified psychological distress (e.g., depression) as another pathway from racial discrimination to alcohol and marijuana use in a sample of 567 African American high school students (mean age = 15.6 years). Perceived racial discrimination led to more depressive symptoms, and more depressive symptoms were associated with greater past-month substance use.

Everyday discrimination and nicotine dependence is related (Kendzor et al., 2014). Using a national sample of African American men (N = 1,271), Parker et al. (2016) assessed the relationship between discrimination and cigarette smoking. Thirty-two percent of the sample were current smokers. Those who experienced major discrimination were more likely to be a current smoker than those who had not experienced major discrimination.

Crack Cocaine–Powdered Cocaine Discrepancy

Previous differences in mandatory minimum sentences for crack cocaine and powdered cocaine illustrate the role of race in convictions and lengths of sentencing. Crack is a form of cocaine whose market is concentrated in urban communities that are largely African American and Hispanic (Banks, 1997). These communities have elevated levels of poverty, unemployment, and other indicators of community distress. The Omnibus Bill, implemented in 1987, imposed mandatory minimum sentences of 5 years for first offenders convicted of trafficking 5 (or more) grams of crack cocaine. In contrast, conviction for possessing powdered cocaine was a misdemeanor with a maximum penalty of 1 year of imprisonment. To obtain a 5-year sentence for powdered cocaine would require trafficking 500 grams. The Omnibus Drug Bill was upheld in 1995, despite efforts to address and overturn the 100-to-1 quantity ratio between sentences for trafficking in crack and powdered cocaine and the penalties for simple possession of crack (Banks, 1997).

These sentencing differentials had a large effect on African Americans' convictions in federal courts (Banks, 1997; Nunn, 2002). For example, in 1993, the racial distribution of all convictions for drug trafficking in the federal courts was fairly even (Whites, 30.8%; African Americans, 33.9%; Hispanics, 33.8%). However, persons convicted of crack cocaine offenses have been overwhelmingly African American (88.3%), as opposed to White (4.1%) or Hispanic (7.1%). Because most drug cases are tried at the state and local levels, mandatory minimum sentences also resulted in an overwhelming majority of those convicted at the state and local level for crack cocaine offenses to be African American. In December 2007, the U.S. Supreme Court ruled that these differences in sentencing for crack and powdered cocaine were unjust, and more parity in sentencing guidelines for crack and powdered cocaine began.

In 2010, President Obama signed the Fair Sentencing Act into legislation. This legislation limits the mandatory minimum sentences for low-level crack cocaine offenses (The Sentencing Project, 2010). The new law significantly reduced the cocaine sentencing quantity disparity from 100 to 1 to 18 to 1 by increasing the amount of crack cocaine necessary to trigger the 5- and 10-year mandatory minimum sentences that were set in 1986. The legislation also eliminated the mandatory minimum for simple possession of crack cocaine. On his last day in office, President Obama commuted 330 drug sentences that were identified as unfair given the nature of the drug offense (Lederman, 2017).

METHODOLOGICAL AND RESEARCH ISSUES

We discuss two methodological issues to consider when conducting research on drugs and African Americans. These issues are (a) the identification of appropriate and relevant constructs and measures in drug research and (b) the recruitment of African American participants in drug research.

Identification of Appropriate and Relevant Constructs and Measures in Drug Research

Identifying the appropriate and relevant constructs and measures to understand predictors of or contributors to drug use are methodological concerns. Most researchers have assumed that the same factors that are correlated with drug use among the general population hold true for African Americans. However, this is not always the case. For example, several studies reviewed earlier in this chapter showed that strong cultural beliefs and values were associated with less drug use and more negative drug attitudes among African Americans (Belgrave et al., 1997, Belgrave, Brome, & Hampton, 2000; Cherry et al., 1998; Zapolski et al., 2017). Other studies have shown an association between drug use and religiosity and spirituality for African Americans (Belgrave et al., 1997; Wallace, Brown, Bachman, & LaVeist, 2003). The relationship between drug use and spirituality may not be as strong for Whites. In analysis of data on African American and White adults, Belgrave (2005) found that spirituality had a stronger negative association with drug use among African Americans than it did among Whites. Another study on ethnic identity showed that ethnic identity correlated differentially with drug use for ethnic minority and White youth (Zapolski et al., 2017). Still other studies have shown that while African Americans are exposed to higher risk factors, they are less vulnerable to some drugs.

Finally, some research suggests that family factors may play a different role in drug use among White and African American youth. Research on White youth has suggested that those who reside within single-parent households are more likely to use drugs than those who reside in two-parent households (Miller & Volk, 2002). However, Belgrave et al. (1997) found no correlation between family structure and drug attitudes or use for African American adolescents. That is, youth who lived with one parent were not any more likely to use drugs than those who lived with two parents. Also, the work of Wallace and Muroff (2002) shows that African American youth differ from other ethnic groups in exposure to drug risk and in vulnerability to drug use. Wallace and Muroff found that African American and White high school seniors differed significantly in their exposure to more than half of 55 risk factors.

Recruitment of African American Participants in Drug Research

Good recruitment and retention is critical to successful drug research and prevention interventions. Research findings will not be valid and effective prevention interventions will not benefit African American participants unless they are recruited and retained. Recruitment efforts begin with identifying the population and using a sampling approach that will ensure that findings are relevant to African Americans. But socioeconomic and contextual factors linked to ethnicity affect sample identification and recruitment. For example, a study on factors that predict drug use among youth who are and are not in school would need to include youth who are both in and out of school.

Sampling the latter will require a different type of identification protocol and recruitment strategy. Another example is a sampling protocol where participants are selected based on random telephone dialing. Participants without landline telephones may be omitted from the sample if only landline telephones are used to identify participants. Household surveys would exclude those who are in nontraditional housing. Although these sampling biases affect the inclusion of individuals from all ethnic groups in substance abuse research, they may more likely affect African Americans because socioeconomic factors affect lower school attendance and access to telephones and housing.

Studies on recruitment have focused on factors that predict family engagement in substance abuse prevention programs, with engagement defined as program attendance or nonattendance (Gorman-Smith, Tolan, & Henry 2002). Zane, Thomson, and Dugan (2004) studied factors that predicted recruitment among African American adolescents and families in a drug prevention program. Of the 257 families that provided permission-to-contact slips, only 99 (38.5%) were enrolled in the project, and 158 (61.5%) were not enrolled in the project. On average, it took six contacts to enroll an adolescent in the study. More research on effective recruitment strategies for engaging African American youth in drug prevention studies is needed.

Other research has found that African Americans are less likely than other ethnic and racial groups to complete substance abuse treatment (Davis & Ancis, 2012; Montgomery, Petry, & Carroll, 2012). In a study of court-referred, marijuana-dependent young adults, African Americans were compared with White participants on treatment completion. African American young adults were significantly less likely to complete treatment than their White counterparts. Montgomery et al. and Davis and Ancis similarly note that African American women are less likely to be retained in a treatment program. The lower completion rate for African Americans may be linked to program and treatment approaches that are not culturally tailored for them.

Research by Guerrero, Fenwich, Kong, Grella, and D'Aunno (2015) suggests that one reason African Americans and other racial and ethnic minorities fare worse than Whites in treatment retention is because African Americans are more likely to be treated in low-capacity programs that are not able to meet their treatment needs. High- versus low-capacity programs have the resources to be responsive to diverse populations served. High-capacity treatment programs have strong leadership, organizational readiness to implement new practices, and usually acceptance of a state Medicaid program. High-capacity treatment programs also provide culturally tailored outreach and engagement. Guerrero et al. found that when African American clients were in high-capacity drug treatment programs, they had longer treatment retention than when they were in low-capacity programs.

To better address substance abuse prevention and treatment among African Americans, more culturally targeted strategies are needed for recruiting and retaining African Americans in research and treatment protocols.

BEST PRACTICES FOR PREVENTING AND TREATING DRUG USE

The best way of dealing with substance and drug use is to prevent it from occurring. Several types of prevention programs have been successfully used to prevent alcohol, tobacco, and other drug use among African Americans. Some of these programs are universal, meaning that they are applicable to all ethnic and cultural groups. Others are more culturally specific, meaning that they are designed specifically for African Americans.

Several approaches have been used for preventing and reducing substance use and abuse among youth. Knowledge-based programs are designed to provide information about drugs and the negative consequences of drugs. Knowledge-based programs, when used alone, have not shown effectiveness in changing drug behaviors. Personal, interpersonal, and enhancement programs promote feelings of self-worth and competence that make the individual less likely to engage in drug use. Life skills and social skills programs teach youth skills for refusing drugs, make youth aware of the social context of drug use, and provide youth with skills for coping with anxiety and interpersonal relationships that may lead to drug use. Family programs improve parenting skills and family cohesiveness and foster competence and connections among children to deter drug use. Community programs target aspects of the environment that affect drug accessibility and attitudes. Actions can include removal of liquor stores, policing of drug trade, and advertising. Alternative programs provide youth with constructive and healthy activities that offset the attractiveness of drugs. These may include community service programs for youth, athletic and recreational programs, and tutoring and educational enhancement programs. Cultural enhancement programs focus on the infusion of cultural values, attitudes, and behaviors that are protective against drug use. Most programs use a combination of these strategies and approaches for drug prevention.

A review of Substance Abuse Mental Health Services Administration's (SAMHSA) National Registry of Evidence-Based Programs and Practices (NREPP) listed 49 substance abuse prevention interventions targeted specifically for African American youth ages 6 through 17 with promising or effective outcomes (SAMHSA, n.d.). The majority of these programs target youth 11–14 years of age or youth in middle school or junior high school. These prevention interventions are most likely to be implemented within school settings, followed by family sessions. These preventive interventions are designed to prevent and delay drug use and also improve (a) drug refusal or resistance skills, (b) negative and intolerant drug attitudes and norms, (c) prosocial behaviors and social competence, (d) intrapersonal and psychological well-being, (e) communication and decision-making skills, and (f) family bonding and cohesion. There were eight substance abuse treatment programs for African American adults 18 and over on SAMHSA's NREPP. These programs (a) address mental health issues along with substance abuse issues; (b) provide an alternative to incarceration; and (c) encourage family and community support.

Culturally Focused Approaches to Drug Prevention and Treatment

Considering how important cultural beliefs and behaviors are in drug prevention and intervention, programs that consider culture in such efforts should be beneficial (Castro & Alarcon, 2002; Longshore, Grills, & Annon, 1999). There has been some recent work in which culturally congruent drug programs have been developed, implemented, and evaluated.

Culturally focused prevention programs funded by the Center for Substance Abuse Prevention can be categorized into three broad categories (Chipungu et al., 2000). The first program type addresses the potential of cultural tradition, values, and spirituality as protective factors. These factors are incorporated in prevention programs. The second program type explores African American and African history and the contributions of Blacks as sources of identity and positive affirmation. This type of program might also include trips to Black museums or exhibits. The third program type focuses on contemporary cultural experiences among African Americans and addresses a range of topics related to external risk. This program may, for example, address racism and discrimination as factors in drug use and incarceration. Most culturally focused prevention programs include a combination of these three program types.

We describe three programs with strong cultural foci: a drug prevention program for African American youth and two drug treatment programs for African American women. Common to all programs is the use of culture, both in content (e.g., topics, lessons, curriculums) and in process (e.g., method by which the program is implemented).

A Culturally Appropriate Drug Prevention Program

The Strong African American Families–Teen (SAAF-T) program is a culturally specific drug prevention program for African American youth (Brody, Chen, et al., 2012). This evidence-based substance abuse prevention program also deters conduct disorders. The program consists of five consecutive meetings held at community centers. Each session involves a separate 1-hour meeting for parents or caregivers and adolescents followed by a 1-hour meeting with both caregivers or parents and adolescents. Topics covered in the parents' session include the importance of monitoring and control; racial socialization, including how to deal with discrimination; establishing norms and expectations about substance use; and cooperative problem solving. Topics covered in the adolescent session include household rules, academic success, and strategies to use when encountering racism. Caregivers or parents and adolescents meet jointly in a subsequent session where they apply the skills they have learned in the previous session. Data collected 22 months after program completion showed that participation in the SAAF-T resulted in a significant decrease in the frequency of conduct problems, substance use, and substance use problems. The SAAF-T program was implemented in community centers but can also be implemented in other organizations and agencies, such as Boys and Girls Clubs, schools, and Churches.

Africentric Approaches to Substance Abuse Treatment

An example of a culturally congruent drug treatment program for African American women was discussed in Chapter 2. Nobles and Goddard's Healer Women Fighting Disease (HWFD) Integrated Substance Abuse and HIV Prevention Program for Black Women (Nobles et al., 2009) used African philosophy for framing and delivering both HIV and substance abuse intervention activities.

Another culturally congruent drug treatment program was implemented by Jackson, Stephens, and Smith (1997). This program, called the Iwo San (Swahili for house of healing; Jackson et al., 1997), was a residential treatment program for drug- and alcohol-abusing African American women and their dependent children. The program was based on the assumption that addiction arises as a coping mechanism for escaping stressors and the problems of daily life.

Iwo San incorporated a rites-of-passage component engendering the African-centered perspective. The rites of passage fostered a sense of responsibility for self, family, and community. Spirituality played a key role in this program and was interwoven throughout the treatment in Iwo San. A council of elders was one component of the rites program. Elders were selected by age, recognition, and standing in the community and consisted of representatives from all program components (staff, residents, community residents, etc.). The Council of Elders expressed wisdom, offered guidance and leadership, and facilitated moral and spiritual development.

The Iwo San program also emphasized respect for tradition. Respect for tradition was reflected in holding ceremonies to celebrate rites of passage and holidays such as

Kwanzaa and by the preparation of traditional African and African American foods. All clients and their children were taught African and African American history. Another feature of the program was to promote harmony within the spiritual, mental, and physical self. Accordingly, each client was taught meditation in order to facilitate self-understanding. The program also focused on the "we," and the entire community shared responsibilities—from chores to problems.

In terms of treatment length, most drug treatment programs establish set days for participation. However, establishment of a set number of days for a client to complete treatment is incompatible with an African-centered perspective. In African-centered tradition, the will of the people, not the clock, defines time. Because the client's treatment progress was individual, so was her period of participation.

Another culturally focused substance abuse prevention program used members of African American Churches as mentors for women in recovery (Stahler et al., 2005). This program, called Bridges, was developed based on the fact that women in recovery from cocaine addiction needed ties or bridges with the natural helping networks within their community. One hundred and eighteen African American women experiencing homelessness and who used cocaine participated. Women who were in a comprehensive residential rehabilitation program received standard treatment or standard treatment plus Bridges. The Bridges program recruited mentors from Churches and other faith-based institutions and trained them as community anchor persons. Each client was matched with a community anchor person whose job was to help in any way needed (i.e., providing clients with group and individual fellowship, being a mentor and friend, assisting with children, and helping to secure housing and furnishings from local donors). Mentors and the women were paired while the women were still in a residential treatment program and communicated daily by phone. An evaluation of the program indicated that women who were in the Bridges program stayed in the residential treatment program longer. After 1 year of program completion, all women in the Bridges program reported no cocaine use in the past 30 days versus 2 days of reported cocaine use by participants who were not in the Bridges program.

Although the research on cultural approaches to prevention and treatment is limited, the few studies that have been conducted are promising. Research suggests that culturally based approaches used in conjunction with other prevention and treatment methods support prevention or reduction of drug use among African Americans.

CRITICAL ANALYSIS

Drug use is less prevalent among African Americans than in most other ethnic groups. Yet African Americans continue to face worse social, economic, and health consequences from such use. A similar analogy is found when we consider other health conditions and outcomes among African Americans. African Americans are less likely to benefit from treatment given the same medical condition and comparable socioeconomic conditions (see Chapter 12). The likely culprit is racism and discrimination: Access to prevention programming and fair and equitable treatment of drug infractions are less likely to occur for African Americans than other ethnic groups. This suggests that changing public policies and criminal justice procedures will need to occur in order for African Americans to receive appropriate treatment when there is drug dependence and abuse.

At the same time, there are promising areas for reducing drug use and the cost of such use. We need to examine closely drug prevention programs that target all types of problem behaviors. In doing so, we simultaneously reduce risk for many problem behaviors, including violence. And we may improve prosocial behaviors, such as academic achievement and community engagement, at the same time. These programs should be culturally congruent in order to be most effective. Understanding the ways in which culturally congruent programming works is also an important continuing research priority.

Also, more research is needed to understand the etiology and consequences of drug use among African Americans. For example, why is it that African Americans who begin drug use later in life (rather than earlier) tend to escalate in use? This is in contrast to other populations whose early use (rather than later use) creates more problems later in life. More research on drug use vulnerabilities is also needed because an identification of these will allow for more effective prevention interventions.

Summary

The proverb at the beginning of the chapter states, "When the cock is drunk, he forgets about the hawk." Similarly, alcohol and other drugs have had devastating consequences for African Americans. In this chapter, we have explored some of the reasons for drug use and abuse and what can be done about the problem.

Africans drank alcohol during celebrations and special events, and alcohol was also used as currency in the slave trade. The use of alcohol and other drugs continued among enslaved Africans in the New World. Following the Civil War, increased use of drugs occurred as African Americans began migrating North and to urban areas.

Surveys of the prevalence of drug use among youth show that African American teenagers use less alcohol, cigarettes, and other drugs than White youth. However, patterns of use change with age, and African Americans increase their drug use as they get older.

Drug initiation begins during early adolescence and tends to co-occur with other social problems. There are several risk and protective factors for drug use.

These include risk and protective factors at the individual, family, peer, school, and community levels. Poverty is a contributor to drug use.

Drug incarceration policies result in higher rates of incarceration among African Americans than among other ethnic groups because of differentials in crack cocaine and powdered cocaine sentencing. While sentencing disparities remain, they are becoming less disparate because of the Fair Sentencing Act.

Cultural beliefs and values may reduce risk for drug use. Strong spirituality, high ethnic identity, and Africentric values correlate with less drug use and more negative drug attitudes. Programs that infuse cultural values, beliefs, and ethnic consciousness enhance these protective factors against drug use.

There are several approaches to preventing and treating substance use including culturally specific programs such as the Strong African American Family Program and the Iwo San rites-of-passage program.

PROSOCIAL AND ANTISOCIAL BEHAVIOR

To fight once shows bravery, but to fight all the time is stupid.

—Oromo proverb

LEARNING OBJECTIVES

- To be able to define prosocial and antisocial behavior and related concepts

- To increase awareness of prosocial behavior, including volunteering, giving, and philanthropy among African Americans

- To become familiar with factors that influence prosocial behavior among children and youth

- To become more aware of how community violence exposure affects youth prosocial and antisocial behavior

- To become familiar with methodological issues when studying prosocial behavior and aggression

- To learn best practices for preventing violence and aggression

A RISING FORCE: ON THE STATE OF BLACK PHILANTHROPY

BY ADE ADENIJI

Thanks to a few hundred years of slavery and Jim Crow, followed by decades of economic exclusion, African American households have far less wealth than whites. In fact, according to a recent study by Demos and the Institute on Assets and Social Policy, the typical black household now has just 6 percent of the wealth of the typical white household.

(Continued)

(Continued)

This deep racial wealth gap wouldn't seem to bode well for black philanthropy. In fact, though, black Americans have a long history of philanthropic commitment. A report by the W. K. Kellogg Foundation a few years ago found that African Americans give away 25 percent more of their income per year than white Americans. With the cohort of people of color growing in size and assets, these populations will likely be even more important down the line. As we recently reported, a number of African Americans, as well as Latinos, are already giving at a substantial level.

This rising philanthropic muscle has been on display in fundraising for the new Smithsonian National Museum of African American History and Culture (NMAAHC), set to open later this month after years in the making. Aside from established foundations like Mellon, Gates and Atlantic Philanthropies, the museum's top donors also include black Americans like billionaires Oprah Winfrey, Michael Jordan and Robert F. Smith, as well as Shonda Rhimes, Kenneth Chenault and Richard Parsons.

To get a better sense of the state of black giving, I recently spoke with the three architects of the Black Philanthropy Month (BPM) campaign. They are Jacqueline Copeland-Carson, who founded BPM in 2011 and is also the co-founder of Pan-African Women's Philanthropy Network; Tracey Webb, who's the founder of Black Benefactors, a giving circle in Washington, D.C.; and Valaida Fullwood, a writer and consultant and author of *Giving Back: A Tribute to Generations of African American Philanthropists*. BPM, which just happened in August, is "an annual, global celebration of African-descent giving."

One point that the trio stressed is that the story of black philanthropy isn't just about a wealthy elite, but the masses of people committed to giving back whatever they can. Sayings like "don't forget where you came from" have long been part of the black lexicon, they reminded me. This tradition is also rooted in the black church, a defining institution which has served not only as an important site of organizing and social change, but also of giving.

The populist nature of black philanthropy underscores the need to look beyond foundations and major donors in thinking about how to spur greater African American giving. Because there are fewer big pots of wealth available, as is the case for white America, efforts to elicit higher levels of mass giving and better-targeted giving are key to nurturing black philanthropy as a rising force.

The main aims of Black Philanthropy Month are to inform, involve, inspire and invest in black philanthropic leadership to strengthen African-American and African-descent giving in all its forms. Each year, BPM has a new theme. This year's theme was "Elevating A Culture of Giving." An event at the Museum of the African Diaspora (MoAD) in San Francisco called "Giving Arts" featured keynote speaker Danny Glover. It examined the critical role of art in the black community and the state of philanthropy and community giving; research suggests that only about 5 percent of the multi-billion-dollar black philanthropy economy gives to the arts.

Other events took place in less obvious regions, like Portland, Oregon, which has a black population in the low single digits. The MRG Foundation, a social justice funder, hosted "Giving Back: The Soul of Philanthropy Reframed and Exhibited" for BPM.

MRG Foundation Major Giving Director Carol Tatch echoed the idea that giving often tends to be baked into the African American experience. Certainly, that was the case for Tatch, who said:

Philanthropy wasn't a late-in-life idea or practice, but it was a foundational way of being, that existed in my childhood, and in my mothers' childhood, in my community and our collective ancestors. From my mother's feet, in my church's pews, at my grandmother's picnics, at school events, I was shown how to be a philanthropist. We never used big fancy words for it—we simply called it giving back because that is exactly what it was.

There's an international dynamic to BPM, as well, which makes sense, given the growing number of blacks in America with recent roots in Africa. One of the BPM events took place in the Minneapolis–Saint Paul area, a region with the most ethnically diverse black community in the U.S., with a population that includes Nigerians, Somalis, Ethiopians and Liberians.

This year's Black Philanthropy Month came at a moment when quite a few foundations are thinking harder about racial equity and how to do more around this issue, as we've reported. The California Endowment and the California Wellness Foundation partnered in the BPM campaign, while other foundations spread the word.

Now that August has come to a close, BPM's leaders tell me that next steps include launching a website called Black Giving United, an information clearinghouse and chat room to get people in touch with resources. BPM also aims to collaborate with the National Museum of African American History and Culture. You can see more about its doings by following hashtag #BPM365.

Source: Adeniji (2016).

INTRODUCTION

Throughout history, there have been examples of individuals and groups who behave in altruistic and positive ways. As the cover story illustrates, giving is well established among African Americans and part of a historical legacy. Altruistic acts range from taking food to an ill neighbor, to contributing millions of dollars to an educational institution, to risking one's life to save another's. At the same time, humankind is filled with aggressive, violent, and unimaginable acts done to one another. These behaviors range from the online social exclusion of middle school girls to a serial killer's apparently senseless murders. Prosocial and antisocial behavior is the focus of this chapter.

Prosocial behavior covers topics such as volunteerism; community, civic, and political engagement; philanthropy; and cooperation and sharing. Antisocial behavior covers topics such as aggression and violence. The first part of this chapter is devoted to prosocial behavior, and the second part is devoted to antisocial behavior. In the section on prosocial behavior, we provide an introduction, a discussion of foundations of prosocial behavior, a history of prosocial behavior in the United States, theoretical perspectives, and then a discussion of selected topics in prosocial behavior (e.g., volunteering and giving, civic engagement, philanthropy). In the section on antisocial behavior, we provide a discussion on violence against enslaved Africans and African Americans. In trying to understand the origin of violence, we examine the theoretical debate over whether aggression is inborn or learned, along with theoretical perspectives on crime and violence. We also discuss community violence and covictimization, youth violence, and violence against African American women. A discussion of methodological and research issues is provided and then a discussion of best practices for improving prosocial behavior and decreasing antisocial behavior. This is followed by a critical analysis and, finally, a chapter summary.

PROSOCIAL BEHAVIOR

Prosocial behavior among African Americans can be seen everywhere, whether in the notable philanthropy of famous African Americans, such as Gladys Knight, Oprah Winfrey, Russell Simmons, and Alicia Keyes, or in the sacrifices of African Americans, such as Frederick Douglass and Harriet Tubman, who risked their lives to free enslaved Africans. Prosocial behavior among children and adolescents is seen in cooperative behaviors, such as sharing, cooperating, and helping others.

Prosocial behavior is defined as a voluntary action intended to benefit another individual or groups of individuals (Mussen & Eisenberg, 2001). Forms of prosocial behavior are varied and include community, civic, and political engagement. Philanthropy, a form of prosocial behavior, is a Greek word that means "love of mankind." *Merriam-Webster's Collegiate Dictionary* (Merriam-Webster, n.d.) defines philanthropy as goodwill to fellow men, especially active effort to promote human welfare. Often, philanthropy brings to mind large contributions by wealthy donors to foundations and institutions. However, Dr. Emmett Carson, a scholar on African American philanthropy, calls for a broadening of the definition of philanthropy. He defines Black philanthropy as the giving of time, talent, goods, and services or money by African Americans for charitable purposes (Carson, 2005). Black philanthropy includes three types of philanthropy: (a) Humanitarian aid is providing aid or assistance to others in need. (b) Self-help involves creating opportunities and systems for individuals and groups to help themselves and to solve their own problems. (c) Social philanthropy involves targeting resources and efforts for social and economic changes.

Foundations of Prosocial Behavior

Universality of Prosocial Behavior

Prosocial behavior is seen in all cultures. Prosocial acts range from the donation of an organ to a complete stranger to small acts of care, such as taking a meal to a sick neighbor. Prosocial behavior is associated with positive emotions, and people feel better when they engage in prosocial behavior. Aknin et al. (2013) examined prosocial behavior across 136 countries. Prosocial behavior was defined as whether money had been donated to a charity in the past month. Data was collected from high- and low-income countries. In 120 of the 136 countries, prosocial behavior and subjective well-being were significantly correlated. This relationship was found in both poor and rich countries.

Prosocial behavior is displayed by very young children and continues to develop as children age. The increasing development of prosocial behavior is also universal (House et al., 2013). One study looked at prosocial behavior among 326 children who were 3–14 years of age. Participants were from six countries, including those located in America, Oceania, and Africa. Results showed that prosocial behavior increased steadily as children grew older. When prosocial behavior involved personal sacrifice, rates of prosocial behavior declined across all cultures.

African-Centered Values and Prosocial Behavior

Prosocial behavior is evident in African culture, as in other cultures. Among people of African descent, prosocial behavior may be linked to communalism, as communalism is associated with a range of prosocial attitudes and behaviors (Humphries, Parker, & Jagers, 2000; Mattis et al., 2004). Individuals who have high communal values tend to be more generous, cooperative, honest, and engaged in social justice than those who do not. Kindness, care, and concern for others are attributes of an African-centered cultural orientation that is expressed through prosocial behavior (Grills et al., 2016). Similarly, an orientation toward social justice and civic and community engagement are consistent with the Africentric cultural orientation of feeling responsible for others in the community. A study of African American youth and prosocial behavior showed that cultural orientation and Africentric values were linked to beliefs that persons should be politically and civically involved (Grills et al., 2016).

Collectivism has been linked to one type of prosocial behavior, public service motivation. Public service motivation encourages behavior that serves the public interest and orients one to provide services that help others and society. Kim (2017) investigated collectivism and individualism and public service motivation using data collected from 43,365 cases across 32 countries. People in collectivist cultures were more likely to report higher levels of public service motivation than people in individualist cultures.

While prosocial behavior is universal, the enactment of prosocial behavior is culturally specific. Research suggests that there may be some unique antecedents of prosocial behavior among Africans. One unique antecedent of prosocial behavior among Africans is traditional beliefs. Traditional beliefs assume that magic can be influential in one's life and that there should be immediate punishment for violating a moral code. Hadnes and Schumacher (2012) primed traditional beliefs of individuals living in Burkina Faso (West Africa). When traditional beliefs were made salient, there were increases in prosocial behavior, as shown in a trust game. Another study showed that making religion salient among North African Muslims increased prosocial behavior. In this study of shopkeepers, prosocial behavior (as indicated by an economic decision-making task) increased when the Islamic call to prayer was audible compared with when it was not (Duhaime, 2015).

Values and beliefs unique to a cultural group are likely to be expressed through emotions and subsequent behaviors. Values such as caring and concern are expressed emotionally as empathy, compassion, and love across cultures (Tamir et al., 2016). One study examined prosocial behavior (defined as spending money on yourself or on someone else) in a Western (Canada) and an African (Uganda) country (Aknin et al., 2013). Participants were randomly assigned to a condition and asked to describe a time they had spent money on themselves (personal spending) versus others (prosocial spending). Responses were coded. Participants from both counties who were asked to recall an experience of spending money on others reported more happiness than those asked to recall an experience of spending money on themselves. Differences were seen in the reasons for spending money on others; a larger percentage of Ugandan participants compared with Canadian participants recalled a purchase made in response to a negative event, especially the need for medical supplies. The relationship between spending money on others and prosocial behavior was replicated using a Canadian and South African sample. Participants reported more positive emotions when they were assigned to purchase a goody bad for a sick child rather than themselves (Aknin et al., 2013).

Africans also engage in volunteering, a type of prosocial behavior. Compion (2017) investigated the extent to which sub-Saharan Africans participate in voluntary groups. She also identified who was more likely to participate in voluntary groups and examined both characteristics of the individual level (e.g., education, individual wealth) and macro-structural characteristics (e.g., countries' gross national product and developmental assistance to the country). The sample included individuals who participated from 20 countries in the west, east, and south of sub-Saharan Africa. Respondents were asked about their involvement in religious organizations and other voluntary organizations or community groups. About 40% of respondents were involved in secular voluntary groups, with 25% being active members and/or leaders. Active membership was associated with higher levels of education, employment, living in a rural area, and beliefs that religion was important. Compion also found that the profile of active members in voluntary organizations is similar to those found in advanced capitalist societies, confirming that there are similarities across cultures in characteristics of people who volunteer.

History of Prosocial Behavior in the United States

Civic, social, and political contributions and engagement among African Americans have a long and significant history in this country. These include the development of national and local mutual aid and beneficent societies and social welfare and community organizations, such as Marcus Garvey's Universal Negro Improvement Association (1920s), Lugenia Burns Hope's Atlanta Neighborhood Union (1908), and W. E. B. Du Bois's National Association for the Advancement of Colored People (NAACP, 1910; Carlton-LaNey, 2007).

Social organizations, such as the National Association of Colored Women's Clubs (NACWC) and the National Urban League, were established in the early 1900s to provide assistance to disenfranchised African Americans. The NACWC and the National Urban League emphasized the importance of participating in civic activities. At the same time, these organizations encouraged African Americans to work on their own behalf to better themselves (Carlton-LaNey, 2007). Other African American social organizations also began around the turn of the 20th century. These included the Eastern Star, the Masons, the Grand United Order of Salem, and the Elks, each of which played important service roles in their communities.

In 1899, the Black Elks were formed, and they have subsequently grown to be the largest African American fraternal organization in the world. The Black Elks are also known as the Improved Benevolent Protective Order of Elks of the World (IBPOEW, n.d.) The Black Elks provided communities with financial, spiritual, and emotional support and served their membership and communities in several ways. Although recently declining in membership and function, the Black Elks have continued to provide programs in education, health, veteran's affairs, and civil liberties. The Black Elks work for the benefit of African Americans and Black Elks worldwide. The Black Elks currently have over 500,000 members in over 1,500 lodges worldwide.

Formed in the early 1900s, African American sororities and fraternities also became popular social organizations that engaged in significant philanthropic activities. Between 1906 and 1924, eight Black fraternities and sororities were established. Sororities and fraternities have a tradition of volunteerism, charitable giving, civic action, and community service. African American fraternities and sororities have historically (and currently) had substantial influence in the African American community (Brown, Parks, & Phillips, 2012). For example, the oldest African American sorority, Alpha Kappa Alpha, founded in 1908, has as its mission to empower communities through service programs (www.aka1908.com). African American sororities and fraternities are known for their service and contribution to educational programming for youth, for work in community service, in health promotion activities, and in disaster relief, such as for Hurricanes Katrina and Harvey.

Many influential African Americans were and are members of African American sororities and fraternities. A few of these include Martin Luther King (Alpha Phi Alpha); George Washington Carver (Phi Beta Sigma); Michael Jordan (Omega Psi Phi); Thurgood Marshall (Alpha Phi Alpha); Shaquille O'Neal (Omega Psi Phi); and Arthur Ashe (Kappa Alpha Psi). Influential African American women in sororities include Coretta Scott King (Alpha Kappa Alpha); Toni Morrison (Alpha Kappa Alpha); Zora Neale Hurston (Zeta Phi Beta); Dr. Lorraine Hale (Sigma Gamma Rho); Dorothy Height (Delta Sigma Theta); Dr. Nikki Giovanni (Delta Sigma Theta); and Aretha Franklin (Delta Sigma Theta).

In the 1930s and 1940s, organizations such as the National Council for Negro Women and the United Negro College Fund were formed. Starting in the 1960s, more formal organizations were formed through which to channel philanthropic efforts.

Contemporary Charitable African American Organizations and Nonprofits

Numerous national organizations were formed over the past 50 years to address social issues and problems within the African American communities. Most of these organizations have state and local chapters. Some notable ones include (1) 100 Black Men of America (works to improve the quality of life within the African American community); (2) National Coalition of 100 Black Women (advocates on behalf of Black women and girls and promotes leadership and gender equity); (3) The Links (volunteer service organization for enriching culture and economic conditions of African Americans); (4) National Black United Fund (invests in organizations that impact children, families, and communities); (5) Jack and Jill of America (provides cultural, education, and social opportunities to children and adolescents); and (6) Jackie Robinson Foundation (named after Jackie Robinson, to provide scholarships and mentorship support to reduce the achievement gap).

Other African American organizations were formed to address social justice issues and the empowerment of African Americans and include (1) Black Lives Matter (formed to address racial injustices after the acquittal of George Zimmerman for Trayvon Martin's murder); (2) National Action Network (led by Al Sharpton to promote social justice); (3) We Are Here (founded by Alicia Keyes as a partnership of organizations devoted to reducing poverty and oppression); (4) The Innocence Project (formed to exonerate those who have been wrongfully convicted of crimes); (5) My Brother's Keeper (developed in the Obama administration to address problems of African American and other racial and ethnic minority boys through mentorship); and (6) Incitel (focuses on ending violence against women of color).

In summary, throughout their history in this country, African Americans have formed organizations, structured mechanisms, and engaged in prosocial behavior to better the lives of individuals, communities, and society.

Theoretical Perspectives on Prosocial Behavior

Several theoretical perspectives account for prosocial behavior, with social learning theory being the most prevalent theory. Other theoretical perspectives highlight the role of empathy and self-regulation.

Social Learning Theory

Social learning theory assumes that people learn from others how to behave in prosocial ways. Individuals learn from watching others that prosocial behavior can bring rewards and reduce negative consequences. Individuals also learn how to carry out prosocial acts from observing others. Just as violent media can increase aggressive and violent behavior, watching prosocial and positive media can increase prosocial behavior (Jin & Li, 2017; Padilla-Walker, Coyne, & Collier, 2016). Cross-cultural studies show that children are more likely to engage in prosocial behavior when their parents engage in prosocial behavior (Blake, Corbit, Callaghan, & Warneken, 2016).

A study conducted across three countries found, among youth from middle school to college, that those who played prosocial video games increased in prosocial behavior (e.g., helping others) more than those in control conditions (Gentile et al., 2009). Engaging in prosocial video games is linked to more positive interpersonal relationships, cooperation, sharing, and empathy among children and youth (Harrington & O'Connell, 2016). On the other hand, competitive video gaming is associated with reductions in prosocial behavior, especially among youth who play video games frequently (Lobel, Engels, Stone, Burk, & Granic, 2017).

Empathy and Perspective Taking

Another theoretical perspective focuses on empathy as a precursor to prosocial behavior. Empathetic arousal is a state in which a person is motivated to reduce arousal by engaging in prosocial behavior. Studies have shown that empathy predicts willingness to help others in different ways (i.e., providing time, money, resources, etc.). Empathetic people who focus on the emotions of others in distress are more likely to help (Pavey, Greitemeyer, & Sparks, 2012). Empathy is associated with several positive life outcomes, such as higher overall life satisfaction, self-esteem, and more rewarding social networks (Chopik, O'Brien, & Konrath, 2017).

Perspective taking is a precursor to empathy and occurs when an individual is able to assess a situation from another person's point of view. Parental empathy can transfer to children: Children of parents who encourage them to consider the perspective of others engage in more prosocial behavior (Farrant, Devine, Maybery, & Fletcher, 2012). In a sample of African American children in Grades 5 through 8, McMahon, Wernsman, and Parnes (2006) found that children higher in empathy exhibited more behavior that was prosocial. MacEvoy and Leff (2012) conducted a study on empathy toward peers among African American youth (mean age = 9.71). Empathy was measured by a scale of sympathy toward peers who were the targets of aggression. Greater empathy toward peers was correlated with less overt and relational aggression and less defiant behavior (MacEvoy & Leff, 2012).

There are individual-level and societal-level differences in empathy. Girls and women tend to be more empathetic than boys and men (Berg et al., 2015). Individuals from collective cultures tend to be more empathetic than those from individualistic cultures. In a cross-cultural study of empathy, Chopik et al. (2017) analyzed data collected from 104,365 adults from 63 countries to examine cross-cultural differences in empathy. Higher levels of empathic concern were found among adults from collectivist countries (such as those found in Africa and Asia) than individualistic countries. Adults in countries with higher levels of empathy reported higher levels of volunteering and helping.

Self-Regulation

A third theoretical perspective is that self-regulation is a precursor to prosocial behavior. Self-regulation is a process that allows one to respond appropriately to the environment by managing and controlling emotions and behavior (Bronson, 2000). In a study of 850 sixth graders (mean age = 11), researchers found that adolescents who were able to engage in self-regulation exhibited more prosocial behavior in the home and with peers (Carlo, Crockett, Wolff, & Beal, 2012). A longitudinal design allowed researchers to determine that the effects of self-regulation of these children on prosocial behavior remained 4 years later.

One dimension of self-regulation is anger management. Anger management affects what is attended to and how it is interpreted; children with more anger management skills are less likely to interpret hostile social cues in an aggressive way (Lemerise & Arsenio, 2000). In a study of mostly urban African American youth in middle school, Sullivan, Helms, Kliewer, and Goodman (2010) found that children's ability to cope by regulating anger led to less physical aggression. Belgrave, Nguyen, Johnson, and Hood (2011) found in a sample of 789 African American adolescents (ages 11–14) that those with higher anger management skills had higher levels of prosocial behavior and lower levels of aggressive behavior.

Volunteering, Giving, and Civic Engagement

Volunteering

A vast amount of prosocial behavior is shown in volunteering. Volunteers are defined as persons who do unpaid work (except for expenses) through or for an organization (Bureau of Labor Statistics, 2016). About 62.6 million people volunteered through or for an organization at least once between September 2014 and September 2015. Women volunteered more than men and people with higher levels of education volunteered more than those with less education. According to the Bureau of Labor Statistics, volunteer rates of racial and ethnic groups were as follows in 2015: Whites (26.4%), Blacks (19.3%), Asians (17.9%), and Hispanics (15.5%).

Demographic factors associated with volunteering among African Americans include gender, age, education, and income. Individuals who are older and who have more education and income are more likely to volunteer than those who are younger with less education and income. It is likely that these individuals have access to more resources that allow them to share their time with others. Overall, African American women are more likely than African American men to volunteer (Mattis et al., 2000). Gutierrez and Mattis (2014) investigated religious involvement and volunteering among African American women recruited in a large city in the northeast part of the United States. Slightly over 50% of the 211 participants reported that they volunteered. Religious involvement had a positive relationship with volunteer engagement, with more religious involvement linked to more volunteering. Members of a religious institution were 3.9 times more likely to volunteer than nonmembers.

Giving and the African American Church

Currently and historically, philanthropy has been conducted through the African American Church or other Black religious institutions (Barnes, 2013a), and the Black Church is the number-one beneficiary of philanthropy (Ball, 2003). During colonial times, it was the newly established Black Churches that provided social services and education to African American community members (Winters, 1999). Many of the resources necessary for supporting community residents have been historically provided by faith-based institutions. Contemporary African American religious institutions help with food and clothing drives, provide shelter, after-school tutoring, and health fairs (see Chapter 10). Most African American Churches operate one or more social and welfare programs. These include programs focusing on child development, family support and aid, financial support, housing support, elder services, and community service development.

Not surprisingly, the vast amount of giving among African Americans is through Churches. Seventy-five percent of philanthropic dollars in the African American community operate through religious institutions, and most volunteer activities are also conducted through the Church (Ball, 2008). This giving encompasses money, time, and services. The Pew Charitable Trusts conducted a study to measure the impact that faith-based organizations have on their communities (Ball, 2008). Of the 401 congregations surveyed, 91% offered at least one social service program, such as food pantries and summer camps. The findings from the survey estimated that it would cost more than $200 million to replace the social and community services provided by these faith-based organizations.

Barnes (2013a) conducted a study of giving patterns among 1,601 Black Churches across seven denominations. Churches were asked about the percentages of tithers (tithers give 10% of their income to the Church) in the congregation, the amount of income received last year from all sources (tithes, pledges, and plate offerings), and how much income was spent for missions (e.g., donations to local shelters, international Churches, schools). The findings showed denominational differences in type of giving. The Church of God in Christ had the higher percentage of tithers. African Methodist Episcopal Zion, Presbyterian, and United Methodist Churches reported higher amounts of Church income and mission giving than Baptists. Baptist Churches tended to have higher rates of Church tithers but not Church incomes or mission donations. Members of larger Churches and Churches with more educated members had higher giving patterns.

One development in giving is seen among African American MegaChurches (see Chapter 10). These Churches have continued the philanthropic tradition substantively by building homes, creating schools, and providing social and health services within their communities.

Civic Engagement and Social Activism

Civic engagement is doing something that makes a positive difference within the community. The Civic Engagement Center at the National Louis University describes civic engagement as working to make a difference in the civic life of our communities and developing the combination of knowledge, skills, values, and motivation to make that difference.

Farmer and Piotrikowski (2009) examined African American and White women and civic engagement and activism. Civic engagement over the past 12 months was measured by asking questions such as whether participants had worked on a community project and whether they had volunteered at their place of worship. Activism was assessed with questions such as whether they had signed a petition or attended a political meeting over the past 12 months. The researchers found that African American and White women did not differ on volunteering for their place of worship but that White women were more likely to have worked on a community project. In terms of activism, White women were more likely to sign petitions, and African American women were more likely to attend political meetings or rallies and to participate in protest activities. Regardless of ethnicity, higher socioeconomic status was linked to more activism.

Civic engagement activities oriented toward social justice and community system change may be attractive activities for promoting civic identity among young African Americans who reside in low-resource communities. Chung and Probert (2011) studied 129 young African American adults whose age ranged from 18 to 25 and who lived in low-resource neighborhoods. The authors examined relationships between participants' outcome expectations (e.g., whether political actions will lead to improvements in the community or system-level changes) and volunteering and political activism. Participants were more engaged in volunteering than in political activism. Almost 64% of the sample had volunteered at least once during the previous year, whereas only 15.5% had participated in political activism. The authors also found that participants' outcome expectations shaped volunteering and participation in political activities.

High racial identity contributes to civic engagement. Racial identity is the meaning an individual attributes to their racial status (Sellers et al., 1998). White-Johnson (2012) studied racial identity and civic engagement among 303 African American college students. Measures included a measure of prosocial attitudes specific to African Americans (e.g., successful Blacks should help other Blacks to succeed) and measures of involvement in civic and social justice behaviors (e.g., volunteered for a political campaign), along with racial identity. High racial identity was associated with both prosocial attitudes and involvement in civic activities.

CONTEMPORARY ISSUES
MORE AFRICAN AMERICAN MALE VOLUNTEERS NEEDED

One of the authors (Belgrave) has been involved in a local collective with several African American female organizations. These organizations and their leaders are dedicating time and resources to mentor and provide a range of activities and programs for African American girls. These women invest a tremendous amount of personal time and resources in programming for African American girls, including empowerment and cultural enrichment programs, physical fitness and recreational programs, and academic and vocational enhancement programs, to name a few. There is no such collective of organizations of African American males that mentor and provide programs for African American boys—at least not at the local level. Why? There is certainly a compelling need, as statistics suggest that African American boys do worse than African American girls on most indicators (e.g., lower academic achievement, more involvement in juvenile justice system, more drug use).

Many African American males would like to be involved in mentoring and working with African American boys, but the infrastructure and models for such programs do not seem readily available and accessible. Would there be higher levels of mentoring if the need for these programs were clear-cut and if there was an infrastructure in which men could be recruited and supported in their efforts. One approach taken by a group in eastern Missouri is to go to barbershops to recruit African American males to volunteer for the Big Brothers and Big Sisters program. Williams (2012) highlights how this recruitment strategy is used in an interesting article titled, "Big Brothers Big Sisters Heads to the Barber Shop to Recruit Volunteers." This news article discusses how Vivian Gibson, director of the Boys and Girls Club in this area, conveys the message in a central place so that more African American men will sign up as mentors. African American men of all ages, socioeconomic classes, and backgrounds go to barbershops. Barbershops are excellent venues in which to recruit men because while men are at barbershops, they are engaged in informal networking that can facilitate learning from each other how to be good mentors and role models. Other venues for recruiting males include African American Churches and fraternities.

Philanthropy

There has been limited research on philanthropy among African Americans and other ethnic minorities. However, as the cover story shows, there is a large amount of philanthropy activity among African Americans. This activity does not just involve wealthy African Americans. Most African American donors do not consider their acts as philanthropic (Winters, 1999). Copeland-Carson (2005) expands the concept of Black philanthropy to include practices originating from African diaspora cultural traditions. Using this framework, philanthropy consists of the voluntary ways in which any social group redistributes financial and other resources for the purposes of promoting the collective good.

The African tradition of philanthropic practices was adapted by African Americans during enslavement and continues today. Copeland-Carson provides, as an example, the practice of sou-sou, which is practiced in African and Caribbean countries and by immigrants and others in this country. Sou-sou is a practice whereby members of a group contribute a set amount of funds on a weekly or monthly basis so that each participating member can rotate to use the entire pool for economic or social projects. The practice is based on trust, as there is no paperwork involved, and every member gets exactly what they put in. According to Copeland-Carson, these funds allow individuals to increase access to large amounts of money in which larger-scale projects can be completed. She argues that this practice is philanthropic because pooled individual resources support collective community needs, along with individual needs. Another example of African-centered practices can be seen in the similarities of rituals of early voluntary groups such as the Masons who developed secret rites-of-passage rituals and communication systems akin to those indigenous to West Africa. While the structure of Black Mason societies was European based, the content and function was based in African American culture and traditions.

Several national organizations are devoted to Black philanthropy. The National Center for Black Philanthropy (NCBP) was established in 1999 to promote and strengthen African American participation in all aspects of modern philanthropy (Wiser, n.d.). NCBP's mission is to encourage giving and volunteerism among African Americans, to promote African Americans' participation in all aspects of philanthropy, and to educate the public about the contributions of Black philanthropy. Annual conferences are held on aspects of African American philanthropy. Similarly, the National Council of Black Philanthropy promotes giving and volunteerism among African Americans and encourages participation by African Americans in all aspects of philanthropy. The National Council of Black Philanthropy is composed of Black executives whose pledge is to be a national resource for the Black community. Black Philanthropy Month as discussed in the cover story was created in August 2011 as an annual celebration of giving among people of African descent.

The Center on Philanthropy and Civil Society at the Graduate Center of the City University of New York conducted a study to address philanthropy among ethnic minorities. The authors were specifically interested in understanding motivations for giving. African American, Asian American, and Latino donors who had given annual gifts of at least $200 (Mottino & Miller, 2004) were interviewed. Participants' names were obtained from organizational lists and referrals. Of the 166 donors interviewed, 58 were African Americans, 53 were Latinos, and 55 were Asian Americans, whose ages ranged from 23 to 94. Seventy percent of the donors had household income of more than $100,000.

The study found that the median giving was $5,000, which surpasses the national average of households that give but do not volunteer at $1,620. Giving ranged from $200 to $1 million. The authors found that older African Americans gave a median of $7,250, with 97% giving at least $1,000. Younger African Americans gave a median of $2,000, with 80% giving at least $1,000. The median level of giving for the other two ethnic groups was slightly less than the median level for African Americans.

The authors found that African Americans were more likely to give to Churches, Latinos to community-based organizations, and Asian Americans to ethnic and cultural institutions. The biggest difference in types of giving was related to age. Researchers looked at donors born before and after the mid-1960s. Older participants tended to focus on their respective ethnic community, whereas younger participants had a broader and less racial view of their community. Overall, older donors tended to give more to organizations in their own ethnic communities, including the Church. Younger donors gave more to educational programs for high school and college students. These participants felt that giving to educational institutions promoted social change.

Other important findings included the following: (a) Participants were committed to social change, but this did not translate to financial support for political candidates and campaigns. (However, this did not cover the Obama presidential campaign, as there were high levels of giving to this campaign.) (b) Volunteering was high: 90% had volunteered in the year preceding the survey. (c) Most of the participants began doing volunteer work while young—before or during college. (d) Donors tended to give to organizations where they had personal connections. (e) There is a need for philanthropic marketing, as participants in this study were not likely to ask for advice regarding their philanthropic activities.

This study was an important one, as it revealed that African Americans and other ethnic minorities do give and provided insight into some of the reasons for giving. At the same time, the study is limited in that it interviewed only donors in the New York City area and individuals with high levels of income.

Net Worth and Giving

Historically, researchers have believed that African Americans give less money than Whites. Conley (2000) argues that net worth should be considered when looking at the giving of African Americans. Net worth is the value of everything owned minus debt. Commenting on the research that shows the giving of African Americans to be less than that of Whites, Conley notes that this is not a valid comparison because the net worth of African Americans is considerably less than that of Whites. Research conducted by Pew found that the median wealth of White households was approximately 13 times that of Black households (Pew, 2016). In 2013, African American households had just $11,200 in wealth (assets minus debts) and the typical White household had $144,200 in wealth (Pew, 2016).

In fact, research suggests that Black people give 25% more of their discretionary income to charity than do other ethnic groups. For example, African Americans who make between $30,000 and $50,000 give an average of $528 annually, compared with $462 donated by their White counterparts in the same income range (Kellogg Foundation, 2012).

In overview, much of the charitable work and giving among African Americans occurs within the Church and other religious institutions. But African Americans also contribute to philanthropic organizations and give money for other causes, including local ethnic organizations and youth and educational service organizations.

ANTISOCIAL BEHAVIOR

We focus on aggression and antisocial behavior in this section of the chapter. Aggression is an intentional behavior aimed at causing physical or emotional pain. Aggression can be instrumental or hostile (Berkowitz, 1993). *Instrumental* aggression is intentional behavior to hurt someone as a means to an end, as for example, between boxers in a boxing match. *Hostile* aggression is a type of aggression that comes from feelings of anger and is aimed at inflicting pain, such as when a person initiates a fight because he or she has been insulted. Aggression can be physical or verbal and direct or indirect. Examples of physical aggression are hitting, using weapons, and kicking. Examples of verbal aggression are gossiping about others, isolating others, and insulting others.

Violence is an extreme form of aggression. Violence is defined by the World Health Organization (n.d.) as "the intentional use of physical force or power, threatened or actual, against oneself, another person, or against a group or community, which either results in or has a high likelihood of resulting in injury, death, psychological harm, maldevelopment, or deprivation."

Violence Against Africans From the Middle Passage to the Present Day

In the popular media and academic literature, considerable attention has been directed at aggressive and violent behavior, especially within inner-city and urban communities whose residents are primarily African Americans or members of other ethnic minority groups. High levels of violence and crime have especially been noted among African American males. In fact, most Americans have an implicit (or unconscious) bias that associates violence with African American males (Greenwald, Poehlman, Uhlmann, & Banaji, 2009). However, violent behavior among African Americans is a fairly recent phenomenon. A discussion of violence and aggression among contemporary African American males must include a consideration of the historical context of violence against Africans and African Americans.

Violence During the Middle Passage

King (1997) provides a thoughtful discussion of the historical context of violence against Africans and African Americans in an article titled "Understanding Violence Among Young African American Males: An Afrocentric Perspective." He begins by discussing violence by Europeans against Africans and then enslaved Africans in the colonies and in the United States. According to King, present-day violent behaviors among young African American males were almost nonexistent in Africa prior to the slave trade. Given this historical framework, how can we account for the violence that appears to be a part of the contemporary African American male experience?

According to King (1997), the enslavement of African people was the single most violent and brutal act committed against any group of people in the history of the world. The roots of violence began with the brutal and inhumane enslavement of millions of Africans on land stolen from Native Americans. The 365 years of enslavement was a violent period. There were more than 40 million (some estimates are as high as 150 million) African people throughout the Americas. Mortality among Africans was very high. One out of every three Africans captured during slave raids died before reaching the coast of Africa where they were loaded onto ships; another third died at sea prior to reaching the coast of the Americas.

Violence During and After Slavery

Following the Middle Passage, violence continued under American slavery. Africans were considered to be property and were forced to work under strenuous conditions for more than 220 years (King, 1997). Male Africans (as compared with female Africans) were treated more violently and received all types of physical punishment, including lynching, beatings, body mutilations, and castration. Violence in the form of rape was directed against African women.

After slavery ended, violence against African Americans, especially males, continued. During the late 19th and early 20th centuries, thousands of African American males were incarcerated, injured, and murdered. Between 1885 and 1921, 4,096 lynchings of African Americans were recorded in the United States, an average of 113 per year (Fishel & Quarles, 1970, as cited in King, 1997). The number of actual lynchings was most likely higher than 4,096, as many were not recorded. Many of the victims of lynchings were accused but rarely confirmed of raping a White female. Burning by mobs was another form of violence. Lynchings were well publicized in newspapers and were cause for celebrations among members of the White community, especially in the Southern states (A. King, 1997).

Police brutality did not begin with the publicized Rodney King incident of 1992. Between 1920 and 1932, out of 479 Blacks killed by White persons in the South, 259, or 54%, were killed by White police officers. According to King (1997), the institutional and legal violence against African Americans has led to an undervaluing of their lives. How does this historical context relate to the violence seen among African American males currently taking place in African American communities, especially inner-city communities? The systemic and institutional expression of violence directed at African Americans has affected African American males' perceptions of opportunities and life course expectations, especially in urban, poor, and low-resource communities. African Americans observe that adult males in their communities have high rates of underemployment, unemployment, poverty, and poor health. High rates of mortality and incarceration leave adolescent males without exposure to adult males who can serve as positive mentors to show them how to be a man and how to succeed in this society. Males who are considered successful may obtain funds illegally through drug sales and other illegal activities. Role models for legitimate routes to success are often lacking. In addition, structural barriers, such as education and transportation, also limit African American males' access to legal employment opportunities. The availability of drugs is a major contributor to violence in urban African American communities. Involvement in the drug culture results in violence, turf wars, and illegal activities.

Current Violence Against African American Men

There have been several notable recent violent acts and hate crimes against African American males spurred by racial bigotry. Since the last edition of this book, in 2013, there have been many shootings of unarmed Black men. Philando Castile was fatally shot July 6, 2016, in a suburb near Minneapolis during a traffic stop while his girlfriend videotaped the shocking incident, which went viral. The police officer Jeronomo Yanez was acquitted of second-degree manslaughter reporting that he thought Castile was reaching for his gun. Charles Kinsey, a mental health therapist taking care of a severely autistic man was shot on July 18, 2016, while lying on the ground. He was trying to get the autistic man back to the group home he had come from. A shocking crime occurred on June 26, 2011, in Jackson, Mississippi, when three White teens beat and ran over James Anderson, a 49-year-old Black man, with a pick-up truck (Caron, 2011). Surveillance footage of the incident showed several White teens beating Anderson and then driving over his body. Race has been identified as the cause for the assault, as one of the teens was recorded during a phone conversation stating, "I ran that ni**a over." The most highly publicized act of violence against an African American male is the Trayvon Martin murder case. On February 26, 2012, 17-year-old Trayvon Martin was shot and killed by a multiracial Hispanic man, George Zimmerman (Roberts, 2012). Martin's death drew increased attention to the dangers of violence many Black males encounter in the United States. The acquittal of Zimmerman spurred the Black Lives Matter Movement.

In overview, a history of violence and oppression against African Americans in the United States, along with limited pathways to adequate economic roles for African American males, have contributed to feelings of hopelessness and lower life course expectations. In turn, these perceptions contribute significantly to aggression and violence among African American males.

Theories of Aggression and Violence

Is aggression learned or inborn? The answer to this question has long been debated. Some researchers point out that the universality of aggression among vertebrates suggests that aggression has been maintained over the years because it has some survival value. However, cultures differ greatly in their degree of aggressiveness. In the history of Europe, there has been one major war after another. In contrast, among cultural groups such as the Pygmies of Central Africa and the Arepesh of New Guinea, acts of aggression are extremely rare (Baron & Richardson, 1994).

Aggression and violence have been viewed from several theoretical perspectives. The innate perspective suggests that aggression is instinctual and that humans are biologically programmed to be aggressive for survival purposes. Another theoretical perspective indicates that aggression occurs under conditions of frustration. Aggression is used to reduce this frustration. A frustration reduction drive theory would account for the riots of the 1960s that took place in several U.S. cities following the assassination of Dr. Martin Luther King Jr. African Americans, frustrated by civil rights injustices and other violations of human rights, dealt with their frustration through rioting. More recent examples include violence that has erupted following deaths of African American males at the hands of police officers. Notable have been the riots and protests following Michel Brown's death in Ferguson, Missouri, and Freddie Gray's death in Baltimore, Maryland. Major theoretical perspectives on aggression and violence are reviewed next.

Social Learning Theory

Social learning theory assumes that we learn aggressive behavior (just as we learn prosocial behavior) by observing others and imitating them. Exposure to media violence leads to aggression and violence (Bushman & Anderson, 2001). Children between the ages of 8 and 18 spend, on average, more than 7 hours per day engaging with media (Anderson, Bushman, Donnerstein, Hummer, & Warburton, 2015). African American and Latino/Hispanic children consume nearly 4.5 hours more of media daily than White children (13 hours for Latino children, 12:59 hours for Black children, and 8:36 hours for White children) (Silva, 2015). Exposure to even short-term media violence causes desensitization to real-world violence. Sixty-one percent of all TV programs contain violence, and of these, 75% do not contain remorse, criticism, or penalty for that violence (Kaiser Family Foundation, 2010; Seppa, 1997). An average American child will see 200,000 violent acts and 16,000 murders on TV by age 18.

Longitudinal studies show that exposure to media violence is associated with physical, verbal, and relational (e.g., using words to hurt others) aggression. Violent media exposure is linked to violent behaviors, including assault, intimate partner violence, and other antisocial behaviors (Anderson et al., 2015) Violent video games lead to physiological changes, such as increased cortisol and cardiovascular arousal, along with the accessibility of aggressive thoughts (Gentile, Bender, & Anderson, 2017).

The literature on exposure to community violence also supports that violence is learned. This literature shows that African American youth who witness violence are more likely to engage in violence themselves (Thomas, Caldwell, Assari, Jagers, & Flay, 2016).

In summary, the social learning perspective can be used to account for violence seen within some African American communities. First, there is the modeling of adult violence by older teens in these communities. Teens, in turn, may serve as models of aggression and violence for younger children. The availability of and display of weapons, as well as the increased exposure to violence through the media, are additional factors that promote violence in these communities.

Social Organizational Theory

Social organization refers to the extent to which residents of a neighborhood are able to achieve and maintain effective social control and realize collective goals. Socially disorganized neighborhoods are characterized by dysfunctional households; ethnic, racial, and class segregation; hostile behavior; and norms tolerant of crime. These neighborhoods are further characterized by high rates of unemployment, poverty, and residential mobility (Bennett & Fraser, 2000).

The social organizational perspective assumes that violence is the result of structural disadvantages that deny African Americans, in general, and African American males, in particular, access to economic opportunities and upward social mobility (Gibbs, 1988).

Social organizational theory also takes into account the relationship between oppositional and destructive behaviors and violence (Bennett & Fraser, 2000). Within many low-income communities, destructive behaviors are tolerated. These behaviors range from littering to destroying property to stealing. Drug addiction and trafficking, along with other criminal activities, are further evidence of social disintegration. These acts contribute to the fear and isolation of residents.

Community violence exposure can be reduced. Brevard, Maxwell, Hood, and Belgrave (2013) found that the presence of intergenerational connections was a protective factor for African American youth living in disorganized neighborhoods characterized by high crime rates, unemployment, and other social problems. Intergenerational connection is the feeling and belief that there are adults in the community who will look out for and take care of you. African American youth who reported high levels of intergenerational connections felt safer in their neighborhoods than did those who reported low levels of intergenerational connections. Similarly, Liu, Mustanski, Dick, Bolland, and Kertes (2017) found that collective efficacy (beliefs that members of a community can control behavior of individual and people in the community) buffered youth experiencing discrimination and other risk factors in poor neighborhoods from behavior problems.

Incarceration and Police Presence. High rates of incarceration in low-income, urban neighborhoods may contribute to social disorganization by creating a heavy reliance on law enforcement to address deviant and criminal behavior (Bennett & Fraser, 2000). When monitoring by law enforcement is high, informal systems of monitoring by community members decreases. High levels of incarceration may undermine informal social, political, and economic systems in a neighborhood. In addition, the presence of law enforcement may reduce neighborhood cohesion. Neighborhood cohesion also may be reduced when law enforcement focuses on arrest and incarceration and not on intervention or preventive measures, such as would be found in community policing.

Residential Segregation. Racial residential segregation has also been suggested as an explanation for higher rates of violence among African Americans (Peterson, Krivo, & Velez, 2001). Racial segregation is associated with racial inequality, and inequality, in turn, is associated with increased violence. Under conditions of racial inequality, deviant and criminal behavior is seen as a response to frustration due to the lack of economic success and socioeconomic resources. Moreover, the expression of such frustration is likely to be enhanced when the inequalities are based on race. Because the residents of segregated neighborhoods tend to have limited social and economic power, racially segregated minorities are not able to organize collective protests (e.g., strikes, boycotts, voting) to address inequities. Instead, protest may be expressed at the individual or group level in other forms, such as aggressive behavior and criminal activity.

African American–White residential segregation is a defining feature of racial inequality in the United States. In many places, African Americans have virtually no contact with Whites in their own or neighboring communities. High levels of segregation are associated with several problems, including concentrated poverty, physical deterioration of housing and business units, poorer schools, high levels of crime, and homicides (Feldmeyer, 2010; Peterson et al., 2001). To African Americans, residential racial segregation symbolizes barriers to upward mobility and life opportunities. Limited opportunities for achievement can lead to frustration, resentment, hopelessness, and alienation, which, in turn, can lead to violence.

In summary, the social organizational theory of violence assumes that violence is a result of structural inequalities in one's neighborhood that prevent access to needed resources and positive role models.

Cultural Theories of Aggression and Violence

Cultural theories of aggression and violence are other ways to account for socialization of aggression and violence among people of African descent in the United States. These theories also recognize the impact of the historical legacy of racism and oppression as a contributor to violence.

Cultural Racism. Cultural racism has been examined as a reason for violence among African Americans. Cultural racism is the systematic manner in which the White majority has established its primary cultural institutions (e.g., education, media, religion) to elevate and promote European physical characteristics, character, and achievement and to denigrate the physical characteristics, character, and achievement of non-White people (Oliver, 2001). An example of cultural racism is the absence of social science curricula that cover the contributions of Africans and African Americans to human civilization. Another example might be the mass media's portrayal of African Americans in a manner that promotes and justifies racial bias and stereotypes (Tyree, 2011). Exposure to cultural racism contributes to the existence of violence, as it influences how African Americans define themselves, others, and their community and how they understand specific interpersonal encounters (Oliver, 2001). Cultural racism has contributed to social disorganization among African Americans, as it influences how African Americans see themselves.

The inability to achieve the status of manhood and adult male social roles through conventional means may lead some African American males to embrace exaggerated and stereotypical images of manhood. These alternative views of manhood are likely to increase one's risk of becoming involved in violence. For example, African American males who define manhood in terms of toughness, sexual conquest, and thrill seeking are most likely to spend time hanging out in the street, using and selling drugs, and committing criminal acts as a way to maintain their lifestyles. These males are attracted to the street because they have been denied access to the conventional opportunity structure.

A study investigated whether the "code of the street" explanation could be used to explain violence and victimization among African American youth. The study involved a longitudinal sample of 720 African American adolescents from 250 neighborhoods (Stewart, Schreck, & Simons, 2006). The code of the street is an informal system that governs the use of violence among young African American males. This code emphasizes that one must maintain the respect of others through a violent and tough identity and be willing to exact retribution in the event of disrespect and/or if physically assaulted (Anderson, 1999). The assumption is that adopting a street code should increase youths' safety during a potential confrontation. Those who fail to adopt the street code may be seen as more vulnerable, less respected, and subject to higher victimization. The authors found that even when controlling for neighborhood characteristics and other factors known to be associated with victimization, adopting the street code increased victimization risk. Adopting street code behaviors as a response to prior victimization increased the risk of victimization, which created a cycle of violence.

Community and Youth Violence

Community Violence

Community violence includes both experiences and exposure. Exposure is defined as experiencing, seeing, or hearing about violence in one's home, school, or neighborhood. Covictimization is the indirect experience of violence by directly observing the assault of another person (Garrett, 1997; Shakoor & Chalmers, 1991; Subašić, Schmitt, & Reynolds, 2011). Several studies have examined prevalence of violence exposure, the effects of violence exposure, and factors that reduce some of the negative effects of violence exposure.

Prevalence of Exposure to Community Violence. African Americans living in inner cities experience a high degree of exposure to community violence (Voisin, 2007). Across many studies and different regions of the country, African American youth report high community violence exposure. African American youth are exposed to more violence than other groups. Almost 97% of urban youth (N = 110) in West/Southwest Philadelphia reported some type of community violence expose (McDonald, Deatrick, Kassam-Adams, & Richmond, 2011). Similarly, among mostly African American adolescents (N = 312; 71% African Americans) (mean age = 14.5) enrolled in a multiyear child development project, almost 80% experienced community violence exposure. This included seeing someone get beaten up (72%), seeing someone get badly hurt (44.4%), seeing someone pull a gun on someone else (22.7%), and seeing someone pull a knife on someone else (18.3%) (Hardaway, Sterrett-Hong, Larkby, & Cornelius, 2016).

Effects of Exposure to Community Violence. Exposure to violence results in both short- and long-term negative effects, including increased depression and anxiety, low self-esteem, post-traumatic stress disorder, fear, and sleep disturbance (Kilpatrick et al., 2000). Exposure is also associated with behavioral problems, such as aggression, delinquency, and drug abuse (McMahon et al., 2013; Voisin, 2007; Wallace et al., 2017). Youth who are exposed to community violence are more likely to be violent themselves and experience emotional desensitization (Gaylord-Harden, So, Bai, Henry, & Tolan, 2017; Mrug, Madan, & Windle, 2016).

Studies have also shown an association between community violence exposure and physical symptoms and risky health practices, such as HIV sexual risk behaviors, across multiple samples of youth (Jones, Foster, Forehand, & O'Connell, 2005; McMahon et al., 2013; Voisin, 2003, 2007; Wilson, Donenberg, & Emerson, 2014). Academic difficulties are another by-product of exposure to violence. Children who are exposed to violence concentrate less well and learn less (Thompson & Massat, 2005; Voisin, 2007; Wallace et al., 2017) and have lower educational aspirations (Stoddard, Heinze, Choe, & Zimmerman, 2015).

Exposure to community violence is a precursor to youth violence. In a study of mostly African American (71%) low-income youth, participants were asked about exposure to community violence (defined as witnessing violence and violent victimization) at age 14 and then later at age 16. A linear relationship was seen between violence exposure and expression of violence (Hardaway et al., 2016). Youth were also asked about internalizing (e.g., anxiety, depression) and externalizing (e.g. aggressive behaviors toward others) problems. Violence exposure and externalizing behaviors were moderated by high levels of kinship support and high parental involvement. High levels of emotional and tangible support from the extended family and parental involvement buffered youth from community violence exposure, thus lowering their aggression and violence.

The relationship between community violence exposure and aggressive and prosocial behavior was explored among 266 African American youth (McMahon et al., 2013). Factors that protected (e.g. beliefs about aggression, self-efficacy, lack of impulsivity) against community violence were also explored. Participants were in fifth through eighth grade, and ages ranged from 11 to 14. Data were collected at four time periods from students, peers, and teachers. Exposure to community violence at one time predicted future aggressive behavior, as reported by youth. Moreover, students who reported more community violence had lower levels of prosocial behavior, as reported by peers. This finding is important because it linked community violence exposure to prosocial as well as aggressive behavior. Impulsivity, as reported by both youth and teachers, also predicted aggressive behavior. Impulsivity involves not thinking of the consequences of behavior.

What Protects Children Against Exposure to Community Violence? Not every child from a disorganized neighborhood engages in violence; in fact, most do not. One factor is resilience, and other attributes of the child, including self-esteem, self-efficacy, cultural identity, and social competence, may buffer the individual from community-level risks for violence.

One attribute that moderates the negative effect of violence exposure is emotional regulation. Children who are able to regulate their emotions and who have the ability to take a different perspective are less likely to be affected by community violence (Kliewer, 2016). This is because these youth are more likely to think through problems associated with violence instead of acting out aggressively.

Family relationships and cohesion are another set of variables that help children who live in violent communities. Children who feel valued, accepted, and loved are less likely to be negatively affected by community violence than those children in households without good family relationships. In addition, parenting involvement and monitoring are protective factors against violence for children exposed to community violence (Hardaway et al., 2016).

Racial socialization attenuates the effects of community violence. When parents racially socialize their children, they are less likely to have poor outcomes even when there are high levels of violence exposure. In a study of African American urban youth, Henry, Lambert, and Smith Bynum (2015) found that racial socialization messages from mothers about cultural pride reduced the effects of community violence exposure and aggressive behaviors among youth.

At the neighborhood level, youths' perception of neighborhood cohesion affects perception of and reactions to community violence. When resources are available in a community, youth are less likely to experience the stress of community violence. These resources include other adults to talk to and community centers, playgrounds, recreational facilities, and Churches. Neighborhood resources in the form of people and access to buildings and safe spaces generate feelings of collective efficacy. Collective efficacy is defined as beliefs that members of a community are connected to each other and share common goals (Sampson, 2011). In contexts of high violence, high neighborhood collective efficacy helps the youth feel safer and represents a source of protection (Thomas et al., 2016). Feeling that someone is available to turn to other than parents and immediate family members contributes to collective efficacy among children and adolescents. In a study of 553 African American males (mean age = 10.8), youth who believed that their neighborhood is a place where people are supported and encouraged to adopt prosocial behavior reported feeling safer (Thomas et al., 2016).

Racial respect is a cultural attribute that protects youth from the effects of community violence (DeGruy, Kjellstrand, Briggs, & Brennan, 2012). Racial respect is defined as a prosocial attitude that comes from one's awareness of self-worth and the honoring of one's racial origins by the self, peers, and others in society (DeGruy et al., 2012). DeGruy et al. examined exposure to community violence, violent behavior, and racial respect. The sample consisted of 100 African American males who had been detained in the juvenile justice system and 100 African American males who were members of a community youth development program. Youth were 14 to 18 years old. Consistent with the findings from other studies, a history of witnessing violence predicted the intensity of violent behavior. However, endorsing positive attitudes toward racial respect reduced the effects of chronic exposure to violence.

Jones (2007) used an Africentric perspective to better understand exposure to community violence and resilience among African American children. She examined the relationship between exposure to chronic community violence and the development of symptoms of post-traumatic stress disorder in the context of specific African American cultural beliefs and values that are used as coping mechanisms. Specifically, African-centered coping strategies such as the use of formal and informal kinships and spirituality were investigated as moderators of the relationship between exposure to community violence and post-traumatic stress disorder. Seventy-one African American children (ages 9–11) from a low-income area in a large urban city participated in the study. The prevalence of exposure to community violence was high in the sample: 19% had witnessed people they knew being shot or stabbed, and 10% had witnessed people they knew being killed. Jones found a significant moderating effect for both kinship networks and spirituality such that students high in these reported less traumatic stress in the context of community violence.

In overview, several types of factors protect against the negative effects of exposure to community violence. Self-esteem and competence, cohesive families, and caregivers who coach and model good behaviors buffer the negative effects of exposure to community violence. Cultural variables, such as spirituality, ethnic identity, and racial respect, also serve as protective factors, as do community resources. Although these protective factors are important, creating safe communities where there are lower levels of violence and children and youth have lower exposure is clearly the priority.

Youth Violence

Youth are both perpetrators and victims of violence. A national survey of youth 14–17 reported that almost 60% had been exposed to violence in the past year (Finkelhor, Turner, Shattuck, Hamby, & Kracke, 2015). African American youth are more likely to be victims of homicide than are other racial and ethnic groups. Among 10- to 24-year-olds, homicide is the leading cause of death for African Americans (CDC, 2014).

Gang Membership. More adults belong to gangs than juveniles (under 18) and 3 out of every 5 gang members are adults. Males are much more likely to be in gangs than females (92.6% versus 7.4%) (National Gang Center, n.d.). Gangs are in larger cities, suburban counties, smaller cities, and rural counties. In terms of race and ethnicity of gang members, 46.2% are Hispanic/Latino, 35.2% are Black or African American, 11.5% are White, and 7% are other.

Membership in gangs has serious consequences for all youth, including death, injury, and incarceration, not to mention the additional toll on families and communities. Gang members also experience high levels of mental health problems, including post-traumatic stress disorder (Brunson, Jackson, Christson, Miller, Pender, & David, 2017).

Factors contributing to gang membership include intrapersonal and psychological factors such as conduct disorder, parental and family factors, peer and school factors, and community-level factors. Table 15.1 shows some of the risk and protective factors

TABLE 15.1 ■ Risk and Protective Factors for Gang Involvement Among Youth	
Risk Factors	**Protective Factors**
Individual Factors	
Juvenile delinquency	Prosocial behaviors
Drug use	No drug use
Seeking power and attention	Good interpersonal skills
Conduct disorder	Anger management skills
Low self-esteem	High self-efficacy
Family Factors	
Lack of parenting monitoring and supervision	Parental involvement and monitoring
Siblings and kin who are in gangs	No family and kin involvement in gangs
Family disorganization	Stable family structure
Peer Factors	
Peers who are in gangs	Nondelinquent peers
Delinquent peers	Positive social connections
Friends who use drugs	Non-drug-using friends
School Factors	
Low academic achievement	Academic achievement
Frequent school transitions	School bonding
School suspension and dropout	High educational expectations
Community Factors	
Exposure to gang activity	Community resources
Community violence and crime	Feeling safe in community
Poverty	Employment

for gang membership. One reason youth may join gangs is that gang members provide social affiliation (Li et al., 2002). However, data support the fact that although youth who join gangs may be seeking affiliation, they do not always find social support from the gang, as there is a strong correlation between gang membership and feeling a lack of belongingness.

Voisin, King, Kelly, DiClemente, and Carry (2014) investigated correlates of gang involvement among African American adolescent females detained in a juvenile detention center. Participants were 13–17 years of age. Individual-level factors that correlated with gang involvement included lower levels of self-esteem and poor emotional regulation skills. Family factors for gang membership included low levels of parenting monitoring, parental communication, and housing instability. Gang membership for girls was associated with having a boyfriend in a gang, higher levels of sexual risky behaviors, and more drug and alcohol use. Finally poorly resourced neighborhoods contribute to gang membership for girls.

Bullying and Victimization

Both bullies and victims have poorer psychosocial functioning. Victims of bullying show increased depression and anxiety, and poor academic performance. Youth who bully others are also at risk for poor developmental outcomes, such as substance abuse, academic problems, and violence exposure later in life (Albdour & Krouse, 2014). Albdour and Krouse conducted a literature review of papers published on bullying and victimization among African American adolescents. Three types of bullying were identified—physical, relational, and verbal assaults. Studies published showed that African American youth were more likely to be both perpetrators of bullying activities as well as victims when compared with adolescents in other racial and ethnic groups. Males were more likely than females to be perpetuators of bullying. The peak time for bullying was during the transition from middle to high school.

Several risk factors increase risk for bullying and victimization. Children who live in poverty are much more likely to bully than those who do not. Youth who live in poverty are likely exposed to more violence, drugs, and guns, which contribute to aggressive behavior. Socioeconomic status could also contribute to bullying as African American youth are more likely than other youth to be teased about their clothing and appearance (Shirley & Cornell, 2012).

Youth whose parents encourage them to stand up and be tough are more likely to bully (Bettencourt & Farrell, 2013). Some other risk factors for bullying include lack of family monitoring and supervision, gun ownership, parental support of violent behavior, peer support of violence and aggressive behaviors, and the youth's beliefs about aggressive behaviors. Some protective factors against bullying include parenting supervision and monitoring, parental support of nonviolent behavior, and peer support of nonaggressive behaviors (Albdour & Krouse, 2014). High levels of academic engagement are linked to less bullying and victimization (Elsaesser, Hong, & Voisin, 2016).

Violence Against African American Women

Despite the myth of the strong and resilient African American woman, she has been subject to violence both historically and contemporarily. In this section, we discuss rape and domestic violence from the perspective of African American girls and women. Although rape and domestic violence are health and social problems that affect women in all ethnic groups, the nature and the extent of the violence may differ qualitatively for African American women compared with women in other ethnic groups.

Rape

Rape is the ultimate expression of aggression and violence. Although men are also victims of rape, we concentrate on females as rape survivors because rape of females is more common than rape of males.

Rape of Enslaved Female Africans. Prior to setting foot on this continent, African women were raped and sexually exploited by Europeans who went to the coast of West Africa to select slaves for transport to the New World. Europeans who went to the West African coast had been at sea and away from home (and wives) for extended periods of time. In a visit to slave castles off the coast of Ghana and the open court-yards that surrounded these castles, one author (Belgrave) was reminded of narratives that told of how female slaves were selected for sexual exploitation. The slave traders would require women to be brought unclothed into an open courtyard, where they could be viewed, in turn, by the captain (slave trader). The captain would select one woman for sex with himself. The selected women would be washed down (as their living quarters were filthy) prior to being taken to the trader.

Extreme sexual exploitation of African women continued throughout the period of slavery (Wyatt, 1992). The rape of enslaved African women was done not only for the pleasure of the slave owner but also for profit. Rape by slave owners that resulted in pregnancy increased slave populations and thus increased the slave owner's property. Justification for the sexual exploitation of enslaved Africans stemmed from 15th-century Christian missionary attitudes about the strong "sexual appetite" of Africans. Stereotypes about Black male sexual prowess and Black female promiscu-ity linger to this day. Until slavery was abolished, enslaved Africans had no legal recourse for rape. After slavery, the American legal system still treated the rape of African American and White women differently. Even in contemporary times, these stereotypes may lead some to believe that Black women are less credible rape victims (George & Martinez, 2002). A national study found that 19% of African American women reported rape in their lifetime (USDOJ, OJP, 2006). The vast majority of African American women who have experienced a rape do not report it.

Krebs et al. (2011) found a lower prevalence of rape among students attend-ing a HBCU than those attending a non-HBCU. The authors analyzed data on sexual assault victimization among 3,951 undergraduate women at an HBCU and among 5,446 female students at a non-HBCU. They found that approximately 9.7% of undergraduate women at the HBCU reported experiencing a completed sexual assault since entering college compared with 13.7% of women from the non-HBCU. These differences were attributed to less alcohol use among women at the HBCU than at the non-HBCU. Prevalence of rape might be lower on an HBCU campus also because African American women are less likely to report rape than women in other racial and ethnic groups. They report fewer rapes because they may feel that no one will believe them, and they also do not want to get the perpetrator in trouble, especially if rape is by an acquaintance.

There are racial differences in response to rape based on scripts, cognitive struc-tures that guide one's thoughts and beliefs. Rape scripts are influenced by sexual scripts. A commonly held sexual script is that men are the initiators of a sexual encounter, and it is up to the women to decide how far the sexual encounter should go (Littleton & Dodd, 2016). This sexual script may normalize aggressive behav-ior from men, as it assumes that men are initiators of sexual activity and women gatekeepers. Nonconsenusal sexual scripts were investigated in a qualitative study of African American (N = 72) and White (N = 99) college women (Littleton & Dodd, 2016). Participants were asked to describe their experiences about a typical rape, including what happens before, during, or after. Analyses showed some similarities in African American and White women's responses. Both groups described three rape scripts, which included the "real rape," "party rape," and the "mismatched inten-tions rape." The party rape was described most by participants. Most participants viewed the real rape as that of a violent stranger attack. Few participants described a rape as occurring between individuals with a prior relationship.

Overall, the rape scripts seen in this study differed from that of most rapes of college women that do not involve violence, are perpetrated against women when intoxicated, and involve the perpetuator and the victim having a prior relationship. The scripts of African American women differed from White women in a few ways. African American women were more likely to describe the victim as resisting in active ways; they were less likely to include content related to the victim's inability to resist the rape (e.g., rape happened in an isolated area, perpetrator was large). African American women were also significantly less likely to include the vulnerable victim theme. The authors note this might be due to African American women's expectations that they should be strong and independent and thus should engage in active resistant strategies if they experience a rape attempt.

In an interesting study, Squires, Kohn-Wood, Chavous, and Carter (2006) used hip-hop to explore how African American adolescents explained violence against women. They conducted six focus groups that involved 35 African American high school students. Focus group participants were presented with three sets of questions that represented controversies from the world of hip-hop culture. The first set of questions was devoted to the discussion of a song by Eve, a popular hip-hop artist, titled "Love Is Blind." The song tells the story of a young woman victimized and killed by a physically and sexually abusive male partner. The second set of questions asked participants questions about the portrayal of African American men and women in hip-hop music and videos. The third set of questions included a hypothetical situation in which a young woman says she was raped after dancing with a famous rap star and then going to his hotel room. Three major themes came from the focus group discussions. The first theme suggested that women were considered at least equally if not predominantly responsible for their violent or abusive relationships with men. Girls believed that women should be self-sufficient in safeguarding themselves against violence. The theme of active resistance and women being responsible for defending themselves was similar to that found for African American women in the Littleton and Dodd study. Boys felt that women were sending mixed messages and that there should be exceptions to the rule of never hitting a woman. A second theme among both male and female students was that they held negative opinions of most women in the world of hip-hop. They believed women depicted in hip-hop engaged in "nasty" behavior, such as dancing and dressing provocatively. The third theme was the ambivalence female students felt about the images of women in hip-hop. These images contained dualistic expectations of both femininity and strength. The authors noted that these findings are consistent with the findings of others concerning acceptance of rape myths.

Intimate Partner Violence

Intimate partner violence (IPV) is a major public health problem. It includes rape and sexual assault, along with physical or psychological harm, by a current or former partner or spouse. Intimate partner violence occurs in heterosexual and same-sex relationships (Niolon et al., 2017). Survivors of IPV display a range of problems, including injury, impaired cardiovascular and reproductive conditions, and poor mental health, including post-traumatic stress disorder. IPV led to missing school or work, needing mental health and medical services, and poor child-rearing practices. It also incurs criminal justice and child welfare costs (Nioloon et al., 2017). Data collected from the National Intimate Partner and Sexual Violence Survey provides data on prevalence of IPV. Twenty-three percent of adult women and 14% of adult men in the U.S. report having experienced severe physical violence (e.g., being beaten, choked, having a weapon used against them) from an intimate partner in their lifetime. Forty-seven percent of men and 47% of women have experienced psychological violence, which includes controlling behavior and emotional abuse.

IPV is more likely to occur among racial and ethnic and sexual minority groups. Lifetime physical violence or stalking by an intimate partner is highest among multiracial women, at 57%. The prevalence among other racial and ethnic groups is as follows: American Indian/Alaska Native women (48%), non-Hispanic Black women (45%), non-Hispanic White women (37%), Hispanic women, 34%, and Asian/Pacific Islander women (18%). Lifetime prevalence for men is as follows: multiracial men (42%), American Indian/Alaska Native men (41%), non-Hispanic Black men (40%), non-Hispanic White men (30%), Hispanic men (30%), and Asian/Pacific Islander men (14%) (Nioloon et al., 2017).

IPV also occurs among youth. In the Youth Risk Behavior Survey, a nationally representative survey of youth in Grades 9 to 12, approximately 1 in 10 students reported being a victim of physical violence from a romantic partner during the previous 12 months (CDC, 2013). African American female adolescents are more likely than White teens to be both victim and perpetrator of teen dating violence (Ahonen & Loeber, 2016). Ahonen and Loeber found high levels of dating violence among girls between the ages 14 and 18. For example, 14.4% of African American girls (N = 2,450) reported physical assault by a partner, compared with 5.8% of White girls (N = 1,009), and 55.4% of African American girls reported verbal aggression by a partner, compared with 46.7% of White girls.

METHODOLOGICAL AND RESEARCH ISSUES

In this section, we comment on methodological issues, including the conceptualization of prosocial behavior and aggression and violence among African Americans. We provide an example of a scale that measures respect, a construct that has cultural significance to African Americans.

Measuring Prosocial and Aggressive Behavior

Prosocial behavior is universal and, among people of African descent, rooted in communal experiences. Yet the literature on prosocial behavior among African Americans has been limited. There is a need to develop culturally relevant indicators and measures of what constitutes prosocial behaviors in African American communities. For example, does baking a cake for a neighbor, giving a coworker a ride to an appointment with a doctor, or providing childcare for an extended family member constitute prosocial behavior? Is the senior citizen on a fixed income who contributes $1.00 to the Church plate exhibiting philanthropy? These examples suggest that there is a need for better ways to assess prosocial behavior in the African American community, including identifying prosocial norms. Yet much of the literature has focused on antisocial behaviors, especially among African American males.

Disproportionately higher rates of incarceration among African Americans add credibility to this portrayal. Understanding the causes of aggression, violence, and crime among African Americans is incomplete without understanding the historical context of violence against Africans, enslaved Africans, and contemporary African Americans. Therefore, one methodological consideration is the way in which data and statistics are analyzed and reported. Analysis and presentation of data that highlight violence and the perpetrators of violence should also take into account the context of violence and aggression in the United States, including present-day violence against African American males.

Another methodological issue that arises when discussing aggression and violence among young African Americans is what constitutes an aggressive and/or violent act. Within the context of some urban communities, not to aggress when one is aggressed against can be problematic. Learning how and when to respond or not respond in aggressive ways is essential to many African American males who reside in urban communities. This type of survival aggressiveness may be qualitatively different (and measured differently) from the type of retaliatory aggressive behavior seen in youth who have been bullied and those responsible for the Virginia Tech killings and the killings of students at Sandy Hook Elementary School in Newtown, Connecticut.

Similarly, there might be some unique cultural nuances in conceptualizing and measuring prosocial behavior among African Americans. Copeland-Carson (2005) called for a broadening of conceptualization of prosocial behavior to include any collective act done to benefit others.

A Measure of Respect

Respect has been described by Leary, Brennan, and Briggs (2005) as one component of prosocial behavior. Respect means to regard and value a person as a unique contributor to society (Lawrence-Lightfoot, 2000). An interesting scale has been developed to measure respect among African American male adolescents. The African American Respect Scale is a 20-item scale that measures prosocial attitudes held by male adolescents. The development of the scale is based on the assumption that respect is very important to African Americans, building on core African values. The roots of respect are grounded in African axiology (Leary et al., 2005), where integrity of relationships is essential. Also, as noted earlier, respect is a critical street norm that is strictly enforced and regulated (Anderson, 1999). The African American Respect Scale was developed to be used with African American male youth to measure prosocial attitudes toward respect. The development of the scale involved a sample of 200 African American male youth who were between 14 and 18 years of age. Youth were both incarcerated and from the community. The scale has three main subscales: (a) societal respect (e.g., "It is difficult to get appreciation as a Black man"), (b) family respect (e.g., "I am proud of my family's achievements"), and (c) peer respect ("No one will respect you unless you demand it"). These subscales have adequate reliability and validity.

Confounding Class and Race

Another methodological consideration is that class is often not considered in research on violence. Race is often used as a proxy for social class and other structural inequalities. For example, research suggests that African American youth are likely to both bully and to be victims of bullying when compared with other racial and ethnic groups. Similar disparities exist for gang membership, with Hispanics/Latinos and African Americans more likely to be gang members than Whites. Poverty is a major contributor to bullying experiences and gang membership. African American (and Hispanic/Latino) youth are more likely to live in poverty than other racial and ethnic groups. When investigating racial and ethnic differences in bullying or other antisocial behavior, participants from similar sociodemographic backgrounds should be included before making inferences about racial and ethnic differences.

BEST PRACTICES FOR INCREASING PROSOCIAL BEHAVIOR AND DECREASING ANTISOCIAL BEHAVIOR

There have been few programs that have targeted increasing prosocial behaviors among African Americans. Many more violence prevention programs for African Americans have been implemented and evaluated. Violence prevention programs typically target children and teens in order to reach youth prior to their engagement in violence. Because early adolescence (ages 11 to 13) is a critical period for instilling skills, beliefs, and values that support nonviolence, and it is the period preceding the largest developmental increases in aggressive behavior, many prevention programs target this age group. The Office of Juvenile Justice and Delinquency Prevention provides a registry of several model programs aimed at deterring violence and delinquency among African Americans and other groups. The programs are oriented at preventing violence and aggression at the individual, school, and community level. More information about these programs can be seen at the Office of Juvenile Justice and Delinquency Prevention's Model Programs Guide (U.S. Department of Justice, n.d.b). We briefly review two of the programs on this registry.

The Aban Aya Youth Project

The Aban Aya Youth Project is a culturally specific social development curriculum targeted at increasing protective factors and decreasing risk factors for violence, early and risky sexual behavior, drug use, and school delinquency. The program uses an Africentric framework and is implemented with African American youth ages 10 to 14 (Flay et al., 2004; Liu, & Flay, 2009; Segawa, Ngwe, Li, & Flay, 2005). The name of the program comes from the Akan language of Ghana. Aban means "fence" and is a symbol of social protection, and Aya means "an unfurling fern" and is a symbol of self-determination.

Aban Aya is implemented in school settings and contains a community component. A social development curriculum is administered in classrooms, and cognitive behavioral skills that address risk and protective factors are taught. Students learn nonviolent conflict resolution, the refusal skills to avoid drugs and alcohol and other problem behaviors while increasing self-esteem and cultural pride. The curriculum engages stakeholders (e.g., parents, local businesses) in the community in order to have long-lasting program effects.

Aban Aya Youth Project is administered in schools over a period of 4 years, starting in the fifth grade and ending in the eighth grade. Sessions lasting for approximately 45 minutes are delivered in the classroom by teachers. The number of sessions varies from year to year. An evaluation of the program showed significant reductions in violence behavior, school delinquency, and substance use among participants in the program when compared with a control group. Additional information about Aban Aya Youth Project can be found at the National Institute of Justice (2011).

Pen or Pencil

Pen or Pencil is an initiative of the National Alliance of Faith and Justice (Pen or Pencil, n.d.). "Pen" stands for penitentiary and "pencil" for education. The program was developed to promote prosocial behavior and to decrease antisocial behavior among youth at risk because of high-risk neighborhoods they live in, parental incarceration, and/or because of involvement in juvenile justice or social welfare systems. The program is delivered in school settings but can also be delivered in community settings, including faith-based institutions and juvenile detention centers. The program targets youth from 8 to 17 years of age.

The objectives of Pen or Pencil are for youth to increase self-competency beliefs by doing something well, to gain a sense of usefulness through service contributions, to establish a positive relationship with caring adults, and to gain a sense of empowerment in learning how to control their destiny. There are several components of the program. The curriculum component consists of a 2-plus-hour enrichment presentation where students are introduced to African American history taken from the videos "The Intolerable Burden" and "Choices" to promote responsibility and ethnic identity. A 10-week extended weekly series of workshops addresses character and prosocial ways of behaving. Youth are also given an opportunity to implement a service learning intervention project, called "The B.U.S. Boycott." For this project, students apply lessons learned from the Montgomery bus boycott to learn about public policy, to reduce negative contact with law enforcement, and to complete service projects in their community. Another component is one-on-one academic mentoring with a trained adult for 1 year. Youth may participate in one or more of these components. Facilitators for Pen or Pencil are recruited from faith and community groups and trained in group facilitation skills. Several nonprofit youth development organizations are affiliated with Pen or Pencil, and the program has been implemented in many cities throughout the United States.

Data collected from over 1,930 African American youth enrolled in the Pen or Pencil program were used to examine relationships between cultural variables and prosocial behaviors. Data were collected from youth in 12 states and the District of Columbia (Grills et al., 2016). Participants included males and females whose age ranged from 9 to 19. Participants completed measures of cultural variables (e.g., Africentric values, racial socialization) and positive youth development variables (e.g., prosocial behavior, community and civic engagement). Grills and colleagues found among Pen or Pencil participants that cultural variables were significantly related to prosocial behavior and other aspects of positive youth development. This study contributes to our understanding of how cultural beliefs and behaviors promote prosocial behaviors in African American youth and can be extended to culturally tailored interventions to promote positive youth development.

CRITICAL ANALYSIS

Throughout our review of the literature and research on prosocial and antisocial behavior among African Americans, we see considerably less on prosocial behavior. Using the search words "African American" and "prosocial behavior" yielded 172 articles in the PsycINFO® database. Deleting the word "behavior" and using just the terms "African American" and "prosocial" identified 204 papers. The search words "African American" and "violence" yielded 2,410 citations alone, and the search words "African American" and "aggression" yielded 817 citations. Despite this imbalance in the literature, it is clear that African Americans are guided by prosocial behavior as much as by antisocial behavior. Clearly, more research is needed to understand prosocial behavior, factors that promote prosocial behavior, and interventions to increase prosocial behaviors. The research of Grills et al. (2016) is a promising start, as their research illustrates the link between cultural factors such as Africentric values and prosocial behavior among African American youth. Similarly informative is the work of Jagers, Sydnor, Mouttapa, and Flay (2007) on factors that protect against violence while simultaneously increasing prosocial behavior. These researchers encourage us to attend to culture in interventions and programs that target both the prevention of antisocial behavior and the promotion of prosocial behavior among African American youth. The Pen or Pencil program is an example of a program that uses African American history as a way to engage and motivate youth.

Scholars who have written on philanthropy suggest using a broader definition of what philanthropy consists of, including the fact that philanthropy includes acts other than providing money and can include all practices and acts to better African Americans individually and collectively. This broader definition of philanthropy is likely to capture the full spectrum of philanthropy among African Americans. The majority of media attention and cited statistics continue to portray African Americans, especially young African American males, as violent. Disproportionately higher rates of incarceration among African Americans add credibility to this portrayal. Understanding the causes of aggression and violence among African Americans is incomplete without understanding the historical context of violence against Africans, enslaved Africans, and contemporary African Americans. We hope more studies will be conducted that will address both historical and contemporary problems that contribute to violence. In addition, culturally specific violence prevention interventions are still needed.

Summary

In this chapter, we have presented psychological perspectives on positive behaviors of African Americans. Prosocial behavior is universal and directed at helping or benefiting others and includes topics such as community and civic engagement, charity, philanthropy, and cooperation. Expressions of prosocial behavior among African Americans may differ from expressions for other ethnic groups. For example, African Americans are more likely to contribute to Churches or other faith-based institutions and may provide goods and services that are not monetary in value. Prosocial behavior among African Americans is linked to communal attitudes. Empathy and religiosity are correlated with prosocial behavior among both African American children and adults.

Antisocial behavior is directed at negative actions toward others and includes topics such as aggression and violence. The study of aggression and violence among African Americans must consider historical and contemporary issues, including enslavement, current discrimination, and segregated neighborhoods. Youth exposure to community violence is associated with a myriad of resulting academic and psychological problems, including increased aggression among those exposed. Programs that prevent or reduce violence include programs that change youths' skills in handling conflict and programs that increase community resources. Youth violence and violence against women are two types of violence that are of particular concern in the African American community.

REFERENCES

Abbo, C., Okello, E., Ekblad, S., Waako, P., & Musisi, S. (2008). Lay concepts of psychosis in Busoga, Eastern Uganda: A pilot study. *World Culture Psychiatry Research Review, 3*(3), 132–145.

Abdou, C. M., Dunkel-Schetter, C., Campos, B., Hilmert, C. J., Dominguez, T. P., Hobel, C. J., . . . Sandman, C. (2010). Communalism predicts prenatal affect, stress, and physiology better than ethnicity and socioeconomic status. *Cultural Diversity and Ethnic Minority Psychology, 16*(3), 395–403.

Abdou, C. M., & Fingerhut, A. W. (2014). Stereotype threat among black and white women in health care settings. *Cultural Diversity and Ethnic Minority Psychology, 20*(3), 316–323.

Abdullah, A. S. (1998). Mammy-ism: A diagnosis of psychological misorientation for women of African descent. *Journal of Black Psychology, 24*(2), 196–210.

Abdullah, T., & Brown, T. L. (2012). Acculturation style and alcohol use among African American college students: An exploration of potential moderators. *Journal of Black Psychology, 38*(4), 421–441.

Aberson, C., & Ettlin, T. (2004). The aversive racism paradigm and responses favoring African Americans: Meta-analytic evidence of two types of favoritism. *Social Justice Research, 17*(1), 25–46.

Abrams, J. A., Maxwell, M., Pope, M., & Belgrave, F. Z. (2014). Carrying the world with the grace of a lady and the grit of a warrior: Deepening our understanding of the "Strong Black Woman" schema. *Psychology of Women Quarterly, 38*(4), 503–518.

Achenbach, T. M., & Edelbrock, C. S. (1984). Psychopathology of childhood. *Annual Review of Psychology, 35,* 227–256.

ACT. (2012). *2012 condition of college and career readiness.* Retrieved from www.act.org/readiness/2012

Adams, E. A., Kurtz-Costes, B. E., & Hoffman, A. J. (2016). Skin tone bias among African Americans: Antecedents and consequences across the life span. *Developmental Review, 40,* 93–116.

Addo, F., Houle, J., & Simon, D. (2016). Young, black, and (still) in the red: Parental wealth, race, and student loan debt. *Race and Social Problems, 8*(1), 64–76.

Adebimpe, V. R., & Cohen, E. (1989). Schizophrenia and affective disorder in black and white patients: A methodologic note. *Journal of the National Medical Association, 81*(7), 761–765.

Adelabu, D. H. (2008). Future time perspective, hope, and ethnic identity among African American adolescents. *Urban Education, 43*(3), 347–360.

Adelman, L., Baynard, J., Chisolm, R., Fortier, J. M., Garcia, R. P., Herbes-Sommers, C., . . . Pacific Islanders in Communications. (2008). *Unnatural causes: Is inequality making us sick?* San Francisco, CA: California Newsreel.

Adeniji, A. (2016). *Insider philanthropy.* Retrieved from https://www.insidephilanthropy.com/home/2016/9/14/a-rising-force-on-the-state-of-black-philanthropy.html

Adewuya, A. O., & Makanjuola, R. O. (2008). Social distance towards people with mental illness in Southwestern Nigeria. *Australian & New Zealand Journal of Psychiatry, 42*(5), 389–395.

Adkison-Bradley, C., DeBose, C. H., Terpstra, J., & Bilgic, Y. K. (2012). Postadoption services utilization among African American, transracial, and white American parents: Counseling and legal implications. *The Family Journal, 20*(4), 392–398.

Adkison-Johnson, C., Terpstra, J., Burgos, J., & Payne, E. D. (2016). African American child discipline: Differences between mothers and fathers. *Family Court Review, 54*(2), 203–220.

Administration on Aging (AOA). (2011). *A profile of older Americans: 2011.* Retrieved from http://www.aoa.gov/Aging_Statistics/Profile/2011/docs/2011profile.pdf

Agrawal, A., & Lynskey, M. T. (2008). Are there genetic influences on addiction?: Evidence from family, adoption and twin studies. *Addiction, 103,* 1069–1081.

Aguirre, C. G., Bello, M. S., Andrabi, N., Pang, R. D., Hendricks, P. S., Bluthenthal, R. N., & Leventhal, A. M. (2016). Gender, ethnicity, and their intersectionality in the prediction of smoking outcome expectancies in regular cigarette smokers. *Behavior Modification, 40*(1–2), 281–302.

Aholou, T. M., Cooks, E., Murray, A., Sutton, M. Y., Gaul, Z., Gaskins, S., & Payne-Foster, P. (2016). "Wake Up! HIV is at Your Door": African American faith leaders in the rural south and HIV perceptions: A qualitative analysis. *Journal of Religion and Health, 55*(6), 1968–1979.

Aikens, N. L., Coleman, C. P., & Barbarin, O. (2008). Ethnic differences in the effects of parental depression on preschool children's socioemotional functioning. *Social Development, 17*(1), 137–160.

Aisenberg, E. (2008). *Evidence-based practice in mental health care to ethnic minority communities: Has its practice fallen short of its evidence?* Farmington Hills, MI: National Association of Social Workers, Gale: Cengage Learning.

Akande, A., Adetoun, B., & Tserere, M. (2006). The South African family. In J. Georgas, J. Berry, F. J. R. van de Vijver, Ç. Kagitçibasi & Y. Poortinga (Eds.), *Families across cultures: A 30-nation psychological study* (pp. 442–449). New York, NY: Cambridge University Press.

Akbar, N. (1981). Mental disorder among African-Americans. *Black Books Bulletin, 7*(2), 18–25.

Akbar, N. (1983). *From miseducation to education.* Jersey City, NJ: New Mind Productions.

Akbar, N. (1991a). The evolution of human psychology for African Americans. In R. Jones (Ed.), *Black psychology* (pp. 99–123). Berkeley, CA: Cobb & Henry.

Akbar, N. (1991b). Mental disorders among African Americans. In R. Jones (Ed.), *Black psychology* (pp. 339–352). Berkeley, CA: Cobb & Henry.

Akbar, N. (1996). African metapsychology of human personality. In D. A. Azibo (Ed.), *African psychology* (pp. 29–46). Trenton, NJ: African World Press.

Akbar, N. (2004). The evolution of human psychology for African Americans. In R. Jones (Ed.), *Black psychology* (pp. 17–40). Hampton, VA: Cobb & Henry.

Akinleye, I., Roberts, J. S., Royal, C. D., Linnenbringer, E., Obisesan, T. O., Fasaye, G. A., & Green, R. C. (2011). Differences between African American and White research volunteers in their attitudes, beliefs and knowledge regarding genetic testing for Alzheimer's disease. *Journal of Genetic Counseling, 209*, 650–659.

Aknin, L. B., Barrington-Leigh, C. P., Dunn, E. W., Helliwell, J. F., Burns, J., Biswas-Diener, R., . . . Norton, M. I. (2013). Prosocial spending and well-being: Cross-cultural evidence for a psychological universal. *Journal of Personality and Social Psychology, 104*(4), 635.

Albdour, M., & Krouse, H. J. (2014). Bullying and victimization among African American adolescents: A literature review. *Journal of Child and Adolescent Psychiatric Nursing, 27*(2), 68–82.

Albury, A. (1998). *Social orientation, learning condition and learning outcomes among low income black and white grade school children* (Unpublished doctoral dissertation). Howard University, Washington, DC.

Alexander, R., & Curtis, C. M. (1996). A review of empirical research involving the transracial adoption of African American children. *Journal of Black Psychology, 22*(2), 223–235.

Alghasham, A. A. (2012). Effect of students' learning styles on classroom performance in problem-based learning. *Medical Teacher, 34*, 14–19.

Ali, M. M., Rizzo, J. A., & Heiland, F. W. (2013). Big and beautiful? Evidence of racial differences in the perceived attractiveness of obese females. *Journal of Adolescence, 36*(3), 539–549.

Allen, A. J., Davey, M. P., & Davey, A. (2010). Being examples to the flock: The role of church leaders and African American families seeking mental health care services. *Contemporary Family Therapy, 32*, 117–134.

Allen, B. A., & Butler, L. (1996). The effects of music and movement opportunity on the reasoning performance of African American and White school children: A preliminary study. *Journal of Black Psychology, 22*(3), 316–327.

Allen, D., & Marshall, E. S. (2010). Spirituality as a coping resource for African American parents of chronically ill children. *MCN The American Journal of Maternal Child Nursing, 35*(4), 232–237.

Alliance for Health Reform. (2004). *Closing the gap 2003: Racial and ethnic disparities in health care.* Retrieved from http://www.allhealth.org/publications/pub_16 .pdf

Allport, G. (1954). *The nature of prejudice.* Reading, MA: Addison-Wesley.

Allport, G. (1988). *The nature of prejudice.* Cambridge, MA: Perseus Books.

Altschul, I., Oyserman, D., & Bybee, D. (2006). Racial-ethnic identity in mid-adolescence: Content and change as predictors of academic achievement. *Child Development, 77*(5), 1155–1169.

Ambler, C. (2003). Alcohol and the slave trade in West Africa, 1400–1850. In W. Jankowiak & D. Bradburd (Eds.), *Drugs, labor, and colonial expansion* (pp. 73–87). Tucson: University of Arizona Press.

American Anthropological Association. (1998, May 17). *American Anthropological Association statement on "race".* Retrieved from http://www.aaanet.org/stmts/racepp.htm

American Association of Suicidology. (2017). Retrieved from http://www.suicidology.org/resources/facts-statistics

American College Testing Program. (2016). Retrieved from https://nces.ed.gov/programs/digest/d16/tables/dt16_302.20.asp

American Council on Education. (2007). *Older adults and higher education.* Washington, DC: Author. Retrieved from http://plus50.aacc.nche.edu/documents/Reinvestingfinal.pdf

American Diabetes Association. (2012). *African Americans and complications.* Retrieved from http://www.diabetes.org/living-with-diabetes/complications/african-americans-and-complications.html

American Diabetes Association. (n.d.). *Diabetes in African American Communities Advocacy Fact Sheet.* . Retrieved from http://main.diabetes.org/dorg/PDFs/Advocacy/fact-sheet-advocacy-african-american.pdf

American Foundation for Suicide Prevention. (n.d.). Retrieved from https://afsp.org/

American Heart Association. (2013). *Statistical fact sheet.* Retrieved from https://www.heart.org/idc/groups/heart-public/@wcm/@sop/@smd/documents/downloadable/ucm_319587.pdf

American Psychiatric Association. (2013). *Diagnostic and statistical manual of mental disorders* (5th ed.). Arlington, VA: American Psychiatric Publishing.

American Psychological Association (APA). (2002). *Guidelines on multicultural education, training, research, and organizational change for psychologists.* Retrieved from http://www.apa.org/pi/oema/resources/policy/multicultural-guidelines.aspx

American Psychological Association (APA). (2015). *Demographics of the U.S. psychology workforce: Findings from the American Community Survey.* Washington, DC: Author. Retrieved from http://www.apa.org/workforce/publications/13-demographics/index.aspx?tab=6

American Psychological Association (APA). (2017a). *About the office of ethnic minority affairs.* Retrieved from http://www.apa.org/pi/oema/about/index.aspx

American Psychological Association (APA). (2017b). *Who we are.* Retrieved from http://www.apa.org/about/apa/index.aspx

American Psychological Association, Task Force on Resilience and Strength in Black Children and Adolescents. (2008). *Resilience in African American children and adolescents: A vision for optimal development.* Washington, DC: Author.

American Religious Identification Survey. (2001). Retrieved from http://commons.trincoll.edu/aris/files/2013/11/ARIS-2001-report-complete.pdf

Amodio, D., Harmon-Jones, E., & Devine, P. (2003). Individual differences in the activation and control of affective race bias as assessed by startle eye blink responses and self-report. *Journal of Personality and Social Psychology, 84*, 738–753.

Anand, V., McGinty, K. L., O'Brien, K., Guenthner, G., Hahn, E., & Martin, C. A. (2015). E-cigarette use and beliefs among urban public high school students in North Carolina. *Journal of Adolescent Health, 57*(1), 46–51

Anderson, C. A., Bushman, B. J., Donnerstein, E., Hummer, T. A., & Warburton, W. (2015). SPSSI research summary on media violence. *Analyses of Social Issues and Public Policy, 15*(1), 4–19.

Anderson, E. (1999). *Code of the street: Decency, violence, and the moral life of the inner city.* New York, NY: Norton.

Anderson, M. (2015). *A rising share of the US Black population is foreign born.* Washington, DC: Pew Research Center.

Anderson, R. P., Williamson, G. A., & Lundy, N. C. (1977). *Relationship between performance-based and observer-based measures of hyperactivity.* Paper presented at the meeting of the Southwestern Psychological Association, Fort Worth, TX.

Andrews, A. M., Zhang, N., Buechley, C., Chapman, R., Guillen, J. L., Magee, J. C., & Resnicow, K. (2016).

Organ donation attitudes and practices among African Americans: An adapted measurement instrument. *Journal of Health Care for the Poor and Underserved, 27*(3), 1397–1410.

Anglin, D. M., & Wade, J. C. (2007). Racial socialization, racial identity, and Black students' adjustment to college. *Cultural Diversity and Ethnic Minority Psychology, 13*(3), 207–215.

Annie E. Casey Foundation. (n.d.). Retrieved from http://datacenter.kidscount.org/data/tables/7752-child-and-teen-death-rate-by-race-and-ethnicity?loc=1&loct=2#detailed/1/any/true/573,133,16/9,1,13/14941,17850

Anstey, E. H., Chen J., Elam-Evans, L. D., & Perrine, C. G. (2017). Racial and geographic differences in breastfeeding: United States, 2011–2015. *MMWR Morbidity and Mortality Weekly Report, 66*, 723–727.

Anyon, Y. (2011). Reducing racial disparities and disproportionalities in the child welfare system: Policy perspectives about how to serve the best interests of African American youth. *Children and Youth Services Review, 33*, 242–253.

Aries, E., & Moorehead, K. (1989). The importance of ethnicity in the development of identity of Black adolescents. *Psychological Reports, 65*, 75–82.

Armstead, C. A., Hébert, J. R., Griffin, E. K., & Prince, G. M. (2014). A question of color: The influence of skin color and stress on resting blood pressure and body mass among African American women. *Journal of Black Psychology, 40*(5), 424–450.

Arnold, L. E., Elliott, M., Sachs, L., Bird, H., Kraemer, H., Wells, K. C., . . . Wigal, T. (2003). Effects of ethnicity on treatment attendance, stimulant response/dose, and 14-month outcome in ADHD. *Journal of Consulting and Clinical Psychology, 71*, 713–727.

Aronson, E., Wilson, T. D., & Akert, R. M. (2002). *Social psychology* (4th ed.). Upper Saddle River, NJ: Prentice Hall.

Aronson, J., Burgess, D., Phelan, S. M., & Juarez, L. (2013). Unhealthy interactions: The role of stereotype threat in health disparities. *American Journal of Public Health, 103*(1), 50–56.

Arrazola, R. A., Singh, T., Corey, C. G., Husten, C. G., Neff, L. J., Apelberg, B. J., . . . McAfee, T. (2015). Tobacco use among middle and high school students-United States, 2011–2014. *MMWR Morbidity and Mortality Weekly Report, 64*(14), 381–385.

Asante, M. K. (2003). *Afrocentricity: The theory of social change.* Chicago, IL: African American Images.

Asare, M., & Sharma, M. (2009). Using the theory of planned behavior to predict safer sexual behavior by Ghanaian immigrants in a large Midwestern U.S. city. *International Quarterly of Community Health Education, 30*, 321–335.

Askenasy, A. R., Dohrenwend, B. P., & Dohrenwend, B. S. (1977). Some effects of social class and ethnic group membership on judgments of the magnitude of stressful life events: A research note. *Journal of Health and Social Behavior, 18*(4), 432–439.

The Association of Theological Schools. (2016). *Annual Data Tables (2015–2016).* Retrieved from http://www.ats.edu/uploads/resources/institutional-data/annual-data-tables/2015-2016-annual-data-tables.pdf

Attaway, N., & Bry, B. H. (2004). Parenting style and black adolescents' academic achievement. *Journal of Black Psychology, 30*(2), 229–247.

Aud, S., Fox, M. A., & Kewal Ramani, A. (2010). *Status and trends in the education of racial and ethnic minorities.* Washington, DC: National Center for Education Statistics.

Aud, S., Hussar, W., Johnson, F., Kena, G., Roth, E., Manning, E., . . . Zhang, J. (2012). *The condition of education 2012 (NCES 2012-045).* Washington, DC: U.S. Department of Education, National Center for Education Statistics. Retrieved from https://nces.ed.gov/pubs2012/2012045.pdf

Auspos, P., & Kubisch, A. C. (2004). *Building knowledge about community change: Moving beyond evaluations.* New York, NY: Aspen Institute Roundtable for Community Change.

Awad, G. H., Norwood, C., Taylor, D. S., Martinez, M., McClain, S., Jones, B., . . . Chapman-Hilliard, C. (2015). Beauty and body image concerns among African American college women. *Journal of Black Psychology, 41*(6), 540–564.

Aycock, D. M., & Clark, P. C. (2016). Incongruence between perceived long-term risk and actual risk of stroke in rural African Americans. *Journal of Neuroscience Nursing, 48*(1), 35–41.

Aymer, S. R. (2016). "I can't breathe": A case study—Helping Black men cope with race-related trauma stemming from police killing and brutality. *Journal of Human Behavior in the Social Environment, 26*(3–4), 367–376.

Azibo, D. A. (1983). Some psychological concomitants and consequences of the black personality: Mental health implications. *Journal of Non-White Concerns in Personnel and Guidance, 11,* 59–66.

Azibo, D. A. (1989). African-centered theses on mental health and a nosology of Black/African personality disorder. *Journal of Black Psychology, 15*(2), 173–214.

Azibo, D. A. (1996). African psychology in historical perspective and related commentary. In D. A. Azibo (Ed.), *African psychology in historical perspective and related commentary* (pp. 1–28). Trenton, NJ: African World Press.

Azibo, D. A. (2006). Empirical exploration of the Azibo theory of diminutional psychological misorientation. *Humboldt Journal of Social Relations, 30,* 9–43.

Azibo, D. A. (2008). *The Azibo nosology.* Presentation at the annual meeting of the Association of Black Psychologists, Oakland, CA.

Azibo, D. A. (2013). Unmasking materialistic depression as a mental health problem: Its effect on depression and materialism in an African–United States undergraduate sample. *Journal of Affective Disorders, 150*(2), 623–628.

Azibo, D. A. (2014). The Azibo Nosology II: Epexegesis and 25th anniversary update—55 culture-focused mental disorders suffered by African descent people. *Journal of Pan African Studies, 7*(5), 137–178.

Azibo, D., & Dixon, P. (1998). The theoretical relationship between materialistic depression and depression: Preliminary data and implications for the Azibo Nosology. *Journal of Black Psychology, 24,* 211–225.

Babb, S., Stewart, C., & Bachman, C. (2012). Gender, ethnic, age, and relationship differences in nontraditional college student alcohol consumption: A tri-ethnic study. *Journal of Ethnicity in Substance Abuse, 11,* 22–47.

Bachman, J. G., Staff, J., O'malley, P. M., Schulenberg, J. E., & Freedman-Doan, P. (2011). Twelfth-grade student work intensity linked to later educational attainment and substance use: New longitudinal evidence. *Developmental Psychology, 47*(2), 344–363.

Bahr, S. J., Hoffman, J. P., & Yang, X. (2005). Parental and peer influences on the risk of adolescent drug use. *Journal of Primary Prevention, 26*(6), 529–551.

Baker, C. E. (2014). African American fathers' contributions to children's early academic achievement: Evidence from two-parent families from the early childhood longitudinal study–birth cohort. *Early Education & Development, 25*(1), 19–35.

Baldwin, D. R., Jackson, D., Okoh, I., & Cannon, R. L. (2011). Resiliency and optimism: An African American senior citizen's perspective. *Journal of Black Psychology, 37*(1), 24–41.

Baldwin, J. A. (1981). Notes on an Africentric theory of black personality. *The Western Journal of Black Studies, 5,* 172–179.

Baldwin, J. A. (1984). African self-consciousness and the mental health of African-Americans. *Journal of Black Studies, 15,* 177–194.

Baldwin, J. A. (1986). Black psychology: Issues and synthesis. *Journal of Black Studies, 16,* 235–249.

Baldwin, J. A. (1991). African (black) psychology: Issues and synthesis. In R. Jones (Ed.), *Black psychology* (pp. 125–135). Berkeley, CA: Cobb & Henry.

Baldwin, J. A., & Bell, Y. R. (1985). The African self-consciousness scale: An Africentric personality questionnaire. *Western Journal of Black Studies, 9*(2), 61–68.

Baldwin, J. A., Duncan, J. A., & Bell, Y. R. (1992). Assessment of African self- consciousness among black students from two college environments. In K. A. Burlew, W. C. Banks, H. P. McAdoo & D. A. Azibo (Eds.), *African American psychology: Theory, research, and practice* (pp. 283–299). Newbury Park, CA: Sage.

Ball, E. L. (2003). African American philanthropy. *Philanthropy.* Retrieved from http://www.philanthropy.org/publications/online_publications/african_american_paper.pdf

Ball, E. L. (2008). *African American philanthropy.* Paper available from the Center on Philanthropy and Civil Society, City University of New York, New York.

Balsam, K. F., Molina, Y., Blayney, J. A., Dillworth, T., Zimmerman, L., & Kaysen, D. (2015). Racial/ethnic differences in identity and mental health outcomes among young sexual minority women. *Cultural Diversity and Ethnic Minority Psychology, 21*(3), 380–390.

Bandura, A. (1977). Self-efficacy: Toward a unifying theory of behavioral change. *Psychological Review, 84,* 191–215.

Banerjee, M., Rowley, S. J., & Johnson, D. J. (2015). Community violence and racial socialization: Their influence on the psychosocial well-being of

African American college students. *Journal of Black Psychology, 41*, 358–383.

Banks, D. E., & Zapolski, T. C. (2017). Racial differences in the link between alcohol expectancies and adolescent drinking. *Addictive Behaviors, 67*, 34–37.

Banks, J. (2006). Improving race relations in schools: From theory and research to practice. *Journal of Social Issues, 62*(3), 607–614.

Banks, K. H. (2010). African American college students' experience of racial discrimination and the role of college hassles. *Journal of College Student Development, 51*(1), 23–34.

Banks, R. (1997). Race, representation, and the drug policy agenda. In C. Herring (Ed.), *African Americans and the public agenda* (pp. 209–223). Thousand Oaks, CA: Sage.

Bannon, W. M., McKay, M. M., Chacko, A., Rodriguez, J. A., & Cavaleri, M. (2009). Cultural pride reinforcement as a dimension of racial socialization protective of urban African American child anxiety. *Family in Society: The Journal of Contemporary Science, 90*, 79–86.

Banton, M. (1987). *Racial theories.* Cambridge, England: Cambridge University Press.

Barke, A., Nyarko, S., & Klecha, D. (2011). The stigma of mental illness in Southern Ghana: Attitudes of the urban population and patients' views. *Social Psychiatry Psychiatric Epidemiology, 46*(11), 1191–1202.

Barna Group. (2005). *African Americans.* Retrieved from http://www.barna.org/

Barna Group. (2011). Major faith shifts evident among Whites, Blacks, and Hispanics since 1991. *Barna Group.* Retrieved from http://www.barna.org/faith-spirituality/510-major-faith-shifts-evident-among-whites-blacks-and-hispanics-since-1991

Barnes, S. (2001). Stressors and strengths: A theoretical and practical examination of nuclear, single-parent, and augmented African American families. *Families in Society, 82*(5), 449–460.

Barnes, S. L. (2013a). Black church giving: An analysis of ideological, programmatic, and denominational effects. *Sage Open, 3*, 1–11.

Barnes, S. L. (2013b). To welcome or affirm: Black clergy views about homosexuality, inclusivity, and church leadership. *Journal of Homosexuality, 60*(10), 1409–1433.

Barnett, W. S. (1995). Long-term effects of childhood programs on cognitive and school outcomes. *The Future of Children, 5*(3), 25–50.

Barnidge, E. K., Baker, E. A., Schootman, M., Motton, F., Sawicki, M., & Rose, F. (2015). The effect of education plus access on perceived fruit and vegetable consumption in a rural African American community intervention. *Health Education Research, 30*(5), 773–785.

Baron, R. A., & Richardson, D. R. (1994). *Human aggression* (2nd ed.). New York, NY: Plenum Press.

Barrantes, R. J., Eaton, A. A., Veldhuis, C. B., & Hughes, T. L. (2017). The role of minority stressors in lesbian relationship commitment and persistence over time. *Psychology of Sexual Orientation and Gender Diversity, 4*(2), 205.

Barrera, M., Jr., Castro, F. G., Strycker, L. A., & Toobert, D. J. (2013). Cultural adaptations of behavioral health interventions: A progress report. *Journal of Consulting and Clinical Psychology, 81*(2), 196–205.

Barrett, D. H., Wisotzek, I. E., Abel, G. G., Rouleau, J. L., Platt, A. F., Pollard, W. E., & Eckman J. R. (1988). Assessment of psychosocial functioning of patients with sickle cell disease. *Southern Medical Journal, 81*, 745–750.

Baumeister, R. F. (Ed.). (1999). *The self in social psychology.* Philadelphia, PA: Psychology Press.

Baumeister, R. F., & Muraven, M. (1996). Identity as adaptation to social, cultural, and historical context. *Journal of Adolescence, 19*(5), 405–416.

Baumgarte, R., & Nelson, D. W. (2009). Preference for same-versus cross-sex friendships. *Journal of Applied Social Psychology, 39*(4), 901–917.

Beadnell, B., Baker, S., Knox, K., Stielstra, S., Morrison, D., Degooyer, E., . . . Oxford, M. I. (2003). The influence of psychosocial difficulties on women's attrition in an HIV/STD prevention program. *AIDS Care, 15*(3), 807–820.

Bean, R. A., Bush, K. R., McKenry, P. C., & Wilson, S. M. (2003). The impact of parental support, behavioral control, and psychological control on the academic achievement and self-esteem of African American and European American adolescents. *Journal of Adolescent Research, 18*, 523–541.

Beaulac, J., Kristjansson, E., & Cummins, S. (2009). A systematic review of food deserts, 1966–2007. *Preventing Chronic Disease, 6*(3), A105.

Bediako, S. M., & King-Meadows, T. (2016). Public support for sickle-cell disease funding: Does race matter? *Race and Social Problems, 8*(2), 186–195.

Bediako, S. M., Lattimer, L., Haywood, J. C., Ratanawongsa, N., Lanzkron, S., & Beach, M. C. (2011). Religious coping and hospital admissions among adults with sickle cell disease. *Journal of Behavioral Medicine, 34*, 120–127.

Bediako, S. M., & Moffitt, K. (2011). Race and social attitudes about sickle cell disease. *Ethnicity & Health, 16*, 4–5.

Bediako, S. M., & Neblett, E. W., Jr. (2011). Optimism and perceived stress in sickle-cell disease: The role of an afrocultural social ethos. *Journal of Black Psychology, 37*(2), 234–253.

Behnke, A., & Allen, W. (2007). Effectively serving low-income fathers of color. *Marriage and Family Review, 42*(2), 29–50.

Behnken, M. P. W., Abraham, T., Cutrona, C. E., Russell, D. W., Simons, R. L., & Gibbons, F. X. (2014). Linking early ADHD to adolescent and early adult outcomes among African Americans. *Journal of Criminal Justice, 42*(2), 95–103.

Belgrave, F. Z. (1998). *Psychosocial aspects of chronic illness and disability among African Americans.* Westport, CT: Auburn House/Greenwood.

Belgrave, F. Z. (2002). Relational theory and cultural enhancement interventions for African American adolescent girls. *Public Health Reports, 117*(Suppl. 1), 76–81.

Belgrave, F. Z. (2005). *Unpublished data.* Richmond, VA: Virginia Commonwealth University.

Belgrave, F. Z., Abrams, J. A., Hood, K. B., Moore, M. P., & Nguyen, A. B. (2016). Development and validation of a preliminary measure of African American women's gender role beliefs. *Journal of Black Psychology, 42*(4), 320–342.

Belgrave, F. Z., Allison, K. W., Wilson, J., & Tademy, R. (2012). *Brothers of Ujima: A cultural empowerment program for adolescent African American males.* Champaign, IL: Research Press.

Belgrave, F. Z., & Brevard, J. K. (2015). *African American boys: Identity, culture, and development.* New York, NY: Springer.

Belgrave, F. Z., Brome, D. R., & Hampton, C. (2000). The contribution of Africentric values and racial identity to the prediction of drug knowledge, attitudes, and use among African American youth. *Journal of Black Psychology, 26*(4), 386–401.

Belgrave, F. Z., Cherry, V., Butler, D., & Townsend, T. (2008). *Sisters of Nia: An empowerment cultural curriculum for African American girls.* Champaign, IL: Research Press.

Belgrave, F. Z., Logan, D., & Tademy, R. (2000). *Africentric Psychology.* Thomson Learning.

Belgrave, F. Z., Nguyen, A. B., Johnson, J. L., & Hood, K. (2011). Who is likely to help and hurt? Profiles of African American adolescents with prosocial and aggressive behavior. *Journal of Youth and Adolescence, 40*(8), 1012–1024.

Belgrave, F. Z., Reed, M. C., Plybon, L. E., Butler, D. S., Allison, K. W., & Davis, T. (2004). An evaluation of sisters of Nia: A cultural program for African American girls. *Journal of Black Psychology, 30*, 329–343.

Belgrave, F. Z., Townsend, T. G., Cherry, V. R., & Cunningham, D. M. (1997). The influence of an Africentric worldview and demographic variables on drug knowledge, attitudes, and use among African American youth. *Journal of Community Psychology, 25*(5), 421–433.

Bell, K., Burton, N. K., & Blount, L. G. (2017). *Black women's mental health: Balancing strength and vulnerability.* Albany, NY: Suny Press.

Bell, Y. R. (1994). A culturally sensitive analysis of black learning style. *Journal of Black Psychology, 20*(1), 47–61.

Bem, S. L. (1993). *The lenses of gender: Transforming the debate on sexual inequality.* New Haven, CT: Yale.

Bennett, G. G., Marcellus, M. M., Sollers, J. J., Edwards, C. L., Whitfield, K. E., Brandom, D. T., & Tucker, R. D. (2004). Stress, coping, and health outcomes among African-Americans: A review of the John Henryism hypothesis. *Psychology and Health, 19*(3), 369–383.

Bennett, M. D., Jr. (2006). Culture and context: A study of neighborhood effects on racial socializations and ethnic identity content in a sample of African American adolescents. *Journal of Black Psychology, 32*, 479–500.

Bennett, M. D., & Fraser, M. W. (2000). Urban violence among African American males: Integrating family, neighborhood, and peer perspectives. *Journal of Sociology and Social Welfare, 27*(3), 93–116.

Bennett, S., Sheridan, M., & Richardson, F. (2014). Caregiving as ministry: Perceptions of African Americans providing care for elders. *Families in Society: The Journal of Contemporary Social Services, 95*(1), 51–58.

Berg, K., Blatt, B., Lopreiato, J., Jung, J., Schaeffer, A., Heil, D., . . . Darby, E. (2015). Standardized patient assessment of medical student empathy: Ethnicity and gender effects in a multi-institutional study. *Academic Medicine, 90*(1), 105–111.

Berkowitz, L. (1993). *Aggression: Its causes, consequences, and control.* New York, NY: McGraw-Hill.

Berlin, L. J., Ispa, J. M., Fine, M. A., Malone, P. S., Brooks-Gunn, J., Brady-Smith, C., . . . Bai, Y. (2009). Correlates and consequences of spanking and verbal punishment for low-income white, African American, and Mexican American Toddlers. *Child Development, 80*(5), 1403–1420.

Berry, J. W. (1980). Acculturation as varieties of adaptation. In A. M. Padilla (Ed.), *Acculturation: Theory, model, and some new findings* (pp. 9–25). Boulder, CO: Westview Press.

Berry, J. W. (1990). Psychology of acculturation. In J. Berman (Ed.), *Cross-cultural perspectives: Nebraska symposium on motivation* (pp. 201–234). Lincoln: University of Nebraska Press.

Berry, J. W. (1992). *Cross-cultural psychology: Research and applications.* Cambridge, England: Cambridge University Press.

Berry, J. W., & Kim, U. (1988). Acculturation and mental health. In P. R. Dasen, J. W. Berry & N. Sarorius (Eds.), *Health and cross-cultural psychology: Toward applications* (pp. 207–236). Newbury Park, CA: Sage.

Berry, R. (2004). *Voices of African American male students: A portrait of successful middle school mathematics students* (Unpublished doctoral dissertation). University of North Carolina, Chapel Hill.

Berscheid, E. (1985). Interpersonal attraction. In G. Lindzey & E. Aronson (Eds.), *The handbook of social psychology* (3rd ed., Vol. 3, pp. 413–484). New York, NY: McGraw-Hill.

Berscheid, E., Snyder, M., & Omoto, A. M. (1989). The relationship closeness inventory: Assessing the closeness of interpersonal relationships. *Journal of Personality and Social Psychology, 57*(5), 792–807.

Bertelson, A. D., Marks, P. A., & May, G. D. (1982). MMPI and race: A controlled study. *Journal of Consulting and Clinical Psychology, 50*(2), 316–318.

Bettencourt, A. F., & Farrell, A. D. (2013). Individual and contextual factors associated with patterns of aggression and peer victimization during middle school. *Journal of Youth and Adolescence, 42*(2), 285–302

Beyers, J. (2012). What is religion? An African understanding. *HTS Teologiese Studies/Theological Studies 66*(1), Art. #341.

Bhagwat, R., Kelly, S., & Lambert, M. C. (2012). Exploratory factor analysis of African self-consciousness scale scores. *Assessment, 19*(1), 65–76.

Bhana, A., Mellins, C. A., Petersen, I., Alicea, S., Myeza, N., Holst, H., . . . Leu, C. S. (2014). The VUKA family program: Piloting a family-based psychosocial intervention to promote health and mental health among HIV infected early adolescents in South Africa. *AIDS Care, 26*(1), 1–11.

Billings, A. C. (2005). Beyond the Ebonics debate: Attitudes about Black and standard American English. *Journal of Black Studies, 36*(1), 68–81.

Billings, D. W., Leaf, S. L., Spencer, J., Crenshaw, T., Brockington, S., & Dalal, R. S. (2015). A randomized trial to evaluate the efficacy of a web-based HIV behavioral intervention for high-risk African American women. *AIDS and Behavior, 19*(7), 1263–1274.

Billingsley, A. C. (1968). *Black families in white America.* Englewood, NJ: Prentice Hall.

Birndorf, S., Ryan, S., Auinger, P., & Aten, M. (2005). High self-esteem among adolescents: Longitudinal trends, sex differences, and protective factors. *Journal of Adolescent Health, 37*(3), 194–201.

Black, A. R., & Woods-Giscombé, C. (2012). Applying the Stress and 'Strength' hypothesis to Black women's breast cancer screening delays. *Stress and Health, 28*(5), 389–396.

Black Demographics. (n.d.). *The African American church.* Retrieved from http://blackdemographics .com/culture/religion/

Blackmon, S. K. M., Coyle, L. D., Davenport, S., Owens, A. C., & Sparrow, C. (2016). Linking racial-ethnic socialization to culture and race-specific coping among African American college students. *Journal of Black Psychology, 42*(6), 549–576.

Blacks Lives Matter. (2017, January 29). *Guiding principles.* Retrieved from http://blacklivesmatter.com/ guiding-principles

Blair, I. V., Judd, C. M., & Chapleau, K. M. (2004). The influence of Afrocentric facial features in criminal sentencing. *Psychological Science, 15*, 674–679.

Blake, P. R., Corbit, J., Callaghan, T. C., & Warneken, F. (2016). Give as I give: Adult influence on children's giving in two cultures. *Journal of Experimental Child Psychology, 152*, 149–160.

Blascovich, J., Mendes, W., Hunter, S., Lickel, B., & Kowai-Bell, N. (2001). Perceived threat in social interactions with stigmatized others. *Journal of Personality and Social Psychology, 80*, 253–267.

Blum, E. J. (2011). "Look, baby, we got Jesus on our flag": Robust democracy and religious debate from the era of slavery to the age of Obama. *The Annals of the American Academy of Political and Social Science, 637*, 17–37.

Blunden, D., Spring, C., & Greenberg, L. M. (1974). Validation of the classroom behavior inventory. *Journal of Consulting and Clinical Psychology, 42*(1), 84–88.

Bocian, D. G., Li, W., & Ernst, K. S. (2010). Foreclosures by race and ethnicity: The demographics of a crisis. *Center for Responsible Lending.* Retrieved from http://www.responsiblelending.org/mort gage-lending/research-analysis/foreclosures-by-race-and-ethnicity.pdf

Bogart, L. M., Galvan, F. H., Wagner, G. J., & Klein, D. J. (2011). Longitudinal association of HIV conspiracy beliefs with sexual risk among black males living with HIV. *AIDS Behavior, 15*(6), 1180–1186.

Bojuwoye, O., & Edwards, S. (2011). Integrating ancestral consciousness into conventional counseling. *Journal of Psychology in Africa, 21*(3), 375–381.

Boltri, J. M., Davis-Smith, Y. M., Seale, J. P., Shellenberger, S., Okosun, I. S., & Cornelius, M. E. (2008). Diabetes prevention in a faith-based setting: Results of translational research. *Journal of Public Health Management Practice, 14*(1), 29–32.

Borders, T. F., Booth, B. M., Stewart, K.E., Cheney, A. M., & Curran, G. M. (2015). Rural/urban residence, access, and perceived need for treatment among African American cocaine users. *The Journal of Rural Health, 31*(1), 98–107.

Botvin, G. J., & Kantor, L. (2000). Preventing alcohol and tobacco use through life skills training. *Alcohol Research and Health, 24*(4), 250–257.

Botvin, G. J., & Scheier, L. M. (1997). Preventing drug abuse and violence. In D. K. Wilson & J. R. Rodriguez (Eds.), *Health-promoting and health-compromising behaviors among minority adolescents: Application and practice in health psychology* (pp. 65–86). Washington, DC: American Psychological Association.

Bowen-Reid, T. L., & Rhodes, W. A. (2003). Assessment of marijuana use and psychosocial behaviors at two historically black universities. *Journal of Black Psychology, 29*, 429–444.

Bowie, J. V., Parker, L. J., Beadle-Holder, M., Ezema, A., Bruce, M. A., & Thorpe, R. J., Jr. (2017). The influence of religious attendance on smoking among Black men. *Substance Use & Misuse, 52*(5), 581–586.

Bowleg, L. (2013). "Once you've blended the cake, you can't take the parts back to the main ingredients": Black gay and bisexual men's descriptions and experiences of intersectionality. *Sex Roles, 68*, 754–767.

Bowleg, L., English, D., del Rio-Gonzalez, A. M., Burkholder, G. J., Teti, M., & Tschann, J. M. (2016). Measuring the pros and cons of what it means to be a Black man: Development and validation of the Black Men's Experiences Scale (BMES). *Psychology of Men & Masculinity, 17*(2), 177–188.

Bowles, J., & Kingston, R. S. (1998). The impact of family function on health of African American elderly. *Journal of Comparative Family Studies, 29*(2), 337–347.

Bowman, N. A. (2012). Promoting sustained engagement with diversity: The reciprocal relationships between informal and formal college diversity experiences. *Review of Higher Education, 36*(1), 1–24.

Boyd, A. S., & Wilmoth, M. C. (2006). An innovative community-based intervention for African American women with breast cancer: The Witness Project. *Health and Social Work, 31*(1), 77–80.

Boyd, R. (2014). African American disproportionality and disparity in child welfare: Toward a comprehensive conceptual framework. *Children and Youth Services Review, 37*, 15–27.

Boyd-Franklin, N. (1989). *Black families in therapy: A multisystems approach.* New York, NY: Guilford.

Boyd-Franklin, N. (2010). Incorporating spirituality and religion into the treatment of African American clients. *Counseling Psychologist, 38*, 976–1000.

Boyd-Franklin, N. (2013). *Black families in therapy: Understanding the African American experience.* New York, NY: Guilford.

Boyd-Starke, K., Hill, O. W., Fife, J., & Whittington, M. (2011). Religiosity and HIV risk behaviors in African-American students. *Psychological Reports, 108*, 528–536.

Boykin, A. W. (1978). Psychological/behavioral verve in academic/task performance: Pre-theoretical considerations. *Journal of Negro Education, 47*(4), 343–354.

Boykin, A. W. (1983). The academic performance of Afro-American children. In J. Spence (Ed.), *Achievement and achievement motives* (pp. 324–371). San Francisco, CA: W. H. Freeman.

Boykin, A. W. (1994). The sociocultural context of schooling for African American children: A proactive deep structural analysis. In E. Hollins (Ed.), *Formulating a knowledge base for teaching culturally diverse learners* (pp. 233–245). Philadelphia, PA: Association for Supervision and Curriculum Development.

Boykin, A. W., & Cunningham, R. T. (2001). The effects of movement expressiveness in story content and learning context on the analogical reasoning performance of African American children. *Journal of Negro Education, 70*(1), 72–83.

Boykin, A. W., & Ellison, C. M. (1995). The multiple ecologies of black youth socialization: An Afrographic analysis. In R. L. Taylor (Ed.), *African American youth: Their social and economic status in the United States* (pp. 33–51). Westport, CT: Praeger.

Boykin, A. W., Jagers, R. J., Ellison, C., & Albury, A. (1997). Communalism: Conceptualization and measurement of an Afrocultural social ethos. *Journal of Black Studies, 27*(3), 409–418.

Boykin, A. W., & Mungai, M. (1997). *The effect of movement/music expressiveness on task and off-task contexts on the prose recall of low-African American and European American children.* Paper presented at the annual meeting of the American Educational Research Association, Chicago, IL.

Boykin, A., & Toms, F. (1985). Black child socialization: A conceptual framework. In H. McAdoo & J. McAdoo (Eds.), *Black children: Social, educational, and parental environment* (pp. 33–51). Beverly Hills, CA: Sage.

Bozionelos, N. (1996). Cognitive spontaneity and learning style. *Perceptual and Motor Skills, 83*(1), 43–48.

Bradley, B., Westen, D., Mercer, K. B., Binder, E. B., Jovanovic, T., Crain, D., . . . Heim, C. (2011). Association between childhood maltreatment and adult emotional dysregulation in a low-income, urban, African American sample: Moderation by oxytocin receptor gene. *Development and Psychopathology, 23*(2), 439–452.

Bradley, C., & Hawkins-Leon, C. (2002). The transracial adoption debate: Counseling and legal implications (practice & theory). *Journal of Counseling and Development, 80*(4), 433–441.

Brady, S. S., Winston, A., & Gockley, S. E. (2014). Stress-related externalizing behavior among African American youth: How could policy and practice transform risk into resilience? *Journal of Social Issues, 70*(2), 315–341.

Braga, A. A., Welsch, B. C., & Schnell, C. (2015). Can policing reduce crime? A systematic review and meta-analysis. *Journal of Research in Crime and Delinquency, 52*, 567–588.

Brannon, T. N., Markus, H. R., & Taylor, V. J. (2015). "Two souls, two thoughts," two self- schemas: Double consciousness can have positive academic consequences for African Americans. *Journal of Personality and Social Psychology, 108*(4), 586–609.

Bratton, C., Chavin, K., & Baliga P. (2015). Racial disparities in organ donation and why. *Current Opinion in Organ Transplantation, 16*, 243–249.

Bratton, S. C., Ceballos, P. L., Sheely-Moore, A. I., Meany-Walen, K., Pronchenko, Y., & Jones, L. D. (2013). Head start early mental health intervention: Effects of child-centered play therapy on disruptive behaviors. *International Journal of Play Therapy, 22*(1), 28–42.

Braveman, P. A., Heck, K., Egerter, S., Marchi, K. S., Dominguez, T. P., Cubbin, C., . . . Curtis, M. (2015). The role of socioeconomic factors in Black-White disparities in preterm birth. *American Journal of Public Health, 105*(4), 694–702.

Breitkopf, C. R., Littleton, H., & Berenson, A. (2007). Body image: A study in a tri-ethnic sample of low income women. *Sex Roles, 56*(5–6), 373–380.

Breland-Noble, A. M. (2013). The impact of skin color on mental and behavioral health in African American and Latina adolescent girls: A review of the literature. In *The melanin millennium* (pp. 219–229). The Netherlands: Springer.

Breland-Noble, A. M., Bell, C. C., Burriss, A., Poole, H. K.; AAKOMA Project Adult Advisory Board. (2012). The significance of strategic community engagement in recruiting African American youth and families for clinical research. *Journal of Child and Family Studies, 21*(2), 273–280.

Breland-Noble, A. M., Bell, C. C., & Nicolas, G. (2006). Family first: The development of an evidence-based family intervention for increasing participation in psychiatric clinical care and research in depressed African American adolescents. *Family Process, 45*(2), 153–169.

Brevard, J., Maxwell, M., Hood, K., & Belgrave, F. (2013). Feeling safe: Intergenerational connections and neighborhood disorganization among urban and rural African American youth. *Journal of Community Psychology, 41*(8), 992–1004.

Brody, G. H., Chen, Y. F., Kogan, S. M., Yu, T., Molgaard, V. K., DiClemente, R. J., & Wingood, G. M. (2012). Family-centered program deters substance use, conduct problems, and depressive symptoms in black adolescents. *Pediatrics, 129*(1), 108–115.

Brody, G. H., Kogan, S. M., & Chen, Y. (2012). Perceived discrimination and longitudinal increases in adolescent substance use: Gender differences in mediational pathways. *American Journal of Public Health, 102*, 1006–1011.

Brody, G. H., Lei, M. K., Chae, D. H., Yu, T., Kogan, S. M., & Beach, S. R. (2014). Perceived discrimination among African American adolescents and allostatic load: A longitudinal analysis with buffering effects. *Child Development, 85*(3), 989–1002.

Brody, G. H., Murry, V. M., Gerrard, M., Gibbons, F. X., Molgaard, V., McNair, L., . . . Chen, Y. F. (2004). The strong African American families program: Translating research into prevention programming. *Child Development, 75*(3), 900–917.

Bronfenbrenner, U. (1977). Toward an experimental ecology of human development. *American Psychologist, 32*(7), 513–531.

Bronfenbrenner, U. (1979). *The ecology of human development*. Cambridge, MA: Harvard University Press.

Bronfenbrenner, U. (1986). Ecology of the family as a context for human development: Research perspectives. *Developmental Psychology, 22*, 723–742.

Bronson, M. B. (2000). *Self-regulation in early childhood: Nature and nurture*. New York, NY: Guilford.

Brook, J. S., Balka, E. B., Brook, D. W., Win, P. T., & Gursen, M. D. (1998). Drug use among African Americans: Ethnic identity as a protective factor. *Psychological Reports, 83*(3 Pt. 2), 1427–1446.

Brook, J. S., Brook, D. W., & Pahl, K. (2006). The developmental context for adolescent substance abuse intervention. In H. A. Liddle & C. L. Row

(Eds.), *Adolescence substance abuse: Research and clinical advances* (pp. 25–51). Cambridge, England: Cambridge University Press.

Brook, J. S., & Pahl, K. (2005). The protective role of ethnic and racial identity and aspects of an Africentric orientation against drug use among African American young adults. *The Journal of Genetic Psychology, 166*(3), 329–345.

Brook, J. S., Pahl, K., & Ning, Y. (2004). Peer and parental influences on longitudinal trajectories of smoking among African Americans and Puerto Ricans. *Nicotine and Tobacco Research, 8*(5), 639–651.

Brook, J. S., Zhang, C., Finch, S. J., & Brook, D. W. (2010). Adolescent pathways to adult smoking: Ethnic identity, peer substance use, and antisocial behavior. *The American Journal on Addictions, 19*, 178–186.

Brookins, C. C. (1994). The relationship between Afrocentric values and racial identity attitudes: Validation of the belief systems analysis scale on African American college students. *Journal of Black Psychology, 20*(2), 128–142.

Brookins, C. C. (1999). Afrikan and community psychology: Synthesizing liberation and social change. In R. L. Jones (Ed.), *Advances in African American psychology: Theory, paradigms, and research* (pp. 27–50). Hampton, VA: Cobb & Henry.

Brooks, J. E., & Neville, H. A. (2017). Interracial attraction among college men: The influence of ideologies, familiarity, and similarity. *Journal of Social and Personal Relationships, 34*(2), 166–183.

Brooks, S. (2016). Staying in the Hood: Black Lesbian and transgender women and identity management in North Philadelphia. *Journal of Homosexuality, 63*(12), 1573–1593.

Brooks-Gunn, J., Duncan, G. J., Klebanov, P. K., & Sealand, N. (1993). Do neighborhoods influence child and adolescent development? *American Journal of Sociology, 99*(2), 353–395.

Brooms, D. R., & Perry, A. R. (2016). "It's simply because we're Black men" Black men's experiences and responses to the killing of Black men. *The Journal of Men's Studies, 24*(2), 166–184.

Brown, A. (2017). Why Black boss women (still) find it hard to find equal mates. *Madamenoire*. Retrieved from http://madamenoire.com/822888/elusive-love-boss-women-find-hard-find-equal-mates/

Brown, D. L. (2008). African American resiliency: Examining racial socialization and social support as protective factors. *Journal of Black Psychology, 34*(1), 32–48.

Brown, D. L., Rosnick, C. B., & Segrist, D. J. (2016). Internalized racial oppression and higher education values the mediational role of academic locus of control among college African American men and women. *Journal of Black Psychology, 22*, 1–23.

Brown, D. L., & Tylka, T. (2011). Racial discrimination and resilience in African American young adults: Examining racial socialization as a moderator. *Journal of Black Psychology, 37*(3), 259–285.

Brown, J. L., Littlewood, R. A., & Vanable, P. A. (2013). Social-cognitive correlates of antiretroviral therapy adherence among HIV-infected individuals receiving infectious disease care in a medium-sized northeastern US city. *AIDS Care, 25*(9), 1149–1158.

Brown, K. M. (2004). Leadership for social justice and equity: Weaving a transformative framework and pedagogy. *Educational Administration Quarterly, 40*, 77–108.

Brown, T. L., Parks, G. S., & Phillips, C. M. (Eds). (2012). *African American fraternities and sororities: The legacy and the vision* (p. 1054). University Press of Kentucky Lexington, KY.

Brown v. Board of Education, 347 U.S. 483 (1954).

Brunson, J., Jackson, M. S., Christson, A. A., Miller, M., Pender, A., & David, S. (2017). Exploring post-traumatic stress syndrome among African-American adolescent gang members in rural areas: Suggestions for therapeutic intervention. *Journal of Gang Research, 24*(2), 23–34.

Bryant-Davis, T., Ellis, M. U., Edwards, N., Adams, T. P., Counts, P., Arline-Bradley, S., & Sadler, K. (2016). The role of the black church in HIV prevention: Exploring barriers and best practices. *Journal of Community & Applied Social Psychology, 26*(5), 388–408.

Bryant-Davis, T., & Ocampo, C. (2006). A therapeutic approach to the treatment of racist-incident-based trauma. *Journal of Emotional Abuse, 6*(4), 1–22.

Bryant-Davis, T. E., & Comas-Díaz, L. E. (2016). Introduction womanist and mujerista psychologies. In T. Bryant-Davis & L. Comas-Díaz (Eds.), *Womanist and mujerista psychologies: Voices of fire, acts of courage* (pp. 3–25). Washington, DC: American Psychological Association.

Burd-Sharps, S., & Rasch, R. (2015). Impact of the US housing crisis on the racial wealth across generations. *Social Science Research Council*. Retrieved from https://www.aclu.org/files/field_document/discrimlend_final.pdf

Bureau of Labor Statistics (BLS). (2001). *Table A-2. Employment status of the civilian population by race, sex, and age.* Retrieved from http://www.bls.gov/news.release/empsit.t02.htm

Bureau of Labor Statistics. (2016). *Volunteering in the United States, 2015.* Retrieved from https://www.bls.gov/news.release/volun.nr0.htm

Bureau of Labor Statistics. (2017). *Unemployment rate and employment-population ratio vary by race and ethnicity.* Retrieved from https://www.bls.gov/opub/ted/2017/unemployment-rate-and-employment-population-ratio-vary-by-race-and-ethnicity.htm

Bureau of Labor Statistics. (n.d.). *Employment status of the civilian population by race, sex, and age.* Retrieved from https://www.bls.gov/news.release/empsit.t02.htm

Burgess, N. J. (1995). Looking back, looking forward: African American families in sociohistorical perspective. In R. B. Ingoldsby & S. Smith (Eds.), *Families in multicultural perspective* (pp. 321–334). New York, NY: Guilford.

Burlew, K., Neely, D., Johnson, C., Hucks, T. C., Purnell, B., Butler, J., . . . Burlew, R. (2000). Drug attitudes, racial identity, and alcohol use among African American adolescents. *Journal of Black Psychology, 26*(4), 402–420.

Burns, J. C., & Caldwell, C. H. (2016). Breaking the ice! Predictors about communication between non-resident African American fathers and sons about sex. *Journal of the American Association of Nurse Practitioners, 28*(2), 84–90.

Burt, C. H., & Simons, R. L. (2013). Interpersonal racial discrimination, ethnic-racial socialization, and offending: Risk and resilience among African American females. *Justice Quarterly, 32*(3), 532–570.

Burton, L. M. (1992). Black grandparents rearing children of drug-addicted parents: Stressors, outcomes, and social service needs. *Gerontologist, 32*(6), 744–751.

Burton, L. M., Allison, K. W., & Obeidallah, D. (1995). Social context and adolescence: Perspectives on development among inner-city African-American teens. In L. J. Crockett & A. C. Crouter (Eds.),

Pathways through adolescence: Individual development in relation to social contexts (pp. 119–138). Hillsdale, NJ: Erlbaum.

Burton, L. M., Price-Spratlen, T., & Spencer, M. B. (1997). On ways of thinking about measuring neighborhoods: Implications for studying context and developmental outcomes for children. In J. Brooks-Gunn, G. Duncan & J. L. Aber (Eds.), *Neighborhood poverty: Context and consequences for children* (Vol. 2, pp. 132–144). New York, NY: Russell Sage.

Bushman, B. J., & Anderson, C. A. (2001). Media violence and the American public: Scientific facts versus media misinformation. *American Psychologist, 56*(6–7), 477–489.

Busseri, M., Willoughby, T., & Chalmers, H. (2007). A rationale and method for examining reasons for linkages among adolescent risk behaviors. *Journal of Youth Adolescence, 36*, 279–289.

Bussey, J., & Trasvina, J. (2003). *Racial preference: The treatment of White and African American job applicants by temporary employment agencies in California.* Berkeley, CA: Discrimination Research Center of the Impact Fund.

Butcher, J. N., Dahlstrom, W. G., Graham, J. R., Tellegen, A., & Kaemmer, B. (1989). *Manual for the restandardized Minnesota multiphasic personality inventory: MMPI-2.* Minneapolis: University of Minnesota Press.

Butcher, J. N., Nezami, E., & Exner, J. (1998). Psychological assessment of people in diverse cultures. In S. S. Kazarian & D. R. Evans (Eds.), *Cultural clinical psychology: Theory, research, and practice* (pp. 61–105). London, England: Oxford University Press.

Butler, J. (1992). Of kindred minds: The ties that bind. In M. A. Orlandi, R. Weston & L. G. Epstein (Eds.), *Cultural competence for evaluators: A guide for alcohol and other drug abuse prevention practitioners working with ethnic/racial communities* (pp. 23–54). Rockville, MD: U.S. Department of Health and Human Services, Office for Substance Abuse Prevention.

Butler-Sweet, C. (2011). "A healthy black identity": Transracial adoption, middle-class families and racial socialization. *Journal of Comparative Family Studies, 42*, 193–212.

Byrd, C. M. (2012). The measurement of racial/ethnic identity in children: A critical review. *Journal of Black Psychology, 38*(1), 3–31.

Byrd, C. M., & Chavous, T. M. (2009). Racial identity and academic achievement in the neighborhood context: A multilevel analysis. *Journal of Youth and Adolescence, 38*(4), 544–559.

Byrd, W. M., & Clayton, L. A. (2001). Race, medicine, and health care in the United States: A historical survey. *Journal of the National Medical Association, 93*(3), 11S–34S.

Byrne, D., Clore, G. L., & Smeaton, G. (1986). The attraction hypothesis: Do similar attitudes affect anything? *Journal of Personality and Social Psychology, 51*, 1167–1170.

Cacioppo, J., & Tassinary, L. (1990). Inferring psychological significance from physiological signals. *American Psychologist, 45*(1), 16–28.

Cain, D., & Combs-Orme, T. (2005). Family structure effects on parenting stress and practices in the African American family. *Journal of Sociology and Social Welfare, 32*(2), 19–40.

Calabrese, S. K., Meyer, I. H., Overstreet, N. M., Haile, R., & Hansen, N. B. (2015). Exploring discrimination and mental health disparities faced by Black sexual minority women using a minority stress framework. *Psychology of Women Quarterly, 39*(3), 287–304.

Calabrese, S. K., Rosenberger, J. G., Schick, V. R., & Novak, D. S. (2015). Pleasure, affection, and love among Black men who have sex with men (MSM) versus MSM of other races: Countering dehumanizing stereotypes via cross-race comparisons of reported sexual experience at last sexual event. *Archives of Sexual Behavior, 44*(7), 2001–2014.

Caldwell, C. H., Rafferty, J., Reischl, T. M., De Loney, E. H., & Brooks, C. L. (2010). Enhancing parenting skills among nonresident African American fathers as a strategy for preventing youth risky behaviors. *American Journal of Community Psychology, 45*, 17–35.

Calhoun-Brown, A. (1998). While marching to Zion: Other worldliness and racial empowerment in the black community. *Journal for the Scientific Study of Religion, 37*(3), 427–439.

Calvin, D., Quinn, L., Dancy, B., Park, C., Fleming, S. G., Smith, E., & Fogelfeld, L. (2011). African Americans' perception of risk for diabetes complications. *The Diabetes Educator, 37*(5), 689–698.

Campbell, C. M., & Edwards, R. R. (2012). Ethnic differences in pain and pain management. *Pain, 2*(3), 219–230.

Campbell, F. A., & Ramey, C. T. (1995). Cognitive and school outcomes for high-risk African-American students at middle adolescence: Positive effects of early intervention. *American Educational Research Journal, 32*(4), 743–772.

Campbell, F. A., Ramey, C. T., Pungello, E., Sparling, J., & Miller-Johnson, S. (2002). Early childhood education: Young adult outcomes from the Abecedarian Project. *Applied Developmental Science, 6*(1), 42–57.

Campbell, M. K., Resnicow, K., Carr, C., Wang, T., & Williams, A. (2007). Process evaluation of an effective church-based diet intervention: Body and soul. *Health Education and Behavior, 34*(6), 864–880.

Campbell, M. M., Sibeko, G., Mall, S., Baldinger, A., Nagdee, M., Susser, E., & Stein, D. J. (2017). The content of delusions in a sample of South African Xhosa people with schizophrenia. *BMC Psychiatry, 17*(1), 41.

Cantrell, J., Kreslake, J. M., Ganz, O., Pearson, J. L., Vallone, D., Anesetti-Rothermel, A., . . . Kirchner, T. R. (2013). Marketing little cigars and cigarillos: Advertising, price, and associations with neighborhood demographics. *American Journal of Public Health, 103*(10), 1902–1909.

Carabello, R. S., Giovino, G. A., Pechacek, T. F., Mowery, P. D., Richter, P. A., Strauss, W. J., . . . Maurer, K. R. (1998). Racial and ethnic differences in serum cotinine levels of cigarette smokers. *Journal of the American Medical Association, 280*, 135–142.

Card, D., & Guiliano, L. (2015). Can universal screening increase the representation of low income and minority students in gifted education? *NBER Working Paper Series*. Retrieved from http://www.nber.org/papers/w21519.pdf

Carlo, G., Crockett, L. J., Wolff, J. M., & Beal, S. J. (2012). The role of emotional reactivity, self-regulation, and puberty in adolescents' prosocial behaviors. *Social Development, 21*(4), 667–685.

Carlton-LaNey, I. (2007). "Doing the Lord's work": African American elders civic engagement. *American Society on Aging, 4*, 47–50.

Caron, C. (2011). *White Mississippi teens may have attacked homeless Blacks in Jackson*. Retrieved from http://abcnews.go.com/US/white-teens-run-black-man-surveillance-video/story?id=14273579#.ULzwP5PjkiU

Carruthers, J. H. (1996). Science and oppression. In D. Azibo (Ed.), *African psychology in historical perspective and related commentary* (pp. 185–192). Trenton, NJ: Africa World Press.

Carson, E. (2005). Black philanthropy's past, present, and future. *New Directions for Philanthropic Fundraising, 48*, 5–12.

Carter, J. R., & Neufeld, R. J. W. (1998). Cultural aspects of understanding people with schizophrenic disorders. In S. S. Kazarian & D. R. Evans (Eds.), *Cultural clinical psychology: Theory, research, and practice* (pp. 246–266). London, England: Oxford University Press.

Carter, N. P., Hawkins, T. N., & Natesan, P. (2008). The relationship between verve and the academic achievement of African American students in reading and mathematics in an urban middle school. *The Journal of Educational Foundations, 22*(1/2), 29–46.

Cartman, O. A. (2016). *More committed to baby mamas than a wife*. Retrieved from https://www.drobaricartman.com/single-post/2016/05/08/More-committed-to-Baby-Mamas-than-a-Wife

Carter, R. T., & Forsyth, J. M. (2009). A guide to the forensic assessment of race-based traumatic stress reactions. *Journal of the American Academy of Psychiatry and the Law*.

Casas, J. M. (1984). Police, training, and research in counseling psychology: The racial/ethnic minority perspective. In S. D. Brown & R. W. Lent (Eds.), *Handbook of counseling psychology* (pp. 785–831). New York, NY: Wiley.

Castilla, E. J. (2008). Gender, race, and meritocracy in organizational careers. *American Journal of Sociology, 113*(6), 1479–1526.

Castro, F. G., & Alarcon, E. H. (2002). Integrating cultural variables into drug abuse prevention and treatment with racial/ethnic minorities. *Journal of Drug Issues, 32*(3), 783–811.

Caughy, M. O., Nettles, S. M., & Lima, J. (2011). Profiles of racial socialization among African American parents: Correlates, context, and outcome. *Journal of Child and Family Studies, 20*, 491–502.

Caughy, M. O., Nettles, S. M., O'Campo, P. J., & Lohrfink, K. F. (2006). Neighborhood matters: Racial socialization of African American children. *Child Development, 77*(5), 1220–1236.

Caughy, M. O., & O'Campo, P. J. (2006). Neighborhood poverty, social capital, and the cognitive development of African American preschoolers. *American Journal of Community Psychology, 37*(1, 2), 141–154.

Caughy, M. O., Randolph, S. M., & O'Campo, P. J. (2002). The Afrocentric home environment inventory: An observational measure of the racial socialization environment of the home for preschool children. *Journal of Black Psychology, 28*, 37–52.

Cazden, C., & Leggett, E. (1981). Culturally responsive education: Recommendations for achieving Lau remedies II. In H. Trueba, G. Guthrie & K. Au (Eds.), *Culture and the bilingual classroom: Studies in classroom ethnography* (pp. 69–86). Rowley, MA: Newbury House.

Centers for Disease Control and Prevention (CDC). (2011a). *Health United States, 2010. With special feature on death and dying* (DHHS Publication 2011–1232).

Centers for Disease Control and Prevention (CDC). (2011b). *HIV among African Americans.* Retrieved from http://www.cdc.gov/hiv/topics/aa/pdf/aa.pdf

Centers for Disease Control and Prevention (CDC). (2013a). *Best practices of youth violence prevention: A sourcebook for community action.* Retrieved from http://www.cdc.gov/ncipc/dvp/bestpractices.htm

Centers for Disease Control and Prevention (CDC). (2013b). *Fact sheet: HIV and AIDS among African Americans.* Retrieved from http://www.cdc.gov/nchhstp/newsroom/docs/CDC-HIV-AA-508.pdf

Centers for Disease Control and Prevention (CDC). (2013c). *National suicide statistics at a glance.* Retrieved from http://www.cdc.gov/violenceprevention/suicide/statistics/leading_causes.html

Centers for Disease Control and Prevention. (2014). Surveillance summaries: Youth risk behavior surveillance—United States. *MMWR, 63*(4), 1-168.

Centers for Disease Control and Prevention. (2015a). Diagnoses of HIV infection in the United States and dependent areas, 2014. *HIV Surveillance Report, 26,* 1-123.

Centers for Disease Control and Prevention. (2015b). Infant mortality statistics from the 2013 period linked birth/infant death data set. *National Vital Statistics Reports. Table A.* Retrieved from http://www.cdc.gov/nchs/data/nvsr/nvsr64/nvsr64_09.pdf [PDF | 994KB]

Centers for Disease Control and Prevention (CDC). (2016). *HIV among women.* Retrieved from http://www.cdc.gov/hiv/pdf/group/gender/women/cdc-hiv-women.pdf

Centers for Disease Control and Prevention. (2016, Feb. 23). Lifetime risk of HIV diagnosis. *Half of black gay men and a quarter of Latino gay men projected to be diagnosed within their lifetime.* Retrieved from https://www.cdc.gov/nchhstp/newsroom/2016/croi-press-release-risk.html

Centers for Disease Control and Prevention. (2016, June 10). *Morbidity and mortality weekly report.* Retrieved from https://www.cdc.gov/healthyyouth/data/yrbs/pdf/2015/ss6506_updated.pdf

Centers for Disease Control and Prevention. (2017, May 2). *African-American death rate drops 25 percent.* Retrieved from https://www.cdc.gov/media/releases/2017/p0502-aa-health.html

Central Intelligence Agency (CIA). (2014). *World factbook.* Retrieved from http://www.indexmundi.com/map/?v=29

Central Intelligence Agency. (2017). Retrieved from https://www.cia.gov/library/publications/the-world-factbook/rankorder/2091rank.html

Chae, D. H., Nuru-Jeter, A. M., & Adler, N. E. (2012). Implicit racial bias as a moderator of the association between racial discrimination and hypertension: a study of Midlife African American men. *Psychosomatic medicine, 74*(9), 961–964.

Chae, D. H., Nuru-Jeter, A. M., Adler, N. E., Brody, G. H., Lin, J., Blackburn, E. H., & Epel, E. S. (2014). Discrimination, racial bias, and telomere length in African-American men. *American Journal of Preventive Medicine, 46*(2), 103–111.

Chao, R. C. L., Mallinckrodt, B., & Wei, M. (2012). Co-occurring presenting problems in African American college clients reporting racial discrimination distress. *Professional Psychology Research and Practice, 43*(3), 199–207.

Chase-Lansdale, P. L., & Gordon, R. A. (1996). Economic hardship and the development of five- and six-year-olds: Neighborhood and regional perspectives. *Child Development, 67*(6), 3338–3367.

Chase-Lansdale, P. L., Gordon, R. A., Brooks-Gunn, J., & Klebanov, P. K. (1997). Neighborhood and family influences on the intellectual and behavioral competence of preschool and early school-age children. In J. Brooks-Gunn, G. J. Duncan & J. L. Aber (Eds.), *Neighborhood poverty: Context and consequences for children* (Vol. 1, pp. 79–118). New York, NY: Russell Sage.

Chaskin, R. J. (1998). Neighborhood as a unit of planning and action: A heuristic approach. *Journal of planning Literature, 13*(1), 11–30.

Chaskin, R. J., & Richman, H. A. (1992). Concerns about school-linked services: Institution-based versus community-based models. *The Future of Children, 2*(1), 107–117.

Chatters, L. M., Mattis, J. S., Woodward, A. T., Taylor, R. J., Neighbors, H. W., & Grayman, N. A. (2011). Use of ministers for a serious personal problem among African Americans: Findings from the National Survey of American Life. *American Journal of Orthopsychiatry, 81*(1), 118–127.

Chatters, L. M., Taylor, R. J., Bullard, K. M., & Jackson, J. (2009). Race and ethnic differences in religious involvement: African Americans, Caribbean Blacks and non-Hispanic Whites. *Ethnic and Racial Studies, 32*, 1143–1163.

Chatters, L. M., Taylor, R. J., Woodward, A. T., & Nicklett, E. J. (2015). Social support from church and family members and depressive symptoms among older African Americans. *American Journal of Geriatric Psychiatry, 23*(6), 559–567.

Chauhan, P., Reppucci, N. D., Burnette, M., & Reiner, S. (2010). Race, neighborhood disadvantage, and antisocial behavior among female juvenile offenders. *Journal of Community Psychology, 38*(4), 532–540.

Chavous, T. M., Bernat, D. H., Schmeelk-Cone, K., Caldwell, C. H., Kohn-Wood, L., & Zimmerman, M. A. (2003). Racial identity and academic attainment among African American adolescents. *Child Development, 74*(4), 1076–1090.

Chavous, T. M., Rivas-Drake, D., Smalls, C., Griffin, T., & Cogburn, C. (2008). Gender matters, too: The influences of school racial discrimination and racial identity on academic engagement outcomes among African American adolescents. *Developmental Psychology, 44*(3), 637–654.

Chen, J., Fox, S., Cantrell, C., Stockdale, S., & Kagawa-Singer, M. (2007). Health disparities and prevention: Racial/ethnic barriers to flu vaccinations. *Journal of Community Health, 3*, 5–20.

Chen, J., Vargas-Bustamante, A., Mortensen, K., & Ortega, A. N. (2016). Racial and ethnic disparities in health care access and utilization under the Affordable Care Act. *Medical Care, 54*(2), 140.

Cheney, A. M., Booth, B. M., Borders, T. F., & Curran, G. M. (2016). The role of social capital in African Americans's attempts to reduce and quite cocaine use. *Substance Use and Misuse, 51*, 777–787.

Cherng, H., Turney, K., & Kao, G. (2014). Less socially engaged? Participation in friendship and extracurricular activities among racial/ethnic minority and immigrant adolescents. *Teachers College Record, 116*(3), 1–28.

Cherry, V. R., Belgrave, F. Z., Jones, W., Kennon, D. K., Gray, F. S., & Phillips, F. (1998). NTU: An Africentric approach to substance abuse prevention among African American youth. *Journal of Primary Prevention, 18*(3), 319–338.

Chestang, L. W. (1972). *Character development in a hostile environment* (Occasional Paper No. 3). Chicago, IL: University of Chicago, School of Social Service Administration.

Chiachiere, R. (2007). *Imus called women's basketball team "nappy-headed hos"*. Retrieved from http://media matters.org/research/2007/04/04/imus-called-womens-basketball-team-nappy-headed/138497

Chimezie, A. (1988). Black children's characteristics and the school: A selective adaptation approach. *Western Journal of Black Studies, 12*(2), 77–85.

Chipungu, S., Herman, J., Sambrano, S., Nistler, M., Sale, E., & Springer, J. F. (2000). Prevention programming for African American youth: A review of strategies in CSAP's national cross-site evaluation of high risk youth programs. *Journal of Black Psychology, 26*(4), 360–385.

Choi, J. K., & Jackson, A. P. (2012). Nonresident fathers parenting, maternal mastery and child development in poor African American single-mother families. *Race and Social Problems, 4*, 102–111.

Chopik, W. J., O'Brien, E., & Konrath, S. H. (2017). Differences in empathic concern and perspective taking across 63 countries. *Journal of Cross-Cultural Psychology, 48*(1), 23–38.

Chou, T., Asnaani, A., & Hofmann, S. G. (2012). Perception of racial discrimination and psychopathology across three U.S. ethnic minority groups. *Cultural Diversity & Ethnic Minority Psychology, 18*(1), 74–81.

Chow, E. A., Foster, H., Gonzalez, V., & McIver, L. (2012). The disparate impact of diabetes on racial/ethnic minority populations. *Clinical Diabetes, 30*(3), 130–133.

Chow, E. N., Segal, M. T., & Tan, L. (2011). *Analyzing gender, intersectionality, and multiple inequalities: Global, transnational and local contexts* (Advances in Gender Research, Vol. 15). Bingley, England: Emerald.

Chung, H. L., & Probert, S. (2011). Civic engagement in relation to outcome expectations among African American young adults. *Journal of Applied Developmental Psychology, 32*(4), 227–234.

Clark, A. (2013). Honoring the ancestors: Toward an afrocentric theology of liberation. *Journal of Black Studies, 44*(4), 376–394.

Clark, K. B., & Clark, M. K. (1939). The development of consciousness of self and the emergence of identification in Negro preschool children. *Journal of Social Psychology, 10*, 591–599.

Clark, K. B., & Clark, M. K. (1947). Racial identification and preference in Negro children. In T. M. Newcomb & E. L. Hartley (Eds.), *Readings in social psychology* (pp. 169–178). New York, NY: Holt.

Clark, M. S., & Mills, J. R. (2012). A theory of communal (and exchange) relationships. In P. A. M. Van Lange, A. W. Kruglanski & E. T. Higgins (Eds.), *Handbook of theories of social psychology* (Vol. 2, pp. 232–250). Thousand Oaks, CA: Sage.

Clark, R. (2004). Interethnic group and intraethnic group racism: Perceptions and coping in Black University students. *Journal of Black Psychology, 30*, 506–526.

Clark, R., Anderson, N., Clark, V., & Willams, D. (1999). Racism as a stressor for African Americans: A biopsychosocial model. *American Psychologist, 54*(10), 805–816.

Clark, T.C., Norris, T., & Schiller, J.S. (2017). Early Release of Selected estimates based on data from the 2016 National Health Interview Survey. Centers for Disease Control and Prevention, National Center for Health Statistics. Released 5/27. Retrieved from https://www.cdc.gov/nchs/data/nhis/earlyrelease/earlyrelease201705.pdf

Clark, T. T. (2014). Perceived discrimination, depressive symptoms, and substance use in young adulthood. *Addictive Behaviors, 39*(6), 1021–1025.

Clark, T. T., Belgrave, F. Z., & Abell, M. (2012). The mediating and moderating effects of parent and peer influences upon drug use among African American adolescents. *Journal of Black Psychology, 38*, 52–80.

Clark, T. T., Nguyen, A. B., Belgrave, F., & Tademy, R. (2011). Understanding the dimensions of parental influence on alcohol use and alcohol refusal efficacy among African American adolescents. *Social Work Research, 35*(3), 147–158.

Clay, R. A. (2011, July). Ethnically identified psychological associations. *Monitor on Psychology, 42*(7), 66.

Clayton, J. K. (2011). Changing diversity in US schools: The impact on elementary student performance and achievement. *Education and Urban Society, 43*(6), 671–695.

Clement, S., Schauman, O., Graham, T., Maggioni, F., Evans-Lacko, S., Bezborodovs, N., . . . Thornicroft, G. (2015). What is the impact of mental health-related stigma on help-seeking? A systematic review of quantitative and qualitative studies. *Psychological Medicine, 45*(1), 11–27.

Clotfelter, C. T. (1976). School desegregation, "tipping," and private school enrollment. *Journal of Human Resources, 11*(1), 28–50.

Coard, S. I., Foy-Watson, S., Zimmer, C., & Wallace, A. (2007). Considering culturally relevant parenting practices in intervention development and adaptation: A randomized controlled trial of the Black parenting strengths and strategies (BPSS) program. *The Counseling Psychologist, 35*(6), 797–820.

Coard, S. I., & Sellers, R. M. (2005). African American families as a context for racial socialization. In V. C. McLoyd, N. E. Hill & K. A. Dodge (Eds.), *African American family life: Ecological and cultural diversity* (pp. 264–284). New York, NY: Guilford.

Cochran, S. D., & Mays, V. M. (1993). Applying social psychological models to predicting HIV-related sexual risk behaviors among African Americans. *Journal of Black Psychology, 19*(2), 142–154.

Coetzee, P. H., & Roux, A. P. J. (Eds.). (2003). *The African philosophy reader* (2nd ed.). New York, NY: Routledge.

Coker, T. R., Elliott, M. N., Toomey, S. L., Schwebel, D. C., Cuccaro, P., Emery, S. T., Davies, S. L., Visser, S. N., & Schuster, M. A. (2016). Racial and ethnic disparities in ADHD diagnosis and treatment. *Pediatrics, 138*(3). Retrieved from http://pediatrics.aappublications.org/content/138/3/e20160407

Cokley, K., & Chapman, C. (2009). Racial identity theory: Adults. In H. A. Neville, B. M. Tynes & S. O. Utsey (Eds.), *Handbook of African American Psychology* (pp. 283–297). Thousand Oaks, CA: Sage.

Cole, E. R. (2009). Intersectionality and research in psychology. *American Psychologist, 64*, 170–180.

Cole, J. M., & Boykin, A. W. (2008). Examining culturally structured learning environments with different types of music-linked movement opportunity. *Journal of Black Psychology, 34*(3), 331–355.

Coleman, J. D., Lindley, L. L., Annang, L., Saunders, R. P., & Gaddist, B. (2012). Development of a framework for HIV/AIDS prevention programs in African American churches. *AIDS Patient Care and STDs, 26*, 116–124.

Coleman, J. S. (1966). *Equality of educational opportunity*. Retrieved from http://files.eric.ed.gov/fulltext/ED012275.pdf

Coleman, J. S. (1988). Social capital in the creation of human capital. *American Journal of Sociology, 94*(Suppl.), 95–121.

Coleman, K. (1998). *The effects of communal learning contexts on black and white children's problem solving ability* (Unpublished doctoral dissertation). Howard University, Washington, DC.

Coleman, M. N., Butler, E. O., Long, A. M., & Fisher, F. D. (2016). In and out of love with hip-hop: Saliency of sexual scripts for young adult African American women in hip-hop and Black-oriented television. *Culture, Health & Sexuality, 18*(10), 1165–1179.

Coley, R. L., Kull, M. A., & Carrano, J. (2014). Parental endorsement of spanking and children's internalizing and externalizing problems in African American and Hispanic families. *Journal of Family Psychology, 28*(1), 22–31.

Collins, F. (2004). What we do and don't know about "race," "ethnicity," genetics and health at the dawn of the genome era. *Nature Genetics, 11*(Suppl.), 13–15.

Colman, A. M. (1994). *Companion encyclopedia of psychology.* London, England: Routledge.

Comas-Díaz, L. (2016). Racial trauma recovery: A race-informed therapeutic approach to racial. In A. N. Alvarex, C. T. Liang & H. A. Neville (Eds.), *The cost of racism for people of color: Contextualizing experiences of discrimination* (pp. 249–272). Washington, DC: American Psychological Association.

Comer, J. P. (2004). *Leave no child behind: Preparing today's youth for tomorrow's world.* New Haven, CT: Yale University Press.

Common Sense Media. (2015). *Landmark report: U.S. teens use an average of nine hours of media per day, tweens use six hours.* Retrieved from https://www.commonsensemedia.org/about-us/news/press-releases/landmark-report-us-teens-use-an-average-of-nine-hours-of-media-per-da

Compion, S. (2017). The joiners: Active voluntary association membership in twenty African countries. *VOLUNTAS: International Journal of Voluntary and Nonprofit Organizations, 28*(3), 1270–1300.

Cone, J. H. (1970). *A black theology of liberation* (1st ed.). Philadelphia, PA: Lippincott.

Conference on Retroviruses and Opportunistic Infections (CROI) (2016). Retrieved from https://www.cdc.gov/nchhstp/newsroom/2016/croi-2016.html#Graphics2

Conley, D. (2000). The racial wealth gap: Origins and implications for philanthropy in the African American community. *Nonprofit and Voluntary Sector Quarterly, 29*(4), 530–540.

Constantine, M. G., Alleyne, V. L., Wallace, B. C., & Franklin-Jackson, D. C. (2006). Africentric values. Their relation to positive mental health in African American adolescent girls. *Journal of Black Psychology, 32*, 141–154.

Coogan, P. F., Coier, Y. C., Krishnan, S., Wise, L. A., Adams-Campbell, L. L., Rosenberg, L. & Palmer, J. R. (2010). Neighborhood socioeconomic status in relation to 10-year weight gain in the Black Women's Health Study. *Obesity, 18*(10), 2064–2065.

Cook, B. L., Zuvekas, S. H., Carson, N., Wayne, G. F., Vesper, A., & McGuire, T. G. (2014). Assessing Racial/ethnic disparities in treatment across episodes of Mental Health Care. *Health Services Research, 49*(1), 206–229.

Cook, D. (1993). Research in African-American churches: A mental health counseling imperative. *Journal of Mental Health Counseling, 15*(3), 320–333.

Cook, D. A., & Wiley, C. Y. (2000). Psychotherapy with members of African American churches and spiritual traditions. In R. P. Scott & A. E. Bergin (Eds.), *Handbook of psychotherapy and religious diversity* (pp. 369–396). Washington, DC: American Psychological Association.

Cooke, C. L., Bowie, B. H., & Carrère, S. (2014). Perceived discrimination and children's mental health symptoms. *Advances in Nursing Science, 37*(4), 299–314.

Cooley, M. L., & Unger, D. G. (1991). The role of family support in determining developmental outcomes in children of teen mothers. *Child Psychiatry and Human Development, 21*(3), 217–234.

Coon, D. (1997). *Essentials of psychology.* Pacific Grove, CA: Brooks/Cole.

Cooper, B., Cox, D., Lienesch, R., & Jones, R. B. (2016). Beyond same-sex marriage: Attitudes on LGBT non-discrimination laws and religious exemptions from the 2015 American values atlas. Public Religion Research Institute [PRRI]. Retrieved from https://www.prri.org/research/poll-same-sex-gay-marriage-lgbt-nondiscrimination-religious-liberty/

Cooper, D. (2012). *The black church: Where women pray and men prey.* Chicago, IL: Amagination.

Cope, C., Michalski, D. S., & Fowler, G. A. (2017). *Graduate study in psychology, 2017.* Summary report:

Student demographics. Washington, DC: American Psychological Association. Retrieved from http://www.apa.org/education/grad/survey-data/2017-student-demographics.pdf

Copeland-Carson, J. (2005). Promoting diversity in contemporary black philanthropy: Toward a new conceptual model. *New Directions for Philanthropic Fundraising, 48*, 77–87.

Copen, C. E., Daniels, K., Vespa, J., & Mosher, W. (2012). *First marriages in the United States: Data from the 2006-2010 National Survey of Family Growth.* Hyattsville, MD: U.S. Dept. of Health and Human Services, Centers for Disease Control and Prevention, National Center for Health Statistics.

Corneille, M., Ashcraft, A., & Belgrave, F. Z. (2005). What's culture got to do with it: Deconstructing drug and HIV prevention programs for African American youth. *Journal of Health Care for the Poor and Underserved, 16*, 38–47.

Corneille, M., & Belgrave, F. Z. (2007). Ethnic identity, neighborhood risk, and adolescent drug and sex attitudes and refusal efficacy: The urban African American girls' experience. *Journal of Drug Education, 37*(2), 177–190.

Corneille, M., Fife, J., Belgrave, F. Z., & Sims, B. C. (2012). Ethnic identity, masculinity, and healthy sexual relationships among African American men. *Psychology of Men and Masculinity, 13*(4), 393–399.

Corona, R., Turf, E., Corneille, M. A., Belgrave, F. Z., & Nasim, A. (2009). Risk and protective factors for tobacco use among African American 8th and 10th grade students in Virginia. *Preventing Chronic Disease, 6*(2). Retrieved from http://www.ncbi.nlm.nih.gov/pmc/articles/PMC2687851

Corral, I., Landrine, H., Hao, Y., Zhao, L., Mellerson, J. L., & Cooper, D. L. (2012). Residential segregation, health behavior and overweight/obesity among a national sample of African American adults. *Journal of Health Psychology, 17*(3), 371–378.

Correll, J., Park, B., Judd, C. M., & Wittenbrink, B. (2002). The police officer's dilemma: Using ethnicity to disambiguate potentially threatening individuals. *Journal of Personality and Social Psychology, 83*(6), 1314–1329.

Cosby, C., & Poussaint, R. (2004). *A wealth of wisdom: Legendary African American elders speak.* New York, NY: Atria Books.

Costello, E. J., He, J., Sampson, N. A., Kessler, R. C., & Merikangas, K. R. (2014). Services for adolescents with psychiatric disorders: 12-Month data from the National Comorbidity Survey. *Adolescent Psychiatric Services, 65*(3), 359–366.

Cotter, D. A., Hermsen, J. M., Ovadia, S., & Vanneman, R. (2001). *The glass ceiling effect.* Retrieved from http://www.bsos.umd.edu/socy/vanneman/papers/Cotter HOV01.pdf

Cottrell, L. S. (1976). The competent community. In B. H. Kaplan, R. N. Wilson & A. H. Leighton (Eds.), *Further explorations in social psychiatry* (pp. 21–43). New York, NY: Basic Books.

Coulon, S. M., & Wilson, D. K. (2015). Social support buffering of the relation between low income and elevated blood pressure in at-risk African-American adults. *Journal of Behavioral Medicine, 38*(5), 830–834.

Council of Independent Black Institutions (CIBI). (n.d.). Retrieved from http://www.cibi.org/

Cox, D., Navarro-Rivera, J., & Jones, R. P. (2016). Race, religion, and political affiliation of Americans' core social networks. *Public Religion Research Institute (PRRI).* Retrieved from https://www.prri.org/research/poll-race-religion-politics-americans-social-networks/

Cratty, C., Hayes, A., & Gast, P. (2010). DEA wants to hire Ebonics translators, *CNN.* Retrieved from http://www.cnn.com/2010/US/08/24/dea.ebonics/

Craven, J. (2017). *More than 250 black people were killed by police in 2016 [Updated].* Retrieved from http://www.huffingtonpost.com/entry/black-people-killed-by-police-america_us_577da633e4b0c590f7e7fb17

CREDO. (2013). *National charter school study 2013.* Retrieved from http://credo.stanford.edu/documents/NCSS%202013%20Final%20Draft.pdf

CREDO. (2015). *Urban charter school study report on 41 regions 2015.* Retrieved from http://urbancharters.stanford.edu/download/Urban%20Charter%20School%20Study%20Report%20on%2041%20Regions.pdf

Crenshaw, K. (1989). Demarginalizing the intersection of race and sex: A black feminist critique of antidiscrimination doctrine, feminist theory and antiracist politics. *The University of Chicago Legal Fund, 140*, 139–167.

Crespo, C. J., Keteyian, S. J., Heath, G. W., & Sempos, C. T. (1996). Leisure-time physical activity among U.S. adults. *Archives of Internal Medicine, 156*, 93–98.

Crick, N. R., & Grotpeter, J. K. (1995). Relational aggression, gender, and social-psychological adjustment. *Child Development, 66*(3), 710–722.

Crocker, J., & Major, B. (1989). Social stigma and self-esteem: The self-protective properties of stigma. *Psychological Review, 96*(4), 608–630.

Crockett, L. J., Carlo, G., & Temmen, C. (2016). Ethnic and racial minority youth in the rural United States: An overview. In L. Crockett & C. Gustavoe (Eds.), *Rural ethnic minority youth and families in the United States* (pp. 1–12). New York, NY: Springer International.

Crosby, F. J., Iyer, A., & Sincharoen, S. (2006). Understanding affirmative action. *Annual Review Psychology, 57*, 585–611.

Cross, W. E. (1978). The Thomas and Cross models of psychological nigrescence: A review. *Journal of Black Psychology, 5*(1), 13–31.

Cross, W. E. (1991). *Shades of black: Diversity in African-American identity.* Philadelphia, PA: Temple University Press.

Cross, W. E., Parham, T. A., & Helms, J. E. (1998). Nigrescence revisited: Theory and research. In R. Jones (Ed.), *African American identity development* (pp. 3–71). Hampton, VA: Cobb & Henry.

Cubanski, J., Casillas, G., & Damico, A. (2015, June 10). Poverty among seniors: An updated analysis of national and state level poverty rates under the official and supplemental poverty measures. Kaiser Family Foundation. Retrieved from https://www.kff.org/report-section/poverty-among-seniors-issue-brief/

Cuevas, A. G., O'Brien, K., & Saha, S. (2016). African American experiences in healthcare: "I always feel like I'm getting skipped over". *Health Psychology, 35*(9), 987–995.

Cuffee, Y. L., Hargraves, J. L., Rosal, M., Briesacher, B. A., Schoenthaler, A., Person, S., . . . Allison, J. (2013). Reported racial discrimination, trust in physicians, and medication adherence among inner-city African Americans with hypertension. *American Journal of Public Health, 103*(11), e55–e62.

Cullen, M. J., Hardison, C. M., & Sackett, P. R. (2004). Using SAT-grade and ability-job performance relationships to test predictions derived from stereotype threat theory. *Journal of Applied Psychology, 89*(2), 220–230.

Cunningham, M., & Francois, S. (2016). Theoretical perspectives on African American youth and families in rural settings. In L. Crockett & C. Gustavoe (Eds.), *Rural ethnic minority youth and families in the United States* (pp. 57–70). New York, NY: Springer International.

Cunningham, M., Swanson, D. P., & Hayes, D. M. (2013). School- and community-based associations to hypermasculine attitudes in African American adolescent males. *American Journal of Orthopsychiatry, 83*(2–3), 244–251.

Cunningham, M. R., Barbee, A. P., & Pike, C. L. (1990). What do women want? Facialmetric assessment of multiple motives in the perception of male facial physical attractiveness. *Journal of Personality and Social Psychology, 68*, 261–279.

Cunningham, M. R., & Meunier, L. N. (2004). The influence of peer experiences on bravado attitudes among African American males. In N. Way & J. Chu (Eds.), *Adolescent boys in context: Exploring diverse cultures of boyhood* (pp. 219–234). New York: New York University Press.

Cunningham, R. T. (1997). *The effects of contextual differentiation and content imagery on the cognitive performance of African American and Euro-American low-income children: Movement/music explorations* (Unpublished doctoral dissertation). Howard University, Washington, DC.

Cunningham, R. T., & Boykin, A. W. (2004). Enhancing cognitive performance in African American children: Infusing Afro-cultural perspective and research. In R. Jones (Ed.), *Black psychology* (4th ed., pp. 487–507). Berkeley, CA: Cobb & Henry.

Cunningham, T. J., Croft, J. B., Liu, Y., Lu, H., Eke, P. I., & Giles, W. H. (2017). Vital Signs: Racial disparities in age-specific mortality among Blacks or African Americans—United States, 1999–2015. *MMWR Morbidity and Mortality Weekly Reports, 66*, 444–456.

Cutrona, C. E., Clavél, F. D., & Johnson, M. A. (2016). African American couples in rural contexts. In L. Crockett & C. Gustavoe (Eds.), *Rural ethnic minority youth and families in the United States* (pp. 127–142). New York, NY: Springer International.

Cutrona, C. E., Russell, D. W., Brown, P. A., Clark, L. A., Hessling, R. M., & Gardner, K. A. (2005). Neighborhood context, personality, and stressful life events as predictors of depression among African American women. *Journal of Abnormal Psychology, 114*(1), 3–15.

Cutrona, C. E., Russell, D. W., Hessling, R. M., Brown, P. A., & Murry, V. (2000). Direct and moderating effects of community context on the psychological well-being of African American women. *Journal of Personality and Social Psychology, 79*, 1088–1101.

Dale, S. K., Bogart, L. M., Wagner, G. J., Galvan, F. H., & Klein, D. J. (2016). Medical mistrust is related to lower longitudinal medication adherence among African-American males with HIV. *Journal of Health Psychology, 21*(7), 1311–1321.

Dalmida, S. G., Holstad, M. M., Dilorio, C., & Laderman, G. (2012). The meaning and use of spirituality among African American women living with HIV/AIDS. *Western Journal of Nursing Research, 34*(6), 736–765.

Damon, W., & Hart, D. (1982). The development of self-understanding from infancy through adolescence. *Child Development, 53*, 841–864.

Dana, R. H. (1998). Problems with managed mental health care for multicultural populations. *Psychological Reports, 83*(1), 283–294.

Dana, R. H., & Whatley, P. R. (1991). When does a difference make a difference? MMPI scores and African-Americans. *Journal of Clinical Psychology, 47*(3), 400–406.

David-Barrett, T., Rotkirch, A., Carney, J., Izquierdo, I. B., Krems, J. A., Townley, D., . . . Dunbar, R. I. (2015). Women favour dyadic relationships, but men prefer clubs: Cross-cultural evidence from social networking. *PLoS One, 10*(3), e0118329.

Davis, J. L., Buchanan, K. L., & Green, B. L. (2013). Racial/ethnic differences in cancer prevention beliefs: Applying the health belief model framework. *American Journal of Health Promotion, 27*(6), 384–389.

Davis, L., & Wu, S. (2013). *Social comparisons and life satisfaction across racial and ethnic groups: The effects of status, information and solidarity.* Retrieved from https://ssrn.com/abstract=2045902 or http://dx.doi.org/10.2139/ssrn.2045902

Davis, T. A., & Ancis, J. (2012). Look to the relationship: A review of African American women substance users' poor treatment retention and working alliance development. *Substance Use and Misuse, 47*, 662–672.

Davis-Smith, M. (2007). Implementing a diabetic prevention program in a rural African American church. *Journal of the National Medical Association, 99*(4), 440–446.

Debnam, K., Holt, C. L., Clark, E. M., Roth, D. L., & Southward, P. (2012). Relationship between religious social support and general social support with health behaviors in a national sample of African Americans. *Journal of Behavioral Medicine, 35*(2), 179–189.

Decker, D. M., Dona, D. P., & Christenson, S. L. (2007). Behaviorally at-risk African American students: The importance of student-teacher relationships for student outcomes. *Journal of School Psychology, 45*(1), 83–109.

DeGruy, J., Kjellstrand, J. M., Briggs, H. E., & Brennan, E. M. (2012). Racial respect and racial socialization as protective factors for African American male youth. *Journal of Black Psychology, 38*(4), 395–420.

Dempsey, K., Butler, S. K., & Gaither, L. (2016). Black Churches and mental health professionals: Can this collaboration work? *Journal of Black Studies, 47*(1), 73–87.

DeNavas-Walt, C., Cleveland, R. W., & Roemer, M. I. (2001). Money: Income in the United States: 2000. *Current population Reports.* Retrieved from http://www.census.gov/prod/2001pubs/p60-213.pdf

DeNavas-Walt, C., & Proctor, B. D. (2015). *Income and poverty in the United States: 2014* (U.S. Census Bureau. Current Population Reports P60-252). U.S. Government Printing Office, Washington, DC.

Derlan, C. L., & Umana-Taylor, A. J. (2015). Brief report: Contextual predictors of African American adolescents' ethnic-racial identity affirmation-belonging and resistance to peer pressure. *Journal of Adolescence, 41*, 1–6.

Derlega, V. J., Janda, L. H., Miranda, J., Chen, I. A., Goodman, B. M., & Smith, W. (2014). How patients' self-disclosure about sickle cell pain episodes to significant others relates to living with sickle cell disease. *Pain Medicine, 15*(9), 1496–1507.

Desforges, J., Milner, P., Wethers, D. L., & Whitten, C. F. (1978). *Sickle cell disease.* Los Angeles, CA: National Association for Sickle Cell Disease.

Deutsch, M. (1985). *Distributive justice: A social psychological perspective.* New Haven, CT: Yale University Press.

DeVane-Johnson, S., Woods-Giscombé, C., Thoyre, S., Fogel, C., & Williams, R. (2017). Integrative Literature review of factors related to breastfeeding in African American women: Evidence for a potential paradigm shift. *Journal of Human Lactation, 33*(20), 435–447.

Dexter, C. A., Wong, K., Stacks, A. M., Beeghly, M., & Barnett, D. (2013). Parenting and attachment among low-income African American and Caucasian preschoolers. *Journal of Family Psychology, 27*(4), 629–638.

Diabetes Prevention Program Research Group. (2002a). The Diabetes Prevention Program (DPP): Description of lifestyle intervention. *Diabetes Care, 25*(12), 2165–2171.

Diabetes Prevention Program Research Group. (2002b). Reduction in the incidence of Type 2 Diabetes with lifestyle intervention or Metformin. *The New England Journal of Medicine, 446*(6), 393–403.

Dick, D. M., Barr, P., Guy, M., Nasim, A., & Scott, D. (2017). Genetic research on alcohol use outcomes in African American populations: A review of the literature, associated challenges, and implications. *The American Journal on Addictions, 26*(5), 486–493.

Diener, E. D., Emmons, R. A., Larsen, R. J., & Griffin, S. (1985). The satisfaction with life scale. *Journal of Personality Assessment, 49*(1), 71–75.

Dill, L. J., Mahaffey, C., Mosley, T., Treadwell, H., Barkwell, F., & Barnhill, S. (2015). "I Want a Second Chance": Experiences of African American fathers in reentry. *American Journal of Men's Health, 10*(6), 459–465.

DiIorio, C., McCarty, F., Resnicow, K., Lehr, S., & Denzmore, P. (2007). REAL men: A group-randomized trial of an HIV prevention intervention for adolescent boys. *American Journal of Public Health, 97*(6), 1084–1089.

Dilworth-Anderson, P., & Goodwin, P. (2005). A model of extended family support: Care of the elderly in African American families. In V. C. McLoyd, N. E. Hill & K. A. Dodge, (Eds.), *African American family life: Ecological and cultural diversity: Duke Series in Child Development and Public Policy* (pp. 211–223). New York, NY: Guilford.

Dilworth-Anderson, P., & Williams, S. W. (2004). Recruitment and retention strategies for longitudinal African American caregiving research: The family caregiving project. *Journal of Aging and Health, 16*(Suppl. 5), 137S–156S.

Dinwiddie, G. Y., Gaskin, D. J., Chan, K. S., Norrington, J., & McCleary, R. (2013). Residential segregation, geographic proximity and type of services used: Evidence for racial/ethnic disparities in mental health. *Social Science & Medicine, 80*, 67–75.

Dixon, J., Durrheim, K., & Tredoux, C. (2007). Intergroup contact and attitudes toward the principle and practice of racial equality. *Psychological Science, 18*(10), 867–872.

Dixon, P. (2014). AARMS: The African American relationships and marriage strengthening curriculum for African American relationships courses and programs. *Journal of African American Studies, 18*(3), 337–352.

Doamekpor, L. A., & Dinwiddie, G. Y. (2015). Allostatic load in foreign-born and US-born Blacks: Evidence from the 2001–2010 National Health and Nutrition Examination Survey. *American Journal of Public Health, 105*(3), 591–597.

Dobbie, W., & Fryer, R. G., Jr. (2009). *Are high quality schools enough to close the achievement gap? Evidence from a social experiment in Harlem* (No. 15473). Cambridge, MA: National Bureau of Economic Research. Retrieved from http://www.nber.org/papers/w15473

Dodor, B. (2012). The impact of religiosity on health behaviors and obesity among African Americans. *Journal of Human Behavior in the Social Environment, 22*, 451–462.

Doherty, C. (2013, June 28). *For African Americans, discrimination is not dead.* Washington, DC: Pew Research Center.

Doherty, E. E., Robertson, J. A., Green, K. M., Fothergill, K. E., & Ensminger, M. E. (2012). A longitudinal study of substance use and violent victimization in adulthood among a cohort of urban African Americans. *Addiction, 107*, 339–348.

Dolcini, M. M., Harper, G. W., Watson, S., Han, L., Ellen, J., & Catania, J. (2004). *The structure and quality of adolescent friendships in an urban African American neighborhood.* San Francisco: University of California, San Francisco, AIDS Research Institute.

Dolezsar, C. M., McGrath, J. J., Herzig, A. J., & Miller, S. B. (2014). Perceived racial discrimination and hypertension: A comprehensive systematic review. *Health Psychology, 33*(1), 20–34.

Donaldson Report. (2008). *Finding families for African American children: The role or race & law in adoption from foster care.* New York, NY: Evan B. Donaldson Adoption Institute.

Donders, N. C., Correll, J., & Wittenbrink, B. (2008). Danger stereotypes predict racially biased attentional allocation. *Journal of Experimental Social Psychology, 44*(5), 1328–1333.

Doran, N., Luczak, S. E., Bekman, N., Koutsenok, I., & Brown, S. A. (2012). Adolescent substance use and aggression: A review. *Criminal Justice and Behavior, 39*(6), 748–769.

Dorsey, S., & Forehand, R. (2003). The relation of social capital to child psychosocial adjustment difficulties: The role of positive parenting and neighborhood dangerousness. *Journal of Psychopathology and Behavioral Assessment, 25*(1), 11–23.

Doss, R. C., & Gross, A. M. (1992). The effects of Black English on stereotyping in intra-racial perceptions. *Journal of Black Psychology, 18*(2), 47–58.

Dougherty, K., & Huyser, K. R. (2008). Racially diverse congregations: Organizational identity and the accommodation of differences. *Journal for the Scientific Study of Religion, 47*(1), 23–44.

Dovidio, J., Evans, N., & Tyler, R. (1986). Racial stereotypes: The contents of their cognitive representation. *Journal of Experimental Social Psychology, 22*, 22–37.

Dovidio, J., & Gaertner, S. (1991). Changes in the expression and assessment of racial prejudice. In H. J. Knopke, R. J. Norrell, & R. W. Rogers (Eds.), *Opening doors: Perspectives on race relations in contemporary America* (pp. 119–148). Tuscaloosa: University of Alabama Press.

Dovidio, J., & Gaertner, S. (2000). Aversive racism in selection decisions: 1989 and 1999. *Psychological Science, 11*, 315–319.Down, K. (2016). *When black death goes viral, it can trigger PTSD-like trauma.* Retrieved from http://www.pbs.org/newshour/rundown/black-pain-gone-viral-racism-graphic-videos-can-create-ptsd-like-trauma on 1/29/17

Downey, D. B., & Condron, D. J. (2016). Fifty years since the Coleman report: Rethinking the relationship between schools and inequality. *Sociology of Education, 89*(3), 207–220.

Doyle, O., Clark, T. T., Cryer-Coupet, Q., Nebbitt, V. E., Goldston, D. B., Estroff, S. E., & Magan, I. (2015). Unheard voices: African American fathers speak about their parenting practices. *Psychology of Men & Masculinity, 16*(3), 274–283.

Dreger, R. M., & Miller, K. S. (1960). Comparative psychological studies of Negroes and Whites in the United States. *Psychological Bulletin, 57*, 361–340.

Dreyer, J. S. (2015). Ubuntu. *International Journal of Practical Theology, 19*(1), 189–209.

Driscoll, M. W., Reynolds, J. R., & Todman, L. C. (2014). Dimensions of race-related stress and African American life satisfaction: A test of the protective role of collective efficacy. *Journal of Black Psychology, 41*(5), 462–486.

Du Bois, D. L., Holloway, B. E., Valentine, J. C., & Cooper, H. (2002). Effectiveness of mentoring programs for youth: A meta-analytic review. *American Journal of Community Psychology, 30*, 157–197.

Du Bois, W. E. B. (1899). *The Philadelphia Negro.* Philadelphia: University of Pennsylvania.

Du Bois, W. E. B. (1903). *The souls of Black folk.* Chicago, IL: McClurg.

Du Bois, W. E. B. (1908). *The Negro American family.* Atlanta, GA: Atlanta University Press.

Duckworth, A. L., Peterson, C., Matthews, M. D., & Kelly, D. R. (2007). Grit: Perseverance and passion for long-term goals. *Journal of Personality and Social Psychology, 92*(6), 1087–1101.

Duffin, T. P. (2016). The lowdown on the down low: Why some bisexually active men choose to self-identify as straight. *Journal of Bisexuality, 16*(4), 484–506.

Duhaime, E. P. (2015). Is the call to prayer a call to cooperate? *Judgment and Decision Making, 10*(6), 593–596.

Dunbar, A. S., Leerkes, E. M., Coard, S. I., Supple, A. J., & Calkins, S. (2017). An integrative conceptual model of parental racial/ethnic and emotion socialization and links to children's social-emotional development among African American families. *Child Development Perspectives, 11*(1), 16–22.

Duncan, A. E., Lessov-Schlaggar, C. N., Sartor, C. E., & Bucholz, K. K. (2012). Differences in time to onset of smoking and nicotine dependence by race/ethnicity in a Mid-western sample of adolescents and young adults from a high risk family study. *Drug and Alcohol Dependence, 125*, 140–145.

Duncan, G. J. (1994). Families and neighbors as sources of disadvantage in the schooling decisions of white and black adolescents. *American Journal of Education, 103*(1), 20–53.

Duncan, G. J., Brooks-Gunn, J. P., & Klebanov, P. K. (1994). Economic deprivation and early-childhood development. *Child Development, 65*, 296–318.

Duncan, L. E. (2003). Black male college students' atittudes toward seeking psychological help. *Journal of Black Psychology, 29*(1), 68–86.

Duncan, L. E., & Johnson, D. (2007). Black undergraduate students' attitude toward counseling and counselor preference. *College Student Journal, 41*, 696–719.

Dunifon, R. (2013). The influence of grandparents on the lives of children and adolescents. *Child Development Perspectives*, 7: 55–60.

Durkheim, E. (1897/1951). *Suicide: A study in sociology*. New York, NY: The Free Press.

Durodoye, B., & Hildreth, B. (1995). Learning styles and the African American student. *Education, 116*, 241–247.

Durose, M. R., Smith, E. L., & Langan, P. A. (2007). *Contacts between the police and the public, 2005*. Washington, DC: Bureau of Justice Statistics.

Duru, K., Sarkisian, C. A., Leng, M., & Mangione, C. M. (2010). Sisters in motion: A randomized controlled trial of a faith-based physical activity intervention. *Journal of the American Geriatrics Society, 58*(10), 1863–1869.

Eberhardt, J. (2005). Imaging race. *American Psychologist, 60*, 181–190.

Eberhardt, J. L., Davies, P. G., Purdie-Vaughns, V. J., & Johnson, S. L. (2006). Looking deathworthy perceived stereotypicality of black defendants predicts capital-sentencing outcomes. *Psychological Science, 17*(5), 383–386.

Eberhardt, J. L., Goff, P. A., Purdie, V. J., & Davies, P. G. (2004). Seeing black: Race, crime, and visual processing. *Journal of Personality and Social Psychology, 87*(6), 876.

Edkins, V. A. (2011). Defense attorney plea recommendations and client race: Does zealous representation apply equally to all? *Law Human Behavior, 35*, 413–425.

Edwards, K. L. (1999). African American definitions of self and psychological health. In C. C. Yeakey & R. D. Henderson (Eds.), *Surmounting all odds: Education, opportunity, and society in the new millennium* (Vol. 1). Greenwich, CT: Information Age.

Edwards, S. D. (2011). A psychology of indigenous healing in southern Africa. *Journal of Psychology in Africa, 21*(3), 335–348.

Effective Black Parenting Program (EBPP). (n.d.). Retrieved from http://www.cebc4cw.org/program/effective-black-parenting-program/detailed

Egen, O., Beatty, K., Blackley, D. J., Brown, K., & Wykoff, R. (2017). Health and social conditions of the poorest versus wealthiest counties in the United States. *American Journal of Public Health, 107*(1), 130–135.

Eggly, S., Barton, E., Winckles, A., Penner, L. A., & Albrecht, T. L. (2015). A disparity of words: Racial differences in oncologist–patient communication about clinical trials. *Health Expectations, 18*(5), 1316–1326.

Elkington, K. S., Bauemeister, J. A., & Zimmerman, M. A. (2010). Do parents and peers matter?: A prospective socio-ecological examination of substance use and sexual risk among African American youth. *Journal of Adolescence, 34*(5), 1035–1047.

Ellison, C., & Powers, D. (1994). The contact hypothesis and racial attitudes among Black Americans. *Social Science Quarterly, 75*(2), 385–400.

Ellison, C. G., Burdette, A. M., & Wilcox, W. B. (2010). The couple that prays together: Race and ethnicity, religion, and relationship quality among working-age adults. *Journal of Marriage and Family, 72*(4), 963–975.

Ellison, C. G., & Flannelly, K. J. (2009). Religious involvement and risk of major depression in a prospective nationwide study of African American adults. *Journal of Nervous and Mental Disease, 197*, 568–573.

Ellison, C. M., Boykin, A. W., Tyler, K. M., & Dillihunt, M. L. (2005). Examining classroom learning preferences among elementary school students. *Social Behavior and Personality, 33*, 699–708.

El-Mohandes, A. A., Kiely, M., Joseph, J., Subramanian, S., Johnson, A., Blake, S., . . . El-Khorazaty, M. N. (2008). An intervention to improve postpartum outcomes in African American mothers. *Obstetrics and Gynecology, 112*(3), 611–620.

Elmore, C. A., & Gaylord-Harden, N. K. (2013). The influence of supportive parenting and racial socialization messages on African American youth behavioral outcomes. *Journal of Child and Family Studies, 22*(1), 63–75.

Elsaesser, C., Hong, J. S., & Voisin, D. R. (2016). Violence exposure and bullying among African American adolescents: Examining the protective role of academic engagement. *Children and Youth Services Review, 70*, 394–402.

Emerson, M. O., Kimbro, R., & Yancey, G. (2002). Contact theory extended: The effects of prior racial contact on current social ties. *Social Science Quarterly, 83*(3), 745–761.

Engelbrecht, P., & Natzel, S. G. (1997). Cultural variations in cognitive style: Field dependence vs. field independence. *School Psychology International, 18*(2), 155–164.

Ensminger, M. E., Lamkin, R. P., & Jacobson, N. (1996). School leaving: A longitudinal perspective including neighborhood effects. *Child Development, 67*(5), 2400–2416.

Entringer, S., Buss, C., & Wadhwa, P. D. (2015). Prenatal stress, development, health and disease risk: A psychobiological perspective—2015 Curt Richter Award Paper. *Psychoneuroendocrinology, 62*, 366–375.

Epstein, J., Williams, C., & Botvin, G. (2002). How universal are social influences to drink and problem behaviors for alcohol use? A test comparing urban African American and Caribbean American adolescents. *Addictive Behaviors, 27*, 75–86.

Erikson, E. H. (1963). *Childhood and society* (2nd ed.). New York, NY: Norton.

Erikson, E. H. (1968). *Identity: Youth and crisis.* New York, NY: Norton.

Erwin, D. O., Spatz, T. S., Stotts, R. C., Hollenberg, J. A., & Deloney, L. A. (1996). Increasing mammography and breast self-examination in African American women using the Witness Project model. *Journal of Cancer Education, 11*, 210–215.

Evans, G. W. (2006). Child development and the physical environment. *Annual Review of Psychology, 57*, 423–451.

Evans, S. Y., Bell, K., & Burton, N. K. (2017). *Black women's mental health: Balancing strength and vulnerability.* New York: SUNY Press.

Evans, S. Z., Simons, L. G., & Simons, R. L. (2012). The effect of corporal punishment and verbal abuse on delinquency: Mediating mechanisms. *Journal of Youth and Adolescence, 41*(8), 1095–1110.

Evans-Whipp, T., Beyers, J., & Lloyd, S. (2004). A review of school drug policies and their impact on youth substance use. *Health Promotion International, 19*(2), 227–234.

Eveleth, P. B., & Tanner, J. M. (1976). *Worldwide variation in human growth.* New York, NY: Cambridge University Press.

Everhart, R. S., Miadick, S. A., Leiback, G. G., Borschuk, A. P., & Koinis-Mitchell, D. (2016). Acculturation and quality of life in urban, African American caregivers of children with asthma. *Journal of Asthma, 53*(9), 983–988.

Ewing, K. M., Richardson, T. Q., James-Myers, L., & Russell, R. K. (1996). The relationship between racial identity attitudes, worldview, and African American graduate students' experience of the imposter phenomenon. *Journal of Black Psychology, 22*(1), 53–66.

Fagan, A. A., Wright, E. M., & Pinchevsky, G. M. (2014). The protective effects of neighborhood collective efficacy on adolescent substance use and violence following exposure to violence. *Journal of Youth and Adolescence, 43*(9), 1498–1512.

Fairchild, H. H. (1994). Whither liberation? A critique of a critique. *Journal of Black Psychology, 20*(3), 367–371.

Fairchild, H. H. (2000). *African American psychology. Encyclopedia of psychology.* New York, NY: Oxford University Press; The American Psychological Association.

Fairchild, H. H. (2011). On the need for eurocentrics anonymous: An assessment of the July 2000 keynote address. *Psych Discourse, 45*(5).

Fairchild, H. H., Yee, A. H., Wyatt, G. E., & Weizmann, F. M. (1995). Readdressing psychology's problems with race. *American Psychologist, 50*(1), 46–47.

Faith Communities Today. (2015). *2015 National Survey of Congregations.* Retrieved from http://www.faithcommunitiestoday.org/sites/default/files/Faith-Communities-Today-2015-Final-Survey-with-Frequencies.pdf

Fallik, S. W., & Novak, K. J. (2012). Decision to search: Is race or ethnicity important? *Journal of Contemporary Criminal Justice, 28*(2), 146–165.

Fanon, F. (1963). *The wretched of the earth* (C. Farrington, Trans.). New York, NY: Grove Press.

Fanon, F. (1967). *Black skin, white masks.* New York, NY: Grove Press.

Farmer, G. L., & Piotrkowski, C. S. (2009). African and European American Women's volunteerism and activism: Similarities in volunteering and differences in activism. *Journal of Human Behavior in the Social Environment, 19*(2), 196–212.

Farrant, B. M., Devine, T. A. J., Maybery, M. T., & Fletcher, J. (2012). Empathy, perspective taking and prosocial behaviour: The importance of parenting practices. *Infant and Child Development, 21*(2), 175–188.

Feagin, J. (1991). The continuing significance of race: Anti-Black discrimination in public places. *American Sociological Review, 56*, 101–116.

Federal Bureau of Prisons. (n.d.). Retrieved from https://www.bop.gov/about/statistics/statistics_inmate_race.jsp

Federal Reserve Bank of St. Louis. (2014). *Unemployment rate: Black or African American.* Retrieved from https://fred.stlouisfed.org/graph/?g=V0F

Feingold, A. (1990). Gender differences in effects of physical attractiveness on romantic attraction: A comparison across five research paradigms. *Journal of Personality and Social Psychology, 59*, 981–993.

Feldmeyer, B. (2010). The effects of racial/ethnic segregation on Latin and black homicide. *The Sociological Quarterly, 51*(4), 600–623.

Ferguson, G. M., & Bornstein, M. H. (2015). Remote acculturation of early adolescents in Jamaica towards European American culture: A replication and extension. *International Journal of Intercultural Relations, 45*, 24–35.

Ferguson, G. O. (1916). *The psychology of the Negro: An experimental study.* New York, NY: Science Press.

Ferguson, S. L. (1998). Peer counseling in a culturally specific adolescent pregnancy prevention program. *Journal of Health Care for the Poor and Underserved, 9*(3), 322–340.

Fernandes-Alcantara, A. L. (2015). Disconnected youth: A look at 16 to 24 year olds who are not working or in school. *Congressional Research Service.* Retrieved from https://fas.org/sgp/crs/misc/R40535.pdf

Ferre, C., Jones, L., Norris K., & Rowley, D. (2010). The Healthy African American Families (HAAF) project: From community-based participatory research to community partnered participatory research. *Ethnic Diseases, 20*(1 Suppl. 2), S21–S28.

Festinger, L., Schachter, S., & Back, L. (1950). *Social pressures in informal groups: A study of a housing community.* New York, NY: Harper.

Field, C. J., Kimuna, S. R., & Straus, M. A. (2013). Attitudes toward interracial relationships among college students: Race, class, gender, and perceptions of parental views. *Journal of Black Studies, 44*(7), 741–776.

Field, T., Diego, M., Hernandez-Reif, M., Deeds, O., Holder, V., Schanberg, S., & Kuhn, C. (2009). Depressed pregnant black women have a greater incidence of prematurity and low birthweight outcomes. *Infant Behavior and Development, 32*(1), 10–16.

Fife, J. E., McCreary, M., Brewer, T., & Adegoke, A. A. (2011). Family rituals, religious involvement, and drug attitudes among recovering substance abusers. *North American Journal of Psychology, 13*, 87–98.

Fincham, F. D., Ajayi, C., & Beach, S. R. H. (2011). Spirituality and marital satisfaction in African American couples. *Psychology of Religion and Spirituality, 3*, 259–268.

Finkelhor, D., Turner, H. A., Shattuck, A. M., Hamby, S. L., & Kracke, K. (2015). Children's exposure to violence, crime, and abuse: An update. *Juvenile Justice Bulletin, 2015*, 1–13.

Finlay, A. K., White, H. R., Mun, E. Y., Cronley, C. C., & Lee, C. (2012). Racial differences in trajectories of heavy drinking and regular marijuana use from ages 13 to 24 among African-American and White males. *Drug and Alcohol Dependence, 121*, 118–123.

Finn, K. V. (2012). Marijuana use at school and achievement-linked behaviors. *High School Journal, 95*(3), 3–13.

Firebaugh, G., & Acciai, F. (2016). For blacks in America, the gap in neighborhood poverty has declined faster than segregation. *PNAS, 113*(47), 13372–13377.

Firebaugh, G., & Farrell, C. R. (2016). Still large, but narrowing: The sizable decline in racial neighborhood inequality in metropolitan America, 1980–2010. *Demography, 53*(139), 139–164.

Fishbein, M., & Ajzen, I. (1975). *Belief, attitude, intention, and behavior: An introduction to theory and research.* Reading, MA: Addison-Wesley.

Fishel, L. H., & Quarles, B. (1970). *The Black American: A documentary history.* Glenview, IL: Scott, Foresman.

Fisher, K., & Tana Gilmore, T. (2017). *Eposide 11: Matchmaker approved tips to balance success and finding love!* Retrieved from http://www.thematchmakingduo.com/ep-11-matchmaker-approved-tips-to-balance-success-and-finding-love/

Fisher, W. A., Fisher, J. D., & Rye, B. J. (1995). Understanding and promoting AIDS-preventive behavior: Insights from the theory of reasoned action. *Health Psychology, 14*(3), 255–264.

Fiske, S. T. (2014). *Social beings: A core motives approach to social psychology.* Hoboken, NJ: Wiley.

Fiske, S. T., & Taylor, S. E. (1991). *Social cognition.* New York, NY: McGraw-Hill.

Fiske, S. T., & Taylor, S. E. (2013). *Social cognition: From brains to culture.* London, England: Sage.

Flannelly, K. J., Galek, K., Kytle, J., & Silton, N. R. (2010). Religion in America: 1972–2006—Religious affiliation, attendance, and strength of faith. *Psychological Reports, 106*(3), 875–890.

Flay, B. R., Graumlich, S., Segawa, E., Burns, J. L., & Holliday, M. Y.; Aban Aya Investigators. (2004). Effects of 2 prevention programs on high-risk behaviors among African American youth: A randomized trial. *Archives of Pediatrics & Adolescent Medicine, 158*(4), 377–384.

Foner, E. (1988). *Reconstruction: America's unfinished revolution, 1863–1877.* New York, NY: Harper & Row.

Ford, D. Y. (1996). *Reversing underachievement among gifted black students: Promising practices and programs.* New York, NY: Teachers College Press.

Ford, D. Y., Harris, J. J., III, Tyson, C. A., & Frazier Trotman, M. (2002). Beyond deficit thinking: Providing access for gifted African American students. *Roeper Review, 24*(2), 52–58.

Ford, N. D., Narayan, K. V., & Mehta, N. K. (2016). Diabetes among US-and foreign-born blacks in the USA. *Ethnicity & Health, 21*(1), 71–84.

Fordham, S., & Ogbu, J. U. (1986). Black students' school success: Coping with the "burden of acting White". *Urban Review, 18*(3), 176–206.

Forehand, R., & Kotchick, B. A. (2016). Cultural diversity: A wake-up call for parent training. *Behavior Therapy, 47*(6), 981–992.

Forsyth, J., Schoenthaler, A., Chaplin, W. F., Ogedegbe, G., & Ravenell, J. (2014). Perceived discrimination and medication adherence in black hypertensive patients: The role of stress and depression. *Psychosomatic Medicine, 76*(3), 229–236.

Forsyth, J. M., & Carter, R. T. (2014). Development and preliminary validation of the racism-related Coping scale. *Psychological Trauma: Theory, Research, Practice, and Policy, 6*(6), 632–643.

Foster, E. M., & Kalil, A. (2007). Living arrangements and children's development in low-income white, black, and Latino families. *Child Development, 78*(6), 1657–1674.

Foster, M. L., Arnold, E., Rebchook, G. M., & Kegeles, S. M. C. (2011). "It's my inner strength": Spirituality, religion and HIV in the lives of young African American men who have sex with men. *Culture, Health & Sexuality, 13*, 1103–1117.

Foster, P. M., Phillips, F., Belgrave, F. Z., Randolph, S. M., & Braithwaite, N. (1993). An Africentric model for AIDS education, prevention, and psychological services within the African American community. *Journal of Black Psychology, 19*(2), 123–141.

Fouad, M. N., Johnson, R. E., Nagy, M. C., Person, S. D., & Partridge, E. E. (2014). Adherence and retention in clinical trials: A community-based approach. *Cancer, 120*(S7), 1106–1112.

Francis, S. A., & Liverpool, J. (2009). A review of faith-based HIV prevention programs. *Journal of Religion and Health, 48*, 6–15.

Franco, L. M., Pottick, K. J., & Huang, C. C. (2010). Early parenthood in a community context: Neighborhood conditions, race–ethnicity, and parenting stress. *Journal of Community Psychology, 38*(5), 574–590.

Francois, S., Overstreet, S., & Cunningham, M. (2012). Where we live: The unexpected influence of urban neighborhoods on the academic performance of African American adolescents. *Youth & Society, 44*(2), 307–328.

Franklin, A. J. (1999). Invisibility syndrome and racial identity development in psychotherapy and counseling African American men. *The Counseling Psychologist, 27*(6), 761–793.

Frazier, E. F. (1939). *The Negro family in the United States.* Chicago, IL: University of Chicago Press.

Freire, P. (1989). *Pedagogy of the oppressed.* New York, NY: Continuum (Original work published 1970).

French, S., Seidman, E., Allen, L., & Aber, J. (2006). The development of ethnic identity during adolescence. *Developmental Psychology, 42*(1), 1–10.

Frey, D., & Gaertner, S. (1986). Helping and the avoidance of inappropriate interracial behavior: A strategy that perpetuates a nonprejudiced self-image. *Journal of Personality and Social Psychology, 50*, 1035–1090.

Frey, W. H. (2011). *Melting pot cities and suburbs: Racial and ethnic change in metro America in the 2000s.* Washington, DC: Brookings Institution Report, Brookings Institution. Retrieved from http://www.brookings.edu/research/papers/2011/05/04-census-ethnicity-frey

Frey, W. H. (2014). *Diversity explosion: How new racial demographics are remaking America.* Washington, DC: Brookings Institution Press.

Friedman, M. (2016, March 21). *This 20-year-old waitress quit her job after being told her natural hair was "unacceptable".* Retrieved from http://www.newsjs.com/url.php?p=http://www.cosmopolitan.com/career/news/a55516/toronto-waitress-fired-over-natural-hair/

Frumkin, H. (2005). Guest editorial: Health, equity, and the built environment. *Environmental Health Perspectives, 113*(5), A290–A291.

Fu, X., & Heaton, T. B. (2008). Racial and educational homogamy: 1980 to 2000. *Sociological Perspectives, 51,* 735–758.

Fuchs, F. D. (2011). Why do Black Americans have higher prevalence of hypertension? An enigma still unsolved. *Hypertension, 57*(3), 379–380.

FuneralWise. (n.d.). *African American funeral service rituals.* Retrieved from https://www.funeralwise.com/customs/african_american/

Furdyna, H. E., Tucker, M. B., & James, A. D. (2008). Relative spousal warnings and marital happiness among African American and White women. *Journal of Marriage and Family, 70*(2), 332–344.

Furr-Holden, C. D., Lee, M. H., Johnson, R., Milam, A. J., Duncan, A., Reboussin, B. A., . . . Lalongo, N. S. (2015). Neighborhood environment and marijuana use in urban young adults. *Prevention Science, 16*(2), 268–278.

Gadsden, V. L. (1999). Black families in intergenerational and cultural perspectives. In M. E. Lamb (Eds.), *Parenting and child development in "nontraditional" families* (pp. 221–246). Mahwah, NJ: Erlbaum.

Gaertner, S., & Dovidio, J. (2000). The aversive form of racism. In C. Stanger (Ed.), *Stereotypes and prejudice* (pp. 289–304). Ann Arbor, MI: Taylor & Francis.

Gaines, S. O., Larbie, J., Patel, S., Pereira, L., & Sereke-Melake, Z. (2005). Cultural values among African-descended persons in the United Kingdom: Comparisons with European-descended and Asian-descended persons. *Journal of Black Psychology, 31,* 130–151.

Gall, S., Beins, B., & Feldman, A. J. (1996). *The Gale encyclopedia of psychology.* Detroit, MI: Gale Research.

Garb, H. N. (1997). Race bias, social class bias, and gender bias in clinical judgment. *Clinical Psychology: Science and Practice, 4*(2), 99–120.

Garrett, D. (1997). Co-victimization among African-American adolescents. *Adolescence, 32*(127), 635–638.

Gates, G. J. (2013). LGBT parenting in the United States. *The Williams Institute.* Retrieved from http://williamsinstitute.law.ucla.edu/wp-content/uploads/LGBT-Parenting.pdf

Gavin, A. R., Walton, E., Chae, D. H., Alegria, M., Jackson, J. S., & Takeuchi, D. (2010). The associations between socio-economic status and major depressive disorder among Blacks, Latinos, Asians and non-Hispanic Whites: Findings from the Collaborative Psychiatric Epidemiology Studies. *Psychological Medicine, 40*(1), 51–61.

Gay, G. (2000). *Culturally responsive teaching: Theory, practice and research.* New York, NY: Teachers College Press.

Gaylord-Harden, N., Burrows, A. L., & Cunningham, J. A. (2012). A cultural-asset framework for investigating successful adaptation to stress in African American youth. *Child Development Perspectives, 6,* 264–271.

Gaylord-Harden, N. K., So, S., Bai, G. J., Henry, D. B., & Tolan, P. H. (2017). Examining the pathologic adaptation model of community violence exposure in male adolescents of color. *Journal of Clinical Child & Adolescent Psychology, 46*(1), 125–135.

Geller, A., Fagan, J., Tyler, T., & Link, B. G. (2014). Aggressive policing and the mental health of young urban men. *American Journal of Public Health, 104*(12), 2321–2327.

General Accounting Office (GAO). (2003). Distance education: More data could improve education's ability to track technology at minority serving institutions (GAO Report No. GAO-03-900). Washington, DC.

Gentile, D. A., Anderson, C. A., Yukawa, S., Ihori, N., Saleem, M., Ming, L. K., . . . Sakamoto, A. (2009). The effects of prosocial video games on prosocial behaviors: International evidence from correlational, longitudinal, and experimental studies. *Personality & Social Psychology Bulletin, 35*(6), 752–763.

Gentile, D. A., Bender, P. K., & Anderson, C. A. (2017). Violent video game effects on salivary cortisol, arousal, and aggressive thoughts in children. *Computers in Human Behavior, 70,* 39–43.

George, D. S., Holstad, M. M. D., Dilorio, C., & Laderman, G. (2011). Spiritual well-being and health-related quality of life among African-American women with HIV/AIDS. *Applied Research in Quality of Life, 6*(2), 139–157.

George, W. H., & Martinez, L. J. (2002). Victim blaming in rape: Effects of victim and perpetrator race, type of race, and participant racism. *Psychology of Women Quarterly, 26,* 110–119.

Georgie, J., Sean, H., Deborah, M., Matthew, H., & Rona, C. (2016). Peer-led interventions to prevent tobacco, alcohol and/or drug use among young people aged 11–21 years: A systematic review and meta-analysis. *Addiction, 111*(3), 391–407.

Geronimus, A. T. (1991). Teenage childbearing and social and reproductive disadvantage: The evolution of complex questions and the demise of simple answers. *Family Relations, 40*, 463–471.

Geronimus, A. T. (1996). Black/white differences in the relationship of maternal age to birth weight: A population-based test of the weathering hypothesis. *Social Science and Medicine, 42*, 589–597.

Geronimus, A. T., Neidert, L., & Bound, J. (1993). Age patterns of smoking in U.S. black and white women of childbearing age. *American Journal of Public Health, 83*(9), 1258–1264.

Gerrard, M., Stock, M. L., Roberts, M. E., Gibbons, F. X., O'Hara, R. E., Weng, C. Y., & Wills, T. A. (2012). Coping with racial discrimination: The role of substance use. *Psychology of Addictive Behaviors, 26*, 550–560.

Gershoff, E. T., Lansford, J. E., Sexton, H. R., Davis-Kean, P., & Sameroff, A. J. (2012). Longitudinal links between spanking and children's externalizing behaviors in a national sample of White, Black, Hispanic, and Asian American families. *Child Development, 83*(3), 838–843.

Ghandnoosh, N. (2015). *Black lives matter: Eliminating racial inequity in the criminal justice system.* Washington, DC: The Sentencing Project.

Gibbons, F. X., O'Hara, R. E., Stock, M. L., Gerrard, M., Weng, C. Y., & Wills, T. A. (2012). The erosive effects of racism: Reduced self-control mediates the relation between perceived racial discrimination and substance use in African American adolescents. *Journal of Personality and Social Psychology, 102*, 1089–1104.

Gibbs, J. T. (1988). *Young, black and male in America: An endangered species.* Dover, MA: Auburn House.

Gibbs, T. A., Okuda, M., Oquendo, M. A., Lawson, W. B., Wang, S., Thomas, Y. F., & Blanco, C. (2013). Mental health of African Americans and Caribbean blacks in the United States: Results from the national epidemiological survey on alcohol and related conditions. *American Journal of Public Health, 103*(2), 330–338.

Gibson, C. B. (2003). Quality of team service: The role of field independent culture, quality orientation and quality improvement focus. *Small Group Research, 34*(5), 619–646.

Gilbert, D., & Goddard, L. (2007). HIV prevention targeting African American women: Theory, objectives, and outcomes from an African-centered behavior change perspective. *Family and Community Health, 30*(Suppl. 1), S109–S111.

Gilbert, D., Harvey, A. R., & Belgrave, F. Z. (2009). Advancing the Africentric paradigm shift discourse: Building toward evidence-based Africentric interventions in social work practice with African Americans. *Social Work, 54*(3), 243–252.

Giles, M. W. (1978). White enrollment stability and school desegregation: A two level analysis. *American Sociological Review, 43*, 848–865.

Gilliard-Matthews, S., Stevens, R., Nilsen, M., & Dunaev, J. (2015). "You See It Everywhere. It's Just Natural.": Contextualizing the role of peers, family, and neighborhood in initial substance use. *Deviant Behavior, 36*(6), 492–509.

Gillum, F., & Griffith, D. M. (2010). Prayer and spiritual practices for health reasons among American adults: The role of race and ethnicity. *Journal of Religion and Health, 49*, 283–295.

Gingerich, K. J., Turnock, P., Litfin, J. K., & Rosen, L. A. (1998). Diversity and attention deficit hyperactivity disorder. *Journal of Clinical Psychology, 54*(4), 415–426.

Ginther, D. K., Schaffer, W. T., Schnell, J., Masimore, B., Liu, F., Haak, L. L., & Kington, R. (2011). Race, ethnicity and NIH research awards. *Science, 333*(6045), 1015–1019.

Glaeser, E., & Vigdor, J. (2012). The end of the segregated century: Racial separation in America's neighborhoods 1980–2010. *Civic Report*, Manhattan Institute. Retrieved from http://www.manhattaninstitute.org/pdf/cr_66.pdf

Glanville, D. N., & Nowicki, S. (2002). Facial expression recognition and social competence among African American elementary school children: An examination of ethnic differences. *Journal of Black Psychology, 28*(4), 318–329.

Godin, G., Tinka, B. A., Sow, A., Minani, I., Morin, D., & Alary, M. (2008). Correlates of condom use among sex workers and their boyfriends in three West African countries. *AIDS and Behavior, 12*, 441–451.

Goff, P. D., Eberhardt, J. L., Williams, M. J., & Jackson, M. C. (2008). Not yet human: Implicit knowledge, historical dehumanization, and contemporary consequences. *Journal of Personality and Social Psychology, 94*(2), 292–305.

Goldsmith, P. R. (2009). Schools or neighborhoods or both? Race and ethnic segregation and educational attainment. *Social Forces, 87*(4), 1913–1941.

Goldstein, S. B. (2013). Predicting college students' intergroup friendships across race/ethnicity, religion, sexual orientation, and social class. *Equity & Excellence in Education, 46*(4), 502–519.

Gomez, M. A. (1998). *Exchanging our country marks: The transformation of African identities in the colonial and antebellum south.* Chapel Hill: University of North Carolina Press.

Gonzalez, M., Jones, D. J., Kincaid, C. Y., & Cuellar, J. (2012). Neighborhood context and adjustment in African American youths from single mother homes: The intervening role of hopelessness. *Cultural Diversity & Ethnic Minority Psychology, 18*, 109–117.

González, T. (2012). Keeping kids in schools: Restorative justice, punitive discipline, and the school to prison pipeline. *Journal of Law & Education, 41*(2), 281–335.Good, T. L., & Brophy, J. E. (1987). *Looking in classrooms* (4th ed.). New York, NY: Harper & Row.

Goode, W. J. (1982). *The family.* Englewood Cliffs, NJ: Prentice Hall.

Gooden, W. E. (1989). Development of black men in early adulthood. In R. L. Jones (Ed.), *Black adult development and aging* (pp. 63–89). Berkeley, CA: Cobb & Henry.

Goodman, R. M., Speers, M. A., McLeroy, K., Fawcett, S. B., Kegler, M., Parker, E. A., . . . Wallerstein, N. (1998). Identifying and defining the dimensions of community capacity to provide a basis for measurement. *Health Education and Behavior, 25*, 258–278.

Goodman, R. M., Wandersman, A., Chinman, M., Imm, P., & Morrissey, E. (1996). An ecological assessment of community based interventions for prevention and health promotion: Approaches to measuring community coalitions. *American Journal of Community Psychology, 24*(1), 22–61.

Gordon, D. M., Iwamoto, D., Ward, N., Potts, R., & Boyd, E. (2009). Mentoring urban Black middle-school male students: Implications for academic achievement. *The Journal of Negro Education, 78*(3), 277.

Gordon, R. (2003). Inside the Windhoek lager: Liquor and lust in Namibia. In W. Jankowiak & D. Bjradburd (Eds.), *Drugs, labor, and colonial expansion* (pp. 117–134). Tucson: University of Arizona Press.

Gorham, J. (1988). The relationship between verbal teacher immediacy behaviors and student learning. *Communication Education, 37*, 40–53.

Gorman-Smith, D., Tolan, P., & Henry, D. (2002). Predictors of participation in a family-focused preventive intervention for substance use. *Psychology of Addictive Behaviors, 16*(4S), S55–S64.

Goss, D. R., Byrd, W. C., & Hughey, M. W. (2017). Racial authenticity and familial acceptance among transracial adoptees: A bothersome bargain of belonging. *Symbolic Interaction, 40*(2), 147–168.

Govender, K., Penning, S., George, G., & Quinlan, T. (2012). Weighing up the burden of care on caregivers of orphan children: The Amajuba District Child Health and Wellbeing Project, South Africa. *AIDS Care, 24*(6), 712–721.

Governing. (2016). *Governing the states and localities* [State Marijuana Laws in 2016 Map]. Retrieved from http://www.governing.com/gov-data/state-marijuana-laws-map-medical-recreational.html

Goyette, C. H., Conners, C. K., & Ulrich, R. F. (1978). Normative data on revised Conners parent and teacher rating scales. *Journal of Abnormal Child Psychology, 6*(2), 221–236.

Grace, C. M. (2004). Exploring the African American oral tradition: Instructional implications for literacy learning. *Language Arts, 81*, 481–489.

Graham, G., & Gracia, J. N. (2012). Health disparities in boys and men. *American Journal of Public Health, 102*(Suppl. 2), S167.

Grambs, J. D. (1965). The self-concept: Basis for reeducation of Negro youth. In W. C. Kvaraceus, J. S. Gibson, F. K. Patterson, B. Seasholes & J. D. Brambs (Eds.), *Negro self-concept: Implications for school and citizenship* (pp. 11–51). New York, NY: McGraw-Hill.

Gramlich, J. (2017). *Black and white officers see many key aspects of policing differently.* Washington, DC: Pew Research Center.

Granberg, E. M., Simons, L. G., & Simons, R. L. (2015). The role of body size in mate selection among African American young adults. *Sex Roles, 73*(7–8), 340–354.

Grasmuck, S., Martin, J., & Zhao, S. (2009). Ethnoracial identity displays on Facebook. *Journal of Computer-Mediated Communication, 15*(1), 158–188.

Graves, S. L., Jr., & Nichols, K. (2016). *Psychoeducational assessment and intervention for ethnic minority children: Evidence-based approaches.* Washington, DC: American Psychological Association.

Gray-Little, B., & Hafdahl, A. R. (2000). Factors influencing racial comparisons of self-esteem: A quantitative review. *Psychological Bulletin, 126*(1), 26–54.

Grayman-Simpson, N., & Mattis, J. S. (2012). Doing good and feeling good among African Americans: Subjective religiosity, helping, and satisfaction. *Journal of Black Psychology, 39*(4), 411–427.

Greene, B. (1997). Ethnic minority lesbians and gay men: Mental health and treatment issues. In B. Greene (Ed.), *Ethnic and cultural diversity among lesbians and gay men: Psychological perspectives on lesbian and gay issues* (Vol. 3, pp. 216–239). Thousand Oaks, CA: Sage.

Greene, B. (2000). Homophobia. In A. E. Kazdin (Ed.), *Encyclopedia of psychology* (Vol. 4, pp. 146–149). Washington, DC: American Psychological Association.

Greene, B. E. (1997). *Ethnic and cultural diversity among lesbians and gay men.* Thousand Oaks: Sage Publications, Inc.

Greene, J. P., & Forster, G. (2003). *Public high school graduation and college readiness rates in the United States* (Education Working Paper No. 3). New York, NY: Manhattan Institute for Policy Research.

Greene, J. P., & Winters, M. A. (2002). *Public high school graduation and college-readiness rates: 1991–2002* (Education Working Paper No. 8). New York, NY: Manhattan Institute for Policy Research.

Greene, R. L. (1987). Ethnicity and MMPI performance: A review. *Journal of Consulting and Clinical Psychology, 55*(4), 497–513.

Greenwald, A. G., Oakes, M. A., & Hoffman, H. G. (2003). Targets of discrimination: Effects of race on responses to weapons holders. *Journal of Experimental Social Psychology, 39*(4), 399–405.

Greenwald, A. G., Poehlman, T. A., Uhlmann, E. L., & Banaji, M. R. (2009). Understanding and using the implicit association test. *Journal of Personality and Social Psychology, 97*(1), 17–41.

Gregory, S. D., & Phillips, F. B. (1997). "Of mind, body, and spirit": Therapeutic foster care—An innovative approach to healing from an NTU perspective. *Child Welfare, 76*(1), 127–142.

Greig, R. (2003). Ethnic identity development: Implications for mental health in African-American and Hispanic adolescents. *Issues in Mental Health Nursing, 24*(3), 317–332.

Grier, W. H., & Cobbs, P. M. (1968). *Black rage.* New York, NY: Basic Books.

Griffith, D. M., Allen, J. O. J., & Gunter, K. (2011). Social and cultural factors influence African American men's medical help seeking. *Research on Social Work Practice, 21*, 337–347.

Griffith, D. M., Johnson, J. L., Zhang, R., Neighbors, H. W., & Jackson, J. S. (2011). Ethnicity, nativity, and the health of American Blacks. *Journal of Health Care for the Poor and Underserved, 22*(1), 142–156.

Grills, C., Cooke, D., Douglas, J., Subica, A., Villanueva, S., & Hudson, B. (2016). Culture, racial socialization, and positive African American youth development. *Journal of Black Psychology, 42*(4), 343–373.

Grills, C., Villanueva, S., Subica, A. M., & Douglas, J. A. (2014). Communities creating healthy environments: Improving access to healthy foods and safe places to play in communities of color. *Preventive Medicine, 69*, S117–S119.

Grills, C. T. (2004). African psychology. In R. L. Jones (Ed.), *Black psychology* (4th ed., pp. 171–208). Hampton, VA: Cobb & Henry.

Grills, C. T., & Longshore, D. (1996). Africentrism: Psychometric analysis of a self-report measure. *Journal of Black Psychology, 22*, 86–106.

Grissom, J. A., & Redding, C. (2016). Discretion and disproportionality: Explaining the underrepresentation of high-achieving students of color in gifted programs. *AERA Open.* Retrieved from http://journals.sagepub.com/doi/pdf/10.1177/2332858415622175

Grossman, I., Sullivan, P. F., Walley, N., Liu, Y., Dawson, J. R., Gumbs, C., . . . Goldstein, D. B. (2008). Genetic determinants of variable metabolism have little impact on the clinical use of leading antipsychotics in the CATIE study. *Genetics in Medicine, 10*(10), 720–729.

Grover, P. L. (1998). *Preventing substance abuse among children and adolescents: Family-centered approaches* (DHHS Publication No. 3223). Washington, DC: Substance Abuse and Mental Health Services Administration, Center for Substance Abuse Prevention.

Guerrero, E. G., Fenwick, K., Kong, Y., Grella, C., & D'Aunno, T. (2015). Paths to improving engagement among racial and ethnic minorities in addiction health services. *Substance Abuse Treatment, Prevention, and Policy, 10*(1), 40.

Gum, A. M., Watson, M. A., Briscoe, R., Goldsmith, J., Henley, B., & Smith, B. A. (2012). Collaborative design of a church-based, multidimensional senior wellness program by older adults, church leaders, and researchers. *Journal of Religion, Spirituality and Aging, 24*(3), 213–234.

Gureje, O., Lasebikan V., Ephraim-Oluwanuga, O., Olley, B., & Kola, L. (2005). Community study of knowledge and attitude to mental illness in Nigeria. *British Journal of Psychiatry, 186*, 436–444.

Gurin, P., Dey, E. L., Hurtado, S., & Gurin, G. (2002). Diversity and higher education: Theory and impact on educational outcomes. *Harvard Educational Review, 72*(3), 330–366.

Guthrie, R. V. (1998). *Even the rat was white: A historical view of psychology* (2nd ed.). Needham Heights, MA: Allyn & Bacon (Original work published 1976).

Gutierrez, I. A., & Mattis, J. S. (2014). Factors predicting volunteer engagement among urban-residing African American women. *Journal of Black Studies, 45*(7), 599–619.

Gutman, H. G. (1976). *The black family in slavery and freedom, 1750–1925.* New York, NY: Pantheon.

Gutman, L. M., & Eccles, J. (2007). Stage-environment fit during adolescence: Trajectories of family relations and adolescent outcomes. *Developmental Psychology, 43*(2), 522–537.

Gutman, L. M., Eccles, J. S., Peck, S., & Malanchuk, O. (2011). The influence of family relations on trajectories of cigarette and alcohol use from early to late adolescence. *Journal of Adolescence, 34*, 119–128.

Gyekye, K. (1996). *African cultural values.* Accra, Ghana: Sankofa.

Ha, J. H., Greenberg, J. S., & Seltzer, M. M. (2011). Parenting a child with a disability: The role of social support for African American parents. *Families in Society, 92*, 405–411.

Hadden, B. R., Tolliver, W., Snowden, F., & Brown-Manning, R. (2016). An authentic discourse: Recentering race and racism as factors that contribute to police violence against unarmed Black or African American men. *Journal of Human Behavior in the Social Environment, 26*(3–4), 336–349.

Hadnes, M., & Schumacher, H. (2012). The Gods are watching: An experimental study of religion and traditional belief in Burkina Faso. *Journal for the Scientific Study of Religion, 51*(4), 689–704.

Hagen, E. (2009). Biological aspects of race. *AAPA statement on biological aspects of race.* Retrieved from http://www.physanth.org/association/position-statements/biological-aspects-of-race

Hagiwara, N., Penner, L. A., Gonzalez, R., & Albrecht, T. L. (2013). Within-group health disparities among Blacks: The effects of Afrocentric features and unfair treatment. *Cultural Diversity and Ethnic Minority Psychology, 19*(4), 477–480.

Hahn, E. J., & Rado, M. (1996). African American head start parent involvement in drug prevention. *American Journal of Health Behavior, 20*, 41–51.

Halbert, C. H., Bellamy, S., Briggs, V., Bowman, M., Delmoor, E., Kumanyika, S., . . . Johnson, J. C. (2014). Collective efficacy and obesity-related health behaviors in a community sample of African Americans. *Journal of Community Health, 39*(1), 124–131.

Hale, J. E. (1982). *Black children: Their roots, culture, and learning styles.* Provo, UT: Brigham Young University.

Hale, J. E. (2016). Thirty-year retrospective on the learning styles of African American children. *Education and Urban Society, 48*(5), 444–459.

Hale-Benson, J. (1986). *Black children: Their roots, culture, and learning styles* (2nd ed.). Baltimore, MD: Johns Hopkins University Press.

Hale-Benson, J. (1990). *African American children: Their socialization, culture and education* (pp. 1–54). Kansas City, MO: Monograph of the Mid-Continental Regional-Educational Laboratory.

Hall, C. J. (2013). Resilience despite risk: Understanding African-American ACOA's kin and fictive kin relationships. In D. S. Becvar (Ed.), *Handbook of family resilience* (pp. 481–494). New York, NY: Springer.

Hall, D. L., Lattie, E. G., McCalla, J. R., & Saab, P. G. (2016). Translation of the Diabetes Prevention program to ethnic communities in the United States. *Journal of Immigrant Minority Health, 18*, 479–489.

Hall, R. E. (2005). The Euro-Americanization of race: Alien perspective of African Americans vis-á-vis trivialization of skin color. *Journal of Black Studies, 36*(1), 116–128.

Hall, R. E. (2007). Racism as health risk for African-American males: Correlations between hypertension and skin color. *Journal of African American Studies, 11*(3–4), 204–213.

Hallam, J. (2004). *The slave experience: Family. Slavery and the making of America.* New York, NY: Educational Broadcasting Network. Retrieved from http://www.pbs.org/wnet/slavery/experience/family/history.html

Halpern, J., Johnson, M. D., Miranda, J., & Wells, K. B. (2004). The partners in care approach to ethics outcomes in quality improvement programs for depression. *Psychiatric Services, 55*(5), 532–539.

Halpern-Felsher, B. L., Connell, J. P., Spencer, M. B., Aber, J. L., Duncan, G. P., Clifford, E., . . . Cole, S. S. (1997). Neighborhood and family factors predicting educational risk and attainment in African American and white children and adolescents. In J. Brooks-Gunn, G. Duncan & J. L. Aber (Eds.), *Neighborhood poverty: Context and consequences for children* (Vol. 1, pp. 146–173). New York, NY: Russell Sage.

Hamilton, B. E., Martin, J. A., & Ventura, S. J. (2010). Births: Preliminary data for 2009 [online]. *National Vital Statistics Reports, 59*(3). National Center for Health Statistics.

Hamilton, B. E., Rossen, L. M., & Branum, A. M. (2016). Teen birth rates for urban and rural areas in the United States, 2007–2015. *NCHS Data Brief, 264,* 1.

Hamilton, D., Goldsmith, A. H., & Darity, W. (2009). Shedding "light" on marriage: The influence of skin shade on marriage for black females. *Journal of Economic Behavior and Organization, 72*(1), 30–50.

Hamilton, K. (2005). The dialect dilemma. *Black Issues in Higher Education, 22,* 34–36.

Hamilton, K. (2006, June). Hampton steps on cultural nerves with no braids policy. *Diverse Issues in Higher Education, 3*(10).

Hamlat, E. J., Strange, J. P., Alloy, L. B., & Abramson, L. Y. (2014). Early pubertal timing as a vulnerability to depression symptoms: Differential effects of race and sex. *Journal of Abnormal Child Psychology, 42*(4), 527–538.

Hamlet, J. D. (1998). *Afrocentric visions: Studies in culture and communication.* Thousand Oaks, CA: Sage.

Hamm, J. V. (2000). Do birds of a feather flock together? The variable bases for African American, Asian American, and European American adolescents' selection of similar friends. *Developmental Psychology, 36*(2), 209–219.

Hamm, L., & McDonald, S. (2015). Helping hands: Race, neighborhood context, and reluctance in providing job-finding assistance. *Sociological Quarterly, 56*(3), 539–557.

Haney, W., Madaus, G., Abrams, L., Wheelock, A., Miao, J., & Gruia, I. (2004). *The education pipeline in the United States, 1970–2000.* Chestnut Hill, MA: National Board on Educational Testing and Public Policy, Boston College.

Hankerson, S. H., & Weissman, M. M. (2012). Church-based health programs for mental disorders among African Americans: A review. *Psychiatric Services, 63*(3), 243–249.

Hanlon, C., Eshetu, T., Alemayehu, D., Fekadu, A., Semrau, M., Thornicroft, G., . . . Alem, A. (2017). Health system governance to support scale up of mental health care in Ethiopia: A qualitative study. *International Journal of Mental Health Systems, 11*(1), 38.

Hannon, L., DeFina, R., & Bruch, S. (2013). The relationship between skin tone and school suspension for African Americans. *Race and Social Problems, 5*(4), 281.

Hannon, L., Sawyer, P., & Allman, R. M. (2012). The influence of community and the built environment on physical activity. *Journal of Aging and Health, 24*(3), 384–406.

Hansen, B. R., Hodgson, N. A., & Gitlin, L. N. (2016). It's a matter of trust older African Americans speak about their health care encounters. *Journal of Applied Gerontology, 35*(10), 1058–1076.

Hardaway, C. R., Sterrett-Hong, E., Larkby, C. A., & Cornelius, M. D. (2016). Family resources as protective factors for low-income youth exposed to community violence. *Journal of Youth and Adolescence, 45*(7), 1309–1322.

Hardy, K. (2015). Capturing the spirit: Validation of the attitudes toward religious help-seeking scale (ATRHSS) among African-American Christians. *Social Work and Christianity, 42*(3), 385–395.

Hardy, K. V. (2013). Healing the Hidden Wounds of Racial Trauma. *Reclaiming Children And Youth, 22*(1), 24–28.

Harnois, C. E. (2005). Different paths to different feminisms? Bridging multiracial feminist theory and quantitative sociological gender research. *Gender and Society, 19*(6), 809–828.

Harper, S. R., Davis, R. J., Jones, D. E., Mcgowan, B. L., Ingram, T. N., & Spencer, P. C. (2011). Race and racism in the experiences of black male resident assistants at predominantly white universities. *Journal of College Student Development, 52*(2), 180–200.

Harrell, S., Coleman, A., & Adams, T. (2014). Toward a positive womanist psychospirituality: Strengths, gifts, and optimal well-being among women of African descent. In T. Bryant-Davis, A. Austria, D. Kawahara & D. Willis (Eds.), *Religion and spirituality for diverse women: Foundations of strength and resilience* (pp. 49–70). Santa Barbara, CA: Praeger.

Harrington, B., & O'Connell, M. (2016). Video games as virtual teachers: Prosocial video game use by children and adolescents from different socioeconomic groups is associated with increased empathy and prosocial behaviour. *Computers in Human Behavior, 63*, 650–658.

Harrington, E. F., Shipherd, J. C., & Crowther, J. H. (2010). Trauma, binge eating, and the "Strong Black Woman". *Journal of Consulting and Clinical Psychology, 78*(4), 469–479.

Harris, A. C. (1996). African American and Anglo-American gender identities: An empirical study. *Journal of Black Psychology, 22*(2), 182–194.

Harris, M. I., Flegal, K. M., Cowie, C. C., Eberhardt, M. S., Goldstein, D. E., Little, R. R., . . . Byrd-Holt, D. D. (1998). Prevalence of diabetes, impaired fasting glucose, and impaired glucose tolerance in U.S. adults. The Third National Health and Nutrition Examination Survey, 1988–1994. *Diabetes Care, 21*(4), 518–524.

Hart, A. J., Whalen, P. J., Shin, L. M., McInerney, S. C., Fischer, H., & Rauch, S. L. (2000). Differential response in the human amygdala to racial outgroup vs. in-group face stimuli. *Neuroreport, 11*(11), 2351–2354.

Hart, B. M., Wicherski, M., & Kohout, J. L. (2011). *Faculty in U.S. and Canadian Graduate Departments of Psychology 2010-2011*. Washington, DC: APA, Center for Workforce Studies.

Harvey, A. R., & Hill, R. B. (2004). Africentric youth and family rites of passage program: Promoting resilience among at-risk African American youths. *Social Work, 49*, 65–74.

Harvey, I. S., & Cook, L. (2010). Exploring the role of spirituality in self-management practices among older African-American and non-Hispanic White women with chronic conditions. *Chronic Illness, 6*(2), 111–124.

Harwood, S. A., Huntt, M. B., Mendenhall, R., & Lewis, J. A. (2012). Racial microaggressions in the residence halls: Experiences of students of color at a predominantly White university. *Journal of Diversity in Higher Education, 5*, 159–173.

Hatfield, E., & Walster, G. W. (1978). *A new look at love*. Reading, MA: Addison-Wesley.

Hathaway, S. R., & McKinley, J. C. (1940). A multiphasic personality schedule (Minnesota): I. Construction of the schedule. *Journal of Psychology, 10*, 249–254.

Hausmann, L. R. M., Schofield, J. W., & Woods, R. L. (2007). Sense of belonging as a predictor of intentions to persist among African American and white first-year college students. *Research in Higher Education, 48*(7), 803–839.

Hawkins, D. J., Catalano, R. F., & Miller, J. Y. (1992). Risk and protective factors for alcohol and other drug problems in adolescence and early adulthood: Implications for substance abuse prevention. *Psychological Bulletin, 112*, 64–105.

Hayes, W. A. (1982). Radical black behaviorism. In R. L. Jones (Ed.), *Black psychology* (2nd ed., pp. 37–47). Cambridge, MA: Harper & Row.

Haynes, N. (1995). How skewed is The Bell Curve? *Journal of Black Psychology, 21*(3), 275–292.

Haynes, V., Escoffery, C., Wilkerson, C., Bell, R., & Flowers, L. (2014). Adaptation of a cervical cancer education program for African Americans in the faith-based community, Atlanta, Georgia. *Preventing Chronic Disease, 11*, 1–9.

Hayward, C., Gotlib, I. H., Kchraedley, P. K., & Litt, I. F. (1999). Ethnic differences in the association between pubertal status and symptoms of depression in adolescent girls. *Journal of Adolescent Health, 25*(2), 143–149.

Hayward, L. E., Tropp, L. R., Hornsey, M. J., & Barlow, F. K. (2017). Toward a comprehensive understanding of intergroup contact: Descriptions and mediators of positive and negative contact among majority and minority Groups. *Personality and Social Psychology Bulletin, 43*(3), 347–364.

Hayward, R. D., & Krause, N. (2015). Religion and strategies for coping with racial discrimination among African Americans and Caribbean Blacks. *International Journal of Stress Management, 22*(1), 70–91.

Heigi, K. E., & Bergner, R. M. (2010). What is love? An empirically-based essentialist account. *Journal of Social and Personal Relationships, 27*, 620–636.

Helms, J. (2008). *A race is a nice thing to have: A guide to being a white person or understanding the white persons in your life.* Hanover, MA: Microtraining Associates.

Helms, J. E. (1990). *Black and white racial identity: Theory, research and practice.* New York, NY: Greenwood Press.

Helms, J. E., & Cook, D. A. (1999). *Using race and culture in counseling and psychotherapy: Theory and process.* Needham Heights, MA: Allyn & Bacon.

Helms, J. E., Jernigan, M., & Mascher, J. (2005). The meaning of race in psychology and how to change it: A methodological perspective. *American Psychologist, 60*(1), 27–36.

Henderson, L. (2017). Racial discrimination, religion, and the African American drinking paradox. *Race and Social Problems, 9*(1), 79–90.

Henriksen, L., Schleicher, N. C., Dauphinee, A. L., & Fortmann, S. P. (2011). Targeted advertising, promotion, and price for menthol cigarettes in California high school neighborhoods. *Nicotine & Tobacco Research, 14*(1), 116–121.

Henry J. Kaiser Family Foundation. Retrieved online at http://kff.org/medicare/issue-brief/poverty-among-seniors-an-updated-analysis-of-national-and-state-level-poverty-rates-under-the-official-and-supplemental-poverty-measures/

Henry, J. S., Lambert, S. F., & Smith Bynum, M. (2015). The protective role of maternal racial socialization for African American adolescents exposed to community violence. *Journal of Family Psychology, 29*(4), 548–557.

Henry, P., & Sears, D. (2002). The symbolic racism 2000 scale. *Political Psychology, 23*, 253–283.

Herrnstein, R. J., & Murray, C. (1994). *The bell curve: Intelligence and class structure in American life.* New York, NY: Free Press.

Hervet, B. N. (2014). *African American women in the urban Black church: The experience of black female clergy* (Doctoral dissertation). Capella University.

Hicken, M. T., Lee, H., Morenoff, J., House, J. S., & Williams, D. R. (2014). Racial/ethnic disparities in hypertension prevalence: Reconsidering the role of chronic stress. *American Journal of Public Health, 104*(1), 117–123.

Hickson, D. M. A., Lewis, T. T., Mount, D. L., Mount, D. L., Younge, S. N., Jenkins, W. C., . . . Williams, D. R. (2012). The associations of multiple dimensions of discrimination and abdominal fat in African American adults: The Jackson Heart Study. *Annals of Behavioral Medicine, 43*(1), 4–14.

Hill, D., & Mrug, S. (2015). School-level correlates of adolescent tobacco, alcohol, and marijuana use. *Substance use & Misuse, 50*(12), 1518–1528.

Hill, J. L., Mance, G. A., Anderson, R. E., & Smith, E. P. (2012). The role of ethnic identity in interventions to promote positive adolescent development. *Global Journal of Community Psychology Practice, 2*(3), 1–12. Retrieved from http://www.gjcpp.org/

Hill, K. D. (2009). Code-switching pedagogies and African American student voices: Acceptance and resistance. *Journal of Adolescent & Adult Literacy, 53*(2), 120–131.

Hill, L. K., Hoggard, L. S., Richmond, A. S., Gray, D. L., Williams, D. P., & Thayer, J. F. (2017). Examining the association between perceived discrimination and heart rate variability in African Americans. *Cultural Diversity and Ethnic Minority Psychology, 23*(1), 5–14.

Hill, M. E. (2002). Skin color and the perception of attractiveness among African Americans: Does gender make a difference? *Social Psychology Quarterly, 65*(1), 77–91.

Hill, P. D., & Hood, R. W. (1999). *Measures of religiosity.* Birmingham, AL: Religious Education Press.

Hill, R. B. (1971). *The strengths of black families.* New York, NY: Emerson Hall.

Hill, R. B. (1998). Understanding black family functioning: A holistic perspective. *Journal of Comparative Family Studies, 29*(1), 15–25.

Hill, S. A. (1999). Racial socialization. In S. A. Hill (Ed.), *African American children* (pp. 89–111). Thousand Oaks, CA: Sage.

Hilliard, A. G. (1983). IQ and the courts: Larry P. vs. Wilson Riles and PASE vs. Hannon. *Journal of Black Psychology, 10*(1), 1–18.

Hilliard, A. G. (1992). Behavioral style, culture, and teaching and learning. *Journal of Negro Education, 61*(3), 370–377.

Himle, J. A., Baser, R. E., Taylor, R. J., Campbell, R. D., & Jackson, J. S. (2009). Anxiety disorders among African Americans, blacks of Caribbean descent, and non-Hispanic whites in the United States. *Journal of Anxiety Disorders, 23*(5), 578.

Hofferth, S. L., & Reid, R. (2002). Early childbearing and children's achievement and behavior over time. *Perspectives on Sexual and Reproductive Health, 34*(1), 41–49.

Hofferth, S. L., Reid, L., & Mott, F. L. (2001). The effects of early childbearing on schooling over time. *Family Planning Perspectives, 33*(6), 259–267.

Hoffman, A. (2017). Embracing new approach, African-American families help kids deal with racism. *WHY*. Retrieved from http://www.newsworks .org/index.php/local/education/104725-embracing-new-approach-african-americans-helping-kids-deal-with-racism-

Hoffmann, N., & Metz, T. (2017). What can the capabilities approach learn from an Ubuntu ehic? A relational approach to development theory. *World Development, 97*, 153–164.

Hofstede, G. H. (2001). *Culture's consequences: Comparing values, behaviors, institutions, and organizations across nations* (2nd ed.). Thousand Oaks, CA: Sage.

Hokanson, J. E., & Calden, G. (1960). Negro-white differences on the MMPI. *Journal of Clinical Psychology, 16*, 32–33.

Holbrook, C. T., & Phillips, G. (1994). Natural history of sickle cell disease and the effects on biopsychosocial development. *Journal of Health and Social Policy, 5*(3/4), 7–18.

Holley, L. C., Tavassoli, K. Y., & Stromwall, L. K. (2016). Mental illness discrimination in mental health treatment programs: Intersections of race, ethnicity, and sexual orientation. *Community Mental Health Journal, 52*(3), 311–322.

Hollie, S. (2001). Acknowledging the language of African American students: Instructional strategies. *English Journal, 90*, 54–59.

Hollingshead, A. B., & Redlich, F. (1958). *Social class and mental illness.* New York, NY: Wiley.

Holt, C. L., Clark, E. M., Debnam, K. J., & Roth, D. L. (2014). Religion and health in African Americans: The role of religious coping. *American Journal of Health Behavior, 38*(2), 190–199.

Holt, C. L., Clark, E. M., Roth, D. L., Crowther, M., Kohler, C., Fouad, M., . . . Southward, P. L. (2010). Development and validation of an instrument to assess perceived social influence on health behaviors. *Journal of Health Psychology, 15*(8), 1225–1235.

Holt, C. L., Schulz, E., Williams, B., Clark, E. M., Wang, M. Q., & Southward, P. L. (2012). Assessment of religious and spiritual capital in African American Communities. *Journal of Religion and Health, 51*(4), 1061–1074.

Hood, K., Hart, A., Belgrave, F. Z., Tademy, R., & Jones, R. A. (2012). Health decision-making among African American men recruited from urban barbershops: The role of trust. *Journal of the National Medical Association, 104*, 351–359.

hooks, b. (1999). *Happy to be nappy.* New York, NY: Hyperion.

Hooper, M. W., Zhao, W., Byrne, M. M., Caban-Martinez, A., Dietz, N. A., Lee, D. J., . . . Messiah, A. (2011). Menthol cigarette smoking and health, Florida 2007 BRFSS. *American Journal of Health Behavior, 35*, 3–14.

Horton, J. O., & Horton, L. E. (1997). *In hope of liberty: Culture, community and protest among northern free blacks, 1700–1860.* New York, NY: Oxford University Press.

House, B. R., Silk, J. B., Henrich, J., Barrett, H. C., Scelza, B. A., Boyette, A. H., . . . Laurence, S. (2013). Ontogeny of prosocial behavior across diverse societies. *Proceedings of the National Academy of Sciences, 110*(36), 14586–14591.

Houston, L. N. (1990). *Psychological principles and the Black experience.* Lanham, MD: University Press of America.

Howard, T. C. (2008). "Who really cares?" The disenfranchisement of African American males in PreK-12 schools: A critical race theory perspective. *Teachers College Record, 110*(5), 954–985.

Howden, L. M., & Meyer, J. A. (2011). *Age and sex composition: 2010.* Washington, DC: U.S. Department of Commerce, Economics and Statistics Administration, U.S. Census Bureau.

Hudson, C. G. (1988). The social class and mental illness correlation: Implications of the research for policy and practice. *Journal of Sociology and Social Welfare, 15*(1), 27–54.

Hudson, D. L., Eaton, J., Lewis, P., Grant, P., Sewell, W., & Gilbert, K. (2016). "Racism? Just look at our neighborhoods" Views on racial discrimination and coping among African American men in Saint Louis. *The Journal of Men's Studies, 24*(2), 130–150.

Huebschmann, A. G., Campbell, L. J., Brown, C. S., & Dunn, A. L. (2016). "My hair or my health":

Overcoming barriers to physical activity in African American women with a focus on hairstyle-related factors. *Women & Health, 56*(4), 428–447.

Hughes, D., & Johnson, D. (2001). Correlates in children's experiences of parents' racial socialization behaviors. *Journal of Marriage and Family, 63*(4), 981–995.

Hughes, D., Rodriguez, J., Smith, E. P., Johnson, D. J., Stevenson, H. C., & Spicer, P. (2006). Parents' ethnic-racial socialization practices: A review of research and directions for future study. *Developmental Psychology, 42*(5), 747–770.

Hughes, D., Witherspoon, D., Rivas-Drake, D., & West-Bey, N. (2009). Received ethnic–racial socialization messages and youths' academic and behavioral outcomes: Examining the mediating role of ethnic identity and self-esteem. *Cultural Diversity and Ethnic Minority Psychology, 15*(2), 112–124.

Hughes, M., & Hertel, B. R. (1990). The significance of color remains: A study of life chances, mate selection, and ethnic consciousness among black Americans. *Social Forces, 68*(4), 1105–1120.

Hughes, M., Kiecolt, K. J., Keith, V. M., & Demo, D. H. (2015). Racial identity and well-being among African Americans. *Social Psychology Quarterly, 78*(1), 25–48.

Humphries, M. L., Parker, B. L., & Jagers, R. J. (2000). Predictors of moral reasoning among African American children: A preliminary study. *Journal of Black Psychology, 26*(1), 51–64.

Hunt, J. B., Eisenberg, D., Lu, L., & Gathright, M. (2015). Racial/ethnic disparities in mental health care utilization among U.S. college students: Applying the Institution of Medicine definition of health care disparities. *Academic Psychiatry, 39*(5), 520–526.

Hunt, L. L., & Hunt, M. O. (1999). Regional patterns of African American church attendance: Revisiting the semi-involuntary thesis. *Social Forces, 78*(2), 779–791.

Hunter, A. G., & Davis, J. E. (1994). Hidden voices of Black men: The meaning, structure, and complexity of manhood. *Journal of Black Studies, 25*, 20–40.

Hunter, B. A., Mohatt, N. V., Prince, D. M., Thompson, A. B., Matlin, S. L., & Tebes, J. K. (2017). Sociopsychological mediators of the relationship between behavioral health stigma and psychiatric symptoms. *Social Science & Medicine, 181*, 177–183.

Hunter, M. L. (2002). "If you're light you're alright": Light skin color as social capital for women of color. *Gender and Society, 16*(2), 175–193.

Hunter, M. L. (2005). *Race, gender, and the politics of skin tone.* New York, NY: Routledge.

Hurd, N. M., Sellers, R. M., Cogburn, C. D., Butler-Barnes, S. T., & Zimmerman, M. A. (2012). Racial identity and depressive symptoms among black emerging adults: The moderating effects of neighborhood racial composition. *Developmental Psychology, 49*(5), 938–950.

Hurd, N. M., & Zimmerman, M. (2010). Natural mentors, mental health, and risk behaviors: A longitudinal analysis of African American adolescents transitioning into adulthood. *American Journal of Community Psychology, 46*(1), 36–48.

Huyser-Honig, J. (n.d.), Why Churches are engaging hip hop culture. *Calvin Institute of Christian Worship.* Retrieved from http://worship.calvin.edu/resources/resource-library/why-churches-are-engaging-hip-hop-culture

Hyers, L. L. (2001). A secondary survey analysis study of African American ethnic identity orientations in two national samples. *Journal of Black Psychology, 27*(2), 139–171.

Ibarra, R. A. (2001). *Beyond affirmative action: Reframing the context of higher education.* Madison: University of Wisconsin Press.

IBPOEW (Improved Benevolent and Protective Order Elks of the World, Inc). (n.d.). Retrieved from http://ibpoew.org/our-brief-history.html

Ihrke, D. K., & Faber, C. S. (2012). *Geographical mobility: 2005 to 2010.* Washington, DC: United States Census Bureau.

Institute for Social Research. (n.d.). *The National Survey of American Life: Coping with stress in the 21st century.* Ann Arbor, MI: Author. Retrieved from http://rcgd.isr.umich.edu/prba/nsal.htm.

Institute of Medicine. (1991). *Disability in America.* Washington, DC: National Academy Press.

Irvine, J. J. (2012). Complex relationships between multicultural education and special education. *Journal of Teacher Education, 63*(4), 268–274.

Iscoe, I. (1974). Community psychology and the competent community. *American Psychologist, 29*, 607–613.

Izadi, E. (2015). *The incidents that led to the University of Missouri president's resignation.* Retrieved from https://www.washingtonpost.com/news/grade-point/wp/2015/11/09/the-incidents-that-led-to-the-university-of-missouri-presidents-resignation/?utm_term=.edbe0f83d649 on 1/29/17

Jaccard, J., Blanton, H., & Dodge, T. (2005). Peer influences on risk behavior: An analysis of the effects of close friends. *Developmental Psychology, 41*, 135–147.

Jackson, J. S., & Antonucci, T. C. (2005). Physical and mental health consequences of aging in place and aging out of place among black Caribbean immigrants. *Research in Human Development, 2*(4), 229–244.

Jackson, M., Barth, J. M., Powell, N., & Lochman, J. E. (2006). Classroom contextual effects of race on children's peer nominations. *Child Development, 77*(5), 1325–1337.

Jackson, M., Stephens, R., & Smith, R. (1997). Afrocentric treatment in residential substance abuse care. *The Iwo San Journal of Substance Abuse Treatment, 14*(1), 87–92.

Jacob, S., Byrne, M., & Keenan, K. (2009). Neonatal physiological regulation is associated with perinatal factors: A study of neonates born to healthy African American women living in poverty. *Infant Mental Health Journal, 30*(1), 82–94.

Jagers, R. J., Smith, P., Mock, L. O., & Dill, E. (1997). An Afrocultural social ethos: Component orientations and some social implications. *Journal of Black Psychology, 23*(4), 328–343.

Jagers, R. J., Sydnor, K., Mouttapa, M., & Flay, B. R. (2007). Protective factors associated with pre-adolescent violence: Preliminary work on a cultural model. *American Journal of Community Psychology, 40*, 138–145.

James, W. H., & Johnson, S. L. (1996). *Doing drugs: Patterns of African American addiction.* Austin: University of Texas Press.

James-Todd, T., Senie, R., & Terry, M. B. (2011). Racial/ethnic differences in hormonally-active hair product use: A plausible risk factor for health disparities. *Journal of Immigrant and Minority Health, 14*(3), 506–511.

Jamison, D. F. (2016). Kobi K. K. Kambon (Joseph A. Baldwin) portrait of an African-Centered Psychologist. *Journal of Black Studies, 47*(6), 592–609.

Jarrett, R. L. (1999). Successful parenting in high-risk neighborhoods. *The Future of Children, 9*(2), 45–50.

Jaynes, G. (1982, September 30). Suit of race recalls lines drawn under slavery. *New York Times,* p. 18.

Jemmott, L. S., & Jemmott, J. B. (2007). Applying the theory of reasoned action to HIV risk-reduction behavioral interventions. In I. Ajzen, D. Albarracín & R. Hornik (Eds.), *Prediction and change of health behavior: Applying the reasoned action approach* (pp. 243–263). Mahwah, NJ: Erlbaum.

Jencks, C., & Mayer, S. (1990). The social consequences of growing up in a poor neighborhood. In L. E. Lynn & M. F. H. McGeary (Eds.), *Inner-city poverty in the United States* (pp. 111–186). Washington, DC: National Academy Press.

Jenkins, A. H. (1995). *Psychology and African Americans: A humanistic approach.* Boston, MA: Allyn & Bacon.

Jenkins, M. (2006). Gullah Island dispute resolution: An example of Afrocentric restorative justice. *Journal of Black Studies, 37*(2), 299–319.

Jensen, A. R. (1969). How much can we boost I.Q. and scholastic achievement? *Harvard Educational Review, 39*(1), 1–123.

Jerald, C. D. (2001). *Dispelling the myth revisited.* Washington, DC: The Education Trust. Retrieved from http://www.eric.ed.gov/ERICWebPortal/search/detailm ini.jsp?_nfpb=true&_&ERICExtSearch_SearchValue_0=ED462485&ERICExtSearch_SearchType_0=no&accno=ED462485.

Jessor, R., & Jessor, S. L. (1977). *Problem behavior and psychosocial development: A longitudinal study of youth.* San Diego, CA: Academic Press.

Jiang, G., Sun, F., & Marsiglia, F. F. (2016). Rural-urban disparities in adolescent risky behaviors: Family social capital perspective. *Journal of Community Psychology, 44*(8), 1027–1039.

Jimenez, D. E., Cook, B. L., Bartels, S. J., & Alegria, M. (2013), Disparities in mental health service use among racial and ethnic minority elderly adults. *Journal of the American Geriatric Society, 61*(1), 18–25.

Jin, Y., & Li, J. (2017). When newbies and veterans play together: The effect of video game content, context and experience on cooperation. *Computers in Human Behavior, 68*, 556–563.

Johnson, A. M., Godsil, R., MacFarlane, J., Tropp, L., & Goff, P. A. (2016). The "Good Hair" study: Explicit and implicit attitudes toward Black women's hair. *Perception Institute.* Retrieved from https://perception.org/goodhair/

Johnson, J. H., & Kasarda, J. D. (2011). *Six disruptive demographic trends: What the census 2010 will reveal.* Retrieved from http://www.kenanflagler.unc.edu/~/media/files/kenaninstitute/UNC_KenanInstitute_2010Census

Johnson, K. A., Dolan, M. K., & Sonnett, J. (2011). Speaking of looting: An analysis of racial propaganda in national television coverage of Hurricane Katrina. *Howard Journal of Communications, 22*(3), 302–318.

Johnson, P. L., & Flake, E. M. (2007). Maternal depression and child outcomes. *Psychiatric Annals Online, 37*(6). Retrieved from http://www.psychiatricannalsonline.com/view.asp?rid=22202

Jones, D., Zalot, A., Foster, S., Sterrett, E., & Chester, C. (2007). A review of childrearing in African-American single mother families: The relevance of a coparenting framework. *Journal of Child and Family Studies, 16,* 671–683.

Jones, D. J., Foster, S, Forehand, G., & O'Connell, C. (2005). Neighborhood violence and psychosocial adjustment in low-income urban African American children: Physical symptoms as a marker of distress. *Journal of Child and Family Studies, 14,* 237–259.

Jones, H. L., Cross, W. E., & DeFour, D. C. (2007). Race-related stress, racial identity attitudes, and mental health among Black women. *Journal of Black Psychology, 33*(2), 208–231.

Jones, J. (1997). *Prejudice and racism.* New York, NY: McGraw-Hill (Originally published in 1972).

Jones, J. (2003). TRIOS: A psychological theory of the African legacy in American culture. *Journal of Social Issues, 59*(1), 217–243.

Jones, J. (2007). Exposure to chronic community violence: Resilience in African American children. *Journal of Black Psychology, 33*(2), 125–149.

Jones, J. M., Dovidio, J. F., & Vietze, D. L. (2013). *The psychology of diversity: Beyond prejudice and racism.* Hoboken, NJ: Wiley.

Jones, R. (1972). *Black psychology.* New York, NY: Harper & Row.

Jones, R. (Ed.). (1989). *Black adolescents.* Hampton, VA: Cobb & Henry.

Jones, R. (Ed.). (1996). *Handbook of tests and measurements for black populations.* Hampton, VA: Cobb & Henry.

Jones, R. (Ed.). (1998a). *African American children, youth, and parenting.* Hampton, VA: Cobb & Henry.

Jones, R. (Ed.). (1998b). *African American identity development.* Hampton, VA: Cobb & Henry.

Jones, R. (Ed.). (1998c). *African American mental health.* Hampton, VA: Cobb & Henry.

Jones, R. (Ed.). (1999). *Advances in African American psychology.* Hampton, VA: Cobb & Henry.

Jones, R. (2004). *Black psychology* (4th ed.). Hampton, VA: Cobb & Henry.

Jones, S. C., & Neblett, E. W. (2016). Racial-ethnic protective factors and mechanisms in psychosocial prevention and intervention programs for Black youth. *Clinical Child and Family Psychology Review, 19*(2), 134–161.

Jones, S. C., & Neblett, E. W. (2017). Future directions in research on racism-related stress and racial-ethnic protective factors for Black youth. *Journal of Clinical Child & Adolescent Psychology, 46*(5), 754–766.

Jordi, R. (2011). Reframing the concept of reflection: Consciousness, experiential learning, and reflective learning practices. *Adult Education Quarterly: A Journal of Research and Theory, 61*(2), 181–197.

Journal of Black Psychology. (1995). Various articles. *21*(3).

Journal of Black Psychology. (2004). Various articles. *30*(1).

Juniper, K. C., Oman, R. F., Hamm, R. M., & Kerby, D. S. (2004). The relationships among constructs in the health belief model and the transtheoretical model among African-American college women for physical activity. *American Journal of Health Promotion, 8,* 354–357.

Kahlenberg, R. D. (2001). *All together now: Creating middle-class schools through public school choice.* Washington, DC: Brookings Institution Press.

Kain, J. F., & Singleton, K. (1996, May–June). Equality of educational opportunity revisited. *New England Economic Review,* (Special Issue), 87–112.

Kaiser Family Foundation. (2010). *Generation M2: Media in the lives of 8- to 18-year-olds.* Menlo Park, CA: Kaiser Family Foundation.

Kambon, K. (1998). *African-black psychology in the American context: An African-centered approach.* Tallahassee, FL: Nubian Nation.

Kambon, K. (2003). *Cultural misorientation.* Tallahassee, FL: Nubian Nation.

Kambon, K., & Bowen-Reid, T. (2009). Africentric theories of African American personality: Basic constructs and assessments. In H. A. Neville, B. M. Tynes, & S. O. Utsey (Eds.), *Handbook of African American Psychology* (pp. 61–74). Thousand Oaks, CA: Sage.

Kandel, D. (2006, November 13). *Developmental trajectories of drug use among African Americans.* Presentation at the National Institute of Drug Abuse Conference on Drug Use Trajectories among African Americans, Bethesda, MD.

Kann, L., McManus, T., Harris, W. A., Shanklin, S. L., Flint, K. H. Hawkins, J., ... Zaza, S. (2016). Youth risk behavior surveillance: United States, 2015. *Morbidity and Mortality Weekly Report, 65*(6), 1–174.

Kaphagawani, D. N., & Malherbe, J. S. (1998). African epistemology. In P. H. Coetzee & A. P. J. Roux (Eds.), *Philosophy from Africa* (pp. 205–216). London, England: Oxford University Press.

Kardiner, A., & Ovesey, L. (1951). *The mark of oppression: A psychosocial study of the American Negro.* New York, NY: Norton.

Kardiner, A., & Ovesey, L. (1962). *The mark of oppression: Explorations in the personality of the American Negro.* Cleveland, OH: Meridian Books.

Karenga, M. (1988). *Introduction to black studies.* Los Angeles, CA: University of Sankore Press.

Kastanis, A., & Gates, G. J. (2013). LGBT African-American individuals and African-American same-sex couples. *The Williams Institute.* Retrieved from https://williamsinstitute.law.ucla.edu/research/census-lgbt-demographics-studies/lgbt-african-american-oct-2013/

Katz, I., & Hass, G. (1988). Racial ambivalence and American value conflict: Correlational and priming studies of dual cognitive structures. *Journal of Personality and Social Psychology, 55*(6), 893–905.

Kaufman, J., & Rosenbaum, J. (1992). The education and employment of low-income black youth in white suburbs. *Educational Evaluation and Policy Analysis, 14*(3), 229–240.

Keels, M., Duncan, G. J., Deluca, S., Mendenhall, R., & Rosenbaum, J. (2005). Fifteen years later: Can residential mobility programs provide a permanent escape from neighborhood segregation, crime and poverty? *Demography, 42*(1), 51–73.

Keenan, K., Culbert, K. M., Grimm, K. J., Hipwell, A. E., & Strepp, S. D. (2014). Timing and tempo: Exploring the complex association between pubertal development and depression in African American and European American girls. *Journal of Abnormal Psychology, 123*(4), 725–736.

Keith, F. M., & Herring, C. (1991). Skin tone and stratification in the black community. *American Journal of Sociology, 97,* 760–778.

Keith, V. M., Lincoln, K. D., Taylor, R. J., & Jackson, J. S. (2010). Discriminatory experiences and depressive symptoms among African American women: Do skin tone and mastery matter? *Sex Roles, 62*(1), 48–59.

Kekwaletswe, T. C. (2008). Africentric values and ethnic identity as predictors of HIV risk behavior, substance use, and psychopathology among African American girls seeking outpatient psychiatric services. *Dissertation Abstracts International: Section B: The Sciences and Engineering, 68*(7-B), 4829.

Kelley, S. J., Whitley, D. M., & Campos, P. E. (2011). Behavior problems in children raised by grandmothers: The role of caregiver distress, family resources, and the home environment. *Children and Youth Services Review, 33,* 2138–2145.

Kellogg Foundation. (2012). *Cultures of giving: Energizing and expanding philanthropy by and for communities of color.* Retrieved from http://foundationcenter.org/pnd/connections/conn_item.jhtml;jsessionid=ZTYCOGPKHMNKXLAQBQ4CGXD5AAAACI2F?id=366500014

Kendzor, D. E., Businelle, M. S., Reitzel, L. R., Rios, D. M., Scheuermann, T. S., Pulvers, K., & Ahluwalia, J. S. (2014). Everyday discrimination is associated with nicotine dependence among African American, Latino, and White smokers. *Nicotine & Tobacco Research, 16*(6), 633–640.

Kennamer, J. D., Honnold, J., Bradford, J., & Hendricks, M. (2000, December). Differences in disclosure of sexuality among African American and White gay/bisexual men: Implications for HIV/AIDS prevention. *AIDS Education and Prevention, 12*(6), 519–531.

Kennedy, S. B., Nolen, S., Applewhite, J., Pan, Z., Shamblen, S., & Vanderhoff, K. J. (2007). A quantitative study on the condom-use behaviors of eighteen- to twenty-four-year-old urban African American males. *AIDS Patient Care and STDs, 21,* 306–320.

Kerpelman, J. L., Eryigit, S., & Stephens, C. J. (2008). African American adolescents' future education orientation: Associations with self-efficacy, ethnic identity, and perceived parental support. *Journal of Youth and Adolescence, 37*(8), 997–1008.

Kessler, R. C., & Neighbors, H. W. (1986). A new perspective on the relationships among race, social class, and psychological distress. *Journal of Health and Social Behavior, 27*(2), 107–115.

Keyes, C. L. (2002). *Rap music and street consciousness.* Champaign: University of Illinois.

Keyser, V., Gamst, G., Meyers, L. S., Der-Karabetian, A., & Morrow, G. (2014). Predictors of self-perceived cultural competence among children's mental health providers. *Cultural Diversity and Ethnic Minority Psychology, 20*(3), 324–335.

Khalifa, M. A., Gooden, M. A., & Davis, J. E. (2016). Culturally responsive school leadership: A synthesis of the literature. *Review of Educational Research, 86*(4), 1272–1311.

Kids Count. (n.d.). *Children in poverty by race and ethnicity.* Retrieved from https://www.khanacademy.org/about; http://datacenter.kidscount.org/data/tables/44-children-in-poverty-by-race-and-ethnicity#detailed/1/any/false/573,869,36,868,867/10,11,9,12,1,185,13/324,323

Kiecolt, K. J., Momplaisir, H., & Hughes, M. (2016). Racial identity, racial discrimination, and depressive symptoms among African Americans and Afro-Caribbeans. In J. E. Stets & R. T. Serpe (Eds.), *New directions in identity theory and research* (pp. 369–393). New York, NY: Oxford University Press.

Killen, M., Kelly, M., Richardson, C., Crystal, D., & Ruck, M. (2010). European American children's and adolescents' evaluations of interracial exclusion. *Group Processes and Intergroup Relations, 13,* 283–300.

Kilpatrick, D. G., Acierno, R., Saunders, B., Resnick, H. S., Best, C. L., & Schnurr, P. P. (2000). Risk factors for adolescent substance abuse and dependence: Data from a national sample. *Journal of Consulting and Clinical Psychology, 68*(1), 19–30.

Kim, S. (2017). National culture and public service motivation: Investigating the relationship using Hofstede's five cultural dimensions. *International Review of Administrative Sciences, 83*(Suppl. 1), 23–40.

Kim, Y. K., Park, J. J., & Koo, K. K. (2015). Testing self-segregation: Multiple-group structural modeling of college students' interracial friendship by race. *Research in Higher Education, 56*(1), 57.

Kimmel, A. D., Masiano, S. P., Bono, R. S., Martin, E. G., Belgrave, F. Z. Adimora, A. A., . . . Sabik, L. M. (under revisions). Structural barriers to comprehensive, coordinated HIV care: Geographic accessibility in the U.S. South.

King, A. C. (2001). Interventions to promote physical activity by older adults. *The Journals of Gerontology Series A: Biological Sciences and Medical Sciences, 56*(suppl_2), 36–46.

King, A. E. O. (1997). Understanding violence among young African American males: An Afrocentric perspective. *Journal of Black Studies, 28*(1), 79–96.

King, A. E. O., & Allen, T. T. (2009). Personal characteristics of the ideal African American marriage partner: A survey of adult black men and women. *Journal of Black Studies, 39,* 570–588.

King, J. E. (1994). The purpose of schooling for African American children: Including cultural knowledge. In E. R. Hollins, J. E. King & W. C. Hayman (Eds.), *Teaching diverse populations: Formulating a knowledge base* (pp. 25–56). Albany: State University of New York Press.

King, M. L., Jr. (1963). Letter from a Birmingham jail. In J. M. Washington (Ed.), *A testament of hope: The essential writings and speeches of Martin Luther King, Jr.* (pp. 289–302). San Francisco, CA: Harper.

King, W. R., Holmes, S. T., Henderson, M. L., & Latessa, E. J. (2001). The community corrections partnership: Examining the long-term effects of youth participation in Afrocentric diversion program. *Crime and Delinquency, 47*(2), 558–572.

Klag, M. J., Whelton, P. K., Coresh, J., Grim, C. E., & Kuller, L. H. (1991). The association of skin color with blood pressure in U.S. blacks with low socioeconomic status. *Journal of the American Medical Association, 265*(5), 5990–6002.

Klepinger, D. H., Lundberg, S., & Plotnick, R. D. (1995). Adolescent fertility and the educational attainment of young women. *Family Planning Perspectives, 27,* 23–28.

Kliewer, W. (2016). Victimization and biological stress responses in urban adolescents: Emotion regulation as a moderator. *Journal of Youth and Adolescence, 45*(9), 1812–1823.

Klonoff, E. A., & Landrine, H. (2000). Is skin color a marker for racial discrimination? Explaining the skin color-hypertension relationship. *Journal of Behavioral Medicine, 23*(4), 329–338.

Knettel, B. A. (2016). Exploring diverse mental illness attributions in a multinational sample: A mixed-methods survey of scholars in international psychology. *International Perspectives in Psychology: Research, Practice, Consultation, 5*(2), 128–140.

Knott, T., & Giwa, S. (2012). African American disproportionality within CPS and disparate access to support services: Review and critical analysis of the literature. *Residential Treatment for Children & Youth, 29*(3), 219–230.

Knowledge is Power Program. (n.d.). Retrieved from http://www.kipp.org/kipp-foundation/history/

Knox, D., & Schacht, C. (2010). *Choices in relationships: An introduction to marriage and the family* (10th ed.). Belmont, CA: Wadsworth.

Knuckey, J., & Kim, M. (2015). Racial resentment, old-fashioned racism, and the vote choice of Southern and nonsouthern Whites in the 2012 US presidential election. *Social Science Quarterly, 96*(4), 905–922.

Koch, L. M., & Gross, A. (1997). Children's perceptions of Black English as a variable in intraracial perception. *Journal of Black Psychology, 23*(3), 215–226.

Kochhar, R., Fry, R., & Taylor, P. (2011). Wealth gaps rise to record highs between Whites, Blacks, Hispanics. *Pew Research. Social and Demographic Trends*. Retrieved from http://www.pewsocialtrends .org/2011/07/26/wealth-gaps-rise-to-record-highs-between-whites-blacks-hispanics/

Kochman, T. (1981). *Black and white styles in conflict.* Chicago, IL: University of Chicago Press.

Kogan, S. M., Lei, M. K., Grange, C. R., Simons, R. L., Brody, G. H., Gibbons, F. X., & Chen, Y. (2013). The contribution of community and family contexts to African American young adults' romantic relationship health: A prospective analysis. *Journal of Youth and Adolescence, 42*(6), 878–890.

Kogan, S. M., Yu, T., & Brown, G. L. (2016). Romantic relationship commitment behavior among emerging adult African American men. *Journal of Marriage and Family, 78*(4), 996–1012.

Kohn, L., Oden, T., Munoz, R. F., Robinson, A., & Leavitt, D. (2002). Adapted cognitive behavioral group therapy for depressed low-income African American women. *Community Mental Health, 38*(6), 497–504.

Kohrt, B. A., Rasmussen, A., Kaiser, B. N., Haroz, E. E., Maharjan, S. M., Mutamba, B. B., . . . Hinton, D. E. (2014). Cultural concepts of distress and psychiatric disorders: Literature review and research recommendations for global mental health epidemiology. *International Journal of Epidemiology, 43*, 365–406.

Komarraju, M., & Cokley, K. O. (2008). Horizontal and vertical dimensions of individualism-collectivism: A comparison of African Americans and European Americans. *Cultural Diversity and Ethnic Minority Psychology, 14*, 336–343.

Komar-Samardzija, M., Braun, L. T., Keithley, J. K., & Quinn, L. T. (2012). Factors associated with physical activity levels in African-American women with type 2 diabetes. *Journal of the American Academy of Nurse Practitioners, 24*, 209–217.

Kong, G., Camenga, D., Cavallo, D., Connell, C. M., Pflieger, J. C., & Krishnan-Sarin, S. (2012). The role of ethnic pride and parental disapproval of smoking on smoking behaviors among minority and White adolescents in a suburban high school. *American Journal on Addictions, 21*(5), 424–434.

Korry, E. (2017). San Francisco seeks to ban sale of menthol cigarettes, flavored tobacco products. *Keiser Health News*.

Kosberg, J. I., Kaufman, A. V., Burgio, L. D., Leeper, J. D., & Sun, F. (2007). Family caregiving to those with dementia in rural Alabama: Racial similarities and differences. *Journal of Aging and Health, 19*(1), 3–21.

Kovacs, M. (1985). The children's depression inventory (CDI). *Psychopharmacology Bulletin, 21*, 995–998.

Kowalski, B., & Lundman, R. (2007). Vehicle stops by police for driving while Black: Common problems and some tentative solutions. *Journal of Criminal Justice, 35*(2), 165–181.

Kozol, J. (1991). *Savage inequalities.* New York, NY: Crown.

Krause, N. (2003). Race, religion, and abstinence from alcohol in late life. *Journal of Aging and Health, 15*(3), 508–533.

Krebs, C. P., Barrick, K., Lindquist, C. H., Crosby, C. M., Boyd, C., & Bogan, Y. (2011). The sexual assault of undergraduate women at historically Black colleges and universities (HBCUs). *Journal of Interpersonal Violence, 26*(18), 3640–3666.

Krentzman, A. R., Farkas, K. J., & Townsend, A. L. (2010). Spirituality, religiousness, and alcoholism treatment outcomes: A comparison between black and white participants. *Alcoholism Treatment Quarterly, 28*, 128–150.

Kretzmann, J. P., & McKnight, J. L. (1993). *Building communities from the inside out: A path toward finding and mobilizing a community's assets.* Chicago, IL: Northwestern University, Institute for Policy Research.

Kretzschmar, J. W. A. (2008). Public and academic understandings about language: The intellectual history of Ebonics. *English World-Wide, 29*(1), 70–95.

Krieger, N. (2000). Social epidemiology. In L. F. Berkman & I. Kawachi (Eds.), *Discrimination and health* (pp. 36–75). New York, NY: Oxford University Press.

Kuentzel, J. G., Arble, E., Boutros, N., Chugani, D., & Barnett, D. (2012), Nonsuicidal self-injury in an ethnically diverse college sample. *American Journal of Orthopsychiatry, 82*, 291–297.

Kunjufu, J. (1984). *Developing positive self-images and discipline in black children.* Chicago, IL: African American Images.

Kunjufu, J. (1985). *Countering the conspiracy to destroy black boys.* Chicago, IL: African American Images.

Kupchik, A., & Ward, G. (2014). Race, poverty, and exclusionary school security: An empirical analysis of U.S. elementary, middle, and high schools. *Youth Violence and Juvenile Justice, 12*(4), 332–354.

Kwate, N. O. A., Meyer, I. H., Eniola, F., & Dennis, N. (2010). Individual and group racism and problem drinking among African American women. *Journal of Black Psychology, 36*, 446–457.

Lacey, K. K., Mouzon, D. M., Govia, I. O., Matusko, N., Forsythe-Brown, I., Abelson, J. M., & Jackson, J. S. (2016). Substance abuse among blacks across the diaspora. *Substance Use & Misuse, 51*(9), 1147–1158.

Lambert, S., Brown, L., Phillips, C., & Ialongo, N. (2004). The relationship between perception of neighborhood characteristics and substance use among African American adolescents. *American Journal of Community Psychology, 34*(3/4), 205–218.

Landor, A., Gordon, S. L., Simons, R. L., Brody, G. H., & Gibbons, F. X. (2011). Role of religiosity in the relationship between parents, peers, and adolescent risky sexual behavior. *Journal of Youth and Adolescence, 40*(3), 296–309.

Landor, A., & Halpern, C. (2016). The enduring significance of skin tone: Linking skin tone, attitudes toward marriage and cohabitation, and sexual behavior. *Journal of Youth and Adolescence, 45*(5), 986–1002.

Landor, A. M., Simons, L. G., Simons, R. L., Brody, G. H., Bryant, C. M., Gibbons, F. X., . . . Melby, J. N. (2013). Exploring the impact of skin tone on family dynamics and race-related outcomes. *Journal of Family Psychology, 27*(5), 817–826.

Landrine, H., & Klonoff, E. A. (1996a). *African American acculturation: Deconstructing race and reviving culture.* Thousand Oaks, CA: Sage.

Landrine, H., & Klonoff, E. A. (1996b). The schedule of racist events: A measure of racial discrimination and a study of its negative physical and mental health consequences. *Journal of Black Psychology, 22*(2), 144–168.

Landrine, H., & Klonoff, E. A. (1999). Do blacks believe that HIV/AIDS is a government conspiracy against them? *Preventive Medicine, 28*(5), 451–457.

Langford, A. T., Resnicow, K., & Beasley, D. D. (2015). Outcomes from the Body & Soul Clinical Trials Project: A university-church partnership to improve African American enrollment in a clinical trial registry. *Patient Education and Counseling, 98*(2), 245–250.

Langley, C. (2016). Father knows best: Paternal presence and sexual debut in African-American adolescents living in poverty. *Family Process, 55*(1), 155–170.

Langreth, R. (1998, July 8). Black smokers' health may be affected as more nicotine is inhaled, studies say. *Wall Street Journal,* p. B6.

Lansford, J., Deater-Deckard, K., & Dodge, K. (2004). Ethnic differences in the link between physical discipline and later adolescent externalizing behaviors. *Journal of Child Psychology and Psychiatry, 45*, 801–812.

Lanson-Billings, G. (1999). Preparing teachers for diverse student populations: A critical race theory perspective. In A. Iran-Nejad & D. Pearson (Eds.), *Review of research in education* (Vol. 24, pp. 211–248). Washington, DC: American Educational Research Association.

LaPollo, A. B., Bond, L., & Lauby, J. L. (2014). Hypermasculinity and sexual risk among black and white men who have sex with men and women. *American Journal of Men's Health, 8*(5), 362–372.

Lashley, M. B., Marshall, V., & McLaurin-Jones, T. (2017). African American women seeking strength in romance and family relationships. In N. R. Silton (Ed.), *Family dynamics and romantic relationships in a changing society* (pp. 193–211). Hershey, PA: IGI Global.

Lassiter, R. F. (1987). Child rearing in black families: Child-abusing discipline? In R. L. Hampton (Ed.), *Violence in the black family: Correlates and consequences* (pp. 39–54). Lexington, MA: Lexington Books.

Laughlin, L. (2013, April). Who's minding the kids? Child care arrangements: Spring 2011. *U.S. Census Bureau.* Retrieved from https://www.census.gov/prod/2013pubs/p70-135.pdf

LaVeist, T. A. (1993). Segregation, poverty, and empowerment: Health consequences for African Americans. *Milbank Quarterly, 71*(1), 41–64.

LaVeist, T. A. (2003). Racial segregation and longevity among African Americans: An individual-level analysis. *Health Services Research, 38*(6), 1719–1734.

Lawrence-Lightfoot, S. (2000). *Respect.* New York: Basic Books.

Lazarus, R. S., & Folkman, S. (1984). *Stress, appraisal, and coping.* New York, NY: Springer.

Leary, J. D., Brennan, E. M., & Briggs, H. E. (2005). The African American adolescent respect scale: A measure of prosocial attitude. *Research on Social Work Practice, 15*(6), 462–469.

Lease, S. H. (2006). Factors predictive of the range of occupations considered by African American juniors and seniors in high school. *Journal of Career Development, 32*(4), 333–350.

Leavell, A. S., Tamis-LeMonda, C. S., Ruble, D. N., Zosuls, K. M., & Cabrera, N. J. (2012). African American, White and Latino fathers' activities with their sons and daughters in early childhood. *Sex Roles, 66,* 53–65.

LeCuyer, E. A. (2014). African American and European American mothers' limit-setting with their 36 month-old children. *Journal of Child and Family Studies, 23*(2), 275–284.

Lederman, J. (2017). Obama commutes 330 drug sentences on last day as president. *Washington Associated Press.* Retrieved from http://bigstory.ap.org/article/965eeb2830bd4f84811b684567c9b897/final-act-president-obama-commutes-330-drug-sentences

Lee, B. A., & Campbell, K. E. (1990). *Common ground? Urban neighborhoods as survey respondents see them.* Paper presented at the annual meeting of the American Sociological Association, Washington, DC.

Lee, D. B., Kim, E. S., & Neblett, E. W., Jr. (2017). The link between discrimination and telomere length in African American adults. *Health Psychology, 36*(5), 458–467.

Lee, E. B. (2012). Young, Black, and connected: Facebook usage Among African American college students. *Journal of Black Studies, 43*(3), 336–354.

Lee, J. G., Henriksen, L., Rose, S. W., Moreland-Russell, S., & Ribisl, K. M. (2015). A systematic review of neighborhood disparities in point-of-sale tobacco marketing. *American Journal of Public Health, 105*(9), e8–e18.

Leman, P. J., Smith, E. P., & Petersen, A. C.; SRCD Ethnic–Racial Issues and International Committees. (2017). Introduction to the special section of child development on positive youth development in diverse and global contexts. *Child Development, 88*(4), 1039–1044.

Lemanek, K. L., & Ranalli, M. (2009). Sickle cell disease. In M. C. Roberts & R. Steele (Eds.), *Handbook of pediatric psychology* (Vol. 4, pp. 303–318). New York, NY: Guilford.

Lemerise, E. A., & Arsenio, W. (2000). An integrated model of emotion processes and cognition in social information processing. *Child Development, 71,* 107–118.

Lepore, L., & Brown, R. (2000). Category and stereotype activation: Is prejudice inevitable? In C. Stangor (Ed.), *Stereotypes and prejudice* (pp. 119–138). Philadelphia, PA: Taylor & Francis.

Leventhal, H., Leventhal, E. A., & Cameron, L. (2001). Representations, procedures, and affect in illness self-regulation: A perceptual-cognitive model. In A. Baum, T. A. Revenson & J. E. Singer (Eds.), *Handbook of health psychology* (pp. 19–48). Mahwah, NJ: Erlbaum.

Leventhal, T., & Brooks-Gunn, J. (2000). The neighborhoods they live in: Effects of neighborhood residence on child and adolescent outcomes. *Psychological Bulletin, 126*(2), 309–337.

Levin, J. S., & Taylor, R. J. (1997). Age differences in patterns and correlates of the frequency of prayer. *The Gerontologists, 37*(1), 75–88.

Levine, D. S., Taylor, R. J., Nguyen, A. W., Chatters, L. M., & Himle, J. A. (2015). Family and friendship informal support networks and social anxiety disorder among African Americans and Black Caribbeans. *Social Psychiatry and Psychiatric Epidemiology, 50*(7), 1121–1133.

Levine, J. A., Emery, C. R., & Pollack, H. (2007). The well-being of children born to teen mothers. *Journal of Marriage and Family, 69*(1), 105–122.

Levine, J. A., Pollack, H., & Comfort, M. E. (2001). Academic and behavioral outcomes among the children of young mothers. *Journal of Marriage and the Family, 63*(2), 355–369.

Levine, L. W. (1977). *Black culture and Black consciousness: Afro-American folk thought from slavery to freedom.* New York, NY: Oxford University Press.

Levinson, D. J., Darrow, C. N., Klein, E. B., Levinson, M. H., & McKee, B. (1978). *The seasons of a man's life.* New York, NY: Knopf.

Lewis, A. E. (2001). There is no "race" in the schoolyard: Color-blind ideology in an (almost) all-white school. *American Education Research Journal, 38*(4), 781–811.

Lewis, J. R., & Ford-Robertson, J. (2010). Understanding the occurrence of interracial marriage in the United States through differential assimilation. *Journal of Black Studies, 41*, 405–420.

Lewis, K. M., Andrews, E., Gaska, K., Sullivan, C., Bybee, D., & Ellick, K. L. (2012). Experimentally evaluating the impact of a school-based African-centered emancipatory intervention on the ethnic identity of African American adolescents. *Journal of Black Psychology, 38*(3), 259–289.

Lewis, L. M. (2008). Spiritual assessment in African-Americans: A review of measures of spirituality used in health research. *Journal of Religious Health, 47*, 458–475.

Lhila, A., & Long, S. (2012). What is driving the black-white difference in low birthweight in the US? *Health Economics, 21*(3), 301–315.

Li, N. P., Yong, J. C., Tov, W., Sng, O., Fletcher, G. J., Valentine, K. A., . . . Balliet, D. (2013). Mate preferences do predict attraction and choices in the early stages of mate selection. *Journal of Personality and Social Psychology, 105*(5), 757.

Li, W., Dorstyn, D. S., & Denson, L. A. (2016). Predictors of mental health service use by young adults: A systematic review. *Psychiatric Services, 67*, 946–956.

Li, X., Stanton, B., Pack, R., Harris, C., Cottrell, L., & Burns, J. (2002). Risk and protective factors associated with gang involvement among urban African American adolescents. *Youth and Society, 34*(2), 172–194.

Lichter, D. T., Parisi, D., & Taquino, M. C. (2012). The geography of exclusion: Race, segregation, and concentrated poverty. *Social Problems, 59*, 364–388.

Lincoln, C. E., & Mamiya, L. H. (1990). *The black church in the African-American experience.* Durham, NC: Duke University Press.

Lindsey, K. P., & Paul, G. L. (1989). Involuntary commitments to public mental institutions: Issues involving the overrepresentation of blacks and assessment of relevant functioning. *Psychological Bulletin, 106*(2), 171–183.

Linnehan, F. (2001). The relation of a work-based mentoring program to the academic performance and behavior of African American students. *Journal of Vocational Behavior, 59*, 310–325.

Linton, S. L., Cooper, H. L., Luo, R., Karnes, C., Renneker, K., Haley, D. F., . . . Rothenberg, R. (2016). People and places: Relocating to neighborhoods with better economic and social conditions is associated with less risky drug/alcohol network characteristics among African American adults in Atlanta, GA. *Drug and Alcohol Dependence, 160*, 30–41.

Lipman, P. (2002). Making the global city, making inequality: The political economy and cultural politics of Chicago school policy. *American Educational Research Journal, 39*(2), 379–419.

Little, A. C. (2014). Facial attractiveness. *Wiley Interdisciplinary Reviews: Cognitive Science, 5*(6), 621–634.

Littlefield, A., Lieberman, L., & Reynolds, L. (1982). Redefining race: The potential demise of a concept in physical anthropology. *Current Anthropology, 23*, 641–656.

Littlefield, M. B. (2003). Gender role identity and stress in African American women. *Journal of Human Behavior in the Social Environment, 8*(4), 93–104.

Littleton, H. L., & Dodd, J. C. (2016). Violent attacks and damaged victims: An exploration of the rape scripts of European American and African American US college women. *Violence Against Women, 22*(14), 1725–1747.

Liu, J., Mustanski, B., Dick, D., Bolland, J., & Kertes, D. A. (2017). Risk and protective factors for comorbid internalizing and externalizing problems among economically disadvantaged African American youth. *Development and Pychopathology, 29*(3), 1043–1056.

Liu, L. C., & Flay, B. R.; Aban Aya Investigators. (2009). Evaluating mediation in longitudinal multivariate data: Mediation effects for the Aban Aya Youth Project drug prevention program. *Prevention Science, 10*(3), 197–207.

Livingston, G., & Brown, A. (2017). Intermarriage in the U.S. 50 years after loving v. Virginia. *Pew Research Center.* Retrieved from http://www.pewsocialtrends.org/2017/05/18/intermarriage-in-the-u-s-50-years-after-loving-v-virginia/

Llanos, A. A., Rabkin, A., Bandera, E. V., Zirpoli, G., Gonzalez, B. D., Xing, C. Y., . . . Ambrosone, C. B. (2017). Hair product use and breast cancer risk among African American and White women. *Carcinogenesis, 38*(9), 883–892.

Lobel, A., Engels, R. C., Stone, L. L., Burk, W. J., & Granic, I. (2017). Video gaming and children's psychosocial wellbeing: A longitudinal study. *Journal of Youth and Adolescence, 46*(4), 884–897.

Logan, J. R., & Stults, B. (2011). *The persistence of segregation in the metropolis: New findings from the 2010 Census* [Census Brief prepared for Project US2010]. Retrieved from http://www.s4.brown.edu/us2010

Loggins, S., & Andrade, F. C. D. (2014). Despite an overall decline in US infant mortality rates, the black/white disparity persists: Recent trends and future projections. *Journal of Community Health, 39*(1), 118–123.

Lombe, M., Saltzman, L. Y., Chu, Y., Sinha, A., & Nebbitt, V. E. (2017). Cumulative risk and resilience: The roles of comorbid maternal mental health conditions and community cohesion in influencing food security in low-income households. *Social Work in Mental Health, 16*(1), 74–92.

Long, E., Ponder, M., & Bernard, S. (2016). Knowledge, attitudes, and beliefs related to hypertension and hyperlipidemia self-management among African-American men living in the southeastern United States. *Patient Education and Counseling, 100*(5), 1000–1006.

Longshore, D., & Grills, C. (2000). Motivating illegal drug use recovery: Evidence for a culturally congruent intervention. *Journal of Black Psychology, 26*(3), 288–301.

Longshore, D., Grills, C., & Annon, K. (1999). Effects of a culturally congruent intervention on cognitive factors related to drug-use recovery. *Substance Use and Misuse, 34*(9), 1223–1241.

Lorber, M. F., O'Leary, S. G., & Smith, S. A. M. (2011). An initial evaluation of the role of emotion and impulsivity in explaining racial/ethnic differences in the use of corporal punishment. *Developmental Psychology, 47*, 1744–1749.

Losen, D. J., & Orfield, G. (2002). Introduction. In D. J. Losen & G. Orfield (Eds.), *Racial inequity in special education.* Cambridge, MA: Harvard Education Press.

Lowen, L. (2016). The role of African American women in the Black Church. *ThoughtCo.* Retrieved from https://www.thoughtco.com/african-american-women-black-church-3533748

Loyd, B. A., & Williams, B. V. (2017). The potential for youth programs to promote African American youth's development of ethnic and racial identity. *Child Development Perspectives, 11*(1), 29–38.

Luebbert, R., & Perez, A. (2016). Barriers to clinical research participation among African Americans. *Journal of Transcultural Nursing, 27*(5), 456–463.

Luhby, T. (2012). *Worsening wealth inequality by race.* Retrieved from http://money.cnn.com/2012/06/21/news/economy/wealth-gap-race/index.htm

Lumpkins, C. Y., Greiner, K. A., Daley, C., Mabachi, N. M., & Neuhaus, K. (2013). Promoting healthy behavior from the pulpit: Clergy share their perspectives on effective health communication in the African American church. *Journal of Religion and Health, 52*(4), 1093–1107.

Lundy, G. F. (2003). The myths of oppositional culture. *Journal of Black Studies, 33*(4), 450–467.

Lung Cancer Fact Sheet. (n.d.). Retrieved from http://www.lung.org/lung-disease/lung-cancer/resources/facts-figures/lung-can cer-fact-sheet.html

Lutfi, K., Trepka, M. J., Fennie, K. P., Ibanez, G., & Gladwin, H. (2015). Racial residential segregation and risky sexual behavior among non-Hispanic blacks, 2006–2010. *Social Science & Medicine, 140*, 95–103.

Lynch, E. B., & Kane, J. (2014). Body size perception among African American women. *Journal of Nutrition Education and Behavior, 46*(5), 412–417.

Lynn, B., Yoo, G. J., & Levine, E. G. (2014). "Trust in the Lord": Religious and spiritual practices of African American breast cancer survivors. *Journal of Religion and Health, 53*(6), 1706–1716.

Lynn, M., Bacon, J. N., Totten, T. L., Bridges, T. L., & Jennings, M. (2010). Examining teachers' beliefs about African American male students in a low-performing high school in an African American school district. *Teachers College Record, 112*(1), 289–330.

Macapagal, K., Greene, G. J., Rivera, Z., & Mustanski, B. (2015). "The best is always yet to come": Relationship stages and processes among young LGBT couples. *Journal of Family Psychology, 29*(3), 309.

Macartney, S., Bishaw, A., & Fontenot, K. (2013). *Poverty rates for selected detailed race and Hispanic groups by state and place: 2007–2011.* US Department of Commerce, Economics and Statistics Administration, US Census Bureau.

MacEvoy, J. P., & Leff, S. S. (2012). Children's sympathy for peers who are the targets of peer aggression. *Journal of Abnormal Child Psychology, 40*(7), 1137–1148.

Maddox, K. B., & Gray, S. A. (2002). Cognitive representations of Black Americans: Reexploring the role of skin tone. *Personality and Social Psychology Bulletin, 28*(2), 250–259.

Maddux, J. E., & Lewis, J. (1995). Self-efficacy and adjustment: Basic principles and issues. In J. E. Maddux (Ed.), *Self-efficacy, adaptation, and adjustment* (pp. 37–68). New York, NY: Plenum Press.

Madsen, J. A., & Mabokela, R. O. (2002). Introduction: Leadership and diversity: Creating inclusive schools. *Peabody Journal of Education, 77*(1), 1–6.

Madu, S. N., Baguma, P. K., & Pritz, A. (Eds.). (2000). *Psychotherapy and African reality.* Sovinga, South Africa: University of the North Press.

Magnus, K. B., Cowen, E. L., Wyman, P. A., Fagen, D. B., & Work, W. C. (1999). Parent-child relationship qualities and child adjustment in highly stressed urban black and white families. *Journal of Community Psychology, 27*(1), 55–71.

Magnuson, K. A., & Waldfogel, J. (2005). Early childhood care and education: Effects on ethnic and racial gaps in school readiness. *The Future of Children, 15*(1), 169–196.

Maiello, S. (1999). Encounter with an African healer: Thinking about the possibilities and limits of cross-cultural psychotherapy. *Journal of Child Psychotherapy, 25*(2), 217–238.

Makanjuola, V., Esan, Y., Oladeji, B., Kola, L., Appiah-Poku, J., Harris, B., . . . Gureje, O. (2016). Explanatory model of psychosis: Impact on perception of self-stigma by patients in three sub-saharan African cities. *Social Psychiatry and Psychiatric Epidemiology, 51*(12), 1645–1654.

Malmberg, M., Kleinjan, M., Vermulst, A. A., Overbeek, G, Monshouwer, K., Lammers, J., . . .

Engels, R. C. (2012). Do substance use risk personality dimensions predict the onset of substance use in early adolescence? A variable- and person-centered approach. *Journal of Youth and Adolescence, 41*(11), 1512–1525.

Mama, S. K., McNeill, L. H., McCurdy, S. A., Evans, A. E., Diamond, P. M., Adamus-Leach, H. J., & Lee, R. E. (2015). Psychosocial factors and theory in physical activity studies in minorities. *American Journal of Health Behavior, 39*(1), 68–76.

Mandara, J., Gaylord-Harden, N. K., Richards, M. H., & Ragsdale, B. L. (2009). The effects of changes in racial identity and self-esteem on changes in African American adolescents' mental health. *Child Development, 80*(6), 1660–1675.

Man-in-the-House Rule. (2008). *West's Encyclopedia of American Law* (2nd ed.). Retrieved August 15, 2017 from http://legal-dictionary.thefreedictionary.com/Man-in-the-House+Rule

Mannes, S. (2016). The power of the pen: The impact of knowledge of defendant's character present in pretrial publicity varies by defendant race. *Applied Psychology in Criminal Justice, 12*(1), 36–53.

Marcia, J. E. (1966). Development and validation of ego identity status. *Journal of Personality and Social Psychology, 3*(5), 551–558.

Marcia, J. E. (1980). Identity in adolescence. In J. Adelson (Ed.), *Handbook of adolescent psychology* (pp. 159–187). New York, NY: Wiley.

Marin, G., Burhansstipanox, L., Connell, C. M., Gielen, A. C., Helitzer, A. D., Lorig, K., & Morisky D. E. (1995). A research agenda for health education among underserved populations. *Health Education Quarterly, 22,* 346–363.

Marjoribanks, K. (1995). Educational and occupational aspirations of "common man" boys: Kahl's study revisited. *Journal of Genetic Psychology, 156*(2), 205–216.

Marks, G., Crepaz, N., & Janssen, R. S. (2006). Estimating sexual transmission of HIV from persons aware and unaware that they are infected with the virus in the USA. *AIDS, 20*(10), 1447–1450.

Marks, L. (2012). Same-sex parenting and children's outcomes: A closer examination of the American psychological association's brief on lesbian and gay parenting. *Social Science Research, 41*(4), 735–751.

Marks, L. D., Nesteruk, O., Swanson, M., Garrison, M. E. B., & Davis, T. (2005). Religion and health among African Americans: A qualitative examination. *Research on Aging, 27*, 447–474.

Markus, H., & Kitayama, S. (1999). Culture and the self: Implications for cognition, emotion, and motivation. In R. F. Baumeister (Ed.), *The self in social psychology* (pp. 339–368). Cleveland, OH: Taylor & Francis.

Martin, A. C. (2008). Television media as a potential negative factor in the racial identity development of African American youth. *Academic Psychiatry, 32*(4), 338–342.

Martin, J. A., Hamilton, B. E., Ostermam, M. J. K., Driscoll, A. K., & Matthews, T. J. (2017). Births: Final data for 2015. *National Vital Statistics Reports, 66*(1). Retrieved from https://www.cdc.gov/nchs/data/nvsr/nvsr66/nvsr66_01.pdf

Martin, J. A., Hamilton, B. E., & Ventura, S. J. (2015). *Births: Final data for 2014*. Retrieved from https://www.hhs.gov/ash/oah/adolescent-development/reproductive-health-and-teen-pregnancy/teen-pregnancy-and-childbearing/trends/index.html

Martin, J. J., Kulinna, P. H., McCaughtry, N., Cothran, D., Dake, J., & Fahoome, G. (2005). The theory of planned behavior: Predicting physical activity and cardiorespiratory fitness in African American children. *Journal of Sport and Exercise Psychology, 27*(4), 456–469.

Martin, N. D., Tobin, W., & Spenner, K. I. (2014a). Interracial friendships across the college years: Evidence from a longitudinal case study. *Journal of College Student Development, 55*(7), 720–725.

Martin, S. P., Astone, N. M., & Peters, E. (2014b). Fewer marriages, more divergence: Marriage projections for millennials to age 40. *Urban Institute*. Retrieved from http://www.ebony.com/wp-content/uploads/2014/05/413110-Fewer-Marriages-More-Divergence.pdf

Mason, M. A., Skolnick, A., & Sugarman, S. D. (2002). *All our families: New policies for the new century.* New York, NY: Oxford University Press.

Masten, A. S., & Coatsworth, J. D. (1998). The development of competence in favorable and unfavorable environments: Lessons from research on successful children. *American Psychologist, 53*, 205–220.

Mather, M., & Adams, D. (2006). *The risk of negative child outcomes in low-income families.* Baltimore,

MD: The Annie E. Casey Foundation, Population Reference Bureau.

Mathews, T. J., Curtin, S. C., & MacDorman, M. F. (2000). Infant mortality statistics from the 1998 period linked birth/infant death data set. *National Vital Statistical Report, 48*(12), 1–25.

Matsea, T. C. (2017). Strategies to destigmatize mental illness in South Africa: Social work perspective. *Social Work in HealthCare, 56*(5), 367–380.

Matsumoto, D., & Juang, K. (2013). *Culture and psychology.* Belmont, CA: Wadsworth.

Matthews, A., Berrios, N., Darnell, J., & Calhoun, E. (2006). A qualitative evaluation of a faith-based breast and cervical cancer screening intervention for African American women. *Health Education and Behavior, 33*(5), 643–663.

Matthews, T. J., & MacDorman, M. F. (2013). Infant mortality statistics from the 2009 period linked birth/infant death data set. *National Vital Statistics Report, 61*(8). Retrieved from http://www.cdc.gov/mattinchs/data/nvsr/nvsr61/nvsr61_08.pdf

Matthews, T. J., MacDorman, M. F., & Thoma, M. E. (2015). Infant mortality statistics from the 2013 period linked birth/infant death data set. *Division of Vital Statistics. National Vital Statistics Report, 64*(9). Retrieved from https://www.cdc.gov/nchs/data/nvsr/nvsr64/nvsr64_09.pdf

Matthie, N., Hamilton, J., Wells, D., & Jenerette, C. (2015). Perceptions of young adults with sickle cell disease concerning their disease experience. *Journal of Advanced Nursing, 72*(6), 1441–1451.

Mattis, J. S. (2000). African American women's definitions of spirituality and religiosity. *Journal of Black Psychology, 26*(1), 101–122.

Mattis, J. S., Beckham, W. P., Saunders, B. A., Williams, J. E., McAllister, D., Myers, V., . . . Dixon, C. (2004). Who will volunteer? Religiosity, everyday racism, and social participation among African American men. *Journal of Adult Development, 11*(4), 261–272.

Mattis, J. S., & Grayman-Simpson, N. (2013). Faith and the sacred in African American life. In K. I. Pargament, J. J. Exline & J. W. Jones (Eds.), *Handbook of religion, spirituality, and psychology* (pp. 547–564). Washington, DC: American Psychological Association.

Mattis, J. S., Jagers, R. J., Hatcher, C. A., Lawhon, G. D., Murphy, E. J., & Murray, Y. F. (2000). Religiosity, volunteerism, and community involvement among African American men: An exploratory analysis. *Journal of Community Psychology, 28*(4), 391–406.

Mattis, J. S., & Watson, C. (2009). Religion and spirtuality. In H. A. Neville, B. M. Tynes & S. O. Utsey (Eds.), *Handbook of African American psychology* (pp. 91–102). Thousand Oaks, CA: Sage.

Mausbach, B. T., Semple, S. J., Patterson, T. L., & Strathdee, S. A. (2009). Predictors of safer sex intentions and protected sex among heterosexual HIV-negative methamphetamine users: An expanded model of the theory of planned behavior. *AIDS Care: Psychological and Socio-Medical Aspects of AIDS/HIV, 21*, 17–24.

Maxwell, M., Abrams, J., & Belgrave, F. Z. (2017). It's bigger than pictures: The influence of social media on young African American adults' perceptions of racism and anger expression. Manuscript under review.

Maxwell, M. L., Abrams, J. A., & Belgrave, F. Z. (2016). Redbones and earth mothers: The influence of rap music on African American girls' perceptions of skin color. *Psychology of Music, 44*(6), 1488–1499.

Mayberry, M. L., Espelage, D. L., & Koenig, B. (2009). Multilevel modeling of direct effects and interactions of peers, parents, school, and community influences on adolescent substance use. *Journal of Youth and Adolescence, 38*, 1038–1049.

Mayfield, V. M., & Garrison-Wade, D. (2015). Culturally responsive practices reform. *Journal of Instructional Pedagogies, 16*, 1.Mbiti, J. S. (1970). *African religions and philosophy.* Garden City, NY: Anchor Books.

Mbiti, J. S. (1991). *African religions and philosophy* (2nd ed.). Portsmouth, NH: Heinemann.

McAdoo, H. P. (1998). African-American families: Strengths and realities. In H. I. McCubbin, E. A. Thompson, A. I. Thompson & J. A. Futrell (Eds.), *Resiliency in African-American families* (pp. 17–30). Thousand Oaks, CA: Sage.

McAdoo, H. P. (2007). *Black families.* Thousand Oaks, CA: Sage.

McAdoo, J. (1988). The roles of black fathers in the socialization of black children. In H. P. McAdoo (Ed.), *Black families* (pp. 257–269). Newbury Park, CA: Sage.

McCluskey, C. P., Krohn, M. D., Lizotte, A. J., & Rodriguez, M. L. (2002). Early substance abuse and school achievement: An examination of Latino, White, and African American youth. *Journal of Drug Issues, 2*(3), 921–944.

McConahay, J. (1982). Self-interest versus racial attitudes as correlates of anti-busing attitudes in Louisville: Is it the buses or the blacks? *Journal of Politics, 44*, 692–720.

McDonald, C. C., Deatrick, J. A., Kassam-Adams, N., & Richmond, T. S. (2011). Community violence exposure and positive youth development in urban youth. *Journal of Community Health, 36*(6), 925–932.

McDowell, J., & Carter-Francique, A. (2017). An intersectional analysis of the workplace experiences of African American female athletic directors. *Sex Roles, 77*(5-6), 393-408.

McGlothlin, H., & Killen, M. (2005). Children's perceptions of intergroup and intragroup similarity and the role of social experience. *Journal of Applied Developmental Psychology, 26*(6), 680–698.

McHale, S., Crouter, A., Kim, J., Burton, L., Davis, K., Dotterer, A., & Swanson, D. (2006). Mothers' and fathers' racial socialization in African American families: Implications for youth. *Child Development, 77*(5), 1387–1402.

McLean, R. (2003). Deconstructing Black gay shame: A multicultural perspective on the quest for a healthy ethnic and sexual identity. In G. Roysircar, D. S. Sandhu & V. E. Bibbins, Sr. (Eds.), *Multicultural competencies: A guidebook of practices* (pp. 109–118). Alexandria, VA: Association for Multicultural Counseling & Development.

McLoyd, V. C. (1991). What is the study of African American children the study of? The conduct, publication, and changing nature of research on African American children. In R. L. Jones (Ed.), *Black psychology* (3rd ed., pp. 419–440). Berkeley, CA: Cobb & Henry.

McLoyd, V. C., Kaplan, R., Hardaway, C., & Wood, D. (2007). Does endorsement of physical discipline matter? Assessing moderating influences on the maternal and child psychological correlates of physical discipline in African American families. *Journal of Family Psychology, 21*(2), 165–175.

McMahon, S. D., Todd, N. R., Martinez, A., Coker, C., Sheu, C. F., Washburn, J., & Shah, S. (2013). Aggressive and prosocial behavior: Community violence, cognitive, and behavioral predictors among urban African American youth. *American Journal of Community Psychology, 51*(3-4), 407–421.

McMahon, S. D., Wernsman, J., & Parnes, A. L. (2006). Understanding prosocial behavior: The impact of empathy and gender among African American adolescents. *Journal of Adolescent Health, 39*(1), 135–137.

McMillan, D. W., & Chavis, D. M. (1986). Sense of community: A definition and theory. *American Journal of Community Psychology, 14*(1), 6–23.

McRoy, R., Mica, M., Freundlich, M., & Kroll, J. (2007). Making MEPA-IEP work: Tools for professionals (Multiethnic Placement Act of 1994—Interethnic Adoption Provisions of 1996). *Child Welfare, 86*(2), 49–67.

Meehan, R. (2007, December 23). Court surprises with ruling about crack cocaine sentences. *Gannett News Service.*

Meezan, W., & Rauch, J. (2005). Gay marriage, same-sex parenting, and American children. *The Future of Children, 15*(2), 97–115.

Mehta, N. K., Elo, I. T., Ford, N. D., & Siegel, K. R. (2015). Obesity among US-and foreign-born Blacks by region of birth. *American Journal of Preventive Medicine, 49*(2), 269–273.

Meinert, J. A., Blehar, M. C., Peindl, K. S., Neal-Barnett, A., & Wisner, K. L. (2003). Bridging the gap. Recruitment of African American women into mental health research studies. *Academic Psychiatry, 27*(1), 21–28.

Mendez, D. D., Hogan, V. K., & Culhane, J. F. (2014). Institutional racism, neighborhood factors, stress, and preterm birth. *Ethnicity and Health, 19*(5), 479–499.

Mennis, J., & Stahler, G. J. (2016). Racial and ethnic disparities in outpatient substance use disorder treatment episode completion for different substances. *Journal of Substance Abuse Treatment, 63,* 25–33.

Meraviglia, M. G. (1999). Critical analysis of spirituality and its empirical indicators. *Journal of Holistic Nursing, 17*(1), 18–33.

Meredith v. Jefferson County Board of Education (2006). No. 05-915. Retrieved from: http://supreme.findlaw.com/supreme_court/docket/2006/december/05-915-meredith-v-jefferson-county-school-board.html

Merriam-Webster. (2003). *Merriam-Webster's collegiate dictionary* (11th ed.). Springfield, MA: Author.

Merz, J. P. (1997). The role of Churches in helping adolescents prevent HIV/AIDS. *Journal of HIV/AIDS Prevention & Education for Adolescents & Children, 1*(2), 45–55.

Messing, J. T. (2006). From the child's perspective: A qualitative analysis of kinship care placements. *Children and Youth Services Review, 28*(12), 1415–1434.

Meyer, I. H., Frost, D. M., & Nezhad, S. (2014). Minority stress and suicide in lesbians, gay men, and bisexuals. In P. Goldblum, D. L. Espelage, J. Chu & B. Bongar (Eds.), *Youth suicide and bullying.* New York, NY: Oxford University Press.

Mezuk, B., Rafferty, J. A., Kershaw, K. N., Hudson, D., Abdou, C. M., Lee, H., . . . Jackson, J. S. (2010). Reconsidering the role of social disadvantage in physical and mental health: Stressful life events, health behaviors, race, and depression. *American Journal of Epidemiology, 172*(11), 1238–1249.

Mickelson, R. A. (1990). The attitude-achievement paradox among black adolescents. *Sociology of Education, 63*(1), 44–61.

Milam, A. J., Furr-Holden, C. D., & Leaf, P. J. (2010). Perceived school and neighborhood safety, neighborhood violence and academic achievement in urban school children. *The Urban Review, 42*(5), 458–467.

Milam, A. J., Furr-Holden, C. D., Whitaker, D., Smart, M., Leaf, P., & Cooley-Strickland, M. (2012). Neighborhood environment and internalizing problems in African American children. *Community Mental Health Journal, 48*(1), 1–6.

Miller, T. Q., & Volk, R. J. (2002). Family relationships and adolescent cigarette smoking: Results from a national longitudinal survey. *Journal of Drug Issues, 2*(3), 945–972.

Miller, T. R., Lawrence, B. A., Carlson, N. N., Hendrie, D., Randall, S., Rockett, I. R., & Spicer, R. S. (2017). Perils of police action: A cautionary tale from US data sets. *Injury Prevention, 23,* 27–32.

Millsap, M. A., Chase, A., Obeidallah, D., Perez-Smith, A., Brigham, N., & Johnston, K. (2000). *Evaluation of Detroit's Comer schools and families initiative: Final report.* Cambridge, MA: Abt Associates.

Miniño, A. M., Murphy, S. L., Xu, J., & Kochanek, K. D. (2011). *Deaths: Final data for 2008.* Hyattsville, MD: Dept. of Health and Human Services, Centers for Disease Control and Prevention, National Center for Health Statistics.

Miranda, J., Bernal, G., Lau, A., Kohn, L., Hwang, W. C., & LaFromboise, T. (2005). State of the science on psychosocial interventions for ethnic minorities. *Annual Review of Clinical Psychology, 1,* 113–142.

Mitchell, C., Hobcraft, J., McLanahan, S. S., Siegel, S. R., Berg, A., Jeanne Brooks-Gunn, J., . . . Notterman, D. (2014). Social disadvantage, genetic sensitivity, and children's telomere length. *Proceedings of the National Academy of Sciences, 111*(1), 5944–5949.

Miyamoto, Y., Nisbett, R. E., & Masuda, T. (2006). Culture and the physical environment: Holistic versus analytic perceptual affordances. *Psychological Science, 17*(2), 113–119.

Mobley, M. C., & Chun, H. (2013). Testing Jessor's problem behavior theory and syndrome: A nationally representative comparataive sample of Latino and African American adolescents. *Cultural Diversity and Ethnic Minority Psychology, 19*(2), 190–199.

Mohai, P., Kweon, B. S., Lee, S., & Ard, K. (2011). Air pollution around schools is linked to poorer student health and academic performance. *Health Affairs, 30*(5), 852–862.

Mollborn, S., & Dennis, J. A. (2012). Investigating the life situations and development of teenage mothers' children: Evidence from the ECLS-B. *Population Research and Policy Review, 31*(1), 31–66.

Mollborn, S., Fomby, P., & Dennis, J. A. (2012). Extended household transitions, race/ethnicity, and early childhood cognitive outcomes. *Social Science Research, 41*(5), 1152–1165.

Molock, S. D., Matlin, S., Barksdale, C., Puri, R., & Lyles, J. (2008). Developing suicide prevention programs for African American youth in African American churches. *Suicide and Life-Threatening Behavior, 38*, 323–333.

Monk, E. P., Jr. (2015). The cost of color: Skin color, discrimination, and health among African-Americans. *American Journal of Sociology, 121*(2), 396–444.

Montgomery, B. E., Stewart, K. E., Bryant, K. J., & Ounpraseuth, S. T. (2014). Dimensions of religion, depression symptomatology, and substance use among rural African American cocaine users. *Journal of Ethnicity in Substance Abuse, 13*(1), 72–90.

Montgomery, D. E., Fine, M. A., & James-Myers, L. (1990). The development and validation of an instrument to assess an optimal Afrocentric world view. *Journal of Black Psychology, 17*(1), 37–54.

Montgomery, L. (2015). Marijuana and tobacco use and co-use among African Americans: Results from the 2013, National Survey on Drug Use and Health. *Addictive Behaviors, 51*, 18–23.

Montgomery, L., & Marinos, D. A. (2016). The influence of potentially traumatic household characteristics on blunt use among Black youth. *Journal of Prevention & Intervention in the Community, 44*(2), 101–111.

Montgomery, L., Petry, N. M., & Carroll, K. M. (2012). Moderating effects of race in clinical trial participation and outcomes among marijuana-dependent young adults. *Drug Alcohol Dependence, 126*(3), 333–339.

Moon, H. (2012). Productive activities and perceived well-being in an African American older adult urban sample. *Activities, Adaptation & Aging, 36*(2), 107–130.

Moore, A. D., Hamilton, J. B., Knafl, G., Godley, P. A., Carpenter, W. R., Bensen, J. T., . . . Mishel, M. (2013). The influence of mistrust, racism, relgious participation, and access to care on patient satisfaction for African Amerian men: The North Caroline-Louisiana Prostate Cancer Project. *Journal of the National Medical Association, 105*(1), 59–68.

Moore, K. A., Morrison, D. R., & Greene, A. D. (1997). Effects on the children born to adolescent mothers. In R. A. Maynard (Ed.), *Kids having kids: Economic costs and social consequences of teen pregnancy* (pp. 145–180). Washington, DC: The Urban Institute.

Moore, T. J., & Mattison, D. R. (2017). Adult utilization of psychiatric drugs and differences by sex, age, and race. *JAMA Internal Medicine, 177*(2), 274–275.

Morales, E. S. (1989). Ethnic minority families and minority gays and lesbians. *Marriage & Family Review, 14*(3–4), 217–239.

Moreno, M. A., Furtner, F., & Rivara, F. P. (2011). Breastfeeding as obesity prevention. *Archives of Pediatrics and Adolescent Medicine, 165*(8), 772.

Morin, R., Parker, K., Stepler, R., & Mercer, A. (2017). Police views, public views: Behind the badge. *Pew Research Center.* Retrieved from http://www.pewsocialtrends.org/2017/01/11/police-views-public-views/

Morris, E. M., & Perry, B. L. (2016). The punishment gap: School suspension and racial disparities in achievement. *Social Problems, 63*(1), 68–86.

Moscou-Jackson, G., Finan, P. H., Campbell, C. M., Smyth, J. M., & Haythornthwaite, J. A. (2015). The effect of sleep continuity on pain in adults with sickle cell disease. *The Journal of Pain, 16*(6), 587–593.

Moskowitz, G. B., Stone, J., & Childs, A. (2012). Implicit stereotyping and medical decisions: Unconscious stereotype activation in practitioners' thoughts about African Americans. *American Journal of Public Health, 102*(5), 996–1001.

Mottino, F., & Miller, E. D. (2004, September). *Pathways for change: Philanthropy among African American, Asian American, and Latino donors in the New York metropolitan region.* New York: Center on Philanthropy and Civil Society at the Graduate Center, The City University of New York in Partnership with Coalition for New Philanthropy.

Mouzon, D. M., Taylor, R. J., Keith, V. M., Nicklett, E. J., & Chatters, L. M. (2017). Discrimination and psychiatric disorders among older African Americans. *International Journal of Geriatric Psychiatry, 32*(2), 175–182.

Mowbray, O., Ryan, J. P., Victor, B. G., Bushman, G., Yochum, C., & Perron, B. E. (2017). Longitudinal trends in substance use and mental health service needs in child welfare. *Children and Youth Services Review, 73*, 1–8.

Moynihan, D. P. (1965). *The Negro family: The case for national action.* Washington, DC: U.S. Department of Labor, Office of Policy, Planning, and Research.

Mpofu, E. (2002). Psychology in Sub-Saharan Africa: Challenges, prospects and promises. *International Journal of Psychology, 37*(3), 179–186.

Mrug, S., King, V., & Windle, M. (2016). Brief report: Explaining differences in depressive symptoms between African American and European American adolescents. *Journal of Adolescence, 46*, 25–29.

Mrug, S., Madan, A., & Windle, M. (2016). Emotional desensitization to violence contributes to adolescents' violent behavior. *Journal of Abnormal Child Psychology, 44*(1), 75–86.

Murdock, G. P. (1949). *Social structure.* New York, NY: Free Press.

Murphy, M. (2008). Variations in kinship networks across geographic and social space. *Population and Development Review, 34*(1), 19–49.

Murphy, S. Y., Hunter, A. G., & Johnson, D. J. (2008). Transforming caregiving: African American custodial grandmothers and the child welfare system. *Journal of Sociology and Social Welfare, 53*(2), 67–89.

Murray, M. S., Neal-Barnett, A., Demmings, J. L., & Stadulis, R. E. (2012). The acting White accusation, racial identity, and anxiety in African American adolescents. *Journal of Anxiety Disorders, 26*(4), 526–531.

Murty, K. S., & Roebuck, J. B. (2016). African American Students preferred characteristics in marital mates. *Race, Gender & Class, 23*(3/4), 42–67.

Mussen, P., & Eisenberg, N. (2001). Prosocial development in context. In A. C. Bohart & D. J. Stipek (Eds.), *Constructive and destructive behavior: Implications for family, school, and society* (pp. 103–126). Washington, DC: American Psychological Association.

Musser, D. W., & Price, J. L. (1992). *A new handbook of Christian theology.* Nashville, TN: Abington Press.

Musyimi, C. W., Mutiso, V. N., Ndetei, D. M., Unanue, I., Desai, D., Patel, S. G., . . . Bunders, J. (2017). Mental health treatment in Kenya: Task-sharing challenges and opportunities among informal health providers. *International Journal of Mental Health Systems, 11*(1), 45.

Muus, R. (1988). *Theories of adolescence* (5th ed.). New York, NY: Random House.

Mwendwa, D. T., Sims, R. C., Madhere, S., Thomas, J., Keen, L. D., Callender, C. O., & Campbell, A. L. J. (2011). The influence of coping with perceived racism and stress on lipid levels in African Americans. *Journal of the National Medical Association, 103*(7), 594–601.

Myers, H. F., Wyatt, G. E., Ullman, J. B., Loeb, T. B., Chin, D., Prause, N., . . . Liu, H. (2015). Cumulative burden of lifetime adversities: Trauma and mental health in low-SES African Americans and Latino/as. *Psychological Trauma, 7*(3), 243–251.

Myers, L. J. (1985). Transpersonal psychology: The role of the Afrocentric paradigm. *Journal of Black Psychology, 12*(1), 31–42.

Myers, L. J. (1988). *Understanding an Afrocentric world view: Introduction to an optimal psychology.* Dubuque, IA: Kendall/Hunt.

Myers, L. J. (1991). Expanding the psychology of knowledge optimally: The importance of worldview revisited. In R. L. Jones (Ed.), *Black psychology* (3rd ed., pp. 15–28). Berkeley, CA: Cobb & Henry.

Myers, L. J. (1992). Transpersonal psychology: The role of the Afrocentric paradigm. In A. K. H. Burlew & W. C. Banks (Eds.), *African American psychology: Theory, research, and practice* (pp. 5–17). Thousand Oaks, CA: Sage.

Myers, L. J. (2009). Theoretical and conceptual approaches to African American psychology. In H. Neville, S. Utsey & B. Tynes (Eds.), *Handbook of African American Psychology* (pp. 35–46). Thousand Oaks, CA: Sage.

Nadal, K. L., Griffin, K. E., Wong, Y., Hamit, S., & Rasmus, M. (2014). The impact of racial microaggressions on mental health: Counseling implications for clients of color. *Journal of Counseling & Development, 92*(1), 57–66.

Na'poles, A. M., Chadiha, L., Eversley, R., & Moreno-John, G. (2010). Developing culturally sensitive dementia caregiver interventions: Are we there yet? *American Journal of Alzheimer's Disease and Other Dementias, 25*(5), 398–406.

Nasim, A., Belgrave, F. Z., Jagers, R. J., Wilson, K. D., & Owens, K. (2007). The moderating effects of culture on peer deviance and alcohol use among high-risk African-American adolescents. *Journal of Drug Education, 37*(3), 335–363.

Nasim, A., Corona, R., Belgrave, F., Utsey, S. O., & Fallah, N. (2007). Cultural orientation as a protective factor against tobacco and marijuana smoking for African American young women. *Journal of Youth and Adolescence, 36*(4), 503–516.

Nasim, A., Guy, M. C., Soule, E. K., Cobb, C. O., Blank, M. D., & Eissenberg, T. (2015). Characteristics and patterns of Black & Mild use among African American smokers. *Nicotine & Tobacco Research, 18*(5) 842–849.

Nasim, A., Utsey, S., Corona, R., & Belgrave, F. (2006). Religiosity, refusal efficacy, and substance use among African American adolescents and young adults. *Journal of Ethnicity in Substance Abuse, 5*(2), 27–48.

Nasir, N., Mclaughlin, M., & Jones, A. (2009). What does it mean to be African American? Constructions of race and academic identity in an urban public high school. *American Educational Research Journal, 46*(1), 73–114.

Nasir, N. S., & Shah, N. (2011). On defense: African American males making sense of racialized narratives in mathematics education. *Journal of African American Males in Education, 2*(1), 24–45.

National African Religion Congress (NARC). (2013). *Mission statement.* Retrieved from http://www.narc-world.com/mission.html

National Black Home Educators (NBHE). (n.d.). Retrieved from http://www.nbhe.net/

National Cancer Institute. (2013). *The witness project.* Retrieved from http://rtips.can cer.gov/rtips/programDetails.do?program Id=270521

National Center for Education Statistics (NCES). (2013). *A first look: 2013 mathematics and reading.* https://nces.ed.gov/nationsreportcard/subject/publications/main2013/pdf/2014451.pdf

National Center for Education Statistics (NCES). (2015). *2015 mathematics and reading assessments.* Retrieved from https://www.nationsreportcard.gov/reading_math_2015/#?grade=4

National Center for Education Statistics (NCES). (2016a). U.S. Department of Education, National Center for Education Statistics, Higher Education General Information Survey (HEGIS), "Fall Enrollment in Colleges and Universities," 1976 through 1985 surveys; Integrated Postsecondary Education Data System (IPEDS), "Fall Enrollment Survey" (IPEDS-EF:86-99); and IPEDS Spring 2001 through Spring 2015, Fall Enrollment component.

National Center for Education Statistics (NCES). (2016b). U.S. Department of Education, National Center for Education Statistics, Common Core of Data (CCD), "Public Elementary/Secondary School Universe Survey," 2014–15. See Digest of Education Statistics 2016, table 216.50.

National Center for Health Statistics (NCHS). (2011). *Health, United States: With special features on socioeconomic status and health.* Hyattsville, MD: U.S. Dept. of Health and Human Services, Centers for Disease Control and Prevention, National Center for Health Statistics.

National Center for Health Statistics (NCHS). (2013). *Page 14, Series 10, Number 259.* Hyattsville, MD: National Center for Health Statistics (NCHS).

National Center for Health Statistics (NCHS). (2015a). *Health, United States: With special features on socioeconomic status and health.* Hyattsville, MD: U.S. Dept. of Health and Human Services, Centers for Disease Control and Prevention, National Center for Health Statistics.

National Center for Health Statistics (NSHS). (2015b). *Health, United States, 2015: With special feature on racial and ethnic health disparities.* Hyattsville, MD: U.S. Dept. of Health and Human Services, Centers for Disease Control and Prevention, National Center for Health Statistics.

National Center for Health Statistics. (2017). *Health, United States, 2016: With Chartbook on long-term trends in health.* Hyattsville, MD. Retrieved from https://www.cdc.gov/nchs/data/hus/hus16.pdf#015

National Diabetes Information Clearinghouse. (2002). *Diabetes prevention program.* Retrieved from http://diabetes.niddk.nih.gov/dm/pubs/prevention program

National Gang Center. (n.d.). *National youth gang survey analysis.* Retrieved from https://

www.nationalgangcenter.gov/Survey-Analysis/Demographics

National Institutes of Health (NIH). (2001). *Outreach notebook for the NIH guidelines on inclusion of women and minorities as subjects in clinical research.* Retrieved from http://grants.nih.gov/grants/funding/women_min/guidelines_amended_10_2001.htm

National Institutes of Health (NIH). (2016). *PHS inclusion enrollment report.* Retrieved from https://grants.nih.gov/grants/forms/phs-inclusion-enrollment-report.htm

National Institute of Justice. (2011). *Program profile: Aban Aya youth project.* Retrieved from https://www.crimesolutions.gov/ProgramDetails.aspx?ID=129

National Institute on Drug Abuse (NIDA). (2000). *The brain: Understanding neurobiology through the study of addiction* (NIG Pub. No. 00–4871). Bethesda, MD: NIDA, NIH, DHHS.

National Institute on Drug Abuse (NIDA). (2002, February 18). *NIDA research report: Cocaine abuse and addiction* (PHD813, NIH Publication No. 99–4342). Washington, DC: U.S. Government Printing Office.

National Institute on Drug Abuse. (2016a). Understanding drug use and addiction. Retrieved from https://docs.google.com/document/d/19xuKE2ryJ8Md3GzcOSyvhA3gEIC9G6hrBUmHgcci8wo/edit

National Institute on Drug Abuse. (2016b). *Electronic cigarettes.* Retrieved from https://www.drugabuse.gov/publications/drugfacts/electronic-cigarettes-e-cigarettes

National Institute on Minority Health and Health Disparities (NIMHD). (n.d.). *Vision and mission.* Retrieved from http://www.nimhd.nih.gov/about_ncmhd/mission.asp

National Survey of American Life, 2001-2003. (n.d.). *ICPSR.* Retrieved from https://www.icpsr.umich.edu/icpsrweb/ICPSR/studies/00190

Nebbitt, V. E., Lombe, M., & Lindsey, M. (2007). Perceived parental behavior and peer affiliations among urban African American adolescents. *Social Work Research, 31*(3), 163–169.

Neblett, E. W., Jr., & Carter, S. E. (2012). The protective role of racial identity and Africentric worldview in the association between racial discrimination and blood pressure. *Psychosomatic Medicine, 74*(5), 509–516.

Neblett, E. W., Jr., Chavous, T. M., Nguyen, H. X., & Sellers, R. M. (2009). "Say It Loud: I'm Black and I'm Proud"—Parents' messages about race, racial discrimination, and academic achievement in African American boys. *Journal of Negro Education, 78*(3), 246–259.

Neblett, E. W., Jr., Hammond, W. P., Seaton, E. K., & Townsend, T. G. (2010). Underlying mechanisms in the relationship between Africentric worldview and depressive symptoms. *Journal of Counseling Psychology, 57*(1), 105.

Neblett, E. W., Jr., Philip, C. L., Cogburn, C. D., & Sellers, R. M. (2006). African American adolescents' discrimination experiences and academic achievement: Racial socialization as a cultural compensatory and protective factor. *Journal of Black Psychology, 32*(2), 199–218.

Neblett, E. W., Jr., Rivas-Drake, D., & Umaña-Taylor, A. J. (2012). The promise of racial and ethnic protective factors in promoting ethnic minority youth development. *Child Development Perspectives, 6*(3), 295–303.

Neblett, E. W., Jr., White, R. L., Ford, K. R., Philip, C. L., Nguyên, H. X., & Sellers, R. M. (2008). Patterns of racial socialization and psychological adjustment: Can parental communications about race reduce the impact of racial discrimination? *Journal of Research on Adolescence, 18*(3), 477–515.

Negy, C., Shreve, T. L., Jensen, B. J., & Uddin, N. (2003). Ethnic identity, self-esteem, and ethnocentrism: A study of social identity versus multicultural theory of development. *Cultural Diversity and Ethnic Minority Psychology, 9*(4), 333–344.

Nehl, E. J., Blanchard, C. M., Peng, C. Y. J., Rhodes, R. E., Kupperman, J., Sparling, P. B., . . . Baker, F. (2009). Understanding nonsmoking in African American and Caucasian college students: An application of the theory of planned behavior. *Behavioral Medicine, 35,* 23–29.

Nehl, E. J., Elifson, K., DePadilla, L., & Sterk, C. (2016). Sex partner type, drug use and condom with consistent condom use moderated by gender? *The Journal of Sex Research, 53*(7), 805–815.

Neighbors, H. W., Caldwell, C., Williams, D. R., Nesse, R., Taylor, R. J., Bullard, K. M., . . . Jackson, J. S. (2007). Race, ethnicity, and the use of services for mental disorders: Results from the National Survey of American Life. *Archives of General Psychiatry, 64*(4), 485–494.

Neighbors, H. W., Jackson, J. S., Bowman, P. J., & Gurin, G. (1983). Stress, coping, and black mental health: Preliminary findings from a national study. *Prevention in Human Services, 2*(3), 5–29.

Neighbors, H. W., Jackson, J. S., Campbell, L., & Williams, D. (1989). The influence of racial factors on psychiatric diagnosis: A review and suggestions for research. *Community Mental Health Journal, 25*(4), 301–311.

Neighbors, H. W., Woodward, A. T., Bullard, K. M., Ford, B. C., Taylor, R. J., & Jackson, J. S. (2008). Mental health service use among older African Americans: The National Survey of American Life. *American Journal of Geriatric Psychiatry, 16*(12), 948–956.

Nellis, A. (2016). *The color of justice: Racial and ethnic disparities in state prisons.* Washington, DC: The Sentencing Project.

Nellis, A., Green, J., & Mauer, M. (2008). *Reducing racial disparity in the criminal justice system.* Washington, DC: The Sentencing Project. Retrieved from http://www.sentencingproject.org/doc/publications/rd_reducingracialdisparity.pdf

Nelson, J. A., Leerkes, E. M., O'Brien, M., Calkins, S. D., & Marcovitch, S. (2012). African American and European American mothers' beliefs about negative emotions and emotion socialization practices. *Parenting, 12*(1), 22–41.

Nelson, J. A., Leerkes, E. M., Perry, N. B., O'brien, M., Calkins, S. D., & Marcovitch, S. (2013). European-American and African-American mothers' emotion socialization practices relate differently to their children's academic and social-emotional competence. *Social Development, 22*(3), 485–498.

Netter, S. (2010). Wanted: Ebonics translator for Federal DEA Job. *ABC News.* Retrieved from http://abcnews.go.com/US/wanted-ebonics-translator-federal-dea-job/story?id=11462206

Neubeck, K. J., & Cazenave, N. A. (2001). *Welfare racism: Playing the race card against America's poor.* New York, NY: Psychology Press.

Neufeldt, V., & Guralnik, D. B. (Eds.). (1996). *Webster's New World college dictionary.* New York, NY: Macmillan.

Neuliep, J. W. (2002). *Intercultural communication: A contextual approach.* Boston, MA: Houghton Mifflin.

Neville, H. A., Tynes, B. M., & Utsey, S. O. (Eds.). (2008). *Handbook of African American psychology.* Thousand Oaks, CA: Sage.

Newman, F. (2012). *An empowering curriculum for the African American student: Depaul University, School for New Learning Advanced Project.* Retrieved from http://snl.depaul.edu/writing/NewmanAPpaper2012.pdf

Newport, F. (2008). Blacks as conservative as Republicans on some moral issues. *Gallup.* Retrieved from http://www.gallup.com/poll/112807/blacks-conservative-republicans-some-moral-issues.aspx

Nguyen, A. W., Chatters, L. M., Taylor, R. J., & Mouzon, D. M. (2016a). Social support from family and friends and subjective well-being of older African Americans. *Journal of Happiness Studies, 17*(3), 959–979.

Nguyen, A. W., Taylor, R. J., Chatters, L. M., Taylor, H. O., Lincoln, K. D., & Mitchell, U. A. (2016b). Extended family and friendship support and suicidality among African Americans. *Social Psychiatry and Psychiatric Epidemiology, 52*(3), 299–309.

Nichols, T. M., Kotchick, B. A., Barry, C. M., & Haskins, D. G. (2010). Understanding the educational aspirations of African American adolescents: Child, family, and community factors. *Journal of Black Psychology, 36*(1), 25–48.

Nickerson, K. J., Helms, J. E., & Terrell, F. (1994). Cultural mistrust: Opinions about mental illness, and black students' attitudes toward seeking psychological help from white counselors. *Journal of Counseling Psychology, 41*(3), 378–385.

Niolon, P. H., Kearns, M. C., Dills, J., Rambo, K., Irving, S. M., Armstead, T. L., & Gilbert, L. K. (2017). Preventing intimate partner violence across the lifespan: a technical package of programs, policies, and practices. National Center for Injury Prevention and Control, Centers for Disease Control and Prevention.

Nisbett, R. E., & Miyamoto, Y. (2005). The influence of culture: Holistic versus analytic perception. *Trends in Cognitive Sciences, 9*(10), 467–473.

Nisbett, R. E., Peng, K., Choi, I., & Norenzayan, A. (2001). Culture and systems of thought: Holistic vs. analytic cognition. *Psychological Review, 108,* 291–310.

Nkosi, B., & Daniels, P. (2007). Family strengths: South Africa. *Marriage and Family Review, 41*(1–2), 11–26.

Nobles, W. W. (1976). Extended-self: Rethinking the so-called Negro self- concept. *Journal of Black Psychology, 11*(2), 15–24.

Nobles, W. W. (1980). African philosophy: Foundations for black psychology. In R. Jones (Ed.), *Black psychology* (pp. 23–36). New York, NY: Harper & Row.

Nobles, W. W. (1986). *African psychology: Towards its reclamation, reascension, and revitalization.* Oakland, CA: Black Family Institute.

Nobles, W. W. (1991). African philosophy: Foundations of black psychology. In R. Jones (Ed.), *Black psychology* (pp. 47–63). Berkeley, CA: Cobb & Henry.

Nobles, W. W. (2004). African philosophy: Foundations for black psychology. In R. Jones (Ed.), *Black psychology* (pp. 47–63). Berkeley, CA: Cobb & Henry.

Nobles, W. W. (2015). From black psychology to Sakhu Djaer implications for the further development of a Pan African black psychology. *Journal of Black Psychology, 41*(5), 399–414.

Nobles, W. W., Goddard, L. L., & Gilbert, D. J. (2009). Culturecology, women, and African-centered HIV prevention. *Journal of Black Psychology, 35*(2), 228–246.

Noguera, P. A. (2003). The trouble with black boys: The role and influence of environmental and cultural factors on the academic performance of African American males. *Urban Education, 38*(4), 431–459.

Noguera, P. A. (2012). Saving black and Latino boys: What schools can do to make a difference. *Phi Delta Kappan, 93*(5), 8–12.

Non, A. L., Gravlee, C. C., & Mulligan, C. J. (2012). Education, genetic ancestry, and blood pressure in African Americans and Whites. *American Journal of Public Health, 102*(8), 1559–1565.

Norbeck, J., Dejoseph, J. F., & Smith, R. T. (1996). A randomized trial of an empirically-derived social support intervention to prevent low birthweight among African American women. *Social Science Medicine, 43*(6), 947–954.

Norwalk, K. E., Vandiver, B. J., White, A. M., & Englar-Carlson, M. (2011). Factor structure of the gender role conflict scale in African American and European American men. *Psychology of Men & Masculinity, 12*(2), 128–143.

Nunn, A., Zaller, N., Cornwall, A., Mayer, K. H., Moore, E., Dickman, S., . . . Kwakwa, H. (2011). Low perceived risk and high HIV prevalence among a predominantly African American population participating in Philadelphia's rapid HIV testing program. *AIDS Patient Care and STDs, 25*(4), 229–235.

Nunn, K. B. (2002). Race, crime, and the pool of surplus criminality: Or why the "war on drugs" was a "war on blacks." *Journal of Gender, Race and Justice, 6,* 381–445.

Obasi, E. M., & Smith, A. J. (2009). African psychology, or Sahku Sheti: An application of the art of spiritual liberation and illumination of African people. In Neville, H. A., Tynes, B. M. & Utsey, S. O. (Eds.), *Handbook of African American Psychology* (pp. 47–60). Thousand Oaks, CA: Sage.

Odgerel, Z., Talati, A., Hamilton, S. P., Levinson, D. F., & Weissman, M. M. (2013). Genotyping serotonin transporter polymorphisms 5-HTTLPR and rs25531 in European- and African-American subjects from the National Institute of Mental Health's Collaborative Center for Genomic Studies. *Translational Psychiatry, 3*(9), 307.

O'Donnell, S., Meyer, I. H., & Schwartz, S. (2011). Increased risk of suicide attempts among black and Latino lesbians, gay men, and bisexuals. *American Journal of Public Health, 101*(6), 1055–1059.

O'Donnell, S. M. (1996). Urban African American community development practice. In I. Carlton-LaNey & N. Y. Burwell (Eds.), *African American community practice models* (pp. 7–26). New York, NY: Haworth Press.

Odulana, A., Kim, M. M., Green, M., Taylor, Y., Howard, D. L., Godley, P., & Corbie-Smith, G. (2014). Participating in research: Attitudes within the African American Church. *Journal of Religion and Health, 53*(2), 373–381.

Oetting, E. R., & Beauvais, F. (1986). Peer cluster theory: Drugs and the adolescent. *Journal of Counseling and Development, 65,* 17–22.

Office of Minority Health and Health Equity. (n.d.). Retrieved from https://www.cdc.gov/healthequity/lcod/men/2014/black/index.htm

Ogbu, J. U. (1999). Beyond language: Ebonics, proper English and identity in a Black-American speech community. *American Educational Research Journal, 36*(2), 147–184.

Ogden, C. L., Carroll, M. D., Kit, B. K., & Flegal, K. M. (2014). Prevalence of childhood and adult obesity in the United States, 2011–2014. *Journal of the American Medical Association, 311*(8), 806–814.

Ojelade, I. I., McCray, K., Ashby, J. S., & Meyers, J. (2011). Use of Ifá as a means of addressing mental health concerns among African American clients. *Journal of Counseling & Development, 89*(4), 406–412.

Ojelade, I. I., McCray, K., Meyers, J., & Ashby, J. (2014). Use of indigenous African healing practices as a mental health intervention. *Journal of Black Psychology, 40*(6), 491–519.

Okolo, C. B. (2003). Self as a problem in African philosophy. In P. H. Coetzee & A. P. J. Roux (Eds.), *The African philosophy reader* (pp. 209–215). New York, NY: Routledge.

Okwumabua, T. M., Walker, K. M., Hu, X., & Watson, A. (2011). An exploration of African American students' attitudes toward online learning. *Urban Education, 46*(2), 241–250.

Olang'o, C. O., Nyamongo, I. K. A., & Nyambedha, E. O. (2012). Children as caregivers of older relatives living with HIV and AIDS in Nyang'oma division of western Kenya. *African Journal of AIDS Research, 11*, 135–142.

Olfson, M., Blanco, C., Wang, S., Laje, G., & Correll, C. U. (2014). National trends in the mental health care of children, adolescents, and adults by office-based physicians. *JAMA Psychiatry, 71*(1), 81–90.

Oliver, J. S., Grindel, C. G., DeCoster, J., Ford, C. D., & Martin, M. Y. (2011). Benefits, barriers, sources of influence, and prostate cancer screening among rural men. *Public Health Nursing, 28*(6), 515–522.

Oliver, W. (2001). Cultural racism and structural violence: Implications for African Americans. *Journal of Human Behavior in the Social Environment, 4*(2–3), 1–26.

O'Neal, C. W., Wickrama, K. K., Ralston, P. A., Ilich, J. Z., Harris, C. M., Coccia, C., . . . Lemacks, J. (2012). Eating behaviors of older African Americans: An application of the theory of planned behavior. *The Gerontologist, 54*(2), 211–220.

Opare-Henaku, A. (2017). *Conceptions of love in Ghana: An exploration among orthodox and charismatic Christians* (Unpublished Paper). University of Ghana, Legon.

O'Reilly, B. (Producer). (2007, September 19). Nationally syndicated radio show. *The Radio Factor* [Audio Broadcast]. New York, NY: Fox Broadcasting. Retrieved from http://mediamatters.org/research/2007/09/21/oreilly-surprised-there-was-no-difference-betwe/139893

Orfield, G., Losen, D., Wald, J., & Swanson, C. (2004). *Losing our future: How minority youth are being left behind by the graduation rate crisis.* Cambridge, MA: Harvard University Civil Rights Project.

Oruka, H. O. (2002). Ideology and culture: The African experience. In P. H. Coetzee & A. P. J. Roux (Eds.), *Philosophy from Africa* (2nd ed., pp. 58–63). New York, NY: Routledge.

Ossana, S. M., Helms, J. E., & Leonard, M. M. (1992). Do "womanist" identity attitudes influence college women's self-esteem and perceptions of environmental bias? *Journal of Counseling and Development, 70*(3), 402–408.

Oyserman, D., Coon, H. M., & Kemmelmeier, M. (2002). Rethinking individualism and collectivism: Evaluation of theoretical assumptions and meta-analyses. *Psychological Bulletin, 128*, 3–72.

Pacek, L. R., Malcolm, R. J., & Martins, S. S. (2012), Race/ethnicity differences between alcohol, marijuana, and co-occurring alcohol and marijuana use disorders and their association with public health and social problems using a national sample. *The American Journal on Addictions, 21*(5), 435–444.

Padilla-Walker, L. M., Coyne, S. M., & Collier, K. M. (2016). Longitudinal relations between parental media monitoring and adolescent aggression, prosocial behavior, and externalizing problems. *Journal of adolescence, 46*, 86–97.

Page, C. (2010). Speak Ebonics? DEA is looking for translators. Federal agency looking for linguists fluent in Ebonics to help agents translate wiretaps. *Chicago Tribune.* Retrieved from http://articles.chicagotribune.com/2010-08-29/news/ct-oped-0829-page-20100829_1_ebonics-dea-translators

Pahilke, E., Hyde, J. S., & Allison, C. M. (2014). The effects of single-sex compared with coeducational schooling on students' performance and attitudes: A meta-analysis. *Psychological Bulletin, 140*(4), 1042–1072.

Palapattu, A. G., Kingery, J. N., & Ginsburg, G. S. (2006). Gender role orientation and anxiety symptoms among African American adolescents. *Journal of Abnormal Child Psychology, 34*(3), 423–431.

Palmer, R., & Gasman, M. (2008). *"It Takes a Village to Raise a Child": The role of social capital in promoting academic success for African American men at a Black college.* Retrieved from http://repository.upenn.edu/gse_pubs/173

Parent, J., Jones, D. J., Forehand, R., Cuellar, J., & Shoulbert, E. K. (2013). The role of coparents in African American single-mother families: The indirect effect of coparent identity on youth psychosocial adjustment. *Journal of Family Psychology, 27*(2), 252–262.

Parents Involved In Community Schools v. Seattle School District No. 1 Et Al. (2007). No. 05-908. Retrieved from http://caselaw.findlaw.com/us-supreme-court/551/701.html

Parham, T. A. (1992a). Cycles of psychological nigrescence. *The Counseling Psychologist, 17*(2), 187–226.

Parham, T. A. (2005). *Working with African American clients* [Video]. Washington, DC: American Psychological Association.

Parham, T. A. (2009). Foundations for an African centered psychology: Extending roots to an ancient Kemetic past. In H. A. Neville, B. M. Tynes & S. O. Utsey (Eds.), *Handbook of African American psychology.* Thousand Oaks, CA: Sage.

Parham, T. A., & Helms, J. E. (1981). The influence of black students' racial identity attitudes on preferences for counselor's race. *Journal of Counseling Psychology, 28*(3), 250–257.

Parham, T. A., White, J. L., & Ajamu, A. (1999). *The psychology of Blacks: An African centered perspective* (3rd ed.). Upper Saddle River, NJ: Prentice Hall.

Parham, T. A., White, J. L., & Ajamu, A. (2008). *The psychology of Blacks: An African centered perspective* (4th ed.). Upper Saddle River, NJ: Prentice Hall.

Parham-Payne, W. (2013). Weight perceptions and desired body size in a national sample of African-American men and women with diabetes. *Journal of African American Studies, 17*(4), 433–443.

Parker, L. J., Kinlock, B. L., Chisolm, D., Furr-Holden, D., & Thorpe, R. J., Jr. (2016). Association between any major discrimination and current cigarette smoking among adult African American men. *Substance Use & Misuse, 51*(12), 1593–1599.

Parks, C. A., Hughes, T. L., & Matthews, A. K. (2004). Race/ethnicity and sexual orientation: Intersecting identities. *Cultural Diversity and Ethnic Minority Psychology, 10*(3), 241–254.

Parks, G., & Hughey, M. W. (2011). *The Obamas and a (post) racial America?* Oxford, England: Oxford University Press.

Pascoe, E. A., & Smart Richman, L. (2009). Perceived discrimination and health: A meta-analytic review. *Psychological Bulletin, 135*(4), 531–554.

Pastore, N. (1946). A comment on "psychological differences as among races". *School and Society, 63*, 136–137.

Patel, N. C., Crismon, M. L., Shafer, A., DeLeon, A., Lopez, M., & Lane, D. C. (2006). Ethnic variation in symptoms and response to risperidone in youth with schizophrenia-spectrum disorders. *Social Psychiatry and Psychiatric Epidemiology, 41*(5), 341–346.

Patterson, C. J. (2005). Lesbian and gay parents and their children: Summary of research findings. In *Lesbian and gay parenting: A resource for psychologists* (2nd ed.). Washington, DC: American Psychological Association.

Patterson, G. E., Ward, D. B., & Brown, T. B. (2013). Relationship scripts: How young women develop and maintain same-sex romantic relationships. *Journal of GLBT Family Studies, 9*, 179–201.

Patterson, K. (2004). A longitudinal study of African American women and the maintenance of a healthy self-esteem. *Journal of Black Psychology, 30*(33), 307–328.

Pavey, L., Greitemeyer, T., & Sparks, P. (2012). "I help because I want to, not because you tell me to": Empathy increases autonomously motivated helping. *Personality & Social Psychology Bulletin, 38*(5), 681–689.

Paxton, R., Valois, R., & Drane, J. (2007). Is there a relationship between family structure and substance use among public middle school students? *Journal of Child and Family Studies, 16*(5), 593–605.

Payne, Y. A., & Gibson, L. R. (2009). Hip-hop music and culture: A site of resiliency for the streets of young Black America. In H. A., Neville, B. M. Tynes & S. O. Utsey (Eds.), *Handbook of African American psychology* (pp. 127–141). Thousand Oaks, CA: Sage.

Pellebon, D. A. (2011). The Asante-based afrocentricity scale: Developing a scale to measure Asante's Afrocentricity paradign. *Journal of Human Behavior in the Social Environment, 21*(1), 35–56.

Pen or Pencil. (n.d.). National alliance of faith and justice. Retrieved from http://www.penorpencilmovement.org/

Penner, L. A., Dovidio, J. F., West, T. V., Gaertner, S. L., Albrecht, T. L., Dailey, R. K., & Markova, T. (2010). Aversive racism and medical interactions with Black patients: A field study. *Journal of Experimental Social Psychology, 46*(2), 436–440.

Peplau, L. A., & Fingerhut, A. W. (2007). The close relationships of lesbian and gay men. *Annual Review of Psychology, 58*, 405–424.

Pérez-Stable, E. J., & Benowitz, N. L. (2011). Do biological differences help explain tobacco-related disparities. *American Journal of Health Promotion, 25*(5), S8–S10. Thousand Oaks, CA: Sage.

Perkins, K. R. (1996). The influence of television images on black females' self-perceptions of physical attractiveness. *Journal of Black Psychology, 22*(4), 453–469.

Perry A., & Lewis, S. (2016). Leaving legacies: African American men discuss the impact of their fathers on the development of their own paternal attitudes and behavior. *Journal of Family Social Work, 19*(1), 3–21.

Peters, M. F., & Massey, G. (1983). Mundane extreme environmental stress in family stress theories: The case of black families in white America. *Marriage and Family Review, 6*(1–2), 193–218.

Peters, R. M., & Templin, T. N. (2010). Theory of planned behavior, self-care motivation, and blood pressure self-care. *Research and Theory for Nursing Practice, 24*(3), 172–186.

Peterson, J. (1923). The comparative abilities of white and negro children. *Comparative Psychology Monographs, 1*(5), 141.

Peterson, J. A., & Cheng, A. L. (2011). Heart and soul physical activity program for African American women. *Western Journal of Nursing Research, 33*(5), 652–670.

Peterson, R. D., Krivo, L. J., & Velez, M. B. (2001). Segregation and youth criminal violence: A review and agenda. In S. O. White (Ed.), *Handbook of youth and justice* (pp. 277–286). Dordrecht, the Netherlands: Kluwer.

Pew. (2010). *Collateral costs: Incarceration's effect on economic mobility.* Washington, DC: The Pew Charitable Trusts.

Pew. (2015). *The American family today. Social & Demographic Trends.* Retrieved from http://www.pewsocialtrends.org/2015/12/17/1-the-american-family-today/

Pew Forum on Religion and Public Life. (2008). U.S. religious landscape survey. *Chapter 3: Religious affiliation and demographic groups* (pp. 40–41). Retrieved from http://religions.pewforum.org/reports#

Pew Forum on Religion and Public Life. (2009, January 30). *A religious portrait of African-Americans: Analysis.* Retrieved from http://www.pewforum.org/A-Religious-Portrait-of-African-Americans.aspx

Pew Research. (2016). *A divided and pessimistic electorate: Voters skeptical of progress in many areas—even jobs—since 2008.* Retrieved from http://www.people-press.org/2016/11/10/a-divided-and-pessimistic-electorate/

Pew Research Center. (2011). *Resources on Islam and Christianity in Sub-Saharan Africa.* Retrieved from http://www.pewforum.org/2011/02/17/resources-on-islam-and-christianity-in-sub-saharan-africa/

Pew Research Center. (2015). *American's changing religious landscape.* Retrieved from file:///C:/Users/Faye/Downloads/RLS-08-26-full-report.pdf

Pew Research Center. (2015). *Multiracial in America: Proud, diverse and growing in numbers.* Washington, DC: Pew. Retrieved from http://www.pewsocialtrends.org/2015/06/11/multiracial-in-america/

Pew Research Center. (2016). *Demographic trends and economic well-being.* Retrieved from http://www.pewsocialtrends.org/2016/06/27/1-demographic-trends-and-economic-well-being/

Pew Research Center, U.S. Politics & Policy. (2011). *Muslim Americans: No signs of growth in alienation or support for extremism.* Retrieved from http://www.people-press.org/2011/08/30/section-1-a-demographic-portrait-of-muslim-americans/

Pezzella, F. S., Thornberry, T. P., & Smith, C. A. (2016). Race socialization and parenting styles: Links to delinquency for African American and White adolescents. *Youth Violence and Juvenile Justice, 14*(4), 448–467.

Phares, V., Fields, S., Watkins-Clay, M. M., Kamboukos, D., & Han, S. (2005). Race/ethnicity and self-esteem in families of adolescents. *Child and Family Behavior Therapy, 27*(3), 13–26.

Phelps, J. (1990). *Black spirituality. Spiritual traditions for the contemporary church.* Nashville, TN: Abingdon Press.

Phinney, J. (1992). The multigroup ethnic identity measure: A new scale for use with diverse groups. *Journal of Adolescent Research, 7*(2), 156–176.

Phinney, J. (1995). Ethnic identity and self-esteem: A review and integration. In A. Padilla (Ed.), *Hispanic psychology: Critical issues in theory and research* (pp. 57–70). Thousand Oaks, CA: Sage.

Pierce, C. M. (1978). *Television and education*. Beverly Hills, CA: Sage.

Pierce-Jones, J., Reid, J. B., & King, F. J. (1964). Adolescent racial and ethnic group differences in social attitudes and adjustment. *Psychological Reports, 5*(3), 549–552.

Pierre, M. R., & Mahalik, J. R. (2005). Examining African self-consciousness and black racial identity as predictors of Black men's psychological well-being. *Cultural Diversity and Ethnic Minority Psychology, 11*(1), 28–40.

Pieterse, A. L., Todd, N. R., Neville, H. A., & Carter, R. T. (2012). Perceived racism and mental health among Black American adults: A meta-analytic review. *Journal of Counseling Psychology, 59*(1), 1–9.

Pietila, A. (2010). *Not in my neighborhood: How bigotry shaped a great American city*. Chicago, IL: Ivan R. Dee.

Piko, B. F., & Kovács, E. (2010). Do parents and school matter? Protective factors for adolescent substance use. *Addictive Behaviors, 35*(1), 53–56.

Pittman, C. T. (2011). Getting mad but ending up sad: The mental health consequences for African Americans using anger to cope with racism. *Journal of Black Studies, 42*(7), 1106–1124.

Plummer, D., & Slane, S. (1996). Patterns of coping in racially stressful situations. *Journal of Black Psychology, 22*(3), 302–315.

Plunkett, D. P. (2014). The Black church, values, and secular counseling: Implications for counselor education and practice. *Counseling and Values, 59*(2), 208–221.

Plybon, L. E., Edwards, L., Butler, D., Belgrave, F. Z., & Allison, K. W. (2003). Examining the link between neighborhood cohesion and school outcomes: The role of support coping among African American adolescent girls. *Journal of Black Psychology, 29*(4), 393–407.

Polakow-Suransky, S. (1999). *Access denied*. Ann Arbor, MI: Student Advocacy Center of Michigan.

Poliakov, L. (1982). Racism from the enlightenment to the age of imperialism. In R. Ross (Ed.), *Racism and colonialism: Essays on ideology and social structure* (pp. 55–64). The Hague, Netherlands: Martinus Nijhoff.

Pomery, E., Gibbons, F., Gerrard, M., Cleveland, M., Brody, G., & Wills, T. (2005). Families and risk: Prospective analyses of familial and social influences on adolescent substance use. *Journal of Family Psychology, 19*(4), 560–570.

Ponterotto, J., Utsey, S., & Pedersen, P. (2006). *Preventing prejudice: A guide for counselors, educators, and parents*. Thousand Oaks, CA: Sage.

Popkin, S., Rosenbaum, J., & Meaden, P. (1993). Labor market experiences of low-income black women in middle-class suburbs: Evidence from a survey of Gautreaux program participants. *Journal of Policy Analysis and Management, 12*(3), 556–573.

Porterfield, E. (1982). Black-American intermarriage in the United States. *Marriage and Family Review, 5*(1), 17–34.

Potts, R. (1991). Spirits in the bottle: Spirituality and alcoholism treatment in African-American communities. *Journal of Training and Practice in Professional Psychology, 5*(1), 53–64.

Potts, R. G. (2003). Emancipatory education versus school-based prevention in African American communities. *American Journal of Community Psychology, 31*(1–2), 173–183.

Powell, J. A. (1999). Achieving racial justice: What's sprawl got to do with it? *Poverty and Race, 8*(5). Retrieved from http://www.prrac.org/full_text.php?text_id= 292&item_id=1841&newsletter_id=46&header=Race+%2F+Racism&kc=1

Powell, T. W., Herbert, A., Ritchwood, T. D., & Latkin, C. A. (2016). "Let me help you help me": Church-based HIV prevention for young black men who have sex with men. *AIDS Education and Prevention, 28*, 202–215.

Powell-Hopson, D., & Hopson, D. S. (1992). Implications of doll color preferences among Black preschool children and White preschool children. In A. K. Burlew, W. C. Banks, H. P. McAdoo & D. A. Azibo (Eds.), *African American Psychology: Theory, research, and practice* (pp. 183–189). Newbury Park, CA: Sage.

Powell-Young, Y. M. (2012). Household income and spiritual well-being but not body mass index as determinants of poor self-rated health among African American adolescents. *Research in Nursing and Health, 35*, 219–230.

Priest, N., Paradies, Y., Trenerry, B., Truong, M., Karlsen, S., & Kelly, Y. (2013). A systematic review of studies examining the relationship between reported racism and health and wellbeing for children and young people. *Social Science & Medicine, 95*, 115–127.

Psych Discourse. (2011). The National Institute of Health and racial discrimination: A response from the Association of Black Psychologists. *Psych*

Discourse, 45(5). Retrieved from http://pd-online. abpsi.org/index.php?option=com_content&view=article&id=409%3Athe-national-institutes-of-health-and-racial-discrimination&catid=110%3Afeatured-news-v45-5&Itemid=262

Purvis, M. (2011). Paternal incarceration and parenting program in prison: A review paper. *Journal of Psychiatry, Psychology, and Law, 20*(1), 9–28.

Putnam, R. D. (1993). The prosperous community: Social capital and economic growth. *Current, 356,* 4–10.

Putnam, R. D. (1995). Bowling alone: America's declining social capital. *Journal of Democracy, 6*(1), 664–665.

Quarcoopome, T. N. O. (1987). *West African traditional religion.* Ibadan, Nigeria: African Universities Press.

Quinn, K., Dickson-Gomez, J., DiFranceisco, W., Kelly, J. A., St. Lawrence, J. S., Amirkhanian, Y. A., & Broaddus, M. (2015). Correlates of internalized homonegativity among black men who have sex with men. *AIDS Education and Prevention, 27*(3), 212–226.

Quinn, K., Dickson-Gomez, J., & Kelly, J. A. (2016). The role of the Black Church in the lives of young Black men who have sex with men. *Culture, Health & Sexuality, 18*(5), 524–537.

Radziszewska, B., Richardson, J. L., Dent, C. W., & Flay, B. R. (1996). Parenting style and adolescent depressive symptoms, smoking, and academic achievement: Ethnic, gender, and SES differences. *Journal of Behavioral Medicine, 19*(3), 289–305.

Rajaram, S. S., & Rashidi, A. (2003). African-American Muslim women and health care. *Women & Health, 37*(3), 81–96.

Raley, R. K., & Sweeney, M. M. (2009). Explaining race and ethnic variation in marriage: Directions for future research. *Race and Social Problems, 1*(3), 132–142.

Ramey, C. T., Bryant, D. M., Wasik, B. H., Sparling, J. J., Fendt, K. H., & LaVange, L. M. (1992). The infant health and development program for low birthweight, premature infants: Program elements, family participation, and child intelligence. *Pediatrics, 89*(3), 454–465.

Ramey, C. T., & Ramey, S. L. (2004). Early learning and school readiness: Can early intervention make a difference? *Merrill-Palmer Quarterly, 50*(4), 471–491.

Ramose, M. B. (2003). The philosophy of ubuntu and ubuntu as a philosophy. In P. H. Coetzee & A. P. J. Roux (Eds.), *The African philosophy reader* (pp. 230–238). New York, NY: Routledge.

Randolph, S. M., & Banks, H. D. (1993). Making a way out of no way: The promise of Africentric approaches to prevention. *Journal of Black Psychology, 19*(2), 204–214.

Rashid, K. (2005). Slavery of the mind: Carter G. Woodson and Jacob H. Carruthers-intergenerational discourse on African education and social change. *Western Journal of Black Studies, 29*(1), 542.

Rastogi, S., Johnson, T. D., Hoeffel, E. M., & Drewery, M. P. (2011). The black population: 2010 (*2010 Census Briefs*). Retrieved from http://www.census.gov/prod/cen2010/briefs/c2010br-06.pdf

Rattan, A., Levine, C. S., Dweck, C. S., & Eberhardt, J. L. (2012). Race and the fragility of the legal distinction between juveniles and adults. *PLoS One, 7*(5), e36680.

Read, J. G., & Emerson, M. O. (2005). Racial context, black immigration and the U.S. Black/White health disparity. *Social Forces, 84*(1), 181–199.

Ready by 21. (n.d.). Retrieved from http://www.readyby21.org/

Reagan, P. B., Salsberry, P. J., Fang, M. Z., Gardner, W. P., & Pajer, K. (2012). African-American/white differences in the age of menarche: Accounting for the difference. *Social Science and Medicine.* doi:10.1016/j.socscimed.2012.05.018

Reardon, S. (2015). Ebola's mental-health wounds linger in Africa. *Nature, 519*(7541), 13–14.

Reboussin, B. A., Ialongo, N. S., & Green, K. M. (2015). Influences of behavior and academic problems at school entry on marijuana use transitions during adolescence in an African-American sample. *Addictive Behaviors, 41,* 51–57.

Redford, J., Battle, D., & Bielick, S. (2016). *Homeschooling in the United States: 2012* (NCES 2016-096). Washington, DC: National Center for Education Statistics, Institute of Education Sciences, U.S. Department of Education. Retrieved from https://nces.ed.gov/pubs2016/2016096rev.pdf

Reeves, E. A., & Woods-Giscombé, C. L. (2015). Infant-feeding practices among African American women. *Journal of Transcultural Nursing, 26*(3), 219–226.

Regan, P. C., Durvasula, R., Howell, L., Ureño, O., & Rea, M. (2004). Gender, ethnicity, and the developmental timing of first sexual and romantic experiences. *Social Behavior and Personality, 32*(7), 667–676.

Reiss, I. (1965). The universality of the family: A conceptual analysis. *Journal of Marriage and the Family, 26,* 443–453.

Resnicow, K., Jackson, A., Blissett, D., Wang, T., McCarty, F., Rahotep, S., & Periasamy, S. (2005). Results of the healthy body healthy spirit trial. *Health Psychology, 24*(4), 339–348.

Reynolds, J. E., & Gonzales-Backen, M. A. (2017). Ethnic-racial socialization and the mental health of African Americans: A critical review. *Journal of Family Theory & Review, 92*(2), 182–200.

Richardson, J. J. B. (2009). Men do matter: Ethnographic insights on the socially supportive role of the African American uncle in the lives of inner-city African American male youth. *Journal of Family Issues, 30*(8), 1041–1069.

Richardson, M. S., Constantine, K., & Washburn, M. (2005). New directions for theory development in vocational psychology. In W. B. Walsh & M. L. Savickas (Eds.), *Handbook of vocational psychology* (3rd ed., pp. 51–83). Mahwah, NJ: Erlbaum.

Richardson, T. Q., & Helms, J. E. (1994). The relationship of the racial identity attitudes of black men to perceptions of "parallel" counseling dyads. *Journal of Counseling and Development, 73*(2), 172–178.

Rickford, J. R. (n.d.). *What is Ebonics? (African American Vernacular English)*. Washington, DC: Linguistic Society of America. Retrieved from http://www.linguisticsociety.org/sites/default/files/Ebonics.pdf

Rickford, J. R. (1999). *African American vernacular English: Features, evolution, educational implications.* New York, NY: Wiley-Blackwell.

Rickford, J. R., & King, S. (2016). Language and linguistics on trial: Hearing Rachel Jeantel (and other vernacular speakers) in the courtroom and beyond. *Language, 92*(4), 948–988.

Ridley, C. R. (1984). Clinical treatment of the non-disclosing black client: A therapeutic paradox. *American Psychologist, 39*(11), 1234–1244.

Riina, E. M., Lippert, A., & Brooks-Gunn, J. (2016). Residential instability, family support, and parent–child relationships among ethnically diverse urban families. *Journal of Marriage and Family, 78*(4), 855–870.

Riina, E. M., Martin, A., Gardner, M., & Brooks-Gunn, J. (2013). Context matters: Links between neighborhood discrimination, neighborhood cohesion and African American adolescents' adjustment. *Journal of Youth and Adolescence, 42*(1), 1–11.

Rivas-Drake, D., Seaton, E. K., Markstrom, C., Quintana, S., Syed, M., Lee, R. M., . . . Yip, T. (2014). Ethnic and racial identity in adolescence: Implications for psychosocial, academic, and health outcomes. *Child Development, 85*(1), 40–57.

Robbins, M., Briones, E., & Schwartz, S. (2006). Differences in family functioning in grandparent and parent-headed households in a clinical sample of drug-using African American adolescents. *Cultural Diversity and Ethnic Minority Psychology, 12*(1), 84–100.

Roberts, C. (2012). *Trayvon Martin killer George Zimmerman has bloody lip in new photo of fateful night.* Retrieved from http://www.nydailynews.com/news/national/new-photo-support-self-defense-claim-trayvon-martin-killer-george-zim merman-article-1.1212539

Roberts, D., Torres, I., & Brown, J. (2016). As natural hair goes mainstream, one high schools' natural hair ban sparks firestorm. *ABC News.* Retrieved from http://abcnews.go.com/US/natural-hair-mainstream-high-schools-policy-sparks-firestorm/story?id=42100267

Roberts, M. E., Berman, M. L., Slater, M. D., Hinton, A., & Ferketich, A. K. (2015). Point-of-sale tobacco marketing in rural and urban Ohio: Could the new landscape of Tobacco products widen inequalities? *Preventive Medicine, 81*, 232–235.

Roberts, R. E., Phinney, J. S., Masse, L. C., Chen, Y. R., Roberts, C. R., & Romero, A. (1999). The structure of ethnic identity of young adolescents from diverse ethnocultural groups. *Journal of Early Adolescence, 19*, 301–322.

Roberts-Douglass, K., & Curtis-Boles, H. (2012). Exploring positive masculinity development in African American men: A retrospective study. *Psychology of Men & Masculinity, 14*(1), 7–15.

Robinson, J., & Biran, M. (2006). Discovering self: Relationships between African identity and academic achievement. *Journal of Black Studies, 37*, 46–68.

Robnett, R. D., & Anderson, K. J. (2017). Feminist identity among women and men from four ethnic groups. *Cultural Diversity and Ethnic Minority Psychology, 23*(1), 134–142.

Rock, P. F., Cole, D. J., Houshyar, S., Lythcott, M., & Prinstein, M. J. (2011). Peer status in an ethnic context: Associations with African American adolescents' ethnic identity. *Journal of Applied Developmental Psychology, 32*(4), 163–169.

Rodgers-Farmer, A. Y. (1999). Parenting stress, depression, and parenting in grandmothers raising their grandchildren. *Children and Youth Services Review, 21*(5), 377–388.

Rodriguez, C. H. (2017). Segregated living linked to higher blood pressure among Blacks. *Kaiser Health News*. Retrieved from http://khn.org/news/segregated-living-linked-to-higher-blood-pressure-among-blacks/

Rodriguez, E., Allen, J. A., Frongillo, E. A., Jr., & Chandra, P. (1999). Unemployment, depression, and health: A look at the African American community. *Community Health, 53*(6), 335–342.

Roebuck, J. B., & Murty, K. S. (1993). *Historically black colleges and universities: Their place in American higher education*. Westport, CT: Praeger.

Roen, S. R. (1961). Personality and Negro-White intelligence. *Journal of Abnormal and Social Psychology, 61*, 148–150.

Roh, S., & Robinson, M. (2009). A geographic approach to racial profiling: The microanalysis and macroanalysis of racial disparity in traffic stops. *Police Quarterly, 12*(2), 137–169.

Rollins, V. B., & Valdez, J. N. (2006). Perceived racism and career self-efficacy in African American adolescents. *Journal of Black Psychology, 32*(2), 176–198.

Rolnick, A., & Grunewald, R. (2003). Early childhood development: Economic development with a high public return. *FedGazette*. Retrieved from http://www.minneapolisfed.org/publications_papers/pub_display.cfm?id=3832

Rosenbaum, J. E., Kulieke, M. J., & Rubinowitz, L. S. (1988). White suburban schools' responses to low-income black children: Sources of successes and problems. *Urban Review, 20*(1), 28–41.

Rosenbaum, J. E., & Popkin, S. J. (1991). Employment and earnings of low-income Blacks who move to middle-class suburbs. In C. Jencks & P. Peterson (Eds.), *The urban underclass* (pp. 342–356). Washington, DC: Brookings Institution.

Rosenthal, R., & Jacobson, L. (1968). *Pygmalion in the classroom*. New York, NY: Holt, Rinehart & Winston.

Ross, M., & Aday, L. (2006). Stress and coping in African American grandparents who are raising their grandchildren. *Journal of Family Issues, 27*(7), 912–932.

Ross, M. W., Essien, E. J., & Torres, I. (2006). Conspiracy beliefs about the origin of HIV/AIDS in four racial/ethnic groups. *Journal of Acquired Immune Deficiency Syndromes, 41*(3), 342–344.

Roth, D. L., Mwase, I., Holt, C. L., Clark, E. M., Lukwago, S. N., & Kreuter, M. W. (2012). Religious involvement measurement model in a national sample of African Americans. *Journal of Religion and Health, 51*(2), 567–578.

Rothe, E. M., Pumariega, A., & Rogers, K. (2008). Cultural aspects of the pharmacological treatment of depression: Factors affecting minority and youth. *Psychiatric Times, 25*(5), 1–2.

Rouland, K., Matthews, J. S., Byrd, C. M., Meyer, R. M., & Rowley, S. J. (2014). Culture clash: Interactions between afrocultural and mainstream cultural styles in classrooms serving African American students. *Interdisciplinary Journal of Teaching and Learning, 4*(3), 186–202.

Rovai, A. P., Gallien, L. B., & Wighting, M. J. (2005). Cultural and interpersonal factors affecting African American academic performance in higher education: A review and synthesis of the research literature. *Journal of Negro Education, 74*(4), 359–370.

Rowland, M. L., & Isaac-Savage, E. P. (2014). As I see it: A study of African American pastors' views on health and health education in the Black church. *Journal of Religion and Health, 53*(4), 1091–1101.

Rowley, S. J., & Camacho, T. C. (2015). Increasing diversity in cognitive developmental research: Issues and solutions. *Journal of Cognition and Development, 16*(5), 683–692.

Rowley, S. J., Cooper, S. M., & Clinton, Y. C. (2005). Family and school support for healthy racial identity development in African American youth. In H. Fitzgerald, R. Zucker & K. Freeark (Eds.), *The crisis in youth mental health*. Westport, CT: Praeger.

Rubin, D. F., & Belgrave, F. Z. (1999). Differences between African American and European American college students in relative and mathematical time orientations: A preliminary study. *Journal of Black Psychology, 25*, 105–113.

Ruffin, J. E. (1989). Stages of adult development in black professional women. In R. L. Jones (Ed.), *Black adult development and aging* (pp. 31–61). Berkeley, CA: Cobb & Henry.

Rugh, J., & Massey, D. (2010). Racial segregation and the American foreclosure crisis. *American Sociological Review, 75*(5), 629–651.

Ruglass, L. M., Hien, D. A., Hu, M., Campbell, A. N. C., Caldeira, N. A., Miele, G. M., & Chang, D. F. (2014). Racial/ethnic match and treatment outcomes for women with PTSD and substance use disorders receiving community-based treatment. *Community Mental Health Journal, 50*(7), 811–822.

Ryabov, I. (2016). Examining the role of residential segregation in explaining racial/ethnic gaps in spending on fruit and vegetables. *Appetite, 98*, 74–79.

Ryan, C. L., & Bauman, K. (2016). *Educational attainment in the United States: 2015*. Retrieved from https://www.census.gov/content/dam/Census/library/publications/2016/demo/p20-578.pdf

Saal, W., & Kagee, A. (2012). The applicability of the theory of planned behaviour in predicting adherence to ART among a South African sample. *Journal of Health Psychology, 17*(3), 362–370.

Sadler, M. S., Correll, J., Park, B., & Judd, C. M. (2012). The world is not black and white: Racial bias in the decision to shoot in a multiethnic context. *Journal of Social Issues, 68*(2), 286–313.

Salas-Wright, C. P., Tirmazi, T., Lombe, M., & Nebbitt, V. E. (2015). Religiosity and antisocial behavior: Evidence from young African American women in public housing communities. *Social Work Research, 39*(2), 82–93.

Sampson, R. J. (2011). 11 Neighborhood effects, causal mechanisms and the social structure of the city. In P. Demeulenaere (Ed.). *Analytical sociology and social mechanisms* (pp. 227–250). New York, NY: Cambridge University Press.

Sampson, R. J., Morenoff, J., & Earls, F. (1999). Beyond social capital: Neighborhood mechanisms and structural sources of collective efficacy for children. *American Sociological Review, 64*(5), 633–660.

Sampson, R. J., & Raudenbush, S. (1999). Systematic social observation of public spaces: A new look at disorder in urban neighborhoods. *American Journal of Sociology, 105*(3), 603–651.

Sampson, R. J., Raudenbush, S. W., & Earls, F. (1997). Neighborhoods and violent crime: A multilevel study of collective efficacy. *Science, 227*, 918–923.

Sampson, R. J., Sharkey, P., & Raudenbush, S. W. (2008). Durable effects of concentrated disadvantage on verbal ability of African-American children. *Proceedings of the National Academy of Science, 105*(3), 845–852.

Sampson, R. J., & Winter, A. (2016). The racial ecology of lead poisoning: Toxic inequality in Chicago neighborhoods, 1995–2013. *DuBois Review: Social Science Research on Race, 13*(2), 261–283.

Sanchez-Hughley, J. (2000). *The first session with African Americans: A step by step guide*. San Francisco, CA: Jossey-Bass.

Sanders-Phillips, K., Kliewer, W., Tirmazi, T., Nebbitt, V., Carter, T., & Key, H. (2014). Perceived racial discrimination, drug use, and psychological distress in African American youth: A pathway to child health disparities. *Journal of Social Issues, 70*(2), 279–297.

Santos, C. E., & VanDaalen, R. A. (2016). The associations of sexual and ethnic–racial identity commitment, conflicts in allegiances, and mental health among lesbian, gay, and bisexual racial and ethnic minority adults. *Journal of Counseling Psychology, 63*(6), 668–676.

Sarno, E. L., Mohr, J. J., Jackson, S. D., & Fassinger, R. E. (2015). When identities collide: Conflicts in allegiances among LGB people of color. *Cultural Diversity and Ethnic Minority Psychology, 21*, 550–559.

Satcher, D., Fryer, G. E., McCann, J., Troutman, A., Woolf, S. H., & Rust, G. (2005). What if we were equal? A comparison of the Black-White mortality gap in 1960 and 2000. *Health Affairs, 24*(2), 459–464.

Saucier, D., & Miller, C. (2003). The persuasiveness of racial arguments as a subtle measure of racism. *Personality and Social Psychology Bulletin, 29*(10), 1303–1315.

Saunders, J. M. (2000). Exposure to chronic community violence: Formal kinship, informal kinship, and spirituality as stress moderators for African American children. *Dissertation Abstracts International, A (Humanities and Social Sciences), 60*(12-A), 4333.

Savickas, M. L. (2002). Reinvigorating the study of careers. *Journal of Vocational Behavior, 61*, 381–385.

Saylor, E. S., & Aries, E. (1999). Ethnic identity and change in social context. *Journal of Social Psychology, 139*(5), 549–566.

Sbrocco, T., Osborn, R., Clark, R. D., Hsiao, C. W., & Carter, M. M. (2012). Assessing the stages of change among African American women in a weight management program. *Journal of Black Psychology, 38*(1), 81–103.

Schaalma, H., Aaro, L. E., Flisher, A. J., Mathews, C., Kaaya, S., Onya, H., . . . Klepp, K. I. (2009). Correlates of intention to use condoms among Sub-Saharan African youth: The applicability of the theory of planned behaviour. *Scandinavian Journal of Public Health, 37*(2), 87–91.

Schatz, J., Schlenz, A., McClellan, C. B., Puffer, E. S., Hardy, S., Pfeiffer, M., & Roberts, C. W. (2015).

Changes in coping, pain and activity following cognitive-behavioral training randomized clinical trial for pediatric sickle cell disease using smartphones. *The Clinical Journal of Pain, 31*(6), 536–547.

Schneider, D. (2011). Wealth and the marital divide. *American Journal of Sociology, 117*(2), 627–667.

Schnur, J., & John, R.M. (2014). Childhood lead poisoning and the new Centers for Disease Control and Prevention guidelines for lead exposure. *Journal of the American Association of Nurse Practitioners, 26*(5), 238–247.

Schofield, J. W. (2001). The colorblind perspective in school: Causes and consequences. In J. A. Banks & C. A. M. Banks (Eds.), *Multicultural education: Issues and perspectives* (4th ed., pp. 327–352). New York, NY: Wiley.

Schulte, L. J., & Battle, J. (2004). The relative importance of ethnicity and religion in predicting attitudes towards gays and lesbians. *Journal of Homosexuality, 47*(20), 127–141.

Schwartz, J. (1998, July 8). Blacks absorb more nicotine, suffer greater smoking toll. *Washington Post*, p. A3.

Schwartz, S., & Meyer, I. H. (2010). Mental health disparities research: The impact of within and between group analyses on tests of social stress hypotheses. *Social Science & Medicine, 70*, 1111–1118.

Schwartz, S., Weisskirch, R. S., Hurley, E. A., Zamboanga, B. L., Park, I. J. K., & Kim, S. Y. (2010). Communalism, familism, and filial piety: Are they birds of a collectivist feather? *Cultural Diversity and Ethnic Minority Psychology, 16*(4), 548–560.

Schweinhart, L. J., Barnes, H. V., & Weikart, D. P. (1993). *Significant benefits: The high/scope Perry preschool study through age 27* (Monographs of the High/Scope Educational Research Foundation, 10). Ypsilanti, MI: High/Scope Press.

Scott, J. W., & Black, A. W. (1989). Deep structures of African American family life: Female and male kin networks. *Western Journal of Black Studies, 13*(1), 17–24.

Scott, K. M., Al-Hamzawi, A. O., Andrade, L. H., Borges, G., Caldas-de-Almeida, J. M., Fiestas, F., . . . Kessler, R. C. (2014). Associations between subjective social status and DSM-IV mental disorders: Results from the World Mental Health Surveys. *JAMA Psychiatry, 71*(12), 1400–1408.

Seaton, E. K., & Douglass, S. (2014). School diversity and racial discrimination among African-American adolescents. *Cultural Diversity and Ethnic Minority Psychology, 20*(2), 156–165.

Seaton, E. K., Yip, T., & Sellers, R. M. (2009). A longitudinal examination of racial identity and racial discrimination among African American adolescents. *Child Development, 80*(2), 406–417.

Seaton, G. (2007). Toward a theoretical understanding of hypermasculine coping among urban Black adolescent males. *Journal of Human Behavior in the Social Environment, 15*(2–3), 367–390.

Sedlak, A. J., & Schultz, D. (2001). *Race difference in risk of maltreatment in the general child population*. Paper presented at the Race Matters forum, Chevy Chase, MD.

Segawa, E., Ngwe, J. E., Li, Y., & Flay, B. R.; Aban Aya Coinvestigators. (2005). Evaluation of the effects of the Aban Aya Youth Project in reducing violence among African American adolescent males using latent class growth mixture modeling techniques. *Evaluation Review, 29*(2), 128–148.

Seiler, G., & Elmesky, R. (2007). The role of communal practices in the generation of capital and emotional energy among urban African American students in science classrooms. *Teachers College Record, 109*(2), 391–419.

Sellers, R. M., Copeland-Linder, N., Martin, P. P., & Lewis, R. L. (2006). Racial identity matters: The relationship between racial discrimination and psychological functioning in African American adolescents. *Journal of Research on Adolescence, 16*(2), 187–216.

Sellers, R. M., Rowley, S. A. J., Chavous, T. M., Shelton, J. N., & Smith, M. (1997). Multidimensional inventory of black identity: Preliminary investigation of reliability and construct validity. *Journal of Personality and Social Psychology, 73*(4), 805–815.

Sellers, R. M., Smith, M. A., Shelton, J. N., Rowledy, S. A., & Chavous, T. M. (1998). Multidimensional model of racial identity: A reconceptualization of African American racial identity. *Personality and Social Psychology Review, 2*, 18–39.

Semaj, L. T. (1996). Towards a cultural science. In D. A. Azibo (Ed.), *African psychology in historical perspective and related commentary* (pp. 193–201). Trenton, NJ: Africa World Press.

Semien, T. (2016). How rap music influences African American girls' perceptions of skin color. *PsyPost*. Retrieved from http://www.psypost.org/2016/08/

how-rap-music-influences-african-american-girls-perceptions-of-skin-color-44632

Sentencing Project. (2010). *Federal crack cocaine sentencing.* Retrieved from http://www.sentencing-project.org/wp-content/uploads/2016/01/Federal-Crack-Cocaine-Sentencing.pdf

Sentencing Project. (2013). *Report of the Sentencing Project to the United Nations Human Rights Committee: Regarding racial disparities in the United States Criminal Justice System.* Washington, DC: The Sentencing Project.

Seppa, N. (1997). Children's TV remains steeped in violence. *APA Monitor, 28,* 36.

Shade, B. J. (1982). Afro-American cognitive style: A variable in school success? *Review of Educational Research, 52*(2), 219–244.

Shade, B. J. (1991). African American patterns of cognition. In R. Jones (Ed.), *Black psychology* (3rd ed., pp. 231–247). Berkeley, CA: Cobb & Henry.

Shade, B. J. (1997). *Creating culturally responsive classrooms.* Washington, DC: American Psychological Association.

Shade, B. J., & Edwards, P. A. (1987). Ecological correlates of the educative style of Afro-American children. *Journal of Negro Education, 56*(1), 88–99.

Shakoor, B. H., & Chalmers, D. (1991). Co-victimization of African-American children who witness violence: Effects on cognitive, emotional, and behavioral development. *Journal of the National Medical Association, 83*(3), 233–238.

Shapiro, D., Dundar, A., Huie, F., Wakhungu, P., Yuan, X., Nathan, A., & Hwang, Y. A. (2017). *A national view of student attainment rates by race and ethnicity: Fall 2010 cohort* (Signature Report No. 12b). Herndon, VA: National Student Clearinghouse Research Center. Retrieved from https://nscresearchcenter.org/wp-content/uploads/Signature12-RaceEthnicity.pdf

Sharkey, P. (2010). The acute effect of local homicides on children's cognitive performance. *Proceedings of the National Academy of Sciences, 107*(26), 11733–11738.

Sharkey, P. (2012). Residential mobility and the reproduction of unequal neighborhoods. *Cityscape, 14*(3), 9–31.

Shaw, C., & McKay, H. (1969). *Juvenile delinquency and urban areas.* Chicago, IL: University of Chicago Press.

Sheir, R. (2012). Do you Speak DC.? Georgetown linguists study Washington-area language. *WAMU, 88*(5), American University. Retrieved from https://wamu.org/story/12/11/30/do_you_speak_dc_georgetown_linguists_study_washington_area_language

Shellnutt, K. (2017). How Black and White christians do discipleship differently. *Christianity Today.*

Shin, A., Surkan, P. J., Coutinho, A. J., Suratkar, S. R., Campbell, R. K., Rowan, M., . . . Gittelsohn, J. (2015). Impact of Baltimore healthy eating zones: An environmental intervention to improve diet among African American youth. *Health Education & Behavior, 42*(Suppl. 1), 97S–105S.

Shin, R. Q. (2011). The Influence of Africentric values and neighborhood satisfaction on the academic self-efficacy of African American elementary school children. *Journal of Multicultural Counseling and Development, 39*(4), 218–228.

Shiraev, E. B., & D. A. Levy. (2010). *Cross-cultural psychology: Critical thinking and contemporary applications.* Boston, MA: Allyn and Bacon.

Shirley, E. L., & Cornell, D. G. (2012). The contribution of student perceptions of school climate to understanding the disproportionate punishment of African American students in a middle school. *School Psychology International, 33*(2), 115–134.

Shuval, K. (2013). Impediments and facilitators to physical activity and perceptions of sedentary behavior among urban community residents: The Fair Park Study. *Preventing Chronic Disease, 10,* 130125.

Siegel, C. E., Laska, E. M., Wanderling, J. A., Hernandex, J. C., & Levenson, R. B. (2016). Prevalence and diagnosis rates of childhood ADHA among racial-ethnic groups in a public mental health system. *Psychiatric Services, 67*(2), 199–205.

Siegel, J. (2006). Language ideologies and the education of speakers of marginalized language varieties: Adopting a critical awareness approach. *Language and Education, 17*(2), 157–174.

Sigelman, L., Bledsoe, T., Welch, S., & Combs, M. (1996). Making contact? Black-White social interaction in an urban setting. *The American Journal of Sociology, 101*(5), 1306–1332.

Silva, J. (2015). *Children and electronic media: How much is too much? In the public interest.* Washington, DC: American Psychological Association.

Simmons, C., Worrell, F. C., & Berry, J. M. (2008). Psychometric properties of scores on three Black racial identity scales. *Assessment, 15*(3), 259–276.

Simon, C. E. (2006). Breast cancer screening: Cultural beliefs and diverse populations. *Health & Social Work, 31*, 36–43.

Simon, R. J., & Alstein, H. (1977). *Transracial adoption.* New York, NY: Wiley.

Sims, M., Diez-Roux, A. V., Dudley, A., Gebreab, S., Wyatt, S. B., Bruce, M. A., . . . James, S. A. (2012). Perceived discrimination and hypertension among African Americans in the Jackson Heart Study. *American Journal of Public Health, 102*(Suppl. 2), S258–S265.

Sims, M., Diez-Roux, A. V., Gebreab, S. Y., Brenner, A., Dubbert, P., Wyatt, S., . . . Taylor, H. (2016). Perceived discrimination is associated with health behaviours among African-Americans in the Jackson Heart Study. *Journal of Epidemiology and Community Health, 70*, 187–194.

Skinner, A. C., & Skelton, J. A. (2014). Prevalence and trends in obesity and severe obesity among children in the United States, 1999–2012. *JAMA Pediatrics, 168*(6), 561–566.

Sklar, R. (2013). Yikes! Controversial *New Yorker* cover shows Muslim, flag-burning, Osama-loving, fist-bumping Obama. *Huffington Post.* Retrieved from http://www.huffingtonpost.com/2008/07/13/yikes-controversial-emnew_n_112429.html

Slaughter, D. T., & Johnson, D. J. (Eds.). (1988). *Visible now: Blacks in private schools.* New York, NY: Greenwood Press.

Slavin, L. A., Rainer, K. L., McCreary, M. L., & Gowda, K. K. (1991). Toward a multicultural model of the stress process. *Journal of Counseling and Development, 70*(1), 156–164.

Sloboda, Z., Glantz, M. D., & Tarter, R. E. (2012). Revisiting the concepts of risk and protective factors for understanding the etiology and development of substance use and substance use disorders: Implications for prevention. *Substance Use & Misuse, 47*(8–9), 944–962.

Smedley, A. (1999). *Race in North America: Origin and evolution of a worldview* (2nd ed.). Boulder, CO: Westview Press.

Smedley, A. (2002, September). *Racializing the human body: Example of the United States.* Paper presented at the meeting of the Inter-Congress of the International Union of Anthropological and Ethnological Sciences, Tokyo, Japan.

Smedley, A., & Smedley, B. D. (2005). Race as biology is fiction, racism as a social problem is real: Anthropological and historical perspectives in the social construction of race. *American Psychologist, 60*, 16–26.

Smedley, B. D. (2012). The lived experience of race and its health consequences. *American Journal of Public Health, 102*(5), 933–935.

Smedley, B. D., Stith, A. Y., & Nelson, A. R. (2003). *Unequal treatment: Confronting racial and ethnic disparities in health care.* Washington, DC: The National Academies Press.

Smith, D., Juarez, B., & Jacobson, C. (2011). White on Black: Can White parents teach Black adoptive children how to understand and cope with racism? *Journal of Black Studies, 42*, 1195–1230.

Smith, E. J., & Harper, S. R. (2015). Disproportionate impact of K-12 school suspension and expulsion on Black students in southern states. *Retrieved from Disproportionate Impact of K-12 School Suspension and Expulsion on Black Students in Southern States.* Retrieved from http://www.gse.upenn.edu/equity/sites/gse.upenn.edu.equity/files/publications/Smith_Harper_Report.pdf

Smith, E. P., & Brookins, C. C. (1997). Toward the development of an ethnic identity measure for African American youth. *Journal of Black Psychology, 23*(4), 358–377.

Smith, M. S., Reynolds, J. E., Fincham, F. D., & Beach, S. R. H. (2016). Parental experiences of racial discrimination and youth racial socialization in two-parent African American families. *Cultural Diversity and Ethnic Minority Psychology, 22*(2), 268–276.

Smith, R., III. (2011). HBCUs must embrace online education. *Diverse issues in higher education.* Retrieved from http://diverseeducation.com/article/14983/#

Smith, R. A., & Nguyen, L. K. (2008). 'Searching for a "generalized social agent" to predict Namibians' intentions to prevent sexual transmission of HIV. *AIDS Care: Psychological and Socio-Medical Aspects of AIDS/HIV, 20*(2), 242–250.

Smith, S. S., Fiore, M. C., & Baker, T. B. (2014). Smoking cessation in smokers who smoke menthol and non-menthol cigarettes. *Addiction, 109*(12), 2107–2117.

Smith, W. H. (2010, February 16). *The impact of racial trauma on African Americans.* Pittsburgh, PA: The Heinz Endowments. Retrieved from http://www.heinz.org/

Smith-Bynum, M. A., Lambert, S. F., English, D., & Ialongo, N. S. (2014). Associations between trajectories of perceived racial discrimination and psychological symptoms among African American adolescents. *Development and Psychopathology, 26,* 1049–1065.

Smitherman, G. (2004). Talkin and testifyin: Black English and the black experience. In R. Jones (Ed.), *Black psychology* (4th ed., pp. 249–267). Berkeley, CA: Cobb & Henry.

Snowden, L. R. (2012). Health and mental health policies' role in better understanding and closing African American–White American disparities in treatment access and quality of care. *American Psychologist, 67*(7), 524–531.

Snowden, L. R., & Thomas, K. (2000). Medicaid and African American outpatient mental health treatment. *Mental Health Services Research, 2*(2), 115–120.

Snyder, T. D., & Dillow, S. A. (2012). *Digest of education statistics 2011* (NCES 2012–001). Washington, DC: National Center for Education Statistics, Institute of Education Sciences, U.S. Department of Education. Retrieved from http://nces.ed.gov/pubs2012/2012001.pdf

Snyder, T. D., & Dillow, S.A. (2015). *Digest of education statistics 2013.* Washington, DC: National Center for Education Statistics.

Snyder, T. D., Dillow, S. A., & Hoffman, C. M. (2009). *Digest of education statistics 2008* (NCES 2009–020). Washington, DC: National Center for Education Statistics, Institute of Education Sciences, U.S. Department of Education.

Somayaji, D., & Cloyes, K. G. (2015). Cancer fear and fatalism: How African American participants construct the role of research subject in relation to clinical cancer research. *Cancer Nursing, 38*(2), 133–144.

Sözcü, Ö. F., İpek, İ., & Kinay, H. (2016). The attitudes of field dependence learners for learner interface design (LID) in e-learning instruction. *Universal Journal of Educational Research, 4*(3), 539–546.

Spencer, M. B. (1982). Preschool children's social cognition and cultural cognition: A cognitive developmental interpretation of race dissonance findings. *Journal of Psychology, 112*(2), 275–286.

Spencer, M. B., Cole, S. P., Jones, S., & Swanson, D. P. (1997a). Neighborhood and family influences on young urban adolescents' behavior problems: A multisample multisite analysis. In J. Brooks-Gunn, G. Duncan & J. L. Aber (Eds.), *Neighborhood poverty: Context and consequences for children* (Vol. 1, pp. 200–218). New York, NY: Russell Sage.

Spencer, M. B., Dupree, D., & Hartmann, T. (1997). A phenomenological variant of ecological systems theory (PVEST): A self-organization perspective in context. *Development and Psychopathology, 9*(4), 817–833.

Spencer, M. B., & Markstrom-Adams, C. (1990). Identity processes among racial and ethnic minority children in America. *Child Development, 61*(2), 290–310.

Spencer, M. B., McDermott, P. A., Burton, L. M., & Kochman, T. J. (1997b). An alternative approach to assessing neighborhood effects on early adolescent achievement and problem behavior. In J. Brooks-Gunn, G. Duncan & J. L. Aber (Eds.), *Neighborhood poverty: Context and consequences for children* (Vol. 2, pp. 145–163). New York, NY: Russell Sage.

Spencer, M. B., Noll, E., Stoltzfus, J., & Harpalani, V. (2001). Identity and school adjustment: Revisiting the "acting white" assumption. *Educational Psychologist, 36*(1), 21–30.

Spencer, R. (2006). Understanding the mentoring process between adolescents and adults. *Youth and Society, 37*(3), 287–315.

Spencer, S. J., Steele, C. M., & Quinn, D. M. (1999). Stereotype threat and women's math performance. *Journal of Experimental Social Psychology, 35,* 4–28.

Spraggins, R. E.; U.S. Census Bureau. (2005). *We the people: Women and men in the United States.* Washington, DC: U.S. Dept. of Commerce, Economics and Statistics Administration, U.S. Census Bureau.

Squires, C. R., Kohn-Wood, L. P., Chavous, T., & Carter, P. L. (2006). Evaluating agency and responsibility in gendered violence: African American youth talk about violence and hip hop. *Sex Roles, 55*(11–12), 725–737.

Stack, C. (1974). *All our kin: Survival strategies.* New York, NY: Harper Torchback.

Stackman, V. R., Reviere, R., & Medley, B. C. (2016). Attitudes toward marriage, partner availability, and interracial dating among Black college students from historically Black and predominantly White institutions. *Journal of Black Studies, 47*(2), 169–192.

Stahler, G., Shipley, T., Kirby, K., Godboldte, C., Kerwin, M., Shandler, I., & Simons, L. (2005). Development and initial demonstration of a community-based intervention for homeless, cocaine-using, African American women. *Journal of Substance Abuse Treatment, 28*(2), 171–179.

Stahre, M., Okuyemi, K. S., Joseph, A. M., & Fu, S. S. (2010). Racial/ethnic differences in menthol cigarette smoking, population quit ratios and utilization of evidence-based tobacco cessation treatments. *Addiction, 105,* 75–83.

Stangor, C. (2000). *Stereotypes and prejudice: Essential readings.* Philadelphia, PA: Taylor & Francis.

Stangor, C., & Lange, J. E. (1994). Mental representations of social-groups: Advances in understanding stereotypes and stereotyping. *Advances in Experimental Social Psychology, 26,* 357–416.

Stansbury, K. L., Beecher, B., & Clute, M. A. (2011). African American clergy's perceptions of mental health and pastoral care to elder congregants. *Journal of Religion & Spirituality in Social Work: Social Thought, 30*(1), 34–47.

Stanton, B., Li, X., Cottrell, L., & Kaljee, L. (2001). Early initiation of sex, drug-related risk behaviors, and sensation-seeking among urban low-income African American adolescents. *Journal of the National Medical Association, 93*(4), 129–138.

Staples, R. (1999). Sociocultural factors in black family transformation: Toward a redefinition of family functions. In R. Staples (Ed.), *The black family: Essays and studies* (pp. 18–23). Belmont, CA: Wadsworth.

Staton-Tindall, M., Duvall, J., Stevens-Watkins, D., & Oser, C. B. (2013). The roles of spirituality in the relationship between traumatic life events, mental health, and drug use among African American women from one southern state. *Substance Use & Misuse, 48*(12), 1246–1257.

Stearns, E., Buchmann, C., & Bonneau, K. (2009). Interracial friendships in the transition to college: Do birds of a feather flock together once they leave the nest? *Sociology of Education, 82*(2), 175.

Steckel, R. H. (1998). Demography of slaves in the United States. In P. Finkelman & J. C. Miller (Eds.), *Macmillan encyclopedia of world slavery* (pp. 248–250). New York, NY: Simon & Schuster Macmillan.

Steele, C. (2011). *Whistling Vivaldi: How stereotypes affect us and what we can do (issues of our time).* New York, NY: WW Norton & Company.

Steele, C. M. (1992, April). Race and the schooling of black Americans. *Atlantic Monthly, 269*(4), 68–78.

Steele, C. M. (1997). A threat in the air: How stereotypes shape intellectual identity and performance. *American Psychology, 52*(6), 613–629.

Steele, C. M., & Aronson, J. (1995). Stereotype threat and the intellectual test performance of African Americans. *Journal of Personality and Social Psychology, 69*(5), 797–811.

Steele, R. G., Anderson, B., Rindel, B., Dreyer, M. L., Perrin, K., Christensen, R., . . . Flynn, P. M. (2001). Adherence to antiretroviral therapy among HIV-positive children: Examination of the role of caregiver health beliefs. *AIDS Care, 13*(5), 617–629.

Steele, R. G., Little, T. D., Hardi, S. S., Forehand, R., Brody, G. H., & Hunter, H. L. (2006). A confirmatory comparison of the factor structure of the children's depression inventory between European American and African American youth. *Journal of Child and Family Studies, 15*(6), 779–794.

Steffen, P. R., McNeilly, M., Anderson, N., & Sherwood, A. (2003). Effects of perceived racism and anger inhibition on ambulatory blood pressure in African Americans. *Psychosomatic Medicine, 65*(5), 746–750.

Steinberg, L., Dornbusch, S. M., & Brown, B. B. (1992). Ethnic differences in adolescent achievement: An ecological perspective. *American Psychologist, 47*(6), 723–729.

Steinman, K., & Zimmerman, M. (2004). Religious activity and risk behavior among African American adolescents: Concurrent and developmental effects. *American Journal of Community Psychology, 33*(3/4), 151–161.

Stephan, W. (1999). *Reducing prejudice and stereotyping in schools.* New York, NY: Teachers College Press.

Stephan, W., & Stephan, C. (2004). Intergroup relations in multicultural education programs. In J. A. Banks & C. A. McGee Banks (Eds.), *Handbook of research on multicultural education* (pp. 782–798). San Francisco, CA: Jossey-Bass.

Stephens, D. P., & Phillips, L. D. (2003). Freaks, gold diggers, divas, and dykes: The sociohistorical development of adolescent African American women's sexual script. *Sexuality and Culture: An Interdisciplinary Quarterly, 7*(1), 3–49.

Sternthal, M. J., Jun, H. J., Earls, F., & Wright, R. J. (2010). Community violence and urban childhood asthma: A multilevel analysis. *European Respiratory Journal, 36*(6), 1400–1409.

Stevenson, H. C. (1995). Relationship of adolescent perceptions of racial socialization to racial identity. *Journal of Black Psychology, 21*(1), 49–70.

Stevenson, H. C., Cameron, R., Herrero-Taylor, T., & Davis, G. Y. (2002). Development of teenage experiences of racial socialization scale: Correlates of race-related socializations frequency from the perspectives of black youth. *Journal of Black Psychology, 28*(2), 84–106.

Stevens-Watkins, D., Perry, B., Harp, K. L., & Oser, C. B. (2012). Racism and illicit drug use among African American women: The protective effects of ethnic identity, affirmation, and behavior. *Journal of Black Psychology, 38*(4), 471–496.

Stevens-Watkins, D., & Rostosky, S. (2010). Binge drinking in African American males from adolescence to young adulthood: The protective influence of religiosity, family connectedness, and close friends' substance use. *Substance Use & Misuse, 45*(10), 1435–1451.

Stewart, E. B., Stewart, E. A., & Simons, R. L. (2007). The effect of neighborhood context on the college aspirations of African American adolescents. *American Educational Research Journal, 44*(4), 896–919.

Stewart, E. Z., Schreck, C. J., & Simons, R. L. (2006). "I aint gonna let no one disrespect me": Does the code of the street reduce or increase violent victimization among African American adolescents. *Journal of Research in Crime and Delinquency, 43*(4), 427–458.

Stewart, P. (2007). Who is kin? Family definition and African American families. *Journal of Human Behavior in the Social Environment, 15*(2–3), 163–181.

Stiel, L., Adkins-Jackson, P. B., Clark, P., Mitchell, E., & Montgomery, S. (2016). A review of hair product use on breast cancer risk in African American women. *Cancer Medicine, 5*(3), 597–604.

Stockard, J., & Johnson, M. (1980). *Sex roles.* Englewood Cliffs, NJ: Prentice Hall.

Stoddard, S. A., Heinze, J. E., Choe, D. E., & Zimmerman, M. A. (2015). Predicting violent behavior: The role of violence exposure and future educational aspirations during adolescence. *Journal of Adolescence, 44*, 191–203.

Stone, A. L., Becker, L. G., Huber, A. M., & Catalano, R. F. (2012). Review of risk and protective factors of substance use and problem use in emerging adulthood. *Addictive Behavior, 37*(7), 747–775.

Stout, M. J., Zhou, Y., Wylie, K. M., Tarr, P. I., Macones, G. A., & Tuuli, M. G. (2017). Early pregnancy vaginal microbiome trends and preterm birth. *American Journal of Obstetrics & Gynecology, 217*(3), 356–e1.

Strayhorn, T. L. (2008). The role of supportive relationships in facilitating African Amerian males' success in college. *NASPA Journal, 45*(1), 26–48.

Strayhorn, T. L. (2010). When race and gender collide: Social and cultural capital's influence on the academic achievement of African American and Latino males. *Review of Higher Education: Journal of the Association for the Study of Higher Education, 33*(3), 307–332.

Strayhorn, T. (2014). What role does grit play in the academic success of Black Male collegians at predominantly White institutions? *Journal of African American Studies, 18*(1), 1–10.

Subašić, E., Schmitt, M. T., & Reynolds, K. J. (2011). Are we all in this together?: Co-victimization, inclusive social identity and collective action in solidarity with the disadvantaged. *The British Journal of Social Psychology/The British Psychological Society, 50*(4), 707–725.

Substance Abuse and Mental Health Administration (NREPP). (n.d.). *National registry of evidenced-based programs and practices.* Retrieved from http://nrepp.samhsa.gov/landing.aspx

Substance Abuse and Mental Health Services Administration (SAMHSA). (2005a). *National survey of drug use and health.* Rockville, MD: U.S. Department of Health and Human Services.

Substance Abuse and Mental Health Services Administration (SAMHSA). (2005b, November 10). *Substance abuse treatment and dependence among veterans.* Rockville, MD: Author. Retrieved December 12, 2008 from http://www.oas.samhsa.gov/2k5/vets/vets.pdf

Substance Abuse and Mental Health Services Administration (SAMHSA). (2005c). *Use of marijuana and blunts among adolescents.* Rockville, MD: U.S. Department of Health and Human Services.

Substance Abuse and Mental Health Services Administration (SAMHSA). (2006). *Age at first use of marijuana and past year serious mental illness.* Rockville, MD: Author. Retrieved from http://www.oas.samhsa.gov/2k5/MJageSMI/MJageSMI.cfm

Substance Abuse and Mental Health Services Administration (SAMHSA). (2011). *Treatment Episode*

Data Set (TEDS): 1999–2009. National admissions to substance abuse treatment services (DASIS Series: S-56, HHS Publication No. SMA 11–4646). Rockville, MD: Author.

Substance Abuse and Mental Health Services Administration, Center for Behavioral Health Statistics and Quality. (2013). Need for and receipt of substance use treatment among blacks. Rockville, MD. Retrieved from https://www.samhsa.gov/data/sites/default/files/NSDUH124/NSDUH124/sr124-african-american-treatment.htm

Substance Abuse and Mental Health Services Administration. (2014). Results from the 2013 National Survey on Drug Use and Health: Summary of National Findings (NSDUH Series H-48, HHS Publication No. (SMA) 14-4863). Rockville, MD: Substance Abuse and Mental Health Services Administration. Retrieved from https://www.samhsa.gov/data/sites/default/files/NSDUHresultsPDFWHTML2013/Web/NSDUHresults2013.pdf

Sue, D. W., Capodilupo, C. M., Torino, G. C., Bucceri, J. M., Holder, A., Nadal, K. L., & Esquilin, M. (2007). Racial microaggressions in everyday life: Implications for clinical practice. American Psychologist, 62(4), 271–286.

Sue, D. W., & Constantine, M. G. (2007). Racial microaggressions as instigators of difficult dialogues on race: Implications for student affairs educators and students. College Student Affairs Journal, 26(2), 136.

Sue, S. (1983). Ethnic minority issues in psychology. American Psychologist, 38, 583–592.

Suggs, D. N., & Lewis, S. A. (2003). Alcohol as a direct and indirect labor enhancer: In the mixed economy of the BaTswana, 1800–1900. In W. Jankowiak & D. Bjradburd (Eds.), Drugs, labor, and colonial expansion (pp. 135–148). Tucson: University of Arizona Press.

Sullivan, L., Meschede, T., Dietrich, L., & Shapiro, T. (2015). The racial wealth gap. Retrieved from http://www.demos.org/sites/default/files/publications/RacialWealthGap_1.pdf

Sullivan, S., Pyne, J. M., Cheney, A. M., Hunt, J., Haynes, T. F., & Sullivan, G. (2014). The pew versus the couch: Relationship between mental health and faith communities and lessons learned from a VA/Clergy partnership project. Journal of Religion and Health, 53(4), 1267–1282.

Sullivan, T. N., Helms, S. W., Kliewer, W., & Goodman, K. L. (2010). Associations between sadness and anger regulation coping, emotional expression, and physical and relational aggression among urban adolescents. Social Development, 19(1), 30–51.

Sumo, J. N., Dancy, B., Julion, W., & Wilbur, J. (2015). Rationales for support that African American grandmothers provide to their children who are parenting adolescents. The Journal of School Nursing, 31(6), 441–449.

Sun, F., Kosberg, J. I., Leeper, J., Kaufman, A. V., & Burgio, L. (2010). Racial differences in perceived burden of rural dementia caregivers: The mediating effect of religiosity. Journal of Applied Gerontology, 29(3), 290–307.

Sun, S. S., Schubert, C. M., Chumlea, W. C., Roche, A. F., Kulin, H. E., Lee, P. A., . . . Ryan, A. S. (2002). National estimates of the timing of sexual maturation and racial differences among U.S. children. Pediatrics, 110(5), 911–919.

Sunkel, C. (2014). Mental health services: Where do we go from here? The Lancet Psychiatry, 1(1), 11–13.

Super, C. M., Harkness, S., Barry, O., & Zeitlin, M. (2011). Think locally, act globally: Contributions of African research to child development. Child Development Perspectives, 5(2), 119–125.

Swami, V., Frederick, D. A., Aavik, T., Alcalay, L., Allik, J., Anderson, D., . . . Zivcic-Becirevic, I. (2010). The attractive female body weight and female body dissatisfaction in 26 countries across 10 world regions: Results of the International Body Project I.

Swanson, D. P., Spencer, M. B., Dell'Angelo, T., Harpalani, V., & Spencer, T. R. (2002). Identity processes and the positive development of African Americans: An explanatory framework. In R. M. Lerner, C. S. Taylor & A. Von Eye (Eds.), Pathways to positive development among diverse youth (pp. 73–99). San Francisco, CA: Jossey-Bass.

Swanson, J., Swartz, M., Van Dorn, R. A., Monahan, J., McGuire, T. G., Steadman, H. J., & Robbins, P. C. (2009). Racial disparities in involuntary outpatient commitment: Are they real? Health Affairs, 28(3), 816–826.

Sweeney, K. A., & Borden, A. L. (2009). Crossing the line online: Racial preference of internet daters. Marriage & Family Review, 45, 740–760.

Swim, J., Hyers, L., & Cohen, L. (2003). African American college students' experiences with everyday racism: Characteristics of and responses to these incidents. Journal of Black Psychology, 29(1), 38–67.

Swinburn, B. A., Caterson, I., Seidell, J. C., & James, W. P. (2004). Diet, nutrition and the prevention of excess weight gain and obesity. *Public Health Nutrition, 7*, 123–146.

Tait, E. M., Laditka, S. B., Laditka, J. N., Nies, M. A., & Racine, E. F. (2011). Praying for health by older adults in the United States: Differences by ethnicity, gender, and income. *Journal of Religion, Spirituality and Aging, 23*, 338–362.

Tajfel, H. (1981). *Human groups and social categories.* Cambridge, England: Cambridge University Press.

Tajfel, H. (2010). Social identity and intergroup behaviour. In T. Postmes & N. R. Branscombe (Eds.), *Key readings in social psychology: Rediscovering social identity* (pp. 77–96). New York, NY: Psychology Press.

Tamir, M., Schwartz, S. H., Cieciuch, J., Riediger, M., Torres, C., Scollon, C., . . . Vishkin, A. (2016). Desired emotions across cultures: A value-based account. *Journal of Personality and Social Psychology, 111*(1), 67.

Taylor, O. D., & Williams-Salisbury, E. (2015). Coping skills and the self-efficacy of substance-using women versus non-substance-using women. *Journal of Human Behavior in the Social Environment, 25*(4), 351–359.

Taylor, R. J., Chatters, L. M., & Jackson, J. S. (2007). Religious and spiritual involvement among older African Americans, Caribbean blacks, and non-Hispanic whites: Findings from the national survey of American life. *Journals of Gerontology: Series B: Psychological Sciences and Social Sciences, 62B*(4), S238–S250.

Taylor, R. J., Chatters, L. M., Lincoln, K. D., & Woodward, A. T. (2017). Church-based exchanges of informal social support among African Americans. *Race and Social Problems, 9*(1), 53–62.

Taylor, R. J., Chatters, L. M., Woodward, A. T., & Brown, E. (2013). Racial and ethnic differences in extended family, friendship, fictive kin, and congregational informal support networks. *Family Relations, 62*(4), 609–624.

Taylor, R. J., & Johnson, W. E. (1997). Family roles and family satisfaction among black men. In R. J. Taylor, J. S. Jackson & L. M. Chatters (Eds.), *Family life in black America* (pp. 248–261). Thousand Oaks, CA: Sage.

Taylor, R. J., Mattis, J., & Chatters, L. M. (1999). Subjective religiosity among African Americans: A synthesis of findings from five national samples. *Journal of Black Psychology, 25*(4), 524–543.

Taylor, R. J., Mouzon, D. M., Nguyen, A. W., & Chatters, L. M. (2016). Reciprocal family, friendship and church support networks of African Americans: Findings from the National Survey of American Life. *Race and Social Problems, 8*(4), 326–339.

Taylor, S. (2014). *Health psychology.* New York, NY: McGraw-Hill.

Taylor-Harris, D., & Zhan, H. J. (2011). The third-age African American seniors: Benefits of participating in senior multipurpose facilities. *Journal of Gerontological Social Work, 54*(4), 351–371.

Teasley, M. L. (2014). Shifting from zero tolerance to restorative justice in schools. *Children & Schools, 36*(3), 131–133.

Teasley, M. L., McRoy, R. G., Joyner, M., Armour, M., Gourdine, R. M., Crewe, S. E., . . . Fong, R. (2017). Increasing success for African American children and youth. *Grand Challenges for Social Work Initiative* (Working Paper No. 21). American Academy of Social Work & Social Welfare. Available from http://aas-wsw.org/wp-content/uploads/2016/09/WP21.pdf

Techakesari, P., Barlow, F. K., Hornsey, M. J., Sung, B., Thai, M., & Chak, J. L. (2015). An investigation of positive and negative contact as predictors of intergroup attitudes in the United States, Hong Kong, and Thailand. *Journal of Cross-Cultural Psychology, 46*(3), 454–468.

Tedin, K. L., & Weiher, G. R. (2004). Racial/ethnic diversity and academic quality as components of school choice. *Journal of Politics, 66*(4), 1109–1133.

Teffo, L. J., & Roux, A. P. J. (2003). Metaphysical thinking in Africa. In P. H. Coetzee & A. P. J. Roux (Eds.), *The African philosophy reader* (pp. 161–174). New York, NY: Routledge.

Temple, J. R., & Freeman, J. D. H. (2011). Dating violence and substance use among ethnically diverse adolescents. *Journal of Interpersonal Violence, 26*(4), 701–718.

Tendulkar, S. A., Koenen, K. C., Dunn, E. C., Buka, S., & Subramanian, S. V. (2012). Neighborhood influences on perceived social support among parents: Findings from the Project on Human Development in Chicago Neighborhoods. *PLoS One, 7*(4), 1–9.

Terrell, F., & Terrell, S. (1984). Race of counselor, client sex, cultural mistrust level, and premature termination from counseling among black clients. *Journal of Counseling Psychology, 31*(3), 371–375.

Tetey, N. S., Duran, P. A., Andersen, H. S., Washington, N., & Boutin-Foster, C. (2016). "It's like backing up science with scripture": Lessons learned from the implementation of HeartSmarts, a faith-based cardiovascular disease health education program. *Journal of Religion and Health, 55*(3), 1078–1088.

Teti, D. M., Black, M. M., Viscardi, R., Glass, P., O'Connell, M. A., Baker, L., . . . Hess, C. R. (2009). Intervention with African American premature infants four-month results of an early intervention program. *Journal of Early Intervention, 31*(2), 146–166.

Thomas, A., Caldwell, C. H., Assari, S., Jagers, R. J., & Flay, B. (2016). You do what you see: How witnessing physical violence is linked to violent behavior among male African American adolescents. *The Journal of Men's Studies, 24*(2), 185–207.

Thomas, A. J., Barrie, R., & Tynes, B. M. (2009). Intimate relationships of African Americans. In H. A. Neville, B. M. Tynes & S. O. Utsey (Eds.), *Handbook of African American psychology* (pp. 117–125). Thousand Oaks, CA: Sage.

Thomas, A. J., & Blackmon, S. K. M. (2015). The influence of the Trayvon Martin shooting on racial socialization practices of African American parents. *Journal of Black Psychology, 41*(1), 75–89.

Thomas, A. J., & King, C. (2007). Gendered racial socialization of African American mothers and daughters. *The Family Journal: Counseling and Therapy for Couples and Families, 15*(2), 137–142.

Thomas, D. E., Townsend, T. G., & Belgrave, F. Z. (2003). The influence of cultural and racial identification on the psychosocial adjustment of inner-city African American children in school. *American Journal of Community Psychology, 32*(3–4), 217–228.

Thomas, K. A., & Dettlaff, A. J. (2011). African American families and the role of physical discipline: Witnessing the past in the present. *Journal of Human Behavior in the Social Environment, 21*, 963–977.

Thomas, O., Davidson, W., & McAdoo, H. (2008). An evaluation study of the Young Empowered Sisters (YES!) program: Promoting cultural assets among African American adolescent girls through a culturally relevant school-based intervention. *Journal of Black Psychology, 34*(3), 281–308.

Thompson, A. B., Goodman, M. S., & Kwate, N. O. A. (2016). Does learning about race prevent substance abuse? Racial discrimination, racial socialization and substance use among African Americans. *Addictive Behaviors, 61*, 1–7.

Thompson, S. N., & Chambers, J. W. (2000). African self-consciousness and health-promoting behaviors among African American college students. *Journal of Black Psychology, 26*(3), 330–346.

Thompson, T. J., & Massat, C. R. (2005). Experiences in violence, post-traumatic stress, academic achievement and behavior problems of urban African American children. *Child and Adolescent Social Work Journal, 22*(5–6), 367–393.

Thornhill, T. E. (2016). Resistance and assent: How racial socialization shapes black students' experience learning African American history in high school. *Urban education, 51*(9), 1126–1151.

Thornton, M. C. (1997). Strategies of racial socialization among black parents: Mainstream, minority, and cultural messages. In R. J. Taylor, J. S. Jackson & L. M. Chatters (Eds.), *Family life in black America* (pp. 201–215). Thousand Oaks, CA: Sage.

Thornton, M. C. (1998). Indigenous resources and strategies of resistance. In H. I. McCubbin, E. A. Thompson, A. I. Thompson & J. A. Futrell (Eds.), *Resiliency in African American families* (pp. 49–66). Thousand Oaks, CA: Sage.

Thornton, M. C., Chatters, L., Taylor, R. J., & Allen, W. (1990). Sociodemographic and environmental correlates to racial socialization by black parents. *Child Development, 61*, 401–409.

Threlfall, J. M., Seay, K. D., & Kohl, P. L. (2013). The parenting role of African-American fathers in the context of urban poverty. *Journal of Children and Poverty, 19*, 45–61.

Thurston, B. (2012). *How to be Black.* New York, NY: HarperCollins.

Tilahun, D., Hanlon, C., Araya, M., Davey, B., Hoekstra, R. A., & Fekadu, A. (2017). Training needs and perspectives of community health workers in relation to integrating child mental health care into primary health care in a rural setting in sub-Saharan Africa: A mixed methods study. *International Journal of Mental Health Systems, 11*(1), 15.

Tillyer, R., Klahm, C. F., & Engel, R. S. (2012). The discretion to search: A multilevel examination of driver demographics and officer characteristics. *Journal of Contemporary Criminal Uustice, 28*(2), 184–205.

Timmons, S. M. (2015). Review and evaluation of faith-based weight management interventions that target African American women. *Journal of Religion and Health, 54*(2), 798–809.

Tiwary, C. M. (1998). Premature sexual development in children following the use of estrogen- or placenta-containing hair products. *Clinical Pediatrics, 37*(12), 733–739.

Toldson, I. A. (2013). Retire the myth: Black men, jail, and College. *The Root.*

Tomes, Y. I. (2008). Ethnicity, cognitive styles, and math achievement: Variability within African-American post-secondary students. *Multicultural Perspectives, 10*(1), 17–23.

Tonnies, F. (1925). The concept of Gemeinschaft. In W. J. Cahnman & R. Heberle (Eds.), *Ferdinand Tonnies on sociology: Pure, applied and empirical— Selected writings* (pp. 62–72). Chicago, IL: University of Chicago Press.

Townsend, B. L. (2000). The disproportionate discipline of African American learners: Reducing school suspensions and expulsions. *Exceptional Children, 66*(3), 381–391.

Townsend, T. G., & Belgrave, F. Z. (2000). The impact of personal identity and racial identity on drug attitudes and use among African American children. *Journal of Black Psychology, 76*(4), 421–436.

Townsend, T. G., Grange, C., Belgrave, F. Z., Wilson, K., Fitzgerald, A., & Owens, K. (2007). Understanding HIV risk among African American adolescents: The role of Africentric values and ethnic identity in the theory of planned behavior. *Social Relations, 30*(2), 89–120.

Townsend, T. G., & Hargrove, S. (2016). Implementing community-based research and prevention programs to decrease health disparities. In S. L. Graves & J. J. Blake (Eds.), *Psychoeducational assessment and intervention for ethnic minority children: Evidence-based approaches* (pp. 213–230). Washington, DC: American Psychological Association.

Townsend, T. G., & Lanphier, E. (2007). Family influences on racial identity among African American youth. *Journal of Black Psychology, 33*(3), 278–298.

Trahan, D. P., Jr., & Goodrich, K. M. (2015). "You think you know me, but you have no idea": Dynamics in African American families following a son's or daughter's disclosure as LGBT. *The Family Journal, 23*(2), 147–157.

Trent, W. L. (1997). Outcomes of school desegregation: Findings from longitudinal research. *Journal of Negro Education, 66*(3), 255–257.

Trenz, R. C., Dunne, E. M., Zur, J., & Latimer, W. W. (2015). An investigation of school-related variables as risk and protective factors associated with problematic substance use among vulnerable urban adolescents. *Vulnerable Children and Youth Studies, 10*(2), 131–140.

Triandis, H. C. (1989). The self and social behavior in differing cultural contexts. *Psychological Review, 96*(3), 506–520.

Triandis, H. C. (1995). *Individualism and collectivism.* Boulder, CO: Westview Press.

Troiano, R. P., Flegal, K. M., Kuczmarski, R. J., Campbell, S. M., & Johnson, C. L. (1995). Overweight prevalence and trends for children and adolescents. *Archives of Pediatrics and Adolescent Medicine, 149*(10), 1085–1091.

Troiden, R. (1993). The formation of homosexual identities. In L. Garnets & D. Kimmel (Eds.), *Psychological perspectives on lesbian and gay male experiences.* New York, NY: Columbia University Press.

Trotman S. M., & Moss-Bouldin, S. (2014). We need more drama: A comparison of Ford, Hurston, and Boykin's African American characteristics and instructional strategies for the culturally different classroom. *Interdisciplinary Journal of Teaching and Learning, 4*(2), 68–80.

Tsa-Tsala. (1997). Beliefs and disease in Cameroon. In S. N. Madu, P. K. Baguma & A. Pritz (Eds.), *Psychotherapy in Africa: First investigation* (p. 44). Vienna, Austria: World Council for Psychotherapy.

Tuck, K., & Boykin, A. W. (1989). Verve effects: The relationship of task performance to stimulus preference and variability in low income black and white children. In A. Harrison (Ed.), *The eleventh conference on empirical research in black psychology* (pp. 84–95). Washington, DC: National Institute of Mental Health.

Tucker, C. M., Moradi, B., Wall, W., & Nghiem, K. (2014). Roles of perceived provider cultural sensitivity and health care justice in African American/ black patients' satisfaction with provider. *Journal of Clinical Psychology in Medical Settings, 21*(3), 282–290.

Tucker, C. M., Rice, K. G., Marsiske, M., Nielson, J. J., & Herman, K. (2011). Patient-centered culturally sensitive health care: Model testing and refinement. *Health Psychology, 30*(3), 342–350.

Tucker, M. B., & Mitchell-Kernan, C. (1999). Mate availability among African Americans: Conceptual and methodological issues. In R. L. Jones (Ed.), *Advances in African American psychology* (pp. 129–163). Hampton, VA: Cobb & Henry.

Tucker-Worgs, T. M. (2011). *The Black Megachurch.* Waco, TX: Baylor University Press.

Turner, E. A., Jensen-Doss, A., & Heffer, R. W. (2015). Ethnicity as a moderator of how parents' attitudes and perceived stigma influence intentions to seek child mental health services. *Cultural Diversity and Ethnic Minority Psychology, 21*(4), 613–618.

Turner, E. A. & Richardson, J. (2016, July 14). Racial trauma is real: The impact of police shootings on African Americans. *Psychology Benefits Society Blog from the APA Public Interest Directorate.* Retrieved from https://psychologybenefits.org/2016/07/14/racial-trauma-police-shootings-on-african-americans/

Turner, E. A., & Turner, T. (2015). Diversity in the psychology workforce: Challenges and opportunities to increase the presence of African-American males in psychology graduate programs. *National Register of Health Service Psychologists.* Retrieved from https://www.nationalregister.org/pub/the-national-regis-ter-report-pub/the-register-report-spring-2015/diversity-in-the-psychology-workforce-challenges-and-opportunities-to-increase-the-presence-of-african-american-males-in-psychology-graduate

Turner, M. A., Santos, R., Levy, D. K., Wissoker, D., Aranda, C., & Pitingolo, R.; The Urban Institute. (2013). *Housing discrimination against racial and ethnic minorities 2012: Executive summary.* Washington, DC: U.S. Department of Housing and Urban Development.

Tyler, F. B., Brome, D. R., & Williams, J. E. (1991). *Ethnic validity, ecology, and psychotherapy: A psychological competence model.* New York, NY: Plenum Press.

Tynes, B. M., Umaña-Taylor, A. J., Rose, C. A., Lin, J., & Anderson, C. J. (2012). Online racial discrimination and the protective function of ethnic identity and self-esteem for African American adolescents. *Developmental Psychology, 48*(2), 343.

Tyree, T. (2011). African American stereotypes in reality television. *Howard Journal of Communications, 22*(4), 394–413.

Tyson, K., Darity, W., Jr., & Castellino, D. R. (2005). It's not "a black thing": Understanding the burden of acting white and other dilemmas of high achievement. *American Sociological Review, 70*(4), 582–605.

Ulbrich, P. M., Warheit, G. J., & Zimmerman, R. S. (1989). Race, socioeconomic status, and psychological distress: An examination of differential vulnerability. *Journal of Health and Social Behavior, 30*(1), 131–146.

Unger, J. B., Soto, D. W., & Leventhal, A. (2016). E-cigarette use and subsequent cigarette and marijuana use among Hispanic young adults. *Drug & Alcohol Dependence, 163,* 261–264.

United Church of Christ Commission for Racial Justice. (1987). *Toxic wastes and race in the United States: A national report on the racial and socio-economic characteristics of communities with hazardous waste sites.* New York, NY: Author.

Urrutia-Rojas, X., Ahmad, N., Bayona, M., Bae, S., Rivers, P. A., & Singh, K. P. (2008). Risk factors associated with obesity in children of different racial backgrounds. *Health Education Journal, 67*(2), 121–133.

U.S. Census (2018a). Race. Retrieved from https://www.census.gov/topics/population/race/about.htm

U.S. Census (2018b). Hispanic Origin. Retrieved from https://www.census.gov/topics/population/hispanic-origin/about.html

U.S. Census. (2016a). *Population.* Retrieved from https://www.census.gov/quickfacts/table/PST045215/00

U.S. Census. (2016b). *Historical living arrangements of children.* Retrieved from https://www.census.gov/data/tables/time-series/demo/families/children.html

U.S. Census (2016c) Grandparents and grandchildren. Retrieved from grhttps://census.gov/newsroom/blogs/random-samplings/2016/09/grandparents-and-grandchildren.htmlandchildren.

U.S. Census (2016d). *POV-02. People in families by family structure, age, and sex, iterated by income-to poverty ratio and race.* Retrieved from https://www.census.gov/data/tables/time-series/demo/income-poverty/cps-pov/pov-02.html

U.S. Census. (2016e). *Historical marital status tables. Current population survey, march and annual social and economic supplements.* Retrieved from https://www.census.gov/data/tables/time-series/demo/families/marital.html

U.S. Census (2016f). *Percentage of persons 25 to 29 years old with selected levels of educational attainment, by race/ethnicity and sex: Selected years, 1920 through 2016.* Retrieved from https://nces.ed.gov/programs/digest/d16/tables/dt16_104.20.asp

U.S. Census. (2016g). *Percentage of high school drop-outs among dropout rate), by sex and race/ethnicity: Selected years, 1960 through 2015.* Retrieved from https://nces.ed.gov/programs/digest/d16/tables/dt16_219.70.asp?current=yes

U.S. Census (2016h), Department of Commerce, Current Population Survey (CPS), Annual Social and Economic Supplement, 1996 through 2016. (This table was prepared November 2016.) Retrieved from: https://nces.ed.gov/programs/digest/d16/tables/dt16_502.30.asp

U.S. Census (2016i). Poverty Thresholds for 2015 by Size of Family and Number of Related Children Under 18 years. Retrieved from: https://census.gov/library/publications/2016/demo/p60-256.html

U.S. Census. (2015). Poverty Thresholds for 2015 by Size of Family and Number of Related Children Under 18 years. Retrieved from: https://census.gov/library/publications/2016/demo/p60-256.html

U.S. Census Bureau. (2010a). *Annual social and economic supplements 2010.*

U.S. Census Bureau. (2010b). Measuring America: People, places, and our economy. *Age groups and sex: 2010.* Retrieved from http://factfinder2.census.gov/faces/tableservices/jsf/pages/productview.xhtml ?pid=DEC_10_SF2_QTP1&prod Type=table/

U.S. Census Bureau. (n.d.). *Historical poverty tables: People.* Retrieved from https://www.census.gov/data/tables/time-series/demo/income-poverty/historical-poverty-people.html

U.S. Department of Education. (2012, December 21). *Secretary Duncan announces seventeen 2012 Promise Neighborhoods winners in school safety address at Neval Thomas Elementary School.* Retrieved from http://www.ed.gov/news/press-releases/secretary-duncan-announces-seventeen-2012-promise-neighborhoods-winners-school-s

U.S. Department of Education. *IDEA section, office of special education and rehabilitative services.* Retrieved from https://www2.ed.gov/about/offices/list/osers/index.html

U.S. Department of Education, Office of Civil Rights. (2014). *Civil rights data collection data snapshot: School discipline.* Retrieved from https://ocrdata.ed.gov/Downloads/CRDC-School-Discipline-Snapshot.pdf

U.S. Department of Education. (n.d.). *Promise neighborhoods.* Retrieved from http://www2.ed.gov/programs/promiseneighborhoods/index.html

U.S. Department of Health and Human Services (DHHS). (1985). *Report of the secretary's task force on black and minority health.* Washington, DC: U.S. Government Printing Office.

U.S. Department of Health and Human Services (DHHS). (2001). *Mental health: Culture, race, and ethnicity* (A supplement to mental health: A report of the Surgeon General). Rockville, MD: DHHS, U.S. Public Health Services, Office of the Surgeon General.

U.S. Department of Health and Human Services. (2012). *Preventing tobacco use among youth and young adults: A report of the Surgeon General.* Centers for Disease Control and Prevention, National Center for Chronic Disease Prevention and Health Promotion, Office on Smoking and Health. Retrieved from https://www.cdc.gov/tobacco/data_statistics/sgr/2012/

U.S. Department of Health and Human Services (DHHS). (2013). *Health, United States, 2012.* Retrieved from http://www.cdc.gov/nchs/data/hus/hus12.pdf#018

U.S. Department of Health and Human Services, Administration for Children and Families. (2015). *Adoption and foster care analysis and reporting system* (The AFCARS Report). Retrieved from https://www.acf.hhs.gov/sites/default/files/cb/afcarsreport22.pdf

U.S. Department of Housing and Urban Development (HUD). (2013). *Public and Indian housing, choice neighborhoods: 2013 summary statement and initiatives.* Retrieved from http://portal.hud.gov/hudportal/documents/huddoc? id=choice-neighb.pdf

U.S. Department of Justice, Office of Juvenile Programs. (2006). *Extent, nature, and consequences of intimate partner violence: Findings from the National Violence Against Women Survey, 2000.*

U.S. Department of Justice. (n.d.a). Aban Aya youth project. *Office of Juvenile Justice and Delinquency Prevention.* Retrieved from http://www.ojjdp.gov/mpg/Aban%20Aya%20Youth%20Project-MPG Program Detail-950.aspx

U.S. Department of Justice. (n.d.b). OJJDP model programs guide. *Office of Juvenile Justice and Delinquency Prevention.* Retrieved from http://www.ojjdp.gov/mpg/programTypesDefinitions.aspx

U.S. Sentencing Commission. (2011). *Overview of federal criminal cases fiscal year 2011.* Washington, DC: U.S. Government Printing Office.

Utsey, S. O. (1999). Development and validation of a short form of the index of race-related stress, brief version. *Measurement and Evaluation in Counseling and Development, 32*(3), 149–166.

Utsey, S. O. (1999). Development and validation of a short form of the Index of Race-Related Stress (IRRS)-Brief Version. *Measurement and evaluation in Counseling and Development, 32*(3), 149.

Utsey, S. O., Abrams, J. A., Opare-Henako, A., Bolden, M. A., & Williams, O. (2015). Assessing the psychological consequences of internalized colonialism on the psychological well-being of young adults in Ghana. *Journal of Black Psychology, 41*(3), 195–220.

Utsey, S. O., Adams, E., & Bolden, M. (2000). Development and initial validation of the Africultural Coping Systems Inventory. *Journal of Black Psychology, 26*(2), 194–215.

Utsey, S. O., Belvet, B., & Fischer, N. (2009). Assessing African-centered (Africentric) psychological constructs: A review of existing instrumentation. In H. A. Neville, B. M. Tynes & S. O. Utsey (Eds.), *Handbook of African American psychology* (pp. 75–88). Thousand Oaks, CA: Sage.

Utsey, S. O., Brown, C., & Bolden, M. A. (2004). Testing the structural invariance of the Africultural Coping Systems Inventory across three samples of African descent populations. *Educational and psychological measurement, 64*(1), 185–195.

Utsey, S. O., & Hook, J. N. (2007). Heart rate variability as a physiological moderator of the relationship between race-related stress and psychological distress in African Americans. *Cultural Diversity and Ethnic Minority Psychology, 13*(3), 250–253.

Utsey, S. O., Lee, A., Bolden, M. A., & Lanzier, Y. (2005). A confirmatory test of the factor validity of scores on the Spiritual Well-Being Scale in a community sample of African Americans. *Journal of Psychology and Theology, 33*(4), 251–257.

Utsey, S. O., & Ponterotto, J. (1996). Development and validation of the index of race-related stress. *Journal of Counseling Psychology, 43*, 490–501.

Valdez, A., Kaplan, C., & Curtis, R. (2007). Aggressive crime, alcohol, and drug use, and concentrated poverty in 24 U.S. urban areas. *American Journal of Drug and Alcohol Abuse, 33*(4), 595–603.

Vanman, E. J., Paul, B. Y., Ito, T. A., & Miller, N. (1997). The modern face of prejudice and structural features that moderate the effect of cooperation on affect. *Journal of Personality and Social Psychology, 73*, 941–959.

Varner, F., & Mandara, J. (2013). Discrimination concerns and expectations as explanations of gendered socialization in African American families. *Child Development, 84*(3), 875–890.

Varnum, M. E., Grossmann, I., Kitayama, S., & Nisbett, R. E. (2010). The origin of cultural differences in cognition: Evidence for the social orientation hypothesis. *Current Directions in Psychological Science, 19*, 9–13.

Vaughn, M., Wallace, J., Perron, B., Copeland, V., & Howard, M. (2008). Does marijuana use serve as a gateway to cigarette use for high-risk African-American youth? *The American Journal of Drug and Alcohol Abuse, 34*(6), 782–791.

Veenstra, G., & Patterson, A. C. (2016). Black–white health inequalities in Canada. *Journal of Immigrant and Minority Health, 18*(1), 51–57.

Venter, E. (2004). The notion of Ubuntu and communalism in African educational discourse. *Studies in Philosophy and Education, 23*(2–3), 149–160.

Vereen, L. (2007). African American family structure: A review of the literature. *The Family Journal: Counseling for Couples and Families, 15*(3), 282–285.

Vernon-Feagans, L., & Cox, M. (2013). The family life project: An epidemiological and developmental study of young children living in poor rural communities. *Monographs of the Society for Research in Child Development, 78*(5), 1–150.

Vignoles, V. L., Owe, E., Becker, M., Smith, P. B., Easterbrook, M. J., Brown, R., . . . Bond, M. H. (2016). Beyond the 'east–west' dichotomy: Global variation in cultural models of selfhood. *Journal of Experimental Psychology: General, 145*(8), 966–1000.

Villablanca, A. C., Warford, C., & Wheeler, K. (2016). Inflammation and cardiometabolic risk in African American Women is reduced by a pilot community-based educational intervention. *Journal of Women's Health, 25*(2), 188–199.

Villanti, A. C., Mowery, P. D., Delnevo, C. D., Niaura, R. S., Abrams, D. B., & Giovino, G. A. (2016). Changes in the prevalence and correlates of menthol cigarette use in the USA, 2004–2014. *Tobacco Control, 25*, 14–20.

Voisin, D. R. (2003). Victims of community violence and HIV sexual risk behaviors among African

American males. *HIV/AIDS Education and Prevention for Adolescents and Children, 5*(3), 111–121.

Voisin, D. R. (2007). The effects of family and community violence exposure among youth: Recommendations for practice and policy. *Journal of Social Work Education, 43*(1), 51–66.

Voisin, D. R., Kim, D., Takahashi, L., Morotta, P., & Bocanegra, K. (2017). Involvement in the Juvenile Justice System for African American adolescents: Examining associations with behavioral health problems. *Journal of Social Service Research, 43*(1), 129–140.

Voisin, D. R., King, K. M., Diclemente, R. J., & Carry, M. (2014). Correlates of gang involvement and health-related factors among African American females with a detention history. *Children and Youth Services Review, 44*, 120–125.

von Hippel, P. T., Powell, B., Downey, D. B., & Rowland, N. J. (2007). The effect of school on overweight in childhood: Gain in body mass index during the school year and during summer vacation. *American Journal of Public Health, 97*(4), 696–702.

Vygotsky, L. (1934/1978). *Mind in society.* (M. Cole, Trans.). Cambridge, MA: Harvard University Press.

Wade, J. C., & Rochlen, A. B. (2012). Introduction: Masculinity, identity, and the health and well-being of African American men. *Psychology of Men & Masculinity, 14*(1), 1–6.

Wade, T. J. (1996). The relationships between skin color and self-perceived global, physical, and sexual attractiveness, and self-esteem for African Americans. *Journal of Black Psychology, 22*(3), 358–373.

Wade, T. J., & Bielitz, Z. (2005). The differential effect of skin color on attractiveness, personality evaluations, and perceived life success on African Americans. *Journal of Black Psychology, 31*(3), 215–236.

Waldron-Perrine, B., Rapport, L. J., Lumley, M., Meachen, S. J., Hubbarth, P., & Hanks, R. A. (2011). Religion and spirituality in rehabilitation outcomes among individuals with traumatic brain injury. *Rehabilitation Psychology, 56*(2), 107–116.

Waldrop, D. P. (2003). Caregiving issues for grandmothers raising their grandchildren. *Journal of Human Behavior in the Social Environment, 7*(3–4), 201–223.

Waldrop, D. P., & Weber, J. A. (2001). From grandparent to caregiver: The stress and satisfaction of raising grandchildren. *Family in Society: The Journal of Contemporary Human Services, 82*(5), 461–472.

Walker, A. (1983). *In search of our mothers' gardens: Womanist prose.* New York, NY: Harcourt.

Wallace, B. C., & Constantine, M. G. (2005). Africentric cultural values, psychological help-seeking attitudes, and self-concealment in African American college students. *Journal of Black Psychology, 31*(4), 369–385.

Wallace, J. M., Brown, T. N., Bachman, J. G., & LaVeist, T. A. (2003). The influence of race and religion on abstinence from alcohol, cigarettes and marijuana among adolescents. *Journal of Studies on Alcohol, 64*(6), 843–848.

Wallace, J. M., & Muroff, J. (2002). Preventing substance abuse among African American children and youth: Race differences in risk factor exposure and vulnerability. *Journal of Primary Prevention, 22*(3), 235–261.

Wallace, S. A., & Fisher, C. B. (2007). Substance use attitudes among urban black adolescents: The role of parent, peer, and cultural factors. *Journal of Youth and Adolescence, 36*(4), 441–451.

Wallace, S. A., Neilands, T. B., & Sanders Phillips, K. (2017). Neighborhood context, psychological outlook, and risk behaviors among urban African American youth. *Cultural Diversity and Ethnic Minority Psychology, 23*(1), 59–69.

Wallston, B. S., & Wallston, K. A. (1984). Locus of control and health: A review of the literature. *Health Education Monographs, 6*(2), 107–117.

Wang, H., Parry, S., Macones, G., Sammel, M. D., Kuivaniemi, H., Tromp, G., . . . Strauss, J. R., III. (2006). From the cover: A functional SNP in the promoter of the SERPINH1 gene increases risk of preterm premature rupture of membranes in African Americans. *Proceedings of the National Academy of Sciences USA, 103*, 13463–13467.

Wang, M. C., Joel Wong, Y., Tran, K. K., Nyutu, P. N., & Spears, A. (2013). Reasons for living, social support, and afrocentric worldview: Assessing buffering factors related to Black Americans' suicidal behavior. *Archives of Suicide Research, 17*(2), 136–147.

Wang, M. T., Hill, N. E., & Hofkens, T. (2014). Parental involvement and African American and European

American adolescents' academic, behavioral, and emotional development in secondary school. *Child Development, 85*, 2151–2168.

Wang, M. T., & Huguley, J. (2012). The buffering role of racial socialization from parents on the association between racial discrimination and adolescents' educational outcomes. *Child Development, 83*, 1716–1731.

Wang, P. S., Lane, M., Olfson, M., Pincus, H. A., Wells, K. B., & Kessler, R. C. (2005). Twelve-month use of mental health services in the United States: Results from the national comorbidity survey replication. *Archives of General Psychiatry, 62*(6), 629–640.

Wang, W., & Parker, K. (2014). *Record share of Americans have never married: As values, economics and gender patterns change*. Washington, DC: Pew Research Center's Social & Demographic Trends Project. Retrieved from http://www.pew-socialtrends.org/ files/2014/09/2014-09-24_Never-Married-Americans.pdf

Ward, E., Wiltshire, J. C., Detry, M. A., & Brown, R. L. (2013). African American men and women's attitude toward mental illness, perceptions of stigma, and preferred coping behaviors. *Nursing Research, 62*(3), 185–194.

Warren, W. (1999). *Black women scientists in the United States*. Bloomington: Indiana University Press.

Warren-Findlow, J. W., Seymour, R. B., & Huber, L. R. B. (2012). The association between self-efficacy and hypertension self-care activities among African American adults. *Journal of Community Health, 37*, 15–35.

Washington, B. T. (1896). The awakening of the Negro. *Atlantic Monthly, 78*, 322–328.

Washington, H. (2006). *Medical apartheid*. New York, NY: Random House.

Washington, J. A. (1996). Issues in assembling the language abilities of African American children. In A. G. Kamhi, K. E. Pollack & J. L. Harris (Eds.), *Communication development and disorders in African American children: Research, assessment, and intervention* (pp. 35–54). Baltimore, MD: Brookes.

Washington, T., Gleeson, J. P., & Rulison, K. L. (2013). Competence and African American children in informal kinship care: The role of family. *Children and Youth Services Review, 35*(9), 1305–1312.

Watkins, A. F. (2002). Learning styles of African American children: A developmental consideration. *Journal of Black Psychology, 28*(1), 3–17.

Watkins, R. C., Barr, J. A., Bryand, J. N., Curtis, W. H., & Moss III, O. (2007). *The gospel remix: Reaching the hip hop generation*. Valley Forge, PA: Judson Press.

Watkins-Lewis, K. M., & Hamre, B. K. (2012). African-American parenting characteristics and their association with children's cognitive and academic school readiness. *Journal of African American Studies, 16*(3), 390–405.

Watson, N. N., & Hunter, C. D. (2015). Anxiety and depression among African American women: The costs of strength and negative attitudes toward psychological help-seeking. *Cultural Diversity and Ethnic Minority Psychology, 21*(4), 604–612.

Watson, S., Thorton, C. G., & Engelland, B. T. (2010). Skin color shades in advertising to ethnic audiences: The case of African Americans. *Journal of Marketing Communications, 16*(4), 185–201.

Way, N. (2013). Boys' friendships during adolescence: Intimacy, desire, and loss. *Journal of Research on Adolescence, 23*(2), 201–213.

Weaver A., Himle J. A., Taylor R. J., Matusko N. N., & Abelson J. M. (2015). Urban vs rural residence and the prevalence of depression and mood disorder among African American women and non-Hispanic White women. *JAMA Psychiatry, 72*(6), 576–583.

Weaver, A. M., Wellenius, G. A., Wu, W. C., Hickson, D. A., Kamalesh, M., & Wang, Y. (2017). Residential distance to major roadways and cardiac structure in African Americans: Cross-sectional results from the Jackson Heart Study. *Environmental Health: A Global Access Science Source, 16*(1), 21.

Webb, H. M., & Kolar, S. K. (2016). Racial/ethnic differences in electronic cigarette use and reasons for use among current and former smokers: Findings from a community-based sample. *International Journal of Environmental Research and Public Health, 13*(10), 1009.

Webb, M., Francis, J., Hines, B., & Quarles, F. (2007). Health disparities and culturally specific treatment: Perspectives and expectancies of African American smokers. *Journal of Clinical Psychology, 63*(6), 567–583.

Weitzer, R., & Tuch, S. A. (2002). Perceptions of racial profiling: Race, class, and personal experience. *Criminology, 40*(2), 435–456.

Weitzman, P. F., Dunigan, R., Hawkins, R., Weitzman, E., & Levkoff, S. (2002). Everyday sources of conflict and stress among older African American women. *Journal of Ethnic and Cultural Diversity in Social Work, 10*(2), 27–44.

Welsing, F. C. (1991). *Isis papers: The keys to the colors.* Chicago, IL: Third World Press.

West, H. C., Sabol, W. J., & Greenman, S. J. (2010). *Prisoners in 2009.* Bureau of Justice Statistics, U.S. Department of Justice. Retrieved from http://bjs.ojp.usdoj.gov/content/pub/pdf/p09.pdf

Westbrook, T. R., Harden, B. J., Holmes, A. K., Meisch, A. D., & Whittaker, J. V. (2013). Physical discipline use and child behavior problems in low-income, high-risk African American families. *Early Education and Development, 24*(6), 923–945.

Whaley, A. L. (1998). Cross-cultural perspective on paranoia: A focus on the black American experience. *Psychiatric Quarterly, 69*(4), 325–343.

Whaley, A. L. (2001). Cultural mistrust of white mental health clinicians among African Americans with severe mental illness. *American Journal of Orthopsychiatry, 71*(2), 252–256.

Wheeler, R. S. (2008). Becoming adept at code-switching. *Educational Leadership, 65*(7), 54–58.

Whitaker, D., Graham, C., Severtson, S. G., Furr-Holden, C. D., & Latimer, W. (2012). Neighborhood and family effects on learning motivation among urban African American middle school youth. *Journal of Child and Family Studies, 21*(1), 131–138.

White, A. M. (2006). African American feminist masculinities: Personal narratives of redemption, contamination, and peak turning points. *Journal of Humanistic Psychology, 46*(3), 255–280.

White, J. L. (1970, September). Toward a Black psychology. *Ebony Magazine.*

White, J. L. (1972). Toward a black psychology. In R. Jones (Ed.), *Black psychology* (pp. 5–13). New York, NY: Harper & Row.

White, J. L. (1984). *The psychology of Blacks.* Englewood Cliffs, NJ: Prentice Hall.

White, J. L., & Parham, T. A. (1990). *The psychology of Blacks* (2nd ed.). Englewood Cliffs, NJ: Prentice Hall.

White-Johnson, R. L. (2012). Prosocial involvement among African American young adults: Considering racial discrimination and racial identity. *Journal of Black Psychology, 38*(3), 313–341.

White-Johnson, R. L., Ford, K. R., & Sellers, R. M. (2010). Parental racial socialization profiles: Association with demographic factors, racial discrimination, childhood socialization and racial identity. *Cultural Diversity and Ethnic Minority Psychology, 16*(2), 237–247.

Whitley, R. (2012). "Thank you God": Religion and recovery from dual diagnosis among low-income African Americans. *Transcultural Psychiatry, 49*(1), 87–104.

Wierzbicki, M., & Pekarik, G. (1993). A meta-analysis of psychotherapy dropout. *Professional Psychology: Research and Practice, 24*(2), 190–195.

Wilder, J. (2010). Revisiting "color names and color notions": A contemporary examination of the language and attitudes of skin color among young black women. *Journal of Black Studies, 41*(1), 184–206.

Wilder, J., & Cain, C. (2011). Teaching and learning color consciousness in Black families: Exploring family processes and women's experiences with colorism. *Journal of Family Issues, 32*(5), 577–604.

Wilford, J. N. (2016, November 7) Ezekiel's wheel ties African spiritual traditions to Christianity. *Science, New York Times.*

Williams, C., & Latkin, C. (2007). Neighborhood socioeconomic status, personal network attributes, and use of heroin and cocaine. *American Journal of Preventive Medicine, 32*(6 Suppl. 1), 203–210.

Williams, D. (2000). Race and health in Kansas: Data, issues, directions. In A. R. Tarlov & R. S. Peter (Eds.), *The society and population health reader* (pp. 236–258). New York, NY: The New Press.

Williams, D. R., González, H. M., Neighbors, H., Nesse, R., Abelson, J. M., Sweetman, J., & Jackson, J. S. (2007). Prevalence and distribution of major depressive disorder in African Americans, Caribbean blacks, and non-Hispanic whites: Results from the National Survey of American Life. *Archives of General Psychiatry, 64*(3), 305–315.

Williams, D. R., & Wyatt, R. (2015). Racial bias in health care and health: Challenges and opportunities. *JAMA, 314*(6), 555–556.

Williams, E. (2012, December 21). Big Brothers Big Sisters heads to the barber shop to recruit volunteers. *News for Saint Louis.* Retrieved from http://news.stlpublicra dio.org/post/big-brothers-big-sisters-heads-barber-shop-recruit-volunteers-0

Williams, M. T. (2016). *The link between racism and PTSD.* Retrieved from https://www.psychology

today.com/blog/culturally-speaking/201509/the-link-between-racism-and-ptsd

Williams, R. A., Williams, R. L., & Mitchell, H. (2004). The testing game. In R. Jones (Ed.), *Black psychology* (pp. 465–485). Hampton, VA: Cobb & Henry.

Williams, R. L. (1997). The Ebonics controversy. *Journal of Black Psychology, 23*(3), 208–214.

Williams, R. L. (2008). A 40-year history of the Association of Black Psychologists (ABPsi). *Journal of Black Psychology, 34*(3), 249–260.

Williams, W. S., & Chung, Y. B. (2013). Do cultural attitudes matter? The role of cultural orientation on academic self-concept among Black/African College students. *Journal of College Counseling, 16*(3), 228–242.

Williams Institute. (2013). *LGBT African-American individuals and African-American same-sex couples.* Retrieved from https://williamsinstitute.law.ucla.edu/wp-content/uploads/Census-AFAMER-Oct-

Wilson, A. N. (1998). *Blueprint for Black power: A moral, political, and economic imperative for the twenty-first century.* Brooklyn, NY: Afrikan World InfoSystems.

Wilson, G. (2005). Race and job dismissal: African American/White differences in their sources during the early work career. *American Behavioral Scientist, 48*(9), 1182–1199.

Wilson, H. W., Donenberg, G. R., & Emerson, E. (2014). Childhood violence exposure and the development of sexual risk in low-income African American girls. *Journal of Behavioral Medicine, 37*(6), 1091–1101.

Wilson, J. Q., & Kelling, G. L. (1982, March). Broken windows: The police and neighborhood safety. *Atlantic Monthly, 249*(3), 29–38.

Wilson, M. N., Green-Bates, C., McCoy, L., Simmons, F., Askew, T., Curry-El, J., & Hinton, I. D. (1995). African American family life: The dynamics of interactions, relationships, and roles. In M. Wilson (Ed.), *African American family life: Its structural and ecological aspects* (pp. 5–21). San Francisco, CA: Jossey-Bass.

Wilson, S. M., Heaney, J. C., Cooper, J., & Wilson, O. W. (2008). Built environment issues in unserved and underserved African-American neighborhoods in North Carolina. *Environmental Justice, 1*(2), 63–72.

Wilson, W. J. (1987). *The truly disadvantaged: The inner city, the underclass, and public policy.* Chicago, IL: University of Chicago Press.

Wilson, W. J. (1997). *When work disappears.* New York, NY: Knopf.

Wilson-Jones, L., & Caston, M. C. (2004). Cooperative learning on academic achievement in elementary African American males. *Journal of Instructional Psychology, 31*(4), 280.

Wimberly, G. L. (2002). *School relationships foster success for African American students* [Policy report]. Iowa City, IA: ACT. Retrieved from http://www.act.org/research/policymakers/pdf/school_relation.pdf

Wingood, G. M., DiClemente, R. J., Bernhardt, J. M., Harrington, K., Davies, S. L., Robillard, A., & Hook, E. W. (2003). A prospective study of exposure to rap music videos and African American female adolescents' health. *American Journal of Public Health, 93*(3), 437–440.

Wingood, G. M., DiClemente, R. J., Robinson-Simpson, L., Lang, D. L., Caliendo, A., & Hardin, J. W. (2013a). Efficacy of an HIV intervention in reducing high-risk human papillomavirus, nonviral sexually transmitted infections, and concurrency among African American women: A randomized-controlled trial. *Journal of Acquired Immune Deficiency Syndromes (1999), 63*(1), S36–S43.

Wingood, G. M., Robinson, L. R., Braxton, N. D., Er, D. L., Conner, A. C., Renfro, T. L., & DiClemente, R. J. (2013b). Comparative effectiveness of a faith-based HIV intervention for African American women: Importance of enhancing religious social capital. *American Journal of Public Health, 103*(12), 2226–2233.

Winslow, E. B., & Shaw, D. S. (2007). Impact of neighborhood disadvantage on overt behavior problems during early childhood. *Aggressive Behavior, 33*(3), 207–219.

Winters, M. F. (1999). *Reflections on endowment building in the African-American community. Chapter in cultures of caring: Philanthropy in diverse American communities.* Washington, DC: Council on Foundations.

Wiredu, K. (2003). On decolonizing African religions. In P. H. Coetzee & A. P. J. Roux (Eds.), *The African philosophy reader* (pp. 20–34), New York, NY: Routledge.

Wise, L. A., Palmer, J. R., Reich, D., Cozier, Y. C., & Rosenberg, L. (2012). Hair relaxer use and risk of uterine leiomyomata in African-American women. *American Journal of Epidemiology, 175*(5), 432–440.

Wise, T. J. (2010). *Colorblind: The rise of post-racial politics and the retreat from racial equity.* San Francisco, CA: City Lights Books.

Wise, T. J. (2012, January 31). Opinion: Tim wise— What is post-racial? Reflections on denial and reality. *CNN.* Retrieved from http://inamerica.blogs.cnn .com/2012/01 /31/

Wiser. (n.d.). *National Center for Black Philanthropy.* Retrieved from https://wiser.directory/organization/ national-center-for-black-philanthrop

Witherspoon, D. P., Daniels, L. L., Mason, A. E., & Smith, E. P. (2016). Racial-ethnic identity in context: Examining mediation of neighborhood factors on children's academic adjustment. *American Journal of Community Psychology, 57*(1–2), 87–101.

Witherspoon, K. M., & Speight, S. L. (2009). An exploration of African Americans' interests and self-efficacy beliefs in traditional and nontraditional careers. *Journal of Black Studies, 39*(6), 888–904.

Witkin, H. A., & Goodenough, D. R. (1977). Field-dependence and interpersonal behavior. *Psychological Bulletin, 84,* 661–689.

Witty, P. (1945). New evidence on the learning ability of the Negro. *Journal of Abnormal and Social Psychology, 40,* 401–404.

Wong, C. A., Eccles, J. S., & Sameroff, A. (2003). The influence of ethnic discrimination and ethnic identification on African American adolescents' school and socioemotional adjustment. *Journal of Personality, 71*(6), 1197–1233.

Woods-Giscombé, C. L. (2010). Superwoman schema: African American women's views on stress, strength, and health. *Qualitative Health Research, 20*(5), 668–683.

Woodson, C. G. (1972). *The mis-education of the Negro* (Reprint). Washington, DC: Associated Publishers. (Original work published 1933)

Woodward A. T., Taylor R. J., Abelson J. M., & Matusko, N. (2013). Major depressive disorder among older African Americans, Caribbean blacks, and non-Hispanic whites: Secondary analysis of the National Survey of American Life. *Depression and Anxiety, 30,* 589–597.

Woolf, S. H., & Braveman, P. (2011). Where health disparities begin: The role of social and economic determinants—and why current policies may make matters worse. *Health Affairs, 30*(10), 1852–1859.

Woolf, S. H., Johnson, R. E., Fryer, G. E., Rust, G., & Satcher, D. (2008). The health impact of resolving racial disparities: An analysis of US mortality data. *American Journal of Public Health, 94*(12), 26–28.

Woolfolk, A. E. (1998). *Educational psychology* (7th ed.). Boston, MA: Allyn & Bacon.

World Health Organization (WHO). (n.d.). *WHO definition of health.* Retrieved from http://www.who.int/ about/defini tion/en/print.html

World Health Organization (WHO). (2012). *Data on the size of the HIV/AIDS epidemic: Prevalence of HIV among adults aged 15 to 49 (%) by country.* Retrieved from http://apps.who.int/gho/data/node.main.622

Worrell, F. C. (2003). Why are there so few African Americans in gifted education programs? In C. C. Yeakey & R. D. Henderson (Eds.), *Surmounting all odds: Education, opportunity, and society in the new millennium* (pp. 423–454). Greenwich, CT: Information Age.

Wyatt, G. E. (1992). The sociocultural context of African American and White American women's rape. *Journal of Social Issues, 48*(1), 77–91.

Wyatt, S. K. (2006). Racial identity attitudes, womanist identity attitudes, and self-esteem in African American college women attending historically Black single-sex and coeducational institutions. *College Student Development, 47*(3), 319–334.

Wyatt, T. (1995). Language development in African-American English child speech. *Linguistics and Education, 7*(1), 7–22.

Yancey, G. (2007). Homogamy over the using internet advertisements to discover who interracially dates. *Journal of Social and Personal Relationships, 24*(6), 913–930.

Yankouskaya, A., Humphreys, G. W., & Rotshtein, P. (2014). Differential interactions between identity and emotional expression in own and other-race faces: Effects of familiarity revealed through redundancy gains. *Journal of Experimental Psychology: Learning, Memory, and Cognition, 40*(4), 1025–1038.

Yasui, M., Dorham, C. L., & Dishion, T. J. (2004). Ethnic identity and psychological adjustment: A validity analysis for European American and African American adolescents. *Journal of Adolescent Research, 19*(6), 807–825.

Yip, T., Seaton, E. K., & Sellers, R. M. (2006). African American racial identity across the lifespan: Identity status, identity content, and depressive symptoms. *Child Development, 77*(5), 1504–1517.

Young-Laing, B. (2003). *African American models of community organization: Toward a culturally competent theory* (Unpublished doctoral dissertation). Richmond, VA: Virginia Commonwealth University.

Zane, D., Thomson, N., & Dugan, M. (2004). The recruitment process: Factors that predict African-American adolescents' initial engagement into an alcohol, tobacco, and other drug prevention study. *Journal of Ethnicity and Substance Abuse, 3*(2), 43–54.

Zapolski, T. C., Fisher, S., Banks, D. E., Hensel, D. J., & Barnes-Najor, J. (2017). Examining the protective effect of ethnic identity on drug attitudes and use among a diverse youth population. *Journal of Youth and Adolescence, 46*(8), 1702–1715.

Zapolski, T. C., Pedersen, S. L., McCarthy, D. M., & Smith, G. T. (2014). Less drinking, yet more problems: Understanding African American drinking and related problems. *Psychological Bulletin, 140*(1), 188–223.

Zea, M. C., Quezada, T., & Belgrave, F. Z. (1996). Limitations of an acultural health psychology: Reconstructing the African influence on Latino culture and health related behaviors. In G. J. Garcia & M. C. Zea (Eds.), *Psychological interventions and research with Latino populations* (pp. 255–266). Boston, MA: Allen & Bacon.

Zhang, M. (2015). Internet use that reproduces educational inequalities: Evidence from big data. *Computers & Education, 86*, 212–223.

Zhao, Y., Kershaw, T., Ettinger, A. S. Higgins, C., Lu, M. C., & Chao, S. M. (2015). Association between life from the 2007 and 2010 Los Angeles Mommy and Baby (LAMB) Surveys. *Maternal and Child Health Journal, 19*(10), 2195–2205.

Ziadni, M. S., Patterson, C. A., Pulgarón, E. R., Robinson, M. R., & Barakat, L. P. (2011). Health-related quality of life and adaptive behaviors of adolescents with sickle cell disease: Stress processing moderators. *Journal of Clinical Psychology in Medical Settings, 18*, 335–344.

Zigler, E., Taussig, C., & Black, K. (1992). Early childhood intervention: A promising preventative for juvenile delinquency. *American Psychologist, 47*(8), 997–1006.

AUTHOR INDEX

SUBJECT INDEX

Page references followed by (figure) indicates an illustrated figure; followed by (table) indicates a table.